W9-AFW-570

peng

GLOBAL STRATEGY

peng

GLOBAL STRATEGY

THIRD EDITION

Mike W. Peng, PhD

Jindal Chair of Global Strategy

Jindal School of Management

University of Texas at Dallas

Chair, Global Strategy Interest Group (2008)

Strategic Management Society

Fellow, Academy of International Business (since 2012)

Australia · Brazil · Japan · Korea · Mexico · Singapore · Spain · United Kingdom · United States

SOUTH-WESTERN
CENGAGE Learning

Global Strategy, 3rd Edition
Mike W. Peng

Senior Vice President, LRS/Acquisitions & Solutions Planning; Jack W. Calhoun

Editorial Director, Business & Economics: Erin Joyner

Senior Acquisitions Editor: Michele Rhoades

Associate Development Editor: Josh Wells

Editorial Assistant: Tamara Grega

Brand Manager: Robin Lefevre

Market Development Manager: Jonathan Monahan

Media Editor: Rob Ellington

Manufacturing Planner: Ron Montgomery

Art and Cover Direction, Production Management, and Composition: Integra

Cover Image: © istockphoto/Alexey Stiop

Rights Acquisitions Director: Audrey Pettengill

Rights Acquisitions Specialist: Amber Hosea

For product information and technology assistance, contact us at **Cengage Learning Customer & Sales Support, 1-800-354-9706**

For permission to use material from this text or product, submit all requests online at **www.cengage.com/permissions** Further permissions questions can be emailed to **permissionrequest@cengage.com**

Library of Congress Control Number: 2012948254

ISBN-13: 978-1-133-96461-2

ISBN-10: 1-133-96461-3

South-Western
5191 Natorp Boulevard
Mason, OH 45040
USA

Cengage Learning is a leading provider of customized learning solutions with office locations around the globe, including Singapore, the United Kingdom, Australia, Mexico, Brazil, and Japan. Locate your local office at: **www.cengage.com/global**

Cengage Learning products are represented in Canada by Nelson Education, Ltd.

For your course and learning solutions, visit **www.cengage.com** Purchase any of our products at your local college store or at our preferred online store **www.cengagebrain.com**

Printed in the United States of America
1 2 3 4 5 6 7 16 15 14 13 12

To Agnes, Grace, and James

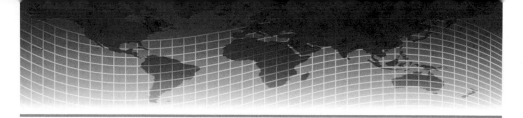

ABOUT THE AUTHOR

Mike W. Peng is the Jindal Chair of Global Strategy at the Jindal School of Management, University of Texas at Dallas, a National Science Foundation CAREER Award winner, and a Fellow of the Academy of International Business. He is also Executive Director of the Center for Global Business, which he founded. At UT Dallas, he has been the number one contributor to the 45 top journals tracked by *Financial Times*, which has ranked UT Dallas as a top 20 school in research worldwide and its MBA and EMBA programs increasingly in the top tier.

Professor Peng holds a bachelor's degree from Winona State University, Minnesota, and a PhD degree from the University of Washington, Seattle. Between 2005 and 2011, he was the first Provost's Distinguished Professor at UT Dallas, a chair position that was created to attract him to join the faculty. He had previously been an associate professor (with tenure) at the Ohio State University. Prior to that he had served on the faculty at the Chinese University of Hong Kong and University of Hawaii. He has taught in five states in the United States (Hawaii, Ohio, Tennessee, Texas, and Washington) as well as China, Hong Kong, and Vietnam. He has also held visiting or courtesy appointments in Australia, Britain, China, Denmark, Hong Kong, and the United States.

Professor Peng is one of the most prolific and most influential scholars in global strategy. During the decade 1996–2006, he was among the top seven contributors to the *Journal of International Business Studies*. His research is also among some of the most widely cited—both the United Nations and the World Bank have cited his work. A *Journal of Management* article found him to be among the top 65 most widely cited management scholars, and an *Academy of Management Perspectives* study found him to be the fourth most influential management scholar both inside and outside of academia (measured by academic citations and non-edu Google webpages) among professors who obtained their PhD since 1991. Overall, Professor Peng has published over 100 articles in leading journals, over 30 pieces in non-refereed outlets, and five books. Since the launch of *Global Strategy*'s second edition, he has published not only in top global strategy journals, such as the *Academy of Management Journal, Journal of International Business Studies,* and *Strategic Management Journal,* but also in leading outlets in operations (*Journal of Operations Management*), entrepreneurship (*Journal of Business Venturing* and *Entrepreneurship Theory and Practice*), and human resources (*International Journal of Human Resource Management*).

Professor Peng's market-leading textbooks, *Global Strategy, Global Business,* and *GLOBAL,* are studied in over 30 countries and have been translated into Chinese, Spanish, and Portuguese. A European adaptation, *International Business* (with Klaus Meyer), has been successfully launched.

Professor Peng is active in leadership positions. He has served on the editorial boards of *AMJ, AMR, JIBS, JMS, JWB,* and *SMJ,* and guest-edited a special issue for the *JMS.* At the Strategic Management Society (SMS), he was elected to be the Global Strategy Interest Group Chair (2008). He also co-chaired the SMS Special Conference on China in Shanghai (2007). At the Academy of International Business (AIB), he was co-chair of the AIB/*JIBS* Frontiers Conference in San Diego (2006), guest-edited a *JIBS* special issue (2010), chaired the Emerging and Transition Economies track for the Nagoya conference (2011), and chaired the Richard Farmer Best Dissertation Award Committee for the Washington conference (2012). He was recently elected to be a Fellow of AIB. He served one term as Editor-in-Chief of the *Asia Pacific Journal of Management.* During his editorial tenure, he managed the doubling of submission numbers and the successful bid to enter the Social Sciences Citation Index (SSCI), which reported *APJM*'s first citation impact to be 3.36 and rated it as the top 18 among 140 management journals for 2010.

Professor Peng is also an active consultant, trainer, and keynote speaker. He has provided on-the-job training to over 300 professors. He has consulted and been a keynote speaker for multinational enterprises (such as AstraZeneca, Berlitz, KOSTA, Nationwide, SAFRAN, and Texas Instruments), nonprofit organizations (such as Greater Dallas Asian American Chamber of Commerce and World Affairs Council of Dallas-Fort Worth), educational and funding organizations (such as Harvard University Kennedy School of Government, National Science Foundation, Social Sciences and Humanities Research Council of Canada, and the University of Memphis), and national and international organizations (such as the US-China Business Council, US Navy, and World Bank).

Professor Peng has attracted close to $1 million in external funding. His honors include a National Science Foundation CAREER Grant, a US Small Business Administration Best Paper Award, a (lifetime) Distinguished Scholar Award from the Southwestern Academy of Management, and a (lifetime) Scholarly Contribution Award from the International Association for Chinese Management Research. He has been quoted in *The Economist, Newsweek, Dallas Morning News, Smart Business Dallas, Atlanta Journal-Constitution, The Exporter Magazine, The World Journal, Business Times* (Singapore), *Sing Tao Daily* (Vancouver), and *Brasil Econômico* (São Paulo), as well as on Voice of America.

BRIEF CONTENTS

About the Author   vii
Preface   xxiii

PART 1 FOUNDATIONS OF GLOBAL STRATEGY   1

1 Strategizing Around the Globe   2
Opening Case: The Global Strategy of *Global Strategy*   3
Closing Case: Emerging Markets: Microsoft's Evolving China Strategy   27

2 Managing Industry Competition   32
Opening Case: Emerging Markets: Competing in the Indian Retail
    Industry   33
Closing Case: Emerging Markets: High Fashion Fights Recession   57

3 Leveraging Resources and Capabilities   62
Opening Case: IBM at 100   63
Closing Case: Emerging Markets: From Copycats to Innovators   85

4 Emphasizing Institutions, Cultures, and Ethics   92
Opening Case: Cut Salaries or Cut Jobs?   93
Closing Case: Facebook Violates Privacy   119

PART 2 BUSINESS-LEVEL STRATEGIES   125

5 Growing and Internationalizing the Entrepreneurial Firm   126
Opening Case: Emerging Markets: Amazon.com of Russia   127
Closing Case: Emerging Markets: Microfinance: Macro Success or Global
    Mess?   149

6 Entering Foreign Markets   154
Opening Case: Enter the United States by Bus   155
Closing Case: Emerging Markets: Pearl River Goes Abroad   182

7 Making Strategic Alliances and Networks Work   188
Opening Case: Emerging Markets: Yum! Brands Teams Up with
    Sinopec   189
Closing Case: Emerging Markets: BP, AAR, and TNK-BP   215

8 Managing Global Competitive Dynamics   222
Opening Case: Patent Wars and Shark Attacks   223
Closing Case: Emerging Markets: HTC Fights Apple   253

PART **3** CORPORATE-LEVEL STRATEGIES 257

9 Diversifying, Acquiring, and Restructuring 258
Opening Case: Emerging Markets: Corporate Diversification Strategy in South Korean Business Groups 259
Closing Case: Emerging Markets: Emerging Acquirers from China and India 288

10 Strategizing, Structuring, and Learning Around the World 294
Opening Case: Emerging Markets: Samsung's Global Strategy Group 295
Closing Case: A Subsidiary Initiative at Bayer MaterialScience North America 321

11 Governing the Corporation Around the World 326
Opening Case: High Drama at Hewlett-Packard (HP) 327
Closing Case: Emerging Markets: The Private Equity Challenge 353

12 Strategizing with Corporate Social Responsibility 360
Opening Case: Launching the Nissan Leaf: The World's First Electric Car 361
Closing Case: Whole Foods' John Mackey on Conscious Capitalism 385

Integrative Cases 389

IC 1   3i Group's Private Equity Investment in China's Little Sheep   391
IC 2   TeliaSonera: A Nordic Investor in Eurasia   404
IC 3   The Indian Business Process Offshoring Industry   409
IC 4   Wynn Macau: Gambling on the Edge of China   412
IC 5   Ryanair   418
IC 6   SolarWorld USA   424
IC 7   SnowSports Interactive: A Global Start-up's Challenges   431
IC 8   Wikimart: Building a Russian Version of Amazon   436
IC 9   Texas Instruments in South Korea: An Educational Opportunity   440
IC 10   Jobek do Brasil's Joint Venture Challenges   448
IC 11   The Antitrust Case on the AT&T–T-Mobile Merger   456
IC 12   Ocean Park Fights Hong Kong Disneyland   460
IC 13   Nomura's Integration of Lehman Brothers' Assets in Asia and Europe   462
IC 14   Baosteel Europe   465
IC 15   Bank of America's Corporate Social Responsibility and the Occupy Wall Street Movement   471

Glossary   477
Index of Organizations   491
Index of Names   499
Index of Subjects   517

CONTENTS

About the Author   vii
Preface   xxiii

PART 1 FOUNDATIONS OF GLOBAL STRATEGY   1

CHAPTER 1

Strategizing Around the Globe   2

Opening Case: The Global Strategy of *Global Strategy*   3
A *Global* Global Strategy Book   4
  Emerging Markets 1.1—Foxconn   6
  Emerging Markets 1.2—GE's Reverse Innovation from the Base of the
  Pyramid   8
Why Study Global Strategy?   9
What Is Strategy?   10
  Origin   10
  Plan versus Action   10
  Strategy as Theory   11
  Strategy in Action 1.1—German and French Military Strategy, 1914   12
Fundamental Questions in Strategy   15
  Why Do Firms Differ?   15
  How Do Firms Behave?   16
  What Determines the Scope of the Firm?   17
  What Determines the Success and Failure of Firms Around the
  Globe?   18
What Is Global Strategy?   19
What Is Globalization?   20
  Three Views on Globalization   20
  The Pendulum View on Globalization   21
  Semiglobalization   22
Global Strategy and the Globalization Debate   23
Organization of the Book   24
Chapter Summary   25
Key Terms   26
Critical Discussion Questions   26
Topics for Expanded Projects   26
Closing Case: Emerging Markets: Microsoft's Evolving China Strategy   27
Notes   29

CHAPTER **2**

Managing Industry Competition 32

Opening Case: Emerging Markets: Competing in the Indian Retail
Industry 33
Defining Industry Competition 34
The Five Forces Framework 35
    From Economics to Strategy 35
    Intensity of Rivalry among Competitors 35
    Threat of Potential Entry 38
    Strategy in Action 2.1—The Cruise Industry: Too Many Love Boats 39
    Bargaining Power of Suppliers 41
    Bargaining Power of Buyers 41
    Threat of Substitutes 42
    Lessons from the Five Forces Framework 43
    Strategy in Action 2.2—From Cardinal Foods to Cardinal Health 44
Three Generic Strategies 45
    Cost Leadership 45
    Strategy in Action 2.3—Ryanair: The Continuous Search for Low Cost 46
    Differentiation 47
    Focus 47
    Lessons from the Three Generic Strategies 48
Debates and Extensions 48
    Clear versus Blurred Boundaries of Industry 48
    Threats versus Opportunities 49
    Five Forces versus a Sixth Force 50
    Stuck in the Middle versus All Rounder 50
    Industry Rivalry versus Strategic Groups 51
    Integration versus Outsourcing 52
    Industry-Specific versus Firm-Specific and Institution-Specific
    Determinants of Performance 54
    Making Sense of the Debates 54
The Savvy Strategist 54
Chapter Summary 55
Key Terms 56
Critical Discussion Questions 56
Topics for Expanded Projects 57
Closing Case: Emerging Markets: High Fashion Fights Recession 57
Notes 59

CHAPTER **3**

Leveraging Resources and Capabilities 62

Opening Case: IBM at 100 63
Understanding Resources and Capabilities 64
    Emerging Markets 3.1—The Ordinary Heroes of the Taj 66

Resources, Capabilities, and the Value Chain 67
From SWOT to VRIO 71
    The Question of Value 71
    The Question of Rarity 72
    The Question of Imitability 72
    Strategy in Action 3.1—ANA: Refreshing the Parts Other Airlines
    Can't Reach 73
    The Question of Organization 74
    Emerging Markets 3.2—Strategic Ambidexterity in Emerging
    Economies 75
Debates and Extensions 76
    Firm-Specific versus Industry-Specific Determinants of Performance 76
    Static Resources versus Dynamic Capabilities 77
    Offshoring versus Non-Offshoring 79
    Domestic Resources versus International (Cross-Border) Capabilities 81
The Savvy Stategist 82
Chapter Summary 83
Key Terms 84
Critical Discussion Questions 84
Topics for Expanded Projects 84
Closing Case: Emerging Markets: From Copycats to Innovators 85
Notes 87

CHAPTER **4**

Emphasizing Institutions, Cultures, and Ethics 92

Opening Case: Cut Salaries or Cut Jobs? 93
Understanding Institutions 94
    Definitions 94
    What Do Institutions Do? 95
    Emerging Markets 4.1—Managing Uncertainty in Pakistan 96
    Emerging Markets 4.2—Binding International Commercial
    Arbitration 97
    How Do Institutions Reduce Uncertainty? 98
An Institution-Based View of Business Strategy 100
    Overview 100
    Two Core Propositions 102
    Emerging Markets 4.3—The Institution-Based Motivation Behind
    Emerging Multinationals 103
The Strategic Role of Cultures 105
    The Definition of Culture 105
    The Five Dimensions of Culture 105
    Cultures and Strategic Choices 107
The Strategic Role of Ethics 108
    The Definition and Impact of Ethics 108
    Managing Ethics Overseas 109
    Ethics and Corruption 110

A Strategic Response Framework for Ethical Challenges 111
Debates and Extensions 113
  Opportunism versus Individualism/Collectivism 113
  Cultural Distance versus Institutional Distance 114
  Bad Apples versus Bad Barrels 115
The Savvy Strategist 115
Chapter Summary 117
Key Terms 117
Critical Discussion Questions 118
Topics for Expanded Projects 118
Closing Case: Facebook Violates Privacy 119
Notes 120

PART 2 BUSINESS-LEVEL STRATEGIES 125

CHAPTER **5**

Growing and Internationalizing the Entrepreneurial Firm 126

Opening Case: Emerging Markets: Amazon.com of Russia 127
Entrepreneurship and Entrepreneurial Firms 128
A Comprehensive Model of Entrepreneurship 129
  Industry-Based Considerations 130
  Resource-Based Considerations 130
  Strategy in Action 5.1—Profiting from the Dirtiest Job Online 131
  Strategy in Action 5.2—Private Military Companies 132
  Institution-Based Considerations 133
Five Entrepreneurial Strategies 134
  Growth 134
  Innovation 134
  Emerging Markets 5.1—Israel: The Start-Up Nation 135
  Network 136
  Financing and Governance 136
  Harvest and Exit 138
Internationalizing the Entrepreneurial Firm 140
  Transaction Costs and Entrepreneurial Opportunities 140
  International Strategies for Entering Foreign Markets 141
  International Strategies for Staying in Domestic Markets 141
Debates and Extensions 142
  Traits versus Institutions 142
  Slow Internationalizers versus Born Global Start-ups 143
  Anti-Failure Biases versus Entrepreneur-Friendly Bankruptcy Laws 144
The Savvy Entrepreneur 146
Chapter Summary 147
Key Terms 147
Critical Discussion Questions 148

Topics for Expanded Projects   148

Closing Case: Emerging Markets: Microfinance: Macro Success or Global
Mess?   149

Notes   150

CHAPTER **6**

Entering Foreign Markets   154

Opening Case: Enter the United States by Bus   155

Overcoming the Liability of Foreignness   156

Emerging Markets 6.1—Russian Firms Spread Their Wings   157

Understanding the Propensity to Internationalize   158

A Comprehensive Model of Foreign Market Entries   159

Industry-Based Considerations   160

Resource-Based Considerations   160

Institution-Based Considerations   161

Where to Enter?   163

Location-Specific Advantages and Strategic Goals   163

Emerging Markets 6.2—Dubai Airport Connects the World   164

Cultural/Institutional Distances and Foreign Entry Locations   166

Emerging Markets 6.3—Emerging Multinationals from South Africa   167

When to Enter?   168

How to Enter?   170

Scale of Entry: Commitment and Experience   170

Modes of Entry: The First Step on Equity versus Non-equity Modes   170

Modes of Entry: The Second Step on Making Actual Selections   174

Debates and Extensions   176

Liability versus Asset of Foreignness   177

Global versus Regional Geographic Diversification   177

Old-line versus Emerging Multinationals: OLI versus LLL   178

The Savvy Strategist   179

Chapter Summary   180

Key Terms   181

Critical Discussion Questions   181

Topics for Expanded Projects   182

Closing Case: Emerging Markets: Pearl River Goes Abroad   182

Notes   183

CHAPTER **7**

Making Strategic Alliances and Networks Work   188

Opening Case: Emerging Markets: Yum! Brands Teams Up with
Sinopec   189

Defining Strategic Alliances and Networks   190

A Comprehensive Model of Strategic Alliances and Networks 191
Strategy in Action 7.1—The Tug of War Over Japan Airlines 192
Industry-Based Considerations 193
Resource-Based Considerations 195
Emerging Markets 7.1—A Local Partner's Perspective: "BP Has Been Treating Russians as Subjects" 197
Institution-Based Considerations 198
Formation 200
Stage One: To Cooperate or Not to Cooperate? 200
Stage Two: Contract or Equity? 200
Stage Three: Positioning the Relationship 202
Evolution 203
Combating Opportunism 203
Evolving from Strong Ties to Weak Ties 203
From Corporate Marriage to Divorce 205
Performance 206
The Performance of Strategic Alliances and Networks 206
The Performance of Parent Firms 207
Debates and Extensions 208
Majority JVs as Control Mechanisms versus Minority JVs as Real Options 208
Alliances versus Acquisitions 209
Emerging Markets 7.2—Embraer's Alliances and Acquisitions 209
Acquiring versus Not Acquiring Alliance Partners 211
The Savvy Strategist 211
Chapter Summary 213
Key Terms 214
Critical Discussion Questions 214
Topics for Expanded Projects 214
Closing Case: Emerging Markets: BP, AAR, and TNK-BP 215
Notes 217

CHAPTER **8**

Managing Global Competitive Dynamics 222

Opening Case: Patent Wars and Shark Attacks 223
Strategy as Action 224
Industry-based Considerations 225
Collusion and Prisoners' Dilemma 225
Industry Characteristics and Collusion vis-à-vis Competition 229
Emerging Markets 8.1—Is a Diamond (Cartel) Forever? 228
Resource-based Considerations 231
Value 231
Rarity 232
Imitability 232
Organization 232

Resource Similarity 232
Strategy in Action 8.1—A Fox in the Hen House 234
Fighting Low-Cost Rivals 235
Institution-based Considerations 236
Formal Institutions Governing Domestic Competition: A Focus on Antitrust 236
Formal Institutions Governing International Competition: A Focus on Antidumping 238
Emerging Markets 8.2—From Trade Wars to Antitrust Wars 239
Attack and Counterattack 241
Three Main Types of Attack 241
Awareness, Motivation, and Capability 242
Cooperation and Signaling 245
Local Firms versus Multinational Enterprises 245
Debates and Extensions 247
Strategy versus IO Economics and Antitrust Policy 247
Competition versus Antidumping 249
The Savvy Strategist 249
Chapter Summary 251
Key Terms 252
Critical Discussion Questions 252
Topics for Expanded Projects 252
Closing Case: Emerging Markets: HTC Fights Apple 253
Notes 255

PART **3** CORPORATE-LEVEL STRATEGIES **257**

CHAPTER **9**

Diversifying, Acquiring, and Restructuring 258

Opening Case: Emerging Markets: Corporate Diversification Strategy in South Korean Business Groups 259
Product Diversification 261
Product-Related Diversification 261
Product-Unrelated Diversification 261
Product Diversification and Firm Performance 262
Geographic Diversification 263
Limited versus Extensive International Scope 263
Geographic Diversification and Firm Performance 264
Combining Product and Geographic Diversification 265
A Comprehensive Model of Diversification 266
Industry-Based Considerations 266
Strategy in Action 9.1—The Evolution of Danisco's Corporate Strategy 267
Resource-Based Considerations 269

Strategy in Action 9.2—Can HondaJet Fly High? 270
Institution-Based Considerations 272
The Evolution of the Scope of the Firm 273
Acquisitions 276
Setting the Terms Straight 276
Motives for Mergers and Acquisitions 277
Emerging Markets 9.1—Brazil's Whopper Deal 278
Performance of Mergers and Acquisitions 280
Restructuring 282
Setting the Terms Straight 282
Motives for Restructuring 282
Debates and Extensions 283
Product Relatedness versus Other Forms of Relatedness 283
Acquisitions versus Alliances 284
The Savvy Strategist 284
Chapter Summary 285
Key Terms 286
Critical Discussion Questions 287
Topics for Expanded Projects 287
Closing Case: Emerging Markets: Emerging Acquirers from China and India 288
Notes 290

CHAPTER **10**

Strategizing, Structuring, and Learning Around the World 294

Opening Case: Emerging Markets: Samsung's Global Strategy Group 295
Multinational Strategies and Structures 296
Pressures for Cost Reduction and Local Responsiveness 296
Four Strategic Choices 297
Emerging Markets 10.1—Citroën Designs Cars in Shanghai 300
Four Organizational Structures 300
The Reciprocal Relationship between Multinational Strategy and Structure 304
A Comprehensive Model of Multinational Strategy, Structure, and Learning 304
Industry-Based Considerations 304
Resource-Based Considerations 306
Institution-Based Considerations 307
Strategy in Action 10.1—Moving Headquarters Overseas 308
Worldwide Learning, Innovation, and Knowledge Management 310
Knowledge Management 310
Knowledge Management in Four Types of Multinational Enterprises 311
Globalizing Research and Development (R&D) 312
Problems and Solutions in Knowledge Management 313

Debates and Extensions   314
    One Multinational versus Many National Companies   315
    Corporate Controls versus Subsidiary Initiatives   315
    Strategy in Action 10.2—Centralized and Decentralized Strategic
    Planning at the Oil Majors   316
    Customer-Focused Dimensions versus Integration, Responsiveness, and
    Learning   317
The Savvy Strategist   318
Chapter Summary   319
Key Terms   319
Critical Discussion Questions   320
Topics for Expanded Projects   320
Closing Case: A Subsidiary Initiative at Bayer MaterialScience North
America   321
Notes   322

CHAPTER **11**

Governing the Corporation Around the World   326

Opening Case: High Drama at Hewlett-Packard (HP)   327
Owners   328
    Concentrated versus Diffused Ownership   328
    Family Ownership   329
    State Ownership   329
Managers   330
    Principal–Agent Conflicts   330
    Principal–Principal Conflicts   331
    Strategy in Action 11.1—The Murdochs versus Minority
    Shareholders   331
Board of Directors   333
    Board Composition   334
    Leadership Structure   334
    Board Interlocks   334
    The Role of Boards of Directors   335
    Directing Strategically   335
Governance Mechanisms as a Package   336
    Internal (Voice-Based) Governance Mechanisms   337
    External (Exit-Based) Governance Mechanisms   337
    Internal Mechanisms + External Mechanisms = Governance Package   338
A Global Perspective   339
A Comprehensive Model of Corporate Governance   340
    Industry-Based Considerations   340
    Resource-Based Considerations   342
    Institution-Based Considerations   342

Debates and Extensions   344
 Opportunistic Agents versus Managerial Stewards   345
 Global Convergence versus Divergence   345
 State Ownership versus Private Ownership   346
 Emerging Markets 11.1—Welcoming Versus Restricting Sovereign
 Wealth Fund Investments   349
The Savvy Strategist   350
Chapter Summary   351
Key Terms   352
Critical Discussion Questions   352
Topics for Expanded Projects   353
Closing Case: Emerging Markets: The Private Equity Challenge   353
Notes   355

CHAPTER **12**

Strategizing with Corporate Social Responsibility   360

Opening Case: Launching the Nissan Leaf: The World's First Electric
Car   361
A Stakeholder View of the Firm   364
 A Big Picture Perspective   364
 Primary and Secondary Stakeholder Groups   364
 A Fundamental Debate   365
 Strategy in Action 12.1—Michael Porter on Creating
 Shared Value   367
A Comprehensive Model of Corporate Social Responsibility   368
 Industry-Based Considerations   370
 Resource-Based Considerations   372
 Institution-Based Considerations   373
Debates and Extensions   378
 Domestic versus Overseas Social Responsibility   378
 Active versus Inactive CSR Engagement Overseas   379
 Race to the Bottom ("Pollution Haven") versus
 Race to the Top   380
The Savvy Strategist   380
 Emerging Markets 12.1—Dow Chemical Company in China   381
Chapter Summary   383
Key Terms   383
Critical Discussion Questions   383
Topics for Expanded Projects   384
Closing Case: Whole Foods' John Mackey on
Conscious Capitalism   385
Notes   386

Integrative Cases   389

IC 1   3i Group's Private Equity Investment in China's Little Sheep
(Lily Fang, INSEAD, and Roger Leeds, Johns Hopkins University, School of Advanced International Studies)   391

IC 2   TeliaSonera: A Nordic Investor in Eurasia
(Canan Mutlu, University of Texas at Dallas)   404

IC 3   The Indian Business Process Offshoring Industry
(Debmalya Mukherjee, University of Akron)   409

IC 4   Wynn Macau: Gambling on the Edge of China
(Javier C. Cuervo, University of Macau)   412

IC 5   Ryanair
(Charles M. Byles, Virginia Commonwealth University)   418

IC 6   SolarWorld USA
(David Darling and Fabia Bourda, University of Texas at Dallas)   424

IC 7   SnowSports Interactive: A Global Start-up's Challenges
(Marilyn L. Taylor, University of Missouri at Kansas City, Xiaohua Yang, University of San Francisco, and Diaswati (Asti) Mardiasmo, Queensland University of Technology.)   431

IC 8   Wikimart: Building a Russian Version of Amazon
(Daniel J. McCarthy and Sheila M. Puffer, Northeastern University)   436

IC 9   Texas Instruments in South Korea: An Educational Opportunity
(Kris Baker, Harold Burman, Andrew Cyders, and Ben Wilson, University of Texas at Dallas, and Yanmin Wu, Texas Instruments)   440

IC 10   Jobek do Brasil's Joint Venture Challenges
(Dirk Michael Boehe, Insper Institute of Education and Research, and Luciano Barin Cruz, HEC Montréal)   448

IC 11   The Antitrust Case on the AT&T–T-Mobile Merger
(Mike W. Peng, University of Texas at Dallas)   456

IC 12   Ocean Park Fights Hong Kong Disneyland
(Michael N. Young, Hong Kong Baptist University)   460

IC 13   Nomura's Integration of Lehman Brothers' Assets in Asia and Europe
(Mike W. Peng, University of Texas at Dallas)   462

IC 14   Baosteel Europe
(Bernd Michael Linke, Friedrich Schiller University of Jena, Germany, and Andreas Klossek, Technical University of Freiberg, Germany)   465

IC 15 **Bank of America's Corporate Social Responsibility and the Occupy Wall Street Movement**
(Cathy Benjamin, Vivian Brown, James Buchanon, Grace Crane, and Michele Harkins, University of Texas at Dallas)   471

Glossary   477
Index of Organizations   491
Index of Names   499
Index of Subjects   517

PREFACE

It has been a decade since I began work on the first edition of *Global Strategy*. While the practice of global strategy has clearly become more important, the research and teaching of global strategy have also scaled new heights. Two landmark events important to the global strategy community in the past decade are (1) the founding of a dedicated Global Strategy Interest Group (GSIG) within the Strategic Management Society (SMS) and (2) the launch of the *Global Strategy Journal* (*GSJ*). I have actively supported these two initiatives, by serving as the first elected officer of GSIG (culminating in my service as the GSIG Chair) and by serving as an inaugural member of *GSJ*'s editorial review board. I believe that the widespread adoption of *Global Strategy*'s first two editions has enhanced the legitimacy of the global strategy field, widened its influence, and helped push the launch of these two exciting initiatives.

Starting from 2002, my goal has been to set a new standard for strategic management and international business textbooks in general and global strategy textbooks in particular. *Global Strategy* serves the needs of three types of undergraduate or MBA courses: (1) global or international strategy courses, (2) strategic management courses (especially those taught by internationally oriented instructors), and (3) international business courses (especially those taught by strategically oriented instructors). Based on the enthusiastic support from students and professors in Angola, Australia, Austria, Brazil, Britain, Canada, Chile, China, Finland, France, Denmark, Germany, Hong Kong, India, Ireland, Macau, Malaysia, Mexico, the Netherlands, Netherlands Antilles, New Zealand, Norway, Portugal, Romania, Singapore, South Korea, Spain, Sweden, Switzerland, Taiwan, Thailand, and the United States, the first two editions achieved unprecedented success and largely accomplished my goal. In addition to English, *Global Strategy* is also available in Chinese, Spanish, and Portuguese. In short, *Global Strategy* is global.

The third edition aspires to do even better. It continues the market-winning framework centered on the "strategy tripod" pioneered in the first edition and has been thoroughly updated to capture the rapidly moving research and events in the past several years. Its most strategic features include (1) a broadened definition of "global strategy," (2) a comprehensive and innovative coverage, (3) an evidence-based, in-depth, and consistent explanation of cutting-edge research, and (4) an interesting and accessible way to engage students.

A Broadened Definition of "Global Strategy"

In this book, "global strategy" is defined not as a particular multinational enterprise (MNE) strategy, but as "strategy around the globe." While emphasizing international strategy, we do not exclusively focus on it. Just like "international business" is about "business" (in addition to being "international"), "global strategy" is most fundamentally about "strategy" before being "global." Most global strategy and international business textbooks take the perspective of the foreign entrant, typically the MNE, often dealing with issues such as how to enter foreign markets and how to look for local partners. Important as these issues are, they only cover one side of international business—namely, the foreign side. The other side, naturally, is how domestic firms strategize by competing against each other and dealing with foreign entrants. Failing to understand the "other side," at best, captures only one side of the coin.

A Comprehensive and Innovative Coverage

With a broadened definition of "global strategy," this book covers the strategies of both large MNEs and smaller entrepreneurial firms, both foreign entrants and domestic firms, and both firms from developed economies and from emerging economies. As a result, this text offers the most comprehensive and innovative coverage of global strategy topics available on the market. In short, it is the world's first *global*, global-strategy book. Its unique features include:

- A chapter on institutions, cultures, and ethics (Chapter 4) and a focus on the emerging institution-based view of strategy (in addition to the traditional industry-based and resource-based views) throughout the book.

- A chapter on entrepreneurship (Chapter 5), especially its internationalization aspects.

- A chapter on global competitive dynamics (Chapter 8), including substantial discussions on cartel, antitrust, and antidumping issues typically ignored by other textbooks.

- A chapter on both product and geographic diversification (Chapter 9), the first time these crucial aspects of corporate strategies appear in the *same* textbook chapter.

- A chapter on corporate governance around the world (Chapter 11), the first time both the principal-agent and principal-principal conflicts are given *equal* "air time."

- A chapter on corporate social responsibility (Chapter 12), an increasingly important area of interest.

- A geographically comprehensive coverage, not only covering firms from the developed economies of the Triad (North America, Western Europe, and Japan) but also those from emerging economies of the world (with a focus on BRIC—Brazil, Russia, India, and China)

- A consistent theme on ethics, which is not only highlighted in Chapters 4 and 12 but also throughout all chapters in the form of Ethical Dilemma features and ethics-based Critical Discussion Questions

An Evidence-Based, In-Depth, and Consistent Explanation

The breadth of the field poses a challenge to textbook authors. My respect and admiration for the diversity of the field have increased tremendously over the past decade. To provide an evidence-based, in-depth explanation, I have leveraged the latest research (including my own forthcoming and ongoing work).[1] Specifically, *every* article published in the past

---

1 All my articles are listed at www.mikepeng.com and www.utdallas.edu/~mikepeng. Go to "Journal Articles."

ten years in leading journals has been consulted. Consequently, the Notes after each chapter are lengthy and comprehensive. While not every publication is cited, I am confident that I have left no major streams of research untouched. Readers—especially contributors to the literature—should feel free to check the Name Index to verify this claim. (Unfortunately, a number of older references have to be deleted to make room for more recent research.)

Given the breadth of the field, it is easy to lose focus. To combat this tendency, I have endeavored to provide a consistent set of frameworks in *all* chapters. This is done in three ways. First, I have focused on the four most fundamental questions in strategic management.[2] These are: (1) Why do firms differ? (2) How do firms behave? (3) What determines the scope of the firm? and (4) What determines the success and failure of firms around the globe? A particular emphasis is on the fourth question on firm performance, which has also been argued to be the leading question guiding global strategy and international business research.[3]

Another way to combat the tendency to lose the sight of the "forest" while scrutinizing various "trees" (or even "branches") is to consistently draw on the strategy tripod—the three leading perspectives on strategy, namely, industry-based, resource-based, and institution-based views. An innovative feature is the development of the institution-based view. In *every* chapter, these three views are integrated to develop a comprehensive model. This provides a great deal of continuity in the learning process.

Finally, I have written a beefy "Debates and Extensions" section for *every* chapter. Virtually all textbooks uncritically present knowledge "as is" and ignore the fact that the field is alive with numerous debates. Because debates drive practice and research ahead, it is imperative that students be exposed to various cutting-edge debates.

An Interesting and Accessible Way To Engage Students

If you fear this book must be very boring because it draws so heavily on current research, you are wrong. I have used a clear, engaging, conversational style to tell the "story." Relative to rival books, my chapters are generally more lively and shorter. Some reviewers commented that reading *Global Strategy* is like reading a "good magazine."

I have woven a large number of interesting anecdotes into the text. In addition to examples from the business world, "outside-the-box" examples range from ancient Chinese military writings to the Roman Empire's import quotas, from quotes from *Anna Karenina* to mutually assured destruction (MAD) strategy during the Cold War.

So what? Many textbooks leave students to struggle with this question at the end of every chapter. In *Global Strategy*, every chapter ends with a section on "The Savvy Strategist" with one teachable table/slide on "Strategic Implications for Action" from a *practical* standpoint. No other competing textbook is so savvy and so relevant.

Students and professors especially enjoyed the wide-ranging and globally relevant cases in previous editions. In the third edition, I have worked hard to bring together a new (and I believe more attractive) set of case materials. The third edition has been blessed by a

2 R. Rumelt, D. Teece, & D. Schendel (eds.), 1994, *Fundamental Issues in Strategy: A Research Agenda*, Boston: Harvard Business School Press.

3 M. W. Peng, 2004, Identifying the big question in international business research, *Journal of International Business Studies*, 35(2): 99–108.

global community of case contributors who are based in Australia, Brazil, Canada, China, Germany, India, Singapore, and the United States. Many are experts who are located in or are from the countries in which the cases take place. For example, we now have an Australia case written by an Australia-based author (see Integrative Case on SnowSports Interactive), a Brazil case penned by a Brazil-based author (see Integrative Case on Jobek do Brasil), two Macau and Hong Kong, China, cases contributed by Macau-based and Hong Kong-based authors (see Integrative Cases on Wynn Macau and Ocean Park fights Hong Kong Disneyland), and a Texas Instruments (TI) case coauthored by a TI executive (see Integrative Case on TI in South Korea). This edition also features a Russia case contributed by the world's top two leading experts on Russian management (see Integrative Case on Wikimart). The end result is an unparalleled, diverse collection of case materials that will significantly enhance the teaching and learning of global strategy around the world.

What's New in the Third Edition?

Most strategically, the third edition has (1) enhanced the executive voice by drawing more heavily from CEOs and other strategic leaders and (2) dedicated more space to emerging economies.

First, if *Global Strategy* aims to train a new generation of global strategists, we need to coach them to think, act, and talk like CEOs. While I have taught a few CEO classes in executive education with *Global Strategy*, most students using the book—even the highest-level Executive MBA (EMBA) students—have not assumed that kind of executive responsibilities. To facilitate strategic thinking, the third edition has featured more extensive quotes and perspectives from CEOs and other strategic leaders. These are longer and more visibly prominent break-out quotes—not merely single quotes typically embedded (or "buried") in paragraphs. In Chapter 1 alone, you will enjoy such insightful quotes from (1) Facebook's founder, chairman, and CEO, (2) GE's chairman and CEO, (3) Microsoft's CEO of Greater China, and (4) P&G's chairman and CEO. In later chapters, the following leaders will share their thoughts with you:

Bayer North America's CEO
Carlyle Group's co-founder and managing director
Dow Chemical's CEO
GE's former chairman and CEO
IBM's CEO
LG's chairman
TNK-BP's chairman and CEO

US Secretary of Justice (representing the Department of Justice's challenge of AT&T's proposed merger with T- Mobile)
US Secretary of Treasury (on the US-China Strategic and Economic Dialogue)
Whole Foods' co-founder and CEO

Second, this edition builds on *Global Strategy*'s previous strengths by more prominently highlighting global strategy challenges in and out of emerging economies. This is both a reflection of the global realities in which emerging economies have played a more important role and a reflection of my own strong research interest in emerging economies. Specifically, in the third edition, (1) a new Emerging Markets in-chapter feature is launched in every chapter, and (2) more than half of the longer Integrative Cases are now devoted to competition in and out of emerging economies (including one case on Brazil, two on Russia, one on India, and five on China).

Of course, in addition to these new features, every chapter has been thoroughly updated. Of the 15 Integrative Cases, 14 (93%) are new to this edition. Of the 60 in-chapter features (each chapter has an Opening Case, a Closing Case, and three boxes), 54 (90%) are new.

Overall, the third edition of *Global Strategy* has packed rigor with relevance, timeliness with excitement, and the strategic with the practical. To see how this book, itself a global product, competes around the world, check out the Chapter 1 Opening Case.

Support Materials

A full set of support materials is available for adopting instructors on the accompanying Instructor Resource CD, ensuring that instructors have the tools they need to plan, teach, and assess their course. These resources include:

- *Instructor's Manual*—This comprehensive manual provides chapter outlines, lecture notes, and sample responses to end-of-chapter questions, providing a complete set of teaching tools to save instructors time in preparing for class and to maximize student success within the class. The Instructor's Manual also includes notes to accompany the Integrative Cases from the text.

- *Testbank*—The robust *Global Strategy* testbank contains a wide range of questions with varying degrees of difficulty in true/false, multiple-choice, and short answer/essay formats. All questions have been tagged to the text's learning objectives and according to AASCB standards to ensure students are meeting necessary criteria for course success. Instructors can use the included ExamView® software package to view, choose, and edit their test questions according to their specific course requirements.

- *PowerPoint® Slides*—Each chapter includes a complete set of PowerPoint slides designed to present relevant chapter material in a way that will allow more visual learners to firmly grasp key concepts.

Acknowledgment

As *Global Strategy* launches its third edition, I first want to thank all the customers—professors, instructors, and students around the world who have made the book's success possible. As my (non-book-related) research not only progresses but also accelerates while I work on the book, I also want to thank my over 90 coauthors around the world for being in action together with me on the research front.

At UT Dallas, I thank my colleagues Dan Bochsler, Larry Chasteen, Tev Dalgic, Van Dam, Greg Dess, Dave Ford, Richard Harrison, Maria Hasenhuttl, Charlie Hazzard, Marilyn Kaplan, Seung-Hyun Lee, Elizabeth Lim, John Lin, Livia Markóczy, Joe Picken, Roberto Ragozzino, Orlando Richard, Jane Salk, Mary Vice, Eric Tsang, and Habte Woldu, as well as the supportive leadership team—Hasan Pirkul (dean), Varghese Jacob (associate dean), and Greg Dess (area coordinator). I also thank my two PhD students, Brian Pinkham (now at Texas Christian University) and Steve Sauerwald, for their research assistance. One PhD student (Canan Mutlu), four MBA students (Kris Baker,

Harold Burman, Andrew Cyders, and Ben Wilson), and seven EMBA students (Cathy Benjamin, Fabia Bourda, Vivian Brown, James Buchanon, Grace Crane, David Darling, and Michele Harkins) authored excellent case materials.

At South-Western Cengage Learning, I thank the "Peng team" that not only publishes *Global Strategy* but also *Global Business* and *GLOBAL.* Our *Global Strategy* team includes Erin Joyner, Publisher; Michele Rhoades, Senior Acquisitions Editor; Josh Wells, Associate Development Editor; Jonathan Monahan, Market Development Manager; Rob Ellington, Media Editor; and Tammy Grega, Editorial Assistant.

In the academic community, I would like to thank the reviewers:

Charles M. Byles (Virginia Commonwealth University)
Sara B. Kimmel (Belhaven College)
Ted W. Legatski (Texas Christian University)
Jun Li (University of New Hampshire)
Carol Sanchez (Grand Valley State University)

In addition, I thank many colleagues who provided informal feedback to me on the book. Over the last decade I have been blessed by such feedback from hundreds of colleagues from around the world. Space constraints here force me to only acknowledge colleagues who wrote me since the second edition, since colleagues who wrote me earlier were thanked in earlier editions. (If you wrote me but I failed to mention your name here, my apologies—blame this on the volume of such emails.)

M. Ambashankar (Gupta College of Management, India)
Hari Bapuji (University of Manitoba, Canada)
Balbir Bhasin (University of Arkansas at Fort Smith, USA)
Murali Chari (Rensselaer Polytechnic Institute, USA)
Tee Yin Chaw (Management and Science University, Malaysia)
Joyce Falkenberg (Norwegian School of Economics and Business Administration, Norway)
Todd Fitzgerald (Saint Joseph's University, USA)
Myles Gartland (Rockhurst University, USA)
Dennis Garvis (Washington and Lee University, USA)
John Gerace (Chestnut Hill College, USA)
Mike Geringer (Ohio University, USA)
Maria Hasenhuttl (University of Texas at Dallas, USA)
Katalin Haynes (Texas A&M University, USA)
Stephanie Hurt (Meredith College, USA)
Anisul Islam (University of Houston, USA)
Basil Janavaras (Minnesota State University, USA)
Marshall Shibing Jiang (Brock University, Canada)
Ferry Jie (University of Technology, Sydney, Australia)
Ben Kedia (University of Memphis, USA)
Aldas Kriauciunas (Purdue University, USA)
Sumit Kundu (Florida International University, USA)
Somnath Lahiri (Illinois State University, USA)
Scung-Hyun Lee (University of Texas at Dallas, USA)
David Liu (George Fox University, USA)
Anoop Madhok (York University, Canada)
Mike Poulton (Dickinson College, USA)
David Pritchard (Rochester Institute of Technology, USA)

Pradeep Kanta Ray (University of New South Wales, Australia)

David Reid (Seattle University, USA)

Al Rosenbloom (Dominican University, USA)

Anne Smith (University of Tennessee, USA)

Clyde Stoltenberg (Wichita State University, USA)

Steve Strombeck (Azusa Pacific University, USA)

Jose Vargas-Hernandez (Universidad de Guadalajara, Mexico)

Loren Vickery (Western Oregon University, USA)

George White (Old Dominion University, USA)

En Xie (Xi'an Jiaotong University, China)

Gracy Yang (University of Sydney, Australia)

Haibin Yang (City University of Hong Kong, China)

Richard Young (Minnesota State University, USA)

Wu Zhan (University of Sydney, Australia)

I also want to thank six very special colleagues: Sun Wei and Lui Xinmei (Xi'an Jiaotong University) in China, Joaquim Carlos Racy (Pontifícia Universidade Católica de São Paulo) and George Bedinelli Rossi (Universidade de Sao Paulo) in Brazil, and Mercedes Munoz (Tecnológico de Monterrey) and Octavio Nava (Universidad del Valle de Mexico) in Mexico. They loved the book so much that they were willing to endure the pain of translating the first and second editions into Chinese, Portuguese, and Spanish. Their hard work has enabled *Global Strategy* to reach wider audiences globally, living up to its self-proclaimed tagline as a "*global*, global-strategy book."

In this edition, 30 colleagues—including one executive from Texas Instruments—graciously contributed cases.

Kris Baker (University of Texas at Dallas, USA)

Cathy Benjamin (University of Texas at Dallas, USA)

Dirk Michael Boehe (Insper Institute of Education and Research, Brazil)

Fabia Bourda (University of Texas at Dallas, USA)

Vivian Brown (University of Texas at Dallas, USA)

James Buchanon (University of Texas at Dallas, USA)

Harold Burman (University of Texas at Dallas, USA)

Charles Byles (Virginia Commonwealth University, USA)

Luciano Barin Cruz (HEC Montreal, Canada)

Grace He Crane (University of Texas at Dallas, USA)

Javier Cuervo (University of Macau, China)

Andrew Cyders (University of Texas at Dallas, USA)

David Darling (University of Texas at Dallas, USA)

Rohit Deshpande (Harvard Business School, USA)

Lily Fang (INSEAD, Singapore)

Michele Harkins (University of Texas at Dallas, USA)

Andreas Klossek (Technical University of Freiberg, Germany)

Roger Leeds (Johns Hopkins University, USA)

Bernd Michael (Friedrich Schiller University of Jena, Germany)

Daniel McCarthy (Northeastern University, USA)

Diaswati (Asti) Mardiasmo (Queensland University of Technology, Australia)

Debmalya Mukherjee (University of Akron, USA)

Canan Mutlu (University of Texas at Dallas, USA)

Sheila Puffer (Northeastern University, USA)

Anjali Raina (HBS India Research Center, India)

Marilyn Taylor (University of Missouri at Kansas City, USA)

Ben Wilson (University of Texas at Dallas, USA)

Yanmin Wu (Texas Instruments, USA)

Xiaohua Yang (University of San Francisco, USA)

Michael Young (Hong Kong Baptist University, China)—*two cases*

In addition, the work of the following global dignitaries was reprinted to grace the pages of our book:

Mikhail Fridman (chairman and CEO of TNK-BP and founder of Alfa Group, Russia)

John Mackey (co-founder and CEO of Whole Foods)

Michael Porter (strategy guru at Harvard Business School)

Last, but no means least, I thank my wife Agnes, my daughter Grace, and my son James—to whom this book is dedicated. I have named Agnes CEO, CFO, CIO, CTO, and CPO for our family, the last of which is coined by me, which stands for "chief parenting officer." Ten years ago Grace was a newborn and James was still waiting for his turn to show up in the world. Now my ten-year-old Grace, already a voracious reader and writer, can help me edit, and my eight-year-old James can assist me to enter grades. Grace is writing and editing her 17th short story called *My Magic Life*, and James is very interested in creating Lego models. For now, Grace wants to be a lawyer and James a banker. As a third-generation professor in my family, I can't help but wonder whether one (or both) of them will become a fourth-generation professor. To all of you, my thanks and my love.

MWP
December 1, 2012

1

Strategizing Around the Globe

2

Managing Industry Competition

3

Leveraging Resources and Capabilities

4

Emphasizing Institutions, Culture, and Ethics

PART **1** | FOUNDATIONS OF GLOBAL STRATEGY

CHAPTER 1

STRATEGIZING AROUND THE GLOBE

© istockphoto/Alexey Stiop

KNOWLEDGE OBJECTIVES

After studying this chapter, you should be able to

1. Offer a basic critique of the traditional, narrowly defined "global strategy"
2. Articulate the rationale behind studying global strategy
3. Define what is strategy and what is global strategy
4. Outline the four fundamental questions in strategy
5. Participate in the debate on globalization with a reasonably balanced view and a keen awareness of your likely bias

The Global Strategy of *Global Strategy*

Launched in 2005, *Global Strategy* has been used by business schools in over 30 countries and is now available in Chinese, Spanish, and Portuguese in addition to English. *Global Strategy* has also spawned two related books: *Global Business* (a more comprehensive, traditional textbook in international business) and *GLOBAL* (a more compact, innovative paperback). Everybody knows global competition is tough. How do *Global Strategy* and its sister books compete around the world? In other words, what is the nature of the global strategy of *Global Strategy*?

Global Strategy and its sister books are published by South-Western Cengage Learning, which is a division of Cengage Learning. Cengage Learning serves students, teachers, and libraries in the secondary and higher education markets, as well as government agencies and corporations. While the copyright page of this book indicates an address in Mason, Ohio (a suburb of Cincinnati), note that this is the address for the specific *division*, South-Western. The corporate headquarters of Cengage Learning is in Stamford, Connecticut. Cengage Learning is a global company, which is owned by Apax Partners of the UK and OMERS Capital Partners of Canada, two private equity groups. Overall, the global nature of Cengage Learning permeates the organization: it is UK- and Canadian-owned and US-headquartered. With annual sales of over $2 billion, Cengage Learning has approximately 5,800 employees worldwide across 35 countries.

In business and economics textbooks, South-Western Cengage Learning vies for number one in the world in terms of market share with McGraw-Hill Irwin and Pearson Prentice Hall, the other two members of the Big Three in this industry. While competition historically focused on the United States and other English-speaking countries, it is now worldwide. *Global Strategy* targets courses in strategic management and international business. While there is no shortage of textbooks in these two areas, *Global Strategy* broke new ground by being the first to specifically address their *intersection*. Thanks to enthusiastic students and professors in Angola, Australia, Austria, Brazil, Britain, Canada, Chile, China, Finland, France, Denmark, Germany, Hong Kong, India, Ireland, Japan, Macau, Malaysia, Mexico, the Netherlands, Netherlands Antilles, New Zealand, Norway,

Portugal, Romania, Singapore, South Korea, Spain, Sweden, Taiwan, Thailand, and the United States, *Global Strategy* achieved unprecedented success.

While competition is primarily among the Big Three, *Global Strategy* has also attracted new entrants—competing textbooks published by smaller, historically more specialized academic publishers such as Cambridge, Oxford, and Wiley that are interested in breaking into the mainstream textbook market. In addition to new entrants, the publishing industry has also been experiencing another challenge: the digital revolution. E-books have emerged as a viable substitute to the printed version. Amazon now sells more Kindle versions than printed versions of books. To keep up with this movement, the Kindle version of *Global Strategy* has been available since the second edition.

Although competition, in theory, is global, in practice Cengage Learning needs to win one local market after another—literally, one course taught by one instructor in one school in one country. Obviously, no instructor teaches globally, and no student studies globally. Teaching and learning remain very local. For the company as a whole, the motto is: "Think global, act local." The hard truth is: *Global Strategy* does not have a "global strategy" (!). While this statement is provocative, what it really means is that *Global Strategy* does not have a grand strategic plan around the globe. What defines its strategy is a relentless process to be in touch with the rapidly evolving market and an unwavering commitment to aspire to meet and exceed customer expectations around the world. In other words, Cengage Learning embraces a "strategy as action" perspective, as opposed to a "strategy as plan" perspective. Every step of the way, Cengage Learning literally learns, tests the market, engages customers, and aspires to improve in the next edition. For instance, the Portuguese edition has been developed by two professors in Brazil, who are not mere translators but "revisers" who enhance the local flavor. In the third edition, *Global Strategy* builds on the already strong coverage of emerging economies in the two previous editions and introduces a new feature on emerging markets in *every* chapter. This edition has also expanded coverage on the previously under-covered regions such as Latin America and Africa, thus making *Global Strategy* more global.

Finally, to successfully compete around the globe, a good understanding of the rules of the game is a must. In some countries, foreign publishers are free to publish whatever they please. In other countries, foreign publishers are not allowed to publish anything at all. For example, Brazil allows Cengage Learning to set up a wholly owned subsidiary that can publish the Portuguese version. However, China does not allow foreign publishers to publish books on their own. Therefore, Cengage Learning licensed the translation of *Global Strategy* to a leading Chinese publisher: Posts and Telecom Press. Further, Chinese rules dictate that all books published in China—regardless of foreign or domestic origin—have to pass political censorship. A thorough understanding of these rules is crucial. Experienced editors at Posts and Telecom Press advised that the title be changed to *Global Business Strategy* (*Quanqiu Qiye Zhanlue*), to avoid potential confusion in the eyes of the political censors that this might be a book about "global military strategy." Such important but subtle local knowledge helped avoid misunderstandings and troubles down the road, and helped a global company to successfully turn a page locally.

Sources: Based on (1) author's interviews with Cengage Learning executives in Brazil, China, and the United States; (2) *Economist*, 2010, The future of publishing, April 3: 65–66; (3) M. W. Peng, 2009, *Global Strategy*, 2nd ed., Cincinnati: South-Western Cengage Learning; (4) M. W. Peng, 2007, *Quanqiu Qiye Zhanlue*, translated by W. Sun & X. Lui, Beijing, China: Posts & Telecom Press; (5) M. W. Peng, 2008, *Estratégia Global*, translated by J. C. Racy & G. B. Rossi, São Paulo, Brazil: Cengage Learning; (6) M. W. Peng, 2010, *Estrategia Global*, segunda edición, translated by A. Alcérreca & M. Muñoz, Mexico City, Mexico: Cengage Learning.

A *Global* Global-Strategy Book

How do firms, such as Cengage Learning, McGraw-Hill, and Pearson, compete around the globe? In the publishing industry in each country, how do various foreign entrants and local firms interact, compete, and/or sometimes collaborate? What determines their success and failure? Since strategy is about competing and winning, this book on global strategy will help current and would-be strategists answer these and other important questions. Setting an example by itself, the book you are reading is a real global product that leverages its strengths, engages rivals, and competes around the world (see Opening Case).

However, this book does *not* focus on a particular form of international (cross-border) strategy, which is characterized by the production and distribution of standardized products and services on a worldwide basis. For over two decades, this strategy, commonly referred to as "global strategy" for lack of a better term, has often been advocated by traditional global-strategy books.[1] However, there is now a great deal of rumbling and soul-searching among managers frustrated by the inability of their "world car," "world drink," or "world commercial" to conquer the world.

multinational enterprise (MNE)

A firm that engages in foreign direct investment (FDI) by directly controlling and managing value-adding activities in other countries.

foreign direct investment (FDI)

A firm's direct investment in production and/or service activities abroad.

In reality, **multinational enterprises (MNEs)**, defined as firms that engage in **foreign direct investment (FDI)** by directly controlling and managing value-adding activities in other countries,[2] often have to adapt their strategies, products, and services for local markets. For example, the Opening Case clearly shows that in the publishing industry, one size does not fit all. In the automobile industry, there is no "world car." Cars popular in one region are often rejected by customers elsewhere. The Volkswagen Golf and the Ford Mondeo (marketed as the Contour in the United States), which have dominated Europe, have little visibility in the streets of Asia and North America. The so-called "world drink," Coke Classic, actually tastes different around the world (with varying sugar content). The Coca-Cola Company's effort in pushing for a set of "world commercials" centered on the polar bear cartoon character presumably appealing to some worldwide values and interests has been undermined by uncooperative TV viewers around the world. Viewers in warmer weather countries had a hard time relating to the furry polar bear. In response, Coca-Cola switched to more costly but more effective country-specific advertisements. For instance, the Indian subsidiary launched an advertising campaign that equated Coke with "thanda," the Hindi word for "cold." The German subsidiary developed a series of commercials that showed a "hidden" kind of eroticism (!).[3]

It is evident that the narrow notion of "global strategy" in vogue over the past two decades (in other words, the "one-size-fits-all" strategy), while useful for some firms in certain industries, is often incomplete and unbalanced.[4] This is reflected in at least three manifestations:

- Too often, the quest for worldwide cost reduction, consolidation, and restructuring in the name of "global strategy" has sacrificed local responsiveness and global learning. The results have been unsatisfactory in many cases and disastrous in others. Many MNEs have now pulled back from such a strategy. MTV has switched from standardized (American) English-language programming to a variety of local languages. With over 5,000 branches in 79 countries, HSBC is one of the world's largest and most global banks. Yet, instead of highlighting its "global" power, HSBC brags about being "the world's *local* bank."

- Almost by definition, the narrow notion of "global strategy" focuses on how to compete internationally, especially on how global rivals, such as Coca-Cola and Pepsi, Toyota and Honda, and Boeing and Airbus, meet each other in one country after another. As a result, the issue of how domestic companies compete with each other and with foreign entrants seems to be ignored. Does anyone know the nationalities and industries of the following companies: Cemex, Embraer, Foxconn, Huawei, and Tata? Based in Mexico, Brazil, Taiwan, China, and India, these five firms are world-class competitors in, respectively, cement, aerospace, electronics manufacturing, telecommunications equipment, and cars. They represent some of the top MNEs from emerging economies. If such firms are outside your strategic radar screen, then perhaps the radar has too many blind spots (see Emerging Markets 1.1).

Triad

Three primary regions of developed economies: North America, Europe, and Japan.

emerging economies (emerging markets)

A label that describes fast-growing developing economies since the 1990s.

- The current brand of "global strategy" seems relevant only for MNEs from developed economies, primarily North America, Europe, and Japan—commonly referred to as the **Triad**—to compete in other developed economies, where income levels and consumer preferences may be similar. **Emerging economies** (or **emerging markets**), a term that has gradually replaced the term developing economies since the 1990s, now command half of the worldwide FDI inflow and nearly half of the global gross domestic product

EMERGING MARKETS 1.1 〉 〉 ETHICAL DILEMMA

Foxconn

Until 2010, the vast majority of the endusers of Apple iPhones and iPads, Hewlett-Packard laptops, Amazon Kindles, and Microsoft Xboxes around the world had no clue about the firm that manufactured their beloved gadgets. The firm is Foxconn, which is headquartered in Taipei, Taiwan. Foxconn's shares (under the name of Hon Hai) are not only listed in Taipei (TWSE: 2317), but also in Hong Kong (SEHK: 2038), London (LSE: HHPD), and NASDAQ (HNHPF). With $110 billion in annual revenue, Foxconn is the global leader in contract manufacturing services. In other words, everybody has heard that leading electronics firms such as Cisco, Dell, Ericsson, Intel, Motorola, Nintendo, Nokia, and Sony—in addition to those named in the first three lines of this box above—have outsourced a large chunk of their manufacturing to "low-cost producers." But to whom? Only a small number of people know the answer: Foxconn has been scooping up a tremendous number of outsourcing orders.

Starting in 1975 in Taipei with a meager $7,500, Foxconn was founded by Taiwanese entrepreneur Terry Gou, who still serves as its chairman. As Foxconn becomes a giant, of course, industry insiders know and respect it. But outside the industry Foxconn lives in relative obscurity. It is likely to be the largest firm many people around the world have never heard of. Just how big is Foxconn? Worldwide, it has 1.3 million employees. In China alone, it employs over 920,000 workers (300,000 on one factory campus in Shenzhen). To put these mind-boggling numbers in perspective, its worldwide headcount is large as the entire US military, and its headcount in China is three times the size of the Taiwanese military. In addition to China, Foxconn has factories in 12 countries: Australia, Brazil, the Czech Republic, India, Japan, Mexico, the Netherlands, Poland, Russia, Slovakia, Singapore, and the United States. Foxconn is the largest private employer and the largest exporter in China and the second largest exporter in the Czech Republic.

In 2010, Foxconn stumbled into the media spotlight, not because of its accomplishments, but because a dozen employees in Shenzhen, China, committed suicide in a span of several months, most of them by jumping from high-rise Foxconn dormitories. Here comes one of the biggest paradoxes associated with such an emerging multinational. What are Foxconn's secrets for being so successful? Just like 100 years ago when Henry Ford created the mass assembly line by standardizing each worker's job, Foxconn has pioneered a business model that it calls e-enabled Components, Modules, Moves, and Services (eCMMS) that can help its clients save a ton of money. But why were there so many worker suicides that shocked the world? The business model is certainly a culprit. Working at Foxconn demands a great deal of concentration and repetition that breed enormous stress. *Bloomberg Businessweek* described Gou as "a ruthless taskmaster." Although the media and corporate social responsibility gurus criticize Foxconn for treating workers like machines and exploiting cheap labor, there is no evidence that Foxconn has mistreated or abused employees. In fact, in China, labor watchdogs actually give Foxconn credit for exceeding the norms, by paying workers (relatively) higher salaries, on time, and for overtime. In both 2005 and 2006, it was among the Best Employers in China, according to a ChinaHR.com poll. In response to the suicides, Foxconn increased Shenzhen factory workers' pay by 30% to $176 a month in 2010. Such raises cut earnings per share by about 5% in 2010 and by 12% in 2011. As a result, Gou recently scaled back his annual growth target from 30% to 15%. Despite the setback, this intriguing (and until recently largely hidden) emerging multinational continues to deserve your attention, especially the next time you turn on your iPad.

Sources: Based on (1) *Bloomberg Businessweek*, 2010, Chairman Gou, September 13: 58–69; (2) *Bloomberg Businessweek*, 2011, How to beat the high cost of happy workers, May 9: 39–40; (3) www.foxconn.com.

BRIC

Brazil, Russia, India, and China.

BRICS

Brazil, Russia, India, China, and South Africa

(GDP) measured at purchasing power parity.[5] Brazil, Russia, India, and China—now known as **BRIC** in the new jargon—command more attention. **BRICS** (that is: BRIC + South Africa) has become a newer buzzword. Many local firms rise to the challenge, not only effectively competing at home but also launching offensives abroad.[6] Overall, more than a quarter of the worldwide FDI outflows are now generated by these emerging multinationals from emerging economies.

As a result, modifying (or even abandoning) the traditional "global strategy" has increasingly been entertained.[7] Figure 1.1 illustrates the global economy as a pyramid. The top consists of about one billion people with annual per capita income greater than $20,000. These are mostly people in the Triad and a small percentage of rich people in the rest of the world. Another billion people, making $2,000 to $20,000 a year, make up the second tier. The vast majority of humanity—about five billion people—make less than $2,000 a year and comprise the **base of the pyramid (BOP)**, which has been ignored by traditional "global strategy." Many MNEs from developed economies believed that there was no money to be made in BOP markets. Recent developments in the global economy have shaken this erroneous belief. General Motors (GM) now sells more cars in China than in the United States, and China has surpassed the United States as the world's largest car market. If MNEs from developed economies do not pay serious attention to BOP markets in emerging economies, local competitors such as India's Tata Motors and China's Geely will (see Emerging Markets 1.2). From the bottom (BOP) up, these new competitors increasingly go after the second and top tier markets overseas, creating serious competitive challenges to MNEs from developed economies.

base of the pyramid (BOP)

The vast majority of humanity, about five billion people, who make less than $2,000 a year.

FIGURE 1.1 The Global Economic Pyramid

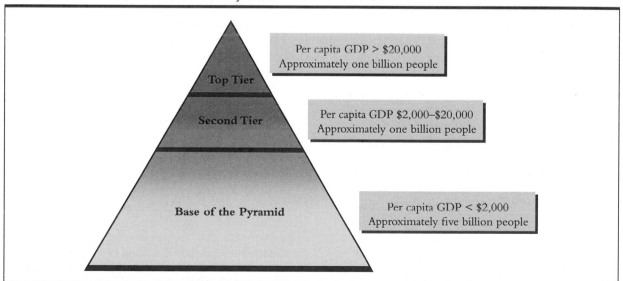

Sources: Adapted from (1) C. K. Prahalad & S. Hart, 2002, The fortune at the bottom of the pyramid, *Strategy+Business*, 26: 54–67; (2) S. Hart, 2005, *Capitalism at the Crossroads* (p. 111), Philadelphia: Wharton School Publishing.

EMERGING MARKETS 1.2 〉 〉

GE's Reverse Innovation from the Base of the Pyramid

Mulitnationals such as General Electric (GE) historically innovate new products in developed economies and then localize these products by tweaking and simplifying them for customers in emerging economies. Unfortunately, a lot of these expensive products meant for well-off customers at the top of the global economic pyramid flop at the base of the pyramid. This is not only because of the products' price tag, but also due to the lack of consideration for the specific needs and wants of local customers. Being the exact opposite, **reverse innovation** turns innovative products created for emerging economies into low-cost offerings for developed economies.

Take a look at GE's conventional ultrasound machines, originally developed in the United States and Japan and sold for $100,000 and up (as much as $350,000). In China, these expensive, bulky devices sold poorly because not every sophisticated hospital imaging center could afford them. GE's team in China realized that more than 80% of China's population relies on rural hospitals or clinics that are poorly funded. Conventional ultrasound machines are simply out of reach for these facilities. Patients thus have to travel to urban hospitals to access ultrasound. However, transportation to urban hospitals, especially for the sick and the pregnant, is challenging. Since most Chinese patients could not come to the ultrasound machines, the machines have to go to the patients. Scaling down its existing bulky, expensive, and complex ultrasound machines was not going to serve that demand. GE realized that it needed a revolutionary product—a compact, portable ultrasound machine. In 2002, GE in China launched its first compact ultrasound, which combined a regular laptop computer with sophisticated software. The machine sold for only $30,000. In 2008, GE introduced a new model that sold for $15,000, less than 15% of the price tag of its high-end conventional ultrasound models. While portable ultrasounds have naturally become a hit in China, especially in rural clinics, they have also generated dramatic growth throughout the world, including *developed* economies. These machines combine a new dimension previously unavailable to ultrasound machines—portability— with an unbeatable price in developed economies where

containing health care cost is increasingly paramount. Before the global recession hit, portable ultrasounds by 2008 were a $278 million global product line for GE, growing at 50% to 60% annually. Even in the midst of a severe global recession, this product line has been growing 25% annually in China.

GE's experience in developing portable ultrasound machines in China is not alone. For rural India, it has pioneered a $1,000 handheld electrocardiogram (ECG) device that brings down the cost by a margin of 60% to 80%. In the Czech Republic, GE developed an aircraft engine for small planes that slashes its cost by half. This allows GE to challenge Pratt & Whitney's dominance of the small turboprop market in developed economies.

Why is GE so enthusiastic about reverse innovation? GE's chairman and CEO Jeffrey Immelt wrote in a *Harvard Business Review* article:

> *To be honest, the company is also embracing reverse innovation for defensive reasons. If GE doesn't come up with innovations in poor countries and take them global, new competitors from the developing world—like Mindray, Suzlon, Goldwind, and Haier—will... GE has tremendous respect for traditional rivals like Siemens, Philips, and Rolls-Royce. But it knows how to compete with them; they will never destroy GE. By introducing products that create a new price-performance paradigm, however, the emerging giants very well could. Reverse innovation isn't optional; it's oxygen.*

Sources: Based on (1) *Economist*, 2011, Frugal healing, January 22: 73–74: (2) *Economist*, 2011, Life should be cheap, January 22: 16; (3) V. Govindarajan & R. Ramamurti, 2011, Reverse innovation, emerging markets, and global strategy, *Global Strategy Journal*, 1: 191–205; (4) J. Immelt, V. Govindarajan, & C. Trimble, 2009, How GE is disrupting itself, *Harvard Business Review*, October: 56–65; (5) C. K. Prahalad & R. Mashelkar, 2010, Innovation's holy grail, *Harvard Business Review*, July: 132–141; (6) *Wall Street Journal*, 2011, Medicine on the move, March 28.

reverse innovation
Low-cost innovation from emerging economies that has potential in developed economies.

Overall, this book can be considered as part of this broad movement in search of a better understanding of how to effectively strategize and compete around the globe, not being merely about "global strategy" per se. This book differentiates itself from existing global-strategy books by providing a more balanced coverage, not only in terms of the traditional "global strategy" and "non-global strategy," but also in terms of both MNEs' and local firms' perspectives. In addition to developed economies, this book also devotes extensive space to competitive battles waged in and out of emerging economies. In every chapter, at least one box deals with "emerging markets" that refer to competition within emerging economies or multinationals emerging from these economies that enhance your understanding of this new breed of global competitors. No other global-strategy book does this. In a nutshell, this is truly a *global* global-strategy book.

Why Study Global Strategy?

Strategy courses in general—and global strategy courses in particular—are typically the most valued courses in a business school.[8] Why study global strategy? Three compelling reasons emerge. First, the most sought-after and highest-paid business school graduates (both MBAs and undergraduates) are typically strategy consultants with global expertise. You can be one of them. Outside the consulting industry, if you aspire to join the top ranks of large firms, expertise in global strategy is often a prerequisite. While eventually international experience may be required to become an expatriate (expat) manager, knowledge of and interest in global strategy during your education will eventually make you a more ideal candidate to be selected.[9] So, don't forget to add a line on your resume that you have studied this strategically important course.

Second, even for graduates at large companies with no interest in working for the consulting industry and no aspiration to compete for top jobs, as well as those individuals who work at small firms or are self-employed, you may find yourself dealing with foreign-owned suppliers and buyers, competing with foreign-invested firms in your home market, and perhaps even selling and investing overseas. Or alternatively, you may find yourself working for a foreign-owned corporation, your previously domestic employer acquired by a foreign player, or your unit ordered to shut down for global consolidation. Approximately 80 million people worldwide, including six million Americans, one million British, and 18 million Chinese, are directly employed by foreign-owned firms. For example, in Africa, the largest private sector employer is Coca-Cola, with 65,000 employees. In the UK, the largest private sector employer is Tata with 45,000 employees. Understanding how strategic decisions are made may facilitate your own career in such organizations. If there is a strategic rationale to downsize your unit, you would want to be able to figure this out as soon as possible and be the first to post your resume online, instead of being the first to receive a pink slip. In other words, you want to be more *strategic*. After all, it is your career that is at stake. Don't be the last in the know!

Overall, in this age of globalization, "how do you keep from being Bangalored? Or Shanghaied?"[10] (That is, have your job outsourced to India or China.) To do this, you must first understand what strategy is, which is discussed next.

What Is Strategy?

Origin

strategic management
A way of managing the firm from a strategic, "big picture" perspective.

strategy
A firm's theory about how to compete successfully.

strategy as plan
A perspective that suggests that strategy is most fundamentally embodied in explicit, rigorous formal planning as in the military.

Derived from the ancient Greek word *strategos*, the word "strategy" originally referred to the "art of the general" or "generalship." Strategy has very strong military roots.[11] The oldest book on strategy, *The Art of War*, dates back to around 500 BC. It was authored by Sun Tzu, a Chinese military strategist.[12] Sun Tzu's most famous teaching is "Know yourself, know your opponents; encounter a hundred battles, win a hundred victories." The application of the principles of military strategy to business competition, known as **strategic management** (or **strategy** in short), is a more recent phenomenon developed since the 1960s.[13]

Plan versus Action

Because business strategy is a relatively young field (despite the long roots of military strategy), what defines strategy has been a subject of intense debate.[14] Three schools of thought have emerged (Table 1.1). The first "**strategy as plan**" school is the oldest. Drawing on the work of Carl von Clausewitz, a Prussian (German) military strategist of the 19th century,[15] this school suggests that strategy is embodied in the same explicit rigorous formal planning as in the military.

TABLE 1.1   What Is Strategy?

Strategy as plan
- "Concerned with drafting the plan of war and shaping the individual campaigns and, within these, deciding on the individual engagements" (von Clausewitz, 1976)[1]
- "A set of concrete plans to help the organization accomplish its goal" (Oster, 1994)[2]

Strategy as action
- "The art of distributing and applying military means to fulfill the ends of policy" (Liddel Hart, 1967)[3]
- "A pattern in a stream of actions or decisions" (Mintzberg, 1978)[4]
- "The creation of a unique and valuable position, involving a different set of activities ... making trade-offs in competing ... creating fit among a company's activities" (Porter, 1996)[5]

Strategy as integration
- "The determination of the basic long-term goals and objectives of an enterprise, and the adoption of courses of action and the allocation of resources necessary for carrying out these goals" (Chandler, 1962)[6]
- "The major intended and emergent initiatives undertaken by general managers on behalf of owners, involving utilization of resources to enhance the performance of firms in their external environments" (Nag, Hambrick, and Chen, 2007)[7]
- "The analyses, decisions, and actions an organization undertakes in order to create and sustain competitive advantages" (Dess, Lumpkin, and Eisner, 2008)[8]

Sources: Based on (1) C. von Clausewitz, 1976, *On War*, vol. 1 (p. 177), London: Kegan Paul; (2) S. Oster, 1994, *Modern Competitive Analysis*, 2nd ed. (p. 4), New York: Oxford University Press; (3) B. Liddell Hart, 1967, *Strategy*, 2nd rev. ed. (p. 321), New York: Meridian; (4) H. Mintzberg, 1978, Patterns in strategy formulation (p. 934), *Management Science*, 24: 934–948; (5) M. Porter, 1996, What is strategy? (pp. 68, 70, 75), *Harvard Business Review*, 74: 61–78; (6) A. Chandler, 1962, *Strategy and Structure* (p. 13), Cambridge, MA: MIT Press; (7) R. Nag, D. Hambrick, & M. Chen, 2007, What is strategic management, really? *Strategic Management Journal*, 28: 935–955; (8) G. Dess, G. T. Lumpkin, & A. Eisner, 2008, *Strategic Management*, 4th ed. (p. 8), Chicago: McGraw-Hill Irwin.

However, the planning school has been challenged by the likes of Liddell Hart, a British military strategist of the early 20th century, who argued that the key to strategy is a set of flexible goal-oriented actions.[16] Hart favored an indirect approach, which seeks rapid flexible actions to avoid clashing with opponents head-on. Within the field of business strategy, this "**strategy as action**" school has been advocated by Henry Mintzberg, a Canadian scholar. Mintzberg posited that in addition to the **intended strategy** that the planning school emphasizes, there can be an **emergent strategy** that is not the result of "top down" planning but rather the outcome of a stream of smaller decisions from the "bottom up."[17] For example, Mark Zuckerberg, Facebook's founder, shared with a journalist in an interview:

> *We build things quickly and ship them. We get feedback. We iterate, we iterate, we iterate. We have these great signs around: "Done is better than perfect."*[18]

Each of these two schools of thought has merits and drawbacks. Strategy in Action 1.1 compares and contrasts them by drawing on real strategies used by the German and French militaries in 1914. The Opening Case suggests that the very book you are reading now comes from a multinational publisher that embraces the "strategy as action" school.

Strategy as Theory

Although the debate between the planning school and action school is difficult to resolve, many managers and scholars have realized that, in reality, the essence of strategy is likely to be a *combination* of both planned deliberate actions and unplanned emergent activities, thus leading to a "**strategy as integration**" school. First advocated by Alfred Chandler,[19] an American business historian, this more balanced "strategy as integration" school of thought has been adopted in many textbooks and is the perspective we embrace here. Following Peter Drucker, an Austrian-American management guru, we extend the "strategy as integration" school by defining strategy as *a firm's theory about how to compete successfully*. In other words, if we have to define strategy with one word, our choice is neither plan nor action—it is *theory*.

According to Drucker, "a valid theory that is clear, consistent, and focused is extraordinarily powerful."[20] Table 1.2 outlines the four advantages associated with our "strategy as theory" definition. First, it capitalizes on the insights of both planning and action schools. This is because a firm's theory of how to compete will simply remain an idea until it has been translated into action. Thus, formulating a theory (advocated by the planning school as **strategy formulation**) is merely a first step; implementing it through a series of actions (noted by the action school as **strategy implementation**) is a necessary second part. Although the cartoon in Figure 1.2 humorously portrays these two activities as separate endeavors, in reality, good strategists do both. Graphically shown in Figure 1.3, a strategy entails a firm's assessment at point A of its own strengths (S) and weaknesses (W), its desired performance levels at point B, and the opportunities (O) and threats (T) in the environment.[21] Such a **SWOT analysis** resonates very well with Sun Tzu's teaching on the importance of knowing "yourself" and "your opponents." After such an assessment, the firm formulates its theory on how to best connect points A and B. In other words, the broad arrow becomes its intended strategy. However, given so many uncertainties, not all intended strategies may prove successful, and some may become unrealized strategies. On the other hand, other unintended actions may become emergent

---

strategy as action
A perspective that suggests that strategy is most fundamentally reflected by firms' pattern of actions.

intended strategy
A strategy that is deliberately planned for.

emergent strategy
A strategy based on the outcome of a stream of smaller decisions from the "bottom up."

strategy as integration
A perspective that suggests that strategy is neither solely about plan nor action and that strategy integrates elements of both schools of thought.

strategy formulation
The crafting of a firm's strategy.

strategy implementation
The actions undertaken to carry out a firm's strategy.

SWOT analysis
A strategic analysis of a firm's internal strengths (S) and weaknesses (W) and the opportunities (O) and threats (T) in the environment.

STRATEGY IN ACTION 1.1

German and French Military Strategy, 1914

Although Germany and France are now the best of friends within the European Union (EU), they had fought for hundreds of years (the last war in which they butted heads was World War II). Prior to the commencement of hostilities that led to World War I in August 1914, both sides had planned for a major clash.

Known as the Schlieffen Plan, the German plan was meticulous. Focusing on the right wing, German forces would smash through Belgium. Every day's schedule of march was fixed in advance: Brussels would be taken by the 19th day, the French frontier crossed on the 22nd, and Paris conquered and a decisive victory attained by the 39th. Heeding Carl von Clausewitz's warning that military plans that left room for the unexpected could result in disaster, the Germans with infinite care had endeavored to plan for every contingency except one—flexibility.

Known as Plan 17, the French plan was a radical contrast to the German plan. Humiliated in the 1870 Franco–Prussian War, during which France lost two provinces (Alsace and Lorraine), the French were determined to regain their lost territories. However, the French had a smaller population and thus a smaller army. Since the French army could not match the German army man for man, the French military emphasized the individual initiatives, actions, and bravery (known as *élan vital*, the all-conquering will). A total of five sentences from Plan 17 was all that was shown to the generals who would

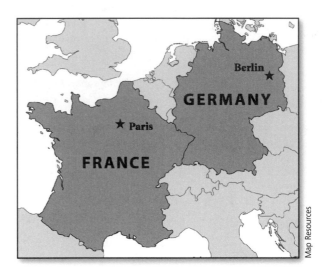

Map Resources

lead a million soldiers into battle. As a strategy exercise, we can speculate that Sentence 1 would be "Target Berlin," Sentence 2 "Recover Alsace and Lorraine," and the last sentence "Good luck!" Now, fill in the blanks for the two other sentences—it won't be too hard.

Sources: Based on (1) B. Tuchman, 1962, *The Guns of August*, New York: Macmillan; (2) US Military Academy, 2008, *Map: Northwest Europe 1914*, Department of History, www.dean.usma.edu.

TABLE 1.2 Four Advantages of the "Strategy as Theory" Definition

- Integrating both planning and action schools
- Leveraging the concept of "theory," which serves two purposes (explanation and prediction)
- Requiring replications and experimentations
- Understanding the difficulty of strategic change

© Cengage Learning

strategies with a thrust toward point B. Overall, this definition of strategy enables us to retain the elegance of the planning school with its more orthodox logical approach, and to entertain the flexibility of the action school with its more dynamic experimental character.

FIGURE 1.2   Strategy Formulation and Strategy Implementation

Source: Harvard Business Review, October 2011 (p. 40).

Second, this new definition rests on a simple but powerful idea, the concept of "theory." The word "theory" often frightens students and managers because it implies an image of "abstract" and "impractical." But it shouldn't.[22] A theory is merely a statement describing relationships between a set of phenomena. At its core, a theory serves two powerful purposes: to *explain* the past and to *predict* the future.[23] If a theory is too complicated, nobody can understand, test, or use it. For example, the theory of gravity explains why some Foxconn employees committing suicide were successful by jumping from a high-rise (see Emerging Markets 1.1). It also predicts that should you (hypothetically) harbor such a dangerous tendency, you will be equally successful by doing the same. Likewise, Wal-Mart's theory, "everyday low prices," captures the essence of all the activities performed by its two million employees in 8,500 stores in 15 countries. This theory explains why Wal-Mart has been successful in the past. After all, who doesn't like "everyday low prices"? It also predicts that Wal-Mart will continue to do well by focusing on low prices.

Third, a theory proven successful in one context during one time period does not necessarily mean it will be successful elsewhere.[24] As a result, a hallmark of theory building and development is **replication**—repeated testing of theory under a variety of conditions to establish its applicable boundaries. In natural sciences, this is known as continuous experimentation. For instance, after several decades of experiments in outer space, we now know that the theory of gravity is earth bound and that it does not apply in outer space. This seems to be the essence of business strategy.[25] Firms successful in one

replication

Repeated testing of theory under a variety of conditions to establish its applicable boundaries.

FIGURE 1.3 The Essence of Strategy

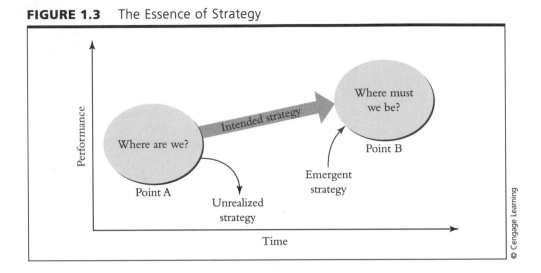

© Cengage Learning

product or country market—that is, having proven the merit of their theory once—constantly seek to expand into newer markets and replicate their previous success. In new markets, firms sometimes succeed and other times fail. As a result, these firms are able to gradually establish the *limits* of their particular theory about how to compete successfully. For instance, Wal-Mart's theory failed in both Germany and South Korea, and the retail giant had to pull out from those markets recently.

Finally, the "strategy as theory" perspective helps us understand why it is often difficult to change strategy.[26] Imagine how hard it is to change an established theory. The reason that certain theories are widely accepted is because of their past success. However, past success does not guarantee future success. Although scientists are supposed to be objective, they are also human. Many scientists may be unwilling to concede the failure of their favorite theories even in the face of repeatedly failed tests. Think about how much resistance from the scientific establishment that Galileo, Copernicus, and Einstein had to face initially. The same holds true for strategists. Bosses were promoted to current positions because of their past success in developing and implementing "old" theories. National heritage, organizational politics, and personal career considerations may prevent many bosses from admitting the evident failure of an existing strategy. Yet, the history of scientific progress suggests that although difficult, it is possible to change established theories. If enough failures in testing are reported and enough researchers raise doubts about certain theories, their views, which may be marginalized initially, gradually drive out failed theories and introduce better ones. The painful process of strategic change in many firms such as Microsoft is similar (see the Closing Case). Usually a group of managers, backed by performance data, challenge the current strategy. They propose a new theory on how to compete more effectively, which initially is often marginalized by top management. But eventually, the momentum of the new theory may outweigh the resistance of the old strategy, thus leading to some strategic change. For example, Wal-Mart recently changed its strategy from "everyday low prices" to "save money, live better" in order to soften its undesirable image as a ruthless cost cutter.

Overall, strategy is not a rulebook, a blueprint, or a set of programmed instructions. Rather, it is a firm's theory about how to compete successfully, a unifying theme that gives coherence to its various actions. Just as military strategies and generals have to be studied simultaneously, an understanding of business strategies around the globe would be incomplete without an appreciation of the role top managers play as strategists. Although mid-level and lower-level managers need to understand strategy, they typically lack the perspective and confidence to craft and execute a *firm-level* strategy. A **top management team (TMT)** led by the chief executive officer (CEO) must exercise leadership by making strategic choices. Since the directions and operations of a firm typically are a reflection of its top managers, their personal preferences based on their own culture, background, and experience may affect firm strategy.[27] Therefore, although this book focuses on firm strategies, it is also about strategists who lead their firms. By definition, strategic work is different from non-strategic (tactical) work. Drawing on the wisdom of A. G. Lafley, chairman and CEO of Procter & Gamble (P&G) between 2000 and 2009, Table 1.3 outlines the nature of the highest level of strategic work that only the CEO can do.

top management team (TMT)

The team consisting of the highest level of executives of a firm led by the CEO.

TABLE 1.3 Strategic Work Only the CEO Can Do

- Identify the meaningful outside and link it with the internal organization
- Define what business the firm is in (and *not* in)
- Balance present and future
- Shape values and standards

Source: Adapted from A. G. Lafley, 2009, What only the CEO can do, *Harvard Business Review*, May: 54–62. Lafley was chairman and CEO of P&G, 2000–2009.

Fundamental Questions in Strategy

Although strategy around the globe is a vast area, we will focus our attention only on the *most fundamental* issues, which act to define a field and to orient the attention of students, practitioners, and scholars in a certain direction. Specifically, we will address the following four fundamental questions:[28]

- Why do firms differ?

- How do firms behave?

- What determines the scope of the firm?

- What determines the success and failure of firms around the globe?

Why Do Firms Differ?

In every modern economy, firms, just like individuals, differ. This question thus seems obvious and hardly generates any debate. However, much of our knowledge about "the firm" is from research on firms in the United States and to a lesser extent the United Kingdom, both of which are embedded in what is known as Anglo-American capitalism.

A smaller literature deals with other Western countries such as Germany, France, and Italy, collectively known as continental European capitalism. While some differences between Anglo-American and continental European firms have been reported (such as a shorter and a longer investment horizon, respectively),[29] the contrast between these Western firms and their Japanese counterparts is more striking.[30] For example, instead of using costly acquisitions typically found in the West, Japanese firms extensively employ a network form of supplier management, giving rise to the term *keiretsu* (interfirm network).[31] The word *keiretsu* is now frequently used in English-language publications without the explanation given in the parentheses—an educated reader of *BusinessWeek*, *Economist,* or *Wall Street Journal* is presumed to already understand it.

More recently, as the strategy radar screen scans the business landscape in emerging economies, more puzzles emerge. For example, it is long established that economic growth can hardly occur in poorly regulated economies. Yet given China's strong economic growth and its underdeveloped formal institutional structures (such as a lack of effective courts), how can China achieve rapid rates of economic growth? Among many answers to this intriguing puzzle, a partial answer suggests that interpersonal networks and relationships (*guanxi*), cultivated by managers, may serve as informal substitutes for formal institutional support. In other words, interpersonal relationships among managers are translated into an interfirm strategy of relying on networks and alliances to grow the firm, which, in the aggregate, contributes to the growth of the economy.[32] As a result, the word *guanxi* has now become the most famous Chinese business word to appear in English-language media, again often without the explanation provided in parentheses. Similarly, the Korean word *chaebol* (large business group) and the Russian word *blat* (relationships) have also entered the English vocabulary. Behind each of these deceptively simple words lie some fundamental differences on how to compete around the world.[33]

How Do Firms Behave?

strategy tripod

A framework that suggests that strategy as a discipline has three "legs" or key perspectives: industry-based, resource-based, and institution-based views.

This question focuses on what determines firms' theories about how to compete. Figure 1.4 identifies three leading perspectives that collectively lead to a **strategy tripod**.[34] The industry-based view suggests that the strategic task is mainly to examine the competitive forces affecting an industry, and to stake out a position that is less vulnerable relative to these five forces. While the industry-based view primarily focuses on the *external* opportunities and threats (the O and T in a SWOT analysis), the resource-based view largely concentrates on the *internal* strengths and weaknesses (S and W) of the firm. This view posits that it is firm-specific capabilities that differentiate successful firms from failing ones.

Recently, an institution-based view has emerged to account for differences in firm strategy.[35] This view argues that in addition to industry-level and firm-level conditions, firms also need to take into account the influences of formal and informal rules of the game. A better understanding of the formal and informal rules of the game explains a great deal behind Microsoft's strategic changes in China (see the Closing Case).

Collectively viewed as a strategy tripod, these three views form the backbone of the first part of this book, Foundations of Global Strategy (Chapters 2, 3, and 4). They shed considerable light on the question "How do firms behave?"[36]

FIGURE 1.4   The Strategy Tripod: Three Leading Perspectives on Strategy

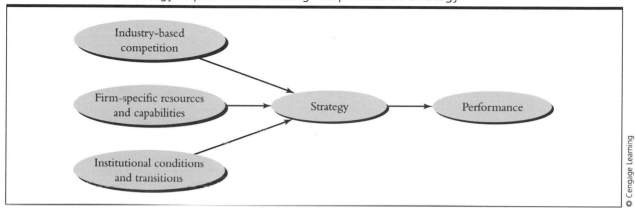

© Cengage Learning

What Determines the Scope of the Firm?

This question first focuses on the growth of the firm. Most firms seem to have a lingering love affair with growth. The motivation to grow is fueled by the excitement associated with such growth. For publicly listed firms, without growth, the share price will not grow. However, there is a limit beyond which further growth may backfire. Then downsizing, downscoping, and withdrawals are often necessary. In other words, answers to the question, "What determines the scope of the firm?" pertain not only to the growth of the firm, but also to the contraction of the firm.

In developed economies, a conglomeration strategy featuring unrelated product diversification, which was in vogue in the 1960s and the 1970s, was found to destroy value and was largely discredited by the 1980s and the 1990s. Witness how many firms are still trying to divest and downsize in the West. However, this strategy seems to be alive and well in many emerging economies. Although puzzled Western media and consultants often suggest that conglomerates destroy value and should be dismantled in emerging economies, empirical evidence suggests otherwise. Recent research in emerging economies reports that some (but not all) units affiliated with conglomerates may enjoy higher profitability than independent firms, pointing out some discernible performance *benefits* associated with conglomeration.[37] One reason behind such a contrast lies in the institutional differences between developed and emerging economies. Viewed through an institutional lens, conglomeration may make sense (at least to some extent) in emerging economies because this strategy and its relatively positive link with performance may be a function of the level of institutional (under)development in these countries.[38]

In addition to product scope, careful deliberation of the geographic scope is important.[39] On the one hand, for companies aspiring to become global leaders, a strong position in *each* of the three Triad markets is often necessary. Expanding market position in key emerging economies, such as BRIC, may also be desirable. But on the other hand, it is not realistic that all companies can, or should, "go global." Given the recent hype to "go global," many companies may have entered too many countries too quickly and may be subsequently forced to withdraw.

What Determines the Success and Failure of Firms Around the Globe?

This focus on performance, more than anything else, defines the field of strategic management and international business.[40] We are not only interested in *acquiring* and *leveraging* competitive advantage, but also in *sustaining* such advantages over time and across regions. All three major perspectives that form the strategy tripod ultimately seek to answer this question.

The industry-based view posits that the degree of competitiveness in an industry largely determines firm performance. Shown in the Opening Case, the structure of the college textbook publishing industry, such as stable brands and high entry barriers, explains a great deal behind the dominance of the top three incumbents in business and economics college textbook publishing around the world.

The resource-based view suggests that firm-specific capabilities drive performance differences. Within the same industry, while some firms win, others struggle. Winning firms such as South-Western Cengage Learning tend to have valuable, unique, and hard-to-imitate capabilities, such as having a "Mr. Global" born in China to author *Global Strategy*, which will inherently have a more global flavor. Rival publishers have a hard time competing with *Global Strategy*, because a majority of other textbook authors were born in the United States and, despite their best efforts to globalize their work, will naturally exhibit a US-centric tendency.

The institution-based view argues that institutional forces also provide an answer to differences in firm performance. As illustrated by our Opening Case, firms must "think global" and "act local" *simultaneously*. Firms that do not do their "homework" by getting to know the various formal and informal rules of the game in overseas markets are unlikely to emerge as winners in the global marketplace.

Overall, although there are many debates among the different schools of thought, the true determinants of firm performance probably involve a *combination* of these three-pronged forces (see Figure 1.4).[41] While these three views present relatively straightforward answers, the reality of global competition often makes these answers more complex and murky. If you survey ten managers from ten countries on what performance exactly is, you may get ten different answers. Long-term or short-term performance?[42] Financial returns or market shares? Profits maximized for shareholders or benefits maximized for **stakeholders** (individuals and organizations that are affected by a firm's actions and thus have a stake in how a firm is managed)? Without consensus on the performance measures, it is difficult to find an easy, uncontroversial answer. Instead of focusing on a single financial or economic bottom line, some firms adopt a **triple bottom line**, which consists of economic, social, and environmental dimensions (see Chapter 12). Another solution is to adopt a **balanced scorecard**, which is a performance evaluation method from the customer, internal, innovation and learning, and financial perspectives. Outlined in Table 1.4, the balanced scorecard can be thought of as the dials in a flight cockpit. To fly an aircraft, pilots simultaneously need a lot of information, such as air speed, altitude, and bearing. To manage a firm, strategists have similar needs. But pilots and strategists also cannot afford **information overload**—too much information. The balanced scorecard summarizes and channels a large volume of information to a relatively small number of crucial dimensions.

stakeholder
Any group or individual who can affect or is affected by the achievement of the organization's objectives.

triple bottom line
A performance yardstick consisting of economic, social, and environmental performance.

balanced scorecard
A performance evaluation method from the customer, internal, innovation and learning, and financial perspectives.

information overload
Too much information to process.

TABLE 1.4   Performance Goals and Measures from the Balanced Scorecard

- From a customer perspective: How do customers see us?
- From an internal business perspectives: What must we excel at?
- From an innovation and learning perspective: Can we continue to improve and create value?
- From a financial perspective: How do we look to shareholders?

Source: Adapted from R. Kaplan & D. Norton, 2005, The balanced scorecard: Measures that drive performance, *Harvard Business Review*, July: 172–180.

In summary, these four questions represent some of the most fundamental puzzles in strategy. While other questions can be raised, they all relate in one way or another to these four. Thus, answering these four questions will be the primary focus of this book and will be addressed in *every* chapter.

What Is Global Strategy?

"Global strategy" has at least two meanings. First, as noted earlier, the traditional and narrowly defined notion of "global strategy" refers to a particular theory on how to compete and is centered on offering standardized products and services on a worldwide basis.[43] This strategy obviously is only relevant for large Triad-based MNEs active in many countries. Smaller firms in developed economies and most firms in emerging economies operating in only one or a few countries may find little use for this definition.

Second, "global strategy" can also refer to "strategy with a comprehensive worldwide perspective."[44] It essentially means any strategy outside one's home country. Americans seem especially fond of using the word "global" this way, which essentially becomes the same as "international." For example, Wal-Mart's first foray outside the United States in 1991 was widely hailed as evidence that Wal-Mart had "gone global." In fact, Wal-Mart had only expanded into Mexico at that time. While this was an admirable first step for Wal-Mart, the action was similar to Singapore firms doing business in Malaysia or German companies investing in Austria. To many internationally active Asian and European firms, there is nothing significantly "global" about these activities in neighboring countries. So why is there the hype about the word "global," especially among Americans? Historically, the vast US domestic markets made it unnecessary for many firms to seek overseas markets. As a result, when many US companies do venture abroad, even in countries as close as Mexico, they are likely to be fascinated about their "discovery of global markets." Since everyone seems to want a more exciting "global" strategy rather than a plain-vanilla "international" one, calling non-US (or non-domestic) markets "global" markets becomes a cliché.

So what do we mean by "global strategy" in *this* book? *Neither* of the preceding definitions will do. Here, **global strategy** is defined as *strategy of firms around the globe*—essentially various firms' theories about how to compete successfully. Seeking to break out of the US-centric straightjacket, this book deals with both the strategy of MNEs (some of which may fit into the traditional narrow global strategy definition)

global strategy

(1) Strategy of firms around the globe. (2) A particular form of international strategy, characterized by the production and distribution of standardized products and services on a worldwide basis.

and the strategy of smaller firms (some of which may have an international presence, while others may be purely domestic). These firms compete in both developed and emerging economies. We do *not* exclusively concentrate on firms doing business abroad, which is the traditional domain of global-strategy books. To the extent that international business involves two sides—namely, domestic firms and foreign entrants—an exclusive focus on foreign entrants only covers one side and, thus, paints a partial picture. The strategy of domestic firms is equally important. As a result, a truly *global* global-strategy book needs to provide a balanced coverage. Like our publisher in the Opening Case, our motto is: Think global, act local.[45] This is the challenge we will take on throughout this book.

What Is Globalization?

globalization

The close integration of countries and peoples of the world.

Globalization, generally speaking, is the close integration of countries and peoples of the world. This abstract five-syllable word is now frequently heard and debated. Those who approve of globalization count its contributions to include greater economic growth and standards of living, increased technology sharing, and more extensive cultural integration. Critics argue that globalization causes the global recession, undermines wages in rich countries, exploits workers in poor countries, and gives MNEs too much power. This section (1) outlines three views on globalization, (2) recommends the pendulum view, and (3) introduces the idea of semiglobalization.

Three Views on Globalization

Depending on what sources you read, globalization could be

- A new force sweeping through the world in recent times

- A long-run historical evolution since the dawn of human history

- A pendulum that swings from one extreme to another from time to time

An understanding of these views helps put the debate about globalization in perspective. First, opponents suggest that it is a new phenomenon beginning in the late 20th century, driven by recent technological innovations and a Western ideology focused on exploiting and dominating the world through MNEs. The arguments against globalization focus on an ideal world free of environmental stress, social injustice, and sweatshop labor but present few clear alternatives to the present economic order. Advocates and anti-globalization protesters often argue that globalization needs to be slowed down, if not stopped.

A second view contends that globalization has always been part of human history. Historians debate whether globalization started 2,000 or 8,000 years ago. MNEs existed for more than two millennia, with their earliest traces discovered in Phoenician, Assyrian, and Roman times.[46] International competition from low-cost countries is nothing new. In the first century AD, the Roman emperor Tiberius was so concerned about the massive quantity of low-cost Chinese silk imports that he imposed the world's first known import quota of textiles.[47] In a nutshell, globalization is nothing new and will always exist.

A third view suggests that globalization is the "closer integration of the countries and peoples of the world which has been brought about by the enormous reduction of the costs of transportation and communication and the breaking down of artificial barriers to the flows of goods, services, capital, knowledge, and (to a lesser extent) people across borders."[48] Globalization is neither recent nor one-directional. It is, more accurately, a process similar to the swing of a pendulum.

The Pendulum View on Globalization

The pendulum view probably makes the most sense because it can help us understand the ups and downs of globalization. The current era of globalization originated in the aftermath of World War II, when major Western countries committed to global trade and investment. However, between the 1950s and the 1970s, this view was not widely shared. Communist countries, such as the former Soviet Union and China, sought to develop self-sufficiency. Many non-communist developing countries such as Brazil, India, and Mexico focused on protecting domestic industries. But refusing to participate in global trade and investment ended up breeding uncompetitive industries. In contrast, four developing economies in Asia—namely, Hong Kong, Singapore, South Korea, and Taiwan—earned their stripes as the "Four Tigers" by participating in the global economy. They became the *only* economies once recognized as less developed (low-income) by the World Bank to have subsequently achieved developed (high-income) status.

Inspired by the Four Tigers, more countries and regions—such as China in the late 1970s, Latin America in the mid 1980s, Central and Eastern Europe in the late 1980s, and India in the 1990s—realized that joining the global economy was a must. As these countries started to emerge as new players in the global economy, they became known as "emerging economies." As a result, globalization rapidly accelerated in the 1990s.

The pendulum view suggests, however, that globalization is unable to keep going in one direction. Rapid globalization in the 1990s saw some significant backlash. First, the rapid growth of globalization led to the historically inaccurate view that globalization is new. Second, it created fear among many people in developed economies that they would lose jobs. Emerging economies not only seem to attract many low-end manufacturing jobs away from developed economies, but also increasingly appear to threaten some high-end jobs. Finally, some factions in emerging economies complained against the onslaught of MNEs, alleging that MNEs not only destroy local companies, but also local cultures, values, and the environment.

While small-scale acts of vandalizing McDonald's restaurants are reported in several countries, the December 1999 anti-globalization protests in Seattle and the September 2001 terrorist attacks in New York and Washington are undoubtedly the most visible and most extreme acts of anti-globalization forces at work. As a result, international travel was curtailed, and global trade and investment flows slowed in the early 2000s. Then in the mid-2000s, worldwide GDP, cross-border trade, and per capita GDP all soared to historically high levels. But starting in 2008, the world was engulfed in a global economic crisis now known as the Great Recession. This recession has been characterized by a painful financial meltdown and numerous government bailouts. Rightly or wrongly, many people have blamed globalization for the recent crisis.

After unprecedented intervention throughout developed economies whose governments ended up being the largest shareholders of many banks, there is growing confidence that the global economy has now turned the corner and that the global recession is now ending. However, economic recovery is likely to be slow in developed economies, whereas emerging economies have rebounded faster.[49]

risk management
The identification and assessment of risks and the preparation to minimize the impact of high-risk, unfortunate events.

The recession reminds all firms and managers of the importance of **risk management**—the identification and assessment of risks and the preparation to minimize the impact of high-risk, unfortunate events.[50] As a technique to prepare and plan for multiple scenarios, **scenario planning** is now used by many firms around the world.[51] As far as the direction of globalization is concerned, the recovery may see more protectionist measures because various governments' stimulus packages and job creation schemes emphasize policies to "hire locals" and "buy national" (such as the "buy American" policy in the United States and the promotion of "indigenous innovation" in China). In short, the pendulum is swinging back.

scenario planning
A technique to prepare and plan for multiple scenarios (either high or low risk).

Like the proverbial elephant, globalization is seen by everyone and rarely comprehended. The suddenness and ferocity of the recent economic crisis surprised everybody, ranging from central bankers to academic experts. Remember, all of us felt sorry when we read the story of a bunch of blind men trying to figure out the shape and form of the elephant. We really shouldn't. Although we are not blind, our task is more challenging than the blind men with a standing animal. Our beast—globalization—does not stand still and is often moving, back and forth (!). Yet, we try to live with it, avoid being crushed by it, and even profit from it. Overall, relative to the other two views, the view of globalization as a pendulum is more balanced and more realistic. In other words, globalization has both rosy and dark sides, and it changes over time.

Semiglobalization

Despite the hype, globalization is not complete. Do we really live in a globalized world? Is doing business abroad just as easy as at home? Obviously not. Most measures of market integration, such as trade and FDI, have recently scaled new heights but still fall far short of becoming a single, globally integrated market. In other words, what we have may be labeled **semiglobalization**, which is more complex than extremes of total isolation and total globalization. Semiglobalization suggests that barriers to market integration at borders are high, but not high enough to completely insulate countries from each other.[52]

semiglobalization
A perspective that suggests that barriers to market integration at borders are high but not high enough to completely insulate countries from each other.

Semiglobalization calls for more than one way of strategizing business around the globe. Total isolation on a nation-state basis would suggest localization—a strategy of treating each country as a unique market. So an MNE marketing products to 100 countries will need to come up with 100 versions of local cars or drinks. This approach is clearly too costly. Total globalization, on the other hand, would lead to standardization, or a strategy of treating the entire world as one market. The MNE in our previous example can just market one version of "world car" or "world drink." The world obviously is not that simple. Between total isolation and total globalization, semiglobalization has no single right strategy, resulting in a wide variety of strategic experimentations and changes (see the Closing Case). Overall, (semi)globalization is neither to be opposed as a menace nor to be celebrated as a panacea; it is to be *engaged*.

Global Strategy and the Globalization Debate

Anti-globalization protests in Seattle (1999). 9/11 terrorist attacks (2001) and the resultant War on Terror (still ongoing). Enron (2001). Global financial crisis (2008) and the Great Recession afterwards. The euro crisis (since 2010). Earthquake in Japan (2011). Occupy Wall Street (2011). These and many other challenges confronting strategists around the globe in the 21st century are enormous. This book is designed to help you make informed strategic choices in this complex and rapidly moving world.

A fundamental reason that many executives, policymakers, and scholars were caught off guard by the anti-globalization protests, the terrorist attacks, and the Occupy Wall Street movement is that they have failed to heed Sun Tzu's most famous maxim: "Know yourself, know your opponents." To know yourself calls for a thorough understanding of not only your strengths, but also your limitations. Many individuals fail to understand their limitations or simply choose to ignore them. Although relative to the general public, executives, policymakers, and scholars tend to be better educated and more cosmopolitan, they are likely to be biased—just like everybody else. Most of them, in both developed and emerging economies in the last two decades, are biased toward acknowledging the benefits of globalization.

Although it has long been known that globalization carries both benefits and costs, many executives, policymakers, and scholars have failed to take into sufficient account the social, political, and environmental costs associated with globalization. However, that these elites share certain perspectives on globalization does *not* mean that most other members of society share the same views. Unfortunately, many elites mistakenly assume that the rest of the world either is, or should be, more like "us." To the extent that powerful economic and political institutions are largely controlled by these elites, it is not surprising that some powerless and voiceless anti-globalization groups end up resorting to unconventional tactics, such as mass protests, to make their point.

nongovernmental organization (NGO)
Organization advocating causes such as the environment, human rights, and consumer rights that are not affiliated with government.

Many of the opponents of globalization are **nongovernmental organizations (NGOs)** such as environmentalists, human rights activists, and consumer groups. Ignoring them will be a grave failure in due diligence when doing business around the globe. Instead of viewing NGOs as opponents, many firms view them as partners. NGOs do raise a valid point when they insist that firms, especially MNEs, should have a broader concern for the various stakeholders affected by the MNEs' actions around the world.[53]

It is certainly interesting and perhaps alarming to note that as would-be business leaders who will shape the global economy in the future, current business school students already exhibit values and beliefs in favor of globalization similar to those held by executives, policymakers, and scholars and different from those held by the general public. Shown in Table 1.5, US business students have significantly more positive (almost one-sided) views toward globalization than the general public. While these data are based on US business students, my teaching and lectures around the world suggest that most business students around the world—regardless of their nationality—seem to share such positive views. This is not surprising. Both self-selection to study business and socialization within the curriculum, in which free trade is widely regarded as positive, may lead to certain attitudes in favor of globalization. Consequently, business students tend to focus more on the economic gains of globalization and be less concerned with its darker sides.

TABLE 1.5 Views on Globalization: American General Public versus Business Students

PERCENTAGE ANSWERING "GOOD" FOR THE QUESTION: OVERALL, DO YOU THINK GLOBALIZATION IS *GOOD* OR *BAD* FOR	GENERAL PUBLIC[1] (N = 1,024)	BUSINESS STUDENTS (AVERAGE AGE 22)[2] (N = 494)
US consumers like you	68%	96%
US companies	63%	77%
The US economy	64%	88%
Strengthening poor countries' economies	75%	82%

Sources: Based on (1) A. Bernstein, 2000, Backlash against globalization, *BusinessWeek*, April 24: 43; (2) M. W. Peng & H. Shin, 2008, How do future business leaders view globalization? *Thunderbird International Business Review* (p. 179), 50 (3): 175–182. All differences are statistically significant.

Current and would-be business leaders need to be aware of their own biases embodied in such one-sided views toward globalization. Since business schools aspire to train future business leaders by indoctrinating students with the dominant values managers hold, these results suggest that business schools may have largely succeeded in this mission. However, to the extent that current managers (and professors) have strategic blind spots, these findings are potentially alarming. They reveal that students already share these blind spots. Despite possible self-selection in choosing to major in business, there is no denying that student values are shaped, at least in part, by the educational experience provided by business schools. Knowing such limitations, professors and students need to work especially hard to break out of this mental straitjacket.

In order to combat the widespread tendency to have one-sided, rosy views, a significant portion of this book is devoted to the numerous debates that surround globalization.[54] Debates are systematically introduced in *every* chapter to provoke more critical thinking and discussion. Virtually all textbooks uncritically present knowledge "as is." The reality is that our field has no shortage of debates.[55] It is imperative that you be exposed to cutting-edge debates and encouraged to form your own views.[56] In addition, ethics is emphasized throughout the book. A featured Ethical Dilemma can be found in every chapter. Two whole chapters are devoted to ethics, norms, and cultures (Chapter 3) and corporate social responsibility (Chapter 14).

Organization of the Book

This book has three parts. The first part concerns *foundations*. Following this chapter, Chapters 2, 3, and 4 introduce the strategy tripod, consisting of the three leading perspectives on strategy: industry-based, resource-based, and institution-based views. Students will be systematically trained to use this tripod to analyze a variety of strategy problems. The second part covers *business-level strategies*. In contrast to most global-strategy books that focus on large MNEs, we start with the internationalization of small entrepreneurial firms (Chapter 5), followed by ways to enter foreign markets (Chapter 6), to leverage alliances and networks (Chapter 7), and to manage global competitive dynamics (Chapter 8). Finally, the third part deals with *corporate-level strategies*. Chapter 9 on diversifying, acquiring, and restructuring starts this part, followed by strategies to structure, learn, and innovate (Chapter 10), to govern the corporation around the world (Chapter 11), and to profit from corporate social responsibility (Chapter 12).

A unique organizing principle is a consistent focus on the strategy tripod and on the four fundamental questions regarding strategy in *all* chapters. Following this chapter, every chapter has a substantial "Debates and Extensions" section, which is followed by "The Savvy Strategist" section culminating a one-slide "Strategic Implications for Action" to drive home the important take-aways.

CHAPTER SUMMARY

1. **Offer a basic critique of the traditional, narrowly defined "global strategy"**
   - The traditional and narrowly defined notion of "global strategy" is characterized by the production and distribution of standardized products and services on a worldwide basis—in short, a "one size fits all" approach. This strategy has often backfired in practice.
   - As a *global* global-strategy book, this book provides a more balanced coverage, not only in terms of the traditional "global strategy" and "non-global strategy," but also in terms of both MNEs' and local firms' perspectives. Moreover, this book has devoted extensive space to emerging economies.

2. **Articulate the rationale behind studying global strategy**
   - To better compete in the corporate world that will appreciate expertise in global strategy.

3. **Define what is strategy and what is global strategy**
   - There is a debate between two schools of thought: "strategy as plan" and "strategy as action." This book, together with other leading textbooks, instead follows the "strategy as integration" school.
   - In this book, strategy is defined as a firm's theory about how to compete successfully, while global strategy is defined as strategy of firms around the globe.

4. **Outline the four fundamental questions in strategy**
   - The four fundamental questions are: (1) Why do firms differ? (2) How do firms behave? (3) What determines the scope of the firm? (4) What determines the success and failure of firms around the globe?
   - The three leading perspectives guiding our exploration are industry-based, resource-based, and institution-based views, which collectively form a strategy tripod.

5. **Participate in the debate on globalization with a reasonably balanced view and a keen awareness of your likely bias**
   - Some view globalization as a recent phenomenon, while others believe that it has been evolving since the dawn of human history.
   - We suggest that globalization is best viewed as a process similar to the swing of a pendulum.
   - Strategists need to know themselves (including their own biases) and know their opponents.

KEY TERMS

Balanced scorecard p. 18

Base of the pyramid (BOP) p. 7

BRIC p. 7

BRICS p. 7

Emergent strategy p. 11

Emerging economies
(emerging markets) p. 5

Foreign direct investment
(FDI) p. 5

Global strategy p. 19

Globalization p. 20

Information overload p. 18

Intended strategy p. 11

Multinational enterprise
(MNE) p. 5

Nongovernmental
organization (NGO) p. 23

Replication p. 13

Reverse innovation p. 9

Risk management p. 22

Scenario planning p. 22

Semiglobalization p. 22

Stakeholder p. 18

Strategic management p. 10

Strategy p. 10

Strategy as action p. 11

Strategy as integration p. 11

Strategy as plan p. 10

Strategy formulation p. 11

Strategy implementation
p. 11

Strategy tripod p. 16

SWOT analysis p. 11

Top management team
(TMT) p. 15

Triad p. 5

Triple bottom line p. 18

CRITICAL DISCUSSION QUESTIONS

1. A skeptical classmate says: "Global strategy is relevant for top executives such as CEOs in large companies. I am just a lowly student who will struggle to gain an entry-level job, probably in a small company. Why should I care about it?" How do you convince her that she should care about global strategy?

2. *ON ETHICS:* Some argue that globalization benefits citizens of rich countries. Others argue that globalization benefits citizens of poor countries. What are the ethical dilemmas here? What do you think?

3. *ON ETHICS:* Critics argue that MNEs, through FDI, allegedly both exploit the poor in poor countries and take jobs away from rich countries. If you were the CEO of an MNE from a developed economy or from an emerging economy, how would you defend your firm?

TOPICS FOR EXPANDED PROJECTS

1. The 2008 global financial crisis and the Great Recession since then have been devastating. However, not all industries and not all firms have suffered. Some may have profited from these events. Write a short paper describing how some industries and firms may have profited from the crisis and the recession.

2. As the CEO of an MNE from an emerging economy, use the strategy tripod to analyze what the leading challenges for your firm's internationalization will be. Present your analysis in the form of a short paper or visual presentation.

3. *ON ETHICS:* What are some of the darker sides (in other words, costs) associated with globalization? How can strategists make sure that the benefits of their various actions outweigh their drawbacks (such as job losses in developed economies and environmental damage in emerging economies)? Working individually or in teams, write a short paper describing at least three examples.

CLOSING CASE   ETHICAL DILEMMA

Emerging Markets: Microsoft's Evolving China Strategy

Microsoft's first decade in China was disastrous. It established a representative office in 1992 and then set up a wholly owned subsidiary, Microsoft (China), in 1995. The firm quickly realized that it didn't have a market share problem—everybody was using Windows. The problem was how to translate that market share into revenue, since everybody seemingly used pirated versions. Microsoft's solution? Sue violators in Chinese courts. But Microsoft lost such lawsuits regularly. Alarmed, the Chinese government openly promoted the free open-source Linux operating systems. For security reasons, the Chinese government was afraid that Microsoft's software might contain spyware for the US government. Internally, Microsoft's executives often disagreed with this confrontational strategy. Its country managers came and went—five in a five-year period. Two of them later wrote books criticizing this strategy. These books revealed that Microsoft's antipiracy policy was excessively heavy-handed. Their authors' efforts to educate their bosses in headquarters in Redmond, Washington (a Seattle suburb), were deeply frustrated.

Fast forward to 2007. President Hu Jintao visited Microsoft and paid Bill Gates a visit at his house as a dinner guest. "You are a friend to the Chinese people, and I am a friend of Microsoft," Hu told Gates. "Every morning I go to my office and use your software." Starting in the mid-2000s, the Chinese government required all government agencies to use legal software and all PC manufacturers to load legal software before selling to consumers. Prior to these

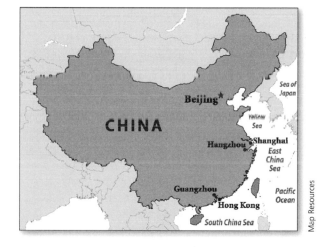

requirements, Lenovo, the leading domestic PC maker, had only shipped about 10% of its PCs that way. Many foreign (and some US) PC makers in China sold numerous machines "naked," implicitly inviting their customers to use cheap illegal software. From a disastrous start, Microsoft today is in a sweet spot in China. So, what happened?

In a nutshell, Microsoft radically changed its China strategy in its second decade in the country. In China, it became the "un-Microsoft": pricing at rock bottom instead of insisting on one very high "global price," abandoning the confrontational, litigious approach in defense of its intellectual property rights (IPR), and closely partnering with the government as opposed to fighting it (as it was doing back home when it was sued by the US government).

To be sure, the strategic changes were gradual. In 1998, Gates sent Craig Mundie, who headed the firm's public policy group, to Beijing. Mundie urged for strategic changes. He brought 25 of Microsoft's 100 vice presidents for a week-long "China Immersion Tour." Also in 1998, in part as a gesture of goodwill, Microsoft set up a research center in Beijing, which emerged to become the premier employer for top-notch software talent in China.

Within Microsoft, debates raged. Given the size of the country, changing the China strategy would inevitably lead to changing the global strategy, which was centered on a globally "one-size-fits-all" set of pricing (such as $560 for the Windows and Office toolset as in the United States). The heart of the question was: "Does Microsoft need China?" As late as in 2004, its CFO John Connors argued "No" publicly. Connors was not alone. On the face of it, nobody needed China less than Microsoft, which became a dynamo without significant China sales. However, in the long run, China's support of Linux could pose dangers to Microsoft. This was because a public infrastructure for a software industry built around Linux could generate an alternative ecosystem with more low-cost rivals that break free from dependence on Windows. By the early 2000s, concerned about this competitive threat, Gates increasingly realized that if the Chinese consumer were going to use pirated software, he would rather prefer it to be Microsoft's.

In 2003, Tim Chen, a superstar China manager at Motorola, was hired as Corporate Vice President and CEO of Greater China Region for Microsoft. Led by Chen, Microsoft quit suing people and tolerated piracy. Instead, it worked with the National Development Reform Commission to build a software industry, with the Ministry of Information Industry to jointly fund labs, and with the Ministry of Education to finance computer classrooms in rural areas. Overall, it elevated its R&D presence, trained thousands of professionals, and invested close to $100 million in local firms. In response to Chinese government concerns about the alleged US government spyware embedded in Microsoft's software, in 2003 the firm offered China (and 59 other countries) the fundamental source code for Windows and the right to substitute certain portions with local adaptation—something Microsoft had never done before. Only after such sustained and

multidimensional efforts did the Chinese government bless Microsoft's business by requiring that only legal software be used by government offices and be loaded by PC makers. Although Microsoft never disclosed how deep the discount it offered to the Chinese government, a legal package of Windows and Office could be bought for $3 (!). In Chen's own words:

> *With all this work, we start changing the perception that Microsoft is the company coming just to do antipiracy and sue people. We changed the company's image. We're the company that has the long-term vision. If a foreign company's strategy matches with the government's development agenda, the government will support you, even if they don't like you.*

Microsoft now has its own five-year plan to match the Chinese government's. But not all is rosy when working closely with the Chinese government. Problems have erupted on two fronts. First, Microsoft continues to be frustrated by the lack of sufficient progress on IPR. While not disclosing country-specific sales numbers, CEO Steve Balmer complained in an interview in 2010 that thanks to IPR problems, "China is a less interesting market to us than India … than Indonesia." Second, Microsoft has been criticized by free speech and human rights activists for its "cozy" relationship with the Chinese government. While largely unscrutinized by the media, the Chinese version of Microsoft MSN has long filtered certain words such as "democracy" and "freedom." In 2010 Google butted heads with the Chinese government and openly called for Microsoft (and other high-tech firms) to join its efforts. Microsoft refused. Instead, Microsoft took advantage of Google's trouble. It set up an alliance with Google's number one rival in China, Baidu, to provide English-language search results for Baidu from its Bing search engine. Such search results, of course, would be subject to political censorship. In 2011, anyone in China searching "jasmine," in either Chinese (on Baidu) or English (on Baidu and routed through Bing), would find this term to be unsearchable—thanks to the Jasmine Revolution (otherwise known as the Arab Spring).

Sources: Based on (1) *CFO*, 2004, Does Microsoft need China? August 10, www.cfo.com; (2) *Fortune*, 2007, How Microsoft conquered China, July 23: 84–90; (3) *Guardian*, 2010, We're staying in China, March 25, www.guardian.co.uk;

(4) *Guardian*, 2011, Microsoft strikes deal with China's biggest search engine Baidu, July 4, www.guardian.co.uk; (5) Microsoft, 2006, Microsoft in China, www.microsoft.com; (6) *South China Morning Post*, 2010, Beijing flexes its economic muscle, July 27: B8.

CASE DISCUSSION QUESTIONS

1. From an industry-based view, why does Microsoft feel threatened by Linux in China and globally?

2. From a resource-based view, what valuable and unique resources and capabilities does Microsoft have in the eyes of the Chinese users and the government?

3. From an institution-based view, what are the major lessons from Microsoft's strategic changes?

4. From a "strategy as theory" perspective, why is it hard to change strategy? How are strategic changes made?

5. *ON ETHICS:* As a Microsoft spokesperson, how do you respond to free speech and human rights critics?

NOTES

[**Journal acronyms**] *AMJ – Academy of Management Journal; AMP – Academy of Management Perspectives; AMR – Academy of Management Review; APJM – Asia Pacific Journal of Management; BW – BusinessWeek (before 2010) or Bloomberg Businessweek (since 2010); ETP – Entrepreneurship Theory and Practice; GSJ – Global Strategy Journal; HBR – Harvard Business Review; IJMR – International Journal of Management Reviews; JEL – Journal of Economic Literature; JEP – Journal of Economic Perspectives; JF – Journal of Finance; JIBS – Journal of International Business Studies; JIM – Journal of International Management; JM – Journal of Management; JMS – Journal of Management Studies; JWB – Journal of World Business; MBR – Multinational Business Review; MIR – Management International Review; OSt – Organization Studies; SMJ – Strategic Management Journal*

1. V. Govindarajan & A. Gupta, 2001, *The Quest for Global Dominance*, San Francisco: Jossey-Bass; S. Tallman, 2009, *Global Strategy*, West Sussex, UK: Wiley; G. Yip, 2003, *Total Global Strategy II*, Upper Saddle River, NJ: Pearson Prentice Hall.
2. J. Dunning, 1993, *Multinational Enterprises and the Global Economy* (p. 30), Reading, MA: Addison-Wesley. Other terms are multinational corporation (MNC) and transnational corporation (TNC), which are often used interchangeably with MNE. To avoid confusion, we will use MNE throughout this book.
3. K. Macharzina, 2001, The end of pure global strategies? (p. 106), *MIR*, 41: 105–108.
4. P. Ghemawat, 2007, *Redefining Global Strategy*, Boston: Harvard Business School Press.
5. M. W. Peng, 2013, *GLOBAL 2* (p. 6), Cincinnati: South-Western Cengage Learning.

6. J. Mathews, 2006, Dragon multinationals as new features of globalization in the 21st century, *APJM*, 23: 5–27; M. W. Peng, 2012, The global strategy of emerging multinationals from China, *GSJ*, 2: 97–107; S. Sun, M. W. Peng, R. Ben, & D. Yan, 2012, A comparative ownership advantage framework for cross-border M&As, *JWB*, 47: 4–16.
7. "Transnational" and "metanational" have been proposed to extend the traditional notion of "global strategy." See C. Bartlett & S. Ghoshal, 1989, *Managing Across Borders*, Boston: Harvard Business School Press; Y. Doz, J. Santos, & P. Williamson, 2001, *From Global to Metanational*, Boston: Harvard Business School Press. A more radical idea is to abandon "global strategy." See A. Rugman, 2005, *The Regional Multinationals*, Cambridge, UK: Cambridge University Press.
8. R. Barker, 2010, No, management is not a profession (p. 58), *HBR*, July: 52–60.
9. Expatriate managers often command significant premium in compensation. In US firms, their average total compensation package is $250,000–300,000. See M. W. Peng, 2011, *Global Business*, 2nd ed., Cincinnati: South-Western Cengage Learning.
10. *BW*, 2007, The changing talent game (p. 68), August 20: 68–71.
11. A. Carmeli & G. Markman, 2011, Capture, governance, and resilience: Strategy implications from the history of Rome, *SMJ*, 32: 322–341.
12. Sun Tzu, 1963, *The Art of War*, translation by S. Griffith, Oxford: Oxford University Press.
13. I. Ansoff, 1965, *Corporate Strategy*, New York: McGraw-Hill; D. Schendel & C. Hofer, 1979, *Strategic Management*, Boston: Little, Brown. D. Hambrick &

M. Chen, 2008, New academic fields as admittance-seeking social movements, *AMR*, 33: 32–54.

14. D. Collis & M. Rukstad, 2008, Can you say what your strategy is? *HBR*, April: 82–90; M. de Rond & R. Thietart, 2007, Choice, chance, and inevitability in strategy, *SMJ*, 28: 535–551.

15. K. Von Clausewitz, 1976, *On War*, London: Kegan Paul.

16. B. Liddell Hart, 1967, *Strategy*, New York: Meridian.

17. H. Mintzberg, 1994, *The Rise and Fall of Strategic Planning*, New York: Free Press. See also J. Bower & C. Gilbert, 2007, How managers' everyday decisions create or destroy your company's strategy, *HBR*, February: 72–79.

18. *BW*, 2011, Charlie Rose talks to Mark Zuckerberg, November 14: 50.

19. A. Chandler, 1962, *Strategy and Structure*, Cambridge, MA: MIT Press.

20. P. Drucker, 1994, The theory of the business (p. 96), *HBR*, September–October: 95–105.

21. S. Julian & J. Ofori-Dankwa, 2008, Toward an integrative cartography of two strategic issue diagnosis frameworks, *SMJ*, 29: 93–114.

22. C. Christensen & M. Raynor, 2003, Why hard-nosed executives should care about management theory, *HBR*, September: 67–74.

23. R. Wiltbank, N. Dew, S. Read, & S. Sarasvathy, 2006, What to do next? *SMJ*, 27: 981–998.

24. J. Camillus, 2008, Strategy as a wicked problem, *HBR*, May: 99–106.

25. E. Anderson & D. Simester, 2011, A step-by-step guide to smart business experiments, *HBR*, March: 98–105; J. Donahoe, 2011, How eBay developed a culture of experimentation, *HBR*, March: 93–97; G. Gavetti & J. Rivkin, 2005, How strategists really think, *HBR*, April: 54–63; C. Zook & J. Allen, 2011, The great repeatable business model, *HBR*, November: 107–114.

26. A. Pettigrew, R. Woodman, & K. Cameron, 2001, Studying organizational change and development, *AMJ*, 44: 697–713; T. Reay, K. Golden-Biddle, & K. Germann, 2006, Legitimizing a new role, *AMJ*, 49: 977–998.

27. D. Hambrick & P. Mason, 1984, Upper echelons, *AMR*, 9: 193–206; M. Porter, J. Lorsch, & N. Nohria, 2004, Seven surprises for new CEOs, *HBR*, October: 62–72.

28. R. Rumelt, D. Schendel, & D. Teece (eds.), 1994, *Fundamental Issues in Strategy* (p. 564), Boston: Harvard Business School Press.

29. C. Carr, 2005, Are German, Japanese, and Anglo-Saxon strategic decision styles still divergent in the context of globalization? *JMS*, 42: 1155–1188.

30. M. Carney, E. Gedajlovic, & X. Yang, 2009, Varieties of Asian capitalism, *APJM*, 26: 361–380.

31. M. W. Peng, S. Lee, & J. Tan, 2001, The *keiretsu* in Asia, *JIM*, 7: 253–276.

32. M. W. Peng & Y. Luo, 2000, Managerial ties and firm performance in a transition economy, *AMJ*, 43: 486–501; H. Yang, S. Sun, Z. Lin, & M. W. Peng, 2011, Behind M&As in China and the United States, *APJM*, 28: 239–255.

33. N. Bloom, C. Genakos, R. Sadun, & J. Van Reenen, 2012, Management practices across firms and countries, *AMP*, February, 12–33; N. Bloom & J. Van Reenen, 2010, Why do management practices differ across firms and countries? *JEP*, 24: 203–224; C. Crossland & D. Hambrick, 2011, Differences in managerial discretion across countries, *SMJ*, 32: 797–819; G. Jackson & R. Deeg, 2008, Comparing capitalisms, *JIBS*, 39: 540–561; C. Luk, O. Yau, L. Sin, A. Tse, R. Chow, & J. Lee, 2008, The effects of social capital and organizational innovativeness in different institutional contexts, *JIBS*, 39: 589–612; R. Whitley, 2006, Understanding differences, *OSt*, 27: 1153–1177.

34. M. W. Peng, S. Sun, B. Pinkham, & H. Chen, 2009, The institution-based view as the third leg for a strategy tripod, *AMP*, 23: 63–81.

35. M. W. Peng, D. Wang, & Y. Jiang, 2008, An institution-based view of international business strategy, *JIBS*, 39: 920–936.

36. K. Meyer, S. Estrin, S. Bhaumik, & M. W. Peng, 2009, Institutions, resources, and entry strategies in emerging economies, *SMJ*. 30: 61–80.

37. M. Carney, E. Gedajlovic, P. Heugens, M. Van Essen, & J. Van Oosterhout, 2011, Business group affiliation, performance, context, and strategy, *AMJ*, 54: 437–460; T. Khanna & Y. Yafeh, 2007, Business groups in emerging markets, *JEL*, 45: 331–372; K. B. Lee, M. W. Peng, & K. Lee, 2008, From diversification premium to diversification discount during institutional transitions, *JWB*, 43: 47–65; D. Yiu, Y. Lu, G. Bruton, & R. Hoskisson, 2007, Business groups, *JMS*, 44: 1551–1579.

38. M. W. Peng, S. Lee, & D. Wang, 2005, What determines the scope of the firm over time? *AMR*, 30: 622–633.

39. G. Qian, T. Khoury, M. W. Peng, & Z. Qian, 2010, The performance implications of intra- and inter-regional

geographic diversification, *SMJ*, 31: 1018–1030; M. Wiersema & H. Bowen, 2011, The relationship between international diversification and firm performance, *GSJ*, 1: 152–170; S. Zaheer & L. Nachum, 2011, Sense of place, *GSJ*, 1: 96–108.

40. M. W. Peng, 2004, Identifying the big question in international business research, *JIBS*, 25: 99–108

41. K. Brouthers, L. Brouthers, & S. Werner, 2008, Resource-based advantage in an international context, *JM*, 34: 189–217; C. Chan, T. Isobe, & S. Makino, 2008, Which country matters? *SMJ*, 29: 1179–1205; G. Gao, J. Murray, M. Kotabe, & J. Lu, 2010, A "strategy tripod" perspective on export behaviors, *JIBS*, 41: 377–396; Y. Yamakawa, M. W. Peng, & D. Deeds, 2008, What drives new ventures to internationalize from emerging to developed economies? *ETP*, 32: 59–82; X. Yang, Y. Jiang, R. Kang, & Y. Ke, 2009, A comparative analysis of the internationalization of Chinese and Japanese firms, *APJM*, 26: 141–162.

42. D. Marginson & L. Macaulay, 2008, Exploring the debate on short-termism, *SMJ*, 29: 273–292.

43. T. Levitt, 1983, The globalization of markets, *HBR*, May: 92–102.

44. S. Tallman & T. Pedersen, 2011, The launch of *Global Strategy Journal, GSJ*, 1: 1–5.

45. B. Greenwald & J. Kahn, 2005, All strategy is local, *HBR*, September: 95–105.

46. K. Moore & D. Lewis, 2009, *The Origins of Globalization*, New York: Routledge.

47. D. Yergin & J. Stanislaw, 2002, *The Commanding Heights* (p. 385), New York: Simon & Schuster.

48. J. Stiglitz, 2002, *Globalization and Its Discontents* (p. 9), New York: Norton.

49. M. W. Peng, R. Bhagat, & S. Chang, 2010, Asia and global business, *JIBS*, 41: 373–376.

50. R. Simons, 2010, Stress test your strategy, *HBR*, November: 93–100; P. Mackay & S. Moeller, 2007, The value of corporate risk management, *JF*, 62: 1379–1419; N. Taleb, D. Goldstein, & M. Spitznagel, 2009, The six mistakes executives make in risk management, *HBR*, October: 78–81.

51. S. Lee & M. Makhija, 2009, The effect of domestic uncertainty on the real options value of international investments, *JIBS*, 40: 405–420.

52. P. Ghemawat, 2003, Semiglobalization and international business strategy, *JIBS*, 34: 138–152.

53. J. Boddewyn & J. Doh, 2011, Global strategy and the collaboration of MNEs, NGOs, and governments for the provisioning of collective goods in emerging markets, *GSJ*, 1: 345–361; T. Devinney, 2011, Social responsibility, global strategy, and the multinational enterprise, *GSJ*, 1: 329–344.

54. M. W. Peng, S. Sun, & D. Blevins, 2011, The social responsibility of international business scholars, *MBR*, 19: 106–119; D. Rodrik, 2011, *The Globalization Paradox*, New York: Norton.

55. J. Barney, 2005, Should strategic management research engage public policy debates? *AMJ*, 48: 945–948; D. Hambrick, 2005, Venturing outside the monastery, *AMJ*, 48: 961–962.

56. M. W. Peng & E. Pleggenkuhle-Miles, 2009, Current debates in global strategy, *IJMR*, 11: 51–68.

CHAPTER 2

MANAGING INDUSTRY COMPETITION

© istockphoto/Alexey Stiop

KNOWLEDGE OBJECTIVES

After studying this chapter, you should be able to

1. Define industry competition
2. Analyze an industry using the five forces framework
3. Articulate the three generic strategies
4. Understand the seven leading debates concerning the industry-based view
5. Draw strategic implications for action

Emerging Markets: Competing in the Indian Retail Industry

India has the world's highest density of retail outlets. It has more than 15 million outlets, compared with 900,000 in the United States, whose market (by revenue) is 13 times bigger. At present, 95% of retail sales in India are made in tiny independent mom-and-pop shops, mostly smaller than 500 square feet (46 square meters). In Indian jargon, this is known, quite accurately, as the "unorganized" sector. The "organized" sector refers to more modern supermarkets and chain stores. The organized sector commands only 5% of the country's $435 billion retail sales. In India, the retail industry is the largest provider of jobs after agriculture, accounting for 6%–7% of jobs and 10% of GDP.

Given the two distinct groups of outlets, competition primarily takes place within the unorganized sector and within the organized sector. Customers tend to be price sensitive and purchase in small quantities. The mom-and-pop shops are too small to negotiate good deals with middleman companies such as wholesalers. But the majority of Indians shop at mom-and-pop shops—often because of a lack of choice. Organized outlets simply do not exist in many rural areas. Because of the scarcity of outlets, competition among supermarkets is relatively tranquil. However, it is heating up. Reliance Group, one of India's largest conglomerates, is now making huge waves by investing $5.5 billion to build 1,000 hypermarkets and 2,000 supermarkets to blanket the country in the next five years.

With a booming economy, a fast-growing middle class, and fragmented local competitors, this industry is the world's biggest untapped retail market. Not surprisingly, foreign giants such as Wal-Mart, Carrefour, Metro, and Tesco are knocking at the door trying to expand the organized sector. However, here is a catch: The door is still officially *closed* to foreign direct investment (FDI) in this industry. Since the post-1991 opening to FDI has brought India to the global spotlight, investing in India has become one of the top items on the corporate to-do list in many multinationals. Yet, there are *industry-specific* restrictions, and the retail industry is conspicuous in being one of the last four still officially closed to FDI—the other three are the more sensitive atomic energy, gambling, and agriculture.

Given the Indian government's and the public's general appreciation of the contributions made by FDI, the retail industry, according to an *Economist* editorial in 2011, is now "the most glaring example of the need for foreign investment." One of the leading arguments is that super-efficient retail operations will enhance efficiency throughout the entire supply chain. At present, about a third of fruits and vegetables spoils while in transit, a catastrophe in a country where so many go hungry. In countries with more modern retail systems, less than a tenth is lost.

For years, a side door has been open to FDI. Until 2011, foreign firms could take up to 51% equity in *single-brand* shops that sell their own products, such as Nike, Nokia, and Starbucks. Foreign firms could also set up wholesale and sourcing subsidiaries that supply local mass retail partners. In 2006, Australia's Woolworths started to supply Croma stores owned by Tata Group. In 2010, Wal-Mart teamed with Bharti by operating nine Best Price joint-venture wholesale stores. But until November 2011, FDI in *multi-brand* stores (such as supermarkets) had been banned.

To attract more FDI, the government in November 2011 announced that foreign firms could now own 51% of multi-brand retailers (up from zero) and foreign firms' stake in single-brand retailers could now reach 100% (up from 51%). The reforms would be very limited—only to be implemented in 53 cities with population of more than one million. Consumers would benefit from increased competition. The shares of listed local retailers soared, on speculation that they might be bought out by foreign firms. Farmers would gain from greater investment in the supply chain. Currently farmers have little bargaining power. They sell to a wholesale market, which dictates prices. The wholesaler then sells the produce to another middleman, which further passes the produce to a distributor. By the time food reaches the consumer, it will have been marked up three to four times, but nearly all of that goes to various middlemen, not farmers. Easy profits provide little incentive for middlemen to enhance efficiency and invest in modern supply chain (such as cold storage), and food spoils along the way. To attract farmers, foreign retailers would have to offer higher prices. Wal-Mart set itself a target of increasing farmer income by 20% over five years. Cost-conscious foreign retailers would then invest in modern supply chain to minimize food spoilage.

A huge political brawl erupted after the announcement. Many shopkeepers, supported by middlemen, protested against the alleged onslaught of multinationals and cited the controversial "Wal-Mart effect" being debated in the United States and elsewhere. Interested in shopkeepers' votes, the government thus faced a dilemma. In December 2011, a mere two weeks after the announcement of the retail reforms, a humiliated government announced that it would suspend the reforms that would

bring lower prices for consumers and better prices for farmers. The incumbents won the day. However, the reforms were "suspended," not "cancelled." So stay tuned for the evolution of this industry.

Sources: Based on (1) Associated Press, 2011, India backtracks on plan to let in foreign retail, December 7; (2) *Economist*, 2011, Fling wide the gates, April 16: 16; (3) *Economist*, 2011, Let Walmart in, December 3: 20; (4) *Economist*, 2011, Send for the supermarketers, April 16: 67–68; (5) *Economist*, 2011, The supermarket's last frontier, December 3: 75–76; (6) *Times*, 2011, Why India should stop fearing Walmart, November 28: http://globalspin.blogs.time.com.

W hy is the Indian retail industry turning from relative peace and tranquility to more heated competition? Why are foreign firms interested in entering? What are the responses of existing players (incumbents) such as unorganized shops, organized supermarkets, and middleman companies? How do farmers and consumers react? Finally, are there any substitutes for retail shopping? This chapter addresses these and other strategic questions. We accomplish this by introducing the industry-based view, which is one of the three leading perspectives on strategy. (The other two, resource-based and institution-based views, will be covered in Chapters 3 and 4, respectively.)

As noted in Chapter 1, a basic strategy tool is SWOT analysis, dealing with internal strengths (S), weaknesses (W), environmental opportunities (O), and threats (T). The focus of this chapter is O and T from the industry environment (S and W will be discussed later). We start by defining industry competition. Then, the five forces framework will be introduced, followed by a discussion of three generic strategies. Finally, we spell out seven leading debates.

Defining Industry Competition

industry
A group of firms producing products (goods and/or services) that are similar to each other.

perfect competition
A competitive situation in which price is set by the "market," all firms are price takers, and entries and exits are relatively easy.

industrial organization (IO) economics
A branch of economics that seeks to better understand how firms in an industry compete and then how to regulate them.

An **industry** is a group of firms producing products (goods and/or services) that are similar to each other. The traditional understanding is based on Adam Smith's (1776) model of **perfect competition**, in which price is set by the invisible hand known as the "market," where all firms are price takers and entries and exits are relatively easy. However, such perfect competition is rarely observed in the real world. Consequently, since the late 1930s, a more realistic branch of economics, called **industrial organization (IO) economics** (or **industrial economics**), has emerged. Its primary contribution is

structure-conduct-performance (SCP) model
An industrial organization economics model that suggests industry structure determines firm conduct (strategy), which in turn determines firm performance.

structure
Structural attributes of an industry such as the costs of entry/exit.

conduct
Firm actions such as product differentiation.

performance
The result of firm conduct.

monopoly
A situation whereby only one firm provides the goods and/or services for an industry.

oligopoly
A situation whereby a few firms control an industry.

duopoly
A special case of oligopoly that has only two players.

five forces framework
A framework governing the competitiveness of an industry proposed by Michael Porter. The five forces are (1) the intensity of rivalry among competitors, (2) the threat of potential entry, (3) the bargaining power of suppliers, (4) the bargaining power of buyers, and (5) the threat of substitutes.

a **structure-conduct-performance (SCP) model**. **Structure** refers to the structural attributes of an industry (such as the costs of entry/exit). **Conduct** is firm actions (such as product differentiation). **Performance** is the result of firm conduct in response to industry structure, which can be classified as (1) average (normal), (2) below-average, and (3) above-average. The model suggests that industry structure determines firm conduct (or strategy), which, in turn, determines firm performance.[1]

However, the goal of IO economics is *not* to help firms compete; instead, it is to help policymakers better understand how firms compete in order to properly regulate them. In terms of the number of firms in one industry, there is a continuum ranging from thousands of small firms in perfect competition to only one firm in a **monopoly**. In between, there may be an **oligopoly** with only a few players or a **duopoly** with two competitors. The numerous small firms can only hope to earn average returns at best, whereas the monopolist may earn above-average returns. Economists and policymakers are usually alarmed by above-average returns, which they label "excess profits." Monopoly is usually outlawed and oligopoly scrutinized.

Such an intense focus on above-average firm performance is shared by IO economics and strategy. However, IO economists and policymakers are concerned with the *minimization* rather than the maximization of above-average profits. The name of the game, from the perspective of strategists in charge of the profit-maximizing firm, is exactly the opposite—to try to earn above-average returns (of course, within legal and ethical boundaries). Therefore, strategists have turned the SCP model upside down, by drawing on its insights to help firms perform better.[2] This transformation comprises the heart of this chapter.

The Five Forces Framework

The industry-based view of strategy is underpinned by the **five forces framework**, first advocated by Michael Porter (a Harvard strategy professor who is an IO economist by training) and later extended and strengthened by numerous others. This section introduces this framework.

From Economics to Strategy

In 1980, Porter "translated" and extended the SCP model for strategy audiences.[3] The result is the well-known five forces framework, which forms the backbone of the industry-based view of strategy. Shown in Figure 2.1, these five forces are (1) the intensity of rivalry among competitors, (2) the threat of potential entry, (3) the bargaining power of suppliers, (4) the bargaining power of buyers, and (5) the threat of substitutes. A key proposition is that firm performance critically depends on the degree of competitiveness of these five forces within an industry. The stronger and more competitive these forces are, the less likely the focal firm will be able to earn above-average returns, and vice versa (Table 2.1).

Intensity of Rivalry among Competitors

Actions indicative of a high degree of rivalry include (1) frequent price wars, (2) proliferation of new products, (3) intense advertising campaigns, and (4) high-cost competitive

FIGURE 2.1   The Five Forces Framework

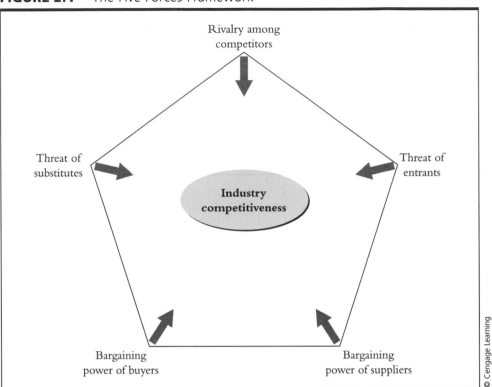

actions and reactions (such as honoring all *competitors'* coupons). Such intense rivalry threatens firms by reducing profits. The key question is: What conditions have led to it?

At least six sets of conditions emerge (Table 2.1). First, the number of competitors is crucial. The more concentrated an industry is, the fewer competitors there will be, and the more likely those competitors will recognize their mutual interdependence and thus restrain their rivalry. For instance, in the automobile industry, the few luxury car competitors such as Ferrari, Lamborghini, and Rolls-Royce historically do not engage in intense competitive actions (such as deep discounts) typically found among mass market competitors.

Second, competitors of similar size, market influence, and product offerings often vigorously compete with each other. This is especially true for firms unable to differentiate their products, such as airlines. How many airlines have flown into the skies of bankruptcy lately? In contrast, the presence of a dominant player lessens rivalry because it can set industrywide prices and discipline behaviors deviating too much from the prices norm. De Beers in the diamond industry is one such example.

Third, in industries whose products are "big tickets" and purchased infrequently (such as mattresses and motorcycles), it may be difficult to establish **dominance**—the market leader has a very large market share. The upshot is more intense rivalry. In contrast, it may be relatively easier for leading firms to dominate in "staple goods" industries with low-price,

dominance

A situation whereby the market leader has a very large market share.

TABLE 2.1 Threats of the Five Forces

FIVE FORCES	THREATS INDICATIVE OF STRONG COMPETITIVE FORCES THAT CAN DEPRESS INDUSTRY PROFITABILITY
Rivalry among competitors	■ A large number of competing firms ■ Rivals are similar in size, influence, and product offerings ■ High-price low-frequency purchases ■ Capacity is added in large increments ■ Industry slow growth or decline ■ High exit costs
Threat of potential entry	■ Little scale-based advantages (economies of scale) ■ Little non-scale-based advantages ■ Inadequate product proliferation ■ Insufficient product differentiation ■ Little fear of retaliation due to the focal firm's lack of excess capacity ■ No government policy banning or discouraging entry
Bargaining power of suppliers	■ A small number of suppliers ■ Suppliers provide unique differentiated products ■ Focal firm is not an important customer of suppliers ■ Suppliers are willing and able to vertically integrate forward
Bargaining power of buyers	■ A small number of buyers ■ Products provide little cost savings or quality-of-life enhancement ■ Buyers purchase standard undifferentiated products from focal firm ■ Buyers are willing and able to vertically integrate backward
Threat of substitutes	■ Substitutes are superior to existing products in quality and function ■ Switching costs to use substitutes are low

more frequently purchased products (such as beers and facial tissues) (see Table 2.2). This is because consumers for "staple goods" are not likely to spend much time to do research on their purchase decisions and find it convenient to stick with well-known brands. On the other hand, consumers for "big ticket" items are more interested in searching for a good deal every time they buy, and may not automatically rely on the reputation of leading firms. For instance, how often do you buy a car? Chances are that the next time you buy a car, you would do some research again. Therefore, the current producer that sold you a car several years ago runs the risk of losing you as a customer.

Fourth, in some industries, new capacity must be added in large increments, thus fueling intense rivalry.[4] If the route between two seaports is currently served by two cruise lines (each with one ship of equal size), any existing company's (or new entrant's) new addition of merely one ship will increase the capacity by 50%. Thus, the two existing cruise lines are often compelled to cut prices (see Strategy in Action 2.1). Industries such as hotels, petrochemicals, semiconductors, and steel often periodically experience over-capacity, leading to price-cutting as a primary coping mechanism.[5]

Fifth, slow industry growth or decline makes competitors more desperate, often unleashing actions not used previously. In the life-and-death fight to remain viable after

TABLE 2.2 Big Tickets versus Staple Goods

PRODUCT	US MARKET LEADER	LEADER'S MARKET SHARE	LEADER'S SHARE AMONG TOP-4 FIRMS
Big tickets: High-price less-frequently purchased products			
Athletic footwear	Reebok	25%	40%
Automobile	General Motors	35%	46%
Mattresses	Sealy	25%	46%
Motorcycles	Honda	33%	42%
Refrigerators	General Electric	34%	38%
Staple goods: Low-price more-frequently purchased products			
Beer	Anheuser Busch (Budweiser)	44%	52%
Facial tissues	Kimberly-Clark (Kleenex)	47%	56%
Laundry detergents	Procter & Gamble	53%	59%
Light bulbs	General Electric	59%	62%
Processed cheese	Kraft	54%	71%

Source: Adapted from J. Shamsie, 2003, The context of dominance: An industry-driven framework for exploiting reputation (pp. 214–215), *Strategic Management Journal*, 24: 199–215.

the 2008 economic crisis, many luxury goods makers had to resort to discounting—a practice they typically avoided before (see the Closing Case).

Finally, industries experiencing high exit costs are likely to see firms continue to operate at a loss. Specialized equipment and facilities that are of little or no alternative use, or that cannot be sold off, pose as exit barriers. In addition, emotional, personal, and career costs, especially on the part of executives admitting failure, may be high. In Japan and Germany, managers may be legally prosecuted if their firms file for bankruptcy.[6] Thus, it is not surprising that these executives will try everything before admitting failure and taking their firms to exit the industry.

Overall, if there are only a small number of rivals led by a few dominant firms, new capacity is added incrementally, industry growth is strong, and exit costs are reasonable, the degree of rivalry is likely to be moderate and industry profits more stable. Conditions opposite from those may unleash intense rivalry. Chapter 8 will discuss more details of interfirm rivalry.

Threat of Potential Entry

incumbents

Current members of an industry that compete against each other.

entry barriers

The industry structures that increase the costs of entry.

In addition to keeping an eye on existing rivals, established firms in an industry, which are called **incumbents**, also have a vested interest in keeping potential new entrants out.[7] New entrants are motivated to enter an industry because of the lucrative above-average returns some incumbents earn.[8] For example, the Amazon Kindle's success has attracted Barnes and Noble to launch its Nook.

Incumbents' primary weapons are **entry barriers**, which refer to industry structures increasing the costs of entry. For instance, Airbus's new A380 burned $12 billion and

> ## STRATEGY IN ACTION 2.1

The Cruise Industry: Too Many Love Boats

The cruise industry is the second life of the ocean liner industry. Eclipsed by jets, the last ocean liners stopped service in the 1980s. The modern cruise industry started in the 1960s, when Norwegian and Carnival cruise lines were founded and dedicated to vacation cruises—not to transportation. In 1977, ABC started its weekly *Love Boat* television series that became a decade-long unpaid commercial for the fledgling industry. The cruise liner was portrayed as a blend of fun and romance. The cruise industry gradually gained popularity, slowly at first but at an increased rate since the 1980s. Initially the industry was serviced by redundant ocean liners. By the 1990s, purpose-built mega ships increasingly entered service. Every year since 2001, nine or more new cruise ships hit the waves, centered around the key markets in the Caribbean, Alaska, Mexico, and Europe. Most of these mega ships were 100,000 tons or greater—larger than the largest, Nimitz-class aircraft carrier. The new ones keep getting bigger. The world's largest are Royal Caribbean's *Oasis of the Seas* and *Allure of the Seas*, each at 225,000 tons with 2,700 cabins and room for 5,400 passengers. Mega ships are more profitable because they enable cruise lines to spread fixed costs across more customers.

Despite the glamour, captains of this industry know that they need a steel stomach to navigate the waters infested by love boats—indeed, too many of them.

Between 1966 and 2008, 88 firms entered the US market but 77 either dropped out or dropped dead. Competition among the survivors now focuses on who can fill an armada of bigger, fancier vessels. In 2000, the US market was served by 111 ships with a capacity of 165,381 lower berths. By 2010, there were 60% more ships and 86% more berths (because of the introduction of larger ships). During the same decade, crises ranged from "9/11" to the recession. To lure passengers, firms slashed prices, eliminated fuel surcharges, repositioned ships from exotic ports to locations that did not require extensive air travel, and launched short (one-day or one-weekend) cruises. In 2010, while the industry carried 15 million passengers (10 million in the United States), an annual increase of 10%, occupancy was still not where it was before the recession. To fill the huge love boats, the key is to reach out to the 80% of Americans who have never taken a cruise.

Sources: Based on (1) the author's interviews; (2) *BusinessWeek*, 2004, Carnival: Plenty of ports in a storm, November 15: 76–78; (3) *BusinessWeek*, 2009, To cruise lines, too many love boats, November 24: 100–102; (4) D. Sull, 2010, Turbulent times and golden opportunities, *Business Strategy Review*, Spring: 34–39.

---

scale-based advantages
Advantages derived from economies of scale (the more a firm produces some products, the lower the unit costs become).

economies of scale
Reduction in per unit costs by increasing the scale of production.

Boeing's new 787 consumed $10 billion before their maiden flights. Facing such sky-high entry barriers, all potential entrants, including those backed by the Japanese and Korean governments, have quit. The key question is: What conditions have created such high entry barriers?

Shown in Table 2.1, at least six structural attributes are associated with high entry barriers. The first is whether incumbents enjoy **scale-based advantages**. The key concept is **economies of scale**, which refer to reductions in *per unit* costs by increasing the scale of production and distribution. For example, Wal-Mart thrives on using its enormous economies of scale in distribution to spread logistics and overhead cost over a large number of outlets, which results in lower prices. In India, it is such economies of scale that the unorganized shop owners are afraid of if Wal-Mart were allowed to enter (see the Opening Case).

non-scale-based advantages
Low-cost advantages that are not derived from the economies of scale.

Another set of advantages that incumbents may enjoy is independent of scale—**non-scale-based advantages**. For example, proprietary technology (such as patents) is helpful. Entrants have to "invent around," the outcome of which is costly and uncertain. Entrants can also directly copy proprietary technology, which may trigger lawsuits by incumbents for patent violations. Another source of such advantages is know-how, the intricate knowledge of how to make products and serve customers that takes years, sometimes decades, to accumulate. It is often difficult for new entrants to duplicate such know-how.

product proliferation
Efforts to fill product space in a manner that leaves little "unmet demand" for potential entrants.

In addition to scale-based and non-scale-based low-cost advantages, another entry barrier is **product proliferation**, which refers to efforts to fill product space in a manner that leaves little "unmet demand" for potential entrants.[9] For example, South-Western Cengage Learning, our multibillion dollar multinational publisher (see Chapter 1 Opening Case), has teamed with your author (whose nickname is "Mr. Global") to not only publish this market-leading text, *Global Strategy*, but also *Global Business* and *GLOBAL* around the world. European students can enjoy a European adaptation titled *International Business* (coauthored with Klaus Meyer). For non-English readers who are dying to arm themselves with the wisdom contained in *Global Strategy*, there are *Quanqiu Qiye Zhanlue* (the Chinese translation), *Estrategia Global* (the Spanish translation), and *Estratégia Global* (the Portuguese translation) (see Chapter 1 Opening Case).

product differentiation
The uniqueness of products that customers value.

Also important is **product differentiation**, which refers to the uniqueness of the incumbents' products that customers value. Its two underlying sources are (1) brand identification and (2) customer loyalty. Incumbents, often through intense advertising, would like customers to identify their brands with some unique attributes. BMW brags about its cars being the "ultimate driving machines." Champagne makers in the French region of Champagne argue that competing products made elsewhere are not really worthy of the name *Champagne*.

A second source of product differentiation is customer loyalty, especially when switching costs for new products are substantial. Many high-tech industries are characterized by

network externalities
The value a user derives from a product increases with the number (or the network) of other users of the same product.

network externalities, whereby the value a user derives from a product increases with the number (or the network) of other users of the same product.[10] These industries have a "winner take all" property, whereby winners (incumbents) whose technology standard is embraced by the market (such as Microsoft Word, Excel, and PowerPoint) are essentially locking out potential entrants. In other words, these industries have an interesting "*increasing* returns" characteristic, as opposed to "*diminishing* returns" taught in basic economics.

excess capacity
Additional production capacity currently underutilized or not utilized.

Another entry barrier is possible retaliation by incumbents. Incumbents often maintain some **excess capacity**, designed to punish new entrants. To think slightly outside the box, perhaps the best example is the armed forces. They cost taxpayers huge sums of money and clearly represent excess capacity in peace time. But they exist for one reason—to deter foreign invasion (or "punish new entrants"). No country has ever unilaterally disbanded its armed forces, and the worst punishment for defeated countries (such as Germany and Japan in 1945 and Iraq in 2003) is to have their military dismantled. In general, the more credible and predictable the retaliation, the more likely new entrants may be deterred. Coca-Cola has been known to retaliate by slashing prices if any competitor (other than Pepsi) crosses the threshold of 10% share in any market. As a result, potential entrants often think twice before proceeding.

Finally, government policy banning or discouraging entries can serve as another entry barrier. For example, the US government does not allow foreign entrants to invest in the defense industry and only allows up to 25% equity injection from foreign carriers in the airline industry. The Indian government bans large-scale entry by foreign retailers such as Wal-Mart (see the Opening Case). In almost every case, the lowering of government-imposed entry barriers leads to a proliferation of new entrants, threatening the profit margins of incumbents. This, of course, is exactly why Indian retail incumbents lobby so hard to prevent the onslaught of foreign entrants.

Overall, if incumbents can leverage scale-based and/or non-scale-based advantages, offer numerous products, provide sufficient differentiation, maintain a credible threat of retaliation, and/or enjoy regulatory protection, the threat of potential entry becomes weak. Thus, incumbents can enjoy higher profits.

Bargaining Power of Suppliers

bargaining power of suppliers

The ability of suppliers to raise prices and/or reduce the quality of goods and services.

Suppliers are organizations that provide inputs, such as materials, services, and manpower, to firms in the focal industry. The **bargaining power of suppliers** refers to their ability to raise prices and/or reduce the quality of goods and services. Four conditions may lead to suppliers' strong bargaining power (Table 2.1). First, if the supplier industry is dominated by a few firms, they may gain an upper hand. To make a point, energy giant Gazprom slowed gas deliveries to Ukraine due to price disputes, leaving customers shivering in winter cold—three times in three years (2007, 2008, and 2009).

Second, the bargaining power of suppliers can become substantial if they provide unique, differentiated products with few or no substitutes. For instance, as a supplier of mission-critical software for most personal computers (PCs), Microsoft is able to extract significant price hikes from PC makers such as Dell, HP, and Lenovo whenever its Windows unleashes a new version.

Third, suppliers enjoy strong bargaining power if the focal firm is *not* an important customer. Boeing and Airbus are not too concerned with losing the business of small airlines, which may only purchase 1–2 aircraft at a time. Consequently, they often refuse to lower prices. But they are intensely concerned about losing large airlines, such as American, Japan, and Singapore Airlines. Thus, lower prices are often offered.

forward integration

Acquiring and owning downstream assets.

Finally, suppliers may enhance their bargaining power if they are willing and able to enter the focal industry by **forward integration**.[11] In other words, suppliers may threaten to become both suppliers *and* rivals. For example, in addition to supplying phones to traditional telecom retail stores, Apple has established a number of Apple Stores in major cities.

In summary, powerful suppliers can squeeze profitability out of firms in the focal industry. Firms in the focal industry, thus, have an incentive to strengthen their own bargaining power by reducing their dependence on certain suppliers. For example, Wal-Mart has implemented a policy of not having any supplier account for more than 3% of its purchases.

bargaining power of buyers

The ability of buyers to reduce prices and/or enhance the quality of goods and services.

Bargaining Power of Buyers

From the perspective of buyers (individual or corporate), firms in the focal industry are essentially suppliers. Therefore, our previous discussion on suppliers is relevant here (Table 2.1). Four conditions lead to the strong **bargaining power of buyers**. First, a small number of buyers leads to strong bargaining power. For example, hundreds of automobile component suppliers try to sell to a small number of automakers, such as BMW, Ford, and Honda. These buyers frequently extract price concessions and quality improvements by playing off suppliers against each other. When these automakers invest abroad, they often encourage or coerce suppliers to invest with them and demand that supplier factories be sited next to the assembly plants—at suppliers' own expenses. Not surprisingly, many suppliers comply.[12] This is how Toyota cloned Toyota City in Guangzhou, China, whose main Toyota-owned factory is surrounded by 30 supplier factories.

Second, buyers may enhance their bargaining power if products of an industry do not clearly produce cost savings or enhance the quality of life for buyers. For example, repeated and frequent upgrades in software packages are causing a buyer fatigue. Heads of information technology (IT) departments are increasingly suspicious of whether the costly new "gadgets" are really able to help their companies save money. The upshot is that reluctant buyers can either refuse to buy or extract significant discounts.

Third, buyers may have strong bargaining power if they purchase standard, undifferentiated commodity products from suppliers. Although automobile components suppliers as a group possess less bargaining power relative to automakers, suppliers are *not* equally powerless. There are usually several tiers. The top tier suppliers are the most crucial, often supplying nonstandard, differentiated key components such as electric systems, steering wheels, and car seats. The bottom tier consists of suppliers making standard, undifferentiated commodity products such as seat belt buckles, cup holders, or simply nuts and bolts. Not surprisingly, top tier suppliers possess more bargaining power than bottom tier suppliers.

Finally, like suppliers, buyers may enhance their bargaining power by entering the focal industry through **backward integration**. Buyers such as COSTCO, Tesco, and Marks & Spencer now directly compete with their own suppliers such as Procter & Gamble (P&G) and Johnson & Johnson by procuring private label (also known as store brand) products.[13] Private label products, such as Kirkland (for COSTCO), Kroger, and Safeway brands, compete side by side with national brands on the shelf space. At present, store brand products command approximately 40% of grocery sales in Spain, 35% in the Netherlands, 30% in Britain, 25% in France, and 20% in the United States.[14] Only leading brand producers such as Frito-Lay (potato chips) can resist the demand made by the powerful stores to make private label goods for the stores. Many mediocre brand producers, when facing the choice of producing private label goods for the stores or being kicked out of shelf space (because their products are replaceable), surrender to the strong bargaining powers of stores.

In summary, powerful or desperate buyers may enhance their bargaining power. Buyers' bargaining power may be minimized if firms can sell to numerous buyers, identify clear value added, provide differentiated products, and enhance entry barriers.

backward integration
Acquiring and owning upstream assets.

Threat of Substitutes

substitutes
Products of different industries that satisfy customer needs currently met by the focal industry.

Substitutes are products of different industries that satisfy customer needs currently met by the focal industry. For instance, while Pepsi is *not* a substitute for Coke (Pepsi is a rival in the same industry), tea, coffee, juice, and water are—that is, they are still beverages but are in a different product category. Two areas of substitutes are particularly threatening (Table 2.1).

First, if substitutes are superior to existing products in quality and function, they may rapidly emerge to attract a large number of customers. For example, music downloads (both legal and illegal kinds) are now rapidly eating into CD sales. Online media has pushed print newspapers to the brink of extinction in many cities. Smartphones (such as iPhone) and tablets (such as iPad) are now substituting some PCs.

Second, substitutes may pose significant threats if switching costs are low. For example, consumers incur virtually no costs when switching from sugar to a sugar substitute like Nutrasweet. Both are readily available in restaurants and grocery stores. On the other hand, no substitutes exist for large passenger jets, especially for transoceanic transportation. The only other way to go to Hawaii or New Zealand seems to be swimming (!). As a result, Boeing and Airbus can charge higher prices than would be the case if there were substitutes for their products.

Overall, the possible threat of substitutes requires firms to vigilantly scan the larger environment, as opposed to the narrowly defined focal industry. Enhancing customer value (such as price, quality, utility, and location) may reduce the attractiveness of substitutes.

Lessons from the Five Forces Framework

Taken together, the five forces framework offers three significant lessons (Table 2.3):

- The framework reinforces the important point that not all industries are equal in terms of their potential profitability. The upshot is that when firms have the luxury to choose (such as diversified companies contemplating entry to new industries or entrepreneurial start-ups scanning new opportunities—see Strategy in Action 2.2), they will be better off if they choose an industry whose five forces are weak. Michael Dell confessed that he probably would have avoided the PC industry had he known how competitive the industry would become.

- The task is to assess the opportunities (O) and threats (T) underlying each competitive force affecting an industry, and then estimate the likely profit potential of the industry.[15]

- The challenge, according to Porter, is "to stake out a position that is less vulnerable to attack from head-to-head opponents, whether established or new, and less vulnerable to erosion from the direction of buyers, suppliers, and substitutes."[16] In other words, the key is to *position* your firm well within an industry and defend its position. Consequently, the five forces framework also becomes known as the **industry positioning** school.

industry positioning
Ways to position a firm within an industry in order to minimize the threats presented by the five forces.

Although the thrust of this framework was put forward over 30 years ago, it has continued to assert strong influence on strategy practice and research today. While it has been debated and modified (introduced later), its core features remain remarkably insightful.

TABLE 2.3 Lessons from the Five Forces Framework

■ Not all industries are equal in terms of potential profitability.
■ The task for strategists is to assess the opportunities (O) and threats (T) underlying each of the five competitive forces affecting an industry.
■ The challenge is to stake out a position that is strong and defensible relative to the five forces.

© Cengage Learning

STRATEGY IN ACTION 2.2

From Cardinal Foods to Cardinal Health

Headquartered in Dublin, Ohio (a suburb of Columbus), Cardinal Health is one of the largest and most successful US firms that many of you probably have never heard of. Cardinal Health is a $99 billion giant that was ranked 19 on the *Fortune* 500 list (by sales) in 2011—yes, it was number 19, not a typo for 190. Named a "stealth empire" by *Fortune*, Cardinal Health produces significantly larger revenues than some of the seemingly more visible health care companies both on the pharmaceutical side (such as Pfizer) and the retail side (such as Walgreens). Cardinal Health today provides products and services to 90% of US hospitals. Every day more than 50,000 deliveries are made to 40,000 hospitals, pharmacies, and other points of care. If you have health care needs in the United States, chances are you have been a Cardinal Health customer without even knowing it.

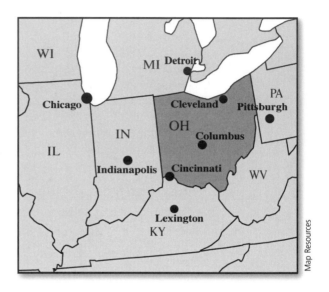

How Cardinal Health chose to focus on health care is an amazing story of the power of the five forces framework. In 1971, the firm was founded by 26-year-old Robert Walter, who earned an MBA from Harvard in the same year. The firm was named Cardinal Foods, which had nothing to do with health care. Walter's father had been a food broker, so Walter knew a little about the food wholesale distribution business. But after peddling ketchup for a few years, it occurred to Walter that Cardinal Foods would never be a big fish in the crowded and competitive food business. Walter then put on his MBA hat and did a classic five forces analysis, scanning various industries. His findings?

- The drug distribution industry had 354 small, independently owned distributors, but only three large, publicly listed firms. In other words, competition was primarily local and not severe. Entry barriers were low. Time was ripe for consolidation.

- Buyers (patients) had little bargaining power. Medicine, when prescribed by a doctor, could not be

substituted—unlike, say, butter. Suppliers (drugmakers) had to rely on drug distributors to get their products to the far corners of the country.

- The drug business was growing faster than the economy, thus presenting more growth opportunities.

Fueled by this powerful insight, Cardinal Foods entered drug distribution by becoming Cardinal Distribution (covering both foods and drugs) in 1980. Finally, the firm, having already sold off its food wholesale business in 1988, renamed itself Cardinal Health in 1994. The rest was history.

Sources: Based on (1) the author's interviews; (2) *Fortune*, 2011, Fortune 500 list; (3) M. W. Peng, 2009, *Global Strategy*, 2nd ed. (pp. 457–458). Cincinnati: South-Western Cengage Learning.

Three Generic Strategies

Having identified the five forces underlying industry competition, the next challenge is how to make strategic choices. Porter suggested three **generic strategies**, (1) cost leadership, (2) differentiation, and (3) focus, all of which are intended to strengthen the focal firm's position relative to the five competitive forces (see Table 2.4).[17]

Cost Leadership

Recall that our definition of strategy (see Chapter 1) is a firm's theory about how to compete successfully. A **cost leadership** strategy suggests that a firm's theory about how to compete successfully centers on low costs and prices. Offering the same value of a product at a lower price—in other words, better value—tends to attract many customers. A cost leader often positions its products to target "average" customers for the mass market with little differentiation. The key functional areas center on efficiency in manufacturing, services, and logistics. The hallmark of this strategy is a *high-volume low-margin* approach.

A cost leader, such as Wal-Mart, can minimize the threats from the five forces. First, it is able to charge lower prices and make better profits compared with higher-cost rivals. Second, its low-cost advantage is a significant entry barrier. Third, the cost leader typically buys a large volume from suppliers, whose bargaining power is reduced. Even Wal-Mart's largest supplier, P&G, is afraid of Wal-Mart's size. In response, P&G acquired Gillette to enhance its size and, hence, its bargaining power. Fourth, the cost leader would be less negatively affected if strong suppliers increase prices or powerful buyers force prices down. Finally, the cost leader challenges substitutes to not only outcompete the utility of its products but also its prices, a very difficult proposition. Thus, a true cost leader is relatively safe from these threats.

However, a cost leadership strategy has at least two drawbacks. First, there is always the danger of being outcompeted on costs. This forces the leader to *continuously* search for lower costs. A case in point is Ryanair's continuous quest for lower cost (but still safe and on time) air travel (see Strategy in Action 2.3). Second, in the relentless drive to cut costs, a cost leader may cut corners that upset customers. Toyota's recalls were caused by its efforts to cut short test procedures when developing software that controlled acceleration. The damage to its reputation was enormous.

Overall, a cost leadership strategy is pursued by most firms, which find little alternative basis for distinction. However, a number of other firms have decided to be different by embracing the second generic strategy discussed next (see the Closing Case).

generic strategies
Strategies intended to strengthen the focal firm's position relative to the five competitive forces, including (1) cost leadership, (2) differentiation, and (3) focus.

cost leadership
A competitive strategy that centers on competing on low cost and prices.

TABLE 2.4 Three Generic Competitive Strategies

	PRODUCT DIFFERENTIATION	MARKET SEGMENTATION	KEY FUNCTIONAL AREAS
Cost leadership	Low (mainly by price)	Low (mass market)	Manufacturing, services, and logistics
Differentiation	High (mainly by uniqueness)	High (many market segments)	R&D, marketing, and sales
Focus	Extremely high	Low (one or a few segments)	R&D, marketing, and sales

© Cengage Learning

> ## STRATEGY IN ACTION 2.3

Ryanair: The Continuous Search for Low Cost

Ryanair is the undisputed king of low cost airlines in Europe. Founded in Dublin, Ireland, in 1985, Ryanair has defied gravity. The past decade since 2001 was devastated by "9/11" attacks, SARS epidemics, the Great Recession, and (in Europe) the complete grounding of air travel due to an Icelandic volcanic eruption (2010). All US legacy airlines flew into the skies of bankruptcy. Most European airlines were struggling. Over the past decade, the global airline industry collectively lost $50 billion. Yet Ryanair turned healthy profits in nine out of the ten years.

What are Ryanair's secrets? Plenty. Like its role model Southwest, Ryanair specializes in short-haul flights using a single type of aircraft, the Boeing 737. Flying point to point allows it to quickly turn around flights. It gets 50% more flying hours per day out of its aircraft than its hub-and-spoke rivals. Ryanair has also rented out overhead storage and seatbacks to advertisers. In-flight food and drinks? Forget it. Baggage fees? Of course. Instead of flying between main airports, Ryanair flies between secondary airports far away from the central city. For example, British Airways (BA) charges $400 for a flight between London (Heathrow) and Munich, Germany, which includes free baggage, food, and drinks. Ryanair only charges $221 between London Stansted (one hour away from central London) and Memmingen (two hours away from Munich proper). Ryanair passengers would cough up another $40 for baggage, food, and drinks. Adding ground transportation from London to Heathrow and from Munich airport to city proper, BA passengers pay $441 for a three-hour journey. In contrast, Ryanair passengers pay $311 (30% savings) for a four-hour trip.

In addition to competing with legacy airlines such as BA, Ryanair also fights with fellow no-frills airlines such as easyJet and Air Berlin. As a result, Ryanair continuously searches for new ways to lower cost. Some of these outside-the-box ideas voiced by its outspoken CEO Michael O'Leary have created huge controversies. For example, O'Leary announced that Ryanair would charge passengers €1 for a trip to use the restroom, and that he was considering offering standing cabins (like a bus) to pack in more passengers. He also suggested that only one pilot would be needed to fly the aircraft. Finally, he argued that the average passenger did not "deserve" the baggage service treatment, which was a high-cost system built during an era when air travel was rare and passengers were affluent. Elsewhere in today's passengers' life, they did not get that kind of treatment. Therefore, today's passengers need to carry their own bags—or pay extra.

"Everytime he opens his mouth," said the head of a nonprofit passenger advocacy group, "he insults the dignity of the flying public." O'Leary has worked hard to be known as the most unpleasant man in Ireland. Ryanair is infamous for its customer service, which some describe as "minimalist" and others say as "hell." Wheelchairs are charged extra. Complaints must be sent by fax—no emails please. A major newspaper, *Guardian*, has created reader competitions dedicated to publicizing Ryanair horror stories.

Enjoying all that publicity, O'Leary has dismissed the notion of bad publicity. He is proud of making provocative (and some say obnoxious) statements about how to further shave a penny from the already minimum cost of no-frills flights. Although passengers have voted Ryanair the "least liked" airline in customer surveys, they continue to flock to its flights. In 2010, Ryanair became the first European airline to fly more than seven million passengers in one month.

Sources: Based on (1) *Bloomberg Businessweek*, 2010, The duke of discomfort, September 6: 58–61; (2) C. Byles, 2014, Ryanair, in M. W. Peng, *Global Strategy*, 3rd ed., Cincinnati: South-Western Cengage Learning (in this book as an Integrative Case); (3) A. Ruddock, 2007, *Michael O'Leary: A Life in Full Flight*, London: Penguin; (4) *Wall Street Journal*, 2009, A lavatory levy, June 3: C16.

Differentiation

A **differentiation** strategy focuses on how to deliver products that customers perceive to be valuable and different (Table 2.4). While cost leaders serve "typical" customers, differentiators target customers in smaller, well-defined segments who are willing to pay premium prices. The key is a *low-volume high-margin* approach. The ability to charge higher prices enables differentiators to outperform competitors unable to do so. A Lexus car is not significantly more expensive to produce than a Chrysler car, yet customers always pay more to get a Lexus. To attract customers willing to pay premiums, differentiated products must have some truly (or perceived) unique attributes, such as quality, sophistication, prestige, and luxury. The challenge is to identify these attributes and deliver value centered on them for *each* market segment. Therefore, in addition to maintaining a strong lineup for its 3-, 5-, and 7-series, BMW is now filling in the "gaps" by adding the new 1- and 6-series as well as sport utility vehicles (SUVs). For differentiators, research and development (R&D) is an important functional area that experiments with new features. Another key function is marketing and sales, focusing on both capturing customers' psychological desires that lure them to buy and satisfying their needs after the sales through excellent services (see the Closing Case).

According to the five forces framework, the less a differentiator resembles its rivals, the more protected its products are. For instance, Disney theme parks advertise the unique experience associated with Disney movie characters. Lingerie queen Victoria's Secret emphasizes her—I mean "its"—seductive secret. Menswear king Ermenegildo Zegna hints at the power and the elegance associated with its style. The bargaining power of suppliers is relatively less of a problem because differentiators may be better able to pass on some (but not unlimited) price increases to customers than cost leaders can. Similarly, the bargaining power of buyers is less problematic because differentiators tend to enjoy relatively strong brand loyalty.

On the other hand, a differentiation strategy has two drawbacks. First, the differentiator may have difficulty sustaining the basis of differentiation in the long run. There is always the danger that customers may decide that the price differential between the differentiator's and cost leader's products is not worth paying for. Second, the differentiator has to confront relentless efforts of imitation. As the overall quality of the industry goes up, brand loyalty in favor of the leading differentiators may decline. For example, the previously high-flying Starbucks has an increasingly hard time differentiating itself. As McDonald's raises its coffee quality and enhances its store image (especially through its newer and hipper McCafé), McDonald's has been able to eat some of Starbucks' lunch (or drink Starbucks' coffee!). In the Great Recession, Starbucks seems to have lost its shine while offerings at McDonald's have become especially valued.

Focus

A **focus** strategy serves the needs of a particular segment or niche of an industry (Table 2.1). The segment can be defined by (1) geographical market, (2) type of customer, or (3) product line. While the breadth of the focus is a matter of degree, focused firms usually serve the needs of a segment so unique that broad-based competitors choose not to serve it. In the coffee industry, while Starbucks is a differentiated player, single-origin coffeemakers such as Discovery, Intelligentsia, and Stumptown deploy a focus strategy by only sourcing premium coffee from a single high-quality region (such as certain farms or villages in Ethiopia, the birthplace of coffee).[18] Compared with Starbucks that mixes coffee from different parts of Ethiopia for its "Ethiopia Sidamo Blend," single-origin coffeemakers are more discriminating and more selective. (In comparison, cost leader Kraft Foods simply labels one of its Maxwell House coffees "South Pacific Blend," without even mentioning any particular farm or even country—conceding that it mixes a lot of low-cost coffee beans from various places.)

Although it sounds like a tongue twister, a specialized differentiator (such as Bentley) is basically more differentiated than the large differentiator (such as BMW). This approach may be successful when a focused firm possesses intimate knowledge about a particular segment. The logic of how a traditional differentiator can dominate the five forces, discussed before, applies here, the only exception being a much smaller and narrower, but sharper, focus. The two drawbacks, namely, the difficulty to sustain such expensive differentiation and the challenge of defending against ambitious imitation, also apply here.

Lessons from the Three Generic Strategies

Recall from Chapter 1 that strategy is about making choices—what to do and what not to do. The essence of the three generic strategic choices is whether to *perform activities differently* or to *perform different activities* relative to competitors.[19] Two lessons emerge. First, cost and differentiation are two fundamental strategic dimensions. The key is to choose one dimension and focus on it consistently. Second, companies that are stuck in the middle—that is, neither having the lowest cost nor sufficient differentiation (or focus)—may be indicative of having either no or a drifting strategy. Their performance may suffer as a consequence. However, the second point is subject to debate, as outlined next.

Debates and Extensions

Although the industry-based view is a powerful strategic tool, it is not without controversies. A new generation of strategists needs to understand some of these debates and thus avoid uncritical acceptance of the traditional view. This section introduces seven leading debates: (1) clear versus blurred boundaries of industry, (2) threats versus opportunities, (3) five forces versus a sixth force, (4) stuck in the middle versus all rounder, (5) industry rivalry versus strategic groups, (6) integration versus outsourcing, and (7) industry-specific versus firm-specific and institution-specific determinants of firm performance.

Clear versus Blurred Boundaries of Industry

The heart of the industry-based view is the identification of a clearly defined industry. However, this concept of an industry may become increasingly elusive. For example, consider the boundaries of the television broadcasting industry. The emergence of cable, satellite, telecommunications, and online technologies has blurred the industry's boundaries. A television in the future may be able to control

TABLE 2.5 Players "Up in the Cloud" (and Their Unofficial Nicknames)

INCUMBENTS	NEW ENTRANTS	ARMS DEALERS
IBM (The eminence)	Amazon (The instigator)	Dell (The gear head)
HP (The question mark)	Google (The needler)	Cisco (The plumber)
VMware (The optimizer)	Microsoft (The late bloomer)	

Source: Based on figure in *Bloomberg Businessweek*, 2011, The power of the cloud (pp. 58–59), March 7: 53–59. The unofficial nicknames were given by the magazine.

household security systems, play interactive games, and place online orders—essentially blending with the functions of a PC. To jockey for advantageous positions in preparation for such a future, there have been a large number of mergers and alliances among television, telecommunications, cable, software, and movie companies in recent years. In other words, the competitors of ABC not only include CBS, NBC, CNN, and Fox, but also AT&T, SkyTV, Microsoft, Apple, YouTube (owned by Google), Sony, and others. So what exactly is this "industry"? Such fuzzy industry boundaries are not alone in television broadcasting. Try to figure out the boundaries of mobile communication or (worse) cloud computing—isn't it mind-boggling to try to define the boundaries of "cloud"? (see Table 2.5). A new concept is to view all the players involved as an "ecosystem."[20] However, it will be challenging to specify the boundaries of such an ecosystem, thus making it extremely difficult to clearly identify the five forces.

Threats versus Opportunities

Even assuming that industry boundaries can be clearly identified, the assumption that all five forces are (at least potential) threats seems too simplistic. This view has been challenged in two areas. First, strategic alliances are on the rise, and even competitors are increasingly exploring opportunities to collaborate. GM and Toyota manufacture cars together. The CEOs of Cisco and Huawei shook hands and discussed collaboration, after Cisco sued Huawei and both firms reached a settlement. In other words, if these rivals do not love each other, they do not hate each other either. Compared with the traditional black-and-white view, this more complicated and realistic view requires a more sophisticated understanding of today's competition *and* collaboration (see Chapters 7 and 8 for more details).

Second, even if firms do not directly collaborate with competitors, intense rivalry within an industry, long considered a "no-no," may become an opportunity instead of a threat. In the IT industry, a number of ambitious firms from India, Israel, and South Korea, instead of staying at home and enjoying the relative tranquility as suggested by the five forces framework, have come to Silicon Valley to seek out the most competitive environment. Their rationale is that only by being closer to where the action is can they hope to become globally competitive.[21] In other words, the new strategic motto seems to be: "Love thy competitors! They make you stronger." Overall, it seems that the five forces model may have overemphasized the threat (T) in SWOT analysis. A more balanced view needs to highlight both O and T.

Five Forces versus a Sixth Force

complementor

A firm that sells products that add value to the products of a focal industry.

The five forces Porter identified in the 1980s are not necessarily exhaustive. In 1990, Porter added related and supporting industries as an important force that affects the competitiveness of an industry.[22] This is endorsed by Andrew Grove, the former CEO of Intel, who coined the term **complementors**.[23] Basically, complementors are firms that sell products that add value to the products of a focal industry. The complementors to the PC industry are firms that produce software applications. When complementors produce exciting products (such as new games), the demand for PCs grows, and vice versa. Therefore, it may be helpful to add complementors as a possible sixth force.[24] However, complementors do not have to be in high-tech industries. For example, sports games directly boost beer sales, which, in turn, fund a lot of commercials aired during sports games. A case can be made that sports and beers are complementors.

Stuck in the Middle versus All Rounder

A key proposition in the industry-based view is that firms must choose either cost leadership or differentiation. Pursuing both may make firms "stuck in the middle" with poor performance prospects.[25] Borders bookstores seemed to be stuck in the middle. Relative to Barnes and Nobles, Borders offered a wider selection. But its selection was nowhere close to the much wider selection offered by Amazon's online list. Crushed by a high cost structure (thanks to the larger inventory cost relative to Barnes and Nobles') and insufficient differentiation (relative to Amazon), Borders closed shops and was liquidated in 2011.[26]

However, some highly successful firms such as Singapore Airlines stand out as both cost leaders *and* differentiators. Widely regarded as the world's premium carrier, Singapore Airlines has won the World's Best Airline Award from *Condé Nast Traveler* 21 out of the 22 times it has been awarded. As a differentiator, Singapore Airlines always buys newer aircraft. It is the launch (first) customer for the new double-decker Airbus A380. It also replaces aircraft more frequently. On average, its fleet is six years old versus an industry average of 13 years old. Customers are willing to pay more for seats on newer aircraft. New aircraft are more fuel efficient and need less repair and maintenance, resulting in lower cost. Singapore Airlines is also renowned for its legendary service. Its cabin crews are trained to interact with American, Chinese, and Japanese passengers differently. However, Singapore Airlines does not pay premium salary. Its wage is average by Singapore standards, which are relatively low by global standards. As a result, its labor costs are about 16% of total costs, whereas United Airlines' are 23%, British Airways' 28%, and American Airlines' 31%. In short, Singapore Airlines is both a world-class differentiator and a cost leader.[27]

As a result, a debate has emerged. First, critics argue that holding technology constant, for firms already operating at the maximum efficiency scale, further cost savings are not possible and differentiation is a must.[28] The king of cost leadership, Wal-Mart, has sought to become more differentiated by experimenting with a more "earth friendly" store in McKinney, Texas; with upscale offerings in Plano, Texas; and with in-store health clinics in Dallas area stores.

Second, critics suggest that technology may not be constant. The idea that differentiators cannot be cost competitive is influenced by manufacturing technology in the

flexible manufacturing technology
Modern manufacturing technology that enables firms to produce differentiated products at low costs (usually on a smaller batch basis than the large batch typically produced by cost leaders).

mass customization
Mass produced but customized products.

strategic groups
Groups of firms within a broad industry.

1970s, whereas more recently, **flexible manufacturing technology** has enabled firms to produce differentiated products at a low cost (usually on a smaller batch basis than the large batch typically produced by cost leaders). Thus, the name of the game may become **mass customization**, pursuing cost leadership and differentiation *simultaneously*.

A review of 17 studies finds that instead of being underdogs, some (but not all) firms "stuck in the middle" may have potential to be "all-rounders," being both cost competitive and differentiated.[29] While not conclusive, these findings do raise questions and enrich the substance of the debate.

Industry Rivalry versus Strategic Groups

While the five forces framework focuses on the industry level, how meaningful it is depends on how an "industry" is defined. In a broadly defined industry, such as the Indian retail industry, obviously not every firm is competing against each other. However, some groups of firms within a broad industry *do* compete against each other, such as the competition among mom-and-pop shops in the unorganized sector and the rivalry among supermarkets in the organized sector in India (see the Opening Case). Likewise, in the automobile industry, we can identify the mass market, luxury, and ultra-luxury groups (Figure 2.2). These different groups of firms are thus known as **strategic groups**. It is argued that strategy within one group tends to be similar: Within the automobile industry, the mass market group pursues a cost leadership strategy, the luxury group a differentiation strategy, and the ultra-luxury group a focus strategy. Members within a strategic group tend to have similar performance.[30]

While this intuitive idea seems uncontroversial, a debate has erupted on two issues. First, how stable are strategic groups?[31] In other words, how easy or difficult is it for firms to change from one strategic group to another? In the automobile industry, strong incentives exist for firms in the mass market group to charge into the luxury group. Can they do it? The launch of Lexus, Acura, and Infiniti by Toyota, Honda,

FIGURE 2.2 Three Strategic Groups in the Global Automobile Industry

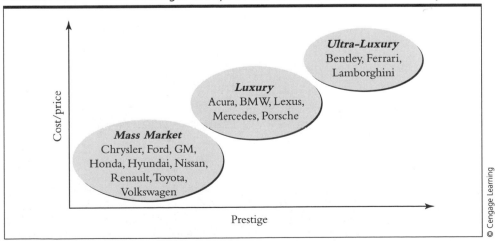

© Cengage Learning

mobility barrier

Within-industry differences that inhibit the movement between strategic groups.

and Nissan, respectively, suggests that despite the challenges, it is possible. However, Mazda entertained the idea of launching its own luxury brand but decided to quit. The root cause is **mobility barriers**, which are within-industry differences that inhibit the movement between strategic groups. Clearly, Mazda was not confident about its ability to overcome mobility barriers. Recently, Hyundai has fought a similar uphill battle by attempting to go upmarket. Will Hyundai succeed or fail?

A second issue centers on the data that classify strategic group memberships. Since strategic group analysis usually requires large quantities of objective data,[32] how useful is it when there is a paucity of data, especially when entering new markets such as emerging economies? Research suggests that while objective data are hard to find, subjective measures tapping into executives' cognitive inclusion and exclusion of certain firms as competitors may provide more reliable clues.[33] This is because executives, when confronting the complexity and chaos of industry competition, are likely to use some *simplifying* schemes to better organize their strategic understanding around some identifiable reference points.[34] In the Chinese electronics industry, executives use ownership type, a simple and easily identifiable reference point, to mentally organize strategic groups.[35] In other words, state-owned enterprises tend to compete with each other, private-owned firms watch each other closely, and foreign entrants view other foreign entrants as a strategic group (Table 2.6). Interviews with these executives find that members within the same self-identified strategic group benchmark intensely against each other, but care less about what is going on in other groups.

Overall, strategic groups have become a useful but somewhat controversial middle ground between industry-level and firm-level analyses. Regardless of whether "real" strategic groups exist, if the idea of strategic groups helps managers simplify the complexity they confront when analyzing an industry, then the strategic group concept seems to have some value.

Integration versus Outsourcing

How to determine the scope of a firm is one of the four most fundamental questions in strategy.[36] As noted earlier, the industry-based view advises the focal firm to consider integrating *backward* (to compete with suppliers) or *forward* (to compete with buyers)—or at least threaten to do so. This strategy is especially recommended when market uncertainty is high, coordination with suppliers/buyers requires tight control, and the number of suppliers/buyers is small.[37] (What if they hold us up, if we don't buy them out?) However,

TABLE 2.6   Strategic Groups and Ownership Types in the Chinese Electronics Industry

STRATEGIC GROUP	DEFENDER	ANALYZER	REACTOR
Ownership type	State ownership	Mixed	Unstable
Customer base	Stable	Mixed	Changing
Growth strategy	Cautious	Mixed	Aggressive
Managers	Older, more conservative	Mixed	Younger, more aggressive

Source: Adapted from M. W. Peng, J. Tan, & T. Tong, 2004, Ownership types and strategic groups in an emerging economy (p. 1110), *Journal of Management Studies*, 41 (7): 1105–1129.

this strategy is very expensive because it takes huge sums of capital to acquire independent suppliers/buyers and most acquisitions end up in failure (see Chapter 9).

In the past two decades, a great debate has erupted challenging the wisdom of integration. Critics make two points. First, they argue that under conditions of uncertainty, *less* integration is advisable. When demand is uncertain, a focal firm with no internal supplier units can simply reduce output by discontinuing or not renewing supply contracts, whereas a firm stuck with its own internal supplier units may keep producing simply to keep these supplier units employed. In other words, integration reduces strategic *flexibility*.[38] Second, internal suppliers, which had to work hard for contracts if they were independent suppliers, may lose high-powered market incentives simply because their business is now taken care of by the "family."[39] Over time, internal suppliers may become less competitive relative to outside suppliers. The focal firm thus faces a dilemma: To go with outside suppliers will keep internal suppliers idle, but to choose internal suppliers will sacrifice cost and quality. In the past two decades, integration has gradually gone out of fashion and outsourcing (turning over an activity to an outside supplier) is in vogue.

The outsourcing movement has been influenced by the Japanese challenge in the 1980s and the 1990s. Given that the five forces framework is a product of prevailing Western strategic practices of the 1970s, the Japanese way of managing suppliers, through what is called a *keiretsu* (interfirm network), seems radically different. In the 1990s, while GM had 700,000 employees, Toyota only had 65,000. A lot of activities performed by GM, such as those in internal supplier units, are undertaken by Toyota's *keiretsu* member firms using non-Toyota employees.

At the same time, Toyota has far fewer suppliers than GM. They tend to be "cherry picked," trusted members of the *keiretsu*. Instead of treating suppliers as adversaries, Toyota treats its suppliers (mostly first-tier ones) as partners by codeveloping proprietary technology with them, relying on them to deliver directly to the assembly line just in time, and helping them when they are in financial difficulty. However, Toyota does not only rely on trust and goodwill. To minimize the potential loss of high-powered market incentive on the part of *keiretsu* members, a dual sourcing strategy—namely, splitting the contract between a *keiretsu* member and a nonmember (often a local company when Toyota moves abroad)—is often practiced.[40] This makes sure that both the internal (*keiretsu*) and external suppliers are motivated to do their best.

Healthy relationships with suppliers may have direct benefits.[41] Overall, similar to the idea discussed earlier that rivalry may represent opportunities instead of threats, solid value-adding relationships with suppliers (and buyers and other partners) are now widely regarded as a source of competitive advantage and are implemented by many non-Japanese firms around the world.[42]

However, this is not the end of the debate. In a curious turn of events, while many US firms have become more "Japanese-like," Japanese firms are increasingly under pressure to become more "American-like" (!). This is because some outsourced activities, crucial to the core business, should not have been outsourced; otherwise, the firm risks becoming a "hollow corporation."[43] Supplier relations that are too close may introduce rigidities, resulting in a loss of much-needed flexibility.[44] In Japan, some previously rock-solid buyer–supplier links have started to fray. There is now less willingness to help troubled suppliers improve. Even *keiretsu* members, previously discouraged (if not outright forbidden) to seek contracts outside the network, are now encouraged to look for work elsewhere, because it is believed that the benefits of learning from dealing with other customers may eventually accrue to the lead firm (such as Toyota).[45] Overall, the rise and fall of these two perspectives in the past two decades suggest very careful analysis is needed when making decisions on the optimal scope of the firm.[46]

Industry-Specific versus Firm-Specific and Institution-Specific Determinants of Performance

The industry-based view argues that firm performance is most fundamentally determined by industry-specific attributes.[47] This view has recently been challenged, from two directions. The first is the resource-based view. Although the five forces framework suggests that particular industries (such as airlines) are highly unattractive, certain firms, such as Southwest, Ryanair, and Singapore Airlines, are highly successful. What is going on? A short answer is that there must be firm-specific resources and capabilities that contribute to the winning firms' performance.

A second challenge comes from the critique that the industry-based view "ignores industry history and institutions."[48] Porter's work, first published in 1980, may have carried some hidden, taken-for-granted assumptions underpinning the way competition was structured in the United States in the 1970s. As "rules of the game" in a society, institutions obviously affect firm strategies. For example, cost leadership as a strategy is *banned* by law in the Japanese bookselling industry. All bookstores have to sell new books at the same price without discount. Thus, Amazon, whose primary weapon was low price, had a hard time elbowing its way into Japan. Clearly, strategists need to understand how institutions affect competition. This view has become known as the institution-based view. Overall, these two views complement the industry-based view,[49] and we will introduce them in Chapters 3 and 4.

Making Sense of the Debates

The seven debates suggest that the industry-based view—and in fact the strategy field as a whole—is alive, exciting, and yet unsettling. All these debates direct their attention to Porter's work, which has become an *incumbent* in the field.[50] When describing his work, Porter deliberately chose the word "framework" rather than the more formal "model." In his own words, "frameworks identify the relevant variables and the questions that the user must answer in order to develop conclusions tailored to a particular industry and company."[51] In this sense, Porter's frameworks have succeeded in identifying variables and raising questions, while not necessarily providing definitive answers. Although the degree of contentiousness among these debates is not the same, it is evident that the last word has not been written on any of them.

The Savvy Strategist

The savvy strategist can draw at least three important implications for action (Table 2.7). (1) You need to understand your industry inside and out by focusing on the five forces.[52] The industry-based view provides a systematic *foundation* for industry analysis and competitor analysis, upon which more detailed examination, introduced in later chapters,

TABLE 2.7   Strategic Implications for Action

> ■ Establish an intimate understanding of your industry by focusing on the five forces.
>
> ■ Be aware that additional forces may influence the competitive dynamics of your industry.
>
> ■ Realize that industry is not destiny. Certain firms may do well in a structurally unattractive industry.

can be added. (2) Be aware that additional forces, some of which are discussed in the "Debates and Extensions" section, may influence the competitive dynamics of your industry. The five forces framework should be a start, but not the end of your strategic analysis. (3) Realize that industry is not destiny. While the industry-based view is a powerful framework to understand the behavior and performance of the "average" firm, you need to be aware that certain firms may do well in a structurally unattractive industry. As a strategist, your job is to lead your firm to become a high-flying outlier despite the pull of gravity of some unattractive attributes of your industry.

In conclusion, we suggest that the industry-based view directly answers the four fundamental questions discussed in Chapter 1. First, why do firms differ? The industry-based view suggests that the five forces in different industries lead to diversity in firm behavior. The answer to the second question, How do firms behave? boils down to how they maximize opportunities and minimize threats presented by the five forces. Third, what determines the scope of the firm? A traditional answer is to examine the relative bargaining power of the focal firm relative to that of suppliers and buyers. Integration would result in an expanded scope of the firm. However, more recent work suggests caution. Firms are advised to leverage opportunities of outsourcing, remain focused on core activities, and be willing to collaborate not only with suppliers and buyers but also possibly their competitors. Finally, what determines the international success and failure of firms? The answer, again, is that industry-specific conditions must have played an important role in determining firm performance around the world.

CHAPTER SUMMARY

1. **Define industry competition**
   • An industry is a group of firms producing similar goods and/or services.
   • The industry-based view of strategy grows out of industrial organization (IO) economics, which helps policymakers better understand how firms compete so policymakers can properly regulate them.
   • Pioneered by Michael Porter, the five forces framework forms the backbone of the industry-based view of strategy, which draws on the insights of IO economics to help firms better compete.

2. **Analyze an industry using the five forces framework**
   • The stronger and more competitive the five forces are, the less likely that firms in an industry are able to earn above-average returns, and vice versa.
   • The five forces are: (1) rivalry within an industry, (2) threat of potential entry, (3) bargaining power of suppliers, (4) bargaining power of buyers, and (5) threat of substitutes.

3. Articulate the three generic strategies
- The three generic strategies are: (1) cost leadership, (2) differentiation, and (3) focus.

4. Understand the seven leading debates concerning the industry-based view
- These debates are: (1) clear versus blurred boundaries of industry, (2) threats versus opportunities, (3) five forces versus a sixth force, (4) stuck in the middle versus all rounder, (5) integration versus outsourcing, (6) industry rivalry versus strategic groups, and (7) industry-specific versus firm-specific and institution-specific determinants of firm performance.

5. Draw strategic implications for action
- Establish an intimate understanding of your industry by focusing on the five forces.
- Be aware that additional forces may influence the competitive dynamics of your industry.
- Realize that industry is not destiny. Certain firms may do well in an unattractive industry.

KEY TERMS

Backward integration p. 42

Bargaining power of buyers p. 41

Bargaining power of suppliers p. 41

Complementor p. 50

Conduct p. 35

Cost leadership p. 45

Differentiation p. 47

Dominance p. 36

Duopoly p. 35

Economies of scale p. 39

Entry barrier p. 38

Excess capacity p. 40

Five forces framework p. 35

Flexible manufacturing technology p. 51

Focus p. 47

Forward integration p. 41

Generic strategies p. 45

Incumbents p. 38

Industrial organization (IO) economics p. 34

Industry p. 34

Industry positioning p. 43

Mass customization p. 51

Mobility barrier p. 52

Monopoly p. 35

Network externalities p. 40

Non-scale-based advantages p. 40

Oligopoly p. 35

Perfect competition p. 34

Performance p. 35

Product differentiation p. 40

Product proliferation p. 40

Scale-based advantages p. 39

Strategic group p. 51

Structure p. 35

Structure-conduct-performance (SCP) model p. 35

Substitutes p. 42

CRITICAL DISCUSSION QUESTIONS

1. Why do price wars often erupt in certain industries (such as the automobile industry), but less frequently in other industries (such as the diamond industry)? What can firms do to discourage price wars or be better prepared for price wars?

2. Compare and contrast the five forces affecting the airline industry, the fast food industry, the beauty products industry, and the pharmaceutical industry (1) on a *worldwide* basis and (2) in *your* country. Which industry holds more promise for earning higher returns? Why?

3. *ON ETHICS:* As a manager, is it ethical to threaten your suppliers? Your buyers?

TOPICS FOR EXPANDED PROJECTS

1. Conduct a five forces analysis of the business school industry or the higher education industry. Identify the strategic group to which your institution belongs. Then write a short paper, using this analysis to explain why your institution is doing well (or poorly) in the competition for better students, professors, donors, and ultimately rankings.

2. *ON ETHICS:* "Excessive profits" coming out of monopoly, duopoly, or any kind of strong market power are often targets for government investigation and prosecution (for example, Microsoft was charged by both US and EU competition authorities). Yet, strategists openly pursue above-average profits, which are argued to be "fair profits." Do you see an ethical dilemma here? Working in pairs, with one person performing the role of an antitrust official and the other acting as a firm strategist (such as Bill Gates), write two statements, each with a rebuttal, to support both sides of the argument.

3. *ON ETHICS:* A powerful new entrant is likely to drive a lot of smaller incumbent firms out of business and their employees out of work. In the Opening Case, this is the heart of the debate on whether the Indian retail industry should be open to FDI. As a manager at Wal-Mart interested in entering India, how do you respond to the political uproar against such entry? As an Indian government official, how do you introduce the new policy to allow such entry to an angry crowd of mom-and-pop shopkeepers? Write a short paper to explain your answers.

❯ CLOSING CASE

Emerging Markets: High Fashion Fights Recession

Pumping out fancy clothing, handbags, jewelry, perfumes, and watches, the high end of the fashion industry—otherwise known as the luxury goods industry—had a challenging time in the Great Recession. In 2008, banks were falling left and right, unemployment rates sky high, and consumer confidence at an all time low. In 2009, total luxury goods industry sales fell by 20%. How did the industry cope?

Of the five forces, the threat of substitutes was relatively insignificant. Potential new entrants were not dying to enter when incumbents were struggling. Suppliers such as leather tanneries were hit hard by cancelled or scaled-down orders from auto companies, shoemakers, and furniture firms. Suppliers thus were eager to work with any order that luxury goods firms could lavish on them. As a result, managing industry competition boiled down to how to manage rivalry among competitors and manage customers.

The high-end fashion industry was dominated by the Big Three: LVMH (with more than 50 brands such as Louis Vuitton handbags, Moët Hennessy liquor, Christian Dior cosmetics, TAG Heuer watches, and Bulgari jewlery), Gucci Group (with nine brands such as Gucci handbags, Yves Saint Laurent clothing, and Sergio Rossi shoes), and Burberry (famous for raincoats and handbags). Next were a number of more specialized players such as king of menswear Ermenegildo Zegna and queen of womenswear Christian Lacroix. Virtually all firms in this industry pursued a differentiation strategy and a smaller number of them engage in a focus strategy. By definition, high fashion means high prices. An informal code of conduct (or norm) permeates the industry: no discount, no coupons, no price wars please—in theory at least. Discounting, so frequently used in the *low-end* fashion industry, is generally viewed as dangerous and poisonous, not only to the occasional firm that unleashes it, but also to the image and margin of the whole world of high fashion. But here is the catch: How do firms survive the Great Recession when such nasty tactics are not advised?

In desperation, many firms cut prices—but quietly. At Tiffany jewelry stores, sales people advised customers about diamond ring price reductions, but otherwise there was no publicity. Gucci and Richemont (with brands such as Cartier jewelry, Vacheron Constantin watches, and Alfred Dunhill menswear) offloaded their excess inventory to discount websites. Coach launched a lower-priced line branded Poppy as a fighter brand without cheapening the image of the Coach brand. During the month prior to Christmas in 2008, American department stores such as Macy's and Saks Fifth Avenue offered some savage price slashing of up to 80% of some luxury goods. The only firm that stood rock solid was the industry leader LVMH, which claimed that it never puts its products on sales at a discount. When the going gets tough, it destroys stock instead. In contrast to many luxury goods firms that rely on department stores, LVMH owns its retail shops, thus allowing it to completely control the fate and price of its own products.

The bloodbath in the Great Recession forced the weaker players such as Christian Lacroix and Escada to file for bankruptcy. But it made stronger players such as LVMH even more formidable. They benefitted from an established pattern in high fashion: the flight to quality. In other words, when people have less money, they spend it on the best. Shoppers go for fewer, more classic items, such as one Burberry raincoat (as opposed to two designer dresses) and one Kelly bag by Hermès (rather than three bags by less prestigious brands). For this reason, LVMH, according to its proud president, "always gains market share in crises." LVMH's sales *grew* from $24 billion in 2008 to $29 billion in 2011, with profit margins at a healthy 40% or so—twice as high as some of its weaker rivals.

In addition to managing interfirm rivalry, how to manage the fickle and capricious customers was tricky. Although the seriously rich were not affected by the Great Recession, their number remained small. Most luxury goods firms had been relying on the "aspirational" customers to fund their growth. As the recession became worse, many middle-class customers in economically depressed, developed economies began to hunt for value instead of triviality and showing off. Japan had been the number one market for luxury goods for years and most Japanese women reportedly owned at least one Louis Vuitton product. But sales were falling since 2005 and dropped sharply since 2008. Young Japanese women seemed more individualistic than their mothers, and often hauled home lesser-known (and cheaper) brands.

Emerging markets, especially China, offered luxury goods firms the best hope while the rest of the world was bleak. Since 2008, while global sales declined, Chinese consumption (both at home and traveling) had been growing between 20% and 30%. In 2009, China surpassed the United States to become the world's second-largest market. In 2011, China rocketed ahead of Japan for the first time as the world's champion consumer of luxury goods—splashing $12.6 billion to command a 28% global market share. Everybody that was somebody in high fashion had been elbowing its way into China, which appears like the New World to old European brands. Interestingly, several years ago it was the Japanese ladies who did the heavy lifting for the top line of luxury goods firms; now it is the Chinese dudes who (are more likely than Chinese women to) eagerly open their wallets to indulge themselves with luxurious trappings. Beyond China, luxury goods firms eagerly chased customers in Brazil, India, Poland, Russia, and Saudi Arabia.

Where did LVMH open one of its newest stores? Ulan Bator, Mongolia.

Sources: Based on (1) *BusinessWeek*, 2009, Coach's new bag, June 29: 41–43; (2) *BusinessWeek*, 2009, When discounting can be dangerous, August 3: 49; (3) *Economist*, 2009, LVMH in the recession, September 19: 79–81; (4) *Economist*, 2010, Fashionably alive, November 13: 76; (5) *Economist*, 2010, Luxury goods in Poland, June 19: 72; (6) *Economist*, 2011, The glossy posse, October 1: 67; (7) J. Li, 2010, *Luxury Brands Management*, Beijing: Peking University Press.

CASE DISCUSSION QUESTIONS

1. Using the five forces framework, how would you characterize the competition in the luxury goods industry?

2. How much bargaining power did consumers as buyers have during the Great Recession?

3. Why was discounting looked down upon by industry peers, all of which were differentiated or focus competitors?

4. What would be the likely challenges in emerging markets for luxury goods firms?

NOTES

[**Journal acronyms**] *AME* – *Academy of Management Executive*; *AMP* – *Academy of Management Perspectives*; *AMJ* – *Academy of Management Journal*; *AMR* – *Academy of Management Review*; *APJM* – *Asia Pacific Journal of Management*; *BW* – *BusinessWeek* (before 2010) or *Bloomberg Businessweek* (since 2010); *ETP* – *Entrepreneurship Theory and Practice*; *HBR* – *Harvard Business Review*; *JBR* – *Journal of Business Research*; *JEP* – *Journal of Economic Perspectives*; *JIBS* – *Journal of International Business Studies*; *JIM* – *Journal of International Management*; *JMS* – *Journal of Management Studies*; *LRP* – *Long Range Planning*; *OSc* – *Organization Science*; *QJE* – *Quarterly Journal of Economics*; *SMJ* – *Strategic Management Journal*

1. L. Einav & J. Levin, 2010, Empirical industrial organization, *JEP*, 24: 145–162.

2. M. Porter, 1981, The contribution of industrial organization to strategic management, *AMR*, 6: 609–620; C. Zott & R. Amit, 2008, The fit between product market strategy and business model, *SMJ*, 29: 1–26.

3. M. Porter, 1980, *Competitive Strategy*, New York: Free Press.

4. D. Simon, 2005, Incumbent pricing responses to entry, *SMJ*, 26: 1229–1248.

5. J. Henderson & K. Cool, 2003, Learning to time capacity expansions, *SMJ*, 24: 393–413; H. Tan & J. Mathews, 2010, Identification and analysis of industry cycles, *JBR*, 63: 454–462.

6. S. Lee, M. W. Peng, & J. Barney, 2007, Bankruptcy law and entrepreneurship development, *AMR*, 32: 257–272.

7. D. Lavie, 2006, Capability reconfiguration, *AMR*, 31: 153–174.

8. G. Dowell, 2006, Product line strategies of new entrants in an established industry, *SMJ*, 27: 959–979; D. Souder & J. M. Shaver, 2010, Constraints and incentives for making long horizon corporate investments, *SMJ*, 31: 1316–1336.

9. A. Mainkar, M. Lubatkin, & W. Schulze, 2006, Toward a product-proliferation theory of entry barriers, *AMR*, 31: 1062–1075.

10. T. Eisenmann, G. Parker, & M. Van Alstyne, 2011, Platform envelopment, *SMJ*, 32: 1270–1285; M. Schilling, 2002, Technology success and failure in winner-take-all markets, *AMJ*, 45: 398–461; P. Soh, 2010, Network patterns and competitive advantage before the emergence of a dominant design, *SMJ*, 31: 438–461.

11. R. Gulati, P. Lawrence, & P. Puranam, 2005, Adaptation in vertical relationships, *SMJ*, 26: 415–440.

12. M. W. Peng, S. Lee, & J. Tan, 2001, The *keiretsu* in Asia, *JIM*, 7: 253–276.

13. S. Chen, 2010, Transaction cost implication of private branding and empirical evidence, *SMJ*, 31: 371–389.

14. *BW*, 2011, Even better than the real thing, November 28: 25–26; *Economist*, 2010, Basket cases, October 16: 79.

15. I. McCarthy, T. Lawrence, B. Wixted, & B. Gordon, 2010, A multidimensional conceptualization of environmental velocity, *AMR*, 35: 604–626.

16. M. Porter, 1998, *On Competition* (p. 38), Boston: Harvard Business School Press.

17. M. Porter, 1985, *Competitive Advantage*, New York: Free Press.

18. *BW*, 2011, A pot of trouble brews in the coffee world, September 8: 13–14.
19. M. Porter, 1996, What is strategy? *HBR*, 74 (6): 61–78.
20. D. Teece, 2007, Explicating dynamic capabilities, *SMJ*, 28: 1319–1350.
21. Y. Yamakawa, M. W. Peng, & D. Deeds, 2008, What drives new ventures to internationalize from emerging to developed economies? *ETP*, 32: 59–82.
22. M. Porter, 1990, *The Competitive Advantage of Nations*, New York: Free Press.
23. A. Grove, 1996, *Only the Paranoid Survive*, New York: Doubleday.
24. D. Yoffie & M. Kwak, 2006, With friends like these, *HBR*, September: 89–98.
25. R. Huckman & D. Zinner, 2008, Does focus improve operational performance? *SMJ*, 29: 178–193; S. Thornhill & R. White, 2007, Strategic purity, *SMJ*, 28: 553–561.
26. *BW*, 2011, The end of Borders is not the end of books, November 14: 94–97.
27. L. Heracleous & J. Wirtz, 2010, Singapore Airlines' balancing act, *HBR*, July: 145–149.
28. C. Hill, 1988, Differentiation versus low cost or differentiation and low cost, *AMR*, 13: 401–412.
29. C. Campbell-Hunt, 2000, What have we learned about generic competitive strategy? *SMJ*, 21: 127–154.
30. W. DeSarbo, R. Grewal, & R. Wang, 2009, Dynamic strategic groups, *SMJ*, 30: 1420–1439; G. Leask & D. Parker, 2007, Strategic groups, competitive groups, and performance within the UK pharmaceutical industry, *SMJ*, 28: 723–745; F. Mas-Ruiz & F. Ruiz-Moreno, 2011, Rivalry within strategic groups and consequences for performance, *SMJ*, 32: 1286–1308; J. Short, D. Ketchen, T. Palmer, & G. T. Hult, 2007, Firm, strategic group, and industry influences on performance, *SMJ*, 28: 147–167.
31. D. Dranove, M. Peteraf, & M. Shanley, 1998, Do strategic groups exist? *SMJ*, 19: 1029–1044
32. R. Hamilton, E. Eskin, & M. Michaels, 1998, Assessing competitors, *LRP*, 31: 406–417; J. D. Osborne, C. Stubbart, & A. Ramaprasad, 2001, Strategic groups and competitive enactment, *SMJ*, 22: 435–454.
33. D. Johnson & D. Hoopes, 2003, Managerial cognition, sunk costs, and the evolution of industry structure, *SMJ*, 24: 1057–1068; B. Kabanoff & S. Brown, 2008, Knowledge structures of prospectors, analyzers, and defenders, *SMJ*, 29: 149–171; J. Kuilman & J. Li, 2009, Grades of membership and legitimacy spillovers, *AMJ*, 52: 229–245.
34. G. McNamara, R. Luce, & G. Tompson, 2002, Examining the effect of complexity in strategic group knowledge structures on firm performance, *SMJ*, 23: 151–170.
35. M. W. Peng, J. Tan, & T. Tong, 2004, Ownership types and strategic groups in an emerging economy, *JMS*, 41: 1105–1129.
36. A. Afuah, 2003, Redefining firm boundaries in the face of the Internet, *AMR*, 28: 34–53; M. Jacobides, 2005, Industry change through vertical disintegration, *AMJ*, 48: 465–498.
37. O. Williamson, 1985, *The Economic Institutions of Capitalism*, New York: Free Press.
38. S. Nadkarni & V. Narayanan, 2007, Strategic schemas, strategic flexibility, and firm performance, *SMJ*, 28: 243–270; G. Pacheco-de-Almeida, J. Henderson, & K. Cool, 2008, Resolving the commitment versus flexibility trade-off, *AMJ*, 51: 517–538.
39. A. Vining, 2003, Internal market failure, *JMS*, 40: 431–457; W. Egelhoff & E. Frese, 2009, Understanding managers' preferences for internal markets versus business planning, *JIM*, 15: 77–91.
40. J. Liker & T. Choi, 2004, Building deep supplier relationships, *HBR*, December: 104–113.
41. D. Griffith & M. Myers, 2005, The performance implications of strategic fit of relational norm governance strategies in global supply chain relationships, *JIBS*, 36: 254–269.
42. J. Dyer & H. Singh, 1998, The relational view, *AMR*, 23: 660–679.
43. J. Barthelemy, 2003, The seven deadly sins of outsourcing, *AME*, 17 (2): 87–98.
44. M. Kotabe, X. Martin, & H. Domoto, 2003, Gaining from vertical partnerships, *SMJ*, 24: 293–316.
45. C. Ahmadjian & J. Lincoln, 2001, *Keiretsu*, governance, and learning, *OSc*, 12: 683–701; R. Lamming, 2000, Japanese supply chain relationships in recession, *LRP*, 33: 757–778; J. McGuire & S. Dow, 2009, Japanese *keiretsu*, *APJM*, 26: 333–351.
46. C. de Fontenay & J. Gans, 2008, A bargaining perspective on strategic outsourcing and supply competition, *SMJ*, 29: 819–839; M. Leiblein, J. Reuer, & F. Dalsace, 2002, Do make or buy decisions matter? *SMJ*, 23: 817–833.
47. A. McGahan & M. Porter, 1997, How much does industry matter, really? *SMJ*, 18: 15–30.
48. S. Oster, 1994, *Modern Competitive Analysis*, 2nd ed. (p. 46), New York: Oxford University Press.

49. J. Bou & A. Satorra, 2007, The persistence of abnormal returns at industry and firm levels, *SMJ*, 28: 707–722; A. van Witteloostujin & C. Boone, 2006, A resource-based theory of market structure and organizational form, *AMR*, 31: 409–426.

50. C. Decker & T. Mellewigt, 2007, Thirty years after Micahel E. Porter, *AMP*, 21: 41–55.

51. M. Porter, 1994, Toward a dynamic theory of strategy, in R. Rumelt, D. Schendel, & D. Teece (eds.), *Fundamental Issues in Strategy* (p. 427), Boston: Harvard Business School Press.

52. X. Lecocq & B. Demil, 2006, Strategizing industry structure, *SMJ*, 27: 891–898; A. McGahan, 2004, How industries change, *HBR*, October: 87–94.

LEVERAGING RESOURCES AND CAPABILITIES

© istockphoto/Alexey Stiop

KNOWLEDGE OBJECTIVES

After studying this chapter, you should be able to

1. Explain what firm resources and capabilities are
2. Undertake a basic SWOT analysis along the value chain
3. Decide whether to keep an activity in-house or outsource it
4. Analyze the value, rarity, imitability, and organizational (VRIO) aspects of resources and capabilities
5. Participate in four leading debates concerning the resource-based view
6. Draw strategic implications for action

IBM at 100

International Business Machines (popularly known as IBM and more affectionately as Big Blue) celebrated its 100th anniversary in 2011. IBM is a multinational information technology (IT) corporation headquartered in Armonk, New York. It manufactures and sells computer hardware and software and offers consulting services in areas ranging from mainframe computers to nanotechnology. IBM is renowned for its innovations. It holds more patents than any other US firm and currently has nine research laboratories worldwide. Its employees have garnered five Nobel Prizes, nine National Medals of Technology, and five National Medals of Science. Its inventions include the automated teller machine (ATM), the floppy disk, the hard disk drive, the magnetic stripe card, the relational database, the Universal Product Code (UPC), the SABRE airline reservation system, DRAM, and Watson artificial intelligence. At present, it employs more than 425,000 employees (often referred to as IBMers) in over 200 countries. In 2010, its sales reached $100 billion, making it the 18th largest corporation in the United States and 31st largest in the world (by sales). Despite the Great Recession, IBM remained highly profitable—ranked 7th most profitable company in the United States. As of September 2011, IBM was the second-largest publicly traded technology company in the world by market capitalization (behind Apple). Other kudos for 2011 included the number one company for leaders (*Fortune*), number two best global brand (Interbrand), number one green company worldwide (*Newsweek*), 12th most admired company (*Fortune*), and 18th most innovative company (*Fast Company*).

In the past century, countless companies came and went. A few countries also appeared and then disappeared—think of the *former* Soviet Union, Yugoslavia, and Czechoslovakia. "Why is IBM still alive and thriving after so long, in an industry characterized perhaps more than any other by innovation and change?" asked the *Economist*. This question is not just academic. Far younger IT giants, such as Dell, Nokia, and Sony, are dying to know the answer in order to prevent their own life span from being much shorter than IBM's.

IBM pioneered in the industry that we now call the IT industry. The intensity of competition in this fast-moving industry is legendary. In essence, this industry can be characterized as never-ending efforts to create "platforms." First came tabulating machines. Then mainframes. These were followed by "distributed" systems, progressing from mini-computers to personal computers (PCs) and then to servers. Now computing clouds and mobile devices are the rage. There has been no shortage of ambitious new entrants. Many of them have flamed out while IBM marches on. Customers in personal and business segments have different needs, and it is hard to please them all. Suppliers of components and services often have a nasty tendency to enter the foray and become direct competitors—think of Acer and Lenovo, which ate IBM's lunch in PCs. Entrepreneurs and incumbents constantly dream up new products and services to substitute what Big Blue has to offer. Michael Dell publicly confessed that had he known how intensely competitive the IT industry had become, he would not have entered this industry.

In such a tough neighborhood, IBM's life is not all smooth sailing. In 1969, during the heydays of its dominance in mainframes, it became the first IT company to be labeled an "evil empire" by antitrust authorities (before the more recently alleged "evil empire," Microsoft, was born). (The US government eventually dropped the case in 1982.) In the 1990s, it narrowly escaped from bankruptcy. IBM has undergone numerous rounds of organizational restructuring since its inception, acquiring companies such as PricewaterhouseCoopers (2002) and selling off businesses such as the printer division Lexmark (1991) and the PC division (2004).

Tons of ink has been spilled on IBM's long history. What are the secrets behind its longevity and success? An innovative culture. A commitment to customer relationships. A willingness to change. A strong leadership team. A multinational presence—it now has 60,000 employees in India and its corporate procurement headquarters is based in China. Many more factors can be nominated. But what exactly is it? Answers to this crucial question are not only important to IBMers and their competitors, but also to executives in other industries as well as interested students, scholars, and reporters around the world. The *Economist* opined that IBM "is unlikely to reach its limits soon." Stay tuned on how far IBM can go in its next 100 years

Sources: Based on (1) *Bloomberg Businessweek*, 2011, Can this IBMer keep Big Blue's edge? October 31: 31–32; (2) *Economist*, 2007, IBM and globalization, April 7: 67–69; (3) *Economist*, 2011, 1100100 and counting, June 11: 67–69; (4) *Economist*, 2011, IBM v. Carnegie Corporation, June 11: 64–66.

W hy is IBM able to stand out in a very crowded and competitive industry? How has IBM consistently delivered value to customers in the past century? Why do most of its rivals fail to match IBM's longevity? The answer is that there must be certain resources and capabilities specific to IBM that are not shared by rivals. This insight has been developed into a **resource-based view**, which has emerged as one of the three leading perspectives on strategy.[1]

While the industry-based view focuses on how "average" firms within one industry compete, the resource-based view sheds considerable light on how individual firms (such as IBM) differ from each other within one industry. In SWOT analysis, the industry-based view deals with the external O and T, and the resource-based view concentrates on the internal S and W.[2] A key question is: How can high-flyers such as IBM defy gravity and sustain competitive advantage?[3] In this chapter, we first define resources and capabilities, and then discuss the value chain analysis. Afterward, we focus on value (V), rarity (R), imitability (I), and organization (O) through a VRIO framework. Debates and extensions follow.

resource-based view

A leading perspective of strategy that suggests that differences in firm performance are most fundamentally driven by differences in firm resources and capabilities.

Understanding Resources and Capabilities

A basic proposition of the resource-based view is that a firm consists of a bundle of productive resources and capabilities.[4] **Resources** are defined as "the tangible and intangible assets a firm uses to choose and implement its strategies."[5] There is some debate regarding the definition of capabilities. Some argue that capabilities are a firm's capacity to dynamically deploy resources. They suggest a crucial distinction between resources and capabilities, and advocate a "dynamic capabilities" view.[6]

While scholars may debate the fine distinctions between resources and capabilities, these distinctions are likely to become blurred in practice.[7] For example, is IBM's long history a resource or capability? How about its multinational presence? How about its willingness to jettison low-margin businesses? For current and would-be strategists, the key is to understand how these attributes help improve firm performance, as opposed to

resource

The tangible and intangible assets a firm uses to choose and implement its strategies.

TABLE 3.1 Examples of Resources and Capabilities

TANGIBLE	INTANGIBLE
Financial	Human
Physical	Innovation
Technological	Reputation

© Cengage Learning

capability

The tangible and intangible assets a firm uses to choose and implement its strategies

tangible resources and capabilities

Observable and more easily quantified resources and capabilities.

figuring out whether they should be labeled as resources or capabilities. Therefore, in this book, we will use the terms "resources" and "capabilities" *interchangeably* and often in *parallel*. In other words, **capabilities** are defined here the same way as resources.

All firms, including the smallest ones, possess a variety of resources and capabilities. How do we meaningfully classify such diversity? A useful way is to separate them into two categories: tangible and intangible ones (Table 3.1). **Tangible resources and capabilities** are assets that are observable and more easily quantified. They can be broadly divided into three categories:

- **Financial resources and capabilities.** Examples include firms' abilities to tap into capital markets.

- **Physical resources and capabilities.** For instance, while many people attribute the success of Amazon to its online savvy (which makes sense), a crucial reason Amazon has emerged as the largest bookseller is because it has built some of the largest physical, *brick-and-mortar* book warehouses in key locations.

- **Technological resources and capabilities.**[8] IBM is renowned for such technological prowess.

intangible resources and capabilities

Hard-to-observe and difficult-to-codify resources and capabilities.

Intangible resources and capabilities, by definition, are harder to observe and more difficult (or sometimes impossible) to quantify (see Table 3.1). Yet, it is widely acknowledged that they must be "there," because no firm is likely to generate competitive advantage by solely relying on tangible resources and capabilities alone.[9] Examples of intangible assets include:

- **Human resources and capabilities.** Emerging Markets 3.1 illustrates how extraordinary human resources (HR) can be crucial assets during crisis.

- **Innovation resources and capabilities.** Some firms are renowned for innovations. For instance, Apple is famous for its cool gadgets.

- **Reputation resources and capabilities.** Reputation can be regarded as an outcome of a competitive process in which firms signal their attributes to constituents.[10] IBM, despite some setbacks, can leverage its reputation and march from strength to strength, while many of its less reputable rivals struggle.

It is important to note that all resources and capabilities discussed here are merely *examples*; they do not represent an exhaustive list. As firms forge ahead, discovery and leveraging of new resources and capabilities are likely.

EMERGING MARKETS 3.1 〉 〉

The Ordinary Heroes of the Taj

On November 26, 2008, Unilever hosted a dinner at the Taj Mahal Palace Hotel in Mumbai. Unilever's directors, senior executives, and their spouses were bidding farewell to a departing CEO and welcoming a new CEO. About 35 Taj employees, led by a 24-year-old banquet manager, Mallika Jagad, were assigned to manage the event in a second-floor banquet room. Around 9:30 PM, as they served the main course, they heard what they thought were fireworks at a nearby wedding. In reality, these were the first gunshots from terrorists who were storming the Taj.

The staff quickly realized something was wrong. Jagad had the doors locked and the lights turned off. She asked everyone to lie down quietly under tables and refrain from using cell phones. She insisted that husbands and wives separate to reduce the risk to families. The group stayed there all night, listening to the terrorists rampaging through the hotel, hurling grenades, firing automatic weapons, and tearing the palace apart. According to the guests, the Taj staff kept calm, and constantly went around offering water and asking people if they needed anything else. Early the next morning, a fire started in the hallway outside, forcing the group to try to climb out the windows. A fire crew spotted them and, with its ladders, helped the trapped people escape quickly. The staff evacuated the guests first, and no casualties resulted.

Elsewhere in the hotel, the upscale Japanese restaurant Wasabi was busy by 9:30 PM. A warning call from a hotel operator alerted the staff that terrorists had entered the building and were heading toward the restaurants. Thomas Varghese, the 48-year-old senior waiter, immediately instructed his 50-odd guests to crouch under tables, and he directed employees to form a human cordon around them. Four hours later, security forces asked Varghese if he could get the guests out of the hotel. He decided to use a spiral staircase near the restaurant to evacuate the customers first and then the staff. The 30-year Taj veteran insisted that he would

Map Resources

be the last man to leave, but he never did get out. The terrorists gunned him down as he exited.

When Karambir Singh Kang, the Taj's general manager, heard about the attacks, he immediately left the conference he was attending off-site. He took charge at the Taj the moment he arrived, supervising the evacuation of guests and coordinating the efforts of firefighters amid the chaos. His wife and two young children were in a sixth-floor suite, where the general manager traditionally lives. When he realized that the terrorists were on the upper floors, he tried to get to his family. It was impossible. By midnight the sixth floor was in flames, and there was no hope of anyone's surviving. Kang led the rescue efforts until noon the next day. Only then did he call his parents to tell them that the terrorists had killed his wife and children. His father, a retired general, told him, "Son, do your duty, do not desert your post." Kang replied, "If the hotel goes down, I will be the last man out."

During the onslaught on the Taj, 31 people died and 28 were hurt, but the hotel received only praise the day after. Its guests were overwhelmed by employees' dedication to duty, their desire to protect guests with little regard to their own personal safety, and their quick thinking. As many as 11 Taj employees—a third of the hotel's casualties—laid down their lives while helping between 1,200 and 1,500 guests escape.

At some level, that isn't surprising. One of the world's top hotels, the Taj is ranked number 20 by *Condé Nast*

Traveler. The hotel is known for the highest levels of quality, its ability to go many extra miles to delight customers, and its staff of highly trained employees. It is a well-oiled machine, where every employee knows his or her job, has encyclopedic knowledge about regular guests, and is comfortable taking orders. Even so, the Taj employees gave customer service a whole new meaning during the terrorist strike.

Source: Excerpted from R. Deshpandé & A. Raina, 2011, The ordinary heroes of the Taj, *Harvard Business Review*, December: 119–123.

Resources, Capabilities, and the Value Chain

value chain

Goods and services produced through a chain of vertical activities that add value.

If a firm is a bundle of resources and capabilities, how do they come together to add value? A value chain analysis allows us to answer this question. Shown in Panel A of Figure 3.1, most goods and services are produced through a chain of vertical activities (from upstream to downstream) that add value—in short, a **value chain**. The value chain typically consists of two areas: primary activities and support activities.[11]

Each activity requires a number of resources and capabilities. Value chain analysis forces managers to think about firm resources and capabilities at a very micro, activity-based level.[12] Given that no firm is likely to be good at all primary and support activities,

FIGURE 3.1 The Value Chain

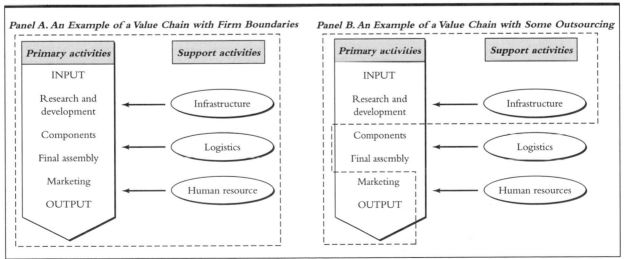

Note: Dotted lines represent firm boundaries.

© Cengage Learning

benchmarking

Examination as to whether a firm has resources and capabilities to perform a particular activity in a manner superior to competitors.

commoditization

A process of market competition through which unique products that command high prices and high margins generally lose their ability to do so—these products thus become "commodities."

the key is to examine whether the firm has resources and capabilities to perform a *particular* activity in a manner superior to competitors—a process known as **benchmarking** in SWOT analysis. If managers find that their firm's particular activity is unsatisfactory, a decision model (shown in Figure 3.2) can remedy the situation. In the first stage, managers ask: "Do we really need to perform this activity in-house?" Figure 3.3 introduces a framework to take a hard look at this question, whose answer boils down to (1) whether an activity is industry-specific or common across industries, and (2) whether this activity is proprietary (firm-specific) or not. The answer is "No" when the activity is found in Cell 2 in Figure 3.3 with a great deal of commonality across industries and little need for keeping it proprietary—known in the recent jargon as a high degree of **commoditization**. The answer may also be "No" if the activity is in Cell 1 in Figure 3.3, which is industry-specific but also with a high level of commoditization. Then, the firm may want to outsource this activity, sell the unit involved, or lease the unit's services to other firms (see Figure 3.2). This is because operating multiple stages of uncompetitive activities in the value chain may be cumbersome and costly.

Think about steel, definitely a crucial component for automobiles. But the question for automakers is: "Do we need to make steel by ourselves?" The requirements for steel are common across end-user industries—that is, the steel for automakers is essentially the same for construction, defense, and other steel-consuming end users (ignoring minor technical differences for the sake of our discussion). For automakers, while it is imperative

FIGURE 3.2 A Decision Model in a Value Chain Analysis

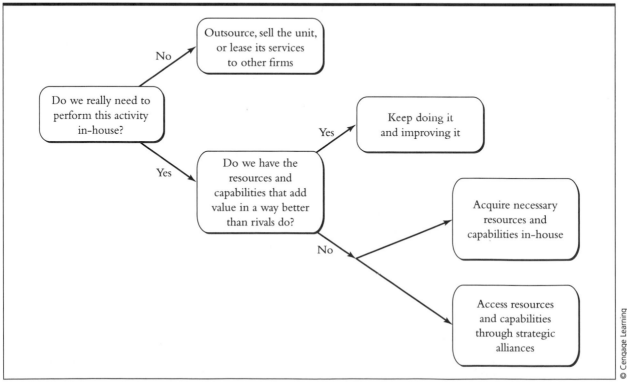

© Cengage Learning

FIGURE 3.3 In-House versus Outsource

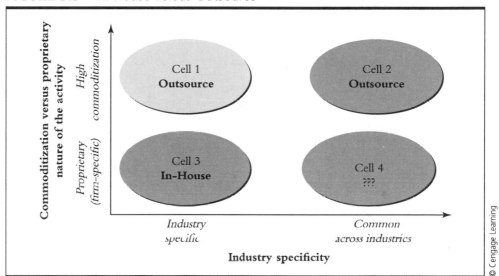

Note: At present, no clear guidelines exist for cell 4, where firms either choose to perform activities in-house or outsource.

to keep the auto making activity (especially engine and final assembly) proprietary (Cell 3 in Figure 3.3), there is no need to keep steel making in-house. Therefore, although many automakers such as Ford and GM historically were involved in steel making, none of them does it now. In other words, steel making is outsourced and steel commoditized. In a similar fashion, Ford and GM no longer make glass, seats, and tires as they did before.

outsourcing

Turning over all or part of an activity to an outside supplier to improve the performance of the focal firm.

Outsourcing is defined as turning over an organizational activity to an outside supplier that will perform it on behalf of the focal firm.[13] For example, many consumer products companies (such as Nike), which possess strong capabilities in upstream activities (such as design) and downstream activities (such as marketing), have outsourced manufacturing to suppliers in low-cost countries. A total of 80% of the value of Boeing's new 787 Dreamliner is provided by outside suppliers. This compares with 51% for existing Boeing aircraft.[14] Recently, not only is manufacturing often outsourced, a number of service activities, such as IT, HR, and logistics, are also outsourced. The driving force is that many firms, which used to view certain activities as a very special part of their industries (such as airline reservations and bank call centers), now believe that these activities have relatively generic attributes that can be shared across industries. Of course, this changing mentality is fueled by the rise of service providers, such as IBM and Infosys in IT, Manpower in HR, Foxconn in contract manufacturing, and DHL in logistics. These specialist firms argue that such activities can be broken off from the various client firms (just as steel making was broken off from automakers decades ago) and leveraged to serve multiple clients with greater economies of scale.[15] Such outsourcing enables client firms to become "leaner and meaner" organizations, which can better focus on their core activities (see Figure 3.1 Panel B).

If the answer to the question, "Do we really need to perform this activity in-house?" is "Yes" (Cell 3 in Figure 3.3), but the firm's current resources and capabilities are not up to the task, then there are two choices (see Figure 3.2). First, the firm may want to acquire

FIGURE 3.4 Location, Location, Location

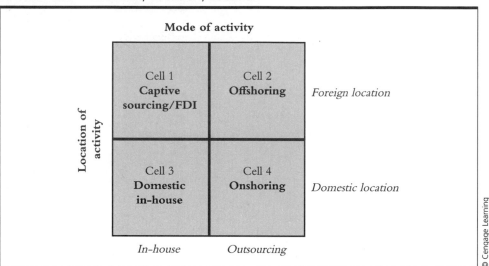

Note: "Captive sourcing" is a new term that is conceptually identical to foreign direct investment (FDI), a term widely used in global strategy.

and develop capabilities in-house so that it can perform this particular activity better.[16] Second, if a firm does not have enough skills to develop these capabilities in-house, it may want to access them through alliances.

Conspicuously lacking in both Figures 3.2 and 3.3 is the *geographic* dimension—domestic versus foreign locations.[17] Because the two terms "outsourcing" and "offshoring" have emerged rather recently, there is a great deal of confusion, especially among some journalists, who often casually equate them as the same. So to minimize confusion, we go from two terms to four terms in Figure 3.4, based on locations and modes (in-house versus outsource):[18]

offshoring

International/foreign outsourcing.

onshoring

Outsourcing to a domestic firm.

captive sourcing

Setting up subsidiaries to perform in-house work in foreign location. Conceptually identical to foreign direct investment (FDI).

- **Offshoring**—international/foreign outsourcing
- **Onshoring**—domestic outsourcing
- **Captive sourcing**—setting up subsidiaries to perform in-house work in foreign locations
- Domestic in-house activity

Outsourcing—especially offshoring—has no shortage of controversies and debates (see the Debates and Extensions section). Despite this set of new labels, we need to be aware that "captive sourcing" is conceptually identical to foreign direct investment (FDI), which is nothing new in the world of global strategy (see Chapters 1 and 6 for details). We also need to be aware that "offshoring" and "onshoring" are simply international and domestic variants of outsourcing, respectively. While offshoring low-cost IT work to India, the Philippines, and other emerging economies has been widely practiced, interestingly, eastern Germany; northern France; and the Appalachian, Great Plains, and southern regions of the United States have emerged as new hotbeds for onshoring.[19] In job-starved regions such as Michigan, high-quality IT workers may accept wages 35% lower than at headquarters in Silicon Valley.

One interesting lesson we can take away from Figure 3.4 is that even for a single firm, value-adding activities may be geographically dispersed around the world, taking advantage of the best locations and modes to perform certain activities. For instance, a Dell laptop may be designed in the United States (domestic in-house activity), its components may be produced in Taiwan (offshoring) as well as the United States (onshoring), and its final assembly may be in China (captive sourcing/FDI). When customers call for help, the call center may be in India, Ireland, Jamaica, or the Philippines, manned by an outside service provider—Dell may have outsourced the service activities through offshoring.

Overall, a value chain analysis engages managers to ascertain a firm's strengths and weaknesses on an activity-by-activity basis, *relative to rivals,* in a SWOT analysis. The recent proliferation of new labels is intimidating, causing some gurus to claim that "21st century offshoring really is different."[20] In reality, it is not. Under the skin of the new vocabulary, we still see the time-honored SWOT analysis at work. The next section introduces a framework on how to do this.

From SWOT to VRIO

Recent progress in the resource-based view has gone beyond the traditional SWOT analysis. The new work focuses on the value (V), rarity (R), imitability (I), and organizational (O) aspects of resources and capabilities, leading to a **VRIO framework**.[21] Summarized in Table 3.2, addressing these four important questions has a number of ramifications for competitive advantage.

VRIO framework

A resource-based framework that focuses on the value (V), rarity (R), imitability (I), and organizational (O) aspects of resources and capabilities.

The Question of Value

Do firm resources and capabilities add value? The preceding value chain analysis suggests that this is the most fundamental question to start with.[22] Only value-adding resources can lead to competitive advantage, whereas non-value-adding capabilities may lead to competitive *disadvantage.* With changes in the competitive landscape, previous value-adding resources and capabilities may become obsolete. The evolution of IBM is a case in

TABLE 3.2   The VRIO Framework: Is a Resource or Capability...

VALUABLE?	RARE?	COSTLY TO IMITATE?	EXPLOITED BY ORGANIZATION?	COMPETITIVE IMPLICATIONS	FIRM PERFORMANCE
No	—	—	No	Competitive disadvantage	Below average
Yes	No	—	Yes	Competitive parity	Average
Yes	Yes	No	Yes	Temporary competitive advantage	Above average
Yes	Yes	Yes	Yes	Sustained competitive advantage	Consistently above average

Sources: Adapted from (1) J. Barney, 2002, *Gaining and Sustaining Competitive Advantage,* 2nd ed. (p. 173), Upper Saddle River, NJ: Prentice Hall; (2) R. Hoskisson, M. Hitt, & R. D. Ireland, 2004, *Competing for Advantage* (p. 118), Cincinnati: South-Western Cengage Learning.

point. IBM historically excelled in making hardware, including tabulating machines in the 1930s, mainframes in the 1960s, and PCs in the 1980s. However, as competition for hardware heated up, IBM's capabilities in hardware not only added little value, but also increasingly stood in the way for it to move into new areas. Since the 1990s, under two new CEOs, IBM has been transformed into focusing on more lucrative software and services, where it has developed new value-adding capabilities, aiming to become an on-demand computing *service* provider for corporations. As part of this new strategy, IBM purchased PricewaterhouseCoopers (PwC), a leading technology consulting firm, in 2002 and sold its PC division to China's Lenovo in 2004 (see the Opening Case).

The relationship between valuable resources and capabilities and firm performance is straightforward. Instead of becoming strengths, non-value-adding resources and capabilities, such as IBM's historical expertise in hardware, may become weaknesses. If firms are unable to get rid of non-value-adding assets, they are likely to suffer below-average performance.[23] In the worst case, they may become extinct, a fate IBM narrowly skirted during the early 1990s. According to IBM's new CEO Ginni Rometty:

> *Whatever business you're in, it's going to commoditize over time, so you have to keep moving it to a higher value and change.*[24]

The Question of Rarity

Simply possessing valuable resources and capabilities may not be enough. The next question asks: How rare are valuable resources and capabilities?[25] At best, valuable but common resources and capabilities will lead to competitive parity but not an advantage. Consider the identical aircraft made by Boeing and Airbus used by numerous airlines. They are certainly valuable, yet it is difficult to derive competitive advantage from these aircraft alone. Airlines have to work hard on how to use these same aircraft *differently* (see Strategy in Action 3.1).

Only valuable and rare resources and capabilities have the potential to provide some temporary competitive advantage. Overall, the question of rarity is a reminder of the cliché: If everyone has it, you can't make money from it. For example, the quality of the American Big Three automakers is now comparable with the best Asian and European rivals. However, even in their home country, the Big Three's quality improvements have not translated into stronger sales. Embarrassingly, in 2009 both GM and Chrysler, despite the decent quality of their cars, had to declare bankruptcy and be bailed out by the US government (and in the case of GM, also by the Canadian government). The point is simple: Flawless high quality is now expected among car buyers, is no longer rare, and thus provides no advantage.

The Question of Imitability

Valuable and rare resources and capabilities can be a source of competitive advantage only if competitors have a difficult time imitating them (see the Closing Case). While it is relatively easier to imitate a firm's *tangible* resources (such as plants), it is a lot more challenging and often impossible to imitate *intangible* capabilities (such as tacit knowledge, superior motivation, and managerial talents).[26]

Imitation is difficult. Why? In two words: **causal ambiguity**, which refers to the difficulty of identifying the causal determinants of successful firm performance.[27] What exactly has

causal ambiguity
The difficulty of identifying the causal determinants of successful firm performance.

STRATEGY IN ACTION 3.1

ANA: Refreshing the Parts Other Airlines Can't Reach

Launched in 2011, the new Boeing 787 Dreamliner is the first plane to introduce a game-changing technology—lightweight plastic composites. As a result, this midsize long-haul jet is regarded as a technological wonder that is 20% more fuel efficient and 30% less costly to maintain than similar-sized planes. Not surprisingly, airlines around the world love it. In the seven years (2004–2011) before the 787 entered service, it became the fastest selling airliner in history, winning over 800 orders. Its launch customer is All Nippon Airways (ANA), Japan's number one airline, which has ordered 55.

The Dreamliner will certainly be valuable to the first airline to fly it. However, its novelty will soon disappear, as more than 800 planes will follow ANA's first 55 to enter service. In other words, the Dreamliner is valuable, not necessarily rare, and relatively easy to imitate—Boeing is happy to produce for any airline that is willing to cough up

$170 million for a copy. What is ANA's response to hold onto its competitive advantage associated with the 787? It plans to install bidet-toilets as standard in its fleet of Dreamliners, in a bid to attract more fastidious passengers from Japan where the washlet is commonplace. Approximately 70% of Japanese households have a bidet. In July 2007, when the Dreamliner was first unveiled at Boeing's plant in Everett, Washington, ANA chief executive Mineo Yamamoto proudly announced at the ceremony that the bidet-toilets onboard the 787 will be a key source of differentiation by "refreshing the parts other airlines cannot reach."

Sources: Based on (1) *Bloomberg Businessweek*, 2011, ANA: First in class, businessweek.com/adsections, (2) *South China Morning Post*, 2007, Boeing unveils new, green 787 jetliner, July 10: A8; (3) All Nippon Airways, 2012, www.ana.co.jp/787.

caused IBM to be such an enduring and continuously relevant company (see the Opening Case)? IBM has no shortage of competitors and imitators. Rumors about IBM's end erupt periodically (and almost became true at least once in the 1990s). Yet, IBM has always been able to turn around by discarding businesses that it once dominated (think of PCs) and constructing a new portfolio of products and services that add value. In 2011, its service businesses had 32% margins, and its software businesses enjoyed 88% margins.[28]

A natural question is: How does IBM do it? Usually a number of resources and capabilities will be nominated, such as an innovative culture, a commitment to customer relationships, a willingness to change, a strong leadership team, and a multinational presence. While all of these resources and capabilities are plausible, what *exactly* is it? This truly is a million (or billion) dollar question, because knowing the answer to this question is not only intriguing to scholars and students, it can also be hugely profitable for IBM's rivals. Unfortunately, outsiders usually have a hard time understanding what a firm does inside its boundaries. We can try, as many rivals have, to identify IBM's recipe for success by drawing up a long list of possible reasons, labeled as "resources and capabilities" in our classroom discussion. But in the final analysis, as outsiders we are not sure.[29]

What is even more fascinating for scholars and students and more frustrating for rivals is that often managers of a focal firm such as IBM do not know exactly what contributes to their firm's success. When interviewed, they can usually generate a long list of what they do well, such as a strong organizational culture, a relentless drive, and many other attributes. To make matters worse, different managers of the same firm may have a different list. When probed as to which resource or capability is "it," they usually suggest that it is all of the above in *combination*. This is probably one of the most interesting and paradoxical aspects of the resource-based view: If insiders have a hard time figuring out what unambiguously contributes to their firm's performance, it is not surprising that outsiders' efforts in understanding and imitating these capabilities are usually flawed and often fail.[30]

Overall, valuable and rare but imitable resources and capabilities may give firms some temporary competitive advantage, leading to above-average performance for some period of time. However, such advantage is not likely to be sustainable. Shown by the example of IBM, only valuable, rare, and *hard-to-imitate* resources and capabilities may potentially lead to sustained competitive advantage.

The Question of Organization

Even valuable, rare, and hard-to-imitate resources and capabilities may not give a firm a sustained competitive advantage if it is not properly organized. Although movie stars represent some of the most valuable, rare, and hard-to-imitate as well as highest-paid resources, *most* movies flop. More generally, the question of organization asks: How can a firm (such as a movie studio) be organized to develop and leverage the full potential of its resources and capabilities?

Numerous components within a firm are relevant to the question of organization.[31] In a movie studio, these components include talents in "smelling" good ideas, photography crews, musicians, singers, makeup artists, animation specialists, and managers on the business side. These components are often called **complementary assets**,[32] because by themselves they are difficult to generate box office hits. For the favorite movie you saw most recently, do you still remember the names of its makeup artists? Of course, not—you probably only remember the stars. However, stars alone cannot generate hit movies, either. It is the *combination* of star resources and complementary assets that create hit movies. "It may be that not just a few resources and capabilities enable a firm to gain a competitive advantage but that literally thousands of these organizational attributes, bundled together, generate such advantage."[33] Emerging Markets 3.2 illustrates how **ambidexterity** to manage both market forces and government forces simultaneously—as a bundle of complementary resources—is key to navigate the competitive waters in emerging economies. In other words, to attain competitive advantage, market-based and nonmarket-based (political) capabilities need to complement each other. Otherwise, strong market performers, such as Ford in Brazil and Tata in India, may nevertheless hit a wall when messing up government relations (see Emerging Markets 3.2).

Another idea is **social complexity**, which refers to the socially complex ways of organizing typical of many firms. Many multinationals consist of thousands of people scattered in many different countries. How they overcome cultural differences and are organized as one corporate entity and achieve corporate goals is profoundly complex. Oftentimes, it is their invisible relationships that add value.[34] Such organizationally embedded capabilities are thus very difficult for rivals to imitate. This emphasis on social complexity refutes what is half-jokingly called the "Lego" view of the firm, in which a firm can be assembled (and dissembled) from modules of technology and people (a la Lego toy

complementary assets

Numerous noncore assets that complement and support the value-adding activities of core assets.

ambidexterity

Ability to use one's both hands equally well. In management jargon, this term has been used to describe capabilities to simultaneously deal with paradoxes (such as exploration versus exploitation).

social complexity

The socially complex ways of organizing typical of many firms.

EMERGING MARKETS 3.2 ⟩ ⟩

Strategic Ambidexterity in Emerging Economies

"Ambidexterity" literally means the ability to use one's both hands equally well. In management jargon, this metaphor has often been used to theorize about organizational capabilities to simultaneously deal with paradoxes, such as the need to explore new but uncertain innovations versus the necessity to exploit existing efficiency in production. In the context of emerging economies, **strategic ambidexterity** is defined as firms' dynamic capabilities to simultaneously manage influences from both governments and markets. Since market competition has intensified, firms obviously have to enhance their market-based capabilities. However, more influence of market forces does not necessarily mean less influence of government forces. Instead of shying away from government forces, firms are advised to embrace them.

In the Brazilian state of Rio Grande do Sul, the election success of a leftist PT Party (Workers Party) created a problem for Dell. Dell had signed a $100 million investment deal with the previous state government that was more friendly to multinationals. Dell obtained a lucrative incentive package consisting of a 75% tax reduction for 12 years and a $16 million loan at a favorable rate. During the election campaign, the PT Party candidate, who would eventually win and become the new governor, attacked such "excessive" concessions granted to Dell (and also to Ford in a similar deal). Once the new governor was in power, Ford chose to go to another Brazilian state.

Sensing that the new governor was criticized for job losses associated with Ford's departure, Dell seized the opportunity by reaching out to renegotiate with the new governor. Dell argued that unlike Ford, Dell's operations would not pollute the environment; instead, Dell would facilitate access to the Internet—a precondition for a more just and egalitarian social order promoted by the new

governor. Not wanting to lose another major investor, the new governor in the end agreed to let Dell keep its lucrative incentive package intact. The only condition was that Dell needed to donate some computers to poor regions in the state, a condition to which Dell readily agreed.

The need to pay attention to political winds is not only relevant to foreign firms such as Dell in Brazil, it is also important to *domestic* firms. Case in point: The Tata Nano, the much-hyped, cheapest car that presumably would allow many Indians to become first-time car owners and create thousands of jobs, could not be made in its originally planned factory in the Indian state of West Bengal. Thousands of farmers who lost their land used to build the Nano factory protested. Pressure from angry politicians forced Tata to abandon the plan and start another plant in another state, Gujarat, at a great cost. The fact that such an influential and otherwise-respected firm can mess up its political relationships *domestically* underscores the importance of managing political calculations as part of the capabilities in strategic ambidexterity in emerging economies. At winning firms such as Dell, market capabilities complement political savvy. At frustrated firms such as Tata, market capabilities are pulled back by political struggles.

Sources: Based on (1) *BusinessWeek*, 2008, Farmers vs. factories, September 8: 30; (2) F. Hermelo & R. Vassolo, 2010, Institutional development and hypercompetition in emerging economies, *Strategic Management Journal*, 31: 1457–1473; (3) Y. Li, M. W. Peng, & C. Macaulay, 2012, Managing strategic ambidexterity during institutional transitions, working paper, University of Texas at Dallas; (4) R. Nelson, 2007, Dell's dilemma in Brazil, in H. Merchant (ed.), *Competing in Emerging Markets*, London: Routledge.

blocks). By treating employees as identical and replaceable blocks, the "Lego" view fails to realize that social capital associated with complex relationships and knowledge permeating many firms can be a source of competitive advantage.

FIGURE 3.5   Strategic Sweet Spot

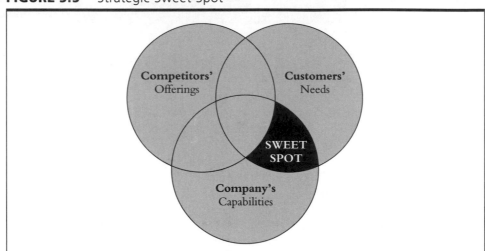

Source: D. Collis & M. Rukstad, 2008, Can you say what your strategy is? (p. 89), *Harvard Business Review,* April: 82–90.

strategic ambidexterity
Firms' dynamic capabilities to simultaneously manage influences from both governments and markets.

Overall, only valuable, rare, and hard-to-imitate capabilities that are organizationally embedded and exploited can possibly lead to sustained competitive advantage and persistently above-average performance. Because capabilities cannot be evaluated in isolation, the VRIO framework presents four interconnected and increasingly difficult hurdles for them to become a source of sustainable competitive advantage (Table 3.2). In other words, these four aspects come together as one "package." Illustrated in Figure 3.5, the VRIO framework urges every firm to search for a strategic sweet spot where it adds value by meeting customer needs in a way that rivals cannot.

Debates and Extensions

Like the industry-based view outlined in Chapter 2, the resource-based view has its fair share of controversies and debates. Here, we introduce four leading debates: (1) firm-specific versus industry-specific determinants of performance, (2) static resources versus dynamic capabilities, (3) offshoring versus non-offshoring, and (4) domestic resources versus international capabilities.

Firm-Specific versus Industry-Specific Determinants of Performance

At the heart of the resource-based view is the proposition that firm performance is most fundamentally determined by firm-specific resources and capabilities, whereas the industry-based view argues that firm performance is ultimately a function of industry-specific attributes. The industry-based view points out persistently different average profit rates of different industries, such as pharmaceutical versus grocery industries. The resource-based view, on the other hand, has documented persistently different performance levels among firms within the same industry, such as IBM and Apple in IT and Southwest and Ryanair in airlines versus other competitors. A number of studies find industry-specific effects to be more significant.[35] However, many studies are supportive of the resource-based view— firm-specific capabilities are stronger determinants of firm performance than industry-specific effects.[36]

While the debate goes on, it is important to caution against an interest in declaring one side to be "winning."[37] There are two reasons for such caution— methodological and practical. First, while industry-based studies have used more observable proxies such as entry barriers and concentration ratios, resource-based studies have to confront the challenge of how to measure *unobservable* firm-specific capabilities, such as organizational learning, knowledge management, and managerial talents. While resource-based scholars have created many innovative measures to "get at" these capabilities, these measures at best are "observable consequences of unobservable resources" and can be subject to methodological criticisms.[38] Critics contend that the resource-based view follows the logic that "show me a success story and I will show you a core competence [resource] (or show me a failure and I will show you a missing competence)."[39] Resource-based theorists readily admit that "the source of sustainable competitive advantage is likely to be found in different places at different points in time in different industries."[40] While such reasoning can insightfully *explain* what happened in the past, it is difficult to *predict* what will happen in the future. For instance, are we going to do better than rivals if we match, say, their equipment?

Second and perhaps more important, there is a good practical reason to believe that it is the *combination* of both industry-specific and firm-specific attributes that collectively drive firm performance. They have in fact been argued to be the two sides of the same "coin" of strategic analysis from the very beginning of the development of the resource-based view.[41] It seems to make better sense when viewing both perspectives as *complementary* to each other. In other words, blending these two insightful frameworks may generate more insight.

Static Resources versus Dynamic Capabilities

Another debate stems from the relatively static nature of the resource-based logic, which essentially suggests "Let's identify S and W in a SWOT analysis and go from there." Such a snapshot of the competitive situation may be adequate for slow-moving industries (such as meat packing), but it may be less satisfactory for dynamically fast-moving industries (such as IT). Critics, therefore, posit that the resource-based view needs to be strengthened by a heavier emphasis on dynamic capabilities.

More recently, as we advance into a "knowledge economy," many scholars argue for a "knowledge-based" view of the firm.[42] Tacit knowledge, probably the most valuable, unique, hard-to-imitate, and organizationally complex resource, may represent the ultimate dynamic capability a firm can have.[43] Such invisible assets range from knowledge about customers through years (and sometimes decades) of interaction to knowledge about product development processes and political connections.

Focusing on knowledge-based dynamic capabilities, recent research suggests some interesting, counter-intuitive findings. Summarized in Table 3.3, while the hallmark for resources in relatively slow-moving industries (such as hotels and railways) is complexity that is difficult to observe and results in causal ambiguity, capabilities in very dynamic high-velocity industries (such as IT) take on a different character. They are "simple (not complicated), experiential (not analytic), and iterative (not linear)."[44] In other words, while traditional resource-based analysis urges firms to rigorously analyze their strengths and weaknesses and then plot some linear application of their resources ("learning before doing"), firms in high-velocity industries have to engage in "learning by doing." The imperative for strategic flexibility calls for simple (as opposed to complicated) routines, which help managers stay focused on broadly important issues without locking them into specific details or the use of inappropriate past experience (see the quote from Facebook's founder Mark Zuckerberg in Chapter 1 on p. 11).

Not all fast-moving industries are high-tech ones. As the pace of competition accelerates, more industries, including many traditional low-tech ones, are becoming fast moving—for example, think of the luxury goods industry (see Chapter 2 Closing Case). The end result is **hypercompetition**, whose hallmark is a shortened window during which a firm may command competitive advantage.[45] In hypercompetition, firms undertake dynamic maneuvering intended to unleash a series of small, unpredictable, but powerful actions to erode rivals' competitive advantage.

Overall, recent research suggests that the current resource-based view may have overemphasized the role of leveraging existing resources and capabilities and underemphasized the role of developing new ones. The assumption that a firm is a tightly bundled collection of resources may break down in high-velocity environments, whereby resources are added, recombined, and dropped with regularity.[46] In such a world of hypercompetition whereby sustainable competitive advantage may be unrealistic, a series of short-term unpredictable advantage seems to be the best a firm can hope for.

hypercompetition

A way of competition centered on dynamic maneuvering intended to unleash a series of small, unpredictable, but powerful actions to erode the rival's competitive advantage.

TABLE 3.3 Dynamic Capabilities in Slow-Moving and Fast-Moving Industries

	SLOW-MOVING INDUSTRIES	FAST-MOVING (HIGH-VELOCITY) INDUSTRIES
Market environment	Stable industry structure, defined boundaries, clear business models, identifiable players, linear and predictable change	Ambiguous industry structure, blurred boundaries, fluid business models, ambiguous and shifting players, nonlinear and unpredictable change
Attributes of dynamic capabilities	Complex, detailed, analytic routines that rely extensively on existing knowledge ("learning before doing")	Simple, experiential routines that rely on newly created knowledge specific to the situation ("learning by doing")
Focus	Leverage existing resources and capabilities	Develop new resources and capabilities
Execution	Linear	Iterative
Organization	A tightly bundled collection of resources with relative stability	A loosely bundled collection of resources, which are frequently added, recombined, and dropped
Outcome	Predictable	Unpredictable
Strategic goal	Sustainable competitive advantage (hopefully for the long term)	A series of short-term (temporal) competitive advantage

Sources: Adapted from (1) K. Eisenhardt & J. Martin, 2000, Dynamic capabilities: What are they? *Strategic Management Journal*, 21: 1105–1121; (2) G. Pisano, 1994, Knowledge, integration, and the locus of learning, *Strategic Management Journal*, 15: 85–100.

Offshoring versus Non-Offshoring

Offshoring—or, more specifically, international outsourcing—has emerged as a leading corporate movement. Outsourcing low end manufacturing is now widely practiced. But increased outsourcing of more high-end services, particularly IT services and all sorts of **business process outsourcing (BPO)**, is controversial. Because digitization and commoditization of service work are enabled only by the very recent rise of the Internet and the reduction of international communication costs, their long-term impact is not known. Thus, it is debatable whether such offshoring proves to be a long-term benefit or hindrance to Western firms and economies.[47]

> **business process outsourcing (BPO)**
>
> Outsourcing of business processes such as loan origination, credit card processing, and call center operations.

Proponents argue that offshoring creates enormous value for firms and economies. Western firms are able to tap into low-cost yet high-quality labor, translating into significant cost savings. Firms can also focus on their core capabilities, which may add more value than dealing with non-core (and often uncompetitive) activities. In turn, offshoring service providers, such as Infosys and Wipro, develop *their* core competencies in IT/BPO. McKinsey reported that for every dollar spent by US firms' offshoring to India, US firms save 58 cents (see Table 3.4). Overall, $1.46 of new wealth is created, of which the US economy captures $1.13. India captures the other 33 cents. While acknowledging that some US employees may lose their jobs, proponents suggest that on balance, offshoring is a win-win solution for both US and Indian firms and economies.

Critics make three points on strategic, economic, and political grounds. Strategically, if "even core functions like engineering, R&D, manufacturing, and marketing can—and often should—be moved outside,"[48] what is left of the firm? US firms have gone down this path before—in manufacturing—with disastrous results. In the 1960s, Radio Corporation of America (RCA) invented the color TV and then outsourced its production to Japan, a low-cost country at that time. Fast-forward to the 2000s and the United States no longer has any US-owned color TV producers. What is the nationality of the RCA brand? French firm Thomson sold it to Chinese firm TCL in 2003. So RCA is now a *Chinese* brand. Overall, critics argue that offshoring nurtures rivals. Why are Indian IT/BPO firms now emerging as strong rivals? It is in part because they built up their capabilities doing work for IBM and EDS in the 1990s, particularly by working to help the IT industry prevent the "millennium bug" (or "Y2K") problem.

TABLE 3.4 Benefit of $1 US Spending on Offshoring to India

BENEFIT TO THE UNITED STATES	$	BENEFIT TO INDIA	$
Savings accruing to US investors/customers	0.58	Labor	0.10
Exports of US goods/services to providers in India	0.05	Profits retained in India	0.10
Profit transfer by US-owned operations in India back to the US	0.04	Suppliers	0.09
Net direct benefit retained in the United States	**0.67**	Central government taxes	0.03
Value from US labor reemployed	0.46	State government taxes	0.01
Net benefit to the United States	**1.13**	**Net benefit to India**	**0.33**

Source: Based on text in D. Farrell, 2005, Offshoring: Value creation through economic change, *Journal of Management Studies*, 42: 675–683. Farrell is director of the McKinsey Global Institute, and she refers to a McKinsey study.

original equipment manufacturer (OEM)
A firm that executes design blueprints provided by other firms and manufactures such products.

original design manufacturer (ODM)
A firm that both designs and manufactures products.

original brand manufacturer (OBM)
A firm that designs, manufactures, and markets branded products.

In manufacturing, many Asian firms, which used to be **original equipment manufacturers (OEMs)** executing design blueprints provided by Western firms, now want to have a piece of the action in design by becoming **original design manufacturers (ODMs)** (see Figure 3.6). Having mastered low-cost and high-quality manufacturing, Asian firms such as BenQ, Flextronics, Foxconn, HTC, and Huawei are indeed capable of capturing some design function from Western firms such as Dell, HP, Kodak, and Nokia. Therefore, increasing outsourcing of design work by Western firms may accelerate their own long-run demise. A number of Asian OEMs, now quickly becoming ODMs, have openly announced that their real ambition is to become **original brand manufacturers (OBMs)**. Thus, according to critics of offshoring, isn't the writing already on the wall?

Economically, critics question whether developed economies, on the whole, actually gain more. While shareholders and corporate highflyers embrace offshoring, it increasingly results in job losses in high-end areas such as design, R&D, and IT/BPO. While white-collar individuals who lose jobs will naturally hate it, the net impact on developed economies may still be negative.

Finally, critics make the political argument that many large Western firms are unethical and are interested only in the cheapest and most exploitable labor. Not only is work commoditized, people are degraded as tradable commodities that can be jettisoned. As a result, large firms that outsource work to emerging economies are often accused of destroying jobs at home, ignoring corporate social responsibility,

FIGURE 3.6   From Original *Equipment* Manufacturer (OEM) to Original *Design* Manufacturer (ODM)

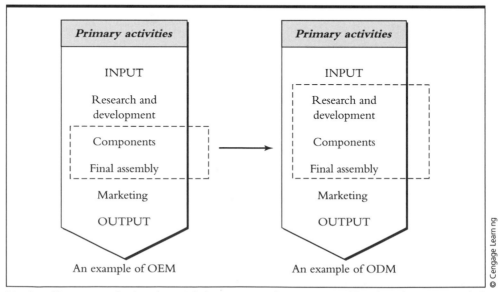

Note: Dotted lines represent firm boundaries. A further extension is to become an original *brand* manufacture (OBM), which would incorporate *brand* ownership and management in the marketing area. For graphic simplicity, it is not shown here.

© Cengage Learning

violating customer privacy (for example, by sending medical records, tax returns, and credit card numbers to be processed overseas), and in some cases undermining national security. Not surprisingly, the debate often becomes emotional and explosive when such accusations are made.

For firms in developed economies, where this debate primarily takes place, the choice is not really offshoring versus non-offshoring, but where to draw the line on offshoring. There is relatively little debate in emerging economies because they clearly stand to gain from offshoring. Taking a page from the Indian playbook, the Philippines, with numerous English-speaking professionals, is trying to eat some of India's lunch. Northeast China, where Japanese is widely taught, is positioning itself as an ideal location for call centers for Japan. Central and Eastern Europe gravitates toward serving Western Europe. Central and South American countries want to grab call center contracts for the large Hispanic market in the United States.

Domestic Resources versus International (Cross-Border) Capabilities

Do firms that are successful domestically have what it takes to win internationally? If you ask managers at The Limited Brands, their answer would be "No." The Limited Brands is the number one US fashion retailer, which has a successful retail empire of 4,000 stores throughout the country with brands such as The Limited, Victoria's Secret, and Bath & Body Works. Yet, it has refused to go abroad—not even Canada. On the other hand, the ubiquitous retail outlets of Zara, LVMH, Gucci, and United Colors of Benetton in major cities around the world suggest that their answer would be "Yes!"

Some domestically successful firms continue to succeed overseas. For example, IKEA has become a global cult brand. The new generation in Russia is known simply as the IKEA Generation. However, many other domestically formidable firms are burned badly overseas. Wal-Mart withdrew from Germany and South Korea. Wal-Mart's leading global rival, France's Carrefour, had to exit the Czech Republic, Japan, Mexico, and Slovakia. Starbucks' bitter brew has also failed to turn into sweet profits overseas.

Are domestic resources and cross-border capabilities essentially the same? The answer can be either "Yes" or "No."[49] This debate is an extension of the larger debate on whether international business is different from domestic business. Answering "Yes" to this question is an excellent argument for having stand-alone international business courses (and for having a global strategy textbook like this one). Answering "No" to this question argues that "international business" fundamentally is about "business," which is well covered by strategy, finance, and other courses (most textbooks in these areas have at least one chapter on international topics). This question is obviously very important for companies and business schools. However, there is no right or wrong answer. It is important to emphasize the advice: *think global, act local*. In practice, this means that despite grand global strategic designs, companies have to concretely win one local market (country) after another (see Chapter 1 Opening Case).

The Savvy Strategist

The savvy strategist can draw at least three important implications for action (Table 3.5). First, there is nothing very novel in the proposition that firms "compete on resources and capabilities." The subtlety comes when managers attempt to distinguish resources and capabilities that are valuable, rare, hard to imitate, and organizationally embedded from those that do not share these attributes. In other words, the VRIO framework can greatly aid the time-honored SWOT analysis, especially the S and W parts. Because managers cannot pay attention to every capability, they must have some sense of what *really* matters. A common mistake that managers often make when evaluating their firms' capabilities is failing to assess them relative to rivals', thus resulting in a mixed bag of both good and mediocre capabilities. The VRIO framework helps managers make decisions on what capabilities to focus on in-house and what to outsource. Capabilities not meeting the VRIO criteria need to be jettisoned or outsourced.

Second, relentless imitation or benchmarking, while important, is not likely to be a successful strategy.[50] By the time Elvis Presley died in 1977, there were a little over 100 Elvis impersonators. After his death, the number skyrocketed.[51] But obviously none of these imitators achieved any fame remotely close to the star status attained by the King of Rock 'n' Roll. Imitators have a tendency to mimic the most visible, the most obvious, and, consequently, the *least* important practices of winning firms (and musicians). At best, follower firms that meticulously replicate every resource possessed by winning firms can hope to attain competitive parity. Firms so well endowed with resources to imitate others may be better off by developing their own unique and innovative capabilities (see the Closing Case).

Third, a competitive advantage that is sustained does not imply that it will last forever, which is not realistic in today's global competition. In fact, competitive advantage has become shorter in duration.[52] All a firm can hope for is a competitive advantage that can be sustained for as long as possible. Over time, all advantages erode.[53] The Opening Case noted that each of IBM's product-related advantages associated with tabulating machines, mainframes, and PCs was sustained for a period of time. But eventually, these advantages disappeared. The lesson for all firms, including current market leaders, is to develop strategic *foresight*—"over-the-horizon radar" is a good metaphor. Such strategic foresight enables firms to anticipate future needs and move early to identify and develop resources and capabilities for future competition.

Finally, how does the resource-based view answer the four fundamental questions in strategy? The idea that each firm is a unique bundle of resources and capabilities directly addresses the first question: Why do firms differ? The answer to the second question— How do firms behave?—boils down to how they take advantage of their strengths embodied in resources and capabilities and overcome their weaknesses. Third, what

TABLE 3.5 Strategic Implications for Action

- Managers need to build firm strengths based on the VRIO framework.
- Relentless imitation or benchmarking, while important, is not likely to be a successful strategy.
- Managers need to build up resources and capabilities for future competition.

determines the scope of the firm? The value chain analysis suggests that the scope of the firm is determined by how a firm performs different value-adding activities relative to rivals. Lastly, what determines firms' international success and failure? Are winning firms lucky or are they smart? The answer, again, boils down to firm-specific resources and capabilities. Although luck certainly helps, it is difficult to believe that IBM's 100-year life span is entirely blessed by luck alone (see the Opening Case).

CHAPTER SUMMARY

1. **Explain what firm resources and capabilities are**
   - "Resources" and "capabilities" are tangible and intangible assets a firm uses to choose and implement its strategies.

2. **Undertake a basic SWOT analysis along the value chain**
   - A value chain consists of a stream of activities from upstream to downstream that add value.
   - A SWOT analysis engages managers to ascertain a firm's strengths and weaknesses on an activity-by-activity basis relative to rivals.

3. **Decide whether to keep an activity in-house or outsource it**
   - Outsourcing is defined as turning over all or part of an organizational activity to an outside supplier.
   - An activity with a high degree of industry commonality and a high degree of commoditization can be outsourced, and an industry-specific and firm-specific (proprietary) activity is better performed in-house.
   - On any given activity, the four choices for managers in terms of modes and locations are (1) offshoring, (2) onshoring, (3) captive sourcing/FDI, and (4) domestic in-house activity.

4. **Analyze the value, rarity, imitability, and organizational (VRIO) aspects of resources and capabilities**
   - A VRIO framework suggests that only resources and capabilities that are valuable, rare, inimitable, and organizationally embedded will generate sustainable competitive advantage.

5. **Participate in four leading debates concerning the resource-based view**
   - (1) Firm-specific versus industry-specific determinants of performance, (2) static resources versus dynamic capabilities, (3) offshoring versus non-offshoring, and (4) domestic resources versus international capabilities.

6. **Draw strategic implications for action**
   - Managers need to build firm strengths based on the VRIO framework.
   - Relentless imitation or benchmarking, while important, is not likely to be a successful strategy.
   - Managers need to build up resources and capabilities for future competition.

KEY TERMS

Ambidexterity p. 74

Benchmarking p. 68

Business process outsourcing (BPO) p. 79

Capability p. 65

Captive sourcing p. 70

Causal ambiguity p. 72

Commoditization p. 68

Complementary assets p. 74

Hypercompetition p. 78

Intangible resources and capabilities p. 65

Offshoring p. 70

Onshoring p. 70

Original brand manufacturer (OBM) p. 80

Original design manufacturer (ODM) p. 80

Original equipment manufacturer (OEM) p. 80

Outsourcing p. 69

Resource p. 64

Resource-based view p. 64

Social complexity p. 74

Strategic ambidexterity p. 76

Tangible resources and capabilities p. 65

Value chain p. 67

VRIO framework p. 71

CRITICAL DISCUSSION QUESTIONS

1. Pick any pair of rivals (such as Boeing/Airbus and Cisco/Huawei), and explain why one outperforms another.

2. *ON ETHICS:* Ethical dilemmas associated with offshoring are plenty. Pick one of these dilemmas and make a case to either defend your firm's offshoring activities or argue against such activities (assuming you are employed at a firm headquartered in a developed economy).

3. *ON ETHICS:* Since firms read information posted on competitors' websites, is it ethical to provide false information on resources and capabilities on corporate websites? Do the benefits outweigh the costs?

TOPICS FOR EXPANDED PROJECTS

1. Conduct a VRIO analysis by ranking your school in terms of the following six dimensions relative to the top three rival schools. If you were the dean with a limited budget, where would you invest precious financial resources to make your school number one among its rivals?

	YOUR SCHOOL	COMPETITOR 1	COMPETITOR 2	COMPETITOR 3
Perceived reputation				
Faculty strength				
Student quality				
Administrative efficiency				
Information systems				
Building maintenance				

2. The Opening Case introduces IBM's 100-year history. Find another firm in any industry and any country that has also survived 100 years. In a short paper, compare and contrast the "secrets" behind the longevity of these two firms.

3. *ON ETHICS:* Illustrated in Strategy in Action 3.2, strategic ambidexterity in emerging economies requires foreign and domestic firms to be not only strong on market competition, but also strong on building relationships with governments. Many governments in emerging economies are known for being corrupt and bureaucratic. Write a short paper to describe some of the ethical dilemmas involved in building good relationships with such governments. Working in small groups, share and discuss your findings.

CLOSING CASE   ETHICAL DILEMMA

Emerging Markets: From Copycats to Innovators

The rise of emerging multinationals from emerging economies—think of Acer, BYD, Cemex, Embraer, Foxconn, Geely, Goldwind, HTC, Lenovo, Mahindra, Suzlon, and Tata—has created tremendous buzz, fear, and disdain around the world. The fear comes from multinationals based in developed economies that are afraid of the disruption brought by this new breed of global competitors. The disdain stems from the characterization of these new multinationals as mere copycats that are good at imitating and bad at innovating.

Although multinationals from developed economies imitate each other all the time, their favorite bragging line is their focus on innovation. In contrast, firms from emerging economies openly confess that they are more interested in learning, which is to say that they are not ashamed of being copycats. In the West, a copycat is defined as one that closely imitates (and even mimics) another, and being a copycat is indicative of a lack of creativity. However, throughout emerging economies, being a copycat is indicative of a conscientious student who intimately learns from the master's every move. For firms in emerging economies, their masters have been good teachers in teaching basic moves. In search for low-cost solutions, Western firms have brought their

original equipment manufacturers (OEM) up to speed—that was how Acer and Lenovo started. In the scramble prior to 2000 to fix the "millennium bug" (otherwise known as the "Y2K" problem), Western IT giants taught Indian firms such as TCS, Infosys, and Wipro a bag of tricks. About a decade ago, the conventional wisdom among Western firms was that firms in emerging economies would indeed become formidable low-cost providers of basic products and services, but as long as they remained behind in the innovation game, they would remain permanently behind leading Western firms. However, such conventional wisdom is now increasingly challenged.

Western firms' emphasis on innovation is consistent with traditional theory, which suggests that a firm's world-class competitive advantage stems from the innovations that it owns—the jargon is "ownership advantage." Owning such innovations allows the GEs, the Siemens, and the Hondas from the Triad to invest globally to teach the rest of the world how to make the stuff. However, a new breed of emerging multinationals has become active global competitors in the *absence* of such world-class capabilities. For example, in semiconductor wafer factories, Chinese technologies are at least two generations behind those of Japan, South Korea, Taiwan, and the United States. In internal-combustion engines, Chinese automakers are still 10 to 20 years behind global leaders. While Indian firms made great progress in IT/BPO, India's lackluster infrastructure seems to undermine the development of more advanced manufacturing and logistics industries.

So what are the core capabilities of the emerging multinationals? While debates rage, one school of thought points to their *learning* abilities. Learning is probably the most unusual aspect among many emerging multinationals. Instead of the "I-will-tell-you-what-to-do" mentality typical of old-line MNEs from developed economies, many emerging multinationals openly profess that they go abroad to learn. Tata expressed a strong interest in learning how to compete in developed economies with high-end products by acquiring Jaguar and Land Rover. Lenovo aspired to learn how to globalize its organization by purchasing IBM's PC division. Geely endeavored to learn to enhance automotive safety and branding capabilities by taking over Volvo.

If you have watched any kung-fu movie (the most recent is *Kung-Fu Panda*), you will remember that a new champion cannot merely be an excellent student—at some point, the student will have to be a master himself by innovating some fancy moves. These moves are not likely to create head-to-head competition against existing masters. Rather, these innovators are likely to leverage their intimate knowledge of the needs and wants of customers in lower-income markets and package it with their learning from world-class competitors. Shown in Table 3.6, the

results may be some "game-changing" or "paradigm-changing" innovations that decisively push advantage to the side of some (while certainly not all) emerging multinationals.

While scholars have long suggested that innovations do not necessarily have to be "high-tech," the hype about "innovation" centers around cutting-edge products and services—many executives and firms daydream about becoming the next Apple. Emerging multinationals tend to focus on "mid-tech" industries and thrive on their capabilities that unleash novel "affordability innovations." For old-line multinationals that traditionally develop high-tech and high-price innovations in developed economies and then manage to let these innovations "trickle down," the learning race now focuses on developing new products and services in emerging economies—known as "reverse innovations." GE's efforts to develop portable ultrasounds and ECG machines in China and India, respectively, represent some successful examples of these new experiments, which are necessitated by the emergence of innovative new multinationals that even the mighty GE has to take seriously (see Emerging Markets 1.2).

Sources: Based on (1) R. Chittoor, M. Sarkar, S. Ray, & P. Aulakh, 2009, Third World copycats to emerging multinationals, *Organization Science*, 20: 187–205; (2) V. Govindarajan & R. Ramamurti, 2011, Reverse innovation, emerging markets, and global strategy, *Global Strategy Journal*, 1: 191–205; (3) Y. Luo, J. Sun, & S. Wang, 2011, Emerging economy copycats, *Academy of*

TABLE 3.6   New Innovations from Emerging Multinationals

AREAS OF INNOVATION	EXAMPLES
Dramatic cost and price reductions that open the vast potential of base-of-the-pyramid markets.	The Tata Nano car, priced at about $2,500, is the world's cheapest mass-produced car.
Leapfrog to latest technologies due to their lack of financial and psychological attachments to legacy technologies.	China's BYD, a battery maker, has little legacy investments in the internal-combustion engine. It is now a leading player in developing electric cars.
Frugal innovations that may have a ready market among poor people in developed economies.	Microfinance, pioneered in Bangladesh, not only revolutionizes entrepreneurial financing in the developing world, but works for the inner-city poor in developed economies.

© Cengage Learning

Management Perspectives, May: 37–56; (4) J. Mathews, 2006, Dragon multinationals as new features of globalization in the 21st century, *Asia Pacific Journal of Management*, 23: 5–27; (5) M. W. Peng, 2012, The global strategy of emerging multinationals from China, *Global Strategy Journal*, 2: 97–107; (6) M. W. Peng, R. Bhagat, & S. Chang, 2010, Asia and global business, *Journal of International Business Studies*, 41: 373–376; (7) O. Shenkar, 2010, *Copycats*, Boston: Harvard Business School Press; (8) S. Sun, M. W. Peng, B. Ren, & D. Yan, 2012, A comparative ownership advantage framework for cross-border M&As, *Journal of World Business*, 47: 4–16.

CASE DISCUSSION QUESTIONS

1. What are the core resources and capabilities of emerging multinationals from emerging economies?

2. What are the core resources and capabilities of most multinationals from developed economies?

3. *ON ETHICS:* Some of the copycat strategies embraced by emerging multinationals have violated the intellectual property rights of their rivals in developed economies. As a new CEO of an emerging multinational brought from the outside, you have just discovered this issue at your new employer. What are you going to do about it?

NOTES

[**Journal acronyms**] *AMJ – Academy of Management Journal;* **AMR** *– Academy of Management Review;* **BW** *– BusinessWeek (before 2010) or Bloomberg Businessweek (since 2010);* **HBR** *– Harvard Business Review;* **JIBS** *– Journal of International Business Studies;* **JIM** *– Journal of International Management;* **JM** *– Journal of Management;* **JMS** *– Journal of Management Studies;* **JWB** *– Journal of World Business;* **MIR** *– Management International Review;* **OSc** *– Organization Science;* **SMJ** *– Strategic Management Journal*

1. J. Barney, 1991, Firm resources and sustained competitive advantage, *JM*, 17: 99–120; M. W. Peng, 2001, The resource-based view and international business, *JM*, 27: 803–829.

2. A. Cuervo-Cazurra & L. Dau, 2002, Promarket reforms and firm profitability in developing countries, *AMJ*, 52: 1348–1368; D. Sirmon, M. Hitt, J. Arregle, & J. Campbell, 2010, The dynamic interplay of capability strengths and weaknesses, *SMJ*, 31: 1386–1409.

3. S. Newbert, 2002, Empirical research on the resource-based view of the firm, *SMJ*, 28: 121–146; D. Sirmon, M. Hitt, & R. D. Ireland, 2007, Managing firm resources in dynamic environments to create value, *AMR*, 32: 273–292.

4. A. Goerzen & P. Beamish, 2002, The Penrose effect, *MIR*, 47: 221–239; J. Steen & P. Liesch, 2007, A note on Penrosian growth, resource bundles, and the Uppsala model of internationalization, *MIR*, 47: 193–206.

5. J. Barney, 2001, Is the resource-based view a useful perspective for strategic management research? (p. 54), *AMR*, 26: 41–56.

6. G. Schreyogg & M. Kliesch-Eberl, 2002, How dynamic can organizational capabilities be? *SMJ*, 28: 913–933; D. Sirmon & M. Hitt, 2009, Contingencies within dynamic managerial capabilities, *SMJ*, 30: 1375–1394; D. Teece, 2007, Explicating dynamic capabilities, *SMJ*, 28: 1319–1350.

7. C. Helfat & S. Winter, 2011, Untangling dynamic and operational capabilities, *SMJ*, 32: 1243–1250.

8. E. Danneels, 2002, The process of technological competence leveraging, *SMJ*, 28: 511–533; A. Phene, K. Fladmoe-Lindquist, & L. Marsh, 2006, Breakthrough innovations in the US biotechnology industry, *SMJ*, 27: 369–388.

9. A. Carmeli & A. Tishler, 2004, The relationships between intangible organizational elements and organizational performance, *SMJ*, 25: 1257–1278.

10. G. Davies, R. Chun & M. Kamins, 2010, Reputation gaps and the performance of service organizations, *SMJ*, 31: 530–546; N. Gardberg & C. Fombrun, 2002, Corporate citizenship, *AMR*, 31: 329–346; M. Rhee, 2009, Does reputation contribute to reducing organizational errors? *JMS*, 46: 676–702; V. Rindova, T. Pollock, & M. Hayward, 2006, Celebrity firms, *AMR*, 31: 50–71.

11. M. Porter, 1985, *Competitive Advantage*, New York: Free Press.

12. A. Parmigiani, 2002, Why do firms both make and buy? *SMJ*, 28: 285–311; M. W. Peng, Y. Zhou, & A. York, 2006, Behind make or buy decisions in export strategy, *JWB*, 41: 289–300.

13. S. Beugelsdijk, T. Pedersen, & B. Petersen, 2009, Is there a trend toward global value chain specialization? *JIM*, 15: 126–141; K. Coucke & L. Sleuwaegen, 2002, Offshoring as a survival strategy, *JIBS*, 39: 1261–1277; J. Hatonen & T. Eriksson, 2009, 30+ years of research and practice of outsourcing, *JIM*, 15: 142–155; P. Jensen, 2009, A learning perspective on the offshoring of advanced services, *JIM*, 15: 181–193; J. Kedia & D. Mukherjee, 2009, Understanding offshoring, *JWB*, 44: 250–261; K. Kumar, P. van Fenema, & M. von Glinow, 2009, Offshoring and the global distribution of work, *JIBS*, 40: 642–667; S. Mudambi & S. Tallman, 2010, Make, buy, or ally? *JMS*, 47: 1434–1456; G. Trautmann, L. Bals, & E. Hartmann, 2009, Global sourcing in integrated network structures, *JIM*, 15: 194–208; C. Weigelt & M. Sarkar, 2012, Performance implications of outsourcing for technological innovations, *SMJ*, 33: 189–216.

14. *BW*, 2006, The 787 encounters turbulence, June 19: 38–40.

15. S. Lahiri, B. Kedia, & D. Mukherjee, 2012, The impact of management capability on the resource-performance linkage, *JWB*, 47: 145–155; R. Mudambi & M. Venzin, 2012, The strategic nexus of offshoring and outsourcing decisions, *JMS*, 47: 1510–1533; H. Safizadeh, J. Field, & L. Ritzman, 2008, Sourcing practices and boundaries of the firm in the financial services industry, *SMJ*, 29: 79–91.

16. D. Gregorio, M. Musteen, & D. Thomas, 2002, Offshore outsourcing as a source of international competitiveness of SMEs, *JIBS*, 40: 969–988; D. Griffith, N. Harmancioglu, & C. Droge, 2009, Governance decisions for the offshore outsourcing of new product development in technology intensive markets, *JWB*, 44: 217–224; C. Grimpe & U. Kaiser, 2010, Balancing internal and external knowledge acquisition, *JMS*, 47: 1483–1509; M. Kenney, S. Massini, & T. Murtha, 2009, Offshoring administrative and technical work, *JIBS*, 40: 887–900; A. Lewin, S. Massini, & C. Peeters, 2009, Why are companies offshoring innovation? *JIBS*, 40: 901–925; Y. Li, Z. Wei, & Y. Liu, 2010 Strategic orientation, knowledge acquisition and firm performance, *JMS*, 47: 1457–1482.

17. J. Doh, K. Bunyaratavej, & E. Hahn, 2009, Separable but not equal, *JIBS*, 40: 926–943; J. Hatonen, 2009, Making the locational choice, *JIM*, 15: 61–76; R. Liu, D. Fails, & B. Scholnick, 2011, Why are different services outsourced to different countries? *JIBS*, 42: 558–571; M. Demirbag & K. Glaister, 2010, Factors determining offshore location choice for R&D projects, *JMS*, 47: 1534–1560; S. Zaheer, A. Lamin, & M. Subramani, 2009, Cluster capabilities or ethnic ties? *JIBS*, 40: 944–968.

18. F. Contractor, V. Kuma, S. Kundu, & T. Pedersen, 2010, Reconceptualizing the firm in a world of outsourcing and offshoring, *JMS*, 47: 1417–1433.

19. A. Pande, 2011, How to make onshoring work, *HBR*, March: 30.

20. D. Levy, 2005, Offshoring in the new global political economy (p. 687), *JMS*, 42: 685–693.

21. J. Barney, 2002, *Gaining and Sustaining Competitive Advantage* (pp. 159–174), Upper Saddle River, NJ: Prentice Hall.

22. R. Adner & R. Kapoor, 2010, Value creation innovation ecosystems, *SMJ*, 31: 306–333; F. Bridoux, R. Coeurderoy, & R. Durand, 2011, Heterogenous motives and the collective creation of value, *AMR*, 36: 711–730; A. Capaldo, 2007, Network structure and innovation, *SMJ*, 28: 585–608; O. Chatain & P. Zemsky, 2011, Value creation and value capture with frictions, *SMJ*, 32: 1206–1231; J. Grahovac & D. Miller, 2009, Competitive advantage and performance, *SMJ*, 30: 1192–1212; T. Holcomb, M. Holmes, & B. Connelly, 2009, Making the most of what you have, *SMJ*, 30: 457–485; M. Kunc & J. Morecroft, 2010, Managerial decision making and firm performance under a resource-based paradigm, *SMJ*, 31: 1164–1182; V. La, P. Patterson, & C. Styles, 2009, Client-perceived performance and value in professional B2B services, *JIBS*, 40: 274–300; M. Leiblein & T. Madsen, 2009, Unbundling competitive heterogeneity, *SMJ*, 30: 711–735; M. Sun & E. Tse, 2009, The resource-based view of competitive advantage in two-sided markets, *JMS*, 46: 45–64.

23. D. Sirmon, S. Gove, & M. Hitt, 2008, Resource management in dyadic competitive rivalry, *AMJ*, 51: 919–935.

24. *BW*, 2011, Can this IBMer keep Big Blue's edge? October 31: 31–32.

25. F. Aime, S. Johnson, J. Ridge, & A. Hill, 2010, The routine may be stable but the advantage is not, *SMJ*, 31: 75–87; D. Tzabbar, 2009, When does scientist

recruitment affect technological repositioning? *AMJ*, 52: 873–896.

26. G. Ray, J. Barney, & W. Muhanna, 2004, Capabilities, business processes, and competitive advantage, *SMJ*, 25: 23–37.

27. A. King, 2007, Disentangling interfirm and intrafirm casual ambiguity, *AMR*, 32: 156–178; T. Powell, D. Lovallo, & C. Caringal, 2006, Causal ambiguity, management perception, and firm performance, *AMR*, 31: 175–196.

28. *BW*, 2011, Can this IBMer keep Big Blue's edge?

29. S. Jonsson & P. Regner, 2009, Normative barriers to imitation, *SMJ*, 30: 517–536; M. Lieberman & S. Asaba, 2006, Why do firms imitate each other? *AMR*, 31: 366–385; F. Polidoro & P. Toh, 2011, Letting rivals come close or warding them off? *AMJ*, 54: 369–392.

30. A. Lado, N. Boyd, P. Wright & M. Kroll, 2006, Paradox and theorizing within the resource-based view, *AMR*, 31: 115–131.

31. M. Chari, S. Devaraj, & P. David, 2007, International diversification and firm performance, *JWB*, 42: 184–197; S. Ethiraj, N. Ramasubbu, & M. Krishnan, 2012, Does complexity deter customer-focus? *SMJ*, 33: 137–161; M. Gruber, F. Heinemann, M. Brettel, & S. Hungeling, 2010, Configurations of resources and capabilities and their performance implications, *SMJ*, 31: 1337–1356; M. Kotabe, R. Parente, & J. Murray, 2007, Antecedents and outcomes of modular production in the Brazilian automobile industry, *JIBS*, 38: 84–106; R. Ployhart, C. Van Iddekinge, & W. Mackenzie, 2011, Acquiring and developing human capital in service contexts, *AMJ*, 54: 353–368; R. Sinha & C. Noble, 2008, The adoption of radical manufacturing technologies and firm survival, *SMJ*, 29: 943–962; K. Srikanth & P. Puranam, 2011, Integrating distributed work, *SMJ*, 32: 849–875.

32. T. Chi & A. Seth, 2009, A dynamic model of the choice of mode for exploiting complementary capabilities, *JIBS*, 40: 365–387; A. Hess & F. Rothaermel, 2011, When are assets complementary? *SMJ*, 32: 895–909; N. Stieglitz & K. Heine, 2007, Innovations and the role of complementarities in a strategic theory of the firm, *SMJ*, 28: 1–15.

33. J. Barney, 1997, *Gaining and Sustaining Competitive Advantage* (p. 155), Reading, MA: Addison-Wesley; J. Jansen, F. Van den Bosch, & H. Volberda, 2005, Managerial potential and related absorptive capacity, *AMJ*, 48: 999–1015.

34. T. Kostova & K. Roth, 2003, Social capital in multinational corporations and a micro-macro model of its formation, *AMR*, 28: 297–317; P. Moran, 2005, Structural vs. relational embeddedness, *SMJ*, 26: 1129–1151.

35. N. Balasubramanian & M. Lieberman, 2010, Industry learning environments and the heterogeneity of firm performance, *SMJ*, 31: 390–412; M. Lenox, S. Rockart, & A. Lewin, 2010, Does interdependency affect firm and industry profitability? *SMJ*, 31: 121–139.

36. J. Hough, 2006, Business segment performance redux, *SMJ*, 27: 45–61; Y. Spanos, G. Zaralis, & S. Lioukas, 2004, Strategy and industry effects on profitability, *SMJ*, 25: 139–165.

37. G. McNamara, F. Aime, & P. Vaaler, 2005, Is performance driven by industry- or firm-specific factors? *SMJ*, 26: 1075–1081; Y. Tang & E. Liou, 2010, Does firm performance reveal its own causes? *SMJ*, 31: 39–57.

38. P. Godfrey & C. Hill, 1995, The problem of unobservables in strategic management research (p. 530), *SMJ*, 16: 519–533.

39. O. Williamson, 1999, Strategy research (p. 1093), *SMJ*, 20: 1087–1108.

40. D. Collis, 1994, How valuable are organizational capabilities (p. 151), *SMJ*, 15: 143–152.

41. B. Wernerfelt, 1984, A resource-based view of the firm (p. 171), *SMJ*, 5: 171–180.

42. T. Reus, A. Ranft, B. Lamont, & G. Adams, 2009, An interpretive systems view of knowledge investments, *AMR*, 34: 382–400; A. von Nordenflycht, 2010, What is a professional service firm? *AMR*, 35: 155–174.

43. S. Berman, J. Down, & C. Hill, 2002, Tacit knowledge as a source of competitive advantage in the National Basketball Association, *AMJ*, 45: 13–32.

44. K. Eisenhardt & J. Martin, 2000, Dynamic capabilities: What are they? (p. 1113), *SMJ*, 21: 1105–1121.

45. R. D'Aveni, 1994, *Hypercompetition*, New York: Free Press. See also E. Chen, R. Katila, R. McDonald, & K. Eisenhardt, 2010, Life in the fast lane, *SMJ*, 31: 1527–1547; C. Lee, N. Venkatraman, H. Tanriverdi, & B. Iyer, 2010, Complementarity-based hypercompetition in the software industry, *SMJ*, 31: 1431–1457,

46. T. Moliterno & M. Wiersema, 2007, Firm performance, rent appropriation, and the strategic resource divestment capability, *SMJ*, 28: 1065–1087; J. Shamsie, X. Martin, & D. Miller, 2009, In with the old, in with the new, *SMJ*, 30: 1440–1452.

47. R. Javalgi, A. Dixit, & R. Scherer, 2009, Outsourcing to emerging markets, *JIM*, 15: 156–168; M. Reitzig & S. Wagner, 2010, The hidden cost of outsourcing, *SMJ*, 31: 1183–1201; S. Swan & B. Allred, 2009, Does "the China Option" influence subsidiary technology sourcing strategy? *JIM*, 15: 169–180.

48. M. Gottfredson, R. Puryear, & S. Phillips, 2005, Strategic sourcing (p. 132), *HBR*, February: 132–139.

49. J. Boddewyn, B. Toyne, & Z. Martinez, 2004, The meanings of "international management," *MIR*, 44: 195–212.

50. K. Kim & W. Tsai, 2012, Social comparison among competing firms, *SMJ*, 33: 115–136.

51. D. Burrus, 2011, *Flash Foresight* (p. 11), New York: HarperCollins.

52. M. Chari & P. David, 2012, Sustaining superior performance in an emerging economy, *SMJ*, 33: 217–229; R. D'Aveni, G. Dagnino, & K. Smith, 2010, The age of temporary advantage, *SMJ*, 31: 1371–1385.

53. G. Pacheco-de-Almeida, 2010, Erosion, time compression, and self-displacement of leaders in hypercompetitive environments, *SMJ*, 31: 1498–1526.

CHAPTER 4

EMPHASIZING INSTITUTIONS, CULTURES, AND ETHICS

© istockphoto/Alexey Stiop

KNOWLEDGE OBJECTIVES

After studying this chapter, you should be able to

1. Explain the concept of institutions

2. Understand the two primary ways of exchange transactions that reduce uncertainty

3. Articulate the two propositions underpinning an institution-based view of strategy

4. Appreciate the strategic role of cultures

5. Identify the strategic role of ethics culminating in a strategic response framework

6. Participate in three leading debates concerning institutions, cultures, and ethics

7. Draw strategic implications for action

Cut Salaries or Cut Jobs?

As a Japanese expatriate, you are the CEO of Yamakawa Corporation's US subsidiary. You scratch your head as you face a difficult decision: Cut salaries across the board or cut jobs when confronting a horrific economic downturn with major losses? Headquarters in Osaka has advised that earnings at home are bad, and that you cannot expect headquarters to bail out your operations. Too bad, US government bailouts are only good for US-owned firms and are thus irrelevant for your unit, which is 100% owned by the Japanese parent company.

As a person brought up in a collectivistic culture, you instinctively feel compelled to suggest an across-the-board pay cut for all 1,000 employees in the United States. You feel an ethical obligation to protect the people working for you, but of course you also feel a grave responsibility to ensure the survival of your business. Personally, as the highest-paid US-based employee, you are willing to take the highest percentage of a pay cut (you are thinking of 30%). If implemented, this plan would call for other executives, who are mostly Americans, to take a 20%–25% pay cut, mid-level managers and professionals a 15%–20% pay cut, and all the rank-and-file employees a 10%–15% pay cut. Indeed, in your previous experience at Yamakawa in Japan, you did this with positive results among all affected Japanese employees. This time, most executive colleagues in Japan are doing the same. However, since you are now managing US operations, headquarters in Osaka, being more globally minded and sensitive, does not want to impose any uniform solutions around the world and asks you to make the call.

A conscientious executive, you have studied all the books on rules, cultures, norms, and ethics—in both Japanese and English—that you can find in preparing for this tough decision. You understand that the formal laws in the United States present few barriers to lay-offs. You have seen frequent announcements in the US media about reduction in force (RIF), which is a euphemism for mass layoffs. You have also noticed that in the recent recession, even "bona-fide" US firms such as AMD, FedEx, HP, and the New York Times have trimmed the base pay for all employees. If there is a time to change the norm and move toward more across-the-board pay cuts in an effort to preserve jobs and avoid RIF, this may be it, according to some US executives quoted in the media.

At the same time, you have also read that some experts note that across-the-board pay cuts are *anathema* to a performance culture enshrined in the United States. "The last thing you want is for your A players—or people in key strategic positions delivering the most value—to leave because you have mismanaged your compensation system," according to Mark Huselid, a Rutgers University professor. You have also read in a *Harvard Business Review* survey that despite the worst recession, 20% of high-potential players in US firms voluntarily jumped ship between 2008 and 2009, in search of greener pastures elsewhere. Naturally, you worry that should you decide to implement the across-the-board pay cuts, you may lose a lot of American star performers and end up with a bunch of mediocre players who cannot go elsewhere—and you may be stuck with them for a long time even after the economy recovers.

After spending two days reading all the materials you have gathered, you still do not have a clear picture. Instead, you have a big headache. You scratch your head again: How should you proceed?

Sources: This case is fictitious. It was inspired by (1) M. Brannen, 2008, Global talent management and learning for the future, *AIB Insights*, 8: 8–12; (2) *BusinessWeek*, 2009, Cutting salaries instead of jobs, June 8: 46–48; (3) *BusinessWeek*, 2009, Pay cuts made palatable, May 4: 67; (4) N. Carter & C. Silva, 2009, High potentials in the downturn: Sharing the pain? *Harvard Business Review*, September: 25; (5) *Wall Street Journal*, 2011, Even hints of layoffs decay morale, September 19, online.wsj.com.

institution-based view
A leading perspective of strategy that argues that in addition to industry- and firm-level conditions, firms also need to take into account wider influences from sources such as the state and society when crafting strategy.

institution
Humanly devised constraints that structure human interaction—informally known as the "rules of the game."

institutional framework
A framework of formal and informal institutions governing individual and firm behavior.

formal institutions
Institutions represented by laws, regulations, and rules.

regulatory pillar
How formal rules, laws, and regulations influence the behavior of individuals and firms.

informal institutions
Institutions represented by norms, cultures, and ethics.

normative pillar
How the values, beliefs, and norms of other relevant players influence the behavior of individuals and firms.

norm
The prevailing practice of relevant players that affect the focal individuals and firms.

How are strategic decisions, such as those associated with cutting salaries or jobs in a recession, made? It is evident that the industry-based and resource-based views introduced in the previous two chapters, while certainly insightful, are not enough to answer such a high-stakes question. To a large degree, firm strategies are enabled and constrained by institutions, popularly known as "the rules of the game" in a society. Different countries have different formal rules regarding the termination of employees. Beyond formal rules, there are informal rules governing these practices. When coping with a recession, in many collectivistic countries such as Japan, across-the-board pay cuts tend to be the norm. In many individualistic countries such as the United States, mass layoffs are often the norm. There are different performance outcomes of these strategic decisions. While across-the-board pay cuts facilitate employee loyalty, they may undermine the morale of star performers. Although mass layoffs keep the star performers, practically everybody else at the firm lives in fear. A workforce living in fear is not likely to show initiative and creativity. Overall, how firms play the game and win (or lose), at least in part, depends on how the rules are made and enforced. Popularized since the 1990s, this **institution-based view**, covering institutions, cultures, and ethics, has emerged as one of the three leading perspectives on strategy.[1] This chapter first introduces the institution-based view. Then we discuss the strategic role of cultures and ethics, followed by a strategic response framework. Debates and implications follow.

Understanding Institutions

Definitions

Building on the "rules of the game" metaphor, Douglass North, a Nobel laureate in economics, more formally defines **institutions** as "the humanly devised constraints that structure human interaction."[2] An **institutional framework** is made up of formal and informal institutions governing individual and firm behavior. These institutions are supported by three "pillars" identified by Richard Scott, a leading sociologist. They are (1) regulatory, (2) normative, and (3) cognitive pillars.[3]

Shown in Table 4.1, **formal institutions** include laws, regulations, and rules. Their primary supportive pillar, the **regulatory pillar**, is the coercive power of governments. For example, while many individuals and companies may pay taxes out of their patriotic duty, a larger number of them pay taxes in fear of the coercive power of the government if they are caught not paying taxes.

On the other hand, **informal institutions** include norms, cultures, and ethics. The two main supportive pillars are normative and cognitive. The **normative pillar** refers to how the values, beliefs, and actions of other relevant players—collectively known as **norms**—influence the behavior of focal individuals and firms.[4] The recent norms

TABLE 4.1 Dimensions of Institutions

DEGREE OF FORMALITY	EXAMPLES	SUPPORTIVE PILLARS
Formal institutions	▪ Laws ▪ Regulations ▪ Rules	▪ Regulatory (coercive)
Informal institutions	▪ Norms ▪ Cultures ▪ Ethics	▪ Normative ▪ Cognitive

© Cengage Learning

centered on rushing to invest in China and India have prompted many Western firms to imitate each other without a clear understanding of how to make such moves work. Cautious managers resisting such "herding" are often confronted by board members and investors: "Why are we not in China and India?" In other words, "Why don't you follow the norm?"

cognitive pillar

The internalized, taken-for-granted values and beliefs that guide individual and firm behavior.

Also supporting informal institutions, the **cognitive pillar** refers to the internalized, taken-for-granted values and beliefs that guide individual and firm behavior.[5] For example, what triggered whistle blowers to report Enron's wrongdoing was their belief in what was right and wrong. While most employees may not feel comfortable with organizational wrongdoing, the norm is to avoid "rocking the boat." Essentially, whistle blowers choose to follow their internalized personal beliefs on what is right by overcoming the norm that encourages silence.

What Do Institutions Do?

While institutions do many things, their key role, in two words, is to *reduce uncertainty*.[6] By signaling which conduct is legitimate and which is not, institutions constrain the range of acceptable actions. In short, institutions reduce uncertainty, which can be potentially devastating.[7] Political uncertainty such as terrorist attacks and ethnic riots may render long-range planning obsolete (see Emerging Markets 1.1). Political deadlocks in Washington have made the US government "less stable, less effective, and less predictable," which led Standard & Poor's to downgrade its triple A crediting rating to AA+.[8] Economic uncertainty such as failure to carry out contractual obligations may result in economic losses. During the Great Recession of 2008–2009, a number of firms, such as Dow Chemical and Trump Holdings, argued that the "unprecedented economic crisis" should let them off the hook.[9] Force majeure is a long-standing legal doctrine that excuses firms from living up to the terms of a deal in the event of natural disasters or other calamities. But is the economic crisis "force majeure"? If the argument prevails, critics contend, then every debtor in a country suffering economic crisis can avoid paying debts. While these arguments are debated in court battles, a great deal of economic uncertainty looms on the horizon.

transaction costs

Costs associated with economic transaction—or more broadly, costs of doing business.

Uncertainty surrounding economic transactions can lead to **transaction costs**, which are defined as the costs associated with economic transactions—or more broadly, the costs of doing business. Nobel laureate Oliver Williamson refers to frictions in mechanical

EMERGING MARKETS 4.1

Managing Uncertainty in Pakistan

Mahummad Azhar Ali, factory manager for National Foods in Karachi, Pakistan, has a set work routine. At dawn he calls his production managers, who live in different parts of this sprawling city of 18 million on the Arabian sea, to find out whether outbreaks of violence have rendered any area dangerous.

If conditions seem especially risky, Ali slips two wallets into his pocket—one real and the other filled with expired credit cards and loose change, ready to hand over if bandits hold him up. He has been held up once. He checks to make sure he isn't riding in the same car as the day before, usually shunning his company-provided Toyota Corolla (a favorite vehicle for Pakistan's upper-middle class) for his own less conspicuous Suzuki Cultus hatchback.

Finally, Ali and his driver head out to meet the 15 buses that have picked up employees at different collection points. Once all the buses have assembled at the rendezvous, Ali heads the convoy 50 kilometers from the city center to National Foods' main plant. When the convoy arrives at 7:45 AM, after a 90-minute ride, the workers line up outside a boundary wall topped with barbed wire and go through a body search as guards armed with shot guns look on. Ali monitors the security check on closed-circuit television from his office. The workday is about to begin. He has been up for more than three hours.

"Anyone else in my position in another country would have half the work I do," says Ali, 49, who has worked at the company, Pakistan's largest maker of spices and pickles, for over 25 years. "If I didn't have to spend so much time figuring all this out, I would be looking at ways to enhance productivity."

Companies across Pakistan's industrial heartland are struggling to cope with rising insecurity, incessant power outages, and government corruption and inefficiency.

Pakistan has lost 35,000 civilians in terrorist attacks since 2006. The war on the Taliban has cost $68 billion in destroyed infrastructure, higher security costs, lost foreign investment, and more.

Some companies still manage to grow. At publicly traded National Foods, sales rose 23% to 7.4 million rupees ($81 million) in the fiscal year ended June 30, 2011. In the company's first year, in 1970, revenue was only 5,000 rupees. "Back then, it was a one-room operation where red chili, coriander, and turmeric were manually ground," says Shakaib Arif, chief operating officer. "Now we make 60 million packets a year with 2,000 employees."

Political violence is not National Foods' worst problem. "The biggest problem by far is energy," says Arif, 38. Demand for electricity in Pakistan is three times the supply. President Asif Ali Zardari is trying to attract independent power producers to Pakistan and has big plans to build hydroelectric plants. Companies cannot wait. "We have created a mix of power we get from the grid, and what we can generate using our gas and diesel generators," Ali says. "It costs three times as much to produce the power through generators."

The country's lack of security takes its toll. "Every time I stop at a light, I look around me and think a gunman is about to come," says Arif, who drives in a small car when visiting the Karachi factory. "I've already been held up three or four times." Ali, the factory manager, has his own way of handling the tension. "When I get into the car in the morning I close my eyes and rest. I don't want to know if any gunman is coming. I let my driver take all the stress."

Source: Excerpted from *Bloomberg Businessweek*, 2011, Convoys and patdowns: A day at the office in Pakistan, July 25: 11–13.

systems: "Do the gears mesh, are the parts lubricated, is there needless slippage or other loss of energy?" He goes on to suggest that transaction costs can be regarded as "the economic counterpart of frictions: Do the parties to exchange operate harmoniously, or are there frequent misunderstandings and conflicts?"[10]

Binding International Commercial Arbitration

Avoiding countries with a weak rule of law is typically advised by textbooks. Yet recent textbooks have also called for firms to invest aggressively in emerging economies, and emerging economies are widely known for their weak rule of law. In Brazil, a limitless number of appeals can be undertaken and the oldest active court case dates back to 1911. In Russia, numerous Russian managers and a small number of foreign managers are in jail, thanks to corrupt prosecutors, police, and courts. In India, there is a shortage of judges—just 11 for every million people, compared with 51 in Britain and 107 in the United States. The number of cases pending before India's courts exceeds 30 *million*. In China, even when foreign firms win intellectual property cases against domestic firms, many court rulings are simply not enforced.

Prior to the recent interest in investing in emerging economies, which country's law would govern the contracts had always been a headache for international investors. Between a host country and a home country, the foreign entrant is understandably afraid of using the host country law—in fear of the local firm's "home court advantage." This fear is magnified in an emerging economy known for its lack of effective rule of law. On the other hand, using the law of the home country of the foreign entrant may not be allowed by the host country of the investment. Are there any institutional mechanisms that can facilitate international investments while addressing the legitimate concerns of both parties?

In response, binding international commercial arbitration (BICA) has emerged as a solution to this seemingly intractable problem. BICA is a process whereby two transacting firms agree a priori to come before a neutral third party (arbitrator) should a dispute arise. As an alternative dispute resolution system, BICA is a means to resolve disputes without entering the domestic court system (in either the home or host country)—thereby creating a neutral middle ground between firms. As a result, BICA has been increasingly used.

For example, why has China been able to attract so much foreign direct investment (FDI) in the past three decades? In addition to the usual suspects such as low cost labor and sizable domestic market, an institution-based rationale, which is typically ignored by reports on China-bound FDI, is that Chinese authorities have actively promoted the use of BICA to alleviate foreign entrants' understandable fear of China's lack of effective rule of law. Specifically, BICA by Stockholm Chamber of Commerce (SCC, a major international arbitration organization) is especially recommended by the Chinese authorities. A case in point: During 2007 and 2009, when Danone and Wahaha engaged in a series of disputes, it was BICA before the SCC that forced both firms to reach a settlement.

Source: This case was based on (1) *Economist*, 2006, India: The long arms of the law, July 1: 40; (2) *Economist*, 2009, Brazil: The self-harming state, November 14: 14–15; (3) *Economist*, 2011, Putin's Russia, December 10: 27–30; (4) B. C. Pinkham & M. W. Peng, 2012, Arbitration and cross-border transaction costs, working paper, University of Texas at Dallas.

opportunism
Self-interest seeking with guile.

An important source of transaction costs is **opportunism**, defined as self-interest seeking with guile. Examples include misleading, cheating, and confusing other parties in transactions that will increase transaction costs. In order to reduce such transaction costs, institutional frameworks increase certainty by spelling out the rules of the game so that violations (such as failure to fulfill a contract) can be mitigated with relative ease (such as through formal arbitration—see Emerging Markets 4.2).

Without stable institutional frameworks, transaction costs may become prohibitively high, to the extent that certain transactions simply would not take place. In the absence of credible institutional frameworks that protect investors, investors may choose to put their money abroad. Rich Russians often choose to purchase a soccer club in London or a seaside villa in Cyprus instead of investing in Russia—in other words, the transaction costs for doing business in Russia may be too high.

How Do Institutions Reduce Uncertainty?

relational contracting

Contracting based on informal relationships (see also informal, relationship-based, personalized exchange).

informal, relationship-based, personalized exchange

A way of economic exchange based on informal relationships among transaction parties. Also known as relational contracting.

Throughout the world, two primary kinds of institutions—informal and formal—reduce uncertainty.[11] Often called **relational contracting**, the first kind of economic transaction is known as an **informal, relationship-based, personalized exchange**. In many parts of the world, there is no need to write an IOU note when you borrow money from your friends. Insisting on such a note, either by you or, worse, by your friends, may be regarded as an insulting lack of trust. While you are committed to paying your friends back, they also *believe* you will—thus, your transaction is governed by informal norms and cognitive beliefs based on what friendship is about. In case you opportunistically take the money and run, your reputation will be ruined and you will not only lose these friends but also, through their word of mouth, lose other friends who may have been willing to loan you money in the future.

However, in addition to the benefits of friendship, there are costs—remember how much time you have spent with friends and how many gifts you have given them? Plotted graphically (Figure 4.1), initially, at time T1, the costs to engage in relational contracting are high (at point A) and the benefits low (at point B), because parties need to build strong social networks through a time- and resource-consuming process to check each other out (such as going to school together). If relationships stand the test of time, then benefits may outweigh costs. Over time, when the scale and scope of informal transactions

FIGURE 4.1 Informal, Relationship-Based, Personalized Exchange

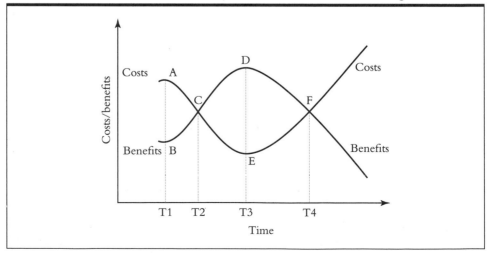

Source: M. W. Peng (2003), Institutional transitions and strategic choices (p. 279), *Academy of Management Review*, 28 (2): 275–296.

expand, the costs per transaction move down (from A to C and then E) and benefits move up (from B to C and then D), because the threat of opportunism is limited by the extent to which informal sanctions may be imposed against opportunists if necessary. There is little demand for costly formal third-party enforcement (such as an IOU note scrutinized by lawyers and notarized by governments). Thus, between T2 and T3, you and your friends—and the economy collectively—are likely to benefit from relational contracting.[12]

Past time T3, however, the costs of such a mode may gradually outweigh its benefits, because "the greater the variety and numbers of exchange, the more complex the kinds of agreements that have to be made, and so the more difficult it is to do so" informally.[13] Specifically, there is a limit as to the number and strength of network ties an individual or firm can possess. In other words, how many good friends can each person (or firm) have? Regardless of how many "Facebook friends" you have, nobody can claim to have 100 real *good* friends. When the informal enforcement regime is weak, trust can be easily exploited and abused. What are you going to do if your (so-called) friends who borrow money from you refuse to pay you back or simply disappear? As a result, the limit of relational contracting is likely to be reached at time T3. Past T4, the costs are likely to gradually outweigh the benefits.

Often termed **arm's-length transaction**, the second institutional mode to govern relationships is a **formal, rule-based, impersonal exchange with third-party enforcement**. As the economy expands, the scale and scope of transactions rise (you want to borrow more money to start up a firm and there are many entrepreneurs like you), calling for the emergence of third-party enforcement through formal market-supporting institutions. Shown in Figure 4.2, the initial costs per transaction are high, because of the high costs of formal institutions. Credit bureaus, courts, jails, police, and lawyers are expensive.

arm's-length transactions

Transactions in which parties keep a distance (see also formal, rule-based, impersonal exchange).

formal, rule-based, impersonal exchange

A way of economic exchange based on formal transactions in which parties keep a distance (see also arm's-length transactions).

FIGURE 4.2 Formal, Rule-Based, Impersonal Exchange

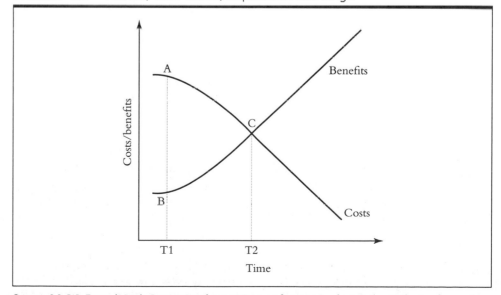

Source: M. W. Peng (2003), Institutional transitions and strategic choices (p. 280), *Academy of Management Review*, 28 (2): 275–296.

Small villages usually cannot afford (and do not need) them. Over time, however, third-party enforcement is likely to facilitate the widening of markets, because unfamiliar parties, people who are not your friends and who would have been deterred to transact with you before, are now confident enough to trade with you (and others). In other words, with an adequate formal institutional framework, you (or your firm) can now borrow from local banks, out-of-state banks, or even foreign banks. Thus, formal market-supporting institutions facilitate more new entries (such as all the new start-ups you and your fellow entrepreneurs can found and all the banks that provide financing) by lowering transaction costs. Consequently, firms are able to grow and economies to expand.

There is no presumption that formal institutions are inherently better than informal ones, because in many situations the demand for formal institutions is not evident. Both forms complement each other. Relational contracting has an advantage when the size of the economy is limited—imagine a small village where everybody knows each other. Its disadvantage is that it may cause firms to stick with established relationships rather than working with new untried players, thus creating barriers to entry. As transaction complexity rises, informal dealings within the group may become difficult—imagine a city or national economy whereby it would be too difficult to impose informal sanctions against opportunists. Arm's-length transactions, on the other hand, help overcome these barriers, by bringing together formerly distant groups (firms, communities, and even countries) to enjoy the gains from complicated long-distance trade. These rule-based transactions thus become increasingly attractive as more new players enter the game. A global economy simply cannot operate on informal institutions alone.

Overall, interactions between institutions and firms that reduce transaction costs shape economic activity. In addition, institutions are not static.[14] **Institutional transitions**, defined as "fundamental and comprehensive changes introduced to the formal and informal rules of the game that affect organizations as players,"[15] are widespread in the world, especially in emerging economies (see Chapter 1). It is evident that managers making strategic choices during such transitions must take into account the nature of institutional frameworks and their transitions, a perspective introduced next.

Institutional transitions
Fundamental and comprehensive changes introduced to the formal and informal rules of the game that affect organizations as players.

firm strategy, structure, and rivalry
How industry structure and firm strategy interact to affect interfirm rivalry.

factor endowments
The endowments of production factors such as land, water, and people in one country.

related and supporting industries
Industries that are related to and/or support the focal industry.

An Institution-Based View of Business Strategy

Overview

Historically, much of the strategy literature, as exemplified by the industry-based and resource-based views, does not discuss the specific relationship between strategic choices and institutional frameworks. To be sure, the influence of the "environment" has been noted. However, much existing work has a "task environment" view that focuses on economic variables such as market demand and technological change.

A case in point is Porter's "diamond" model (Figure 4.3) that argues that competitive advantage of different industries in different nations depends on four factors.[16] According to this model, first, **firm strategy, structure, and rivalry** within one country are essentially the same industry-based view covered in Chapter 2. Second, **factor endowments** refer to the natural and human resource repertoires. Third, **related and supporting industries**

FIGURE 4.3   The Porter Diamond: Determinants of National Competitive Advantage

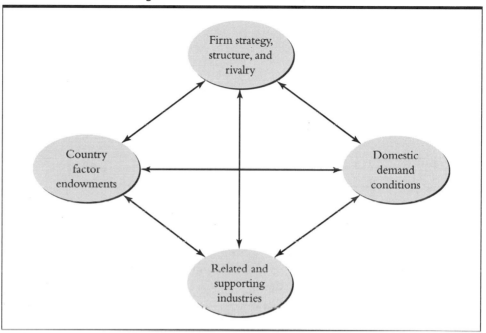

domestic demand

Demand for products and services within a domestic economy.

provide the foundation upon which key industries can excel. Switzerland's global excellence in pharmaceuticals goes hand in hand with its dye industry. Finally, tough **domestic demand** propels firms to scale new heights to satisfy such demand. Why is the American movie industry so competitive worldwide? One reason is that American moviegoers demand the very best. Endeavoring to satisfy such a tough domestic crowd, movie studios unleash *High School Musical 2* and *3* after *High School Musical* and *Spiderman 2* and *3* after *Spiderman*—each time packing more excitement to go beyond the previous production. Overall, the combination of these four factors explains what is behind the competitive advantage of certain globally leading industries.

Interesting as the "diamond" model is, it has been criticized for ignoring histories and institutions, such as what is *behind* firm rivalry.[17] Among strategists, Porter is not alone. Given that most research focuses on market economies, a market-based institutional framework has been taken for granted—in fact, no other strategy textbook has devoted a full chapter to institutions like this one.

Such an omission is unfortunate, because strategic choices, such as those made by the Japanese CEO in the US subsidiary (see the Opening Case), are obviously selected within and constrained by institutional frameworks. Today, this insight becomes more important as more firms do business abroad, especially in emerging economies. The striking institutional differences between developed and emerging economies have propelled the institution-based view to the forefront of strategy discussions.[18] Shown in Figure 4.4, the

FIGURE 4.4   Institutions, Firms, and Strategic Choices

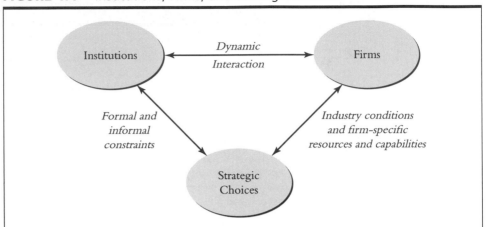

Sources: Adapted from (1) M. W. Peng, 2000, *Business Strategies in Transition Economies* (p. 45), Thousand Oaks, CA: Sage; (2) M. W. Peng, 2002, Towards an institution-based view of business strategy (p. 253), *Asia Pacific Journal of Management*, 19 (2): 251–267.

institution-based view focuses on the dynamic interaction between institutions and firms, and considers strategic choices as the outcome of such interaction. Specifically, strategic choices are not only driven by industry structure and firm-specific resources and capabilities emphasized by traditional strategic thinking, but are also a reflection of the formal and informal constraints of a particular institutional framework.[19]

Overall, it is increasingly acknowledged that institutions are more than background conditions. Instead, "institutions *directly* determine what arrows a firm has in its quiver as it struggles to formulate and implement strategy and to create competitive advantage."[20] At present, the idea that "institutions matter" is no longer novel or controversial. What needs to be better understood is *how* they matter.[21]

Two Core Propositions

The institution-based view suggests two core propositions on how institutions matter (Table 4.2). First, managers and firms *rationally* make strategic choices within institutional constraints.[22] Emerging Markets 4.3 illustrates that one of the main institution-based reasons for emerging multinationals from BRIC to invest overseas is to avoid the bureaucratic, unfriendly, and in some cases predatory policies of their domestic

TABLE 4.2   Two Core Propositions of the Institution-Based View

Proposition 1	Managers and firms *rationally* pursue their interests and make choices within the formal and informal constraints in a given institutional framework.
Proposition 2	While formal and informal institutions combine to govern firm behavior, in situations where formal constraints are unclear or fail, informal constraints will play a *larger* role in reducing uncertainty and providing constancy to managers and firms.

EMERGING MARKETS 4.3

The Institution-Based Motivation Behind Emerging Multinationals

The outward foreign direct investment (OFDI) made by multinationals from emerging economies, especially those from China, has grabbed sensational headlines, such as "China buys the world" (*Fortune*, October 26, 2009) and "Buying up the world" (*Economist*, November 11, 2010). The unmistakable tone is that due to the *strengths* of the Chinese economy, these new multinationals are likely to become strong global contenders and some may become "threats"—resulting in another *Economist* cover story: "America's fear of China" (May 19, 2007). Further digging by scholars reveals that such media sensations are not substantiated by facts on the ground. Two points can be made. First, even among emerging economies, China is *not* the largest generator of OFDI. So what emerging economy has the largest OFDI stock? Not Brazil, not India. Surprise—it is Russia (!). Yet, since 1991, no Western media has ever bothered to report any "Russia threat," despite Russia's much larger OFDI stock (2.1% of world total) versus China's (1.5% of world total). Overall, total Chinese OFDI stock is only 6% of the US OFDI stock. If Chinese multinationals could indeed "buy up" the world with such a tiny sum, then do your own math: US firms would have bought up the world 16 times. The upshot? China's OFDI, while emerging and increasing, certainly does not deserve the media hoopla that does not make a lot of sense.

Second, the actual data reveal that a lot of OFDI made by the emerging multinationals not only from China, but also from Brazil, Russia, and India is a reflection of the institutional *weaknesses* of these economies. A look at the geographic distributions of such OFDI tells why. The number one country receiving Russia's OFDI is tiny Cyprus. Brazil's multinationals love to invest in the British Virgin Islands (BVI). India's OFDI has flooded Mauritius. A full two-thirds of China's OFDI has gone to Hong Kong, and the second largest recipient of China's OFDI is the BVI. How can these relatively small economies known as tax havens absorb so much OFDI from BRIC? The answer: They do not. A substantial chunk of such OFDI is re-invested back to BRIC—this is known as capital round-tripping. The number one foreign investors (by stock) in Brazil, Russia,

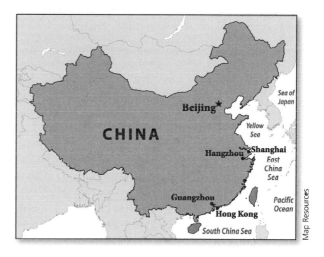

India, and China are the BVI, Cyprus, Mauritius, and Hong Kong, respectively. In China, the BVI has the second largest FDI stock. In other words, instead of using the money overseas to "threaten" host economies, a substantial chunk of such money goes back home to BRIC. The "real" OFDI that is used to acquire local outfits, build factories, and compete with local rivals is much smaller than the total OFDI dollar numbers suggest. Why would managers and firms in BRIC go through such arduous trouble to engage in capital round-tripping? A short answer is that their domestic institutions to protect private property and facilitate investments are *weak*. In Brazil and India, bureaucratic regulations and heavy taxations on domestic earnings have created incentives for firms to invest overseas. In Russia and China, in addition to the above, managers and firms worry about political instability, which may result in the expropriation of their assets. Chinese regulations are more friendly to foreign investors than to domestic firms, especially domestic private firms. In response, a large number of managers and firms in Russia and China have made a rational decision by turning their operations at home into "subsidiaries" of foreign firms registered in the likes of Cyprus and the BVI. Overall, applying some critical thinking skills and probing deeper into institution-based reasoning behind OFDI from emerging economies is so much better and more insightful than blindly believing in the media hoopla.

Sources: Based on (1) *Economist*, 2011, Trouble islands, October 15: 68–69; (2) J. Hines, 2010, Treasure islands, *Journal of Economic Perspectives*, 24: 103–126; (3) A. Kuznetsov, 2011, Outward FDI from Russia and its policy context, update 2011, *Columbia FDI Profiles*, August 2; (4) M. W. Peng, 2012, Why foreign direct investments from China are not a threat, *Harvard Business Review*, February (blogs.hbr.org); (5) M. W. Peng, S. Sun, & D. Blevins, 2011, The social responsibility of international business scholars, *Multinational Business Review*, 19: 106–119; (6) United Nations, 2011, *World Investment Report 2011*, New York: UNCTAD.

---

governments. Why would managers from these firms embrace the challenges of going global while they could have been relatively comfortable and stayed home—after all, their home economies have been growing a lot faster than the rest of the world? The answer has to be that these managers have made a *rational* decision because the institution-based hassles at home outweigh the challenges overseas.

In another example, hundreds of firms and thousands of individuals around the world are involved with counterfeiting. Close to 10% of all world trade is reportedly in counterfeits. Remember that this is not slavery and that everyone involved has voluntarily entered this business. However, no high school graduate anywhere in the world, when filling out a form to determine what would be a desirable career to pursue after graduation, has ever declared an interest in joining counterfeiting. So what happened? Why are so many individuals and firms involved? The key is to realize that managers and entrepreneurs who make such a strategic choice are not amoral monsters but just ordinary people. They have made a *rational* decision (from their standpoint at least) given an institutional environment of weak intellectual protection and the availability of moderately capable manufacturing and distribution skills. Of course, to suggest that a strategy of counterfeiting may be rational does not deny the fact that it is unethical and illegal. However, without an understanding of its institutional basis, it is difficult to devise effective countermeasures.

bounded rationality

The necessity of making rational decisions in the absence of complete information.

Obviously, nobody has perfect rationality—possessing all the knowledge under all circumstances. So Proposition 1 specifically deals with **bounded rationality**, which refers to the necessity of making rational decisions in the absence of complete information.[23] Without prior experience, managers from emerging multinationals from BRIC getting their feet wet overseas and individuals getting involved in counterfeiting do not know exactly what they are getting into. So emerging multinationals often burn cash overseas and counterfeiters sometimes land in jail, which are examples of these decision makers' *bounded* rationality.

The second proposition is that while formal and informal institutions combine to govern firm behavior, in situations where formal constraints fail, informal constraints will play a *larger* role in reducing uncertainty and providing constancy to managers and firms. For example, when the formal institutional regime collapsed with the disappearance of the former Soviet Union, it was largely the informal constraints, based on personal relationships and connections (called *blat* in Russian) among managers and officials, that have facilitated the growth of many entrepreneurial firms.[24]

Many observers have the impression that relying on informal connections is a strategy only relevant to firms in emerging economies and that firms in developed economies only pursue "market-based" strategies. This is far from the truth. Even in developed economies, formal rules only make up a small (although important) part of institutional constraints, and informal constraints are pervasive. Just as firms compete in product markets, firms also fiercely compete in the political marketplace characterized by informal ties.[25] The best-connected firms can reap huge benefits. For every dollar on lobbying spent by US defense firms, they reap $28, on average, in earmarks from Uncle Sam, and more than 20 firms grab $100 or more.[26] Such enviable return on investment (ROI) compares favorably to capital expenditure (where $1 spent brings in $17 in revenues) or direct marketing (where $1 spent barely generates $5 in sales). Basically, if a firm cannot be a cost, differentiation, or focus leader, it may still beat the competition on other grounds—namely, the nonmarket political environment featuring informal relationships.[27] To use the resource-based language, political assets may be very valuable, rare, and hard to imitate. Note that lobbying is not necessarily "corruption"—just a demonstration of certain firms' mastery of the rules of the game.

The Strategic Role of Cultures

The Definition of Culture

culture

The collective programming of the mind that distinguishes the members of one group or category of people from another.

Although hundreds of definitions of culture have appeared, we will use the one proposed by the world's foremost cross-cultural expert, Geert Hofstede, a Dutch professor. He defines **culture** as "the collective programming of the mind which distinguishes the members of one group or category of people from another."[28] Although most international business text-books and trade books talk about culture (often presenting numerous details such as how to present business cards in Japan and how to drink vodka in Russia), virtually all strategy books ignore culture because culture is regarded as "too soft." Such a belief is narrow-minded in today's global economy. Here we will focus on the *strategic* role of culture.

Before proceeding, it is important to make two points to minimize confusion. First, although it is customary to talk about American culture or Brazilian culture, there is no strict one-to-one correspondence between cultures and nation-states. Within the United States, there are numerous sub-cultures such as the Asian American and African American cultures. The same is true for multiethnic countries such as Belgium, Brazil, China, India, Indonesia, Russia, South Africa, and Switzerland. Second, there are many layers of culture, such as regional, ethnic, and religious cultures. Within a firm, one will find a specific organizational culture (such as the Toyota culture). Having acknowledged the validity of these two points, we will follow Hofstede by using the term "culture" when discussing *national* culture—unless otherwise noted. While this is a matter of expediency, it is also a reflection of the institutional realities of the world, which consists of over 200 nation-states imposing different institutional frameworks.

The Five Dimensions of Culture

power distance

The degree of social inequality.

While many ways exist to identify dimensions of culture, the work of Hofstede has become by far the most influential. He and his colleagues have proposed five dimensions (Figure 4.5). First, **power distance** is the extent to which less powerful members within a country expect and accept that power is distributed unequally. For example, in high power distance Brazil, the richest 10% of the population receives approximately 50% of the

FIGURE 4.5 Examples of Hofstede Dimensions of Culture

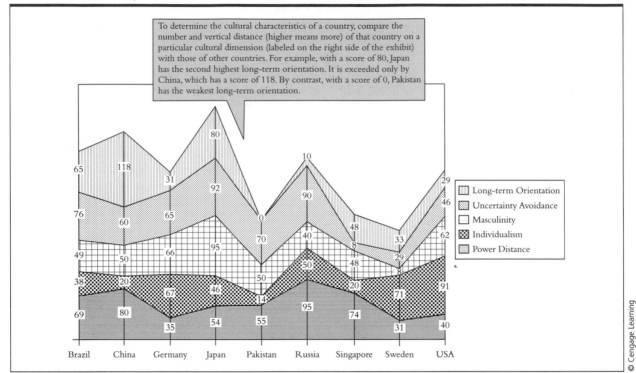

national income and everybody accepts this as "the way it is." In low power distance Sweden, the richest 10% only gets 22% of the national income. In the United States, subordinates often address their bosses on a first-name basis, a reflection of a relatively low power distance. While this boss, Mary or Joe, still has the power to fire you, the distance appears to be shorter than if you have to address this person as Mrs. Y or Dr. Z. In low power distance American universities, all faculty members, including the lowest-ranked assistant professors, are commonly addressed as "Professor A." In high power distance British universities, only full professors are allowed to be called "Professor B." Everybody else is called "Dr. C" or "Ms. D" (if D does not have a PhD). German universities are perhaps more extreme: Full professors with PhDs need to be honored as "Prof. Dr. X."

Second, **individualism** refers to the perspective that the identity of an individual is fundamentally his or her own, whereas **collectivism** refers to the idea that the identity of an individual is primarily based on the identity of his or her collective group (such as family, village, or company). In individualistic societies, ties between individuals are relatively loose and individual achievement and freedom are highly valued. In contrast, in collectivist societies, ties between individuals are relatively close and collective accomplishments are often sought after. This difference in part explains why mass layoffs are widely used in the United States, whereas across-the-board pay cuts are frequently undertaken in Japan (see the Opening Case).

Third, the **masculinity** versus **femininity** dimension refers to sex role *differentiation*. In every traditional society, men tend to have occupations that reward assertiveness, such as

individualism

The perspective that the identity of an individual is most fundamentally based on his or her own individual attributes (rather than the attributes of a group).

collectivism

The perspective that the identity of an individual is most fundamentally based on the identity of his or her collective group (such as family, village, or company).

masculinity

A relatively strong form of societal-level sex role differentiation whereby men tend to have occupations that reward assertiveness and women tend to work in caring professions.

femininity

A relatively weak form of societal-level sex role differentiation whereby more women occupy positions that reward assertiveness and more men work in caring professions.

uncertainty avoidance

The extent to which members in different cultures accept ambiguous situations and tolerate uncertainty.

long-term orientation

A perspective that emphasizes perseverance and savings for future betterment.

politicians, soldiers, and executives. Women, on the other hand, usually work in caring professions such as teachers and nurses in addition to being homemakers. High masculinity societies (led by Japan) continue to maintain such a sharp role differentiation along gender lines. In low masculinity societies (led by Sweden), women increasingly become politicians, scientists, and soldiers, and men frequently assume the role of nurses, teachers, and *househusbands*.[29]

Fourth, **uncertainty avoidance** refers to the extent to which members in different cultures accept ambiguous situations and tolerate uncertainty. Members of high uncertainty avoidance cultures (led by Greece) place a premium on job security, career patterns, and retirement benefits. They also tend to resist change, which, by definition, is uncertain. Low uncertainty avoidance cultures (led by Singapore) are characterized by a greater willingness to take risk and less resistance to change.

Finally, **long-term orientation** emphasizes perseverance and savings for future betterment. China, which has the world's longest continuous written history of approximately 5,000 years and the highest contemporary savings rate, leads the pack. On the other hand, members of short-term orientation societies (led by Pakistan) prefer quick results and instant gratification.

Overall, Hofstede's dimensions are interesting and informative. They are also largely supported by subsequent work.[30] It is important to note that Hofstede's dimensions are not perfect and have attracted some criticisms.[31] However, it is fair to suggest that these dimensions represent a *starting point* for us in trying to figure out the role of culture in global business.

Cultures and Strategic Choices

A great deal of strategic choices is consistent with Hofstede's cultural dimensions. For example, solicitation of subordinate feedback and participation, widely practiced in low power distance Western countries, is regarded as a sign of weak leadership and low integrity in high power distance countries.[32]

Individualism and collectivism also affect strategic choices. Because entrepreneurs are usually willing to take more risk, individualistic societies tend to foster relatively higher levels of entrepreneurship, whereas collectivism may result in relatively lower levels of entrepreneurship.

Likewise, masculinity and femininity have strategic implications. The stereotypical manager in masculine societies is "assertive, decisive, and 'aggressive' (only in masculine societies does this word carry a positive connotation)," whereas the stylized manager in feminine societies is "less visible, intuitive rather than decisive, and accustomed to seeking consensus."[33] At the economy level, masculine countries (such as Japan) may have an advantage in mass manufacturing that focuses on efficiency and speed. Feminine countries (such as Denmark) may have an advantage in small-scale customized manufacturing.

Uncertainty avoidance also has a bearing on strategic behavior. Managers in low uncertainty avoidance countries (such as Great Britain) rely more on experience and training, whereas managers in high uncertainty avoidance countries (such as China) rely more on rules and procedures.

In addition, cultures with a long-term orientation are likely to nurture firms with long horizons. Japanese and Korean firms are known to be willing to forego short-term profits and focus more on market share, which, in the long term, may translate into financial gains. In comparison, Western firms focus on relatively short-term profits.

TABLE 4.3 Some Cross-Cultural Blunders

- Electrolux, a major European home appliance maker, advertised its powerful vacuum machines in the United States using the slogan "Nothing sucks like an Electrolux!"
- A Japanese subsidiary CEO in New York, at a staff meeting consisting of all American employees, informed everyone of the firm's grave financial losses and passed on a request from headquarters in Japan that everyone redouble efforts. The staff immediately redoubled their efforts—by sending their resumes out to other employers.
- In Malaysia, an American expatriate was introduced to an important potential client he thought was named "Roger." He proceeded to call this person "Rog." Unfortunately, this person was a "Rajah," which is an important title of nobility in high power distance Malaysia. Upset, the Rajah walked away from the deal.
- In the United States, some Brazilian and Japanese expatriates treated American secretaries as personal servants, insisting that they serve coffee.
- Shortly after arrival in the US subsidiary, a British expatriate angered minority employees by firing several black middle managers (including the head of the affirmative action program). He was later sued by these employees.

Sources: Based on text in (1) P. Dowling & D. Welch, 2005, *International Human Resource Management*, 4th ed., Cincinnati: South-Western Cengage Learning; (2) M. Gannon, 2008, *Paradoxes of Culture and Globalization*, Thousand Oaks, CA: Sage; (3) D. Ricks, 1999, *Blunders in International Business*, 3rd ed., Oxford, UK: Blackwell.

Overall, there is strong evidence pointing out the strategic importance of culture.[34] Sensitivity to cultural differences can not only help strategists better understand what is going on in other parts of the world, but can also avoid strategic blunders (see Table 4.3 for examples). In addition, while "what is different" cross-culturally can be interesting, it can also be unethical and illegal—all depending on the institutional frameworks in which firms are embedded. Thus, it is imperative that current and would-be strategists be aware of the importance of business ethics, as introduced next.

The Strategic Role of Ethics

The Definition and Impact of Ethics

ethics
The norms, principles, and standards of conduct governing individual and firm behavior.

code of conduct (code of ethics)
Written policies and standards for corporate conduct and ethics.

Ethics refers to the norms, principles, and standards of conduct governing individual and firm behavior. Ethics is not only an important part of *informal* institutions, but is also deeply reflected in *formal* laws and regulations. Recent corporate scandals have pushed ethics to the forefront of global strategy discussions, with numerous firms introducing a **code of conduct**—a set of guidelines for making ethical decisions. There is a debate on what motivates firms to become ethical.

- A *negative* view suggests that some firms may simply jump onto the ethics "bandwagon" under social pressures to appear more legitimate without necessarily becoming more ethical.

- A *positive* view maintains that some (although not all) firms may be self-motivated to "do it right" regardless of social pressures.

- An *instrumental* view believes that good ethics may represent a useful instrument to help make good profits.

All sides of the debate, however, agree that it is increasingly clear that ethics can make or break a firm. Firms with an ethical, trustworthy reputation will not only earn kudos, but may gain significant competitive advantage by attracting more investors, customers, and employees. Perhaps the best way to appreciate the strategic value of ethics is to examine what happens after some crisis. As a "reservoir of goodwill," the value of an ethical reputation can be *magnified* during crisis. After the November 26, 2008, terrorist attacks on the Taj Mahal Palace Hotel in Mumbai that killed 31 people (including 20 guests), the hotel received only praise. Why? The surviving guests were overwhelmed by employees' dedication to duty and their desire to protect guests in the face of terrorist attacks. Eleven employees laid down their lives while helping between 1,200 and 1,500 guests safely escape (see Emerging Markets 3.1). Paradoxically, catastrophes may allow more ethical firms such as the Taj that are renowned for their integrity and customer service to shine. The upshot seems to be that ethics pays (see Figure 4.6).

Managing Ethics Overseas

Managing ethics overseas is challenging, because what is ethical in one country may be unethical elsewhere.[35] Think about the headache that the Japanese expatriate experienced in our Opening Case. Facing such differences, how can managers prepare themselves?

FIGURE 4.6 Integrity Can Command a Premium

"Jenny, can we charge the client extra because of our reputation for integrity?"

Source: Reprinted with permission from Nick Hobart.

ethical relativism
The relative thinking that ethical standards vary significantly around the world and that there are no universally agreed upon ethical and unethical behaviors.

ethical imperialism
The imperialistic thinking that one's own ethical standards should be applied universally around the world.

Two schools of thought exist.[36] First, **ethical relativism** refers to an extension of the cliché, "When in Rome, do as the Romans do." If women in Muslim countries are discriminated against, so what? Likewise, if industry rivals in China can fix prices, who cares? Isn't that what "Romans" do in "Rome"? Second, **ethical imperialism** refers to the absolute belief that "There is only one set of Ethics (with the big E), and we have it." Americans are especially renowned for believing that their ethical values should be applied universally. For example, since sexual discrimination and price fixing are wrong in the United States, they must be wrong everywhere else. In practice, however, neither of these schools of thought is realistic. At the extreme, ethical relativism would have to accept any local practice, whereas ethical imperialism may cause resentment and backlash among locals.

Three "middle-of-the-road" guiding principles have been proposed by Thomas Donaldson, a business ethicist (Table 4.4). First, respect for human dignity and basic rights (such as those concerning health, safety, and the needs for education instead of working at a young age) should determine the absolute minimal ethical thresholds for *all* operations around the world.

Second, respect for local traditions suggests cultural sensitivity. If gifts are banned, foreign firms can forget about doing business in China and Japan. While hiring employees' children and relatives instead of more qualified applicants is illegal according to US equal opportunity laws, Indian companies routinely practice such nepotism, which would strengthen employee loyalty. What should US companies setting up subsidiaries in India do? Donaldson advises that such nepotism is not necessarily wrong—at least in India.

Finally, respect for institutional context calls for a careful understanding of local institutions. Codes of conduct banning bribery are not very useful unless accompanied by guidelines for the scale of appropriate gift giving/receiving. Citigroup allows employees to accept noncash gifts whose nominal value is less than $100. The *Economist* lets its journalists accept any noncash gift that can be consumed in a single day—thus, a bottle of wine is acceptable but a *case* of wine is not. Overall, these three principles, although far from perfect, can help managers improve the quality of their decisions.

Ethics and Corruption

corruption
The abuse of public power for private benefit usually in the form of bribery.

Ethics helps to combat **corruption**, often defined as the abuse of public power for private benefits usually in the form of bribery (in cash or in kind).[37] Corruption distorts the basis for competition that should be based on products and services, thus causing misallocation of resources and slowing economic development.[38] Some evidence reveals that corruption

TABLE 4.4   Managing Ethics Overseas: Three "Middle-of-the-Road" Approaches

- Respect for human dignity and basic rights
- Respect for local traditions
- Respect for institutional context

Sources: Based on text in (1) T. Donaldson, 1996, Values in tension: Ethics away from home, *Harvard Business Review*, September-October: 4–11; (2) J. Weiss, 2006, *Business Ethics*, 4th ed., Cincinnati: South-Western Cengage Learning.

discourages foreign direct investment (FDI).[39] If the level of corruption in Singapore (very low) increases to the level in Mexico (in the middle range), it reportedly would have the same negative effect on FDI inflows as raising the tax rate by 50%.[40]

However, there are exceptions. China is an obvious case, where corruption is often reported. Another exception seems to be Indonesia, whose former president Suharto was known as "Mr. Ten Percent," which refers to the well-known (and transparent!) amount of bribes foreign firms were expected to pay him or members of his family. Why are these two countries popular FDI destinations? Two reasons emerge. First, the vast potential of these two economies may outweigh the drawbacks of corruption. Second, overseas Chinese (mainly from Hong Kong and Taiwan) and Japanese firms are leading investors in mainland China and Indonesia, respectively. While Hong Kong, Taiwan, and Japan may be relatively "cleaner," they are not among the "cleanest" countries. It is possible that "acquiring skills in managing corruption [at home] helps develop a certain competitive advantage [in managing corruption overseas]."[41]

If that is indeed the case, it is not surprising that many US firms complain that they are unfairly restricted by the **Foreign Corrupt Practices Act (FCPA)**, a law enacted in 1977 that bans bribery to foreign officials. They also point out that overseas bribery expenses were often tax-deductible (!) in many EU countries such as Austria, France, Germany, and the Netherlands—at least until the late 1990s. However, even with the FCPA, there is no evidence that US firms are inherently more ethical than others. The FCPA itself was triggered by investigations in the 1970s of many corrupt US firms. Even the FCPA makes exceptions for small "grease" payments to get goods through customs abroad. Most alarmingly, a World Bank study reports that despite over two decades of FCPA enforcement, US firms actually "exhibit systematically *higher* levels of corruption" than other OECD firms (original italics).[42]

Overall, the FCPA can be regarded as an institutional weapon in the fight against corruption.[43] Recall that every institution has three supportive pillars: regulatory, normative, and cognitive (Table 4.1). Despite the FCPA's formal *regulatory* "teeth," for a long time, there was neither a *normative* pillar nor a *cognitive* pillar. The norms among other OECD firms used to be to pay bribes first and get a tax deduction later (!)—a clear sign of ethical relativism. Only in 1997 did the OECD Convention on Combating Bribery of Foreign Public Officials commit all 30 member countries (essentially all developed economies) to criminalize bribery. It went into force in 1999. A more ambitious campaign is the UN Convention against Corruption, signed by 106 countries in 2003 and activated in 2005. If every country criminalizes bribery and every investor resists corruption, their combined power will eradicate it. However, this will not happen unless FCPA-type legislation is institutionalized *and* enforced in every country.

A Strategic Response Framework for Ethical Challenges

At its core, the institution-based view focuses on how certain strategic choices, under institutional influences, are diffused from a few firms to many.[44] In other words, the attention is on how certain practices (such as from paying bribes to refusing to pay) become *institutionalized*. Such forces of institutionalization are driven by a combination

Foreign Corrupt Practices Act (FCPA)

A US law enacted in 1977 that bans bribery of foreign officials.

TABLE 4.5   **Strategic Responses to Ethical Challenges**

STRATEGIC RESPONSES	STRATEGIC BEHAVIORS	EXAMPLES IN THE TEXT
Reactive	Deny responsibility; do less than required	*Ford Pinto fire (the 1970s)*
Defensive	Admit responsibility but fight it; do the least that is required	*Nike (the 1990s), Facebook (2011)*
Accommodative	Accept responsibility; do all that is required	*Ford Explorer rollovers (the 2000s)*
Proactive	Anticipate responsibility; do more than is required	*BMW (the 1990s)*

© Cengage Learning

of regulatory, normative, and cognitive pillars. How firms strategically respond to ethical challenges, thus, leads to a strategic response framework. It features four strategic choices: (1) reactive, (2) defensive, (3) accommodative, and (4) proactive strategies (Table 4.5).

A reactive strategy is passive. Even when problems arise, firms do not feel compelled to act, and denying is usually the first line of defense. The need to take necessary action is neither internalized through cognitive beliefs, nor becoming any norm in practice. That only leaves formal regulatory pressures to compel firms to act. For example, Ford marketed the Pinto car in the early 1970s, knowing that its gas tank had a fatal design flaw that could make the car susceptible to exploding in rear-end collisions. Citing high costs, Ford decided not to add an $11 per car improvement. Sure enough, accidents happened and people were killed and burned in Pintos. Still, for several years Ford refused to recall the Pinto, and more lives were lost. Only in 1978, under intense formal pressures from the government and court cases and informal pressures from the media and consumer groups, did Ford belatedly recall all 1.5 million Pintos.[45]

A defensive strategy focuses on regulatory compliance. In the absence of regulatory pressures, firms often fight informal pressures coming from the media and activists. In the 1990s, Nike was criticized for running "sweatshops," while these incidents took place in its contractors' factories in Indonesia and Vietnam. Although Nike did not own these factories, its initial statement, "We don't make shoes," failed to convey any ethical responsibility. Only when several senators began to suggest legislative solutions did Nike become more serious. Similarly, Facebook defended its behavior when the Federal Trade Commission found that it engaged in unethical (and potentially illegal) conduct (see the Closing Case).

An accommodative strategy features emerging organizational norms to accept responsibility and a set of increasingly internalized cognitive beliefs and values toward making certain changes. These normative and cognitive values may be shared by a number of firms, thus leading to new industry norms. In other words, it becomes legitimate to accept a higher level of ethical and moral responsibility beyond what is minimally required legally. In this fashion, Nike became more accommodative toward the late 1990s.

In another example, in 2000, when Ford Explorer vehicles equipped with Firestone tires had a large number of fatal rollover accidents, Ford evidently took the painful lesson from its Pinto fire fiasco in the 1970s. It aggressively initiated a speedy recall, launched a media campaign featuring its CEO, and discontinued the 100-year-old relationship with Firestone. While critics argue that Ford's accommodative strategy was to place blame squarely on Firestone, the institution-based view (especially Proposition 1) suggests that such highly rational actions are to be expected. Even if Ford's public relations campaign was only "window dressing," publicizing a set of ethical criteria opens doors for scrutiny by concerned stakeholders. It is fair to argue that Ford became a better corporate citizen in 2000 than what it was in 1975.

Finally, proactive firms anticipate institutional changes and do more than is required. For example, BMW anticipated its emerging responsibility associated with the German government's proposed "take-back" policy, requiring automakers to design cars whose components can be taken back by the same manufacturers for recycling. BMW not only designed easier-to-disassemble cars, but also signed up the few high-quality dismantler firms as part of an exclusive recycling infrastructure. Further, BMW actively participated in public discussions and succeeded in establishing its approach as the German national standard for automobile disassembly. Other automakers were thus required to follow BMW's lead. However, they had to fight over smaller lower-quality dismantlers or develop in-house dismantling infrastructure from scratch.[46] Through such a proactive strategy, BMW has facilitated the emergence of new environmentally friendly norms in both car design and recycling. In brief, proactive firms go beyond the current regulatory requirements to do the "right thing." While there is probably an element of "window dressing," the fact that proactive firms are going beyond the current regulatory requirements is indicative of the normative and cognitive beliefs held by many managers on the importance of doing the "right thing."

Debates and Extensions

Similar to the industry-based and resource-based views, the institution-based view has also attracted some significant debates. This section focuses on: (1) opportunism versus individualism/collectivism, (2) cultural distance versus institutional distance, and (3) "bad apples" versus "bad barrels."

Opportunism versus Individualism/Collectivism[47]

Opportunism is a major source of uncertainty, and transaction cost theorists maintain that institutions emerge to combat opportunism. However, critics argue that emphasizing opportunism as "human nature" may backfire in practice.[48] If a firm assumes that employees will steal and thus places surveillance cameras everywhere, then employees who otherwise would not steal may feel alienated enough to do exactly that. If firm A insists on specifying minute details in an alliance contract in order to prevent firm B from behaving opportunistically *in the future*, A is likely to be regarded by B as being not trustworthy and being opportunistic *now*. This is especially the case if B is from a collectivist society. Thus, attempts to combat opportunism may beget opportunism.

Transaction cost theorists acknowledge that opportunists are a minority in any population. However, theorists contend that because of the difficulty to identify such a minority of opportunists *before* they cause any damage, it is imperative to place safeguards that, unfortunately, treat everybody as a potential opportunist. For example, thanks to the work of only 19 terrorists, millions of air travelers around the world since September 11,

2001, now have to go through heightened security. Everybody hates it, but nobody argues that it is unnecessary. This debate, therefore, seems deadlocked.

One cultural dimension, individualism/collectivism, may hold the key to an improved understanding of opportunism. A common stereotype is that players from collectivist societies (such as China) are more collaborative and trustworthy, and that those from individualist societies (such as the United States) are more competitive and opportunistic.[49] However, this superficial understanding is *not* necessarily the case. Collectivists are more collaborative *only* when dealing with **in-group** members—individuals and firms regarded as a part of their own collective. The flip side is that collectivists discriminate more harshly against **out-group** members—individuals and firms not regarded as a part of "us." On the other hand, individualists, who believe that every person (firm) is on his/her (its) own, make less distinction between in-group and out-group. Therefore, while individualists may indeed be more opportunistic than collectivists when dealing with in-group members (this fits the stereotype), collectivists may be *more* opportunistic when dealing with out-group members. Thus, on balance, the average Chinese is not inherently more trustworthy than the average American. The Chinese motto regarding out-group members is: "Watch out for strangers. They will screw you!"

This helps explain why the United States, the leading individualist country, is among societies with a higher level of spontaneous trust, whereas there is greater interpersonal and interfirm *distrust* in the large society in China than in the United States.[50] This also explains why it is important to establish *guanxi* for individuals and firms in China; otherwise, life can be very challenging in a sea of strangers.

While this insight is not likely to help improve airport security screening, it can help managers and firms better deal with each other. Only through repeated social interactions can collectivists assess whether to accept newcomers as in-group members. If foreigners who, by definition, are from an out-group refuse to show any interest in joining the in-group, then it is fair to take advantage of them. For instance, don't refuse the friendly offer of coffee from a Saudi businessman. Most of us do not realize that "Feel free to say no when offered food or drink" reflects the cultural underpinning of individualism, and folks in collectivist societies do not view this as an option (unless one wants to offend the host). This misunderstanding, in part, explains why many cross-culturally naïve Western managers often cry out loud for being taken advantage of in collectivist societies—they are simply being treated as "deserving" out-group members.

Cultural Distance versus Institutional Distance

Given cross-cultural differences and conflicts, it is not surprising that, for instance, Japanese–US joint ventures are shorter lived than Japanese–Japanese joint ventures.[51] Basically, when disputes and misunderstandings arise, it is difficult to ascertain whether the other side is deliberately being opportunistic or is simply being (culturally) different. Firms in general may prefer to do business with culturally close countries because of the shorter **cultural distance**.

However, critics make four arguments.[52] First, they point out a number of findings inconsistent with the cultural distance hypothesis.[53] For example, one study reports

in-group
Individuals and firms regarded as part of "us."

out-group
Individuals and firms not regarded as part of "us."

cultural distance
The difference between two cultures along some identifiable dimensions.

that joint ventures between Chinese and Western firms outperform those between Chinese and Asian firms.[54] Second, critics contend that given the complexity of foreign entry decisions, cultural distance, while important, is but one of many factors to consider. For instance, relative to national culture, organizational culture may be equally important.[55]

Finally, some argue that perhaps cultural distance can be complemented (but not replaced) by the **institutional distance** concept, which is "the extent of similarity or dissimilarity between the regulatory, normative, and cognitive institutions of two countries."[56] For example, the cultural distance between Canada and China is virtually as huge as the cultural distance between Canada and Hong Kong (where 98% of the population is ethnic Chinese). However, the institutional distance between Canada and Hong Kong is much *shorter*: Both use common law, speak English as an official language, and share a common heritage of being former British colonies. Therefore, before entering mainland China, Canadian firms may have a preference to enter Hong Kong first. Overall, this emerging idea on institutional distance is gathering some momentum, as scholars start to look beyond the cultural dimensions and investigate the intricacies of other institutional differences around the world.

institutional distance

The extent of similarity or dissimilarity between the regulatory, normative, and cognitive institutions of two countries.

Bad Apples versus Bad Barrels

This debate focuses on the root cause of unethical business behavior. One argument suggests that people may have ethical or unethical predispositions *before* joining firms. Another side of the debate argues that while there are indeed some opportunistic "bad apples," many times people commit unethical behavior not because they are "bad apples" but because they are spoiled by "bad barrels." Some firms not only condone but may even expect unethical behavior. For example, Siemens has recently been criticized for breeding a "bad barrel" and paid record fines to German, US, and other authorities for engaging in thousands of illegal acts of bribing officials around the world.

The debate on "bad apples" versus "bad barrels" is an extension of the broader debate on "nature versus nurture." Are we who we are because of our genes (nature) or our environments (nurture)? Most studies report that human behavior is the result of both nature *and* nurture. Although individuals and firms (staffed by people) do have some ethical or unethical predispositions that influence their behavior, the institutional environment (such as organizational norms and national institutions) can also have a profound impact. In a nutshell, even "good apples" may turn bad in "bad barrels."

The Savvy Strategist

Strategy is about choices. When seeking to understand how these choices are made, practitioners and scholars usually "round up the usual suspects"—namely, industry structures and firm-specific capabilities. While these views are very insightful, they usually

TABLE 4.6   Strategic Implications for Action

- When entering a new country, do your homework by having a thorough understanding of the formal and informal institutions governing firm behavior.
- Strengthen cross-cultural intelligence by building awareness, expanding knowledge, and leveraging skills.
- Integrate ethical decision making as part of the core strategy processes of the firm—faking it does not last very long.

© Cengage Learning

do not pay adequate attention to the underlying *context*. A contribution of the institution-based view is to emphasize the importance of institutions, cultures, and ethics as the bedrock propelling or constraining strategic choices. Overall, if strategy is about the "big picture," then the institution-based view reminds current and would-be strategists not to forget the "bigger picture."

The savvy strategist draws at least three important implications for action (Table 4.6). First, when entering a new country, do your homework by having a thorough understanding of the formal and informal institutions governing firm behavior. While you don't necessarily have to do "as the Romans do" when in "Rome," you need to understand *why* Romans do things in a certain way.[57] In countries that emphasize informal relational exchanges, insisting on formalizing the contract right away may backfire.

Second, strengthen cross-cultural intelligence by building awareness, expanding knowledge, and leveraging skills.[58] In cross-cultural encounters, while you may not share (or may disagree) with the values held by others, you will need to at least obtain a roadmap of the informal institutions governing their behavior. Of course, culture is not everything. It is advisable not to read too much into culture, which is one of many variables affecting global strategy. But it is imprudent to ignore culture.

Third and finally, integrate ethical decision making as part of the core strategy processes of the firm—faking it does not last very long. The best managers expect norms to shift over time by constantly deciphering the changes in the informal "rules of the game" and by taking advantage of new opportunities—how BMW managers proactively shaped the automobile recycling norms serves as a case in point. Failing to understand and adapt to the changing norms by "sticking one's neck out" in an insensitive and unethical way may lead to unsatisfactory or disastrous results, as Facebook found out (see the Closing Case).

We conclude this chapter by revisiting the four fundamental questions. First, why do firms differ? The institution-based view points out the institutional frameworks that shape firm differences. Second, how do firms behave? The answer also boils down to institutional differences. Third, what determines the scope of the firm? Chapter 9 will have more details on how institutions have shaped the scope of the firm. Finally, what determines the international success and failure of firms? The institution-based view argues that firm performance is, at least in part, determined by the institutional frameworks governing strategic choices.

CHAPTER SUMMARY

1. **Explain the concept of institutions**
   - Commonly known as "the rules of the game," institutions have formal and informal components, each with different supportive pillars (the regulatory, normative, and cognitive pillars).

2. **Understand the two primary ways of exchange transactions that reduce uncertainty**
   - Institutions reduce uncertainty in two primary ways: (1) informal relationship-based personalized exchanges (known as relational contracting), and (2) formal rule-based impersonal exchanges with third-party enforcement (known as arm's-length transaction).

3. **Articulate the two propositions underpinning an institution-based view of strategy**
   - Proposition 1: Managers and firms rationally pursue their interests and make strategic choices within formal and informal institutional constraints.
   - Proposition 2: In situations where formal constraints fail, informal constraints will play a *larger* role.

4. **Appreciate the strategic role of cultures**
   - According to Hofstede, national culture has five dimensions: (1) power distance, (2) individualism/collectivism, (3) masculinity/femininity, (4) uncertainty avoidance, and (5) long-term orientation. Each has some significant bearing on strategic choices.

5. **Identify the strategic role of ethics culminating in a strategic response framework**
   - When managing overseas, two schools of thought are (1) ethical relativism and (2) ethical imperialism.
   - Three "middle of the road" principles focus on respect for (1) human dignity and basic rights, (2) local traditions, and (3) institutional context.
   - When confronting ethical challenges, a strategic framework suggests four strategic choices: (1) reactive, (2) defensive, (3) accommodative, and (4) proactive strategies.

6. **Participate in three leading debates on institutions, cultures, and ethics**
   - (1) Opportunism versus individualism/collectivism, (2) cultural distance versus institutional distance, and (3) "bad apples" versus "bad barrels."

7. **Draw strategic implications for action**
   - When entering a new country, do your homework.
   - Strengthen cross-cultural intelligence.
   - Integrate ethical decision making as part of the core strategy processes of the firm.

KEY TERMS

Arm's-length transactions p. 99

Bounded rationality p. 104

Code of conduct (code of ethics) p. 108

Cognitive pillar p. 95

Collectivism p. 106

Corruption p. 110

Cultural distance p. 114

Culture p. 105

Domestic demand p. 101

Ethical imperialism p. 110

Ethical relativism p. 110

Ethics p. 108

Factor endowments p. 100

Femininity p. 107

Firm strategy, structure, and rivalry p. 100

Foreign Corrupt Practices Act (FCPA) p. 111

Formal institutions p. 94

Formal, rule-based, impersonal exchange p. 99

In-group p. 114

Individualism p. 106

Informal institutions p. 94

Informal, relationship-based, personalized exchange p. 98

Institution p. 94

Institution-based view p. 94

Institutional distance p. 115

Institutional framework p. 94

Institutional transitions p. 100

Long-term orientation p. 107

Masculinity p. 107

Norm p. 94

Normative pillar p. 94

Opportunism p. 97

Out-group p. 114

Power distance p. 105

Regulatory pillar p. 94

Related and supporting industries p. 100

Relational contracting p. 98

Transaction cost p. 95

Uncertainty avoidance p. 107

CRITICAL DISCUSSION QUESTIONS

1. How does the institution-based view complement and differ from the industry-based and resource-based views? Why has the institution-based view become a third leg in the strategy tripod?

2. Find one example of institutional transitions from developed economies and one example from emerging economies. What are their similarities and differences?

3. *ON ETHICS:* Assuming you work for a New Zealand company exporting a container of kiwis to Haiti. The customs official informs you that there is a delay in clearing your container and it may last a month. However, if you are willing to pay an expediting fee of US$200, he will try to make it happen in one day. What are you going to do?

TOPICS FOR EXPANDED PROJECTS

1. If you were the CEO of National Foods in Pakistan, how would you manage uncertainty other than those outlined in Emerging Markets 4.1? If you were the CEO of a foreign electricity utility company looking for opportunities around the world, would President Zardari's call for FDI in the power sector attract you to consider investing in Pakistan? Write a short paper to explain your answers.

2. Some argue that *guanxi* (relationships and connections) is a unique Chinese-only phenomenon embedded in the Chinese culture. As evidence, they point out that the word *guanxi* has now entered the English language and is often used in mainstream media (such

as the *Wall Street Journal*) without explanations provided in brackets. Others disagree, arguing that every culture has a word or two describing what the Chinese call *guanxi*, such as *blat* in Russia, *guan he* in Vietnam, and "old boys' network" in the English-speaking world. They suggest that the intensive use of *guanxi* in China (and elsewhere) is a reflection of the lack of formal institutional frameworks. Write a short paper to explain which side of the debate you would join and why.

3. ***ON ETHICS:*** Why has the FCPA not ended corruption in global business? Working in groups of three or four, research the FCPA, its implementation, and enforcement. Present your findings in a short paper or visual presentation.

CLOSING CASE ETHICAL DILEMMA

Facebook Violates Privacy

Facebook has been playing with fire and has got its fingers burned, again. On November 29, 2011, the US Federal Trade Commission (FTC) announced that it had reached a draft settlement with the giant social network over allegations that it had misled people about its use of their personal data.

The details of the settlement made clear that Facebook, which boasts over 800 million users, betrayed its users' trust. It is also notable because it appears to be part of a broader attempt by the FTC to craft a new privacy framework to deal with the swift rise of social networks in the world.

The regulator's findings come at a sensitive time for Facebook, which is preparing for an initial public offering next year that could value it at around $100 billion. To clear the way for its blockbuster floatation, the firm first needs to resolve its privacy tussles with regulators in America and Europe. Hence its willingness to negotiate the settlement unveiled this week, which should be finalized at the end of December 2011 after a period for public comment.

Announcing the agreement, the FTC said it had found a number of cases where Facebook had made claims that were "unfair and deceptive, and violated federal law." For instance, Facebook passed on personally identifiable information to advertisers, even though it said it would not do

so. And it failed to keep a promise to make photos and videos on deactivated and deleted accounts inaccessible.

The settlement does not constitute an admission by Facebook that it has broken the law. But the regulator's findings are deeply embarrassing for the firm nevertheless. In a blog post published the same day, Mark Zuckerberg, Facebook's boss, tried to play down the impact of the deal. First he claimed that "a small number of high-profile mistakes" were overshadowing the social network's "good history" on privacy. Then he confessed that it could still do better and said he had hired two new "chief privacy officers."

The FTC is not relying on Facebook to police itself. Among other things, the firm will now have to seek consumers' approval before it changes the way it shares their data. And it has agreed to an independent privacy audit every two years for the next 20 years. Jeff Chester of the Center for Digital Democracy reckons that it will make it somewhat easier for privacy activists to hold the social network to account.

There is a clear pattern here. In separate cases over the past couple of years the FTC had insisted that Twitter and Google accept regular external audits, too, after each firm was accused of violating its customers' privacy. The intent seems to be to create a regulatory regime that is tighter than the status quo, but one that still gives social networks plenty of room to innovate. The audits can be used to tweak the framework in the light of new developments.

Some observers reckon web firms have agreed to all this in the hope that it will deflect a push for more onerous privacy legislation in America. But outrage over Facebook's behavior could spur Congress into action anyway. And it will certainly not be lost on regulators in Europe who are scrutinizing the social network's privacy record too. Mr. Zuckerberg's latest *mea culpa* (admission of error and formal apology) is unlikely to be his last.

Source: Economist, 2011, Facebook and privacy: Sorry, friends, December 3: 79.

CASE DISCUSSION QUESTIONS

1. **ON ETHICS:** Supporters of Facebook argue that Facebook's contributions to mankind—think of its positive role behind the Arab Spring of 2011—outweigh its ethical imperfections. Overly harsh regulations will suffocate its capacity to innovate. Do you agree or disagree?

2. **ON ETHICS:** Critics of Facebook argue that its business model is built on violating user privacy. Without selling sensitive personal information to advertisers, how can it make money? Therefore, Facebook must be on a tight regulatory leash. Do you agree or disagree?

3. **ON ETHICS:** Are some of Facebook employees "bad apples" or is Facebook a "bad barrel"?

NOTES

[**Journal acronyms**] *AME – Academy of Management Executive;* **AMJ** *– Academy of Management Journal;* **AMP** *– Academy of Management Perspectives;* **AMR** *– Academy of Management Review;* **APJM** *– Asia Pacific Journal of Management;* **BW** *– BusinessWeek* (before 2010) or *Bloomberg Businessweek* (since 2010); **HBR** *– Harvard Business Review;* **JBV** *– Journal of Business Venturing;* **JIBS** *– Journal of International Business Studies;* **JIM** *– Journal of International Management;* **JM** *– Journal of Management;* **JMS** *– Journal of Management Studies;* **JWB** *– Journal of World Business;* **MIR** *– Management International Review;* **RES** *– Review of Economics and Statistics;* **SMJ** *– Strategic Management Journal.*

1. M. W. Peng, S. Sun, B. Pinkham, & H. Chen, 2009, The institution-based view as a third leg for a strategy tripod, *AMP,* 23: 63–81; M. W. Peng, D. Wang, & Y. Jiang, 2008, An institution-based view of international business strategy, *JIBS,* 39: 920–936.

2. D. North, 1990, *Institutions, Institutional Change, and Economic Performance* (p. 3), New York: Norton.

3. W. R. Scott, 1995, *Institutions and Organizations,* Thousand Oaks, CA: Sage.

4. D. Philippe & R. Durand, 2011, The impact of norm-conforming behaviors on firm reputation, *SMJ,* 32: 969–993.

5. S. Hannah, B. Avolio, & D. May, 2011, Moral maturation and moral conation, *AMR,* 36: 663–685; S. Nadkarni & P. Barr, 2008, Environmental context, managerial cognition, and strategic action, *SMJ,* 29: 1395–1427; B. Tyler & D. Gnyawali, 2009, Managerial collective cognitions, *JMS,* 46: 93–126.

6. M. W. Peng, 2000, *Business Strategies in Transition Economies* (pp. 42–44), Thousand Oaks, CA: Sage.

7. O. Branzai & S. Abdelnour, 2010, Another day, another dollar, *JIBS,* 41: 804–825; M. Czinkota, G. Knight, P. Liesch, & J. Steen, 2010, Terrorism and international business, *JIBS,* 41: 826–843; H. de Soto, 2011, The destruction of economic facts, *BW,* May 2: 60–63; T. Khoury & M. W. Peng, 2011, Does institutional reform of intellectual property rights lead to more inbound FDI? *JWB,* 46: 337–345; S. Lee, Y. Yamakawa, M. W. Peng, & J. Barney, 2011, How do bankruptcy laws affect entrepreneurship development around the world? *JBV,* 28: 505–520.

8. *Economist,* 2011, Looking for someone to blame, August 13: 25–26.

9. *BW,* 2009, The financial crisis excuse, February 23: 32.

10. O. Williamson, 1985, *The Economic Institutions of Capitalism* (pp. 1–2), New York: Free Press.

11. J. Zhou & M. W. Peng, 2010, Relational exchanges versus arm's-length transactions during institutional transitions, *APJM,* 27: 355–370.

12. M. W. Peng, 2003, Institutional transitions and strategic choices, *AMR*, 28: 275–296. See also S. Li, 1999, The benefits and costs of relation-based governance, working paper, Hong Kong: City University of Hong Kong.

13. North, 1990, *Institutions* (p. 34).

14. S. Puffer & D. McCarthy, 2007, Can Russia's state-managed, network capitalism be competitive? *JWB*, 42: 1–13.

15. Peng, 2003, Institutional transitions and strategic choices (p. 275). See also E. George, P. Chattopadhyay, S. Sitkin, & J. Barden, 2006, Cognitive underpinning of institutional persistence and change, *AMR*, 31: 347–365.

16. M. Porter, 1990, *Competitive Advantage of Nations*, New York: Free Press; B. Snowdon & G. Stonehouse, 2006, Competitiveness in a globalized world, *JIBS*, 37: 163–175.

17. H. Davies & P. Ellis, 2001, Porter's *Competitive Advantage of Nations*, *JMS*, 37: 1189–1215; A. Griffiths & R. Zammuto, 2005, Institutional governance systems and variations in national competitive advantage, *AMR*, 30: 823–842; P. Minford, 2006, Competitiveness in a globalized world: A commentary, *JIBS*, 37: 176–178.

18. A. Cuervo-Cazurra & L. Dau, 2009, Promarket reforms and firm profitability in developing countries, *AMJ*, 52: 1348–1368; G. McDermott, R. Corredoira, & G. Kruse, 2009, Public-private institutions as catalysts of upgrading in emerging market societies, *AMJ*, 52: 1270–1296; M. Wright, I. Filatotchev, R. Hoskisson, & M. W. Peng, 2005, Strategy research in emerging economies, *JMS*, 42: 1–33.

19. M. Carney, E. Gedajlovic, & X. Yang, 2009, Varieties of Asian capitalism, *APJM*, 26: 361–380; M. Witt & G. Redding, 2008, Culture, meaning, and institutions, *JIBS*, 40: 859–885.

20. P. Ingram & B. Silverman, 2002, Introduction (p. 20, added italics), in P. Ingram & B. Silverman (eds.), *The new institutionalism in strategic management*: 1–30. Amsterdam: Elsevier.

21. A. Chacar, W. Newburry, & B. Vissa, 2010, Bringing institutions into performance persistence research, *JIBS*, 41: 1119–1140; R. Coeurderoy & G. Murray, 2008, Regulatory environments and the location decision, *JIBS*, 39: 670–687; K. Huang & F. Murray, 2009, Does patent strategy shape the long-run supply of public knowledge? *AMJ*, 52: 1193–1221; S. Julian, J. Ofori-Dankwa, & R. Justis, 2008, Understanding strategic responses to

interest group pressures, *SMJ*, 29: 963–984; T. Kochan, M. Guillen, L. Hunter, & S. O'Mahony, 2008, Public policy and management research, *AMJ*, 52: 1088–1100; T. Kostova, K. Roth, & M. T. Dacin, 2008, Institutional theory in the study of multinational corporations, *AMR*, 33: 994–1006; B. Lee, 2009, The infrastructure of collective action and policy content diffusion in the organic food industry, *AMJ*, 52: 1247–1269; C. Marquis & Z. Huang, 2009, The contingent nature of public policy and the growth of US commercial banking, *AMJ*, 52: 1222–1246; K. Pajunen, 2008, Institutions and flows of foreign direct investment, *JIBS*, 39: 652–669; T. Tong, T. Alessandri, J. Reuer, & A. Chintakananda, 2008, How much does country matter? *JIBS*, 39: 387–405.

22. S. Elbanna & J. Child, 2007, The influence of decision, environmental, and firm characteristics on the rationality of strategic decision-making, *JMS*, 44: 561–590; M. Peteraf & R. Reed, 2007, Managerial discretion and internal alignment under regulatory constraints and change, *SMJ*, 28: 1089–1112; C. Stevens & J. Cooper, 2010, A behavioral theory of governments' ability to make credible commitments to firms, *APJM*, 27: 587–610.

23. D. Ariely, 2009, The end of rational economics, *HBR*, July: 78–84; P. Rosenzweig, 2010, Robert S. McNamara and the evolution of modern management, *HBR*, December: 87–93.

24. M. W. Peng, 2001, How entrepreneurs create wealth in transition economies, *AME*, 15: 95–108.

25. L. Capron & O. Chatain, 2008, Competitors' resource-oriented strategies, *AMR*, 33: 97–121; G. Holburn & R. Bergh, 2008, Making friends in hostile environments, *AMR*, 33: 521–540; S. Lux, T. Crook, & D. Woehr, 2011, Mixing business with politics, *JM*, 37: 223–247; C. Oliver & I. Holzinger, 2008, The effectiveness of strategic political management, *AMR*, 33: 496–520.

26. *BW*, 2007, Inside the hidden world of earmarks, September 17: 56–59.

27. *BW*, 2011, Pssst … wanna buy a law? December 5: 66–72; R. Lester, A. Hillman, A. Zardkoohi, & B. Cannella, 2008, Former government officials as outside directors, *AMJ*, 51: 999–1013; H. Li & Y. Zhang, 2007, The role of managers' political networking and functional experience in new venture performance, *SMJ*, 28: 791–804; J. Pearce, J. De Castro, & M. Guillen, 2008, Influencing politics and political systems, *AMR*, 33: 493–495; P. Ring, G. Bigley, T. D'Aunno, & T. Khanna, 2005, perspectives on how governments matter, *AMR*, 30: 308–320.

28. G. Hofstede, 1997, *Cultures and Organizations: Software of the Mind* (p. 5), New York: McGraw-Hill; G. Hofstede, 2007, Asian management in the 21st century, *APJM*, 24: 421–428.

29. *BW*, 2012, Behind every great woman: The perfect husband, January 9: 54–59.

30. B. Kirkman, K. Lowe, & C. Gibson, 2006, A quarter century of *Culture's Consequences*, *JIBS*, 37: 285–320; K. Leung, R. Bhagat, N. Buchan, M. Erez, & C. Gibson, 2005, Culture and international business, *JIBS*, 36: 357–378; L. Tang & P. Koveos, 2008, A framework to update Hofstede's cultural value indices, *JIBS*, 39: 1045–1063.

31. T. Fang, 2010, Asian management research needs more self-confidence, *APJM*, 27: 155–170; R. House, P. Hanges, M. Javidan, P. Dorfman, & V. Gupta, 2004, *Culture, Leadership, and Organizations*, Thousand Oaks, CA: Sage; R. Maseland & A. van Hoom, 2009, Explaining the negative correlation between values and practices, *JIBS*, 40: 527–532; R. Tung & A. Verbeke, 2010, Beyond Hofstede and GLOBE, *JIBS*, 41: 1259–1274.

32. G. Hirst, P. Budhwar, B. Cooper, M. West, C. Long, C. Xu, & H. Shipton, 2008, Cross-cultural variations in climate for autonomy, stress, and organizational productivity relationships, *JIBS*, 39: 1343–1358.

33. Hofstede, 1997, *Cultures and Organizations* (p. 94).

34. A. Bhardwaj, J. Dietz, & P. Beamish, 2007, Host country cultural influences on foreign direct investment, *MIR*, 47: 29–50; K. Lee, G. Yang, & J. Graham, 2006, Tension and trust in international business negotiations, *JIBS*, 37: 623–641; J. Salk & M. Brannen, 2000, National culture, networks, and individual influence in a multinational management team, *AMJ*, 43: 191–202.

35. D. McCarthy & S. Puffer, 2008, Interpreting the ethicality of corporate governance decisions in Russia, *AMR*, 33: 11–31; A. Spicer, T. Dunfee, & W. Bailey, 2004, Does national context matter in ethical decision making? *AMJ*, 47: 610–620.

36. This section draws heavily from T. Donaldson, 1996, Values in tension, *HBR*, September–October: 4–11.

37. K. Martin, J. Cullen, J. Johnson, & K. Parboteeah, 2007, Deciding to bribe, *AMJ*, 50: 1401–1422.

38. C. Robertson & A. Watson, 2004, Corruption and change, *SMJ*, 25: 385–396; S. Lee & K. Oh, 2007, Corruption in Asia, *APJM*, 24: 97–114; S. Lee & S. Hong, 2012, Corruption and subsidiary profitability, *APJM* (in press); J. H. Zhao, S. Kim, & J. Du, 2003, The impact of corruption and transparency on foreign direct investment, *MIR*, 43: 41–62; J. Zhou & M. W. Peng, 2012, Does bribery help or hurt firm growth around the world? *APJM* (in press).

39. S. Globerman & D. Shapiro, 2003, Governance infrastructure and US foreign direct investment, *JIBS*, 34: 19–39.

40. S. Wei, 2000, How taxing is corruption on international investors? *RES*, 82: 1–11.

41. M. Habib & L. Zurawicki, 2002, Corruption and foreign direct investment (p. 295), *JIBS*, 33: 291–307.

42. J. Hellman, G. Jones, & D. Kaufmann, 2002, Far from home: Do foreign investors import higher standards of governance in transition economies (p. 20), Working paper, Washington: World Bank (www.worldbank.org).

43. A. Cuervo-Cazzura, 2008, The effectiveness of laws against bribery abroad, *JIBS*, 39: 634–651; C. Kwok & S. Tadesse, 2006, The MNC as an agent of change for host-country institutions, *JIBS*, 37: 767–785.

44. J. Clougherty & M. Grajek, 2008, The impact of ISO 9000 diffusion on trade and FDI, *JIBS*, 39: 613–633; H. Greve, 2011, Fast and expensive, *SMJ*, 32: 949–968; K. Weber, G. Davis, & M. Lounsbury, 2009, Policy as myth and ceremony? *AMJ*, 52: 1319–1347.

45. L. Trevino & K. Nelson, 2004, *Managing Business Ethics*, 3rd ed. (p. 13), New York: Wiley.

46. S. Hart, 2005, *Capitalism at the Crossroads*, Philadelphia, PA: Wharton School Publishing.

47. This section draws heavily from C. Chen, M. W. Peng, & P. Saparito, 2002, Individualism, collectivism, and opportunism, *JM*, 28: 567–583.

48. S. Ghoshal & P. Moran, 1996, Bad for practice, *AMR*, 21: 13–47.

49. J. Cullen, K. P. Parboteeah, & M. Hoegl, 2004, Cross-national differences in managers' willingness to justify ethically suspect behaviors, *AMJ*, 47: 411–421.

50. F. Fukuyama, 1995, *Trust*, New York: Free Press; G. Redding, 1993, *The Spirit of Chinese Capitalism*, New York: Gruyter.

51. J. Hennart & M. Zeng, 2002, Cross-cultural differences and joint venture longevity, *JIBS*, 33: 699–716.

52. Y. Luo & O. Shenkar, 2011, Toward a perspective of cultural friction in international business, *JIM*, 17: 1–14; J. Salk, 2012, Changing IB scholarship via rhetoric or bloody knuckles, *JIBS*, 43: 28–40; K. Singh, 2007, The limited relevance of culture to strategy, *APJM*, 24: 421–428; O. Shenkar, 2012, Beyond

cultural distance, *JIBS*, 43: 12–17; O. Shenkar, Y. Luo, & O. Yoheskel, 2008, From "distance" to "friction," *AMR*, 33: 905–923; S. Zaheer, M. Schomaker, & L. Nachum, 2012, Distance without direction, *JIBS*, 43: 18–27.

53. O. Shenkar, 2012, Cultural distance revisited, *JIBS*, 43: 1–11. See also S. Lee, O. Shenkar, & J. Li, 2008, Culture distance, investment flow, and control in cross-border cooperation, *JIBS*, 29: 1117–1125; L. Tihanyi, D. Griffith, & C. Russell, 2005, The effect of cultural distance on entry mode choice, international diversification, and MNE performance, *JIBS*, 36: 270–283.

54. J. Li, K. Lam, & G. Qian, 2001, Does culture affect behavior and performance of firms? *JIBS*, 32: 115–131.

55. V. Pothukuchi, F. Damanpour, J. Choi, C. Chen, & S. Park, 2002, National and organizational culture differences and international joint venture performance, *JIBS*, 33: 243–265.

56. D. Xu & O. Shenkar, 2002, Institutional distance and the multinational enterprise (p. 608), *AMR*, 27: 608–618. See also H. Berry, M. Guillen, & N. Zhou, 2010, An institutional approach to cross-national distance, *JIBS*, 41: 1460–1480; D. Dow & A. Karunaratna, 2006, Developing a multidimensional instrument to measure psychic distance stimuli, *JIBS*, 37: 578–602; L. Hakanson & B. Ambos, 2010, The antecedents of psychic distance, *JIM*, 16: 195–210.

57. R. Orr & W. R. Scott, 2008, Institutional exceptions on global projects, *JIBS*, 39: 562–588.

58. J. Johnson, T. Lenartowicz, & S. Apud, 2006, Cross-cultural competence in international business, *JIBS*, 37: 525–543; A. Tsui, S. Nifadkar, & A. Ou, 2007, Cross-national, cross-cultural organizational behavior research, *JM*, 33: 426–478; N. Yagi & J. Kleinberg, 2011, Boundary work, *JIBS*, 42: 629–653.

5

Growing and Internationalizing the Entrepreneurial Firm

6

Entering Foreign Markets

7

Making Strategic Alliances and Networks Work

8

Managing Global Competitive Dynamics

PART **2** | BUSINESS-LEVEL
STRATEGIES

GROWING AND INTERNATIONALIZING THE ENTREPRENEURIAL FIRM

© istockphoto/Alexey Stiop

KNOWLEDGE OBJECTIVES

After studying this chapter, you should be able to

1. Define entrepreneurship, entrepreneurs, and entrepreneurial firms

2. Articulate a comprehensive model of entrepreneurship

3. Identify five strategies that characterize a growing entrepreneurial firm

4. Differentiate international strategies that enter foreign markets and that stay in domestic markets

5. Participate in three leading debates concerning entrepreneurship

6. Draw strategic implications for action

Emerging Markets: Amazon.com of Russia

Ozon.ru is frequently called the Amazon.com of Russia. But the differences between the Moscow-based start-up and the US e-commerce giant are more revealing than the similarities. There is no equivalent of FedEx or UPS that covers all of Russia, so Ozon must run its own fleet of hundreds of delivery trucks, which have to get as far as Khabarovsk, nearly 4,000 miles (6,400 kilometers) away on the Chinese border. Most Russians eschew credit cards, so customers typically pay delivery staff in cash. Many of Ozon's customers are also wary of placing orders online, so more than 10% of its transaction occur over the phone. "We do look at Amazon, but we always try to adapt what they are doing to the Russian market," says Maelle Gavet, Ozen's chief executive officer. "Copy and paste never works here."

On September 8, 2011, the company announced it was raising $100 million from a consortium of investors including the Baring Vostok Private Equity Fund and Rakuten, the largest e-commerce company in Japan. Ozon, which has more than 1,100 employees based mostly in Moscow and at an 8,000-square-foot shipping center in Tver, located centrally between Moscow and St. Petersburg, plans to use the money to improve its website and build data centers to compensate for the country's sluggish network infrastructure. "They have delivered millions of packages over the last few years," says Giueppe Zocco, a partner at venture capital firm Index Ventures, which has backed Ozon since 2007 and invested in the last round. "It's a well-oiled machine and poised to keep growing."

The Ozon funding caps an eventful year for the Russian Internet. In November 2010, Mail.ru, the operator of various Russia social network sites and an investor in Facebook, raised $912 million on the London Stock Exchange. Yandex, a Russian search engine, followed in May 2011 with an official public offering on NASDAQ that raised $1.3 billion. As in China, investors are attracted primarily by the sheer size of the opportunity. There are 67 million Internet users in Russia, out of a population of 147 million, and the country's Internet audience is among the fastest-growing in Europe.

Ozon was born nearly 14 years ago, when a St. Petersburg software company called Reksoft saw an Amazon press

Map Resources

release and decided to import the business model to Russia. The fledgling effort caught the attention of Baring Vostok, which moved the company to Moscow and eventually tapped Swiss-born Bernard Lukey, a former marketing executive at Yandex, to run it. Lukey raised capital, expanded the company's revenues fivefold, built a state-of-the-art distribution center, and added a profitable online travel arm. Two years ago he started preparations to step aside to return to his native country (he is still Ozon's president).

That cleared the way for the 33-year-old French-born Gavet. She speaks French, Russian, and English, and is a six-year veteran of the consumer retail practice for Boston Consulting Group. She began taking over Lukey's responsibilities in early 2011 and has quickly made several changes. Ozon had experimented with selling a Kindle-like e-reader called the Ozon Galaxy, but Gavet suspended the effort and is now focused on selling e-books, video games, and other digital content for smartphones and mobile devices. She is also trying to expand Ozon's live, 24/7 customer support operation, because Russians often demand to speak to people over the phone. One of her goals: getting the Ozon customer support staff to be polite. "Russians are not a very friendly people," Gavet says. "It's hard to get them to speak nicely to the customers. It's just not in their culture."

Another challenge for Ozon is finding qualified staff. Good engineers in Russia are scarce and expensive. A web programmer in Moscow demands a higher salary than in San Francisco, Gavet says, which has her joking that perhaps the company should consider outsourcing to the US. If she can solve that problem and get Russians to keep buying online, she may just catch the eye of the man who inspired Ozon, Jeffrey Bezos. In 2004, Amazon acquired a start-up called Joyo in China—another country with byzantine customs, massive terrain, and a poor shipping infrastructure.

Source: Bloomberg Businessweek, 2011, Amazon.com on the Volga, September 19: 43–44.

H ow do entrepreneurial firms such as Ozon grow? What are the challenges and constraints they face? This chapter deals with these important questions. This is different from many strategy textbooks, which only focus on large firms. To the extent that every large firm started small and that some (although not all) of today's **small and medium-sized enterprises (SMEs)** may become tomorrow's multinational enterprises (MNEs), current and would-be strategists will not gain a complete picture of the strategic landscape if they only focus on large firms. SMEs are firms with fewer than 500 employees in the United States and with fewer than 250 employees in the European Union (Ozon is no longer an SME). Most students will join SMEs for employment. Some readers of this book will also start up their own SMEs, thus further necessitating our attention on these numerous "Davids" instead of on the smaller number of "Goliaths."

This chapter will first define entrepreneurship. Next, we outline a comprehensive model of entrepreneurship informed by the three leading perspectives on strategy. Then, we introduce six major entrepreneurial strategies. As before, debates and extensions follow.

small and medium-sized enterprise (SME)
A firm with fewer than 500 employees in the United States or with fewer than 250 employees in the European Union.

Entrepreneurship and Entrepreneurial Firms

Although entrepreneurship is often associated with smaller and younger firms, there is no rule banning larger and older firms from being "entrepreneurial." So what exactly is entrepreneurship? Recent research suggests that firm size and age are *not* defining characteristics of entrepreneurship. Instead, **entrepreneurship** is defined as "the identification and exploitation of previously unexplored opportunities."[1] Specifically, it is concerned with "the sources of opportunities; the processes of discovery, evaluation, and exploitation of opportunities; and the set of individuals who discover, evaluate, and exploit them."[2] These individuals, thus, are **entrepreneurs**. French in origin, the word "entrepreneurs" traditionally means intermediaries connecting others. Today, the word mostly refers to founders and owners of new businesses or managers of existing firms. Consequently, **international entrepreneurship** is defined as "a combination of innovative, proactive, and risk-seeking behavior that crosses national borders and is intended to create wealth in organizations."[3]

Although SMEs are not the exclusive domain of entrepreneurship, the convention that many people use is to associate entrepreneurship with SMEs, because, on average, SMEs tend

entrepreneurship
The identification and exploitation of previously unexplored opportunities.

entrepreneur
An individual who identifies and explores previously unexplored opportunities.

international entrepreneurship
A combination of innovative, proactive, and risk-seeking behavior that crosses national borders and is intended to create wealth in organizations.

to be more entrepreneurial than large firms. To minimize confusion, the remainder of this chapter will follow that convention, although it is not totally accurate. In other words, while we acknowledge that some managers at large firms can be very entrepreneurial, we will limit the use of the term "entrepreneurs" to owners, founders, and managers of SMEs. Further, we will use the term "entrepreneurial firms" when referring to SMEs.

SMEs are important. Worldwide, they account for over 95% of the number of firms, create approximately 50% of total value added, and generate 60%–90% of employment (depending on the country).[4] Obviously, entrepreneurship has both rewarding and punishing aspects.[5] Many entrepreneurs will try; many SMEs will fail.[6] Only a small number of entrepreneurs and SMEs will succeed.

A Comprehensive Model of Entrepreneurship

The strategy tripod consisting of the three leading perspectives on strategy—namely, the industry-based, resource-based, and institution-based views—sheds considerable light on the entrepreneurship phenomenon. This leads to a comprehensive model illustrated in Figure 5.1.

FIGURE 5.1   A Comprehensive Model of Entrepreneurship

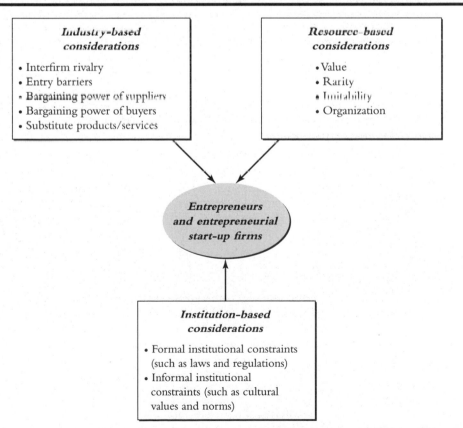

Industry-Based Considerations

The industry-based view, exemplified by the Porter five forces framework first introduced in Chapter 2, emphasizes (1) interfirm rivalry, (2) entry barriers, (3) bargaining power of suppliers, (4) bargaining power of buyers, and (5) threats of substitute products. First, the intensity of *interfirm rivalry* has a direct impact on the probability that a new start-up will be able to make it.[7] The fewer the number of incumbent firms, the more likely they will form some sort of collusion to prevent newcomers from gaining market shares. In a worst-case scenario, a monopoly incumbent, such as Microsoft, may become so dominant that it may potentially stifle new innovation brought about by SMEs—this was the key reason why Microsoft was prosecuted by the US and EU antitrust authorities.

Entry barriers impact entrepreneurship. It is not surprising that new firm entries cluster around low entry-barrier industries, such as restaurants. Conversely, capital-intensive industries hinder the chances of entrepreneurial success. For example, at present no entrepreneurs in their right mind would bet their money on competing against Boeing or Airbus.

When the *bargaining power of suppliers* becomes too large, entrepreneurial solutions can reduce such bargaining power. For instance, Microsoft is the monopoly supplier of operating systems to a majority of personal computer (PC) makers in the world, which feel uncomfortable about being compelled to purchase Microsoft products. As a result, LINUX has become more popular as an emerging alternative.

Similarly, entrepreneurs who can reduce the *bargaining power of buyers* may also find a niche for themselves. For example, a small number of national chain ("brick and mortar") bookstores used to represent the only major outlets through which hundreds of publishers could sell their books. Entrepreneurial Internet bookstores, such as Amazon in the United States and Ozon in Russia (see the Opening Case), have provided more outlets for publishers, thereby reducing the bargaining power of traditional bookstores as buyers.

Substitute products/services may offer great opportunities for entrepreneurs. If entrepreneurs can bring in substitute products that can redefine the game, they can effectively chip away some of the competitive advantages held by incumbents. For example, e-mails and online payments, pioneered by entrepreneurial firms, are now substituting a large portion of faxes, express mails, and paper check printing and processing, whose incumbents are powerless to fight back.

Obviously, entrepreneurs need to carefully understand the nature of the industries they intend to join. However, even when the industry is conducive for entries, there is no guarantee that entrepreneurs will be successful. Firm-specific (and often entrepreneur-specific) resources and capabilities are also important.

Resource-Based Considerations

The resource-based view, first introduced in Chapter 3, sheds considerable light on entrepreneurship, with a focus on its value, rarity, imitability, and organizational (VRIO) aspects (see Figure 5.1). First, entrepreneurial resources must create *value*.[8] For instance, by offering cheap fares, convenient schedules, and Wi-Fi and a power port on every seat, Megabus offers superb value to travelers for medium-haul trips that are too far for a leisurely drive but too close to justify the expenses and the increasing hassle to fly (see Chapter 6 Opening Case). On medium-haul routes, Megabus is rapidly changing the way Americans—especially the young—travel, so much so that it may help kill plans for the new high-speed rail, which after all may not offer that much value.

Second, resources must be *rare*. As the cliché goes, "If everybody has it, you can't make money from it." The best-performing entrepreneurs tend to have the rarest knowledge and deeper insights about business opportunities. For instance, in the 1980s, a small-fry entrepreneur in China, Zong Qinghou, peddled school supplies and ice cream from a bicycle-drawn cart. He noticed that, spoiled by their parents and grandparents, Chinese kids, products of the "one child policy," preferred junk food over more nutritious food. These "little emperors" could benefit from nutritional supplements that supply needed vitamins and minerals. But all the numerous nutritional supplements marketed in China at that time targeted adults, claiming to boost their longevity and sexual potency. Armed by this powerful insight, Zong started up Wahaha that pioneered the category of children's nutritional supplements.[9] Wahaha has now grown to become China's number one beverages company, and Zong one of the richest men in China.

Third, resources must be *inimitable*. For instance, in the ocean of e-commerce companies, the abilities to do the "dirtiest job on the Internet" as online moderators are very hard to imitate. That is why firms such as eModeration and ICUC Moderation can charge up to $50,000 a month to clean up comments and tweets for established organizations (see Strategy in Action 5.1).

STRATEGY IN ACTION 5.1

Profiting from the Dirtiest Job Online

The Internet has enabled some of the most noble human spirit in collaboration to shine—think of Wikipedia. However, the Internet has also unleashed some of the most nasty, disgusting, and hurtful expressions to be used as weapons of choice. In online communities, discussion boards, and social media, the lethal combination of anonymity and opinion have often resulted in discussions going out of control, cussing and swearing increasingly dominating the air. Although such uncivil comments represent less than 10% of online comments, they often command disproportionate attention, resulting in headaches, embarrassments, and disasters for established companies, nonprofits, and government agencies. Such uncivil comments have also presented wonderful opportunities for a new breed of entrepreneurs known as moderators (or "mods").

Moderators delete uncivil comments, scold people behind them (such as "We don't call each other a–holes"), and in the case of repeat offenders ban their accounts from airing their profanity. Working at home (or during vacation), moderators can make between $40,000 to $80,000 annually. But they need to be prepared to daily exposure to extreme racism and bigotry, images of pedophilia, and other undesirable expressions. Such clean-up is arguably the dirtiest job on the Internet. "Sometimes you feel like you need to spend two hours in the shower because it is so disgusting," said Keith Bilous, founder of the Winnipeg, Canada-based ICUC Moderation.

Employing over 200 moderators, ICUC Moderation has emerged as a global leader with $10 million revenue. Its clients include Calvin Klein, Chevron, Intel, Molson, National Public Radio, Scotiabank, Starbucks, and Virgin Group, as well as the Government of Canada. London-based eModeration is another leader, which has 160 moderators with $7 million revenue. Its clients include BBC, the Economist, ESPN, HSBC, Lego, MTV, Oprah, and Sony Ericsson. In 2010, Nestlé's public relations (PR) department attempted to deal with criticisms from Greenpeace on Nestlé's Facebook page, which was not professionally moderated. It turned out to be a PR disaster. The experience, judgment, and expertise of moderators would have contained such fire before it exploded.

Many firms such as New York Times moderate their own websites. But the trend is to increasingly outsource such work to professional online content and community moderation service providers such as ICUC Moderation and eModeration, which typically charges $30 to $40 an hour. However, competition is rapidly becoming global, with Indian and Philippine service providers offering deals to clients at $5 an hour.

Sources: Based on (1) *Bloomberg Businessweek*, 2011, The dirtiest job on the Internet, December 5: 95–97; (2) www.emoderation.com; (3) www.icucmoderation.com.

Fourth, entrepreneurial resources must be *organizationally* embedded.[10] For example, as long as wars are fought, there have been mercenaries for hire. But only in recent times have private military companies (PMCs) become a global industry, thanks to the superb organizational capabilities of entrepreneurial firms such as Blackwater (now known as Xe) (see Strategy in Action 5.2).

STRATEGY IN ACTION 5.2 › › ETHICAL DILEMMA

Private Military Companies

Private military companies (PMCs) form a $100 billion global industry. Although often stereotyped as "mercenaries," modern PMCs are professional firms that offer valuable, unique, and hard-to-imitate organizational capabilities in environments that most individuals, firms, and governments, as well as national militaries, would prefer to avoid. Entrepreneurs thrive on chaos. To PMCs, the war in Iraq and Afghanistan has been a pot of gold. As US forces and allies withdraw, PMCs rush in. In Afghanistan, in 2009, PMCs were the largest military force (130,000 personnel), outnumbering both the Afghan National Army (100,000 personnel) and the US (national) forces (64,000 personnel). In Iraq, in 2009, PMCs were the second largest military contingent (about 113,000 personnel) after the US (national) forces (130,000 personnel). Long after the official withdrawal of the US (national) military in Iraq in 2011, PMCs will remain active in the country. The State Department alone will employ 5,000 PMC personnel in Iraq. Although not every EMC directly engages in the battlefield, this line of work is certainly dangerous. PMCs reported 1,800 dead and 40,000 wounded in Iraq and Afghanistan by 2009.

An ethical challenge confronting PMCs is how to *responsively* deploy their lethal capabilities while getting the job done. In 2007, a furious US Congress held hearings on Blackwater, which, according to the Iraqi government, allegedly killed 17 innocent civilians in Baghdad. Blackwater's staunchest defenders tended to be US officials protected by its private soldiers. US officials preferred PMCs because PMC personnel were regarded as more highly trained than (national) military guards. Blackwater's founder, Erik Prince, told the Congressional committee that "no individual protected by Blackwater has ever been killed or seriously injured," while 30 of its private soldiers died on the job. After the hearing, Blackwater was banned from operating in Iraq. In 2009, Blackwater rebranded itself as Xe Services LLC (pronounced *zee*).

Continuously looking for new entrepreneurial opportunities, some PMCs have recently branched into maritime security services, thanks to Somali pirates who attack ships off the coast of Africa. Most recently, what country has commanded a lot of attention from PMCs? Libya.

Sources: Based on (1) *Bloomberg Businessweek*, 2011, As war winds down in Libya, enter the consultants, September 26: 17–18; (2) *Bloomberg Businessweek*, 2011, For sale, cheap, December 19: 32–35; (3) *Economist*, 2007, Blackwater in hot water, October 13: 51; (4) T. Hammes, 2010, Private contractors in conflict zones, *Strategic Forum of National Defense University*, 260: 1–15; (5) M. W. Peng, 2014, Private military companies, in M. W. Peng, *Global Business*, 3rd ed., Cincinnati: South-Western Cengage Learning; (6) M. Schwartz, 2009, *Department of Defense Contractors in Iraq and Afghanistan*, Washington, DC: Congressional Research Service.

Institution-Based Considerations

First introduced in Chapter 4, both formal and informal institutional constraints, as rules of the game, affect entrepreneurship (see Figure 5.1). Although entrepreneurship is thriving around the globe in general, its development is uneven. Whether entrepreneurship is facilitated or retarded significantly depends on formal institutions governing how entrepreneurs start up new firms.[11] A World Bank survey, *Doing Business*, reports some striking differences in government regulations concerning how easy it is to start up new entrepreneurial firms in terms of registration, licensing, and incorporation (Figure 5.2). A relatively straightforward (or even "mundane") task of connecting electricity to a newly built commercial building illustrates such tremendous differences. In general, governments in developed economies impose fewer procedures (an average of 4.6 procedures for OECD high income countries) and a lower total cost (free in Japan and 5.1% of per capita GDP in Germany). On the other hand, entrepreneurs have to put up with harsher hurdles in poor countries. In a class of its own, Burundi imposes a total cost of 430 times of its per capita GDP for entrepreneurs to obtain electricity. Sierra Leone leads the world in requiring entrepreneurs to spend 441 days to obtain electricity. Overall, it is not surprising that the more entrepreneur-friendly these formal institutional requirements are, the more flourishing entrepreneurship is, and the more developed the economies become—and vice versa. As a result, more countries are now reforming their formal institutions in order to become more entrepreneur-friendly.

FIGURE 5.2 Average Ranking on the Ease of Doing Business

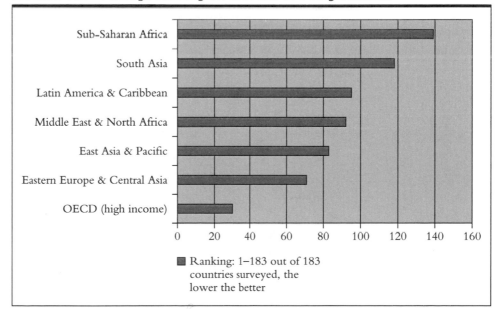

Source: Data extracted from World Bank, 2010, *Doing Business 2010* (database at www.doingbusiness.org).

In addition to formal institutions, informal institutions such as cultural values and norms also affect entrepreneurship.[12] For example, because entrepreneurs necessarily take more risk, individualistic and low uncertainty avoidance societies tend to foster relatively more entrepreneurs, whereas collectivistic and high uncertainty avoidance societies may result in relatively fewer entrepreneurs. Among developed economies, Japan has the lowest rate of start-ups, one-third of America's rate and half of Europe's.[13] In another example, Russians make heavy use of social networks online, averaging 9.8 hours per month—more than double the world average. While spending that much time online makes sense during the long and cold Russian winter, another important reason is the long-held Russian tradition of relying more on informal information networks for daily life. These informal norms help nurture social network entrepreneurs such as Russia's Vkontakte and attract foreign entrants such as Facebook.[14] Overall, the institution-based view suggests that both formal and informal institutions matter. Later sections will discuss *how* they matter.

Five Entrepreneurial Strategies

This section discusses five entrepreneurial strategies: (1) growth, (2) innovation, (3) network, (4) financing/governance, and (5) harvest/exit. A sixth one, internationalization, is covered in the next section.

Growth

For many entrepreneurs, the excitement associated with growing a new company is the very thing that attracts them in the first place.[15] Recall from the resource-based view that a firm can be conceptualized as a bundle of resources and capabilities. The growth of an entrepreneurial firm can thus be viewed as an attempt to more fully use currently under-utilized resources and capabilities. An entrepreneurial firm can leverage its vision, drive, and leadership in order to grow, even though it may be shorter on resources such as financial capital than a larger firm would be.

Innovation

Innovation is at the heart of an entrepreneurial mindset.[16] Israeli SMEs, for example, are known for their formidable innovation capabilities (see Emerging Markets 5.1). Well-known examples include firewalls (Checkpoint) and ICQ instant messaging software (Mirabilis) as well as the Pentium chip (developed by Intel's subsidiary in Israel).[17]

An innovation strategy is a specialized form of differentiation strategy (see Chapter 2). It offers three advantages. First, it allows a potentially more sustainable basis for competitive advantage. Firms first to introduce new goods or services are likely to earn (quasi) "monopoly profits" until competitors emerge. If entrepreneurial firms come up with "disruptive technologies," then they may redefine the rules of competition, thus wiping out the advantages of incumbents.[18]

Second, innovation should be regarded broadly. Not only are technological break-throughs innovations, less novel but still substantially new ways of doing business are also

EMERGING MARKETS 5.1 〉 〉

Israel: The Start-Up Nation

The young must shout if they want to be heard. In a stone hanger in the old port of Jaffa, 30 entrepreneurs have five minutes each to present their start-up companies to a panel of digital luminaries and an audience that includes potential investors. Not everyone in the room is ready to shut up and listen, so the hopefuls must battle against the din. Feng-GUI explains how, by simulating human vision, it can tell advertisers and designers which areas of a web page are most likely to grab people's attention. CopyV promises to send large files quickly and securely. With Fooducate, "a dietician in your pocket," on your smartphone, you can scan bar codes in the supermarket and find out what's really going into your trolley.

Israel's legions of young technology firms clamor for attention and money. Rapid-pitch events like this one, at DLD Tel Aviv, a two-day conference in November, are common. More than 300 firms applied for a slot at DLD; 100 turned up; the lucky 30 were chosen by raffle. Yossi Vardi, a technology entrepreneur who has invested in 75 start-ups since 1996, says that he receives between three and eight approaches every *day*.

Dan Senor and Saul Singer called Israel *The Start-Up Nation* in a book of that name in 2009. The label has stuck

because it fits. Everybody and his brother-in-law seems to be starting a company—with old schoolmates or army colleagues, in a spare room or the parental home. Starting a business is easier than ever, thanks to advances in information technology. Budding designers of smartphone apps can rent space when they need it on a remote server rather than buying huge amounts of computing power. "The Internet has democratized the right to innovate," says Mr. Vardi.

Israelis innovate because they have to. The land is arid, so they excel at water and agricultural technology. They have little oil, so they furrow their brows to find alternatives. They are surrounded by enemies, so their military technology is superb and creates lucrative spin-offs, especially in communications. The relationships forged during military service foster frenetic networking in civilian life. A flood of immigrants in the 1990s gave national brainpower a mighty boost. The results are the envy of almost everyone outside Silicon Valley.

Source: Excerpted from *Economist*, 2012, What next for the start-up nation? January 21: 69–70. © The Economist.

innovations. Most start-ups reproduce existing organizational routines, but *recombine* them to create some novel product/service offerings, such as FedEx's (re)combination of existing air and ground assets to create a new market.

Entrepreneurial firms are uniquely ready for innovation. Owners, managers, and employees at entrepreneurial firms tend to be more innovative and risk taking than those at large firms. In fact, many SMEs are founded by former employees of large firms who were frustrated by their inability to translate innovative ideas into realities at the large firms. A group of programmers at IBM's German affiliate proposed to IBM that standard programming solutions could be profitably sold to clients. After their ideas were turned down, they left and founded SAP, now the number one player in the thriving enterprise resource planning (ERP) market. Innovators at large firms also have limited ability to personally profit from their innovations because property rights usually belong to the corporation. In contrast, innovators at entrepreneurial firms are better able to reap the financial gains associated with innovation, thus fueling their motivation to charge ahead.

Network

A network strategy refers to intentionally constructing and tapping into relationships, connections, and ties that individuals and organizations have.[19] There are two kinds of networks: personal and organizational. Both are important. Prior to and during the founding phase of the entrepreneurial firm, these two networks overlap significantly. In other words, entrepreneurs' personal networks are essentially the same as the firm's organizational networks.[20] The essence of entrepreneurship can be regarded as a process to "translate" personal networks into value-adding organizational networks. Three attributes—namely, urgency, intensity, and impact—distinguish entrepreneurial networking.

First, entrepreneurial firms have a high degree of *urgency* to develop and leverage networks. They confront a **liability of newness**, defined as the inherent disadvantage that entrepreneurial firms experience as new entrants. In the absence of a track record (many start-ups only have an idea), start-ups do not inspire confidence and lack legitimacy in the eyes of suppliers, customers, financiers, and other stakeholders. Therefore, start-ups urgently need to draw upon entrepreneurs' social networks to overcome the liability of newness. Convincing more legitimate and well-established individuals (as co-founders, management team members, investors, or board directors) and organizations (as alliance partners, sponsors, or customers) to lend a helping hand can boost the legitimacy of start-ups. In other words, legitimacy, an intangible but highly important resource, can be transferred.[21]

A second characteristic that distinguishes entrepreneurial networking is its *intensity*. Network relationships can be classified as strong ties and weak ties. **Strong ties** are more durable, reliable, and trustworthy relationships, whereas **weak ties** are less durable, reliable, and trustworthy. Efforts to cultivate, develop, and maintain strong ties are usually more intense than weak ties. Entrepreneurs often rely on strong ties—typically 5–20 individuals—for advice, assistance, and support. Over time, the preference for strong ties may change, and the benefits of weak ties may emerge (see the next section).

Finally, because of the small firm size, the contributions of entrepreneurs' personal networks tend to have a stronger *impact* on firm performance.[22] In comparison, the impact of similar networks cultivated by managers at large firms may be less pronounced because of these firms' sheer size. Moreover, being private owners, entrepreneurs can directly pocket the profits if their firms perform well, thereby motivating them to make these networks work.

Overall, there is strong evidence that networks, both personal and organizational, represent significant resources and opportunities and that successful networking may lead to successful entrepreneurial performance. The most advantageous positions are those well connected to a number of players who are otherwise not connected—in other words, more *centrally* located network positions are helpful. Armed with useful ties and contacts, entrepreneurs, therefore, can literally become "persons who add value by brokering the connection between others."[23] Remember, this indeed is the original meaning of the word entrepreneurs.

Financing and Governance

All start-ups need to raise capital.[24] Here is a quiz (also a joke): Of the "4F" sources of entrepreneurial financing, the first three Fs are founders, family, and friends, but what is

liability of newness
The inherent disadvantage that entrepreneurial firms experience as new entrants.

strong ties
More durable, reliable, and trustworthy relationships cultivated over a long period of time.

weak ties
Relationships that are characterized by infrequent interaction and low intimacy.

the other F source? The answer is… *fools* (!). While this is a joke, it strikes a chord in the entrepreneurial world: Given the well-known failure risks of start-ups (a *majority* of them will fail), why would anybody other than fools be willing to invest in start-ups? In reality, most outside, strategic investors, who can be angels (wealthy individual investors), **venture capitalists (VCs)**, banks, foreign entrants, and government agencies, are *not* fools. They often examine business plans, require a strong management team, and scrutinize financial reviews and analysis. They also demand some assurance (such as collateral) indicating that entrepreneurs will not simply "take the money and run." Entrepreneurs need to develop relationships with these outside investors, some of which are weak ties. Turning weak-tie contacts into willing investors is always challenging.[25]

While dealing with strong-tie contacts can be quite informal (based on handshake deals or simple contracts), working with weak-tie contacts may be more formal. In the absence of a long history of interaction, weak-tie investors such as angels and VCs often demand a more formal governance structure to safeguard their investment, through a significant percentage of equity (such as 20%–40%), a corresponding number of seats on the board of directors, and a set of formal rules and policies.[26] In extreme cases, when business is not going well, VCs may exercise their formal voting power and dismiss the founder CEO. Entrepreneurs, therefore, have to make tradeoffs given the need for larger-scale financing and the necessity to cede a significant portion of ownership and control rights of their "dream" firms.

Given the well-known hazards associated with start-up risks, anything that entrepreneurs can do to improve their odds would be helpful. The odds for survival during the crucial early years are significantly correlated with firm size—the larger, the better (Table 5.1). The upshot is that the faster start-ups can reach a certain size, the more likely they will survive the first few years in the face of the liability of newness. Since it takes a significant amount of capital to reach a large size, entrepreneurs often make the choice of accepting more outside investment and agreeing to give up some ownership and control rights.[27]

venture capitalist (VC)
An investor who invests capital in early-stage, high-potential start-ups.

TABLE 5.1 One-Year and Four-Year Survival Rates by Firm Size

FIRM SIZE (EMPLOYEES)	CHANCES OF SURVIVING AFTER 1 YEAR	FIRM SIZE (EMPLOYEES)	CHANCES OF SURVIVING AFTER 4 YEARS
0–9	78%	0–19	50%
10–19	86%	20–49	67%
20–99	95%	50–99	67%
100–249	95%	100–499	70%
250+	100%		

Source: Adapted from J. Timmons, 1999, *New Venture Creation* (p. 33), Boston: Irwin McGraw-Hill, based on US data.

Internationally, the extent to which entrepreneurs draw on resources of family and friends vis-à-vis formal outside investors (such as VCs) is different. *Global Entrepreneurship Monitor* reported that Sweden, South Africa, Belgium, and the United States lead the world in VC investment as a percentage of GDP.[28] In contrast, Greece and China have the lowest level of VC investment. On the other hand, China leads the world with the highest level of informal investment from family and friends as a percentage of GDP. In comparison, Brazil and Hungary, on the other hand, have the lowest level of informal investment. While there is a lot of noise in such worldwide data, the case of China (second lowest in VC investment and highest in informal investment) is easy to explain: China's lack of formal market-supporting institutions, such as VCs and credit-reporting agencies, requires a high level of informal investment for Chinese entrepreneurs and new ventures, particularly during a time of entrepreneurial boom.[29]

A highly innovative solution, called **microfinance**, has emerged in response to the lack of financing for entrepreneurial opportunities in many countries. Microfinance involves lending small sums ($50–$300) used to start small businesses with the intention of ultimately lifting the entrepreneurs out of poverty. Starting in the 1970s in countries such as Bangladesh and India, microfinance has now become a global movement and has become controversial lately (see the Closing Case).

microfinance

A practice to provide microloans ($50–$300) to start small businesses with the intention of ultimately lifting the entrepreneurs out of poverty.

Harvest and Exit

Outlined in Table 5.2, entrepreneurial harvest and exit can take a number of routes. First, selling an equity stake to outside strategic investors (discussed earlier) can substantially increase the value of the firm and therefore offer an excellent harvest option. However, entrepreneurs must be willing to give up some ownership and control rights.

Second, selling the firm to other private owners or companies may be done with a painful discount if the business is failing, or it may carry a happy premium if the business is booming.[30] Selling the firm is typically one of the most significant and emotionally charged events entrepreneurs confront. It is important to note that "selling out" does not necessarily mean failure. Many entrepreneurs deliberately build up businesses in anticipation of being acquired by larger corporations and profiting handsomely.

Third, when a business is not doing well, merging with another company is another alternative. The drawbacks are that the firm may lose its independence and that some entrepreneurs may have to personally exit the firm to leave room for executives from another company. It is obvious that a lackluster entrepreneurial firm is not in a great position to bargain for a good deal. However, if properly structured and negotiated, a merger will allow entrepreneurs to reap the rewards for which they have worked so hard.

TABLE 5.2 Routes of Entrepreneurial Harvest and Exit

- Selling an equity stake
- Selling the business
- Merging with another firm
- Considering an initial public offering (IPO)
- Declaring bankruptcy

TABLE 5.3   Advantages and Disadvantages of an Initial Public Offering (IPO)

ADVANTAGES	DISADVANTAGES
■ Improved financial condition	■ Subject to the whims of financial market
■ Access to more capital	■ Forced to focus on the short term
■ Diversification of shareholder base	■ Loss of entrepreneurial control
■ Ability to cash out	■ New fiduciary responsibilities for shareholders
■ Management and employee incentives	■ Loss of privacy
■ Enhanced corporate reputation	■ Limits on management's freedom of action
■ Greater opportunity for future acquisitions	■ Demands of periodic reporting

© Cengage Learning

initial public offering (IPO)

The first round of public trading of company stock.

Fourth, entrepreneurs can take their firms through an **initial public offering (IPO)**, which is the goal of many entrepreneurs. An IPO has several advantages and disadvantages (Table 5.3). Among the advantages, first and foremost is financial stability, in that the firm no longer has to constantly "beg" for money. For entrepreneurs themselves, an IPO can potentially result in financial windfalls. For the firm, stock options can be issued as incentives to motivate, attract, and retain capable employees. The IPO is also a great signal indicating that the firm has "made it." Such an enhanced reputation enables it to raise more capital to facilitate future growth such as acquisitions.

On the other hand, an IPO carries a number of nontrivial disadvantages. The firm is being subject to the rational and irrational exuberance (and also pessimism) of the financial market. After the IPO, founding entrepreneurs may gradually lose their majority control. The firm, legally speaking, is no longer "theirs." Instead, founding entrepreneurs have the new fiduciary duty to look after the interests of outside shareholders. As a result, certain constraints restrict entrepreneurs' freedom of action. They are being scrutinized by securities authorities, shareholders, and the media, which often force firms to focus on the short term. There is also a loss of privacy, as information about personal wealth, shareholding, and compensation must be disclosed. In a worst case, the founder can be ousted by new management—a humiliation Apple co-founder Steve Jobs suffered in 1985. Because of these concerns, some entrepreneurs, such as Ingvar Kamprad, founder of the Swedish furniture chain IKEA, and Tadao Yoshida, founder of the Japanese zipper giant YKK, have refused to go public.[31]

Finally, while taking the firm through an IPO is the most triumphant way of harvest, many entrepreneurial firms that are failing do not have such a luxury. The only viable exit is often to declare bankruptcy (see the Debates and Extensions section for some details).

Overall, a number of harvest and exit options are available to entrepreneurs. For instance, they are encouraged to think about the exit plan early in the business cycle and aim at maximizing the gains from the fruits of their labor. Otherwise, they may end up having to eventually declare bankruptcy and face the consequences—definitely not something they planned on.

Internationalizing the Entrepreneurial Firm

There is a myth that only large MNEs do business abroad and that SMEs mostly operate domestically. This myth, based on historical stereotypes, is being increasingly challenged as more SMEs go international.[32] Further, some start-ups attempt to do business abroad from inception. These are often called **born global firms** (or **international new ventures**).[33] This section examines how entrepreneurial firms internationalize.

born global firm (international new venture)

A start-up company that attempts to do business abroad from inception.

Transaction Costs and Entrepreneurial Opportunities

Compared with domestic transaction costs (the costs of doing business), international transaction costs are qualitatively higher. Some costs are high due to numerous innocent differences in formal institutions and informal norms (see Chapter 4). Other costs, however, may be due to a high level of deliberate opportunism that is hard to detect and remedy. For example, when a small manufacturer in Texas with $5 million annual revenues receives an unsolicited order of $1 million from an unknown buyer in Alaska, most likely the Texas firm will fill the order and allow the Alaska buyer to pay within 30 or 60 days after receiving the goods—a typical practice among domestic transactions in the United States. But what if this order comes from an unknown buyer (importer in this case) in Azerbaijan? If the Texas firm ships the goods but foreign payment does not arrive on time (after 30, 60, or even more days), it is difficult to assess whether firms in Azerbaijan simply do not have the norm of punctual payment or that particular importer is being deliberately opportunistic. If the latter is indeed the case, suing the importer in a court in Azerbaijan where Azeri is the official language may be so costly that it is not an option for a small US exporter.

Maybe the Azerbaijani importer is an honest and capable firm with every intention and ability to pay. But because the Texas firm may not be able to ascertain, prior to the transaction, that the Azerbaijani side will pay upon receiving the goods, the Texas firm may simply say "No, thanks!" Conceptually, this is an example of transaction costs being so high that many firms may choose not to pursue international opportunities. Therefore, entrepreneurial opportunities exist to lower transaction costs and bring distant groups of people, firms, and countries together. Table 5.4 shows that while entrepreneurial firms can internationalize by entering foreign markets, they can also add an international dimension without actually going abroad. Next, we discuss how an SME can undertake some of these strategies.

TABLE 5.4 Internationalization Strategies for Entrepreneurial Firms

ENTERING FOREIGN MARKETS	STAYING IN DOMESTIC MARKETS
■ Direct exports ■ Franchising/licensing ■ Foreign direct investment (through greenfield wholly owned subsidiaries, strategic alliances, and/or foreign acquisitions)	■ Indirect exports (through domestic export intermediaries) ■ Supplier of foreign firms ■ Franchisee/licensee of foreign brands ■ Alliance partner of foreign direct investors ■ Harvest and exit (through sell-off to foreign entrants)

© Cengage Learning

International Strategies for Entering Foreign Markets

SMEs can enter foreign markets through three broad modes: (1) direct exports, (2) licensing/franchising, and (3) foreign direct investment (FDI) (see Chapter 6 for more details). First, **direct exports** entail the sale of products made by entrepreneurial firms in their home country to customers in other countries. This strategy is attractive because entrepreneurial firms are able to reach foreign customers directly. When domestic markets experience some downturns, sales abroad may compensate for such drops. However, a major drawback is that SMEs may not have enough resources to turn overseas opportunities into profits.

A second way to enter international markets is through licensing and/or franchising. Usually used in *manufacturing* industries, **licensing** refers to Firm A's agreement to give Firm B the rights to use A's proprietary technology (such as a patent) or trademark (such as a corporate logo) for a royalty fee paid to A by B. Assume (hypothetically) that a US exporter cannot keep up with demand in Turkey. It may consider granting a Turkish firm the license to use its technology and trademark for a fee. **Franchising** is essentially the same idea, except it is typically used in *service* industries such as fast food. A great advantage is that SME licensors and franchisors can expand abroad while risking relatively little of their own capital. Foreign firms interested in becoming licensees or franchisees have to put their own capital up front. For example, a McDonald's franchise now costs the franchisee approximately $1 million. But licensors and franchisors also take a risk because they may suffer a loss of control over how their technology and brand names are used. If a (hypothetical) McDonald's licensee in Finland produces sub-standard products that damage the brand and refuses to improve quality, McDonald's has two difficult choices: (1) sue its licensee in an unfamiliar Finnish court or (2) discontinue the relationship. Either choice is complicated and costly.

A third entry mode is FDI, which may involve greenfield wholly owned subsidiaries (see Chapter 6), strategic alliances with foreign partners (see Chapter 7), and acquisitions of foreign firms (see Chapter 9). By planting some roots abroad, a firm becomes more committed to serving foreign markets. It is physically and psychologically closer to foreign customers. Relative to licensing and franchising, a firm is better able to control how its proprietary technology is used. However, FDI has a major drawback: its cost and complexity. It requires both a nontrivial sum of capital and a significant managerial commitment.

While many entrepreneurial firms have aggressively gone abroad, it is probably true that a majority of SMEs will be unable to do so; they already have enough headaches struggling with the domestic market. However, as discussed next, some SMEs can still internationalize by staying at home.

International Strategies for Staying in Domestic Markets

Table 5.4 also shows a number of strategies for entrepreneurial SMEs to internationalize without leaving their home country. The five main strategies are (1) export indirectly, (2) become suppliers for foreign firms, (3) become licensees or franchisees of foreign brands, (4) become alliance partners of foreign direct investors, and (5) harvest and exit through sell-offs.

direct exports
Directly selling products made in the home country to customers in other countries.

licensing
Firm A's agreement to give Firm B the rights to use A's proprietary technology (such as a patent) or trademark (such as a corporate logo) for a royalty fee paid to A by B. This term is typically used in manufacturing industries.

franchising
Firm A's agreement to give Firm B the rights to use A's proprietary technology (such as a patent) or trademark (such as a corporate logo) for a royalty fee paid to A by B. This term is typically used in service industries.

indirect exports

Exporting indirectly through domestic-based export intermediaries.

export intermediary

A firm that performs an important middleman function by linking domestic sellers and foreign buyers that otherwise would not have been connected.

First, whereas direct exports may be lucrative, many SMEs simply do not have the resources to handle such work. But they can still reach overseas customers through **indirect exports**, which involve exporting through domestic-based export intermediaries. **Export intermediaries** perform an important middleman function by linking domestic sellers and overseas buyers who otherwise would not have been connected.[34] Being entrepreneurs themselves, export intermediaries facilitate the internationalization of many SMEs.[35]

A second strategy is to become a supplier for a foreign firm that is doing business in the domestic market. For example, when Subway opened restaurants in Northern Ireland, it secured a contract for chilled part-bake bread with a domestic bakery. This relationship was so successful that the firm now supplies Subway franchisees throughout Europe. SME suppliers thus may be able to internationalize by piggybacking on the larger foreign entrants.

Third, an entrepreneurial firm may consider becoming licensee or franchisee of a foreign brand. Foreign licensors and franchisors provide training and technology transfer—for a fee, of course. Consequently, an SME can learn a great deal about how to operate at world-class standards. Further, if enough learning has been accomplished, it is possible to discontinue the relationship and to reap greater entrepreneurial profits. In Thailand, Minor Group, which had held the Pizza Hut franchise for 20 years, broke away from the relationship. Then its new venture, The Pizza Company, became the market leader in Thailand.[36]

A fourth strategy is to become an alliance partner of a foreign direct investor.[37] Facing an onslaught of aggressive MNEs, many entrepreneurial firms may not be able to successfully defend their market positions. Then it makes great sense to follow the old adage, "If you can't beat them, join them!" While dancing with the giants is tricky, it is better than being crushed by them.

Finally, as a harvest and exit strategy, entrepreneurs may sell an equity stake or the entire firm to foreign entrants.[38] An American couple, originally from Seattle, built a Starbucks-like coffee chain in Britain called Seattle Coffee. When Starbucks entered Britain, the couple sold the chain of 60 stores to Starbucks for a hefty $84 million. In light of the high failure rates of start-ups (see the next section), being acquired by foreign entrants may help preserve the business in the long run.

Debates and Extensions

The entrepreneurial boom throughout the world has attracted significant controversies and debates. This section introduces three leading debates: (1) traits versus institutions, (2) slow versus rapid internationalization, and (3) anti-failure biases versus entrepreneur-friendly bankruptcy laws.

Traits versus Institutions

This is probably the oldest debate on entrepreneurship. It focuses on the question: What motivates entrepreneurs to establish new firms, while most others are simply content to work for bosses? The "traits" school of thought argues that it is personal traits that matter. Compared with non-entrepreneurs, entrepreneurs seem more likely to possess a stronger desire for achievement and are more willing to take risks and tolerate ambiguities. Overall,

serial entrepreneur

An entrepreneur who starts, grows, and sells several businesses throughout his/her career.

entrepreneurship inevitably deviates from the norm to work for others, and this deviation may be in the "blood" of entrepreneurs.[39] For instance, **serial entrepreneurs** are people who start, grow, and sell several businesses throughout their career. One example is David Neeleman, who as a serial entrepreneur has founded four airlines in three countries (Morris Air and JetBlue in the United States, WestJet in Canada, and Azul in Brazil).[40]

Critics, however, argue that some of these traits, such as a strong achievement orientation, are not necessarily limited to entrepreneurs, but instead are characteristic of many successful individuals. The diversity among entrepreneurs makes any attempt to develop a standard psychological or personality profile futile. Critics suggest what matters is institutions—namely, the environments that set formal and informal rules of the game. Consider the ethnic Chinese, who have exhibited a high degree of entrepreneurship throughout Southeast Asia. As a minority group (usually less than 10% of the population in countries such as Indonesia and Thailand), ethnic Chinese control 70%–80% of the wealth in the region. Yet, in mainland China, for three decades (the 1950s to the 1970s), there had been virtually no entrepreneurship, thanks to harsh communist policies. Over the past three decades, however, as government policies became relatively more entrepreneur friendly, the institutional transitions have opened the floodgates of entrepreneurship in China.[41]

A high-profile case documents how institutions constrain or enable entrepreneurship. In 2005, Chinese Internet start-up Baidu listed on NASDAQ and its shares surged 354% on the same day (from $27 to $154), scoring the biggest one-day stock surge in US capital markets since 2000. While there might be some "irrational exuberance" among US investors chasing "China's Google," it is evident that they did not discriminate against Baidu. The sad reality for Baidu is that, at home, it was blatantly discriminated against by the Chinese securities authorities. As a private start-up, it was not allowed to list its stock on China's stock exchanges—only state-owned firms need apply. Essentially, Baidu was pushed out of China to list in the United States, whose entrepreneur-friendly institutional frameworks, such as NASDAQ regulations, are able to facilitate more entrepreneurial success.[42] In a nutshell, it is not what is in people's "blood" that makes or breaks entrepreneurship—it is institutions that encourage or constrain entrepreneurship.

Beyond the macro societal-level institutions, more micro institutions also matter. Family background and educational attainment have been found to correlate with entrepreneurship. Children of wealthy parents, especially those who own businesses, are more likely to start their own firms. So are people who are better educated. Taken together, informal norms governing one's socioeconomic group, in terms of whether starting a new firm is legitimate or not, assert some powerful impact on the propensity to create new ventures. Overall, this debate is an extension of the broader debate on "nature versus nurture." Most scholars now agree that entrepreneurship is the result of both nature *and* nurture.

Slow Internationalizers versus Born Global Start-ups

stage model

Model that suggests firms internationalize by going through predictable stages from simple steps to complex operations.

Two components should be considered here: (1) Can SMEs internationalize faster than what has been suggested by traditional **stage models** (models that portray SME internationalization as a slow, stage-by-stage process)? (2) Should they rapidly internationalize? The dust has largely settled on the first component: it is possible for some (but not all) SMEs to make very rapid progress in internationalization. Consider Logitech, now a global leader in computer peripherals. It was established by entrepreneurs from Switzerland and the United States, where the firm set up dual headquarters. Research and development (R&D) and manufacturing were initially split between these two countries and then quickly spread to Ireland and Taiwan through FDI. Its first commercial contract was with a Japanese company. Logitech is not alone among such born global firms.

What is currently being debated is the second component.[43] On the one hand, advocates argue that every industry has become "global" and that entrepreneurial firms need to rapidly go after these opportunities.[44] On the other hand, stage models suggest that firms need to enter culturally and institutionally close markets first, spend enough time there to accumulate overseas experience, and then gradually move from more primitive modes such as exports to more sophisticated strategies such as FDI in distant markets. Consistent with stage models, Sweden's IKEA waited 20 years (1943–1963) before entering a neighboring country, Norway. Only more recently has it accelerated its internationalization. Stage models caution that inexperienced swimmers may drown in unfamiliar foreign waters.

A key issue, therefore, is whether it is better for entrepreneurs to start the internationalization process soon after founding (as born global firms do) or to postpone until the firm has accumulated significant resources (as IKEA did). One view supports rapid internationalization. Specifically, firms following the prescription of stage models, when eventually internationalizing, must overcome substantial inertia because of their domestic orientation.[45] In contrast, firms that internationalize earlier need to overcome fewer of these barriers. Therefore, SMEs without an established domestic orientation (such as Logitech discussed earlier) may outperform their rivals that wait longer to internationalize.[46] In other words, contrary to the inherent disadvantages in internationalization associated with SMEs as suggested by stage models, there may be "inherent advantages" of being small while venturing abroad.

On the other hand, some scholars argue that "the born-global view, although appealing, is a dangerous half-truth." They maintain that "You must first be successful at home, then move outward in a manner that anticipates and genuinely accommodates local differences."[47] In other words, the teachings of stage models are still relevant. Consequently, indiscriminate advice to "go global" may not be warranted.[48]

Anti-Failure Biases versus Entrepreneur-Friendly Bankruptcy Laws[49]

Corporate bankruptcies have climbed to new heights in the Great Recession (note "bankruptcy" here refers only to corporate bankruptcy; we do *not* consider personal bankruptcy). Firms ranging from huge ones such as General Motors to tiny entrepreneurial outfits have dropped out left and right around the world. Since bankruptcies do not sound too good or inspiring, is there anything that we—the government, financial institutions, consumers, or the society at large—can do to prevent widespread bankruptcies?

Efforts to rescue failing firms from bankruptcies stem from an "anti-failure" bias widely shared among entrepreneurs, scholars, journalists, and government officials. Although a majority of entrepreneurial firms fail, this "anti-failure" bias leads to strong interest in entrepreneurial success (remember how many times Google and Facebook were written up by the press?), and to scant attention devoted to the vast majority of entrepreneurial firms that end up in failure and bankruptcy. However, one perspective suggests that bankruptcies, which are undoubtedly painful to individual entrepreneurs and employees, may be *good* for the society. Consequently, bankruptcy laws need to be reformed to become more entrepreneur-friendly by making it easier for entrepreneurs to declare bankruptcies and to move on. Consequently, financial, human, and physical resources stuck with failed firms can be redeployed in a socially optimal way.

A leading debate is how to treat failed entrepreneurs who file for bankruptcy. Do we let them walk away from debt or punish them? Historically, entrepreneur-friendliness and bankruptcy laws are like an "oxymoron," because bankruptcy laws are usually harsh and even cruel. The very term "bankruptcy" is derived from a harsh practice: In medieval Italy, if bankrupt entrepreneurs did not pay their debt, debtors would destroy the trading bench (booth) of the bankrupt—the Italian word for broken bench, "banca rotta," has evolved into the English word "bankruptcy." The pound of flesh demanded by the creditor in Shakespeare's *The Merchant of Venice* is only a slight exaggeration. The world's first bankruptcy law, passed in England in 1542, considered a bankrupt individual a criminal and penalties ranged from incarceration to death sentence.

Recently, many governments have realized that entrepreneur-friendly bankruptcy laws can not only lower *exit* barriers, but also lower *entry* barriers. Although we are confident that many start-ups will fail, at present it is impossible to predict which ones will go under. Thus, from an institution-based standpoint, if entrepreneurship is to be encouraged, there is a need to ease the pain associated with bankruptcy by means such as allowing entrepreneurs to walk away from debt, a legal right that bankrupt US entrepreneurs appreciate. In contrast, until the recent bankruptcy law reforms, bankrupt German entrepreneurs might remain liable for unpaid debt for up to 30 *years*. Further, German and Japanese managers of bankrupt firms can also be liable for criminal penalties. Numerous bankrupt Japanese entrepreneurs have committed suicide. As rules of the "end game," harsh bankruptcy laws thus become grave exit barriers. They can also be significant entry barriers, as fewer would-be entrepreneurs may decide to launch their ventures.

At a societal level, if many would-be entrepreneurs abandon their ideas in fear of failure, there will not be a thriving entrepreneurial sector. Given the risks and uncertainties, it is not surprising that many entrepreneurs do not make it the first time. However, if they are given second, third, or more chances, some of them will succeed. Approximately 50% of US entrepreneurs who filed bankruptcy resumed a new venture in four years. This high level of entrepreneurialism is, in part, driven by the relatively entrepreneur-friendly bankruptcy laws in the United States (such as the provision of Chapter 11 bankruptcy reorganization, instead of straight liquidation). On the other hand, a society that severely punishes failed entrepreneurs (such as forcing financially insolvent firms to liquidate) is not likely to foster widespread entrepreneurship. Overall, worldwide evidence from 29 countries—involving both developed and emerging economies—has identified a strong linkage between entrepreneur-friendly bankruptcy laws and new firm entries.[50]

Institutionally, there is an urgent need to remove some of our anti-failure bias and design entrepreneur-friendly bankruptcy policies so that failed entrepreneurs are given more chances. At a societal level, entrepreneurial failures may be beneficial, since it is through a large number of entrepreneurial experimentations—although many will fail—that winning solutions will emerge and that economies will develop. In short, the boom in busts is not necessarily bad.[51]

The Savvy Entrepreneur

Entrepreneurs and their firms are quintessential engines of the "creative destruction" process underpinning global capitalism first described by Joseph Schumpeter. All three leading perspectives can shed considerable light on entrepreneurship. The industry-based view suggests that entrepreneurial firms tend to choose industries with lower entry barriers. The resource-based view posits that it is largely intangible resources such as vision, drive, and willingness to take risk that have been fueling entrepreneurship. Finally, the institution-based view argues that the larger institutional frameworks explain a great deal about what is behind the differences in entrepreneurial and economic development around the world.

Consequently, the savvy entrepreneur can draw at least four important implications for action (Table 5.5). (1) Establish an intimate understanding of your industry to identify gaps and opportunities, or, alternatively, to avoid or exit from it if the threats are too strong. (2) Leverage entrepreneurial resources and capabilities, such as entrepreneurial drive, innovative capabilities, and network ties. (3) Push for more entrepreneur-friendly formal institutions, such as rules governing how to set up new firms (Figure 5.2) and how to go through bankruptcy. Entrepreneurs also need to cultivate strong informal norms granting legitimacy to start-ups. Talking to high school and college students, taking on internships, and providing seed money as angels for new ventures are some of the actions that entrepreneurs can undertake. (4) When internationalizing, be bold but not too bold.[52] Being bold does not mean being reckless. One specific insight from this chapter is that it is possible to internationalize without venturing abroad. There are a variety of international strategies that enable entrepreneurial firms to stay in domestic markets. When the entrepreneurial firm is not ready to take on higher risk abroad, this more limited involvement may be appropriate.

We conclude this chapter by revisiting the four fundamental questions. Because start-ups are an embodiment of the personal characteristics of their founders, why firms differ (Question 1) and how they behave (Question 2) can be found in how entrepreneurs differ from non-entrepreneurs. What determines the scope of the firm (Question 3) boils down to how successful entrepreneurs can expand their businesses. Finally, what determines the international success and failure of firms (Question 4) depends on whether entrepreneurs can select the right industry, leverage their capabilities, and take advantage of formal and informal institutional resources—both at home and abroad.[53]

TABLE 5.5   Strategic Implications for Action

- Establish an intimate understanding of your industry to identify gaps and opportunities.
- Leverage entrepreneurial resources and capabilities.
- Push for institutions that facilitate entrepreneurship development—both formal and informal.
- When internationalizing, be bold, but not too bold.

CHAPTER SUMMARY

1. Define entrepreneurship, entrepreneurs, and entrepreneurial firms
- Entrepreneurship is the identification and exploration of previously unexplored opportunities.
- Entrepreneurs may be founders and owners of new businesses or managers of existing firms.
- Entrepreneurial firms in this chapter are defined as SMEs.

2. Articulate a comprehensive model of entrepreneurship
- Five forces of an industry shape entrepreneurship associated with this industry.
- Resources and capabilities largely determine entrepreneurial success and failure.
- Institutions enable and constrain entrepreneurship around the world.

3. Identify five strategies that characterize a growing entrepreneurial firm
- (1) Growth, (2) innovation, (3) network, (4) financing/governance, and (5) harvest/exit.

4. Differentiate international strategies that enter foreign markets and that stay in domestic markets
- Entrepreneurial firms can internationalize by entering foreign markets, through entry modes such as (1) direct exports, (2) licensing/franchising, and (3) FDI.
- Entrepreneurial firms can also internationalize without venturing abroad, by (1) exporting indirectly, (2) supplying foreign firms, (3) becoming licensees/franchisees of foreign firms, (4) joining foreign entrants as alliance partners, and (5) harvesting and exiting through sell-offs to foreign entrants.

5. Participate in three leading debates concerning entrepreneurship
- (1) Traits versus institutions, (2) slow versus rapid internationalization, and (3) anti-failure biases versus entrepreneur-friendly bankruptcy laws.

6. Draw strategic implications for action
- Establish an intimate understanding of your industry to identify gaps and opportunities.
- Leverage entrepreneurial resources and capabilities.
- Push for institutions that facilitate entrepreneurship development.
- When internationalizing, be bold, but not too bold.

KEY TERMS

Born global firm (international new venture) p. 140

Direct export p. 141

Entrepreneur p. 128

Entrepreneurship p. 128

Export intermediary p. 142

Franchising p. 141

Indirect export p. 142

Initial public offering (IPO) p. 139

International entrepreneurship p. 128

Liability of newness p. 136

Licensing p. 141

Microfinance p. 138

Serial entrepreneur p. 143

Small and medium-sized enterprise (SME) p. 128

Stage model p. 143

Strong ties p. 136

Venture capitalist (VC) p. 137

Weak ties p. 136

CRITICAL DISCUSSION QUESTIONS

1. Why is entrepreneurship most often associated with SMEs, as opposed to larger firms?

2. Given that most entrepreneurial start-ups fail, why do entrepreneurs found so many new firms? Why are (most) governments interested in promoting more start-ups?

3. *ON ETHICS:* Your former high school buddy invites you to join a start-up that specializes in making counterfeit products. She offers you the job of CEO and 10% of the equity of the firm. The chances of getting caught are slim. You are currently unemployed. How would you respond to her proposition?

TOPICS FOR EXPANDED PROJECTS

1. Some suggest that foreign markets are graveyards for entrepreneurial firms to overextend themselves. Others argue that foreign markets represent the future for SMEs. If you were the owner of a small, reasonably profitable firm, would you consider expanding overseas? Why or why not? Write a short paper to state your case.

2. *ON ETHICS:* Everything is the same as in Critical Discussion Question 3, except the "counterfeit" products involved are the more affordable generic drugs to combat HIV/AIDS. Providing these drugs at a lower cost would potentially help millions of patients worldwide who cannot afford the high-priced patented drugs. How would you respond? Write a short paper to explain your answer.

3. *ON ETHICS:* Some argue that entrepreneur-friendly bankruptcy laws, which may allow entrepreneurs to walk away from their debt, are *unethical* because they increase the cost of financing for everybody. Review the arguments in the Debates and Extensions section. Working in small groups, discuss the arguments and then decide whether you support or do not support more entrepreneur-friendly bankruptcy laws. Present your answers in a short paper or a visual presentation.

Emerging Markets: Microfinance, Macro Success or Global Mess?

Teach a man to fish, and he'll eat for a lifetime. However, here is a catch: In many poor developing countries, numerous eager fishermen—also known as entrepreneurs—cannot afford a fishing pole. In 1976, Muhammad Yunus, a young economics professor who received his PhD from Vanderbilt University, lent $27 out of his own pocket to a group of poor craftsmen in his native Bangladesh. He also helped found a village-based enterprise called the Grameen Project. It never occurred to Yunus that he would inspire a global movement for entrepreneurial financing, much less that 30 years later, in 2006 he and the Grameen Bank he founded would be awarded the Nobel Peace Prize.

Used to buy everything from milk cows to mobile phones (to be used as pay phones by the entire village), microloans (typically $50–$300) can make a huge difference. The poor tend to have neither assets (necessary for collateral) nor credit history, making traditional loans risky. The innovative, simple solution is to lend to women. On average, women are more likely to use their earnings to support family needs than men, who may be more likely to indulge in drinking, gambling, or drugs. A more sophisticated solution is to organize the women in a village into a collective and lend money to the collective but not to individuals. Overall, 84% of microloan recipients are women. While annual interest rates average a hefty 35%, they are still far below the rates charged by local loan sharks. By 2011, more than 7,000 microfinance institutions (MFIs) had served 120 million borrowers around the world.

However, as microfinance grows from periphery to mainstream, not all is rosy. Two ferocious debates have erupted recently. The first debate deals with how to view the initial public offerings (IPOs) of MFIs (see Table 5.6). The "successful" IPOs of several MFIs have attracted criticisms that these MFIs and their new shareholders, most of whom are rich investors from North America and Europe, have enriched themselves at the expense of very poor people at the base of the pyramid. In short, the rich have literally profited from the poor. Is that right?

Second, with the onslaught of the 2008–2009 global crisis, default rates have skyrocketed. Several competitive MFIs may have dumped several microfinance loans to the same uneducated clients. In a microfinance boom, some lending practices have increasingly become competitive and reckless, similar to subprime lending in the West before the financial crisis. Should crops or ventures fail, clients thus face crushing debt loads. Recovery methods from MFIs sometimes involve intimidation. The Indian government had a list of 85 MFI "victims," who committed suicide. In response, policymakers in some parts of India capped the interest rate at 24%, and called default borrowers to refuse to pay up. Thus, in some parts of India, nearly 80% of borrowers were in default. Because of the high costs of making and collecting payments on millions of tiny loans, MFIs' margins are razor-thin. Such massive defaults quickly pushed some MFIs to go under, and the Indian government reluctantly spent $221 million to bail them out in 2010. Sheikh Hasina, Bangladesh's prime

TABLE 5.6 Initial Public Offerings of Microfinance Institutions

MFI	COUNTRY	CAPITAL RAISED	YEAR
Bank Rakyat	Indonesia	$480 million	2003
Equity Bank	Kenya	$88 million	2006
Banco Compartamos	Mexico	$467 million	2007
SKS Microfinance	India	$1.5 billion	2010

© Cengage Learning

minister, charged MFIs with "sucking blood from the poor" and treating the people of Bangladesh as "guinea pigs." She launched an investigation into Grameen Bank's allegedly questionable operations. Although as managing director of Grameen Bank, Yunus was eventually cleared of wrongdoing, microfinance—and its missionary pioneer—has suffered from a crisis of faith.

Sources: Based on (1) *Bloomberg Businessweek,* 2010, An IPO for India's top lender to the poor, May 10: 16–17; (2) *Bloomberg Businessweek,* 2010, In a microfinance boom, echoes of subprime, June 21: 50–51; (3) G. Bruton, S. Khavul, & H. Chavez, 2011, Microlending in emerging economies, *Journal of International Business Studies,* 42: 718–739; (4) *Economist,* 2010, Leave well alone, November 20: 16; (5) *Economist,* 2010, Under water, December 11: 56; (6) *Economist,* 2011, Saint under siege, January 8: 75; (7) *Newsweek,* 2010, The micromess, December 20: 10; (8) B. Pinkham & P. Nair, 2011, Microfinance: Going global … and global public? case study, University of Texas at Dallas.

CASE DISCUSSION QUESTIONS

1. Why was Yunus awarded the Nobel *Peace* Prize (as opposed to the Nobel *Economics* Prize)?

2. ON ETHICS: As an investor in a developed economy, do you have any problem investing in MFIs?

3. ON ETHICS: As CEO of a leading MFI in Kenya, Indonesia, or Mexico, you have been invited by your country's leading newspaper to write an opinion piece in defense of MFIs. This defense is prompted by the Indian government bailouts of MFIs and the Bangladesh government investigation of Grameen Bank. How would you proceed?

NOTES

[**Journal acronyms**] *AME – Academy of Management Executive;* **AMJ** *– Academy of Management Journal;* **AMP** *– Academy of Management Perspectives;* **AMR** *– Academy of Management Review;* **APJM** *– Asia Pacific Journal of Management;* **ASQ** *– Administrative Science Quarterly;* **BW** *– BusinessWeek (before 2010) or Bloomberg Businessweek (since 2010);* **ETP** *– Entrepreneurship Theory and Practice;* **FEER** *– Far Eastern Economic Review;* **HBR** *– Harvard Business Review;* **JBV** *– Journal of Business Venturing;* **JIBS** *– Journal of International Business Studies;* **JMS** *– Journal of Management Studies;* **JWB** *– Journal of World Business;* **MS** *– Management Science;* **SEJ** *– Strategic Entrepreneurship Journal;* **SMJ** *– Strategic Management Journal;* **SMR** *– MIT Sloan Management Review*

1. M. Hitt, R. D. Ireland, S. M. Camp, & D. Sexton, 2001, Strategic entrepreneurship (p. 480), *SMJ,* 22: 479–491. See also M. Hitt, R. D. Ireland, D. Sirmon, & C. Trahms, 2011, Strategic entrepreneurship, *AMP,* May: 57–75; R. Hoskisson, J. Covin, H. Volberda, & R. Johnson, 2011, Revitalizing entrepreneurship, *JMS,* 48: 1141–1168; J. McMullen & D. Shepherd, 2006, Entrepreneurial action and the role of uncertainty in the theory of the entrepreneur, *AMR,* 31: 132–152; S. Venkataraman, S. Sarasvathy, N. Dew, & W. Forster, 2012, Reflections on the 2010 *AMR* Decade Award: Whither the promise? *AMR,* 37: 21–33.

2. S. Shane & S. Venkataraman, 2000, The promise of entrepreneurship as a field of research (p. 218), *AMR,* 25: 217–226.

3. P. McDougall & B. Oviatt, 2000, International entrepreneurship (p. 903), *AMJ,* 43: 902–906. See also T. Baker, E. Gedajlovic, & M. Lubatkin, 2005, A framework for comparing entrepreneurship processes across nations, *JIBS,* 36: 492–504; Y. Chandra & N. Coviello, 2010, Broadening the concept of international entrepreneurship, *JWB,* 45: 228–236; D. Cumming, H. Sapienza, D. Siegel, & M. Wright, 2009, International entrepreneurship, *SEJ,* 3: 283–296.

4. Z. Acs & C. Armington, 2006, *Entrepreneurship, Geography, and American Economic Growth,* New York: Cambridge University Press.

5. M. Hayward, D. Shepherd, & D. Griffin, 2006, A hubris theory of entrepreneurship, *MS,* 52: 160–172; V. Lau, M. Shaffer, & K. Au, 2007, Entrepreneurial career success from a Chinese perspective, *JIBS,* 38: 126–146; R. Lowe & A. Ziedonis, 2006, Overoptimism and the performance of entrepreneurial firms, *MS,* 52: 173–186.

6. R. Mudambi & S. Zahra, 2007, The survival of international new ventures, *JIBS*, 38: 333–352.

7. S. Bradley, H. Aldrich, D. Shepherd, & J. Wiklund, 2011, Resources, environmental change, and survival, *SMJ*, 32: 486–509; T. Fan, 2010, De novo venture strategy, *SMJ*, 31: 19–38; P. Geroski, J. Mata, & P. Portugal, 2010, Founding conditions and the survival of new firms, *SMJ*, 31: 510–529.

8. A. Arikan & A. McGrahan, 2010, The development of capabilities in new firms, *SMJ*, 31: 1–18; A. Arora & A. Nandkumar, 2012, Insecure advantage? *SMJ*, 33: 231–251; B. Campbell, M. Ganco, A. Franco, & R. Agarwal, 2012, Who leaves, where to, and why worry? *SMJ*, 33: 65–87; A. Chatterji, 2009, Spawned with a silver spoon? *SMJ*, 30: 185–206; G. Knight & D. Kim, 2009, International business competence and the contemporary firm, *JIBS*, 40: 255–273; D. Lepak, K. Smith, & M. S. Taylor, 2007, Value creation and value capture, *AMR*, 32: 180–194; H. Park & H. K. Steensma, 2012, When does corporate venture capital add value for new ventures? *SMJ*, 33: 1–22.

9. D. Sull, 2005, Strategy as active waiting (p. 125), *HBR*, September: 121–129.

10. G. George, 2005, Slack resources and the performance of privately held firms, *AMJ*, 48: 661–676; R. Katila & S. Shane, 2005, When does lack of resources make new firms innovative? *AMJ*, 48: 814–829.

11. S. Anokhin & J. Wincent, 2012, Start-up rates and innovation, *JIBS*, 43: 41–60; H. Bowen & D. De Clercq, 2008, Institutional context and the allocation of entrepreneurial efforts, *JIBS*, 39: 747–767; J. Capelleras, K. Mole, F. Freene, & D. Storey, 2008, Do more heavily regulated economies have poorer performing new ventures? *JIBS*, 39: 688–704; J. Levie & E. Autio, 2011, Regulatory burden, rule of law, and entry of strategic entrepreneurs, *JMS*, 48: 1392–1419; T. Manolova, R. Eunni, & B. Gyoshev, 2008, Institutional environments for entrepreneurship, *ETP*, January: 203–218.

12. D. Kim, E. Morse, R. Mitchell, & K. Seawright, 2010, Institutional environment and entrepreneurial cognitions, *ETP*, 34: 491–516.

13. *Economist*, 2011, Son also rises, November 27: 71–72.

14. *BW*, 2011, In Russia, Facebook is more than a social network, January 3: 32–33.

15. M. Cardon, J. Wincent, J. Singh, & M. Drnovsek, 2009, The nature and experience of entrepreneurial passion, *AMR*, 34: 511–532; J. Clarke, 2011, Revitalizing entrepreneurship, *JMS*, 48: 1365–1391; V. Rindova, D. Barry, & D. Ketchen, 2009, Entrepreneuring

as emancipation, *AMR*, 34: 477–491; D. Souder, Z. Simsek, & S. Johnson, 2012, The differing effects of agent and founder CEOs on the firm's market expansion, *SMJ*, 33: 23–41.

16. G. Dess & G. T. Lumpkin, 2005, The role of entrepreneurial orientation in stimulating effective corporate entrepreneurship, *AME*, 19: 147–156; J. Dyer, H. Gregerson, & C. Christensen, 2008, Entrepreneur behaviors, opportunity recognition, and the origins of innovative ventures, *SEJ*, 2: 317–338; I. Filatotchev & J. Piesse, 2009, R&D, internationalization, and growth of newly listed firms, *JIBS*, 40: 1260–1276; A. Gaur, D. Mukherjee, S. Gaur, & F. Schmid, 2011, Environmental and firm-level influences on inter-organizational trust and SME performance, *JMS*, 48: 1752–1781; B. George, 2011, Entrepreneurial orientation, *JMS*, 48: 1291–1313; F. Golovko & G. Valentini, 2011, Exploring the complementarity between innovation and export for SMEs' growth, *JIBS*, 42: 362–380; S. Kotha, 2010, Spillovers, spill-ins, and strategic entrepreneurship, *SEJ*, 4: 284–306; F. Santos & K. Eisenhardt, 2009, Constructing markets and shaping boundaries, *AMJ*, 52: 643–671; M. Terziovski, 2010, Innovative practice and its performance implications in SMEs in the manufacturing sector, *SMJ*, 31: 892–902.

17. *Economist*, 2009, Lands of opportunity, March 14: 16–17; *Economist*, 2011, Beyond the start-up nation, January 1: 60.

18. C. Christensen, 1997, *The Innovator's Dilemma*, Boston: Harvard Business School Press.

19. D. Gregorio, M. Musteen, & D. Thomas, 2008, International new ventures, *JWB*, 43: 186–196; S. Jack, 2010, Approaches to studying networks, *JBV*, 25: 120–137; R. Ma, Y. Huang, & O. Shenkar, 2011, Social networks and opportunity recognition, *SMJ*, 32: 1183–1205; D. Sullivan & M. Marvel, 2011, Knowledge acquisition, network reliance, and early-stage technology venture outcomes, *JMS*, 48: 1169–1193; B. Vissa, 2011, A matching theory of entrepreneurs' tie formation intentions and initiation of economic exchange, *AMJ*, 54: 137–158; L. Zhou, B. Barnes, & Y. Lu, 2010, Entrepreneurial proclivity, capability upgrading, and performance advantage of newness among international new ventures, *JIBS*, 41: 882–905.

20. M. Colombo, L. Grilli, S. Murtinu, L. Piscitello, & E. Piva, 2009, Effects of international R&D alliances in performance of high-tech start-ups, *SEJ*, 3: 346–368; T. Manolova, I. Manev, & B. Gyoshev, 2010, In good company, *JWB*, 45: 257–265; M. Musteen, J. Francis,

& D. Datta, 2010, The influence of international networks on internationalization speed and performance, *JWB*, 45: 197–205; S. Prashantham & C. Dhanaraj, 2010, The dynamic influence of social capital on the international growth of new ventures, *JMS*, 47: 965–994; L. Riddle, G. Hrivnak, & T. Nielsen, 2010, Transnational diaspora entrepreneurship in emerging markets, *JIM*, 16: 398–411; P. Sonderegger & F. Taube, 2010, Cluster life cycle and diaspora effects, *JIM*, 16: 383–397; J. Yu, B. Gilbert, & B. Oviatt, 2011, Effects of alliances, time, and network cohesion on the initiation of foreign sales by new ventures, *SMJ*, 32: 424–446.

21. G. Chen, D. Hambrick, & T. Pollock, 2008, Puttin' on the Ritz, *AMJ*, 51: 954–975.

22. M. W. Peng & Y. Luo, 2000, Managerial ties and firm performance in a transition economy, *AMJ*, 43: 486–501.

23. R. Burt, 1997, The contingent value of social capital (p. 342), *ASQ*, 42: 339–365.

24. P. Vaaler, 2011, Immigrant remittances and the venture investment environment of developing countries, *JIBS*, 42: 1121–1149.

25. T. Dalziel, R. White, & J. Arthurs, 2011, Principal costs in initial public offerings, *JMS*, 48: 1346–1364; A. Zacharakis, J. McMullen, & D. Shepherd, 2007, Venture capitalists' decision policies across three countries, *JIBS*, 38: 691–708.

26. G. Bruton, I. Filatotchev, S. Chahine, & M. Wright, 2010, Governance, ownership structure, and performance of IPO firms, *SMJ*, 31: 491–509; B. Walters, M. Kroll, & P. Wright, 2010, The impact of TMT board member control and environment on post-IPO performance, *AMJ*, 53: 572–595.

27. D. Hope, D. Thomas, & D. Vyas, 2011, Financial credibility, ownership, and financing constraints in private firms, *JIBS*, 42: 935–951.

28. M. Minniti, W. Bygrave, & E. Autio, 2006, *Global Entrepreneurship Monitor 2006*, Wellesley, MA: Babson College.

29. D. Ahlstrom, G. Bruton, & K. Yeh, 2007, Venture capital in China: Past, present, future, *APJM*, 24: 247–268; K. Au & H. Kwan, 2009, Start-up capital and Chinese entrepreneurs, *ETP*, 33: 889–908; M. Wright, 2007, Venture capital in China: A view from Europe, *APJM*, 24: 269–282.

30. M. Graebner & K. Eisenhardt, 2004, The seller's side of the story, *ASQ*, 49: 366–403.

31. R. Larsson, K. Brousseau, M. Driver, M. Holmqvist, & V. Tarnovskaya, 2003, International growth through cooperation (p. 15), *AME*, 17: 7–21.

32. C. Bingham, 2009, Oscillating improvisation, *SEJ*, 3: 321–345; S. Fernhaber, B. Gilbert, & P. McDougall,

2008, International entrepreneurship and geographic location, *JIBS*, 39: 267–290; M. Giarratana & S. Torrisi, 2010, Foreign entry and survival in a knowledge-intensive market, *SEJ*, 4: 85–104.

33. N. Hashai, 2011, Sequencing the expansion of geographic scope and foreign operations by "born global" firms, *JIBS*, 42: 995–1015.

34. M. W. Peng, 1998, *Behind the Success and Failure of US Export Intermediaries*, Westport, CT: Quorum.

35. M. W. Peng & A. York, 2001, Behind intermediary performance in export trade, *JIBS*, 32: 327–346.

36. *FEER*, 2002, Pepperoni power, November 14: 59–60.

37. V. Aggarwal & D. Hsu, 2009, Modes of cooperative R&D commercialization by start-ups, *SMJ*, 30: 835–864; P. Ozcan & K. Eisenhardt, 2009, Origin of alliance portfolios, *AMJ*, 52: 246–279.

38. M. Graebner, 2009, Caveat venditor, *AMJ*, 52: 435–472.

39. G. Cassar, 2010, Are individuals entering self-employment overly optimistic? *SMJ*, 31: 822–840; D. Gregoire, A. Corbett, & J. McMullen, 2011, The cognitive perspective in entrepreneurship, *JMS*, 48: 1443–1477.

40. *BW*, 2010, Getting over the JetBlues, February 15: 52–54.

41. D. Ahlstrom, S. Chen, & K. Yeh, 2010, Managing in ethnic Chinese communities, *APJM*, 27: 341–354; J. Lu & Z. Tao, 2010, Determinants of entrepreneurial activities in China, *JBV*, 25: 261–273; M. W. Peng, 2001, How entrepreneurs create wealth in transition economies, *AME*, 15: 95–108.

42. Y. Yamakawa, M. W. Peng, & D. Deeds, 2008, What drives new ventures to internationalize from emerging to developed economies?, *ETP*, 32: 59–82.

43. S. Loane, J. Bell, & R. McNaughton, 2007, A cross-national study on the impact of management teams on the rapid internationalization of small firms, *JWB*, 42: 489–504; H. Sapienza, E. Autio, G. George, & S. Zahra, 2006, A capabilities perspective on the effects of early internationalization on firm survival and growth, *AMR*, 31: 914–933.

44. V. Govindarajan & A. Gupta, 2001, *The Quest for Global Dominance*, San Francisco: Jossey-Bass.

45. S. Nadkarni, P. Herrmann, & P. Perez, 2011, Domestic mindset and early international performance, *SMJ*, 32: 510–531.

46. J. Mathews & I. Zander, 2007, The international entrepreneurial dynamics of accelerated internationalization, *JIBS*, 38: 387–403.

47. S. Rangan & R. Adner, 2001, Profits and the Internet (pp. 49–50), *SMR*, summer: 44–53.

48. L. Lopez, S. Kundu, & L. Ciravegna, 2009, Born global or born regional? *JIBS*, 40: 1228–1238.

49. This section draws heavily from S. Lee, M. W. Peng, & J. Barney, 2007, Bankruptcy law and entrepreneurship development, *AMR*, 32: 257–272; M. W. Peng, Y. Yamakawa, & S. Lee, 2010, Bankruptcy laws and entrepreneur-friendliness, *ETP*, 34: 517–530.

50. S. Lee, Y. Yamakawa, M. W. Peng, & J. Barney, 2011, How do bankruptcy laws affect entrepreneurship development around the world? *JBV*, 28: 505–520.

51. A. Knott & H. Posen, 2005, Is failure good? *SMJ*, 26: 617–641.

52. M. W. Peng, C. Hill, & D. Wang, 2000, Schumpeterian dynamics versus Williamsonian considerations, *JMS*, 37: 167–184.

53. D. Ahlstrom & G, Bruton, 2010, Rapid institutional shifts and the co-evolution of entrepreneurial firms in transition economies, *ETP*, 34: 531–554; G. Bruton, D. Ahlstrom, & H. Li, 2010, Institutional theory and entrepreneurship, *ETP*, 34: 421–440; C. Moore, R. G. Bell, & I. Filatotchev, 2010, Institutions and foreign IPO firms, *ETP*, 34: 469–490; R. Nasra & M. T. Dacin, 2010, Institutional arrangements and international entrepreneurship, *ETP*, 34: 583–609; S. Puffer, D. McCarthy, & M. Boisot, 2010, Entrepreneurship in Russia and China, *ETP*, 34: 441–467; J. Webb, G. Kistruck, R. D. Ireland, & D. Ketchen, 2010, The entrepreneurship process in base of the pyramid markets, *ETP*, 34: 555–581; S. Zahra & M. Wright, 2011, Entrepreneurship's next act, *AMP*, November: 67–83.

CHAPTER 6

ENTERING FOREIGN MARKETS

© istockphoto/Alexey Stiop

KNOWLEDGE OBJECTIVES

After studying this chapter, you should be able to

1. Understand the necessity to overcome the liability of foreignness

2. Articulate a comprehensive model of foreign market entries

3. Match the quest for location-specific advantages with strategic goals (*where* to enter)

4. Compare and contrast first-mover and late-mover advantages (*when* to enter)

5. Follow a decision model that outlines specific steps for foreign market entries (*how* to enter)

6. Participate in three leading debates concerning foreign market entries

7. Draw strategic implications for action

Enter the United States by Bus

If you are a college student studying in the Midwest or Northeast parts of the United States, you may have heard of (or taken a ride on) Megabus. Its website announces that it is "the first, low-cost, express bus service to offer city-to-city travel for as low as $1 via the Internet." Currently serving 50 US cities from five hubs (Chicago, New York, Philadelphia, Pittsburgh, and Washington, DC), Megabus, according to *Bloomberg Businessweek*, "has fundamentally changed the way Americans—especially the young—travel."

A generation ago, Greyhound was a national icon for intercity travel. Unfortunately, as Americans fell more in love with cars and the cost of airfares dropped further, intercity bus ridership steadily decreased. Further, as inner cities, where the bus depots (terminals) were situated, decayed, bus travel became the travel mode of last resort. In 1990, Greyhound filed for Chapter 11 bankruptcy.

Yet, the demand for medium-distance trips ideal for intercity bus travel did not go away. For some of the most traveled routes (such as between Chicago and Detroit and between New York and DC), the distance is too far for a leisurely drive but too close to justify the expense (and increasingly the hassle) of air travel. While Greyhound has been in decline, small, entrepreneurial bus operators, known as the "Chinatown buses," emerged. They started by shuttling passengers (primarily recent Chinese immigrants) between Chinatowns in New York and Boston. Such niche operators quickly grabbed the attention of many college students. Despite four decades of decline, overall US intercity bus ridership spiked in 2006, the year when Megabus entered.

Although Megabus is a brand-new, no-frills entrant into the US market, it is backed by the full strength of the second-largest transport firm in the UK, Stagecoach Group, which employs 18,000 people there. Founded in 1980 and headquartered in Perth, Scotland, Stagecoach not only operates buses, but also trains, trams, and ferries throughout the UK, moving 2.5 million people every day. It is listed on the London Stock Exchange, where it is a member of the FTSE 250. Megabus is a brand of Stagecoach's wholly owned US subsidiary, Coach USA.

Stagecoach is not a stranger to international forays, having previously operated in Hong Kong, Kenya, Malawi, New Zealand, Portugal, and Sweden. However, these operations turned out to be lackluster and were all sold. For now, the sole international market it focuses on is North America (Megabus entered Canada in 2008).

Although Megabus is clearly a late mover in North America, its future looks bright. So what allows Megabus to turn a declining national trend of bus ridership around? At least four features stand out. First, tickets are super cheap, starting at $1 (!). Megabus uses a yield management system, typically used by airlines, which offers early passengers dirt-cheap deals and late passengers progressively higher prices. Although only one or two passengers per trip can get the $1 deal, even the "higher" prices are very competitive. In routes where it competes with Amtrak (the railway), Megabus costs about a tenth of Amtrak. All tickets have to be booked online. This not only eliminates the expenses of maintaining ticket booths, but also attracts a more educated demographic group.

Second, instead of using depots, Megabus follows the Chinatown buses by using curbside stops (like regular city bus stops) to board and disembark passengers. Interestingly, dumping the depot model not only saves a lot of money, but also makes Megabus more attractive, because passengers do not have to spend time in the typically poorly maintained (and sometimes filthy and unsafe) bus depots.

Third, all Megabus coaches are equipped with Wi-Fi and power outlets, allowing the time on board to be more productive (or more fun). These features, which are sometimes not available even when flying first class, have made travel by bus totally cool to the online-savvy younger crowd. Among surveyed passengers, 37% said that Wi-Fi and power outlets were central to their decision to travel by Megabus.

Finally, as gas prices and environmental consciousness rise, bus travel offers an unbeatable "green" advantage. At eight cents per mile, a bus is four times more fuel-efficient than a car. US curbside carriers, led by Megabus, have already reduced fuel consumption by 11 million gallons a year, equivalent to taking 24,000 cars off the road.

While politicians like to talk about the "bright future" of high-speed rail and $10 billion has been budgeted to jump-start the new rail projects, not a single mile of high-speed rail tracks has been laid as of this writing. At the same time, Megabus has been charging ahead and carrying more than 13 million passengers since its entry, while requiring zero additional investment in infrastructure. Texas, Florida, and California are some of the markets it may enter soon. Given the cost and political headache to build new high-speed rail, *Bloomberg Businessweek* speculated: "The Megabus approach works so well, it may scuttle plans for high-speed rail."

Sources: Based on (1) *Bloomberg Businessweek*, 2011, How to keep the world moving, December 5: 80–86; (2) *Bloomberg Businessweek*, 2011, The Megabus effect, April 11: 62–67; (2) Magabus, 2012, www.megabus.com; (3) Stagecoach Group, 2012, www.stagecoachgroup.com.

ow do firms such as Stagecoach Group enter foreign markets? Why do they enter certain countries but not others? Why was Stagecoach able to transform a lackluster travel mode to one that attracts a younger and more educated crowd? These are some of the key questions driving this chapter. Entering foreign markets is crucial for global strategy.[1] Focusing on the necessity to overcome the liability of foreignness, this chapter develops a comprehensive model based on the strategy tripod—namely, industry-based, resource-based, and institution-based views.[2] Then we focus on three crucial dimensions: *where*, *when*, and *how*—known as the 2W1H dimensions. Debates and extensions follow.

Overcoming the Liability of Foreignness

liability of foreignness
The inherent disadvantage foreign firms experience in host countries because of their nonnative status.

Why is it so challenging to enter and succeed in overseas markets? This is primarily because of the **liability of foreignness**, which is the *inherent* disadvantage foreign firms experience in host countries because of their non-native status.[3] Such a liability is manifested in at least two ways. First, numerous differences in formal and informal institutions govern the rules of the game in different countries. While local firms are already well versed in these rules, foreign firms have to learn the rules quickly. For example, European firms that have subsidiaries operating in the United States are busy learning the new "Buy American" rules in US stimulus packages that would qualify them as "US firms."[4] Many governments ban foreigners from owning assets in certain strategic sectors. Governments in Central and Eastern Europe are concerned about investments from Russia (see Emerging Markets 6.1).

Second, although customers in this age of globalization *supposedly* no longer discriminate against foreign firms, the reality is that foreign firms are often still discriminated against, sometimes formally and other times informally. For example, activists in India accused both Coca-Cola and PepsiCo of having products that contained higher-than-permitted levels of pesticides but did not test any Indian-branded soft drinks, even though pesticide residues are present in virtually all groundwater in India. Although both Coca-Cola and PepsiCo denied these charges, their sales suffered.

EMERGING MARKETS 6.1 〉 〉 ETHICAL DILEMMA

Russian Firms Spread Their Wings

After the fall of the Berlin Wall in 1989, Russia suffered a decade of turmoil. Since 1999, the Russian economy staged a spectacular comeback, largely thanks to consistently high prices of its main export items, oil and gas. The 2008–2009 global crisis created another setback. But with the Middle East up in flames since 2011 (think of Libya), the more stable oil and gas production from Russia bodes well for the country's economic performance.

Accumulation of earnings and lucrative opportunities abroad have turned a series of Russian firms into multinational enterprises (MNEs), spreading their wings around the globe. Russian firms active in foreign direct investment (FDI) can be found in three categories: (1) One group targets acquisition targets in Western Europe and North America to access technological innovations and advanced management know how. (2) Another group focuses on the "near abroad"—the Commonwealth of Independent States (CIS), whose member countries were all formerly part of the Soviet Union. (3) A third group channels funds through offshore financial centers such as Cyprus and the British Virgin Islands and reinvests back in Russia—a process known as capital round-tripping. Experts estimate that about 10% of the Russian outward FDI is involved in round-tripping, leaving the other 90% to be real FDI.

Thanks to the liability of foreignness, Russian FDI abroad is not without controversies. Host country governments and the media often voice concern that Russian MNEs, especially large energy companies, may represent the "long arm of the Kremlin." The political hard line recently taken by the Russian government (such as the war with Georgia and the decision to cut off gas supply to Ukraine) heightens such concerns, especially in sensitive Central and Eastern European countries such as Hungary, Lithuania, and Poland. Russian MNEs claim that their FDI is solely driven by profit motives. However, host country governments face the dilemma of how to accommodate the legitimate economic interests of Russia MNEs, harness the FDI dollars they bring, and limit the potential damage when dealing with the bears (or eagles) from Russia. In Central and Eastern Europe, this dilemma has intensified after the Great Recession, when traditionally active MNEs from Germany and Austria were pulling back while Russian firms possessed fat checkbooks ready to invest.

Sources: Based on (1) *Bloomberg Businessweek*, 2011, The Russians are buying, and buying, September 19: 17–18; (2) A. Panibratov & K. Kalotay, 2009, Russia outward FDI and its policy context, *Columbia FDI Profiles*, No. 1, www.vcc.columbia.edu; (3) United Nations, 2011, *World Investment Report 2010*, New York: UN.

Against such significant odds, how do foreign firms crack new markets? The answer: to deploy *overwhelming* resources and capabilities so that after offsetting the liability of foreignness, there is still significant competitive advantage. For example, recently the Chinese government seemed to be more assertive and more interested in promoting "indigenous innovation," and GE's CEO openly complained to the press—typically regarded as a bad political move by experienced China hands.[5] Yet, two weeks *after* airing such high-profile complaints, GE still won a major contract to equip China's all-new, 200-seat C919 jetliner with its advanced engines.[6] Evidently, GE's overwhelming capabilities in advanced engines were able to overcome its political incorrectness—an example of liability of foreignness.

Understanding the Propensity to Internationalize

Despite recent preaching by some gurus that every firm should go abroad, the reality is that not every firm is ready for it. Prematurely venturing overseas may be detrimental to overall firm performance, especially for smaller firms whose margin for error is very small. Then, what motivates some firms to go abroad, while others are happy to stay at home?

At the risk of oversimplification, we can identify two underlying factors: (1) size of the firm and (2) size of the domestic market, which lead to a 2×2 framework (Figure 6.1). In Cell 1, large firms in a small domestic market are likely to be very enthusiastic internationalizers, because they can quickly exhaust opportunities in a small country. Consider Nestlé of Switzerland. Given Switzerland's small population (7 million), the demand for Nestlé's food products is rather limited. As a result, a majority of Nestlé's sales and employees are outside of Switzerland.

In Cell 2, many small firms in a small domestic market are labeled "follower internationalizers," because they often follow their larger counterparts such as Nestlé to go abroad as suppliers. Even small firms that do not directly supply large firms may similarly venture abroad, because of the inherently limited size of the domestic market. A considerable number of small firms from small countries such as Austria, Denmark, Finland, New Zealand, Singapore, and Taiwan are active overseas.

In Cell 3, large firms in a large domestic market are labeled "slow internationalizers," because their overseas activities are usually (but not always) slower than those of enthusiastic internationalizers in Cell 1. For example, Wal-Mart's pace of internationalization is slower when compared with its two global rivals based in relatively smaller countries, Carrefour of France and Metro of Germany.

FIGURE 6.1　Firm Size, Domestic Market Size, and Propensity to Internationalize

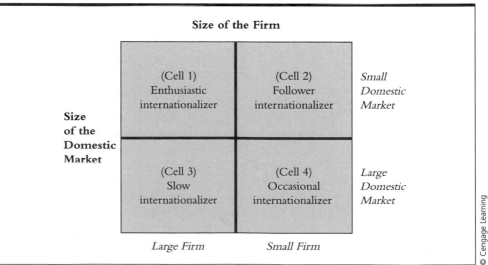

Finally, in Cell 4, most small firms in a large domestic market confront a "double whammy" on the road to internationalization, both because of their relatively poor resource base and the large size of their domestic market. Many small firms in the United States do not feel compelled to go abroad. Overall, small firms in a large domestic market can be labeled "occasional internationalizers" (if they have any international business at all). One joke is that if the United States were divided into 50 independent countries, then the number of US multinational enterprises (MNEs) would skyrocket.[7]

A Comprehensive Model of Foreign Market Entries

Assuming the decision to internationalize is a "go," strategists must make a series of decisions regarding the location, timing, and mode of entry, collectively known as the *where*, *when*, and *how* ("2W1H") aspects, respectively.[8] Underlying each decision is a set of strategic considerations drawn from the three leading perspectives in the strategy tripod, which form a comprehensive model (Figure 6.2).

FIGURE 6.2   A Comprehensive Model of Foreign Market Entries

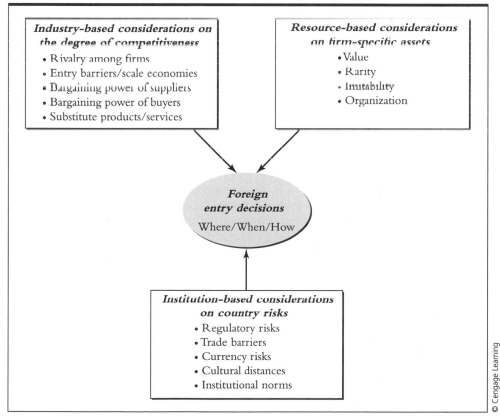

Industry-based considerations on the degree of competitiveness
- Rivalry among firms
- Entry barriers/scale economies
- Bargaining power of suppliers
- Bargaining power of buyers
- Substitute products/services

Resource-based considerations on firm-specific assets
- Value
- Rarity
- Imitability
- Organization

Foreign entry decisions
Where/When/How

Institution-based considerations on country risks
- Regulatory risks
- Trade barriers
- Currency risks
- Cultural distances
- Institutional norms

© Cengage Learning

Industry-Based Considerations

Industry-based considerations are primarily drawn from the five forces framework first introduced in Chapter 2. First, rivalry among established firms may prompt certain moves. Firms, especially those in oligopolistic industries, often match each other in foreign entries. If Komatsu and FedEx enter a new country—let's say Afghanistan—Caterpillar and DHL, respectively, probably would feel compelled to follow. Sometimes, firms may enter foreign markets to retaliate. For example, Texas Instruments (TI) entered Japan not to make money but to *lose* money. The reason was that TI faced the low-price Japanese challenge in many markets, whereas rivals such as NEC and Toshiba were able to charge high prices in Japan and use domestic profits to cross-subsidize their overseas expansion. By entering Japan and slashing prices there, TI retaliated by incurring a loss. This forced the Japanese firms to defend their profit sanctuary at home, whereby they had more to lose.

Second, the higher the entry barriers, the more intense firms will be in attempting to compete abroad. A strong presence overseas in itself can be seen as a major entry barrier. By tapping into wider and bigger markets, international sales can increase scale economies and deter entry. It would be mind-boggling to imagine how high the costs of Boeing and Airbus aircraft would be in the absence of international sales.

Third, the bargaining power of suppliers may prompt certain foreign market entries, often called backward vertical integration because they involve multiple stages of the value chain. Many extractive industries feature extensive backward integration (such as bauxite mining), in order to provide a steady supply of raw materials to late stage production (such as aluminum smelting). Since natural resources are not always found in politically stable countries, many firms have no choice but to enter politically uncertain countries, such as Libya and Venezuela. Why do these Western MNEs go through such troubles to secure oil supplies? Evidently, the costs of such troubles are still less than the costs of having to deal with strong unfriendly suppliers such as OPEC.

Fourth, the bargaining power of buyers may lead to certain foreign market entries, often called forward vertical integration.[9] For example, instead of working with retail chains that as buyers often extract significant price concessions, Apple has established a series of Apple stores in major cities worldwide.

Finally, the market potential of substitute products may encourage firms to bring them abroad. A generation ago, Kodak and Fuji comfortably led the film industry. Their products were substituted by digital camera makers such as Canon. Then cell phone makers such as Nokia and Samsung incorporated the camera function within their devices, which substituted a lot of single-purpose digital cameras. In every round, producers of substitute products had tremendous incentive to hawk their wares globally.

Overall, how an industry is structured and how its five forces are played out significantly affect foreign entry decisions. Next, we examine the influence of resource-based considerations.

Resource-Based Considerations

The VRIO framework introduced in Chapter 3 sheds considerable light on entry decisions (Figure 6.2).[10] First, the value of firm-specific resources and capabilities plays a key role behind decisions to internationalize.[11] It is often the superb value of firm-specific assets that allows foreign entrants such as Stagecoach to overcome the liability of foreignness (see the Opening Case).

Second, the rarity of firm-specific assets encourages firms that possess them to leverage such assets overseas. Patents, brands, and trademarks legally protect the rarity of certain product features. It is not surprising that patented and branded products, such as cars and DVDs, are often aggressively marketed overseas. However, here is a paradox: Given the uneven protection of intellectual property rights, the more countries these products are sold in (becoming less rare), the more likely counterfeits will pop up somewhere around the globe. The question of rarity, therefore, directly leads to the next issue of imitability.

Third, if firms are concerned that their imitable assets may be expropriated in certain countries, they may choose *not* to enter. In other words, the transaction costs may be too high. This is primarily because of **dissemination risks**, defined as the risks associated with the unauthorized imitation and diffusion of firm-specific assets.[12] The worst nightmare is to have nurtured a competitor.

Finally, the organization of firm-specific resources and capabilities as a *bundle* favors firms with strong complementary assets integrated as a system and encourages them to utilize these assets overseas.[13] Many MNEs are organized in a way that protects them against entry and favors them as entrants into other markets—consider the near total vertical integration at ExxonMobil and BP.

In summary, the resource-based view suggests an important set of underlying considerations underpinning entry decisions. In the case of imitability and dissemination risk, it is obvious that these issues are related to property rights protection, which leads to our next topic.

Institution-Based Considerations

Since Chapter 4 has already illustrated a number of *informal* institutional differences such as cultural differences, here we focus on the *formal* institutional constraints confronting foreign entrants: (1) regulatory risks, (2) trade barriers, and (3) currency risks (Figure 6.2).

Regulatory risks are defined as those risks associated with unfavorable government policies (see Emerging Markets 6.1). Some governments may demand that foreign entrants share technology with local firms, essentially *increasing* the dissemination risk. Even as a WTO member, the Chinese government has continued its historical practice of only approving joint ventures for foreign automakers and banned their attempt to set up wholly owned subsidiaries. The government's openly proclaimed goal has been to "encourage" local automakers to learn from their foreign partners.

A well-known regulatory risk is the **obsolescing bargain**, referring to a deal struck by an MNE and a host government, which changes the requirements *after* the entry of the MNE. It typically unfolds in three rounds:

- In Round One, the MNE and the government negotiate a deal. The MNE usually is not willing to enter in the absence of some reasonable government assurance of property rights, earnings, and even some incentives (such as tax holidays).

- In Round Two, the MNE enters and, if all goes well, earns profits that may become visible.

dissemination risks

The risks associated with the unauthorized diffusion of firm-specific assets.

regulatory risks

Risks associated with unfavorable government regulations.

obsolescing bargain

A deal struck by an MNE and a host government, which change the requirements after the entry of the MNE.

- In Round Three, the government, often pressured by domestic political groups, may demand renegotiations of the deal that seems to yield "excessive" profits to the foreign firm (which, of course, regards these as "fair" and "normal" profits). The previous deal, therefore, becomes obsolete.

expropriation

Confiscation of foreign assets invested in one country.

sunk costs

Irrevocable costs incurred and investments made.

The government's tactics include removing incentives, demanding higher taxes, and even confiscating foreign assets—in other words, **expropriation**. The Indian government in the 1970s demanded that Coca-Cola share its secret formula, something that the MNE did not even share with the US government. At this time, the MNE has already invested substantial sums of resources (called **sunk costs**) and often has to accommodate some new demands; otherwise, it may face expropriation or exit at a huge loss (as Coca-Cola did in India). Coca-Cola's experience in India, unfortunately, was not alone. Many governments in Africa, Asia, and Latin America in the 1950s, 1960s, and 1970s expropriated MNE assets through nationalization by turning them over to state-owned enterprises (SOEs).

Recently, some decisive changes have occurred around the world in favor of foreign entries (see Chapter 1). Many governments realize that nationalization of foreign MNE assets does not necessarily maximize their national interests. While expropriation drives MNEs away, SOEs are often unable to run the operations as effectively as did MNEs, and most SOEs end up losing money and destroying value. Therefore, the global trend since the 1980s and 1990s has been privatization, which, being the opposite of nationalization, turns state-owned assets into private firms (see Chapter 11). Interestingly, many private bidders of SOEs are MNEs. Understandably, MNEs often push for the transparency and predictability in host-government decision making *before* committing to new deals. Coca-Cola, for example, agreed to return to India in the 1990s with an explicit commitment from the government that its secret formula would be untouchable.

Overall, there is global competition among host governments (especially those in the developing world) to transform their relationship with MNEs from a confrontational to cooperative one. While regulatory risks, especially those associated with expropriation, have decreased significantly around the world, individual countries still vary considerably, thus calling for very careful analysis of such risks. As recently as 2012, Argentina expropriated the assets of a Spanish MNE, Repsol.

trade barriers

Barriers blocking international trade.

tariff barriers

Taxes levied on imports.

nontariff barriers

Trade and investment barriers that do not entail tariffs.

local content requirements

Government requirements that certain products be subject to higher import tariffs and taxes unless a given percentage of their value is produced domestically.

Trade barriers include (1) tariff and nontariff barriers, (2) local content requirements, and (3) restrictions on certain entry modes. **Tariff barriers**, taxes levied on imports, are government-imposed entry barriers. **Nontariff barriers** are more subtle. For example, the Japanese customs inspectors, in the name of detecting unwanted bacteria from abroad, often insist on cutting *every* tulip bulb exported from the Netherlands vertically down the middle. The Dutch argument that their tulips have been safely exported to just about every other country in the world has not been persuasive. These barriers effectively encourage foreign entrants to produce locally and discourage them from exporting.

However, even after foreign entrants set up factories locally, they can still export completely knocked down (CKD) kits to be assembled in host countries. Such factories are nicknamed "screw driver plants"—only screw drivers plus local labor would be needed. In response, many governments have imposed **local content requirements**, mandating that a "domestically produced" product can still be subject to tariff and nontariff barriers unless a certain fraction of its value (such as 51% in the United States) is truly produced domestically. The Brazilian government, for example, imposed a 70% local content requirement for all the equipment ordered by Petrobras.

Certain entry modes also have restrictions. Many countries limit or even ban wholly owned subsidiaries of MNEs. For example, in the United States, foreign airlines are not allowed to operate wholly owned subsidiaries or acquire US airlines. In Russia, foreign firms are not allowed to operate wholly owned subsidiaries in the strategically important oil and gas industry.

currency risks

Risks stemming from exposure to unfavorable movements of the currencies.

Currency risks stem from unfavorable movements of the currencies to which firms are exposed. For instance, if the Chinese yuan appreciates (as demanded by the US government), domestic and foreign firms producing there may lose a significant chunk of their low-cost advantage. Since a majority of Wal-Mart products are made in China (mostly by non-Chinese-owned producers), a 30% appreciation of the yuan (all else being equal) may result in a 30% cost increase on a lot of Wal-Mart products. Therefore, Wal-Mart and its US-owned suppliers that produce in China face severe currency risks if the yuan appreciates.

currency hedging

A transaction that protects traders and investors from exposure to the fluctuations of the spot rate.

In response, firms can engage in currency hedging or strategic hedging. **Currency hedging** protects firms from exposure to foreign exchange fluctuations. However, this is risky in the case of wrong bets of currency movements. **Strategic hedging** means spreading out activities in a number of countries in different currency zones in order to offset the currency losses in certain regions through gains in other regions. It was one of the key motivations behind Toyota's decision to set up a new factory in France, instead of expanding its existing British operations (which would have cost less in the short run)—France is in the euro zone that the British refused to join.

strategic hedging

Spreading out activities in a number of countries in different currency zones to offset any currency losses in one region through gains in other regions.

In addition to *formal* institutional constraints, firms also need to develop a sophisticated understanding of numerous *informal* aspects such as cultural distances and institutional norms. Since Chapter 4 has already discussed these issues at length, we will not repeat them here other than to stress their importance. We will, however, revisit some of them in the next section.

Overall, the value of the core proposition of the institution-based view, "Institutions matter," is *magnified* in foreign entry decisions.[14] Rushing abroad without a solid understanding of institutional differences can be hazardous and even disastrous.

Where to Enter?

Like real estate, the motto for international business is "Location, location, location." In fact, such a *spatial* perspective (that is, doing business outside of one's home country) is a defining feature of international business.[15] Two sets of considerations drive the location of foreign entries: (1) strategic goals and (2) cultural and institutional distances. Each is discussed next.

Location-Specific Advantages and Strategic Goals

location-specific advantages

Advantages associated with operating in a specific location.

Favorable locations in certain countries may give firms operating there **location-specific advantages**. Certain locations simply possess geographical features that are difficult for others to match. For example, Dubai is an ideal stopping point for air traffic between Europe and Asia and between Africa and Asia. Emirates Airlines has been blessed by being based in Dubai (see Emerging Markets 6.2).

EMERGING MARKETS 6.2 ⟩ ⟩

Dubai Airport Connects the World

As a part of the United Arab Emirates, Dubai has emerged as the undisputed financial, business, and shopping center in the Middle East. Dubai International Airport (DXB) not only positions itself as the aviation center of the region, but also aspires to become the aviation center of the *world*. Geographically, Dubai is indeed the center of the world known as the natural "pinch point" by experts. It is the ideal stopping point for air traffic between Europe and Asia and between Africa and Asia. Two billion people live within four hours of flying time from Dubai, and four billion can be reached within seven hours. Connecting 220 destinations across six continents with 130 airlines, DXB already handles approximately over 40 million passengers a year. New expansion will allow DXB to serve 60 million passengers a year in the near future. Since Dubai's own population is fewer than 4 million (most are expatriates), the majority of the passengers are connecting passengers who are not from or going to Dubai. DXB's expansion will have to rely on customers from the rest of the world. Will they come?

DXB's hometown carrier, Emirates Airlines, is betting that connecting passengers will come. Launched in 1985, Emirates is known as a "super-connecting" airline because the majority of its customers are connecting passengers. One of the world's most powerful carriers, Emirates has an all wide-body fleet of 138 planes and 140 more on firm order (including 50 Airbus A380s). From Dubai, Emirates flies to over 100 cities in over 60 countries. Emirates is the largest customer of the ultra-long-range Boeing 777 and one of the largest users of the A380.

With these capable jets, any two cities in the world can be linked with just one stop via Dubai. Emirates thus has been directly challenging traditional long-haul carriers such as British Airways (BA) and Lufthansa. Emirates has launched services connecting Dubai with secondary (but still very sizable) cities, such as Manchester, Hamburg, and Kolkata. These cities are neglected by BA, Lufthansa, and Air India, respectively, which focus on their own hubs. Passengers flying, for example, from Hamburg to Sydney may not care whether they change planes at Frankfurt or Dubai, especially when Emirates flies newer and quieter planes, offers cheaper tickets, and provides nicer amenities at DXB.

Starting in 1950, DXB has been experiencing an astonishing annual growth rate of 15%. Today it is already the world's third-busiest international passenger airport (after London Heathrow and Hong Kong) and the seventh-busiest cargo airport. Yet it will be replaced by an even larger airport, Dubai World Central-Al Maktoum International (DWC), which partially opened in 2010 (with one runway and with cargo flights only). When completed, the new DWC will be the largest airport in the world, with *five* parallel runways and an annual passenger capacity of 160 million (!).

Sources: Based on (1) *Aviation News*, 2011, Dubai International Airport, December: 34–39; (2) *Bloomberg Businessweek*, 2010, Emirates wins with big planes and low costs, July 5: 18–19; (3) *Economist*, 2010, Rulers of the new silk road, June 5: 75–77; (4) *Economist*, 2010, Super-duper-connectors from the Gulf, June 5: 21.

agglomeration
Clustering economic activities in certain locations.

Beyond geographic advantages, location-specific advantages also arise from the clustering of economic activities in certain locations, usually referred to as **agglomeration**. The basic idea dates back at least to Alfred Marshall, a British economist who first published it in 1890. Essentially, location-specific advantages stem from (1) knowledge spillovers among closely located firms that attempt to hire individuals from competitors, (2) industry demand that creates a skilled labor force whose members may work for different firms without having to move out of the region, and (3) industry demand that facilitates a pool of specialized suppliers and buyers to also locate in the region.[16] For

TABLE 6.1 Matching Strategic Goals with Locations

STRATEGIC GOALS	LOCATION-SPECIFIC ADVANTAGES	EXAMPLES IN THE TEXT
Natural resource seeking	Possession of natural resources and related transport and communication infrastructure	*Oil in the Middle East, Russia, and Venezuela*
Market seeking	Abundance of strong market demand and customers willing to pay	*GM in China*
Efficiency seeking	Economies of scale and abundance of low-cost factors	*Manufacturing in China (especially in Shanghai)*
Innovation seeking	Abundance of innovative individuals, firms, and universities	*IT in Silicon Valley and Bangalore; telecom in Dallas; aerospace in Russia*

© Cengage Learning

example, due to agglomeration, Dallas has the world's heaviest concentration of telecom companies. US firms such as AT&T, HP, Raytheon, TI, and Verizon cluster there. Numerous leading foreign telecom firms such as Alcatel-Lucent, Ericsson, Fujitsu, Huawei, Siemens, and STMicroelectronics have also converged in this region.

Given that different locations offer different benefits, it is imperative that a firm match its strategic goals with potential locations. The four strategic goals are shown in Table 6.1.

- *Natural resource seeking* firms have to go to particular foreign locations where those resources are found. For example, the Middle East, Russia, and Venezuela are all rich in oil. Even when the Venezuelan government became more hostile, Western oil firms had to put up with it.

- *Market seeking* firms go to countries that have a strong demand for their products and services. For example, China is now the largest car market in the world, and practically all the automakers in the world are now elbowing into this fast-growing market. General Motors (GM) has emerged as the leader. It now sells more cars in China than in the United States.

- *Efficiency seeking* firms often single out the most efficient locations featuring a combination of scale economies and low-cost factors. It is the search for efficiency that induced numerous MNEs to enter China. China now manufactures two-thirds of the world's photocopiers, shoes, toys, and microwave ovens; one-half of the DVD players, digital cameras, and textiles; one-third of the desktop computers; and one-quarter of the mobile phones, television sets, and steel. Shanghai alone reportedly has a cluster of over 400 of the *Fortune* Global 500 firms. Approximately one-quarter of all foreign direct investment (FDI) in China has been absorbed by Shanghai.[17] It is important to note that China does not present the absolutely lowest labor costs in the world, and Shanghai is the *highest* cost city in China. However, Shanghai's attractiveness lies in its ability to enhance efficiency for foreign entrants by lowering *total* costs.

- *Innovation seeking* firms target countries and regions renowned for world-class innovations, such as Silicon Valley and Bangalore (in IT), Dallas (in telecom), and Russia (in aerospace).[18] (See Chapter 10 for details.)

It is important to note that location-specific advantages may grow, change, and/or decline, prompting firms to relocate. If policy makers fail to maintain the institutional attractiveness (for example, by raising taxes) and if companies overcrowd and bid up factor costs such as land and talents, some firms may move out of certain locations previously considered advantageous. For example, BMW and Mercedes had proudly projected a 100% "Made in Germany" image until the early 1990s. Now both firms produce in a variety of countries such as Brazil, China, Mexico, South Africa, the United States, and Vietnam and instead boast "Made by BMW" and "Made by Mercedes." Both the relative decline of Germany's location-specific advantages and the rise of other countries' advantages prompted Mercedes and BMW to do this.

Cultural/Institutional Distances and Foreign Entry Locations

In addition to strategic goals, another set of considerations centers on cultural/institutional distances (see also Chapter 4). Cultural distance is the difference between two cultures along some identifiable dimensions (such as individualism).[19] Considering culture as an informal part of institutional frameworks governing a particular country, institutional distance is "the extent of similarity or dissimilarity between the regulatory, normative, and cognitive institutions of two countries."[20] Many Western consumer products firms, such as L'Oreal, have shied away from Saudi Arabia citing its stricter rules of personal behavior—in essence, its cultural and institutional distance being too large.

Two schools of thought have emerged. The first is associated with stage models, arguing that firms will enter culturally similar countries during their first stage of internationalization, and that they may gain more confidence to enter culturally distant countries in later stages.[21] This idea is intuitively appealing: It makes sense for Belgium firms to first enter France, taking advantage of common cultural, language, and historical ties.[22] Business between countries that share a language on average is three times greater than between countries without a common language. Firms from common-law countries (English-speaking countries and Britain's former colonies) are more likely to be interested in other common-law countries. Colony–colonizer links (such as Britain's ties with the Commonwealth and Spain's with Latin America) boost trade significantly. In general, MNEs from emerging economies perform better in other developing countries, presumably because of their closer institutional distance and similar stages of economic development.[23] There is some evidence documenting certain performance benefits of competing in culturally and institutionally adjacent countries.[24]

Citing numerous counter-examples, a second school of thought argues that considerations of strategic goals such as market and efficiency are more important than cultural/institutional considerations.[25] For instance, natural resource seeking firms have compelling reasons to enter culturally and institutionally distant countries (such as Papua New Guinea for bauxite and Zambia for copper). On Sakhalin Island, a remote, oil-rich part of the Russian Far East, Western oil firms have to live with Russia's strong-arm tactics to grab more shares and profits that are described as "thuggish ways" by the *Economist*.[26] Because Western oil firms have few alternatives elsewhere, cultural, institutional, and geographic distance in this case does not seem relevant—they simply have to be there and let the Russians dictate the terms. Overall, in the complex calculus underpinning entry decisions, locations represent but one of several important sets of considerations (see Emerging Markets 6.3). As shown next, entry timing and modes are also crucial.

EMERGING MARKETS 6.3

Emerging Multinationals from South Africa

Since apartheid was removed in 1994, South Africa has brewed a series of multinationals that are increasingly active abroad. While most readers of this book probably have heard about SABMiller (beers) and De Beers (diamonds), how many of you have heard of Didata, MTN, Old Mutual, SAB, SASOL, and Standard Bank? If you have not heard of them, watch out as they may soon come to a city near you (if they have not already arrived).

Naturally, South African firms started by entering sub Saharan African countries. In fact, South Africa is the number one foreign investor in sub-Saharan Africa. South African Breweries (SAB) first pioneered the concept of the pan-African beer market, and then went on to become the global titan known as SABMiller after acquiring Miller Beer of the United States in 2002. As an early mover in cellular (mobile) phones, telecom provider MTN was one of a handful companies to defy conventional wisdom and prove that Africa could be a huge market for mobile services. Retailers such as Massmart, Shoprite, and Game are bringing Western-style shopping to Malawi, Mozambique, Nigeria, Uganda, and others. Standard Bank has charged into 16 African countries that previously often lacked even basic financial services. "Africa is the next China," one South African businessman noted. South African firms have every intention of enjoying first-mover advantages there.

After a short time cutting their teeth in Africa, many South African firms spread their wings beyond the shores of Africa. In the early 1990s, SAB moved into China and Central and Eastern Europe, establishing strong positions in major emerging economies ahead of global rivals. Since becoming SABMiller, it has further globalized. It is now the second-largest brewer in South America. Old Mutual, South Africa's biggest financial services firm, bought Sweden's oldest insurance house in 2005. Dimension Data (Didata), an IT firm, competes in over 30 countries. SASOL, a chemicals and energy firm, operates in over 20 countries.

What explains such a surge of internationalization from South Africa? From an industry-based view, South African multinationals tend to specialize in industries where growth in Africa and elsewhere is strong. From a resource-based standpoint, since South Africa represents 10% of Africa's population but 45% of its GDP, winning firms in South Africa not surprisingly have a competitive edge in other less competitive African countries. Capabilities that serve African customers well can then be leveraged to more effectively compete in more distant emerging economies elsewhere. From an institution-based view, the lifting of anti-apartheid sanctions by other countries and the generally open trade and investment environment worldwide have made such global expansion possible. As Africa is at last enjoying peace and (relatively) decent government, trade barriers have been reduced. Intra Africa trade has gone from 6% to 13% of the total volume in a decade. "South Africans do well when they go elsewhere," noted another expert, "because they're not afraid, having done well in the most difficult continent on earth."

Sources: Based on (1) S. Burgess, 2003, Within-country diversity: Is it key to South Africa's prosperity in a changing world? *International Journal of Advertising*, 22: 157–182; (2) *BusinessWeek*, 2008, Africa's dynamo, December 15: 51–56; (3) *Economist*, 2006, Going global, July 15: 59–60; (4) *Economist*, 2009, Africa's new Big Man, April 18: 11; (5) *Economist*, 2011, The sun shines bright, December 3: 15.

When to Enter?

first-mover advantages
The advantages that first movers enjoy and later movers do not.

Entry timing refers to whether there are compelling reasons to be an early or late entrant in a particular country. Some firms look for **first-mover advantages**, defined as the benefits that accrue to firms that enter the market first and that later entrants do not enjoy.[27] Speaking of the power of first-mover advantages, "Xerox," "FedEx," and "Google" have now become *verbs* such as "Google it." In many African countries, "Colgate" is the generic term for toothpaste. Unilever, a late mover, is disappointed to find out that its African customers call its own toothpaste "the red Colgate" (!). Table 6.2 outlines such advantages.

- First movers may gain advantage through proprietary technology. Think about Apple's iPod, iPad, and iPhone.

- First movers may also make preemptive investments. A number of Japanese MNEs have cherry picked leading local suppliers and distributors in Southeast Asia as new members of the expanded *keiretsu* networks (alliances of Japanese businesses with interlocking business relationships and shareholdings) and have blocked access to the suppliers and distributors by late entrants from the West.[28]

- First movers may erect significant entry barriers for late entrants, such as high switching costs due to brand loyalty. Buyers of expensive equipment are likely to stick with the same producers for components, training, and services for a long time. That is why American,

TABLE 6.2 First-Mover Advantages and Late-Mover Advantages

FIRST-MOVER ADVANTAGES	EXAMPLES IN THE TEXT	LATE-MOVER ADVANTAGES	EXAMPLES IN THE TEXT
Proprietary, technological leadership	*Apple's iPod, iPad, and iPhone*	Opportunity to free ride on first mover investments	*Ericsson won big contracts in Saudi Arabia, free riding on Cisco's efforts*
Preemption of scarce resources	*Japanese MNEs in Southeast Asia*	Resolution of technological and market uncertainties	*GM and Toyota have patience to wait until the Nissan Leaf resolves uncertainties about the electric car*
Establishment of entry barriers for late entrants	*Poland's F-16 fighter jet contract*	First mover's difficulty to adapt to market changes	*Greyhound is stuck with the bus depots, whereas Megabus simply uses curbside stops*
Avoidance of clash with dominant firms at home	*Sony, Honda, and Epson went to the US market ahead of their Japanese rivals*		
Relationships with key stakeholders such as governments	*Citigroup, JP Morgan Chase, and Metallurgical Corporation of China entered Afghanistan*		

© Cengage Learning

British, French, German, and Russian aerospace firms competed intensely for Poland's first post–Cold War order of fighters—America's F-16 eventually won.

- Intense domestic competition may drive some non-dominant firms abroad to avoid clashing with dominant firms head-on in their home market. Matsushita, Toyota, and NEC were the market leaders in Japan, but Sony, Honda, and Epson all entered the United States in their respective industries ahead of the leading firms.

- First movers may build precious relationships with key stakeholders such as customers and governments. For example, Citigroup, JP Morgan Chase, and Metallurgical Corporation of China have entered Afghanistan, earning a good deal of goodwill from the Afghan government that is interested in wooing more FDI.[29]

late-mover advantages
Advantages associated with being a later mover (also known as first-mover disadvantages).

The potential advantages of first movers may be counter-balanced by various disadvantages, which result in **late-mover advantages** (also listed in Table 6.2). Numerous first-mover firms—such as EMI in CT scanners and Netscape in Internet browsers—have lost market dominance in the long run. It is such late-mover firms as GE and Microsoft (Explorer), respectively, that win. Specifically, late-mover advantages are manifested in three ways.

- Late movers can free ride on first movers' pioneering investments. In Saudi Arabia, Cisco invested millions of dollars to rub shoulders of dignitaries, including the king, in order to help officials grasp the promise of the Internet in fueling economic development, only to lose out to late movers such as Ericsson that offered lower cost solutions. For instance, the brand-new King Abdullah Economic City awarded an $84 million citywide telecom project to Ericsson whose bid was more than 20% lower than Cisco's—in part because Ericsson did not have to offer basic education and did not have to entertain that much. "We're very proud to have won against a company that did as much advance work as Cisco did," an elated Ericsson executive noted.[30]

- First movers face greater technological and market uncertainties. Nissan, for example, has launched the world's first all-electric car, the Leaf, which can run without a single drop of gasoline. However, there are tremendous uncertainties. After some of these uncertainties are removed, late movers such as GM and Toyota will join the game with their own electric cars.

- As incumbents, first movers may be locked into a given set of fixed assets or reluctant to cannibalize existing product lines in favor of new ones. Late movers may be able to take advantage of the inflexibility of first movers by leapfrogging them. Although Greyhound, the incumbent in intercity bus service in the United States, is financially struggling, it cannot get rid of the expensive bus depots in inner cities that are often poorly maintained and dreadful. Megabus, the new entrant from Britain, simply has not bothered to build and maintain a single bus depot. Instead, Megabus uses curbside stops (like regular city bus stops), which have made travel by bus more appealing to a large number of passengers (see the Opening Case).

Overall, evidence points out both first-mover advantages and late-mover advantages. Unfortunately, a mountain of research is still unable to conclusively recommend a particular entry timing strategy.[31] Although first movers may have an *opportunity* to win, their pioneering status is not a guarantee of success. For example, among the three first movers into the Chinese automobile industry in the early 1980s, Volkswagen captured significant advantages, Chrysler had very moderate success, and Peugeot failed and had to exit. Although many of the late movers that entered in the late 1990s are struggling, GM, Honda, and Hyundai gained significant market shares. It is obvious that entry timing cannot be viewed in isolation and entry timing *per se* is not the sole determinant of success and failure of foreign entries. It is through *interaction* with other strategic variables that entry timing has an impact on performance.

How to Enter?

This section first focuses on large-scale versus small-scale entries. Then, it introduces a decision model. The first step is to determine whether to pursue equity or non-equity modes of entry. Finally, we outline the pros and cons of various equity and non-equity modes.

Scale of Entry: Commitment and Experience

scale of entry
The amount of resources committed to foreign market entry.

One key dimension in foreign entry decisions is the **scale of entry**, which refers to the amount of resources committed to entering a foreign market. The benefits of large-scale entries are a demonstration of strategic commitment to certain markets. This both helps assure local customers and suppliers ("We are here for the long haul!") and deters potential entrants. The drawbacks are (1) limited strategic flexibility elsewhere and (2) huge losses if these large-scale "bets" turn out to be wrong.

Small-scale entries are less costly. They focus on "learning by doing" while limiting the downside risk.[32] For example, to enter the market of Islamic finance whereby no interest can be charged (per teaching of the Koran), Citibank set up the subsidiary Citibank Islamic Bank, HSBC established Amanah, and UBS launched Noriba. They were all designed to experiment with different interpretations of the Koran on how to make money while not committing religious sins. It is simply not possible to acquire such an ability outside the Islamic world. Overall, the longer foreign firms stay in host countries, the less liability of foreignness they experience. The drawbacks of small-scale entries are a lack of strong commitment, which may lead to difficulties in building market share and in capturing first-mover advantages.

Modes of Entry: The First Step on Equity versus Non-equity Modes

Among numerous modes of entry, managers are unlikely to consider all of them simultaneously. Given the complexity of entry decisions, it is imperative that managers *prioritize*, by considering only a few manageable key variables first and then contemplating other variables later. Therefore, a decision model (shown in Figure 6.3 and explained in Table 6.3) is helpful.[33]

FIGURE 6.3 The Choice of Entry Modes: A Decision Model

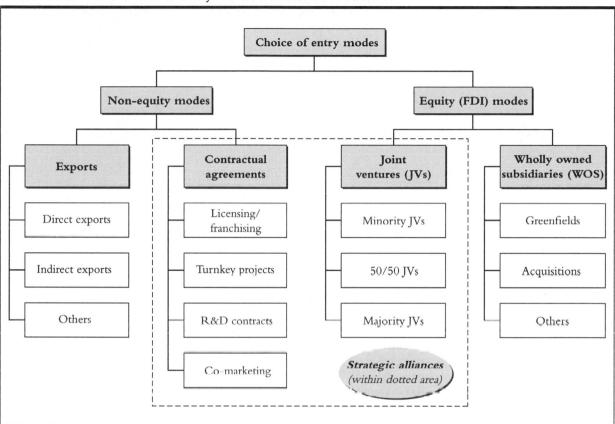

Source: Adapted from Y. Pan & D. Tse, 2000, The hierarchical model of market entry modes (p. 538), *Journal of International Business Studies*, 31: 535–554. The dotted area labeled "strategic alliances," including both non-equity modes (contractual agreements) and equity modes (JVs), is added by the present author. See Chapter 7 for more details on strategic alliances.

non-equity modes

Modes of foreign market entries that do not involve the use of equity.

equity modes

Modes of foreign market entry that involve the use of equity.

In the first step, considerations for small-scale versus large-scale entries usually boil down to the equity (ownership) issue. **Non-equity modes** (exports and contractual agreements) tend to reflect relatively smaller commitments to overseas markets, whereas **equity modes** (joint ventures and wholly owned subsidiaries) are indicative of relatively larger and harder-to-reverse commitments. Equity modes call for the establishment of independent organizations overseas (partially or wholly owned), while non-equity modes do not require such independent establishments.

The distinction between equity and non-equity modes is not trivial. In fact, it is what defines an MNE: An MNE enters foreign markets via equity modes through FDI. A firm that merely exports/imports with no FDI is usually not regarded as an MNE. Why would a firm, say, an oil importer, want to become an MNE by directly investing in the oil-producing country, instead of relying on the market mechanism by purchasing oil from an exporter in that country?

TABLE 6.3 Modes of Entry: Advantages and Disadvantages

ENTRY MODES (EXAMPLES IN THE TEXT)	ADVANTAGES	DISADVANTAGES
1. Non-equity modes: Exports		
Direct exports (*Pearl River piano exports to over 80 countries*)	■ Economies of scale in production concentrated in home country ■ Better control over distribution	■ High transportation costs for bulky products ■ Marketing distance from customers ■ Trade barriers and protectionism
Indirect exports (*commodities trade in textiles and meats*)	■ Concentration of resources on production ■ No need to directly handle export processes	■ Less control over distribution (relative to direct exports) ■ Inability to learn how to operate overseas
2. Non-equity modes: Contractual agreements		
Licensing/franchising (*Pizza Hut in Thailand*)	■ Low development costs ■ Low risk in overseas expansion	■ Little control over technology and marketing ■ May create competitors ■ Inability to engage in global coordination
Turnkey projects (*a German, Italian, and Iranian consortium on a BOT project in Iran*)	■ Ability to earn returns from process technology in countries where FDI is restricted	■ May create efficient competitors ■ Lack of long-term presence
R&D contracts (*IT work in India and aerospace research in Russia*)	■ Ability to tap into the best locations for certain innovations at low costs	■ Difficult to negotiate and enforce contracts ■ May nurture innovative competitors ■ May lose core innovation capabilities
Co-marketing (*McDonald's works with movie studios and toymakers; airline alliances*)	■ Ability to reach more customers	■ Limited coordination
3. Equity modes: Partially owned subsidiaries		
Joint ventures (*Shanghai Volkswagen*)	■ Sharing costs, risks, and profits ■ Access to partners' knowledge and assets ■ Politically acceptable	■ Divergent goals and interests of partners ■ Limited equity and operational control ■ Difficult to coordinate globally

© Cengage Learning

TABLE 6.3 (*Continued*)

ENTRY MODES (EXAMPLES IN THE TEXT)	ADVANTAGES	DISADVANTAGES
4. Equity modes: Wholly owned subsidiaries		
Greenfield operations (*PRPG America; Japanese auto transplants in the United States*)	▪ Complete equity and operational control ▪ Protection of know-how ▪ Ability to coordinate globally	▪ Potential political problems and risks ▪ High development costs ▪ Add new capacity to industry ▪ Slow entry speed (relative to acquisitions)
Acquisitions (*Pearl River's acquisition of Ritmüller*)	▪ Same as greenfield (above) ▪ Do not add new capacity ▪ Fast entry speed	▪ Same as greenfield (above), except adding new capacity and slow speed ▪ Post-acquisition integration problems

ownership advantage

Advantage associated with directly owning assets overseas, which is one of the three key advantages of being a multinational enterprise (the other two are location and internalization advantages).

internalization

The process of replacing a market relationship with a single multinational organization spanning both countries.

internalization advantage

The advantage associated with internalization, which is one of the three key advantages of being a multinational enterprise (the other two are ownership and location advantages).

OLI advantages

Ownership, location, and internalization advantages, which are typically associated with MNEs.

Relative to a non-MNE, an MNE has three principal advantages: ownership (O), location (L), and internalization (I). Since we already discussed location earlier, we focus on ownership and internalization here. By owning assets in both oil-importing and producing countries, the MNE is better able to coordinate cross-border activities, such as delivering crude oil to the oil refinery in the importing country right at the moment its processing capacity becomes available (just-in-time), instead of letting crude oil sit in expensive ships or storage tanks for a long time. This advantage is therefore called **ownership advantage**.

Another advantage stems from the removal of the market relationship between an importer and an exporter, which may suffer from high transaction costs. Using the market, deals have to be negotiated, prices agreed upon, and deliveries verified, all of which entail significant costs. What is more costly is the possibility of opportunism on both sides. For instance, the oil importer may refuse to accept a shipment *after* its arrival, citing unsatisfactory quality, but the real reason could be the importer's inability to sell refined oil downstream (people may drive less due to high oil prices). The exporter is thus forced to find a new buyer for a boatload of crude oil on a last-minute "fire sale" basis. On the other hand, the oil exporter may demand higher-than-agreed-upon prices, citing a variety of reasons ranging from inflation to natural disasters. The importer thus has to either (1) pay more or (2) refuse to pay and suffer from the huge costs of keeping expensive refinery facilities idle. These transaction costs increase international market inefficiencies and imperfections. By replacing such a market relationship with a single organization spanning both countries (a process called **internalization**, basically transforming external markets with in-house links), the MNE thus reduces cross-border transaction costs and increases efficiencies. This advantage is called **internalization advantage**.

Relative to a non-MNE, an MNE that operates in certain desirable locations enjoys a combination of ownership (O), location (L), and internalization (I) advantages (Figure 6.4). These are collectively labeled as the **OLI advantages** by John Dunning, a leading MNE

FIGURE 6.4   The OLI Advantages Associated with Being an MNE through FDI

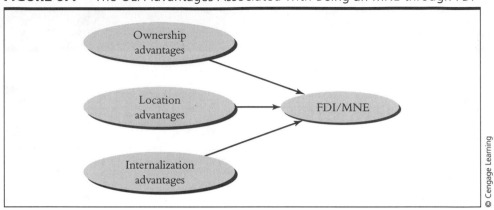

© Cengage Learning

scholar.[34] Overall, the first step in entry mode considerations is extremely critical. A strategic decision must be made in terms of whether to undertake FDI and become an MNE by selecting equity modes.

Modes of Entry: The Second Step on Making Actual Selections

During the second step, managers consider variables within *each* group of non-equity and equity modes. If the decision is to export, then the next consideration is direct exports or indirect exports. Direct exports are the most basic mode of entry, capitalizing on economies of scale in production concentrated in the home country and providing better control over distribution. Pearl River, for example, exports its pianos from China to over 80 countries (see the Closing Case). This strategy essentially treats foreign demand as an extension of domestic demand, and the firm is geared toward designing and producing first and foremost for the domestic market. While direct exports may work if the export volume is small, they are not optimal when the firm has a large number of foreign buyers. Marketing 101 suggests that the firm needs to be closer, both physically and psychologically, to its customers, prompting the firm to consider more intimate overseas involvement such as FDI. In addition, direct exports may provoke protectionism, potentially triggering antidumping actions (see Chapter 8).

Another export strategy is indirect exports—namely, exporting through domestically based export intermediaries. This strategy not only enjoys the economies of scale similar to direct exports but is also relatively worry free. A significant amount of export trade in commodities such as textiles and meats, which compete primarily on price, is indirect through intermediaries.[35] Indirect exports have some drawbacks. For example, third parties such as export trading companies may not share the same objectives as exporters. Exporters choose intermediaries primarily because of information asymmetries concerning foreign markets.[36] Intermediaries with international contacts and knowledge essentially make a living by taking advantage of such information asymmetries. They are not interested in reducing such asymmetries. Intermediaries, for example, may repackage the products under their own brand and insist on monopolizing the communication with overseas customers. If the exporter is interested in knowing more about how its products perform overseas, indirect exports would not provide such knowledge.

The next group of non-equity entry modes involves the following types of contractual agreement: (1) licensing or franchising, (2) turnkey projects, (3) research and development contracts, and (4) co-marketing. In licensing/franchising agreements, the licensor/franchisor sells the rights to intellectual property such as patents and know-how to the licensee/franchisee for a royalty fee. The licensor/franchisor, thus, does not have to bear the full costs and risks associated with foreign expansion. On the other hand, the licensor/franchisor does not have tight control over production and marketing.[37] Pizza Hut, for example, was disappointed when its franchisee in Thailand discontinued the relationship and launched a competing pizza restaurant to eat Pizza Hut's lunch.

In **turnkey projects**, clients pay contractors to design and construct new facilities and train personnel. At project completion, contractors hand clients the proverbial key to facilities ready for operations, hence the term "turnkey." This mode allows firms to earn returns from process technology (such as construction) in countries where FDI is restricted. The drawbacks, however, are twofold. First, if foreign clients are competitors, turnkey projects may boost their competitiveness. Second, turnkey projects do not allow for a long-term presence after the key is handed to clients. To obtain a longer-term presence, build-operate-transfer agreements are now often used, instead of the traditional build-transfer type of turnkey projects. A **build-operate-transfer (BOT) agreement** is a non-equity mode of entry used to build a longer-term presence by building and then operating a facility for a period of time before transferring operations to a domestic agency or firm. For example, a consortium of German, Italian, and Iranian firms obtained a large-scale BOT power-generation project in Iran. After completion of the construction, the consortium will operate the project for 20 years before transferring it to the Iranian government.

Research and development (R&D) contracts refer to outsourcing agreements in R&D between firms. Firm A agrees to perform certain R&D work for Firm B. Firms thereby tap into the best locations for certain innovations at relatively low costs, such as aerospace research in Russia. However, three drawbacks may emerge. First, given the uncertain and multidimensional nature of R&D, these contracts are often difficult to negotiate and enforce. While delivery time and costs are relatively easy to negotiate, quality is often hard to assess. Second, such contracts may cultivate competitors. A number of Indian IT firms, nurtured by such work, are now on a global offensive to take on their Western rivals. Finally, firms that rely on outsiders to perform a lot of R&D may lose some of their core R&D capabilities in the long run.

Co-marketing refers to efforts among a number of firms to jointly market their products and services. Toy makers and movie studios often collaborate in co-marketing campaigns with fast-food chains such as McDonald's to package toys based on movie characters in kids' meals. Airline alliances such as One World and Star Alliance engage in extensive co-marketing through code sharing. The advantage is the ability to reach more customers. The drawback centers on limited control and coordination.

Next are equity modes, all of which entail some FDI and transform the firm to an MNE. A **joint venture (JV)** is a corporate child, a new entity jointly created and owned by two or more parent companies. It has three principal forms: Minority JV (less than 50%

turnkey projects
Projects in which clients pay contractors to design and construct new facilities and train personnel.

build-operate-transfer (BOT) agreement
A special kind of turnkey project in which contractors first build facilities, then operate them for a period of time, and then transfer them back to clients.

research and development (R&D) contracts
Outsourcing agreements in R&D between firms (that is, Firm A agrees to perform certain R&D work for Firm B).

co-marketing
Agreements among a number of firms to jointly market their products and services.

joint venture (JV)
A "corporate child" that is a new entity given birth and jointly owned by two or more parent companies.

equity), 50/50 JV (equal equity), and majority JV (more than 50% equity). JVs, such as Shanghai Volkswagen, have three advantages. First, an MNE shares costs, risks, and profits with a local partner, so the MNE possesses a certain degree of control but limits risk exposure. Second, the MNE gains access to knowledge about the host country; the local firm, in turn, benefits from the MNE's technology, capital, and management. Third, JVs may be politically more acceptable in host countries.

In terms of disadvantages, JVs often involve partners from different backgrounds and with different goals, so conflicts are natural. Furthermore, effective equity and operational control may be difficult to achieve since everything has to be negotiated—in some cases, fought over. Finally, the nature of the JV does not give an MNE the tight control over a foreign subsidiary that it may need for global coordination. Overall, all sorts of non-equity-based contractual agreements and equity-based JVs can be broadly considered as strategic alliances (within the *dotted area* in Figure 6.3). Chapter 7 will discuss them in detail.

The last entry mode is to establish a **wholly owned subsidiary (WOS)**, defined as a subsidiary located in a foreign country that is entirely owned by the parent multinational. There are two primary means to set up a WOS.[38] One is to establish **greenfield operations**, building new factories and offices from scratch (on a proverbial piece of "green field" formerly used for agricultural purposes). For example, PRPG America, Ltd., is a wholly owned greenfield subsidiary of Pearl River Piano Group of China (see the Closing Case). There are three advantages. First, a greenfield WOS gives an MNE complete equity and management control, thus eliminating the headaches associated with JVs. Second, this undivided control leads to better protection of proprietary technology. Third, a WOS allows for centrally coordinated global actions. Sometimes, a subsidiary (such as TI's in Japan, discussed earlier) will be ordered to *lose* money. Local licensees/franchisees or JV partners are unlikely to accept such a subservient role to lose money (!).

In terms of drawbacks, a greenfield WOS tends to be expensive and risky, not only financially but also politically. Its conspicuous foreignness may become a target for nationalistic sentiments. Another drawback is that greenfield operations add new capacity to an industry, which will make a competitive industry more crowded. For example, think of all the Japanese automobile plants built in the United States, which have severely squeezed the market share of US automakers. Finally, greenfield operations suffer from a slow entry speed of at least one to several years (relative to acquisitions).

The other way to establish a WOS is an acquisition. Pearl River's acquisition of Ritmüller is a case in point (see the Closing Case). Acquisition shares all the benefits of greenfield WOS but enjoys two additional advantages: (1) adding no new capacity and (2) faster entry speed. In terms of drawbacks, acquisition shares all of the disadvantages of greenfield WOS except adding new capacity and slow entry speed. But acquisition has a unique disadvantage: post-acquisition integration problems (see Chapter 9 for details).

Debates and Extensions

This chapter has already covered some crucial debates, such as first-mover versus late-mover advantages. Here we discuss three heated *recent* debates: (1) liability versus asset of foreignness, (2) global versus regional geographic diversification, and (3) old-line versus emerging multinationals.

---

wholly owned subsidiary (WOS)
Subsidiary located in a foreign country that is entirely owned by the MNE.

greenfield operation
Building factories and offices from scratch (on a proverbial piece of "greenfield" formerly used for agricultural purposes).

Liability versus Asset of Foreignness

In terms of the "liability of foreignness," one contrasting view argues that under certain circumstances, being foreign can be an *asset* (that is, a competitive advantage).[39] German cars are viewed as of higher quality in the United States and Japan. In China, consumers discriminate against made-in-China luxury goods. Although these made-in-China luxury goods sport Western brands, they are viewed as inferior to made-in-France handbags and made-in-Switzerland watches (see Chapter 2 Closing Case). American cigarettes are "cool" among smokers in Central and Eastern Europe. Anything Korean—ranging from handsets and TV shows to *kimchi* (pickled cabbage)-flavored instant noodles—is considered hip in Southeast Asia. Conceptually, this is known as the **country-of-origin effect**, which refers to the positive or negative perception of firms and products from a certain country. Pearl River's promotion of the Ritmüller brand, which highlights its German origin, suggests that the negative country-of-origin effect can be (at least partially) overcome (see the Closing Case). Pearl River is not alone in this regard. Here is a quiz: What is Häagen-Dazs ice cream's country of origin? My students typically say: Germany, Belgium, Switzerland, and other European countries. Sorry, all wrong. Häagen-Dazs is American and has always been (!).

Whether foreignness is indeed an asset or a liability remains tricky. Tokyo Disneyland became wildly popular in Japan, because it played up its American image. But Paris Disneyland received relentless negative press coverage in France, because it insisted on its wholesome American look. To play it safe, Hong Kong Disneyland endeavored to strike the elusive balance between American image and Chinese flavor. All eyes are now on the forthcoming Shanghai Disneyland in terms of such balance.

Over time, the country-of-origin effect may shift. A number of UK firms used to proudly sport names such as British Telecom and British Petroleum. Recently, they have shied away from being "British" and rebranded themselves simply as BT and BP. In Britain, these changes are collectively known as the "B phenomenon." These costly rebranding campaigns are not casual changes. They reflect less confidence in Britain's positive country-of-origin effect. Recently, BAE Systems, formerly British Aerospace, has complained that its British origin is pulling its legs in its largest market, the US defense market. Only US citizens are allowed to know the details of its most sensitive US contracts, and even its British CEO cannot know such details. This is untenable now that two-fifths of its sales are in the United States. Thus, BAE Systems is seriously considering becoming "American." However, in an interesting twist, an "Americanized" BAE Systems may encounter liability of foreignness in Britain.[40] Not surprisingly, the "B phenomenon" is controversial in Britain. One lesson we can draw is that foreignness can either be a liability or an asset, and that changes are possible. One solution is to *blur* the country of origin. For example, Gucci positions itself as a firm with Italian roots that has a Dutch address (where it is registered) and sells French fashion.

Global versus Regional Geographic Diversification

In this age of globalization, debate continues on the optimal geographic scope for MNEs.[41] Despite the widely held belief that MNEs are expanding "globally," Alan Rugman and colleagues report that, surprisingly, even among the largest *Fortune* Global 500 MNEs, few are truly "global."[42] Using some reasonable criteria (at least 20% of sales in *each* of the three regions of the Triad consisting of Asia, Europe, and North America but less than 50% in any one region), only *nine* MNEs are found to be really "global" (Table 6.4).

country-of-origin effect
The positive or negative perception of firms and products from a certain country.

TABLE 6.4 There Are Only Nine "Global" Multinational Enterprises (MNEs) Measured by Sales

1	2	3	4	5	6	7	8	9
IBM	Sony	Philips	Nokia	Intel	Canon	Coca-Cola	Flextronics	LVMH

Sources: Adapted from A. Rugman & A. Verbeke, 2004, A perspective on regional and global strategies of multinational enterprises (pp. 8–10), *Journal of International Business Studies*, 35: 3–18. "Global" MNEs have at least 20% of sales in each of the three regions of the Triad (Asia, Europe, and North America), but less than 50% in any one region.

Should most MNEs further "globalize"? There are two answers. First, most MNEs know what they are doing, and their current geographic scope is the maximum they can manage. Some of them may have already over-diversified and will need to downscope. Second, these data only capture a snapshot (in the 2000s) and some MNEs may become more "globalized" over time. However, more recent data do not show major changes.[43] While the debate goes on, it has at least taught us one important reason: Be careful when using the word "global." The *majority* of the largest MNEs are not necessarily very "global" in their geographic scope.

Old-line versus Emerging Multinationals: OLI versus LLL

MNEs presumably possess OLI advantages. The OLI framework is based on the experience of MNEs headquartered in developed economies that typically possess high-caliber technology and management know-how. However, emerging multinationals, such as those from China (see the Closing Case), Russia (Emerging Markets 6.1), and South Africa (Emerging Markets 6.3), are challenging some of this conventional wisdom.[44] While these emerging multinationals, like their old-line counterparts, hunt for lucrative locations and internalize transactions—conforming to the L and I parts of the OLI framework—they typically do not own better proprietary technology, and their management capabilities are usually not world class. In other words, the O part is largely missing. How can we make sense of these emerging multinationals?

One interesting new framework is the "linkage, leverage, and learning" (LLL) framework advocated by John Mathews.[45] Linkage refers to emerging MNEs' ability to identify and bridge gaps. Pearl River has identified the gap between what its pianos can actually offer and what price it can command given the negative country-of-origin effect associated with Chinese products. Pearl River's answer has been two-pronged: (1) develop the economies of scale to bring down the unit cost of pianos while maintaining a high standard for quality, and (2) acquire and revive the Ritmüller brand to reduce some of the negative country-of-origin effect. Thus, Pearl River links China and Germany to propel its global push (see the Closing Case).

Leverage refers to emerging multinationals' ability to take advantage of their unique resources and capabilities, which are typically based on a deep understanding of customer needs and wants. For example, Naver enjoys a 76% market share for Internet searches in South Korea. It intends to leverage its deep understanding of Asian languages and cultures by charging into Japan. In the long run, it also has ambition to launch other culturally specific search engines, such as "Naver Korean-American" and "Naver

Chinese-American." On a global scale, Naver's skills obviously pale in comparison with Google's capabilities. But in certain markets such as South Korea, emerging multinationals such as Naver have been beating Google.

Learning probably is the most unusual aspect among the motives behind the internationalization push of many emerging multinationals.[46] Instead of the "I-will-tell-you-what-to-do" mentality typical of old-line MNEs from developed economies, many MNEs from emerging economies openly profess that they go abroad to learn. Skills they need to absorb range from basic English skills to high-level executive skills in transparent governance, market planning, and management of diverse multicultural workforces.

Of course, there is a great deal of overlap between OLI and LLL frameworks. So the debate boils down to whether the differences are fundamental, which would justify a new theory such as **LLL advantages**, or just a matter of degree, in which case OLI would be just fine to accommodate the new MNEs. Given the rapidly moving progress of these emerging multinationals, one thing for certain is that our learning and debate about them will not stop anytime soon.[47]

LLL advantages

Linkage, leverage, and learning advantages, which are typically associated with MNEs from emerging economies.

The Savvy Strategist

Foreign market entries are crucial in global strategy. Without these first steps, firms will remain domestic players. The challenges associated with internationalization are daunting, the complexities enormous, and the stakes high. Consequently, the savvy strategist can draw four implications for action (Table 6.5). First, from an industry-based view, you need to thoroughly understand the dynamism underlying the industry in a foreign market you are looking into. For example, in the early 2000s, a number of European financial services firms such as ABN Amro, HSBC, and ING Group spent billions of dollars to enter the United States through a series of acquisitions. They failed to realize the forthcoming collapse of this industry engulfed in the Great Recession. As a result, they suffered tremendous losses.

Second, from a resource-based view, you and your firm need to develop *overwhelming* capabilities to offset the liability of foreignness. A case in point is the rise of Pearl River illustrated in the Closing Case.

Third, from an institution-based view, you need to understand the rules of the game, both formal and informal, governing competition in foreign markets. Failure to understand these rules can be costly. In the 2000s, managers at Dubai Ports World (DP World) and China National Offshore Oil Corporation (CNOOC) misread the xenophobic US sentiments against foreign acquisitions, which could be regarded as informal norms. As a result, their acquisition attempts were torpedoed politically.

TABLE 6.5   Strategic Implications for Action

- Grasp the dynamism underlying the industry in a host country that you are looking into.
- Develop overwhelming resources and capabilities to offset the liability of foreignness.
- Understand the rules of the game—both formal and informal—governing competition in foreign markets.
- Match efforts in market entry and geographic diversification with strategic goals.

© Cengage Learning

Finally, the savvy strategist matches entries with strategic goals. If the goal is to deter rivals in their home markets by slashing prices there (as TI did when entering Japan), then be prepared to fight a nasty price war and lose money. If the goal is to generate decent returns, then withdrawing from some tough nuts to crack may be necessary (as Wal-Mart withdrew from Germany).

In conclusion, this chapter sheds considerable light on the four fundamental questions. Why firms differ in their propensity to internationalize (Question 1) boils down to the size of the firm and that of the domestic market. How firms behave (Question 2) depends on how considerations for industry competition, firm capabilities, and institutional differences influence market entry decisions. What determines the scope of the firm (Question 3)—in this case, the scope of its international involvement—fundamentally depends on how to acquire and leverage the three-pronged OLI advantages. Firms committed to owning some assets overseas through equity modes of entry and, thus, to becoming MNEs are likely to have a broader scope overseas than those unwilling to do so. Finally, entry strategies obviously have something to do with the international success and failure of firms (Question 4).[48] However, appropriate entry strategies, while certainly important, are only a *beginning*.[49] It takes a lot more to succeed overseas, as we will discuss in later chapters.

CHAPTER SUMMARY

1. Understand the necessity to overcome the liability of foreignness
  - When entering foreign markets, firms confront a liability of foreignness.
  - The propensity to internationalize differs among firms of different sizes and different home market sizes.

2. Articulate a comprehensive model of foreign market entries
  - The industry-based view suggests that industry dynamism in a host country cannot be ignored.
  - The resource-based view calls for the development of capabilities along the VRIO dimensions.
  - The institution-based view focuses on institutional constraints that foreign entrants must confront.

3. Match the quest for location-specific advantages with strategic goals (where to enter)
  - Where to enter depends on certain foreign countries' location-specific advantages and firms' strategic goals, such as seeking (1) natural resources, (2) market, (3) efficiency, and (4) innovation.

4. Compare and contrast first-mover and late-mover advantages (when to enter)
  - Each has pros and cons, and there is no conclusive evidence pointing to one direction.

5. Follow a decision model that guides specific steps for foreign market entries (how to enter)
  - How to enter depends on the scale of entry: Large-scale versus small-scale entries.
  - A decision model first focuses on the equity (ownership) issue.
  - The second step makes the actual selection, such as exports, contractual agreements, JVs, and WOS.

6. Participate in three leading debates on foreign market entries
- (1) Liability versus asset of foreignness, (2) global versus regional geographic diversification, and (3) old-line versus emerging multinationals.

7. Draw strategic implications for action
- Grasp the dynamism underlying the industry in a host country that you are looking into.
- Develop overwhelming resources and capabilities to offset the liability of foreignness.
- Understand the rules of the game governing competition in foreign markets.
- Match efforts in market entry and geographic diversification with strategic goals.

KEY TERMS

Agglomeration p. 164

Build-operate-transfer (BOT) agreement p. 175

Co-marketing p. 175

Country-of-origin effect p. 177

Currency hedging p. 163

Currency risk p. 163

Dissemination risk p. 161

Equity mode p. 171

Expropriation p. 162

First-mover advantage p. 168

Greenfield operation p. 176

Internalization p. 173

Internalization advantage p. 173

Joint venture (JV) p. 175

Late-mover advantage p. 169

Liability of foreignness p. 156

LLL advantages p. 179

Local content requirement p. 162

Location specific advantage p. 163

Non equity mode p. 171

Nontariff barrier p. 162

Obsolescing bargain p. 161

OLI advantages p. 173

Ownership advantage p. 173

Regulatory risk p. 161

Research and development (R&D) contract p. 175

Scale of entry p. 170

Strategic hedging p. 163

Sunk cost p. 162

Tariff barrier p. 162

Trade barrier p. 162

Turnkey project p. 175

Wholly owned subsidiary (WOS) p. 176

CRITICAL DISCUSSION QUESTIONS

1. Pick an industry in which firms from your country are internationally active. What are the top five most favorite foreign markets for firms in this industry? Why?

2. From institution-based and resource-based views, identify the liability of foreignness confronting MNEs from emerging economies interested in expanding overseas. How can such firms overcome them?

3. *ON ETHICS:* Entering foreign markets, by definition, means not investing in a firm's home country. What are the ethical dilemmas here? What are your recommendations as (1) MNE executives, (2) labor union leaders of your domestic (home country) labor forces, (3) host country officials, and (4) home country officials?

TOPICS FOR EXPANDED PROJECTS

1. During the 1990s, many North American, European, and Asian MNEs set up operations in Mexico, tapping into its location-specific advantages such as (1) proximity to the world's largest economy, (2) market-opening policies associated with NAFTA membership, and (3) abundant, low-cost, and high-quality labor. None of these has changed much. Write a short paper explaining whether you think Mexico does or does not enjoy such advantages as it approaches the 30th anniversary of NAFTA.

2. ***ON ETHICS:*** Foreign entrants are often criticized for destroying local firms and cultures. Working in pairs, write a script for an interview between a local TV reporter and the CEO of a leading foreign entrant in a host country discussing this issue.

3. ***ON ETHICS:*** As CEO of a social media firm (such as Facebook), you have been informed that your firm's service will be discontinued in the host country because it allegedly incites social unrest. (Egypt really did that in 2011 and the UK threatened to do that in 2010). Working in small groups, research this situation and write a press release to explain your firm's response.

▶ CLOSING CASE

Emerging Markets: Pearl River Goes Abroad

To many readers of this book, Pearl River is likely to be the world's largest piano maker you have never heard of. It is also the fastest-growing piano maker in North America, with the largest dealer network in Canada and the United States (over 300 dealers). Its website proudly announces that Pearl River is "the world's best selling piano." Although some of you may say, "Sorry, I don't play piano, so I don't know anything about leading piano brands," you most likely have heard about Yamaha and Steinway. Therefore, your excuse for not knowing Pearl River would collapse.

The problem is both yours and Pearl River's. Given the relatively low prestige associated with made-in-China goods, you probably would not associate a fine musical instrument such as a piano with a Chinese firm. Pearl River Piano Group (PRPG) is China's largest piano maker and has recently dethroned Japan's Yamaha to become the world champion by volume. Despite PRPG's outstanding capabilities, it is difficult for one firm to change the negative country-of-origin image associated with made-in-China goods.

PRPG was founded in 1956 in Guangzhou, China, where the Pearl River flows by. Pearl River (the company) in fact exported its very first piano to Hong Kong, yet its center of gravity has remained in China. Pianos have become more affordable with rising incomes. The one-child policy has made families willing to invest in their only child's education. As a result, the Chinese now buy half of the pianos produced in the world.

If you think life will be easy for the leading firm in the largest market in the world, you are wrong. In fact, life is increasingly hard for PRPG. Rising demand has attracted numerous new entrants, many of which compete at the low end in China. These over 140 competitors have pushed PRPG's domestic market share from 70% at its peak a decade ago to about 25% now—although it is still the market leader.

Savage domestic competition has pushed PRPG to increasingly look for overseas opportunities. It now exports to over 80 countries. In North America, PRPG started in the late 1980s by relying on US-based importers. Making its first-ever FDI, it set up a US-based sales subsidiary, PRPG America, Ltd., in Ontario, California, in 1999. Acknowledging the importance of the US market and the limited international caliber of his own managerial rank, PRPG's CEO, Tong Zhi Cheng, attracted Al Rich, an American with long experience in the piano industry, to head the subsidiary. In two years, the greenfield subsidiary succeeded in getting Pearl River pianos into about one-third of the specialized US retail dealers. In ten years, the Pearl River brand became the undisputed leader in the low end of the upright piano market in North America. Efforts to penetrate the high-end market, however, were still frustrated.

Despite the enviable progress made by PRPG itself in general and by its US subsidiary in particular, the Pearl River brand suffers from all the usual trappings associated with Chinese brands. "We are very cognizant that our pricing provides a strong incentive to buy," Rich noted in a media interview, "but $6,000 is still a lot of money." In an audacious move to overcome buyers' reservations about purchasing a high-end Chinese product, PRPG made its second major FDI move in 2000, by acquiring Ritmüller of Germany.

Ritmüller was founded in 1795 by Wilhelm Ritmüller, during the lifetimes of composers Beethoven and Haydn. It was one of the first piano makers in Germany and one of the most prominent in the world. Unfortunately, during the post-WWII era, Ritmüller's style of small-scale, handicraft-based piano making had a hard time surviving the disruptive, mass-production technologies unleashed by Yamaha and more recently by Pearl River. Prior to being acquired by Pearl River, Ritmüller had ended up being inactive. Today, Ritmüller has entered a new era in its proud history and has operated a factory in Germany with full capacity. The entire product line has been re-engineered to reflect a new commitment to a classic heritage and standards of excellence. PRPG has commissioned international master piano designers to marry German precision craftsmanship with the latest piano making technology.

Sources: Based on (1) *Beijing Review*, 2009, The return of the king, May 21, www.bjreview.com; (2) Funding Universe, 2009, Guangzhou Pearl River Piano Group Ltd., www.fundinguniverse.com; (3) Y. Lu, 2009, Pearl River Piano Group's international strategy, in M. W. Peng, *Global Strategy*, 2nd ed. (pp. 437–440), Cincinnati: South-Western Cengage Learning; (4) Pearl River Piano Group, 2012, www.pearlriverpiano.com; (5) Pearl River USA, 2012, www.pearlriverusa.com.

CASE DISCUSSION QUESTIONS

1. Drawing on the industry-based, resource-based, and institution-based views, explain how Pearl River, from its humble roots, became China's and the world's largest piano producer.
2. Why did Pearl River's top management believe that the firm must engage in significant internationalization (beyond the direct export strategy)?
3. Why did Pearl River use different entry modes when entering different markets?

NOTES

[**Journal acronyms**] *AMJ* – *Academy of Management Journal*; *AMR* – *Academy of Management Review*; *APJM* – *Asia Pacific Journal of Management*; *BJM* – *British Journal of Management*; *BW* – *BusinessWeek* (before 2010) or *Bloomberg Businessweek* (since 2010); *CME* – *Construction Management and Economics*; *EJIM* – *European Journal of International Management*; *GSJ* – *Global Strategy Journal*; *HBR* – *Harvard Business Review*; *IBR* – *International Business Review*; *JIBS* – *Journal of International Business Studies*; *JIM* – *Journal of International Management*; *JM* – *Journal of Management*; *JMS* – *Journal of Management Studies*; *JWB* – *Journal of World Business*; *MIR* – *Management International Review*; *SCMP* – *South China Morning Post*; *SMJ* – *Strategic Management Journal*

1. K. Meyer, S. Estrin, S. Bhaumik, & M. W. Peng, 2009, Institutions, resources, and entry strategies in emerging economies, *SMJ*, 30: 61–80.

2. G. Gao, J. Murray, M. Kotabe, & J. Lu, 2010, A strategy tripod perspective on export behaviors, *JIBS*, 41: 377–396; Y. Xie, H. Zhao, Q. Xie, & M. Arnold, 2012, On the determinants of post-entry strategic positioning of foreign firms in a host market: A strategy tripod perspective, *IBR* (in press).

3. A. Cuervo-Carurra, M. Maloney, & S. Manrakhan, 2007, Causes of the difficulties in internationalization, *JIBS*, 38: 709–725; B. Elango, 2009, Minimizing effects of "liability of foreignness", *JWB*, 44: 51–62; J. Johanson & J. Vahlne, 2009, The Uppsala internationalization process model revisited, *JIBS*, 40: 1411–1431; H. Yildiz & C. Fey, 2012, The liability of foreignness reconsidered, *IBR* (in press).

4. *BW*, 2009, Europe's rush to grab US stimulus cash, May 4: 52.

5. *SCMP*, 2010, GE's problem with China, July 6: B14.

6. *SCMP*, 2010, GE boards China's jumbo jet program, July 13: B4.

7. J. Hennart, 2007, The theoretical rationales for a multi-nationality-performance relationship, *MIR*, 47: 423–452.

8. T. Hutzschenreuter, T. Pederson, & H. Volberda, 2007, The role of path dependency and managerial intentionality, *JIBS*, 38: 1055–1068; D. Paul & P. Wooster, 2008, Strategic investments by US firms in transition economies, *JIBS*, 39: 249–266.

9. T. Shervani, G. Frazier, & G. Challagalla, 2007, The moderating influence of firm market power on the transaction cost economics model, *SMJ*, 28: 635–652.

10. A. Kirca et al., 2011, Firm-specific assets, multinationality, and financial performance, *AMJ*, 84: 47–72; M. W. Peng, 2001, The resource-based view and international business, *JM*, 27: 803–829.

11. H. Berry, 2006, Shareholder valuation of foreign investment and expansion, SMJ, 27: 1123–1140; S. Lee & M. Makhija, 2009, Flexibility in internationalization, *SMJ*, 30: 537–555.

12. X. Tian, 2010, Managing FDI technology spillovers, *JWB*, 45: 276–284.

13. W. Lin, K. Cheng, & Y. Liu, 2009, Organizational slack and firm's internationalization, *JWB*, 44: 397–406; N. Malhotra & C. Hinings, 2010, An organizational model for understanding internationalization process, *JIBS*, 41: 300–349.

14. C. Chan & S. Makino, 2007, Legitimacy and multi-level institutional environments, *JIBS*, 38: 621–638;

M. Demirbag, K. Glaister, & E. Tatoglu, 2007, Institutional and transaction cost influence on MNEs' ownership strategies of their affiliates, *JWB*, 42: 418–434; J. Li, J. Yang, & D. Yue, 2007, Identity, community, and audience, *AMJ*, 50: 175–190; C. Oh & J. Oetzel, 2011, Multinationals' response to major disasters, *SMJ*, 32: 658–681; J. Shaner & M. Maznevski, 2011, The relationship between networks, institutional development, and performance in foreign investments, *SMJ*, 32: 556–568; A. Slangen & S. Beugelsdijk, 2010, The impact of institutional hazards on foreign multinational activity, *JIBS*, 41: 980–995.

15. J. Dunning, 2009, Location and the MNE: A neglected factor? *JIBS*, 40: 5–19. See also R. Belderbos, W. Olffen, & J. Zou, 2011, Generic and specific social learning mechanisms in foreign entry location choice, *SMJ*, 32: 1309–1330; J. Cantwell, 2009, Location and the MNE, *JIBS*, 40: 35–41; R. Flores & R. Aguilera, 2007, Globalization and location choice, *JIBS*, 38: 1187–1210; E. Garcia-Canal & M. Guillen, 2008, Risk and the strategy of foreign location choice in regulated industries, *SMJ*, 29: 1097–1115; S. Zaheer & L. Nachum, 2011, Sense of place, *GSJ*, 1: 96–108.

16. A. Arikan & M. Schilling, 2011, Structure and governance in industrial districts, *JMS*, 48: 772–803; S. Bell, P. Tracey, & J. Heide, 2009, The organization of regional clusters, *AMR*, 34: 623–642; S. Manning, J. Ricart, M. Rique, & A. Lewin, 2010, from blind spots to hotspots, *JIM*, 16: 369–382; B. McCann & G. Vroom, 2010, Pricing response to entry and agglomeration effects, *SMJ*, 31: 284–305.

17. *BW*, 2007, Shanghai rising, February 19: 51–55.

18. W. Chung & S. Yeaple, 2008, International knowledge sourcing, *SMJ*, 29: 1207–1224.

19. S. Lee, O. Shenkar, & J. Li, 2008, Cultural distance, investment flow, and control in cross-border cooperation, *SMJ*, 29: 1117–1125; R. Parente, B. Choi, A. Slangen, & S. Ketkar, 2010, Distribution system choice in a service industry, *JIM*, 16: 275–287.

20. D. Xu & O. Shenkar, 2002, Institutional distance and the multinational enterprise (p. 608), *AMR*, 27: 608–618. See also M. Cho & V. Kumar, 2010, The impact of institutional distance on the international diversity-performance relationship, *JWB*, 45: 93–103; G. Delmestri & F. Wezel, 2011, Breaking the wave, *JIBS*, 42: 828–852.

21. H. Barkema & R. Drogendijk, 2007, Internationalizing in small, incremental or larger steps? *JIBS*, 38: 1132–1148.

22. S. Makino & E. Tsang, 2011, Historical ties and foreign direct investment, *JIBS*, 42: 545–557.

23. E. Tsang & P. Yip, 2007, Economic distance and survival of foreign direct investments, *AMJ*, 50: 1156–1168.

24. M. Myers, C. Droge, & M. Cheung, 2007, The fit of home to foreign market environment, *JWB*, 42: 170–183.

25. J. Steen & P. Liesch, 2007, A note on Penrosian growth, resource bundles, and the Uppsala model of internationalization, *MIR*, 47: 193–206.

26. *Economist*, 2006, Don't mess with Russia, December 16: 11.

27. A. Delios, A. Gaur, & S. Makino, 2008, The timing of international expansion, *JMS*, 45: 169–195; J. G. Frynas, K. Mellahi, & G. Pigman, 2006, First mover advantages in international business and firm-specific political resources, *SMJ*, 27: 321–345.

28. M. W. Peng, S. Lee, & J. Tan, 2001, The *keiretsu* in Asia, *JIM*, 7: 253–276.

29. *BW*, 2011, Land of war and opportunity, January 10: 46–54.

30. *BW*, 2008, Cisco's brave new world (p. 68), November 24: 56–68.

31. S. Dobrev & A. Gotsopoulos, 2010, Legitimacy vacuum, structural imprinting, and the first mover disadvantage, *AMJ*, 53: 1153–1174; J. Gomez & J. Maicas, 2011, Do switching costs mediate the relationship between entry timing and performance? *SMJ*, 32: 1251–1269; G. Lee, 2008, Relevance of organizational capabilities and its dynamics, *SMJ*, 29: 1257–1280; M. Semadeni & B. Anderson, 2010, The follower's dilemma, *AMJ*, 53: 1175–1193; F. Suarez & G. Lanzolla, 2005, The half-truth of first-mover advantage, *HBR*, April: 121–128; J. Woo, R. Reed, S. Shin, & D. Lemak, 2009, Strategic choice and performance in late movers, *JMS*, 46: 308–335.

32. G. Gao & Y. Pan, 2010, The pace of MNEs' sequential entries, *JIBS*, 41: 1572–1580; L. Lages, S. Jap, & D. Griffith, 2008, The role of past performance in export ventures, *JIBS*, 39: 304–325; P. Li & K. Meyer, 2009, Contextualizing experience effects in international business, *JWB*, 44: 370–382; A. Nadolska & H. Barkema, 2007, Learning to internationalize, *JIBS*, 38: 1170–1187; L. Qian & A. Delios, 2008, Internationalization and experience, *JIBS*, 39: 231–248; J. Xia, K. Boal, & A. Delios, 2009, When experience meets national institutional environmental change, *SMJ*, 30: 1286–1309.

33. G. Benito, B. Petersen, & L. Welch, 2009, Towards more realistic conceptualizations of foreign operation modes, *JIBS*, 40: 1455–1470; Y. Pan & D. Tse, 2000, The hierarchical model of market entry modes, *JIBS*, 31: 535–554.

34. J. Dunning, 1993, *Multinational Enterprises and the Global Economy*, Reading, MA: Addison-Wesley. See also L. Brouthers, S. Mukhopadhyay, T. Wilkinson, & K. Brouthers, 2009, International market selection and subsidiary performance, *JWB*, 44: 262–273; J. Galan & J. Gonzalez-Benito, 2006, Distinctive determinant factors of Spanish foreign direct investment in Latin America, *JWB*, 41: 171–189; K. Ito & E. Rose, 2010, The implicit return on domestic and international sales, *JIBS*, 41: 1074–1089.

35. M. W. Peng, Y. Zhou, & A. York, 2006, Behind make or buy decisions in export strategy, *JWB*, 41: 289–300.

36. A. Chintakananda, A. York, H. O'Neill, & M. W. Peng, 2009, Structuring dyadic relationships between export producers and intermediaries, *EJIM*, 3: 302–327.

37. A. Akremi, K. Mignonac, & R. Perrigot, 2011, Opportunistic behaviors in franchise chains, *SMJ*, 32: 930–948; P. Aulakh, M. Jiang, & Y. Pan, 2010, International technology licensing, *JIBS*, 41: 587–605; J. Barthelemy, 2008, Opportunism, knowledge, and the performance of franchise chains, *SMJ*, 29: 1451–1463.

38. A. Slangen, 2011, A communication-based theory of the choice between greenfield and acquisition entry, *JMS*, 48: 1699–1726.

39. D. Kronborg & S. Thomsen, 2009, Foreign ownership and long-term survival, *SMJ*, 30: 207–219.

40. *Economist*, 2006, BAE Systems: Changing places, October 28: 66–67.

41. E. Banalieva & K. Eddleston, 2011, Home-region focus and performance of family firms, *JIBS*, 42: 1060–1072; L. Cardinal, C. C. Miller, & L. Palich, 2011, Breaking the cycle of iteration, *GSJ*, 1: 175–186; J. Cuervo & L. Pheng, 2004, Global performance measures for transnational construction corporations, *CME*, 22: 851–860; J. Dunning, J. Fujita, & N. Yakova, 2007, Some macro-data on the regionalization/globalization debate, *JIBS*, 38: 177–199; J. Hennart, 2011, A theoretical assessment of the empirical literature on the impact of multinationality on performance, *GSJ*, 1: 135–151; T. Osegowitsch & A. Sammartino, 2008, Reassessing (home-) regionalization, *JIBS*, 39: 184–196; G. Qian, T. Khoury, M. W. Peng, & Z. Qian, 2010, The performance implications of intra- and inter-regional geographic diversification, *SMJ*, 31: 1018–1030; M. Wiersema & H. Bowen, 2011, The relationship between international diversification and firm performance, *GSJ*, 1: 152–170.

42. S. Collinson & A. Rugman, 2007, The regional character of Asian multinational enterprises, *APJM*, 24: 429–446; A. Rugman & A. Verbeke, 2004, A perspective on regional and global strategies of multinational enterprises, *JIBS*, 35: 3–18.

43. A. Rugman & C. Oh, 2012, Why the home region matters, *BJM* (in press).

44. M. W. Peng, 2012, The global strategy of emerging multinationals from China, *GSJ*, 2: 97–107.

45. J. Mathews, 2006, Dragon multinationals: Emerging players in 21st century globalization, *APJM*, 23: 5–27.

46. Y. Luo & R. Tung, 2007, International expansion of emerging market enterprises, *JIBS*, 38: 481–498.

47. M. W. Peng, R. Bhagat, & S. Chang, 2010, Asia and global business, *JIBS*, 41: 373–376.

48. M. Chari, S. Devaraj, & P. David, 2007, International diversification and firm performance, *JWB*, 42: 184–197; F. Contractor, V. Kumar, & S. Kundu, 2007, Nature of the relationship between international expansion and performance, *JWB*, 42: 401–417.

49. S. Chang & J. Rhee, 2011, Rapid FDI expansion and firm performance, *JIBS*, 42: 979–994; W. Hejazi & E. Santor, 2010, Foreign asset risk exposure, DOI, and performance, *JIBS*, 41: 845–860; S. Li & S. Tallman, 2011, MNC strategies, exogenous shocks, and performance outcomes, *SMJ*, 32: 1119–1127; T. Pedersen & J. M. Shaver, 2011, Internationalization revisited, *GSJ*, 1: 263–274; J. Puck, D. Holtbrugge, & A. Mohr, 2009, Beyond entry mode choice, *JIBS*, 40: 388–404; J. M. Shaver, 2011, The benefits of geographic sales diversification, *SMJ*, 32: 1046–1060; D. Tan, 2009, Foreign market entry strategies and post-entry growth, *JIBS*, 40: 1046–1063.

CHAPTER 7

MAKING STRATEGIC ALLIANCES AND NETWORKS WORK

© istockphoto/Alexey Stiop

LEARNING OBJECTIVES

After studying this chapter, you should be able to

1. Define strategic alliances and networks
2. Articulate a comprehensive model of strategic alliances and networks
3. Understand the decision processes behind the formation of alliances and networks
4. Gain insights into the evolution of alliances and networks
5. Identify the drivers behind the performance of alliances and networks
6. Participate in three leading debates concerning alliances and networks
7. Draw strategic implications for action

Emerging Markets: Yum! Brands Teams Up with Sinopec

Gas stations do everything they can to avoid heat and fire. But in 2011 competition in gas stations operated by China Petroleum and Chemical Corporation (known as Sinopec) was heating up. It was triggered by a strategic alliance agreement signed between Sinopec and Yum! Brands, the number one fast food chain in China with about 3,500 Kentucky Fried Chicken (KFC) and 560 Pizza Hut restaurants in 650 Chinese cities. The agreement announced that KFC and Pizza Hut restaurants would open inside Sinopec's gas stations. By revenue, Sinopec is the largest firm in China and the fifth largest in the world (with $273 billion sales in 2011). It operates over 30,000 gas stations throughout China. As car ownership takes off in China, the growth potential for both Sinopec and for Yum! Brands seems enormous.

> *Both companies expect this important cooperation to have a significant and far-reaching impact on the development and strategic growth of their businesses. Through the complementary advantages of both companies, the combination of the strengths will offer better service for customers, promote both brands, generate more economic returns, and improve their capabilities for sustainable development.*

This sounds like a quote from the press release from Sinopec and Yum! Brands—except, it is not (!). This is actually a quote from a strategic alliance announcement between Sinopec and Yum! Brands' archrival, McDonald's, which was signed in 2007. In their homeland, McDonald's beat Yum! Brands, and KFC was struggling. But in China, McDonalds' 1,000 restaurants were no match to the much larger number and wider spread of KFC, Pizza Hut, and their Chinese cousin East Dawning, a new chain restaurant brand that only sells Chinese fast food. In an effort to catch up, McDonald's set up an alliance with Sinopec.

As a result, Yum! Brands was a late mover in teaming up with Sinopec. Because the deal between Sinopec and McDonald's was a 20-year deal, Yum! Brands restaurants could not displace McDonald's at Sinopec gas stations. Yum! Brands could operate either in new stations not having McDonald's or in established stations alongside McDonald's. In response to such "polygamy," McDonald's announced that it was the first "spouse," with all the rights and privileges to pick high-priority locations. Emphasizing "healthy competition," Yum! Brands highlighted its advantages in two ways: (1) Its multiple restaurant brands could cater to different demographic groups, and (2) its supply chain was far more widespread, thus enabling it to team with Sinopec to reach the far corners of inland China.

As the king of fast food in China, Yum! Brands has not only constantly faced smaller local competitors, but also increasingly confronted capable multinational rivals eager to eat its lunch. In addition to McDonald's, these included Asian chains, such as Dicos, owned by Taiwanese company Ting Hsin International Group; Yoshinoya, owned by Japanese firm Yoshinoya Holdings; and Yonghe King and Hongzhuanqyuan, both owned by Manila-based Jollibee, a powerful regional chain that beats both McDonald's and Yum! in the Philippines.

It was such intense competitive pressure that drove Yum! Brands into Sinopec gas stations. As a late entrant into this tricky three-way relationship, Yum! Brands will have to wait to see whether the Sinopec alliance can deliver the growth it seems to promise. Stay tuned for the evolution of this intriguing relationship.

Sources: Based on (1) *21st Century Business Insights,* 2011, KFC and McDonald's fight over Chinese gas stations, December 16: 60–61; (2) Bloomberg, 2011, McDonald's no match for KFC in China as colonels rules fast food, January 26, www.bloomberg.com; (3) *China Daily,* 2011, Yum! Brands signs deal with Sinopec, November 23, www.chinadaily.com.cn; (4) Sinopec, 2007, The first "drive-through" restaurant and gas station complex is opened collaboratively by Sinopec and McDonald's, January 19, english.sinopec.com.

W hy do both Yum! Brands and McDonald's establish strategic alliances with Sinopec? How do they navigate the complexities of such a tricky three-way relationship? Will these alliances become successful or end up in divorce? These are some of the key questions driving this chapter. As globalization intensifies, "the least attractive way to try to win on a global basis," according to GE's former chairman and CEO Jack Welch, "is to think you can take on the world all by yourself."[1] Proliferation of strategic alliances and networks can now be seen in just about every industry and every country, yet 30%–70% of all alliances and networks fail, thus necessitating our attention to the causes of their failures.

This chapter will first define strategic alliances and networks, followed by a comprehensive model drawing upon the strategy tripod. Then, we discuss the formation, evolution, and performance of alliances and networks, followed by debates and extensions.

Defining Strategic Alliances and Networks

Strategic alliances are voluntary agreements of cooperation between firms.[2] As noted in Chapter 6, the dotted area in Figure 6.3 consisting of non-equity-based contractual agreements and equity-based joint ventures (JVs) can all be broadly considered strategic alliances. Figure 7.1 illustrates this further, visualizing alliances as a *compromise* between pure market transactions and mergers and acquisitions (M&As). **Contractual (non-equity-based) alliances** include co-marketing, research and development (R&D) contracts, turnkey projects, strategic suppliers, strategic distributors, and licensing/franchising. **Equity-based alliances** include **strategic investment** (one partner invests in another), **cross-shareholding** (both partners invest in each other), and JV. A JV is one form of equity-based alliance. It involves the establishment of a new legally independent entity (in other words, a new firm) whose equity is provided by two (or more) partners (see the Closing Case).

Strategic networks are strategic alliances formed by *multiple* firms to compete against other such groups and against traditional single firms.[3] For example, the airline industry has three multipartner alliances—Star Alliance (consisting of United Airlines, Lufthansa, Air Canada, SAS, and others), SkyTeam (Delta Airlines, Air France-KLM, Korean Air, and others), and Oneworld (American Airlines, British Airways, Cathay Pacific, Qantas, Japan Airlines, and others). These strategic networks are sometimes called **constellations**. Shown in Strategy in Action 7.1, such multilateral strategic networks are inherently more complex than single alliance relationships between two firms.[4] Overall, we will use the terms "strategic alliances" and "strategic networks" to refer to cooperative interfirm relationships.

strategic alliance
A voluntary agreement of cooperation between firms

contractual (non-equity-based) alliance
A strategic alliance that is based on contracts and does not involve the sharing of ownership

equity-based alliance
A strategic alliance that involves the use of equity.

strategic investment
One partner invests in another as a strategic investor.

cross-shareholding
Both partners invest in each other to become cross-shareholders.

strategic network
A strategic alliance formed by multiple firms to compete against other such groups and against traditional single firms (also known as a constellation).

constellation
A multipartner strategic alliance (also known as strategic network).

FIGURE 7.1   The Variety of Strategic Alliances

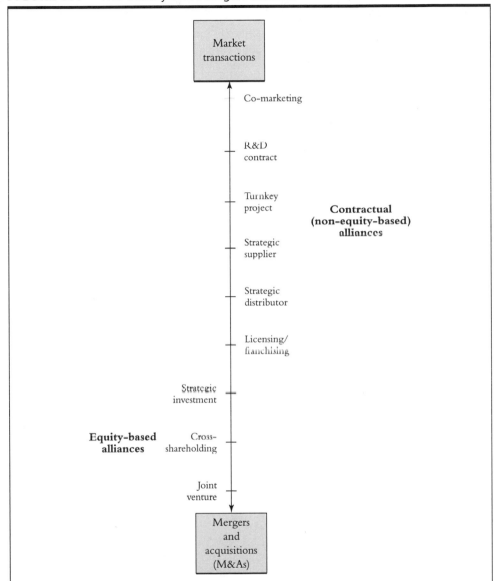

A Comprehensive Model of Strategic Alliances and Networks

Despite the diversity of cooperative interfirm relationships, underlying each decision to engage in alliances and networks is a set of strategic considerations drawn from the strategy tripod discussed earlier. These considerations lead to a comprehensive model (Figure 7.2).

STRATEGY IN ACTION 7.1

The Tug of War Over Japan Airlines

Since 2000, the skies of the world have been dominated by three global airline alliances: Oneworld (American Airlines [AA], British Airways, Cathay Pacific, Qantas, Japan Airlines [JAL], and others); SkyTeam (Delta, Air France-KLM, Korean Air, and others); and Star Alliance (United, Lufthansa, Air Canada, SAS, and others). While the high drama of switching alliance memberships did take place for smaller airlines, the tug of war between Oneworld (led by AA) and SkyTeam (led by Delta) to fight over JAL's loyalty was probably the most dramatic.

The largest Asian carrier by revenue, JAL had been battered by a severe drop in passenger traffic in the aftermath of the 2008 global crisis, huge pension obligations, an aging fleet, and dozens of unprofitable routes. JAL filed for bankruptcy under the Corporate Rehabilitation Law (the Japanese equivalent of a US Chapter 11 bankruptcy filing) in January 2010, and its shares were delisted in February 2010. Positioning as "white knights," Delta and its SkyTeam partners proposed that they be strategic investors in JAL and put $1 billion on the table—the catch was that JAL would need to defect from its existing Oneworld alliance relationship. Why were Delta and its partners trying to get involved with an airline that appeared to head for a crash landing?

Although saddled with debt, JAL was attractive because of its strong position in the Asia Pacific, whose air traffic growth would far outpace the rest of the world. Japanese government officials were pushing JAL to accept Delta's (and SkyTeam's) offer, primarily because SkyTeam was a larger (and thus financially less risky) alliance. In 2010, SkyTeam flew 384 million passengers, while Oneworld flew 333 million (including JAL's 53 million). In response, AA and its Oneworld partners coughed up $1.4

billion to rescue the desperate JAL. While highlighting the $500 million JAL had benefitted annually from its Oneworld alliance, AA pointed out that of the $1 billion Delta and its partners offered, a sizable chunk would be used to pay for the financial penalty for leaving Oneworld. Therefore, the bang for the buck was actually much less than $1 billion. After intense negotiations, JAL announced that it would stay loyal to AA and Oneworld. "The biggest reason for our decision to strengthen our alliance with American is to avoid inconvenience to our customers as much as we can," announced a JAL executive. Although the $1.4 billion that AA and its partners offered was never mentioned in the announcement, everybody knew that money talks.

Thanks in part to the cash injection from AA and its partners, JAL emerged from bankruptcy protection in March 2011. Unfortunately, in part because of such lavish expenditure, AA itself entered Chapter 11 bankruptcy reorganization in November 2011. There were no reports about JAL coming to AA's rescue.

Sources: Based on (1) CBC News, 2010, Japan Airlines chooses American over Delta, February 9, www.cbc.ca; (2) *Financial Times*, 2010, Tokyo rejects external funding for JAL, January 10, cachef.ft.com; (3) *New York Times*, 2009, Dueling alliances make aid offers to Japan Airlines, November 18, www.nytimes.com.

Industry-Based Considerations

According to the traditional industry-based view, firms are independent players interested in maximizing their own performance. In reality, most firms in any industry are embedded in a number of competitive and/or collaborative relationships, thus

FIGURE 7.2 A Comprehensive Model of Strategic Alliances and Networks

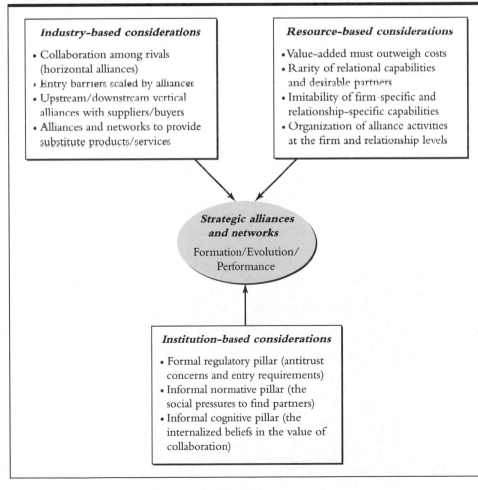

© Cengage Learning

necessitating considerations of their alliance and network ties if we are going to realistically understand the dynamics of the five forces.[5]

horizontal alliance
A strategic alliance formed by competitors.

First, because rivalry reduces profits, many competitors collaborate by forming strategic alliances (often called **horizontal alliances**).[6] For example, BMW and Mercedes are collaborating on green car technology. Pfizer and GSK have pooled HIV/AIDS assets to create ViiV Healthcare, a specialized company focusing on HIV/AIDS drugs. This does not suggest that these pairs of rivals (BMW/Mercedes and Pfizer/GSK) are no longer competing; they still are, in most cases. What is interesting is that they have decided to collaborate on a limited basis.

Second, while high entry barriers may deter individual firms, firms may form strategic alliances to scale these walls. For instance, both Coca-Cola and Nestlé were interested in entering the hot canned drinks market (such as hot coffee and tea) in Japan. However, domestic players led by Suntory built formidable entry barriers and neither Coca-Cola nor Nestlé, despite their global experience, had any expertise in this particular segment largely unknown outside of Japan. Although Suntory was better than Coca-Cola at soluble coffee and tea and had a larger distribution network than Nestlé, Suntory was unable to match the combined strengths of these two giants once they formed an alliance. Overall, combining forces allows for lower cost and lower risk entries into new markets for partner firms.

upstream vertical alliance
A strategic alliance with firms on the supply side (upstream).

Third, although suppliers in the five forces framework are traditionally regarded as a threat, that is not necessarily the case. As introduced in Chapter 2, it is possible to establish strategic alliances with suppliers (often called **upstream vertical alliances**), as exemplified by the Japanese *keiretsu* networks. In essence, strategic supply alliances transform the relationship from an adversarial one centered on hard bargaining to a collaborative one featuring knowledge sharing and mutual assistance. Instead of dealing with a large number of suppliers that are awarded contracts on a frequent short-term basis (such as 2.3 years, the average length of US auto supply contracts in the 1990s), strategic supply alliances rely on a smaller number of key suppliers that are awarded longer-term contracts (such as 8 years, the average length of Japanese auto supply contracts in the 1990s).[7] This helps align the interests of the focal firm with those of suppliers, which, in turn, are more willing to make specialized investments to produce better components. This is not to say that bargaining power becomes irrelevant. Instead, buyer firms increase their dependence on a smaller number of strategic suppliers, whose bargaining power may, in turn, *increase*. However, collaboration softens some rough edges of bargaining power by transforming a zero-sum game into a win-win proposition.

downstream vertical alliance
A strategic alliance with firms in distribution (downstream).

Fourth, similarly, instead of treating buyers and distributors as a possible threat, establishing strategic distribution alliances (also called **downstream vertical alliances**) may bind the focal firm and buyers and distributors together. For example, numerous hotels, publishers, airlines, and car rental companies find that alliances with leading Internet distributors such as Amazon, Expedia, Priceline, and Travelocity enable them to reach more customers.

Finally, the market potential of substitute products may encourage firms to form strategic alliances and networks to materialize the commercial potential of these new products. For instance, smartphones developed by the Android alliance centered on Google and its partners such as HTC and Samsung have now substituted some personal computers (PC).

Resource-Based Considerations

The resource-based view, embodied in the VRIO framework, sheds considerable light on strategic alliances and networks (Figure 7.2).[8]

VALUE. Alliances must create value.[9] The three global airline alliance networks create value by reducing 18%–28% of the ticket costs booked on two-stage flights compared with separate flights on the same route if these airlines were not allied.[10] Table 7.1 identifies three broad categories of value creation in terms of how advantages outweigh disadvantages. First, alliances may reduce costs, risks, and uncertainties.[11] As Google rises to preeminence, Microsoft for its Bing search engine has set up alliances with Baidu, Facebook, Firefox/Mozilla, Nokia, RIM, and Yahoo!. Second, alliances allow firms such as McDonald's, Yum! Brands, and Sinopec to tap into complementary assets of partners and facilitate learning (see the Opening Case).[12] In another case, when Renault entered Turkey via a JV, its Turkish partner that held 49% of the JV was Oyak (Turkish Armed Forces Pension Fund).[13] What complementary resources would Oyak bring to this JV that manufactured cars? In addition to capital, political connections in a country where the military enjoyed a good deal of prestige were clearly helpful.

Finally, an important advantage of alliances lies in their value as real options.[14] Conceptually, an option is the right, but not the obligation, to take some action in the future. Technically, a financial option is an investment instrument permitting its holder, having paid for a small fraction of an asset (often known as a deposit), the right to increase investment to eventually acquire it if necessary. A **real option** is an investment in real operations as opposed to financial capital.[15] A real options view has two propositions:

real option

An option investment in real operations as opposed to financial capital.

- In the first phase, an investor makes a relatively small, initial investment to buy an option, which leads to the right to future investment without being obligated to do so.

- The investor holds the option until a decision point arrives in the second phase, and then decides between exercising the option or abandoning it.

TABLE 7.1 Strategic Alliances and Networks: Advantages and Disadvantages

ADVANTAGES	DISADVANTAGES
■ Reduce costs, risks, and uncertainties	■ Possibilities of choosing the wrong partners
■ Gain access to complementary assets	■ Costs of negotiation and coordination
■ Opportunities to learn from partners	■ Possibilities of partner opportunism
■ Possibilities to use alliances and networks as real options	■ Risks of helping nurture competitors (learning race)

© Cengage Learning

For firms interested in eventually acquiring other companies but not sure about such moves, working together in alliances thus affords an insider view to evaluate the capabilities of partners. This is similar to trying on new shoes to see if they fit before buying them.[16] Since acquisitions are not only costly but also very likely to fail, alliances permit firms to *sequentially* increase their investment should they decide to pursue acquisitions. On the other hand, after working together as partners, if firms find that acquisitions are not a good idea, there is no obligation to pursue them. Overall, alliances have emerged as great instruments of real options because of their flexibility to sequentially scale *up* or scale *down* the investment.

On the other hand, alliances have a number of nontrivial drawbacks. First, there is always a possibility of being stuck with the wrong partner(s).[17] Firms are advised to choose a prospective mate with caution. The mate should be sufficiently differentiated to provide some complementary (non-overlapping) capabilities.[18] Just like many individuals who have a hard time figuring out the true colors of their spouses before they get married, many firms find it difficult to evaluate the true intentions and capabilities of their prospective partners until it is too late.

A second disadvantage is potential partner opportunism. While opportunism is likely in any kind of economic relationship, the alliance setting may provide especially strong incentives for some (but not all) partners to be opportunistic. Cooperative relationships always entail some elements of trust, which may be easily abused.[19] For example, BP's JV partners in Russia alleged that BP treated them not as equal partners, but as lowly subjects (see Emerging Markets 7.1 and the Closing Case).

Finally, alliances, especially those between rivals, can be dangerous, because they may help competitors. By opening "doors" to outsiders, alliances make it *easier* to observe and imitate firm-specific capabilities. In alliances between competitors, there is a potential "**learning race**" in which partners aim to outrun each other by learning the "tricks" from the other side as fast as possible.

RARITY. The second component in the VRIO framework has two dimensions: (1) capability rarity and (2) partner rarity. First, the capabilities to successfully manage interfirm relationships—often called **relational** (or **collaborative**) **capabilities**—may be rare. Managers involved in alliances require relationship skills rarely covered in the traditional business school curriculum that emphasizes competition as opposed to collaboration.[20] To truly derive benefits from alliances, managers need to foster trust with partners, while at the same time being on guard against opportunism.[21]

As much as alliances represent a strategic and economic arrangement, they also constitute a social, psychological, and emotional phenomenon: words such as "courtship," "marriage," and "divorce" often surface. Given that the interests of partner firms do not fully overlap and are often in conflict, managers involved in alliances live a precarious existence, trying to represent the interests of their respective firms while attempting to make the complex relationship work. Given the general shortage of good relationship skills in the human population (remember: 50% of marriages in the United States fail), it is not surprising that sound relational capabilities to successfully manage alliances are in short supply.

A second aspect of rarity is **partner rarity**, defined as the difficulty to locate partners with certain desirable attributes. This stems from two sources: (1) industry structure and

learning race

A race in which alliance partners aim to outrun each other by learning the "tricks" from the other side as fast as possible.

relational (collaborative) capabilities

The capabilities to successfully manage interfirm relationships.

partner rarity

The difficulty to locate partners with certain desirable attributes.

EMERGING MARKETS 7.1 > > ETHICAL DILEMMA

A Local Partner's Perspective: "BP Has Been Treating Russians as Subjects"

The following are excerpts from an article published in London's *Financial Times* on July 7, 2008, by Mikhail Fridman, chairman of the board of TNK-BP and founder of Alfa Group, which owns 25% of TNK-BP.

- We see a long-term future for the joint venture and have no intention of selling out of a business with great prospects.

- We want to build TNK-BP into a great international oil business.

- But we can only do this if BP treats us as its partners, not its subjects.

Source: M. Fridman, 2008, BP has been treating Russians as subjects, *Financial Times*, July 7: 11. © Financial Times

network centrality

The extent to which a firm's position is pivotal with respect to others in the interfirm network.

(2) network position. First, from an *industry structure* standpoint, in many oligopolistic industries, the number of available players as potential partners is limited. In some emerging economies whereby only a few local firms may be worthy partners, latecomers may find that potential partners have already been "cherry picked" by rivals. In the Chinese automobile industry (where wholly owned subsidiaries [WOS] are not allowed), Ford, as a late mover, ended up allying with second-tier partners in China and suffered from mediocre performance.

Second, from a *network position* perspective, firms located in the center of interfirm networks may have access to better and more opportunities (such as information, access, capital, goods, and services) and consequently may accumulate more power and influence.[22] The upshot is that firms with a high degree of **network centrality**—defined as the extent to which the position occupied by a firm is pivotal with respect to others in the interfirm network—are likely to be more attractive partners. Unfortunately, such firms are rare, and they are often very choosy in the kind of relationships they enter. Cisco, Citigroup, and Carrefour, for example, routinely turn down alliance proposals coming from all over the globe.

IMITABILITY. The issue of imitability pertains to two levels: (1) firm level and (2) alliance level. First, as noted earlier, one firm's resources and capabilities may be imitated by partners. For instance, in the late 1980s, McDonald's set up a JV with the Moscow Municipality Government that helped it enter Russia. However, during the 1990s, the Moscow mayor set up a rival fast food chain, The Bistro. The Bistro tried to eat McDonald's' lunch by replicating numerous products and practices. There was very little that McDonald's could do, because nobody sues the mayor in Moscow and hopes to win.

Another imitability issue refers to the trust and understanding among partners in successful alliances. Firms without such "chemistry" may have a hard time imitating such activities. CFM International, a JV set up by GE and Snecma to produce jet engines in France, has successfully operated for over 30 years. Rivals would have a hard time imitating such a successful relationship.

ORGANIZATION. Similarly, the organizational issues affect two levels: (1) firm level and (2) alliance/network level. First, at the firm level, how firms are organized to benefit from alliances and networks is an important issue.[23] When the number of such relationships is small, many firms adopt a trial-and-error approach. Not surprisingly, "misses" are often frequent. What is problematic is that even for the successful "hits," this ad hoc approach does not allow for systematic learning from these experiences. This obviously is a hazardous way of organizing for large MNEs engaging in numerous alliances and networks around the globe. In response, many firms have been developing a dedicated alliance function (parallel with traditional functions such as finance and marketing), often headed by a vice president or director with his/her own staff and resources. Such a dedicated function acts as a focal point for leveraging lessons from prior and ongoing relationships. HP has developed a 300-page decision-making manual on alliances, including 60 different tools and templates (such as alliance contracts, metrics, and checklists). It also organizes a two-day course three times a year to disseminate such learning about alliances to its managers worldwide.

At the alliance/network level, some alliance relationships are organized in a way that makes it difficult for others to replicate. There is much truth behind Tolstoy's opening statement in *Anna Karenina*: "All happy families are like one another; each unhappy family is unhappy in its own way." Given the difficulty for individuals in unhappy marriages to improve their relationship (despite an army of professional marriage counselors, social workers, friends, and family members), it is not surprising that firms in unsuccessful alliances (for whatever reason) often find it exceedingly challenging, if not impossible, to organize and manage their interfirm relationships better.

Institution-Based Considerations

FORMAL INSTITUTIONS SUPPORTED BY A REGULATORY PILLAR. Strategic alliances and networks function within formal legal and regulatory frameworks.[24] The impact of these formal institutions can be found along two dimensions: (1) antitrust concerns and (2) entry mode requirements. First, many firms establish alliances with competitors. Cooperation between competitors is usually suspected of at least some tacit collusion by antitrust authorities (see Chapter 8). However, because integration within alliances is usually not as tight as acquisitions (which would eliminate one competitor), antitrust authorities are more likely to approve alliances as opposed to acquisitions.[25] For instance, the proposed merger between American Airlines and British Airways was blocked by both US and UK antitrust authorities. However, they have been allowed to form an alliance that has eventually grown to become the multipartner Oneworld. In another example, the proposed merger between AT&T and T-Mobile (a WOS of Deutsche Telekom in the United States) was torpedoed by the US antitrust authorities. But the US government *blessed* AT&T and T-Mobile's collaboration in roaming.

Second, formal requirements on market entry modes affect alliances and networks. In many countries, governments discourage or simply ban acquisitions to establish WOS, thereby leaving some sort of alliances with local firms to be the only entry choice for FDI. For instance, the Indian government dictates the maximum ceiling of foreign firms' equity position in the retail sector to be 51%, forcing foreign entrants to set up alliances such as JVs with local firms. For example, Wal-Mart formed a 50/50 JV with Bharti—Bharti Wal-Mart Private Limited.

Recently, two characteristics have arisen concerning formal government policies on entry mode requirements. First is the general trend toward more liberal policies. Many governments (such as those in Mexico and South Korea) that historically only approved JVs have now allowed WOS as an entry mode. As a result, there is now a noticeable decline of JVs and a corresponding rise of acquisitions in emerging economies.[26] A second characteristic is that many governments still impose considerable requirements, especially when foreign firms acquire domestic assets. Only JVs are permitted in the strategically important Chinese automobile assembly industry and the Russian oil industry (see the Closing Case), thus eliminating acquisitions as a choice. US regulations only permit up to 25% of the equity of any US airline to be held by foreign carriers, and EU regulations limit non-EU ownership to 49% of EU-based airlines.

INFORMAL INSTITUTIONS SUPPORTED BY NORMATIVE AND COGNITIVE PILLARS. The first set of informal institutions centers on collective norms, supported by a normative pillar. A core idea of the institution-based view is that because firms act to enhance or protect their legitimacy, copying other reputable organizations—even without knowing the direct performance benefits of doing so—may be a low-cost way to gain legitimacy. Therefore, when competitors have a variety of alliances, jumping on the alliance "bandwagon" may be perceived as a cool way to join the norm as opposed to ignoring industry trends.[27] In other words, informal but powerful normative pressures from the business press, investment community, and board deliberations probably drove late-mover firms such as Ford to ally with relatively obscure partners in China (discussed earlier) as opposed to having no partner and hence no presence there. For the same reason unmarried adults tend to experience some social pressure to get married, firms insisting on "going alone," especially when they experience performance problems, often confront similar pressures and criticisms from peers, analysts, investors, and the media. The flipside of such a behavior is that many firms rush into interfirm relationships without adequate **due diligence** (investigation prior to signing contracts) and then get burned.

A second set of informal institutions stresses the cognitive pillar, which centers on the internalized taken-for-granted values and beliefs that guide firm behavior. BAE Systems (formerly British Aerospace) announced in the 1990s that *all* its future aircraft

due diligence
Investigation prior to signing contracts

development programs would involve alliances, evidently believing that an alliance strategy was the right thing to do.

Overall, both of the two core propositions that underpin the institution-based view (first introduced in Chapter 4) are applicable. The first proposition—individuals and firms rationally pursue their interests and make strategic choices within institutional constraints—is illustrated by the constraining and enabling power of the formal regulatory pillar, the informal but powerful normative pillar, and the internalized but evident cognitive pillar. The second proposition—when formal constraints fail, informal constraints may play a larger role—is also evident. Similar to the institutions governing human marriages, formal regulations and contracts can only govern a small (although important) portion of alliance/network behavior, and the success and failure of such relationships, to a large degree, depend on the day-in-day-out interaction between partners influenced by informal norms and cognitions. This point will be expanded in more detail in the next three sections on the formation, evolution, and performance of strategic alliances and networks.

Formation

How are alliances formed? Figure 7.3 illustrates a three-stage model to address this question.[28]

Stage One: To Cooperate or Not to Cooperate?

In Stage One, a firm must decide if growth can be achieved strictly through market transactions, acquisitions, or alliances.[29] To grow by pure market transactions, the firm has to confront competitive challenges independently. This is highly demanding, even for resource-rich multinationals. As noted earlier in the chapter, acquisitions have some unique drawbacks, leading many managers to conclude that alliances are the way to go. For example, Dallas-based Sabre Travel Network has used alliances to enter Australia, Bahrain, India, Israel, Japan, and Singapore.

Stage Two: Contract or Equity?

In Stage Two, a firm must decide whether to take a contract or an equity approach. As noted in Chapter 6, the choice between contract and equity is crucial. Table 7.2 identifies four driving forces. The first driving force is shared capabilities. The more tacit (that is, hard to describe and codify) the capabilities, the greater the preference for equity involvement. Although not the only way, the most effective way to learn *complex* processes is through **learning by doing.** A good example of this is learning to cook by actually cooking and not by simply reading cookbooks. Many business processes are the same way. A firm that wants to produce cars will find that the codified knowledge in books or reports is not enough. Much tacit knowledge can only be acquired via learning by doing, preferably with experts as alliance partners.

learning by doing
A way of learning not by reading books but by engaging in hands-on activities.

FIGURE 7.3   Alliance Formation

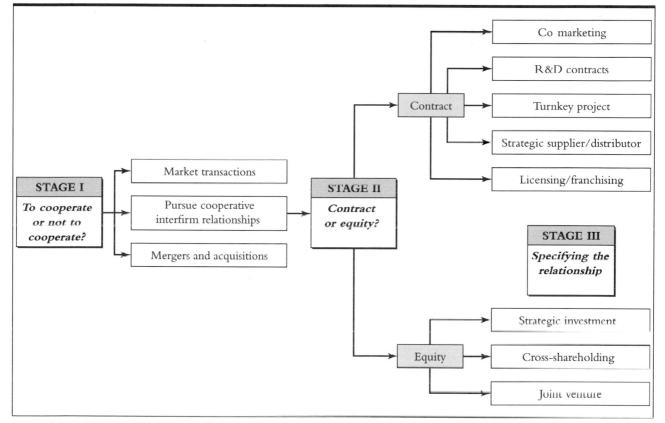

Source: Adapted from S. Tallman & O. Shenkar, 1994, A managerial decision model of international cooperative venture formation (p. 101), *Journal of International Business Studies,* 25(1): 91–113.

A second driving force is the importance of direct monitoring and control. Equity relationships allow firms to have some direct control over joint activities on a continuing basis, whereas contractual relationships usually do not. In general, firms that fear their intellectual property may be expropriated prefer equity alliances (and a higher level of equity).

A third driver is real options thinking. Some firms prefer to first establish contractual relationships, which can be viewed as real options (or stepping stones) for possible upgrading into equity alliances should the interactions turn out to be mutually satisfactory.

Finally, the choice between contract and equity also boils down to institutional constraints. As noted earlier, some governments eager to help domestic firms climb the technology ladder either require or encourage the formation of JVs between foreign and domestic firms. The Chinese auto industry is a case in point.

TABLE 7.2   Equity-Based versus Non-Equity-Based Strategic Alliances and Networks

DRIVING FORCES	EQUITY-BASED ALLIANCES/NETWORKS	NON-EQUITY-BASED ALLIANCES/NETWORKS
Nature of shared resources (degree of tacitness and complexity)	High	Low
Importance of direct organizational monitoring and control	High	Low
Potential as real options	High (for possible upgrading to M&As)	High (for possible upgrading to equity-based relationships)
Influence of formal institutions	High (when required or encouraged by regulations)	High (when required or encouraged by regulations)

© Cengage Learning

Stage Three: Positioning the Relationship

Although the formation of strategic alliances has historically been assumed to be between two partners, the proliferation of interfirm relationships suggests that such thinking needs to be expanded. Given that each firm is likely to have multiple interfirm relationships, it is important to manage them as a corporate *portfolio* (or network) (see Table 7.3). The combination of several individually "optimal" relationships may not create an optimal relationship portfolio for the entire firm, in light of some tricky alliances with competitors.[30] In a world of multilateral intrigues, one step down the alliance path, which may open some doors, may foreclose other opportunities. In other words, "my friend's enemy is my enemy, and my enemy's enemy is my friend." Thus, to prevent an "alliance gridlock," carefully assessing the impact of each individual relationship *prior to its formation* on the firm's other relationships becomes increasingly important (see the Opening Case and the Closing Case).

TABLE 7.3   Cisco's Top Strategic Alliance Partners

Platform companies	HP, IBM, Intel, EMC, Microsoft, SAP
Telecom solutions companies	Fujitsu, Italtel, Motorola, Nokia, Nokia Siemens Networks
Services companies	Accenture, Bearing Point, Capgemini, EDS, Wipro

Source: www.cisco.com

Evolution

All relationships evolve—some grow, others fail.[31] This section deals with three aspects: (1) combating opportunism, (2) evolving from strong ties to weak ties, and (3) going through a divorce.

Combating Opportunism

The threat of opportunism looms large on the horizon. Most firms want to make their relationship work, but also want to protect themselves in case the other side is opportunistic (see the Closing Case).[32] While it is difficult to completely eliminate opportunism, it is possible to minimize its threat by (1) walling off critical capabilities or (2) swapping critical capabilities through credible commitments.

First, both sides can contractually agree to wall off critical skills and technologies not meant to be shared. For example, GE and Snecma cooperated to build jet engines, yet GE was not willing to share its proprietary technology fully with Snecma. GE thus presented sealed "black box" components (the inside of which Snecma had no access to), while permitting Snecma access to final assembly. This type of relationship, in human marriage terms, is like couples whose premarital assets are protected by prenuptial agreements. As long as both sides are willing to live with these deals, these relationships can prosper.

The second approach, swapping skills and technologies, is the exact *opposite* of the first approach. Both sides not only agree not to hold critical skills and technologies back, but also make credible commitments to hold each other as a "hostage."[33] Motorola, for instance, licensed its microprocessor technology to Toshiba, which, in turn, licensed its memory chip technology to Motorola. Setting up a reciprocal relationship may increase the incentives for both partners to cooperate.

In human marriage terms, mutual "hostage taking" is similar to the following commitment: "Honey, I will love you forever. If I betray you, feel free to kill me. But if you dare to betray me, I'll cut your head off!" To think slightly outside the box, the precarious peace during the Cold War can be regarded as a case of mutual "hostage taking" that worked. Because both the United States and Soviet Union held each other as a "hostage," nobody dared to launch a first nuclear strike. As long as the victim of the first strike had only *one* nuclear ballistic missile submarine left (such as the American Ohio class or the Soviet Typhoon class), this single submarine would have enough retaliatory firepower to wipe the top 20 US or Soviet cities off the surface of earth, an outcome that neither of the two superpowers found acceptable (see the movie *The Hunt for Red October*). The Cold War did not turn hot in part because of such a "mutually assured destruction" (MAD) strategy—a real military jargon.

Evolving from Strong Ties to Weak Ties

First introduced in Chapter 5, strong ties are more durable, reliable, and trustworthy relationships cultivated over a long period of time. Strong ties have two advantages:

- Strong ties are associated with the exchange of finer-grained and higher-quality information.

- Strong ties serve as an informal social-control mechanism that is an alternative to formal contracts and thus act to combat opportunism. It is not surprising that many strategic alliances and networks are initially built upon strong ties among individuals and firms.

Defined as relationships characterized by infrequent interaction and low intimacy, weak ties, paradoxically, are likely to provide more opportunities. Weak ties enjoy two advantages:

- Weak ties are less costly (requiring less time, energy, and money) to maintain.

- Weak ties excel at connecting with distant others possessing unique and novel information for strategic actions—often regarded as the *strength* of weak ties. This may be especially critical as firms search for new knowledge for cutting-edge technologies and practices.

In the same way that individuals tend to have a combination of a small number of good friends (strong ties) and a large number of acquaintances (weak ties), firms at any given point in time are likely to have a combination of strong ties and weak ties in their interfirm relationships. Both strong and weak ties are beneficial, but under different conditions. One of the conditions influencing the types of advantages that firms require is the degree to which their strategies are designed to *exploit* current resources (such as existing connections) or *explore* new opportunities (such as future technologies).

Of particular interest to us is the distinction between "exploitation" and "exploration" noted by James March, a leading organization theorist. **Exploitation** refers to "such things as refinement, choice, production, efficiency, selection, and execution," whereas **exploration** includes "things captured by terms such as search, variation, risk taking, experimentation, play, flexibility, discovery, and innovation."[34] While both kinds of strategic activities are important and often occur simultaneously, there is a trade-off between the two because of the limited resources firms possess.[35] Thus, an *emphasis* on either set of the ties is often necessary during a particular period. In environments conducive for exploitation, strong ties may be more beneficial. Conversely, in environments suitable for exploration, weak ties may be preferred.

Many strong ties evolve to become weak ties. Examples from two contexts illustrate these dynamics. First, a new start-up often first concentrates on dense strong ties because it seeks to exploit the current external networks of the founding entrepreneur(s) to ensure its survival. In the next phase, having largely exploited (and exhausted) the initial set of opportunities, the firm needs to search for new opportunities. Therefore, it shifts to exploration in order to seek new opportunities, thus calling for more weak ties with greater diversity. Amazon's changing alliance portfolio is indicative of such evolution. Initially, Amazon established strong ties with a few key publishing and distributing firms. As Amazon expanded to cover new products (toys and CDs) and new business models (auctions), it formed numerous weak ties with a variety of large suppliers, small merchants, and auction houses.

A second example is a JV formed by two partners. Over time as the initial set of opportunities are exploited and exhausted by the JV, partners, as they embark on new searches, may prefer to establish some weak-ties-based relationships with a diverse set of players. In other words, the strong ties within the JV may become too limiting. However, original partners will naturally become upset. In a human marriage, it is easy to appreciate

exploitation

Actions captured by terms such as refinement, choice, production, efficiency, selection, and execution.

exploration

Actions captured by terms such as search, variation, risk taking, experimentation, play, flexibility, discovery, and innovation.

the fury of one spouse when the other spouse is exploring other relationships (although only weak ties!). In the case of the BP-AAR dispute over TNK-BP, AAR was upset by the "extramarital" relationship that BP developed with Rosneft in a new alliance (see the Closing Case).

From Corporate Marriage to Divorce[36]

Alliances are often described as corporate marriages and, when terminated, as corporate divorces. Figure 7.4 portrays an alliance dissolution model. To apply the metaphor of divorce, we focus on the two-partner alliance. Following the convention in research on human divorce, the party who begins the process of ending the alliance is labeled the initiator, while the other party is termed the partner—for lack of a better word. We will draw on our Closing Case to explain this process.

The first phase is initiation. The process begins when the initiator starts feeling uncomfortable with the alliance (for whatever reason). Wavering begins as a quiet, unilateral process by the initiator, which seemed to be AAR in this case. After repeated requests to modify BP's behavior failed, AAR began to escalate its demands. At this point, its display of discontent became bolder. Initially, BP, the partner, may simply not "get it." The initiator's "sudden" dissatisfaction may confuse the partner. Thus, initiation tends to escalate.

FIGURE 7.4   Alliance Dissolution

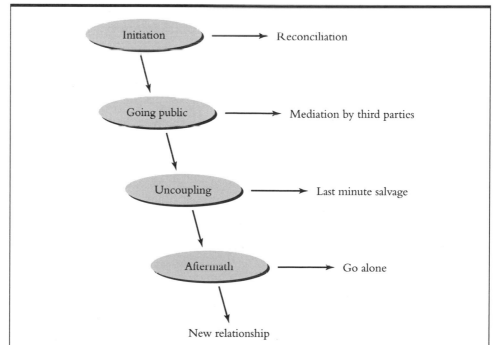

Source: Adapted from M. W. Peng & O. Shenkar, 2002, Joint venture dissolution as corporate divorce (p. 95), *Academy of Management Executive*, 16(2): 92–105.

The second phase is going public. The party that breaks the news first has a first-mover advantage. By presenting a socially acceptable reason in favor of its cause, this party is able to win sympathy from key stakeholders, such as parent company executives, investors, and journalists. Not surprisingly, the initiator is likely to go public first. Alternatively, the partner may pre-empt by blaming the initiator and establishing the righteousness of its position—this was exactly what BP did. Eventually, both AAR and BP were eager to publicly air their grievances (see Emerging Markets 7.1).

The third phase is uncoupling. Like human divorce, alliance dissolution can be friendly or hostile. In uncontested divorces, both sides attribute the separation more on, say, a change in circumstances. For example, Eli Lilly and Ranbaxy phased out their JV in India and remained friendly with each other. In contrast, contested divorces involve a party that accuses another. The worst scenario is "death by a thousand cuts" inflicted by one party at every turn. A case in point is the numerous lawsuits and arbitrations filed in many countries (such as the British Virgin Islands, China, France, Italy, and the United States) by Danone and Wahaha accusing each other of wrongdoing.

The last phase is aftermath. Like most divorced individuals, most (but not all) "divorced" firms are likely to search for new partners. Understandably, the new alliance is often negotiated more extensively.[37] One Italian executive reportedly signed *each* of the 2,000 pages (!) of an alliance contract.[38] However, excessive formalization may signal a lack of trust—in the same way that prenuptials may scare away some prospective human marriage partners.

Figure 7.4 illustrates that for every phase of the dissolution process, there is a way out. In the case of the BP-AAR dispute over TNK-BP, while both sides went public to accuse each other, they managed to stay "married" and did not dissolve their important alliance relationship (see the Closing Case).

Performance

Performance is a central focus for strategic alliances and networks.[39] This section discusses (1) the performance of alliances and networks and (2) the performance of parent firms.

The Performance of Strategic Alliances and Networks

Although managers naturally focus on alliance performance, opinions vary on how to measure it.[40] Table 7.4 shows that a combination of objective measures (such as profit and market share) and subjective measures (such as managerial satisfaction) can be used. Figure 7.5 illustrates four factors that may influence alliance performance: (1) equity, (2) learning and experience, (3) nationality, and (4) relational capabilities.

First, the level of equity may be crucial in how an alliance performs. A greater equity stake may mean that a firm is more committed, which is likely to result in higher performance. Second, whether firms have successfully learned from partners is important when assessing alliance performance. Since learning is abstract, experience is often used as a proxy because it is relatively easy to measure.[41] While experience certainly helps, its impact on performance is not linear. There is a limit beyond which further increase in experience may not enhance performance.[42] Third, nationality may affect performance. For the same reason that marriages where both parties have similar backgrounds are more

TABLE 7.4 Alliance- and Network-Related Performance Measures

ALLIANCE/NETWORK LEVEL	PARENT FIRM LEVEL
Objective	*Objective*
■ Financial performance (e.g., profitability)	■ Financial performance (e.g., profitability)
■ Product market performance (e.g., market share)	■ Product market performance (e.g., market share)
■ Stability and longevity	■ Stock market reaction
Subjective	*Subjective*
■ Level of top management satisfaction	■ Assessment of goal attainment

© Cengage Learning

stable, dissimilarities in national culture may create strains in alliances. Not surprisingly, international alliances tend to have more problems than domestic ones (see the Closing Case). Finally, alliance performance may fundamentally boil down to soft, difficult-to-measure relational capabilities. The art of relational capabilities, which are firm specific and difficult to codify and transfer, may make or break alliances.

However, none of these factors asserts an unambiguous, direct impact on performance.[43] Research has found that they may have some *correlations* with performance. It would be naïve to think that any of these single factors would guarantee success. It is their *combination* that jointly increases the odds for the success of strategic alliances.

The Performance of Parent Firms

Do parent firms benefit from strategic alliances and networks?[44] This goes back to the value-added aspect of these relationships (discussed earlier). Compared with the relative

FIGURE 7.5 What Is Behind Alliance Performance?

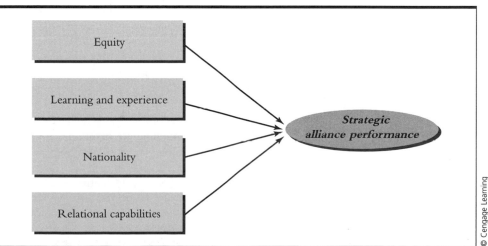

© Cengage Learning

lack of consensus on alliance/network performance, there has been some convergence on the benchmarks of firm performance (such as profitability, product market share, and stock market reaction), in addition to the more subjective measure of goal attainment as perceived by management (see Table 7.4).

A number of studies report that a higher level of collaboration and shared technology is associated with better profitability and product market share for parent firms.[45] Another group of studies focus on stock market reactions by treating each decision to enter or exit a relationship as an "event." If the event window is short enough (several days prior to and after the event), it is possible to view the "abnormal" stock returns as directly caused by that particular event. A number of such event studies indeed find that stock markets respond favorably to alliance activities, but only under certain circumstances, such as (1) complementarities of resources, (2) previous alliance experience, and (3) ability to manage host country political risks.[46] Overall, it is evident that strategic alliances and networks can create value for their parent firms, although how to make that happen remains a challenge.

Debates and Extensions

The rise of alliances and networks has generated a number of debates. Three of them are introduced here: (1) majority JVs as control mechanisms versus minority JVs as real options, (2) alliances versus acquisitions, and (3) acquiring versus not acquiring alliance partners.

Majority JVs as Control Mechanisms versus Minority JVs as Real Options

A long-standing debate focuses on the appropriate level of equity in JVs. While the logic of having a higher level of equity control in majority JVs is straightforward, its actual implementation is often problematic. Asserting one party's control rights, even when justified based on a majority equity position and stronger bargaining power, may irritate the other party. This is especially likely in international JVs in emerging economies, whereby local partners often resent the dominance of Western MNEs (see Emerging Markets 7.1). Some authors advocate a 50/50 share of management control even when the MNE has majority equity.[47] However, a 50/50 JV has its own headaches (see the Closing Case).

In addition to the usual benefits associated with being a minority partner in JVs (such as low cost and less demand on managerial resources and attention), an additional benefit alluded to earlier is exercising real options. In general, the more uncertain the conditions, the higher the value of real options. In highly uncertain but potentially promising industries and countries, M&As or majority JVs may be inadvisable, because the cost of failure may be tremendous. Therefore, minority JVs are recommended *toehold* investments, seen as possible stepping stones for future scaling up—if necessary—while not exposing partners too heavily to the risks involved.

Since the real options thinking is relatively new, its applicability is still being debated. While the real options logic is straightforward, its practice—when applied to acquisitions of JVs—is messy. This is because most JV contracts do not specify a previously agreed upon price for one party to acquire the other's assets. Most contracts only give the rights of first refusal to the parties, which agree to negotiate in "good faith." It is understandable that "neither party will be willing to buy the JV for more than or sell the JV for less than its own expectation of the venture's wealth generating potential."[48] As a result, how to reach an agreement on a "fair" price is tricky.

Alliances versus Acquisitions

An alternative to alliances is M&As (see Chapter 9). Many firms seem to pursue M&As and alliances in isolation. While many large MNEs have an M&A function and some have set up an alliance function (discussed earlier), few firms have established a combined "mergers, acquisitions, *and* alliance" function. In practice, it may be advisable to explicitly consider alliances vis-à-vis acquisitions within a single decision framework.[49] See Emerging Markets 7.2 for an example.

EMERGING MARKETS 7.2

Embraer's Alliances and Acquisitions

Embraer is a Brazilian manufacturer of small commercial and military aircraft. It was established in 1960 as a state-owned enterprise. It was privatized in 1994 with 60% of shares owned by private Brazilian interests (though the government retains a controlling "golden share"). It invested overseas prior to privatization (the United States in 1979, Europe in 1988) primarily to offer sales and technical support to customers in developed markets. However, after 1994—and especially in 1999—it entered into a series of strategic alliances with European groups such as EADS and Thales (France) in order to gain technology (and to reduce risk by pooling resources). Later it made acquisitions to ensure brand recognition in specialist aerospace markets. In 2004, it established a manufacturing affiliate in China (in which it owns a 51% stake), which assembles final aircraft for the Chinese and regional market. With 90% of its global sales overseas, Embraer can be regarded as one of Brazil's (indeed Latin America's) few truly global players.

Source: Excerpts from United Nations, 2006, *World Investment Report 2006: FDI from Developing and* *Transition Economies* (p. 159), New York and Geneva: United Nations/UN Conference on Trade and Development (UNCTAD). © United Nations, 2006.

TABLE 7.5 Alliances versus Acquisitions

	ALLIANCES	ACQUISITIONS
Resource interdependence	Low	High
Ratio of soft to hard assets	High	Low
Source of value creation	Combining complementary resources	Eliminating redundant resources
Level of uncertainty	High	Low

Source: Based on text in J. Dyer, P. Kale, & H. Singh, 2003, Do you know when to ally or acquire? Choosing between acquisitions and alliances, Working paper, Brigham Young University.

Shown in Table 7.5, alliances, which tend to be loosely coordinated among partners, do not work well in a setting that requires a high degree of interdependence. Such a setting would call for acquisitions. Alliances work well when the ratio of soft to hard assets is relatively high (such as a heavy concentration of tacit knowledge), whereas acquisitions may be preferred when such a ratio is low. Alliances create value primarily by combining complementary resources, whereas acquisitions derive most of their value by eliminating redundant resources. Finally, consistent with real options thinking, alliances are more suitable under conditions of uncertainty, and acquisitions are more preferred when the level of uncertainty is low.[50]

While these rules are not exactly "rocket science," "few companies are disciplined to adhere to them."[51] Consider the 50/50 JV between Coca-Cola (Coke) and Procter and Gamble (P&G) that combined their fruit drink businesses (such as Coke's Minute Maid and P&G's Sunny Delight) in 2001. The goal was to combine Coke's distribution system with P&G's R&D capabilities in consumer products. However, the stock market sent a mixed signal in response, pushing P&G's stock 2% *higher* and Coke's 6% *lower* on the day of the announcement. For three reasons, Coke probably could have done better by simply acquiring P&G's fruit drink business. First, a higher degree of integration would be necessary to derive the proposed synergies. Second, because Coke's distribution assets were relatively easy-to-value hard assets, while P&G's R&D capabilities were hard-to-value soft assets, the risk was higher for Coke. Finally, little uncertainty existed regarding the popularity of fruit drinks, so investors found it difficult to understand why Coke would share 50% of this fast-growing business with P&G, a laggard in the industry. Not surprisingly, the JV was quickly terminated within six months.

On the other hand, many M&As (such as DaimlerChrysler) would have probably been better off had the firms pursued alliances, at least initially. Overall, acquisitions may be overused as a first step to access resources in another firm, whereas alliances, guided by a real options logic, can provide a great deal of flexibility to scale up or scale down investments.

Acquiring versus Not Acquiring Alliance Partners

As noted earlier, alliance partners with a high degree of network centrality benefit from being centrally located in a network of players. One debate deals with whether such centrally located firms should acquire other more peripheral (less centrally located) and typically smaller alliance partners in the network. Recent comparative research involving US and Chinese firms reveals interesting contrasts. In the United States, centrally located firms in an alliance network seem to enjoy the benefits of high centrality and are not eager to acquire alliance partners—this finding is consistent with the predictions made from standard network theory.[52] However, in China, centrally located firms, to derive benefits from their high centrality, seem to more aggressively and more quickly acquire partners—this finding is *opposite* to standard predictions.[53]

Why are there such differences? Researchers speculate that due to the dynamic, fast-moving institutional transitions unfolding in China, any competitive advantage associated with high centrality is likely to erode very rapidly, prompting centrally located firms to quickly acquire alliance partners. In the United States, the pace of competitive dynamics is not as fast-moving, thus enabling some centrally located firms to enjoy the benefits and not having to acquire alliance partners.[54] In other words, if the real options logic is in play, it is played out over a longer period of time in the United States than in China.

In addition to Chinese firms, firms from other emerging economies such as Brazil and India also seem to have little patience and have often been found to indulge on a "buying binge" in acquiring alliance partners overseas. Used to their dynamic and fast-moving *domestic* competition, firms from emerging economies may be interested in aggressively and quickly acquiring partner firms *overseas*—out of fear that any competitive advantage associated with the acquisition moves may erode rapidly if they do not act quickly.[55]

Whether rapidly acquiring alliance partners results in better parent firm performance remains to be seen. Two lessons out of this debate are: (1) Alliance partner firms in developed economies need to get used to the more "rapid fire" acquisitions initiated by firms in emerging economies, and (2) firms from developed economies need to speed up their partner acquisition process when competing in emerging economies.[56]

The Savvy Strategist

Traditionally firm strategy is, by definition, about how a single firm strategizes and competes. Instead of concentrating on competition only, a new generation of strategists needs to be savvy at *both* competition and cooperation—in other words, "co-opetition."[57] For example, Google's CEO Eric Schmidt responded to a reporter who asked (in 2010, before Apple's CEO Steve Jobs passed away): "You no longer serve on the Apple board. It is said Steve Jobs got very upset with you, his friend. I didn't go into the search business, he said. Why are you going into the phone business?"

> *Apple is a company we both partner and compete with. We do a search deal with them, recently extended, and we're doing all sorts of things in maps and things like that. So the sum of all this is that two large corporations, both of which are important, both of which I care a lot about, will remain pretty close. But Android was around earlier than iPhone.*[58]

TABLE 7.6   Strategic Implications for Action

- ■ Improve relational (collaborative) capabilities crucial for the success of strategic alliances and networks.
- ■ Understand and master the rules of the game governing alliances and networks around the world.
- ■ Carefully weigh the pros and cons of alliances vis-à-vis those of acquisitions.

© Cengage Learning

The savvy strategist draws three important implications for action (Table 7.6). First, improving relational (collaborative) capabilities is crucial for the success of strategic alliances and networks. Given that excellent relational skills are rare among the population in general (think of the high divorce rates) and that the business school curriculum often emphasizes competition at the expense of collaboration, you need to work extra hard to be good at collaboration. The do's and don'ts in Table 7.7 will provide a useful start.

Second, you need to understand the rules of the game governing alliances and networks—both formal and informal—around the world. Formal rules dictating alliances to be the preferred mode of entry and banning WOS would make it necessary to embark on an alliance strategy, as Eli Lilly did when entering India in the 1990s. Over time, such rules have been relaxed and WOS allowed, thus enabling some reconsideration of Eli Lilly's JV strategy. Informal norms and values are also important. In the absence of a legal mandate for alliances, the norms for entering emerging economies used to be in favor of alliances (see the Opening and Closing Cases). However, the recent trend has moved toward phasing out alliances and establishing stronger controls over subsidiaries in emerging economies.

TABLE 7.7   Improving the Odds for Alliance Success

AREAS	DO'S AND DON'TS
Contract versus "chemistry"	No contract can cover all elements of the relationship. Relying on a detailed contract does not guarantee a successful relationship. It may indicate a lack of trust.
Warning signs	Identify symptoms of frequent criticism, defensiveness (always blaming others for problems), and stonewalling (withdrawal during a fight).
Invest in the relationship	Like married individuals working hard to invigorate their ties, alliances require continuous nurturing. Once a party starts to waver, it is difficult to turn back the dissolution process.
Conflict resolution mechanisms	"Good" married couples also fight. Their secret weapon is to find mechanisms to avoid unwarranted escalation of conflicts. Managers need to handle conflicts— inevitable in any alliance—in a credible, responsible, and controlled fashion.

Source: Based on text in M. W. Peng & O. Shenkar, 2002, Joint venture dissolution as corporate divorce (pp. 101–102), *Academy of Management Executive*, 16 (2): 92–105.

Third, you need to carefully weigh the pros and cons associated with alliances and acquisitions. Diving into alliances (or acquisitions) without considering the other option may be counterproductive, as Coca-Cola found out after it established a JV with P&G on fruit drinks. Considering alliances vis-à-vis acquisitions within an *integrated* decision framework may be necessary.

Overall, this chapter sheds considerable light on the four fundamental questions in strategy. The answers to Questions 1 (Why firms differ?) and 2 (How firms behave?) boil down to how different industry-based, resource-based, and institution-based considerations drive alliance and network actions. What determines the scope of the firm (Question 3)—or more specifically, the scope of the alliance in this context—can be found in the strategic goals behind these relationships. Some alliances may have a wide scope in anticipation of an eventual merger (such as the Renault–Nissan alliance), while other alliances may have a limited scope, keeping the partners fiercely competitive in other aspects (such as the GM–Toyota JV). Finally, the international success and failure of strategic alliances and networks (Question 4) are fundamentally determined by how firms develop, possess, and leverage "soft" relational capabilities when managing their interfirm relationships, in addition to "hard" assets such as technology and capital. In conclusion, there is no doubt that strategic alliances and networks are difficult to manage. But managing is hardly ever simple, whether managing external relationships or internal units.

CHAPTER SUMMARY

1. **Define strategic alliances and networks**
   - Strategic alliances are voluntary agreements of cooperation between firms.
   - Strategic networks are strategic alliances formed by multiple firms.

2. **Articulate a comprehensive model of strategic alliances and networks**
   - Industry-based, resource-based, and institution-based considerations form the backbone of a comprehensive model of strategic alliances and networks.

3. **Understand the decision processes behind the formation of alliances and networks**
   - Principal phases of alliance and network formation include (1) deciding whether to cooperate or not, (2) determining whether to pursue contractual or equity modes, and (3) positioning the particular relationship.

4. **Gain insights into the evolution of alliances and networks**
   - Three aspects of evolution highlighted are (1) combating opportunism, (2) evolving from strong ties to weak ties, and (3) turning from corporate marriages to divorces.

5. **Identify the drivers behind the performance of alliances and networks**
   - At the alliance/network level, (1) equity, (2) learning and experience, (3) nationality, and (4) rational capabilities are found to affect alliance and network performance.

6. **Participate in three leading debates concerning alliances and networks**
   - (1) Majority JVs as control mechanisms versus minority JVs as real options, (2) alliances versus acquisitions, and (3) acquiring versus not acquiring alliance partners.

7. *Draw strategic implications of action*
- Improve relational (collaborative) capabilities.
- Understand and master the rules of the game governing alliances and networks around the world.
- Carefully weigh the pros and cons of alliances vis-à-vis those of acquisitions.

KEY TERMS

Constellation p. 190

Contractual (non-equity-based) alliance p. 190

Cross-shareholding p. 190

Downstream vertical alliance p. 194

Due diligence p. 199

Equity-based alliance p. 190

Exploitation p. 204

Exploration p. 204

Horizontal alliance p. 194

Learning by doing p. 200

Learning race p. 196

Network centrality p. 197

Partner rarity p. 196

Real option p. 195

Relational (collaborative) capability p. 196

Strategic alliance p. 190

Strategic investment p. 190

Strategic network p. 190

Upstream vertical alliance p. 194

CRITICAL DISCUSSION QUESTIONS

1. Pick any recent announcement of the formation of an international alliance. Predict its likely success or failure.

2. *ON ETHICS:* During the courtship and negotiation stages, managers often emphasize "equal partnerships" and do not reveal (and try to hide) their true intentions. What are the ethical dilemmas here?

3. *ON ETHICS:* Some argue that engaging in a "learning race" is unethical. Others believe that a "learning race" is part and parcel of alliance relationships, especially those with competitors. What do you think?

TOPICS FOR EXPANDED PROJECTS

1. Some argue that at a 30%–70% failure rate (depending on different studies), strategic alliances and networks have a strikingly high failure rate and that firms need to scale down their alliance and network activities. Others suggest that this failure rate is not particularly higher than the failure rate of new entrepreneurial start-ups, internal corporate ventures, new products launched by single companies, and M&As. Therefore, such a failure rate is not of grave concern. Write a short paper describing how you would join this debate.

2. Working in pairs, find the longest-running alliance relationship your research can find. Present its secrets for such longevity in a short paper or visual presentation.

3. What are the similarities and differences between human marriages and interfirm alliances? How can the lessons behind the success and failure of human marriages enhance the odds of alliance success? State your answers in a short paper.

> ## CLOSING CASE   **ETHICAL DILEMMA**

Emerging Markets: BP, AAR, and TNK-BP
(also see Emerging Markets 7.1)

TNK-BP is a joint venture (JV) company that is 50% owned by BP and 50% owned by the AAR consortium, which represents three major Russian business groups: Alfa, Access, and Renova. Founded in 2003, TNK-BP is a major oil company in its own right. It is Russia's third largest oil producer and among the ten largest private oil companies in the world. Producing about 1.9 million barrels of oil per day, TNK-BP provides about 25% of BP's oil production and 40% of its reserves. It pays about $2 billion dividends each year to BP. Such a cash cow with huge reserves would seem to be—in the words of *Bloomberg Businessweek*—a "godsend." Unfortunately, TNK-BP has turned out to be an unending saga of headaches, conflicts, and intrigue between BP and its three Russian oligarch partners: Mikhail Fridman (founder of Alfa Group and chairman of the board of TNK-BP), Len Blavatnik (founder of Access Industries), and Viktor Vekselberg (founder of Renova Group). Two episodes stand out.

Episode I

In 2008, the Russian partners publicly aired two grievances. First, TNK-BP relied on too many BP's expatriate (expat) consultants, whose fees were a "rip off"—extra dividends to BP but excessive costs to TNK-BP. Second, and more importantly, the Russians wanted TNK-BP to pursue opportunities outside of Russia and Ukraine, but BP insisted on fencing TNK-BP within Russia and Ukraine to prevent TNK-BP from becoming a global competitor. A memo from the American CEO of TNK-BP at that time,

Bob Dudley, barred managers from entertaining deals in countries blacklisted by the US State Department, such as Cuba, Iran, and Syria. "TNK-BP is an independent Russian company," noted Fridman, "and should be subject to Russian laws," which would bless deals in these countries. In fact, given its Russian background, TNK-BP might be particularly well-suited to exploit opportunities in these "rogue" countries labeled by the US government. The board room dispute quickly spilled out to grab media headlines. The Russian partners claimed that TNK-BP should be free to grow into an independent, global oil company (at least the JV agreement did not ban this).

Rapid-fire developments took place in 2008. In January, the visas of BP's 148 expats working at TNK-BP were declared invalid. In March, the Moscow offices of both BP and TNK-BP were raided by police. Shortly after, a TNK-BP manager was arrested for alleged espionage. In April, a little-known minority shareholder filed a court case blocking BP's expats from working at TNK-BP. In June, the high drama on who was in charge in this 50/50 JV reached a bizarre climax. In a Moscow hearing with Russian immigration officials regarding the proper number of visas for TNK-BP's foreign workers, two delegations showed up, both claiming to represent TNK-BP (!). Tim Summers, TNK-BP's chief operating officer and a BP representative, claimed that visas for 150 foreign workers would be needed. But Vekselberg, a director and 12.5% shareholder of TNK-BP, said that only 71 visas would be necessary. Officials supported Vekselberg's case and thus forced some expat employees to leave Russia almost immediately for good.

BP framed the dispute as oligarchs' time-honored practice to grab control of companies by political pressures and argued that the outcome would be a test of the rule of law in Russia. BP also implied that the Russian government might be behind the oligarchs' aggressive moves. In an article published in *Financial Times* on July 7, 2008, Fridman dismissed political motivations and characterized the dispute as "a traditional, commercial dispute about different ambitions of the strategic development of the business" (see Emerging Markets 7.1). Accusing BP of being opportunistic, Fridman wrote that BP treated TNK-BP as if it had been a wholly owned subsidiary instead of a JV. BP allegedly treated Russians as "subjects," as opposed to shareholders of equal rights. The article noted that BP cared more about its oil reserves than costs or profits. The punch line? Dudley's ouster as TNK-BP's CEO. Under such tremendous pressures, Dudley had to quickly flee the country. A Russian court even barred him from performing his job for two years for allegedly violating local labor laws. In September 2008, Fridman, in addition to his position as chairman of the board, became interim CEO of TNK-BP.

In the end, while the Russians needed BP's expertise, BP also needed to access TNK-BP's crude in Siberia, which was far easier and safer to get at than the complicated and unsafe deep water drilling in places such as the Gulf of Mexico. In April 2010, the devastating oil spill took place. In July 2010, Dudley—although disgraced in Russia—was promoted to become the new BP CEO. As the new CEO, Dudley quickly flew to Moscow and became more accommodating to the Russian partners. With a changed attitude, BP now agreed that TNK-BP could expand abroad. In October 2010, BP sold assets worth $1.8 billion in Venezuela and Vietnam to TNK-BP—a milestone for TNK-BP that finally broke out of Russia and Ukraine. As a Russian company, TNK-BP might indeed be better positioned to do well in "tricky" countries such as Venezuela and Vietnam. To BP, these sales raised immediate cash to help defray the cleanup and compensation costs in the Gulf of Mexico, and it did not have to sell to competitors. Overall, Episode I seemed to have a (relatively) happy ending.

Episode II

Only a couple of months after the ending of Episode I, Episode II began. In January 2011, BP announced a new $16 billion strategic alliance with Russia's state-owned Rosneft. Creating the first cross-shareholding alliance between international and Russian oil companies, the deal would enable BP to own 9.5% of Rosneft's shares and Rosneft to own 5% of BP's shares. Both sides would jointly explore a new offshore oil field on the Russian Arctic continental shelf in the Kara Sea. Rosneft is Russia's second largest oil company, which produces 2.4 million barrels of oil a day (behind Gazprom but ahead of TNK-BP). This new alliance had the full support of the Russian government—after all, Rosneft's chairman of the board Igor Sechin was the sitting Deputy Prime Minister. All seemed well . . . but here was the catch: The Russian partners at TNK-BP jumped out and sought to block the deal. Their argument was that per the TNK-BP JV agreement, BP could only pursue further business in Russia through the JV. In other words, AAR's rights of first refusal were violated. In simple terms, "if you want to marry a new wife," a furious Fridman argued, "you have to divorce the old one first." The Russian government was mad about BP too. "I met with BP's head and he did not say a word about it," said (then) Prime Minister Vladimr Putin. Basically, BP had lied to Rosneft that it had no third-party obligations. According to the *Economist*,

> *At the least, it seems a woeful misjudgment on BP's part. The company says it had no idea that its deal with Rosneft would result in such a legal tussle, so it felt no need to mention the terms of its shareholder agreement with TNK-BP to its new Russian partners. Perhaps Mr. Dudley gambled that getting into bed with Rosneft would silence TNK-BP.*

Such a gamble backfired badly. AAR initiated legal challenges by initiating arbitration proceedings to block BP's deal with Rosneft.* In March 2011 a Swedish arbitration tribunal supported AAR and dealt a blow to the Rosneft deal, which became known as "Ros-nyet." In May 2011, BP admitted failure and reaffirmed that it remained fully committed to TNK-BP as its "primary business vehicle in Russia"—which, in human marriage terms,

---

Arbitration is a private form of dispute resolution that bypasses the court systems of the host country and the home country. In this case, parties to the TNK-BP JV agreed when they signed the contract that neither Russian law nor British law would govern the contractual relationship. Instead they agreed to use arbitration done in a third, neutral country (Sweden in this case) to resolve their disputes.

sounded like acknowledging AAR as its legally married spouse after being caught for indulging in an extramarital affair.

However, BP's headache did not end. In September 2011, its frustrated other partner Rosneft struck a new strategic alliance deal with Exxon Mobil. They would jointly explore the same icy blocks of the Arctic Kara Sea that slipped from BP's hand. Things then got worse. The very next day, BP's Moscow offices were raided by police again. Having managed to alienate *both* the Russian government and Rosneft—just imagine Kremlin's fury after the collapse of the deal—on the one hand and AAR on the other hand, "BP appears to have little protection against being pushed around in Russia," noted the *Economist*. In October 2011, a severely weakened BP agreed to let Fridman to formally serve as CEO, thus enabling him and AAR partners to essentially run the show at TNK-BP.

Despite the ordeals, challenges, and hard feelings, both BP and AAR remained committed to the success of TNK-BP. One has to be totally naïve to believe that they would live "happily ever after." So stay tuned for Episode III...

Sources: Based on (1) *BusinessWeek*, 2008, BP: Roughed up in Russia, June 16: 69; (2) *Bloomberg Businessweek*, 2010, How BP learned to dance with the Russian bear, September 27: 19–20; (3) BP, 2010, BP to sell Venezuela and Vietnam businesses to TNK-BP, October 18, www.bp.com; (4) BP, 2011, BP and AAR agree on new management structure for TNK-BP, October 21, www.bp.com; (5) BP, 2011, BP and AAR reaffirm commitment to growth and success of TNK-BP, May 17, www.bp.com; (6) BP, 2011, BP remains committed to partner with Russia, March 24, www.bp.com; (7) BP, 2011, Rosneft and BP form global and Arctic strategic alliance, January 14, www.bp.com; (8) *Economist*, 2008, At war with itself, July 5: 74; (9) *Economist*, 2008, Crude tactics, June 7: 74–75; (10) *Economist*, 2011, Dudley do-wrong, April 2: 60; (11) *Economist*, 2011, Exxonerated, September 3: 64; (12) M. Fridman, 2008, BP has been treating Russians as subjects, *Financial Times*, July 7: 11.

CASE DISCUSSION QUESTIONS

1. From an industry-based view, explain why alliances are a frequent mode of entry for the oil industry in Russia.

2. From a resource-based view, what are the complementary resources and capabilities both sides brought to TNK-BP?

3. From an institution-based view, what are the formal and informal rules of the game governing this industry in Russia?

4. **ON ETHICS:** As an ethics consultant to BP, how would you advise it during both episodes of the conflicts with AAR?

5. **ON ETHICS:** If you were an arbitrator in Stockholm, Sweden, which side would you support in both episodes?

NOTES

[**Journal acronyms**] *AME – Academy of Management Executive;* *AMJ – Academy of Management Journal;* *AMP – Academy of Management Perspectives;* *AMR – Academy of Management Review;* *APJM – Asia Pacific Journal of Management;* *BW – BusinessWeek* (before 2010) or *Bloomberg Businessweek* (since 2010); *GSJ – Global Strategy Journal;* *HBR – Harvard Business Review;* *JIBS – Journal of International Business Studies;* *JIM – Journal of International Management;* *JM – Journal of Management;* *JMS – Journal of Management Studies;* *JWB – Journal of World Business;* *MS – Management Science;* *OSc – Organization Science;* *SMJ – Strategic Management Journal*

1. Cited in J. Reuer, 2004, Introduction (p. 2), in J. Reuer (ed.), *Strategic Alliances,* New York: Oxford University Press.

2. P. Beamish & N. Lupton, 2009, Managing JVs, *AMP*, May, 75–94; P. Kale & H. Singh, 2009, Managing strategic alliances, *AMP*, August: 45–62.

3. T. Das & B. Teng, 2002, Alliance constellations, *AMR*, 27: 445–456; S. Nambisan & M. Sawhney, 2011, Orchestration processes in network-centric innovation, *AMP*, August: 40–56.

4. S. Lazzarini, 2007, The impact of membership in competing alliance constellations, *SMJ*, 28: 345–367.

5. X. Yin & M. Shanley, 2008, Industry determinants of the "merger versus alliance" decision, *AMR*, 33: 473–491.

6. B. Garrette, X. Castaner, & P. Dussauge, 2009, Horizontal alliances as an alternative to autonomous production, *SMJ*, 30: 885–894.

7. J. Dyer, 1997, Effective interfirm collaboration, *SMJ*, 18: 543–556.

8. L. Mesquita, J. Anand, & T. Brush, 2008, Comparing the resource-based and relational views, *SMJ*, 29: 913–941; M. Schreiner, P. Kale, & D. Corsten, 2009, What really is alliance management capability and how does it impact alliance outcomes and success? *SMJ*, 30: 1395–1419.

9. J. Adegbesan & M. Higgins, 2010, The intra-alliance division of value created through collaboration, *SMJ*, 32: 187–211; R. Agarwal, R. Croson, & J. Mahoney, 2010, The role of incentives and communication in strategic alliances, *SMJ*, 31: 413–437; R. Z. Ainuddin, P. Beamish, J. Hulland, & M. Rouse, 2007, Resource attributes and firm performance in IJVs, *JWB*, 42: 47–60; F. Castellucci & G. Ertug, 2010, What's in it for them? *AMJ*, 53: 149–166; E. Fang & S. Zou, 2009, Antecedents and consequences of marketing dynamic capabilities in IJVs, *JIBS*, 40: 742–761; A. Joshi & A. Nerkar, 2011, When do strategic alliances inhibit innovation by firms? *SMJ*, 32: 1139–1160; M. Srivastava & D. Gnyawali, 2011, When do relational resources matter? *AMJ*, 54: 797–810.

10. *Economist*, 2003, Open skies and flights of fancy (p. 67), October 4: 65–67.

11. S. Ang, 2008, Competitive intensity and collaboration, *SMJ*, 29: 1057–1075; R. Sampson, 2007, R&D alliances and firm performance, *AMJ*, 50: 364–386.

12. B. Bourdeau, J. Cronin, & C. Voorhees, 2007, Modeling service alliances, *SMJ*, 28: 609–622; H. Mitsuhashi & H. Greve, 2009, A matching theory of alliance formation and organizational success, *AMJ*, 52: 975–995; A. Tiwana & M. Keil, 2007, Does peripheral knowledge complement control? *SMJ*, 28: 623–634.

13. M. Koza, S. Tallman, & A. Ataay, 2011, The strategic assembly of global firms (p. 38), *GSJ*, 1: 27–46.

14. A. Chintakananda & D. McIntyre, 2012, Market entry in the presence of network effects, *JM* (in press); I. Cuypers & X. Martin, 2010, What makes and what does not make a real option? *JIBS*, 41: 47–69.

15. B. Kogut, 1991, JVs and the option to expand and acquire, *MS*, 37: 19–33; T. Tong, J. Reuer, & M. W. Peng, 2008, International joint ventures and the value of growth options, *AMJ*, 51: 1014–1029.

16. M. McCarter, J. Mahoney, & G. Northcraft, 2011, Testing the waters, *AMR*, 36: 621–640.

17. L. Hsieh, S. Rodrigues, & J. Child, 2010, Risk perception and post-formation governance in IJVs in Taiwan, *JIM*, 16: 288–303; M. Meuleman, A. Lockett, S. Manigart, & M. Wright, 2010, Partner selection decisions in interfirm collaborations, *JMS*, 47: 995–1018.

18. M. Jensen & A. Roy, 2008, Staging exchange partner choices, *AMJ*, 51: 495–516; D. Li, L. Eden, M. Hitt, & R. D. Ireland, 2008, Friends, acquaintances, or strangers? *AMJ*, 51: 315–334; X. Luo & L. Deng, 2009, Do birds of a feather flock higher? *JMS*, 46: 1005–1030; F. Rothaermel & W. Boeker, 2008, Old technology meets new technology, *SMJ*, 29: 47–77; R. Shah & V. Swaminathan, 2008, Factors influencing partner selection in strategic alliances, *SMJ*, 29: 471–494.

19. A. Arino & P. Ring, 2010, The role of fairness in alliance formation, *SMJ*, 31: 1054–1087.

20. D. Zoogah & M. W. Peng, 2011, What determines the performance of strategic alliance managers? *APJM*, 28: 483–508.

21. C. Jiang, R. Chua, M. Kotabe, & J. Murray, 2011, Effects of cultural ethnicity, firm size, and firm age on senior executives' trust in their overseas business partners, *JIBS*, 42: 1150–1173; Y. Luo, 2009, Are we on the same page? *JWB*, 44: 383–396; L. Mesquita, 2007, Starting over when the bickering never ends, *AMR*, 32: 72–91; F. Molina-Morales & M. Martinez-Fernandez, 2009, Too much love in the neighborhood can hurt, *SMJ*, 30: 1013–1023; A. Phene & S. Tallman, 2012, Complexity, context, and governance in biotechnology alliances, *JIBS*, 43: 61–83.

22. G. Ahuja, F. Polidoro, & W. Mitchell, 2009, Structural homophily or social asymmetry? *SMJ*, 30: 941–958; B. Koka & J. Prescott, 2008, Designing alliance networks, *SMJ*, 29: 639–661; C. Phelps, 2010, A longitudinal study of the influence of alliance network structure and composition on firm exploratory innovation, *AMJ*, 53: 890–913; H. Yang, Z. Lin, & Y. Lin, 2010, A multilevel framework of firm boundaries, *SMJ*, 31: 237–261; A. Zaheer, R. Gozubuyuk, & H. Milanov, 2010, It's the connections, *AMP*, February: 62–76.

23. V. Aggarwal, N. Siggelkow, & H. Singh, 2011, Governing collaborative activity, *SMJ*, 32: 705–730.

24. D. Chen, Y. Paik, & S. Park, 2010, Host-country policies and MNE management control in IJVs, *JIBS*, 41: 526–537; W. Shi, S. Sun, & M. W. Peng, 2013, Sub-national institutional contingencies, network positions, and IJV partner selection, *JMS* (in press).

25. Federal Trade Commission, 2000, *Antitrust Guidelines for Collaborations among Competitors*, Washington: FTC; T. Tong & J. Reuer, 2010, Competitive consequences of interfirm collaboration, *JIBS*, 41: 1056–1073.

26. M. W. Peng, 2006, Making M&As fly in China, *HBR*, March: 26–27. See also H. K. Steensma, L. Tihanyi, M. Lyles, & C. Dhanaraj, 2005, The evolving value of foreign partnerships in transitioning economies, *AMJ*, 48: 213–235; J. Xia, J. Tan, & D. Tan, 2008, Mimetic entry and bandwagon effect, *SMJ*, 29: 195–217.

27. M. T. Dacin, C. Oliver, & J. Roy, 2007, The legitimacy of strategic alliances, *SMJ*, 28: 169–187.

28. This section draws heavily from S. Tallman & O. Shenkar, 1994, A managerial decision model of international cooperative venture formation, *JIBS*, 25: 91–113.

29. G. Lee & M. Lieberman, 2010, Acquisition versus internal development, *SMJ*, 31: 140–158.

30. W. Hoffmann, 2007, Strategies for managing a portfolio of alliances, *SMJ*, 28: 827–856; D. Lavie, C. Lechner, & H. Singh, 2007, The performance implications of timing of entry and involvement in multipartner alliances, *AMJ*, 50: 578–604; J. Reuer & R. Ragozzino, 2006, Agency hazards and alliance portfolios, *SMJ*, 27: 27–43.

31. S. Makino, C. Chan, T. Isobe, & P. Beamish, 2007, Intended and unintended termination of IJVs, *SMJ*, 28: 1113–1132; H. Ness, 2009, Governance, negotiations, and alliance dynamics, *JMS*, 46: 451–480; H. K. Steensma, J. Barden, C. Dhanaraj, M. Lyles, & L. Tihanyi, 2008, The evolution and internalization of IJVs in a transitioning economy, *JIBS*, 39: 491–507.

32. S. White & S. Lui, 2005, Distinguishing costs of cooperation and control in alliances, *SMJ*, 26: 913–932.

33. Y. Zhang & N. Rajagopalan, 2002, Inter-partner credible threat in IJVs, *JIBS*, 33: 457–478.

34. J. March, 1991, Exploration and exploitation in organizational learning (p. 71), *OSc*, 2: 71–87.

35. D. Lavie & L. Rosenkopf, 2006, Balancing exploration and exploitation in alliance formation, *AMJ*, 49: 797–818.

36. This section draws heavily from M. W. Peng & O. Shenkar, 2002, JV dissolution as corporate divorce, *AME*, 16: 92–105. See also H. Greve, J. Baum, H. Mitsuhashi, & T. Rowley, 2010, Built to last but falling apart, *AMJ*, 53: 302–322.

37. D. Faems, M. Janssens, A. Madhok, & B. Looy, 2008, Toward an integrative perspective on alliance governance, *AMJ*, 51: 1053–1078; N. Pangarkar, 2009, Do firms learn from alliance terminations? *JMS*, 46: 982–1004; J. Reuer & A. Arino, 2007, Strategic alliance contracts, *SMJ*, 28: 313–330.

38. A. Arino & J. Reuer, 2002, Designing and renegotiating strategic alliance contracts (p. 44), *AME*, 18: 37–48.

39. A. Goerzen, 2007, Alliance networks and firm performance, *SMJ*, 28: 487–509.

40. R. Kaplan, D. Norton, & B. Rugelsjoen, 2010, Managing alliances with the balanced scorecard, *HBR*, January: 114–120; J. Li, C. Zhou, & E. Zajac, 2009, Control, collaboration, and productivity, *SMJ*, 30: 865–884; J. Lu & D. Xu, 2006, Growth and survival of IJVs, *JM*, 32: 426–448; A. Shipilov, 2006, Network strategy and performance of Canadian investment banks, *AMJ*, 49: 590–604.

41. M. Cheung, M. Myers, & J. Mentzer, 2011, The value of relational learning in global buyer-supplier exchanges, *SMJ*, 32: 1061–1082; F. Evangelista & L. Hau, 2009, Organizational context and knowledge acquisition in IJVs, *JWB*, 44: 63–73; E. Fang & S. Zou, 2010, The effects of absorptive and joint learning on the instability of IJVs in emerging economies, *JIBS*, 41: 906–924; R. Gulati, D. Lavie, & H. Singh, 2009, The nature of partnering experience and the gains from alliances, *SMJ*, 30: 1213–1233; P. Kale & H. Singh, 2007, Building firm capabilities through learning, *SMJ*, 28: 981–1000; J. Lai, S. Chang, & S. Chen, 2010, Is experience valuable in international strategic alliances? *JIM*, 16: 247–261; C. Liu, P. Ghauri, & R. Sinkovics, 2010, Understanding the impact of relational capital and organizational learning on alliance outcomes, *JWB*, 45: 237–249; M. Lyles & J. Salk, 2007, Knowledge acquisition from foreign parents in IJVs, *JIBS*, 38: 3–18; K. Meyer, 2007, Contextualizing organizational learning, *JIBS*, 38: 27–37; B. Nielsen & S. Nielsen, 2009, Learning and innovation in international strategic alliances, *JMS*, 46: 1031–1058; S. Tallman & A. Chacar, 2011, Communities, alliances, networks, and knowledge in multinational firms, *JIM*, 17: 201–210; G. Vasudeva & J. Anand, 2011, Unpacking absorptive capacity, *AMJ*, 54: 611–623; M. Zollo & J. Reuer, 2010, Experience spillovers across corporate development activities, *OSc*, 21: 1195–1212.

42. Y. Luo & M. W. Peng, 1999, Learning to compete in a transition economy, *JIBS*, 30: 269–296.

43. A. Gaur & J. Lu, 2007, Ownership strategies and survival of foreign subsidiaries, *JM*, 33: 84–110; A.

Madhok, 2006, How much does ownership really matter? *JIBS*, 37: 4–11; J. Xia, 2011, Mutual dependence, partner substitutability, and repeated partnership, *SMJ*, 32: 229–253.

44. D. Lavie, 2007, Alliance portfolios and firm performance, *SMJ*, 28: 1187–1212.

45. A. Afuah, 2000, How much do your co-opetitors' capabilities matter in the face of technological change?, *SMJ*, 21: 387–404; J. Baum, T. Calabrese, & B. Silverman, 2000, Don't go it alone, *SMJ*, 21: 267–294.

46. M. Kunar, 2010, Are JVs positive sum games? *SMJ*, 32: 32–54; S. Yeniyurt, J. Townsend, S. T. Cavusgil, & P. Ghauri, 2009, Mimetic and experiential effects in international marketing alliance formations of US pharmaceutical firms, *JIBS*, 40: 301–320.

47. C. Choi & P. Beamish, 2004, Split management control and IJV performance, *JIBS*, 35: 201–215; H. K. Steensma & M. Lyles, 2000, Explaining IJV survival in a transition economy, *SMJ*, 21: 831–851.

48. T. Chi, 2000, Option to acquire or divest a JV, *SMJ* (p. 671), 21: 665–687.

49. L. Wang & E. Zajac, 2007, Alliance or acquisition? *SMJ*, 28: 1291–1317.

50. K. Brouthers & D. Dikova, 2010, Acquisitions and real options, *JMS*, 47: 1048–1070.

51. J. Dyer, P. Kale, & H. Singh, 2004, When to ally and when to acquire, *HBR* (p. 113), July–August: 109–115.

52. R. Burt, 1992, *Structural Holes*, Cambridge, MA: Harvard University Press; H. Yang, Z. Lin, & M. W. Peng, 2011, Behind acquisitions of alliance partners, *AMJ*, 54: 1069–1080.

53. Z. Lin, M. W. Peng, H. Yang, & S. Sun, 2009, How do networks and learning drive M&As? *SMJ*, 30: 1113–1132.

54. H. Yang, S. Sun, Z. Lin, & M. W. Peng, 2011, Behind M&As in China and the United States, *APJM*, 28: 239–255.

55. S. Sun, M. W. Peng, B. Ren, & D. Yan, 2012, A comparative ownership advantage framework for cross-border M&As, *JWB*, 47: 4–16.

56. M. W. Peng, 2012, The global strategy of emerging multinationals from China, *GSJ*, 2: 97–107.

57. A. Brandenburger & B. Nablebuff, 1996, *Co-opetition*, New York: Doubleday.

58. *BW*, 2010, Charlie Rose talks to Eric Schmidt, September 27: 39.

CHAPTER **8**

MANAGING GLOBAL COMPETITIVE DYNAMICS

© istockphoto/Alexey Stiop

KNOWLEDGE OBJECTIVES

After studying this chapter, you should be able to

1. Articulate the "strategy as action" perspective
2. Understand the industry conditions conducive for cooperation and collusion
3. Explain how resources and capabilities influence competitive dynamics
4. Outline how antitrust and antidumping laws affect domestic and international competition
5. Identify the drivers for attacks, counterattacks, and signaling
6. Discuss how local firms fight multinational enterprises (MNEs)
7. Participate in two leading debates concerning competitive dynamics
8. Draw strategic implications for action

Patent Wars and Shark Attacks

The number of worldwide patent applications has shot up from about 800,000 a year in the 1980s to close to 2 million a year in the 2000s. The number of patent lawsuits has also skyrocketed. In the hotly contested mobile arena, Apple sued Samsung, Nokia, and HTC for patent violations. In retaliation, Samsung, Nokia, and HTC countersued Apple, also for patent violations. Kodak also sued Apple as well as Blackberry's maker, Research In Motion (RIM). Oracle and Xerox sued Google. Hardly a week goes by without a new lawsuit in "patent wars."

In many rapidly developing but patent-choked industries, inadvertently tripping over someone else's patents is a real danger. The open secret, according to the *Economist*, is that "everyone infringes everyone else's patents in some way." This creates an incentive for firms to engage in an "arms race" in filing and hoarding patents. In patent wars, patents are both defensive and offensive weapons.

Contrary to popular thinking, many patents are not truly novel and nonobvious. *BusinessWeek* opined that the United States is now "awash in a sea of junk patents. Some are just plain silly, such as a patent for 'a method of exercising and entertaining cats' (basically teasing them with a laser pointer)." Such "massive overpatenting," according to critics, has resulted in a "patent epidemic." Escalation of patenting obviously costs firms a lot of money: on average, one patent costs half a million dollars. But firms are rational. Strategically patenting a portfolio of inventions around some core technologies allows them to gain an upper hand in patent lawsuits and negotiations. Patent lawsuits are becoming very predictable. Firm A sues Firm B for patent infringement. B digs through its own patent portfolio and discovers that some of its own patents are infringed by A. So B countersues A. To avoid costly and mutually destructive exchange of endless patent lawsuits, both typically reach cross-licensing deals that, after exchanging small sums of money, give each other the rights to the patents.

But here is a catch: to be a party to such exchange, a firm needs to have a sufficiently large hoard of patents. As a young firm, Google, prior to 2011, only had applied for or received 307 mobile-related patents. As a result, Google was vulnerable when compared with RIM's 3,134 mobile-related patents, Nokia's 2,655, and Microsoft's 2,594. That was a key reason behind Google's colossal $12.5 billion purchase of Motorola Mobility, a handset maker that was losing money. But Google was not primarily interested in the handset business; instead, it was buying Motorola's rich hoard of over 1,000 mobile-related patents.

Among large firms clashing in emerging industries such as mobile devices, patent fights are normal or even (somewhat) predictable. What are less predictable but no less damaging are attacks by patent "sharks" (or "trolls"). Trolls are patent-holding individuals or (often small) firms that legally challenge manufacturers for patent infringement in order to receive damage awards for the illegitimate use of trolls' patents. While sharks and trolls are colorful labels, the jargon for them is "non-operating entities" (NOEs). In contrast to all the "operating entities" named in the first four paragraphs above, NOEs, by definition, had neither capability nor intention to commercialize their patents. Traditionally, most NOEs would license their patents to manufacturers that would pay a licensing fee. But many of today's trolls *hope* to be infringed and do everything they can to keep patents as invisible as possible (the jargon is to be a "submarine") until the patents are illegitimately used by manufacturers. Trolls then pounce in surprise attacks demanding compensation exceeding what they would reasonably expect from real licensing fees up front. In 1990, individual inventor Jerome Lemelson sued toymaker Mattel for infringing a coupling technology used in toy trucks. Although the court determined that Mattel inadvertently (not willfully) infringed Lemelson's patent, the court nevertheless awarded him $24 *million*— that was a lot of toy trucks (!). Most experts agreed that if Lemelson and Mattel had negotiated up front, Lemelson would not have been able to extract a licensing fee close to this astronomical sum. Cases of this kind have motivated a lot of trolls, eventually opening the floodgates for the "troll business." Although ethically dubious, such a strategy is not only profitable but also perfectly legal.

Executives at "operating entities" (manufacturers), especially high-tech ones, are well advised to prepare for shark attacks. Beefing up patent law expertise is crucial. One joke in high-tech industries is that firms must spend most of their R&D budgets on patent lawyers. Devoting more resources to monitor patents is another obvious solution. However, this solution will not be perfect, because given the mushrooming volume of patents, patent monitoring costs have increased massively. The overall risk of simply neglecting prior art has risen. On the other hand, most of the troll patents are relatively marginal and can be invented around. This further adds more incentive to have a number of alternative patents in a firm's portfolio—just in case.

Sources: Based on (1) *Bloomberg Businessweek*, 2011, Android's dominance is patent pending, August 8: 36–37; (2) *BusinessWeek*, 2006, The patent epidemic, January 9: 60–62; (3) *Economist*, 2005, Patent sense, October 22: 5; (4) *Economist*, 2010, The great patent battle, October 23: 75–76; (5) *Economist*, 2011, Inventive warfare, August 20: 57–58; (6) *Economist*, 2011, Patent applications, November 19: 105; (7) M. Reitzig, J. Hendel, & C. Heath, 2007, On sharks, trolls, and their patent prey, *Research Policy*, 36: 134–154; (8) R. Ziedonis, 2004, Don't fence me in, *Management Science*, 50: 804–820.

competitive dynamics

Actions and responses undertaken by competing firms.

competitor analysis

The process of anticipating rivals' actions in order to both revise a firm's plan and prepare to deal with rivals' responses.

Why do firms take certain actions such as patent lawsuits? Once one side initiates an action, how does the other respond? These are some of the strategic questions we address in this chapter, which focuses on such **competitive dynamics**—actions and responses undertaken by competing firms.[1] Since one firm's actions are rarely unnoticed by rivals, the initiating firm would naturally like to predict rivals' responses *before* making its own move.[2] This process is called **competitor analysis**, advocated a long time ago by ancient Chinese strategist Sun Tzu's teaching to not only know "yourself" but also "your opponents."

Recall that Chapter 1 introduced the "strategy as plan" and "strategy as action" schools. As military officers have long known, a good plan never survives the first contact with the enemy because the enemy does not act according to our plan (!). Thus, strategy's defining feature is action, not planning. This chapter first highlights the "strategy as action" perspective, followed by a comprehensive model. Then, attack, counterattack, and signaling are outlined, with one interesting extension on how local firms fight multinational enterprises (MNEs) in emerging economies. Debates and extensions follow.

Strategy as Action

The heart of this chapter is the "strategy as action" perspective (Figure 8.1). It suggests that the essence of strategy is interaction, which is actions and reactions that lead to competitive advantage. Firms, like militaries, often compete aggressively. Note the military tone of terms such as "attacks," "counterattacks," and "price wars."[3] General Motors (GM) runs a war game among its top 60 executives. Six teams with 10 executives each play GM's major rivals trying to crush GM.[4]

So, business is war—or is it? It is obvious that military principles cannot be completely applied, because the marketplace, after all, is not a battlefield whose motto is "Kill or be killed."

FIGURE 8.1 Strategy as Action

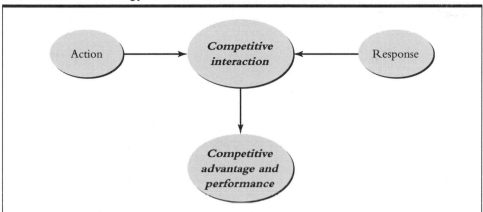

Source: C. M. Grimm & K. G. Smith, 1997, *Strategy as Action: Industry Rivalry and Coordination* (p. 62), Cincinnati: South-Western Thomson (now Cengage Learning).

If fighting to the death destroys the "pie," there will be nothing left. In business, it is possible to compete and win without killing the opposition. In a nutshell, business is simultaneously war *and* peace. Alternatively, most competitive dynamics concepts can also be explained in terms of sports analogies, such as "offense" and "defense."

While militaries fight over territories, waters, and air spaces, firms compete in markets along product dimensions and geographic dimensions. **Multimarket competition** occurs when firms engage the same rivals in multiple markets.[5] Because a multimarket competitor can respond to an attack not only in the attacked market but also in other markets in which both firms meet, its challenger has to think twice before launching an attack. In other words, while firms "act local," they have to "think global." Because firms recognize their rivals' ability to retaliate in multiple markets, such multimarket competition may result in *reduction* of competitive intensity among rivals, an outcome known as **mutual forbearance**,[6] which we will discuss in more detail next.

Overall, the strategy tripod sheds considerable light on competitive dynamics, leading to a comprehensive model (Figure 8.2). The next three sections discuss the three "legs" for the tripod.

Industry-based Considerations

Collusion and Prisoners' Dilemma

Industry-based considerations focus on the very first of the Porter five forces, rivalry among competitors in an industry (see Chapter 2). Most firms in an industry, if given a choice, would probably prefer a reduced level of competition. "People of the same trade seldom meet together, even for merriment and diversion," wrote Adam Smith in *The Wealth of Nations* (1776), "but their conversation often ends in a conspiracy against the public." In modern jargon, this means that competing firms in an industry may have an incentive to engage in **collusion**, defined as collective attempts to reduce competition.

multimarket competition
Firms engage the same rivals in multiple markets.

mutual forbearance
Multimarket firms respect their rivals' spheres of influence in certain markets and their rivals reciprocate, leading to tacit collusion.

collusion
Collective attempts between competing firms to reduce competition.

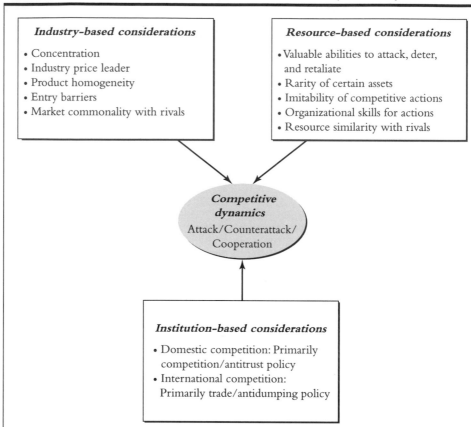

FIGURE 8.2 A Comprehensive Model of Global Competitive Dynamics

tacit collusion

Firms indirectly coordinate actions to reduce competition by signaling to others their intention to reduce output and maintain pricing above competitive levels.

explicit collusion

Firms directly negotiate output, fix pricing, and divide markets.

cartel

An entity that engages in output- and price-fixing, involving multiple competitors. Also known as a trust.

antitrust laws

Laws that attempt to curtail anticompetitive business practices such as cartels and trusts.

prisoners' dilemma

In game theory, a type of game in which the outcome depends on two parties deciding whether to cooperate or to defect.

game theory

A theory that focuses on competitive and cooperative interaction (such as in a prisoners' dilemma situation).

Because managers (and students) generally do not like to discuss "collusion," another "C" word, coordination, is now frequently used in preference over collusion.[7] However, given the legal battles centered on collusion, managers (and students) cannot shy away from it; instead they need to confront the legal definitions and debates about collusion, which can be tacit or explicit. Firms engage in **tacit collusion** when they *indirectly* coordinate actions by signaling their intention to reduce output and maintain pricing above competitive levels. **Explicit collusion** exists when firms *directly* negotiate output and pricing and divide markets. Explicit collusion leads to a **cartel**—an output-fixing and price-fixing entity involving multiple competitors. A cartel is also known as a trust, whose members have to trust each other in honoring agreements. Since the Sherman Act of 1890, cartels have often been labeled "anticompetitive" and outlawed by **antitrust laws** in many countries.

In addition to antitrust laws, collusion often suffers from a **prisoners' dilemma**, which underpins **game theory**. The term "prisoners' dilemma" derives from a simple game in which two prisoners suspected of a major joint crime (such as burglary) are separately interrogated and told that if either one confesses, the confessor will get a one-year sentence while the other will go to jail for ten years. Since the police do not have strong incriminating evidence for the more serious burglary charges, if neither confesses, both will be convicted of a lesser charge (such as trespassing) and each jailed for two years. If both confess, both will go to jail for ten years. At a first glance, the solution to this problem seems clear enough. The maximum *joint* payoff would be for neither of them to confess. However, even if both parties agree not to confess before they are arrested, there are still tremendous incentives to confess.

Translated to an airline setting, Figure 8.3 illustrates the payoff structure for both airlines A and B in a given market—let's say—between Sydney, Australia, and Auckland, New Zealand. Assuming a total of 200 passengers, Cell 1 represents the most ideal outcome for both airlines to maintain the price at $500; each gets 100 passengers and makes $50,000—the "industry" revenue reaches $100,000. In Cell 2, if B maintains its price at $500 while A drops it to $300, B is likely to lose all customers. Assuming perfectly transparent pricing information on the Internet, who would want to pay $500 when you can get a ticket for $300? Thus, A may make $60,000 on 200 passengers and B gets nobody. In Cell 3, the situation is reversed. In both Cells 2 and 3, although the industry *decreases* revenue by 40%, the price dropper *increases* its revenue by 20%. Thus, both A and B have strong incentives to reduce price and hope for the other side to become a "sucker." However, neither likes to be a "sucker." Thus, both A and B may want to chop prices, as in Cell 4, whereby each still gets 100 passengers. But both firms as well as the industry end up with a 40% reduction of revenue. A key insight of game theory is that even if A and B have a prior agreement to fix the price at $500, both still have strong incentives to cheat, thus pulling the industry to Cell 4 in which both are clearly worse off.[8]

FIGURE 8.3 A Prisoners' Dilemma for Airlines and Payoff Structure (assuming a total of 200 passengers)

		Airline A	
		Action 1 A keeps price at $500	Action 2 A drops price to $300
Airline B	Action 1 B keeps price at $500	(Cell 1) A: $50,000 B: $50,000	(Cell 2) A: $60,000 B: 0
	Action 2 B drops price to $300	(Cell 3) A: 0 B: $60,000	(Cell 4) A: $30,000 B: $30,000

© Cengage Learning

Industry Characteristics and Collusion vis-à-vis Competition

concentration ratio

The percentage of total industry sales accounted for by the top four, eight, or 20 firms.

Given the benefits of collusion and incentives to cheat, what industries are conducive for collusion vis-à-vis competition? Five factors emerge (Table 8.1). The first relevant factor is the number of firms or—more technically—the **concentration ratio**, defined as the percentage of total industry sales accounted for by the top four, eight, or 20 firms. In general, the higher the concentration, the easier it is to organize collusion. Because the top four concentration in mobile wireless telecommunications services in the United States accounted for more than 90% of market share, the antitrust authorities blocked the second largest firm AT&T's merger with the fourth largest firm T-Mobile. Specifically, the US Department of Justice argued:

> *The substantial increase in concentration that would result from this merger, and the reduction in the number of nationwide providers from four to three, likely will lead to lessened competition due to an enhanced risk of anticompetitive coordination. Certain aspects of mobile wireless communications services markets, including transparent pricing, little buyer-side market power, and high barriers to entry and expansion, make them particularly conductive to coordination.*[9]

price leader

A firm that has a dominant market share and sets "acceptable" prices and margins in the industry.

capacity to punish

Having sufficient resources to deter and combat defection.

Second, the existence of a **price leader**—a firm that has a dominant market share and sets "acceptable" prices and margins in the industry—helps maintain order and stability needed for tacit collusion. The price leader can signal to the entire industry, with its own pricing behavior, when it is appropriate to raise or reduce prices without jeopardizing the overall industry structure. The price leader also possesses the **capacity to punish**, defined as sufficient resources to deter and combat defection. To combat cheating, the most frequently used punishment entails undercutting the defector by flooding the market with deep discounts, thus making the defection fruitless. Such punishment is very costly because it will bring significant financial losses in the short run. However, if small-scale cheating is not dealt with, defection may become endemic. Thus, the price leader needs to have both the willingness and the capability to carry out punishments and bear the costs (see Emerging Markets 8.1). On the other hand, an industry without an acknowledged price leader is likely to be more chaotic. Prior to the 1980s, GM played the price leader role, announcing in advance the percentage of price increases and expecting Ford and Chrysler to follow (which they often did). Should the latter two have stepped "out of bounds," GM would have punished them. However, more recently, when Asian and

TABLE 8.1   Industry Characteristics and Possibility of Collusion vis-à-vis Competition

COLLUSION POSSIBLE	COLLUSION DIFFICULT (COMPETITION LIKELY)
■ Few firms (high concentration)	■ Many firms (low concentration)
■ Existence of an industry price leader	■ No industry price leader
■ Homogeneous products	■ Heterogeneous products
■ High entry barriers	■ Low entry barriers
■ High market commonality (mutual forbearance)	■ Lack of market commonality (no mutual forbearance)

© Cengage Learning

Is a Diamond (Cartel) Forever?

The longest-running cartel in the modern world is the international diamond cartel headed by De Beers of South Africa. The cartel system underpinning the $64 billion a year industry is, according to the *Economist*, "curious and anomalous—no other market exists, nor would anything similar be tolerated in a serious industry."

A key reason diamonds were so expensive was because of the deeply ingrained perception of scarcity. If there was an oversupply, prices could plummet. Cecil Rhodes, an English tycoon who founded the De Beers Mines in South Africa in 1875, sought to solve this problem by focusing on two areas. First, Rhodes realized that supply from South Africa, the only significant producer in the world at that time, should be limited. Second, because producers (diggers) had little control over the quality and quantity of their output, they preferred to deal with an indiscriminate buyer willing to purchase both spectacular and mediocre stones. Since most output would be mediocre stones, producers preferred to remove any uncertainty and to be able to sell *all* of their output. On the other hand, buyers (merchants) preferred to secure a steady supply of stones (both high and low ends). Rhodes's solution was to create an ongoing agreement between a single producer and a single buyer in which supply was kept low and prices high.

Putting his idea in action, Rhodes bought out all the major South African mines in the 1890s and formed a diamond merchants' association in the country, called the Diamond Syndicate, to which he would sell his output. In such "single-channel marketing," all members of the Syndicate pledged to buy diamonds from Rhodes and sell them in specific quantities and prices. With such an explicit scheme of quantity- and price-fixing, the diamond cartel was born.

Most cartels collapse due to organizational and incentive problems. The longevity of the De Beers cartel, now running for more than 100 years, is very unusual. At least three attributes contribute to its longevity. First, the industry has an extraordinarily high concentration. In

Rhodes's day, De Beers controlled all of South African (and hence virtually worldwide) production. Today, De Beers still controls approximately 40% of the world's rough diamond production, and its London-based wholly owned subsidiary Diamond Trading Company (DTC) sorts, values, and sells about 70% of the world's rough diamonds by value.

Second, De Beers is the undisputed price leader. Ten times a year, sales of rough diamonds (called "sights") are managed by the DTC to an exclusive group of cherry picked "sightholders" from cities such as Antwerp, Johannesburg, Mumbai, New York, and Tel Aviv. Sightholders inform the DTC of their preferences, and the DTC then matches them with inventory. During each sight, the DTC offers each sightholder a preselected parcel. The buyer either takes it or leaves it—no bargaining is permitted. Buyers usually take the parcel. If buyers repeatedly decline to take the parcel, they will not be invited again. This tactic allows De Beers to control, down to the carat, exactly what and how many stones enter the market and at what price. To maintain the exclusivity of the sightholders, their number has reduced from about 350 in the 1970s to less than 100 in the 2000s.

Third, De Beers possesses both the willingness and the capability to enforce cartel arrangements. As in all cartels, the incentives to cheat are tremendous: Both producers and buyers are interested in cutting De Beers out of the process. As a price leader with a significant capacity to punish, De Beers's reactions are typically swift and powerful. In 1981, President Mobutu Seko of Zaire (now the Democratic Republic of Congo) announced that his country would break away from De Beers by directly marketing its diamonds. Although only 3% of De Beers' sales were lost, its world order would be at stake if such actions went unpunished. Consequently, De Beers drew on its stockpiles to flood the market, driving the price of Zairian industrial diamonds from $3 per carat to $1.8 and wiping out any gains the Zairians hoped to grab. While incurring disproportional losses, De Beers made its point and Zaire crawled back on its knees.

In another example, many sightholders in Tel Aviv began to hoard diamonds purchased from the DTC in the 1970s, hoping to combat Israel's rampant inflation. The disappearance of a substantial amount of diamonds from global circulation tightened supply, leading to skyrocketing prices and encouraging merchants elsewhere also to hoard and profit. While De Beers actually benefited from such higher prices in the short run, it realized that in the long run such an uncontrolled speculative bubble would burst. In response, De Beers purged one third of sightholders and kicked out the most aggressive Israeli speculators. Cut off from their supplies, speculative merchants were forced to draw down their stockpiles, thus restoring prices to normal levels.

Finally, De Beers faces one major institutional headache. The US government argued that De Beers was in clear violation of US antitrust laws and unsuccessfully tried to prosecute it in 1945, 1974, and 1994. De Beers managed to stay beyond the extraterritorial reach of US laws since it had no legal presence and no (direct) sales in the US. All its diamonds were sold in London, with sightholders then exporting them to the US, which is legal. However, with 50% of the retail diamond buyers in the US, these legal actions had prevented De Beers executives from being able to visit their buyers and retailers in the US in fear of being arrested. In 2008, De Beers settled the US charges for a total of $295 million and agreed to operate in accordance with competition laws around the world. A question thus looms large on the

horizon for De Beers executives and antitrust officials: Has the longest-running cartel really come to an end? This truly is a billion-dollar question.

Sources: Based on (1) *Chicago Tribune*, 2008, Diamond refunds are a consumer's best friend, January 21, www.chicagotribune.com; (2) A. Cockburn, 2002, Diamonds: The real story, *National Geographic*, March: 2–35; (3) *Economist*, 2004, The cartel isn't forever, July 17: 60–62; (4) *Economist*, 2011, Betting on De Beers, November 12: 73; (5) D. Spa, 1994, *The Cooperative Edge: The Internal Politics of International Cartels*, Ithaca, NY: Cornell University Press; (6) www.debeersgroup.com.

European challengers have refused to follow GM's lead, GM has no longer been willing and able to play this role. Thus, the industry has become much more competitive and chaotic. From the Big Three, the US auto industry is now mostly populated by the Magnificent Seven (the other four are Toyota, Honda, Nissan, and Hyundai/Kia).[10]

Third, an industry with homogeneous products, in which rivals are forced to compete on price (rather than differentiation), is likely to lead to collusion.[11] Because price competition is often "cut throat," firms may have stronger incentives to collude. Since the 1990s, many firms in commodity industries around the globe, such as shipping and vitamins, have been convicted of price fixing.

Fourth, an industry with high entry barriers for new entrants (such as shipbuilding) is more likely to facilitate collusion than an industry with low entry barriers (such as restaurants). New entrants are likely to ignore the existing industry norms by introducing less homogeneous products with newer technologies (in other words, "disruptive technologies").[12] As "mavericks," new entrants "can be thought of as loose cannons in otherwise placid and calm industries."[13] Incumbents have collective interest in resisting such new entrants.

market commonality
The degree to which two competitors' markets overlap.

Finally, **market commonality**, defined as the degree of overlap between two competitors' markets, also has a significant bearing on the intensity of rivalry.[14] Multimarket firms may respect rivals' spheres of influence in certain markets, and their rivals may reciprocate, leading to tacit collusion. To make that happen, firms need to establish multimarket contact by following each other to enter new markets.[15] Thus, when Carlsberg enters a new country, Heineken will not be far behind.

cross-market retaliation
Retaliation in other markets when one market is attacked by rivals.

Mutual forbearance, due to a high degree of market commonality, primarily stems from two factors: (1) deterrence and (2) familiarity.[16] Deterrence is important because a high degree of market commonality suggests that if a firm attacks in one market, its rivals may engage in **cross-market retaliation**, leading to a costly all-out war nobody can afford. Familiarity is the extent to which tacit collusion is enhanced by a firm's awareness of the actions, intentions, and capabilities of rivals.[17] Repeated interactions lead to such familiarity, resulting in more mutual respect. In the words of GE CEO Jeff Imelt:

> *GE has tremendous respect for traditional rivals like Siemens, Philips, and Rolls-Royce. But it knows how to compete with them; they will never destroy GE. By introducing products that create a new price-performance paradigm, however, the emerging giants [such as Mindry, Suzlon, Goldwind, and Haier] very well could.*[18]

Overall, the industry-based view, underpinned by industrial organization (IO) economics (see Chapter 2), has generated a voluminous body of insights on competitive dynamics. IO economics has been influential in antitrust policy. For example, concentration ratios used to be mechanically applied by US antitrust authorities. For many years (until 1982), if an industry's top-four firm concentration ratio exceeded 20%, it would *automatically* trigger an antitrust investigation. However, since the 1980s, such a mechanical approach has been abandoned, in part because "cartels have formed in markets that bear few of the suggested structural criteria and have floundered in some of the supposedly ideal markets."[19] Evidently, industry-based considerations, while certainly insightful, are unable to tell the complete story, thus calling for contributions from resource-based and institution-based views, as outlined in the next two sections.

Resource-based Considerations

A number of resource-based imperatives, informed by the VRIO framework first outlined in Chapter 4, drive decisions and actions associated with competitive dynamics (see Figure 8.2).

Value

Firm resources must create value when engaging rivals.[20] One way to add value is patenting. Firms are rapidly expanding their scale and scope of patenting (see the Opening Case). Also, the ability to attack in multiple markets—of the sort Gillette (now part of P&G) possessed when launching its Sensor razors in 23 countries *simultaneously*—throws rivals off balance, thus adding value. Likewise, the ability to rapidly respond to challenges also adds value.[21] Another example is a dominant position in key markets (such as flights in and out of Dallas/Fort Worth for American Airlines). Such a strong sphere of influence poses credible threats to rivals, which understand that the firm will defend its core markets vigorously.

Rarity

Either by nature or nurture (or both), certain assets are very rare, thus generating significant advantage. Singapore Airlines, in addition to claiming one of the best locations connecting Europe and Asia as its home base, has often been rated as the world's best airline. This combination of both geographic advantage and man-made reputation advantage is rare, thus allowing Singapore Airlines to always charge higher prices and equip itself with newer and better equipment. It is the first airline in the world to fly the all-new A380.

Imitability

Most rivals watch each other and probably have a fairly comprehensive (although not necessarily accurate) picture of how their rivals compete. However, the next hurdle lies in how to imitate successful rivals. Slow-moving firms often find it difficult to do so. Many major airlines have sought to imitate discount carriers such as Southwest and Ryanair but have failed repeatedly.

Organization

Some firms are better organized for competitive actions, such as stealth attacks and answering challenges "tit-for-tat."[22] An intense "warrior-like" culture not only requires top management commitment, but also employee involvement down to the "soldiers in the trenches." It is such a self-styled "wolf" culture that has propelled Huawei to become Cisco's leading challenger. It is difficult for slow-moving firms to suddenly wake up and become more aggressive.[23]

On the other hand, more centrally coordinated firms may be better mutual forbearers than firms whose units are loosely controlled. For an MNE competing with rivals across many countries, a mutual forbearance strategy requires some units, out of respect for rivals' sphere of influence, to sacrifice their maximum market gains by withholding some efforts. Of course, such coordination helps other units with dominant market positions to maximize performance, thus helping the MNE as a whole. Successfully carrying out such mutual forbearance calls for organizational reward systems (such as those concerning bonuses and promotions) that encourage cooperation between units. Conversely, if a firm has competitive reward systems (for example, bonuses linked to unit performance), unit managers may be unwilling to give up market gains for the greater benefits of the whole firm, thus undermining mutual forbearance.[24]

resource similarity
The extent to which a given competitor possesses strategic endowments comparable to those of the focal firm.

Resource Similarity

Resource similarity is defined as "the extent to which a given competitor possesses strategic endowment comparable, in terms of both type and amount, to those of the focal firm."[25] Firms with a high degree of resource similarity are likely to have similar competitive actions. For instance, Apple and IBM used to have a lot of resource similarity in the 1990s, so they fought a lot. Why did they not fight a lot recently? One reason is that their level of resource similarity decreased.

If we put together resource similarity and market commonality (discussed earlier), we can yield a framework of competitor analysis for any pair of rivals (Figure 8.4). In Cell 4, because two firms have a high degree of resource similarity but a low degree of market commonality (little mutual forbearance), the intensity of rivalry is likely to be the highest. Conversely, in Cell 1, since both firms have little resource similarity but a high degree of market commonality, the intensity of their rivalry may be the lowest. Cells 2 and 3 present an intermediate level of competition.

For example, the high-flying Starbucks and the down-to-earth McDonald's used to have little resource similarity. Both had high market commonality—in the United States, both blanketed the country with chain stores. In other words, they were in Cell 1 with the lowest intensity of rivalry. However, recently, McDonald's aspired to go "up market" and offered products such as iced coffee designed to eat some of Starbucks' lunch (or drink some of Starbuck's coffee). Due to profit pressures, Starbucks seemed to go "down market" by offering cheaper drinks and instant coffee. We can say that their resource similarity has increased. Given that they still maintain high market commonality, their rivalry has migrated to Cell 2, whose intensity of rivalry is higher than that in Cell 1. To further illustrate, Strategy in Action 8.1 describes how Fox's entry into the US broadcasting industry intensified the rivalry. Overall, conscientious mapping along the dimensions outlined in Figure 8.4 can help managers sharpen their analytical focus, allocate resources in proportion to the degree of threat each rival presents, and avoid nasty surprises.

FIGURE 8.4   A Framework for Competitor Analysis between a Pair of Rivals

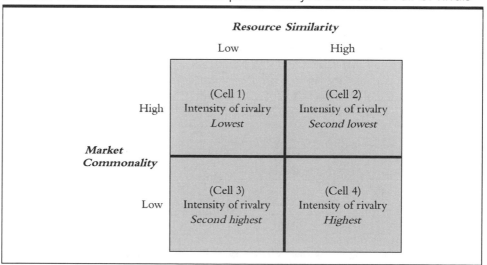

Sources: Adapted from (1) M. Chen, 1996, Competitor analysis and interfirm rivalry: Toward a theoretical integration (p. 108), *Academy of Management Review*, 21: 100–134; (2) J. Gimeno & C. Y. Woo, 1996, Hypercompetition in a multimarket environment: The role of strategic similarity and multimarket contact in competitive de-escalation (p. 338), *Organization Science*, 7: 322–341.

STRATEGY IN ACTION 8.1

A Fox in the Hen House

Prior to 1996, the US TV broadcasting industry could be viewed as a relatively tranquil "hen house." The Big Three networks (ABC, NBC, and CBS) dominated mainstream programming and CNN ran its 24-hour news show. Like hens sharing a house, there was some rivalry. But there were well-understood rules of engagement, such as not raiding each other's affiliate stations. Overall, competition was gentlemanly.

However, the 1996 arrival of Fox News Channel, a subsidiary of Rupert Murdoch's News Corporation, has transformed the industry. First, Fox violated industry norms by raiding Big Three affiliate stations. Fox convinced some affiliates to switch and become Fox stations. In some markets, affiliate defections gave Fox *overnight* success at the expense of one of the Big Three. Second, Fox paid up to $11 per subscriber to cable operators. This violated another norm where cable operators only paid stations carriage fees for programming. Having outfoxed the Big Three, Fox turned its guns to CNN. When it bought CNN, Time Warner was required by an antitrust consent to carry a second news channel in addition to CNN. Time Warner chose MSNBC instead of Fox; Fox sued Time Warner. The media war became dirty: CNN owner Ted Turner publicly compared Murdoch to Hitler while Murdoch's *New York Post* questioned Turner's sanity. Perhaps controversy was exactly what Fox wanted. Critics repeatedly accused Fox of promoting a conservative (allegedly Republican) point of view. Viewers did not care. By 2006, Fox was the most watched news channel in the United States, reaching 96% of US households.

Using Figure 8.4, we can suggest that the pre-1996 industry was in Cell 2. The intensity of rivalry was the second *lowest* because the Big Three and CNN had high market commonality (all focusing on the US) and high resource similarity (TV programming). However, Fox's entry has transformed the game. News Corporation is a global player that was historically headquartered in

Australia but is now headquartered and listed in New York. In addition to its Australian roots, News Corporation has a major presence in Asia, Canada, and Europe. Its first US acquisition took place in 1973, and Murdoch became an American citizen in 1985 to satisfy a requirement that only US citizens could own American TV stations. In other words, while Fox shares high resource similarity with the Big Three and CNN, it has low market similarity with the Big Three because they have little non-US presence. The upshot? The industry is now in Cell 4 with the *highest* intensity of rivalry. Fox can beat up the Big Three because it has little fear of retaliation against its non-US markets. The Big Three thus pay a heavy price for their US-centric mentality. Being more international, CNN is in a better position to fight Fox. In 1997, Turner and Murdoch settled, with Time Warner agreeing to carry Fox and News Corporation giving Time Warner access to News Corporation's satellites in Asia and Europe. In other words, they have established some mutual forbearance.

Sources: Based on (1) *BusinessWeek*, August 21/28, 2006: 82; (2) www.newscorp.com.

Fighting Low-Cost Rivals

A leading challenge for incumbents is how to deal with low-cost rivals.[26] By the 1990s, Dell, Southwest Airlines, and Wal-Mart showed their low-cost teeth. Now, low-cost rivals pop up around the world, such as Israel's Teva in generic drugs, China's Huawei and ZTE in telecom equipment, and Taiwan's HTC in smartphones (see the Closing Case). For incumbents, ignoring them will be dangerous, but do incumbents have the necessary capabilities to fight low-cost rivals?

Figure 8.5 suggests a framework for responding to low-cost rivals. It shows that incumbents need to resist the urge to initiate price wars in an effort to drive out low-cost rivals. From an institution-based view, predatory pricing may be illegal in many countries (see next section). From a resource-based view, in a race to the bottom, incumbents *usually* lose, because low-cost rivals have much better capabilities in the

FIGURE 8.5 How to Fight a Low-Cost Rival

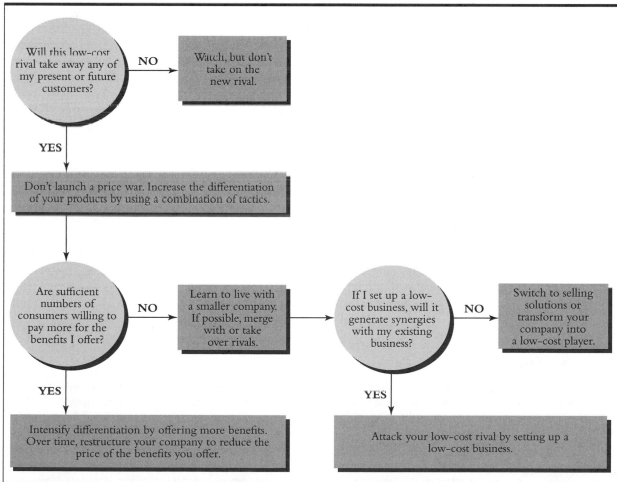

Source: Adapted from N. Kumar, 2006, Strategies to fight low-cost rivals, *Harvard Business Review* (p. 107), December: 104–112.

low-cost game. K-Mart not only failed to beat Wal-Mart on price, but also dragged itself into bankruptcy. Similarly, American Airlines dueled its cross-town rival Southwest (both are headquartered in the Dallas/Forth Worth area, but in different airports). In the end, Southwest soared but American crash-landed into bankruptcy. One piece of advice for incumbents is to enhance differentiation and convince customers to pay for such benefits (see Chapter 2). Apple designs cool gadgets. Target charges a small premium above Wal-Mart prices, as opposed to trying to beat Wal-Mart prices.

However, when differentiation fails and incumbents are forced to go down market, they need to take a hard look at the O aspect from a VRIO standpoint: Do they have the necessary organizational capabilities to compete against low-cost rivals? Incumbents tend to have the delusion that based on their experience, they can easily replicate low-cost operations. In the 1990s, most major airlines launched no-frills operations, such as BA's Go, Continental Lite, Delta Express, KLM's Buzz, SAS's Snowflake, and United's Shuttle. Since then, *all* of them have failed, indicating both a lack of organizational capabilities and a lack of ability to learn "new tricks." In the Great Recession, Coach launched a "fighter brand" Poppy with lower prices for handbags and accessories while maintaining the high prices of its Coach line. Does Coach have what it takes to make Poppy bloom? Stay tuned.

Eventually, while incumbents may (hopefully) transform themselves to become successful low-cost players, they may also switch to selling solutions. For example, IBM switched from selling hardware, whose markets are eroded by low-cost rivals, to selling high-end solutions. The leading piano maker Steinway now focuses on the "experience" and sells a large number of pianos made by its low-cost rival, Pearl River from China, which has formidable manufacturing firepower but limited branding capabilities.

Institution-based Considerations

In a nutshell, the institution-based view advises managers to be well versed in the "rules of the game" governing domestic and international competition. Surprisingly, existing strategy textbooks often have relatively little (or sometimes no) coverage on the institutions governing competitive dynamics. This is unfortunate because a lack of understanding of these institutions may land otherwise successful firms (such as Microsoft) in deep trouble. In a nutshell, the institution-based view argues that free markets are not necessarily free. This section shows why this is the case.

Formal Institutions Governing Domestic Competition:
A Focus on Antitrust

Formal institutions governing domestic competition are broadly guided by **competition policy**, which "determines the institutional mix of competition and cooperation that gives rise to the market system."[27] Of particular relevance to us is one branch called **antitrust policy**, which is designed to combat monopolies and cartels. Competition and antitrust policy seeks to balance efficiency and fairness. While efficiency is relatively easy to understand, it is often hard to agree on what is fair. In the United States, fairness means equal opportunities for incumbents and new entrants. It is "unfair" for incumbents to fix prices and raise entry barriers to shut out new entrants. However, in Japan, fairness means the *opposite*—that is, incumbents that have

competition policy

Policy governing the rules of the game in competition, which determine the institutional mix of competition and cooperation that gives rise to the market system.

antitrust policy

Competition policy designed to combat monopolies, cartels, and trusts.

invested in and nurtured an industry for a long time deserve to be protected from new entrants. What Americans approvingly describe as "market dynamism" is negatively labeled by Japanese as "market turbulence." The Japanese ideal is "orderly competition," which may be labeled "collusion" by Americans. Overall, the American antitrust policy is *pro-competition* and *pro-consumer*, while the Japanese approach is *pro-incumbent* and *pro-producer*. It is difficult to argue who is right or wrong here, but we need to be aware of such crucial differences.

As examples, Table 8.2 outlines the three major US antitrust laws and five landmark cases. Competition and antitrust policy focuses on (1) collusive price setting and (2) predatory pricing. **Collusive price setting** refers to price setting by monopolists or collusion parties at a level higher than the competitive level. For example, the global vitamin cartel convicted in the 2000s artificially jacked up prices by 30% to 40%.

collusive price setting
Monopolists or collusion parties setting prices at a level higher than the competitive level.

TABLE 8.2 Major Antitrust Laws and Landmark Cases in the United States

MAJOR ANTITRUST LAWS	LANDMARK CASES
Sherman Act of 1890 ■ It is illegal to monopolize or attempt to monopolize an industry. ■ "Every person who shall monopolize, or attempt to monopolize, or combine or conspire with any person or persons, to monopolize any part of the trade or commerce among the several states, or with foreign nations, shall be deemed guilty of a misdemeanor." ■ Explicit collusion is clearly illegal. ■ Tacit collusion is in a gray area, although the spirit of the law is against it.	**Standard Oil (1911)** ■ Had a US market share exceeding 85%. ■ Found guilty of monopolization. ■ Dissolved into several smaller firms. **Aluminum Company of America (ALCOA) (1945)** ■ Had 90% of the US aluminum ingot market. ■ Found guilty of monopolization. ■ Ordered to subsidize rivals' entry and sold plants. **IBM (1969–1982)** ■ Had 70% US computer market share. ■ Sued by DOJ for monopolization. ■ Case dropped by the Reagan Administration.
Clayton Act of 1914 ■ Created the Federal Trade Commission (FTC) to regulate the behavior of business firms ■ Empowered the FTC to prevent firms from engaging in harmful business practices	**AT&T (1974–1982)** ■ A legal "natural monopoly" since the 1900s. ■ Still sued by DOJ for monopolization, in particular its efforts to block new entrants. ■ Ordered to break up.
Hart-Scott-Rodino (HSR) Act of 1976 ■ Empowered the Department of Justice (DOJ) to require firms to submit internal documents. ■ Empowered state attorneys general (AGs) to initiate triple-damage suits.	**Microsoft (1990–2001)** ■ MS-DOS and Windows had an 85% market share. ■ Sued by DOJ, FTC, and 22 state AGs for monopolization and illegal product bundling. ■ Settled in 1994, ordered to split into two in 2000, judgment to split the firm reversed on appeal in 2001.

predatory pricing
(1) Setting prices below costs in the short run to destroy rivals and (2) intending to raise prices to cover losses in the long run after eliminating rivals.

Another area of concern is **predatory pricing**, which is defined as (1) setting prices below cost *and* (2) intending to raise prices after eliminating rivals to cover its losses in the long run ("an attempt to monopolize"). This is an area of significant contention. First, it is not clear what exactly constitutes "cost." Second, even when firms are found to be selling below cost, US courts have ruled that if rivals are too numerous to eliminate, one firm cannot recoup the losses incurred by charging low prices by later jacking up prices, so its pricing cannot be labeled "predatory." This seems to be the case in most industries. These two legal tests have made it extremely difficult to win a (domestic) predation case in the United States.[28]

extraterritoriality
The reach of one country's laws to other countries.

A third area of concern is **extraterritoriality**, namely, the reach of one country's laws to other countries. US courts have taken it upon themselves to *unilaterally* punish non-US cartels (some of which may be legal elsewhere). One example is the diamond cartel led by De Beers (see Emerging Markets 8.1). Recently, the EU evidently has taken a page from the US antitrust playbook. It threatened to veto the merger between Boeing and McDonnell Douglas, successfully torpedoed the proposed merger between GE and Honeywell, and heavily fined Microsoft and Intel (Emerging Markets 8.2). Without a doubt, in the age of globalization, extraterritorial applications of domestic competition/antitrust laws create tension among governments and firms.[29]

Since the Reagan era, US antitrust enforcement has generally become more permissive. It is not an accident that strategic alliances among competitors have proliferated since the 1980s (see Chapter 7). However, despite improved clarity and permissiveness, the legal standards are still ambiguous. For example, in 1996, Boeing was allowed to acquire McDonnell Douglass, creating a real monopoly in commercial aircraft (at least domestically). However, in 2011, AT&T was not allowed to take over T-Mobile, even though the combined nation-wide market share of the two firms would barely exceed 40%. Given such fluctuating and inconsistent application of antitrust laws within one country, it is easy to understand the unpredictability and the frustration associated with the international application of antitrust laws in different countries. In the absence of international harmonization of antitrust policy, it is crucial that firms be aware of these ambiguities when planning their actions, especially when operating under the jurisdiction of multiple governments (see Emerging Markets 8.2).

Formal Institutions Governing International Competition: A Focus on Antidumping

dumping
An exporter selling below cost abroad and planning to raise prices after eliminating local rivals.

In the same spirit of predatory pricing, **dumping** is defined as (1) an exporter selling below cost abroad and (2) planning to raise prices after eliminating local rivals. While domestic predation is usually labeled "anticompetitive," cross-border dumping is often emotionally accused of being "unfair."

Consider the following two scenarios. First, a steel producer in *Indiana* enters a new market in Texas, where it offers prices lower than those in Indiana, resulting in a 10% market share in Texas. Texas firms have two choices. The first one is to initiate a lawsuit against the Indiana firm for "predatory pricing." However, it is difficult to prove (1) that the Indiana firm is selling below cost *and* (2) that its pricing is an "attempt to monopolize." Under US antitrust laws, a predation case like this will have no chance of succeeding. In other words, domestic competition/antitrust laws offer no hope for protection. Thus, Texas firms are most likely to opt for their second option—to retaliate in kind by offering lower prices to customers in Indiana, benefitting consumers in both Texas and Indiana.

EMERGING MARKETS 8.2 〉 〉 ETHICAL DILEMMA

From Trade Wars to Antitrust Wars

In the 21st century, trade wars are often threatened but seldom fought. However, a new style of trade wars centered on protectionism is on the rise. These new trade wars are increasingly known as antitrust wars, because antitrust policy, which historically focuses on domestic competition, has been used to score international points.

In 2001, the EU antitrust authorities vetoed the proposed merger of two US-based firms, GE and Honeywell. In 2009, the EU fined Intel a record $1.45 billion for alleged anticompetitive conduct against its smaller US-based rival, AMD. In 2004, the EU fined Microsoft $660 million for bundling its own Media Player with Windows and thus excluding market access for RealNetworks, a US-based rival. In 2009, the EU prosecuted Microsoft for tying Windows with its own web browser, Internet Explorer, and stifling competition from other browsers— exactly the same alleged crime pursued by US authorities a decade ago. The only viable US competitor from the earlier US case against Microsoft, Netscape, had essentially vanished by 2009, accounting for less than 1% of browser usage. This time, the EU case against Microsoft was triggered by a complaint from Opera Software, an Oslo, Norway-based browser maker. In comparison with Explorer's 86% global browser market share in 1999, the 2009 case came at a time when Microsoft's dominance in browsers was weakened. In 2009, Explorer only had 68% of the global market, and its nearest competitor, Firefox (developed by US-based Mozilla), enjoyed 20%. In Europe, Microsoft was even weaker, with Explorer accounting for only 60% of the market, followed by Opera's 5% and Firefox's 3%. Overall, the EU antitrust authorities appear to more vigorously pursue leading US firms, suggesting a potential protectionist undertone.

Not to be outdone, the fledgling Chinese antitrust authorities entered the foray by starting to enforce China's new Antimonopoly Law in 2008. Mergers of firms *not* headquartered in China, as long as their combined China turnover reached $120 million in the previous year, had to be cleared by Chinese authorities. For example, the merger between Belgium-based InBev and US-based Anheuser-Busch was approved by the Chinese authorities, subject to some conditions. What was controversial was the very first decision to stop an acquisition announced in 2009: the proposed acquisition of China's leading fruit juice maker Huiyuan by Coca-Cola. At $2.4 billion, the price was 50 times Huiyuan's expected earnings in 2008 and a 200% premium to Huiyuan's share price. Huiyuan's delighted owners agreed to sell. The only party blocking the transaction was the Chinese Ministry of Commerce. The Ministry cited the adverse impact on small and medium-sized domestic juice makers as a major reason—in other words, protectionism. Beyond the antitrust merit of this individual case, there is a possibility that the Chinese authorities used it to signal displeasure to the United States, which recently disallowed high-profile Chinese acquisitions in the United States. Such signals may be mixed. In 2011, Yum! Brands' acquisition of an iconic national chain restaurant, Little Sheep Hot Pot, did receive approval from the Chinese antitrust authorities. Yum! Brands thus could add Little Sheep to its successful restaurants such as Kentucky Fried Chicken (KFC) and Pizza Hut in China.

Sources: Based on (1) M. Bachrack, 2009, Merger control under China's Antimonopoly Law, *China Business Review*, July: 18–21; (2) J. Clougherty, 2005, Antitrust holdup source, cross-national institutional variation, and corporate political strategy implications for domestic mergers in a global context, *Strategic Management Journal*, 26: 769–790; (3) *Wall Street Journal*, 2009, EU hits Microsoft with new antitrust charges, January 17; (4) *Wall Street Journal*, 2011, Yum's proposed Little Sheep takeover approved, November 8, online.wsj.com.

antidumping laws

Laws that punish foreign companies that engage in dumping in a domestic market.

Now in the second scenario, the "invading" firm is not from Indiana but *India*. Holding everything else constant, Texas firms can argue that the Indian firm is dumping. Under US **antidumping laws,** Texas producers "would almost certainly obtain legal relief on the very same facts that would not support an antitrust *claim*, let alone antitrust relief."[30] Note that imposing antidumping duties on Indian imports reduces the incentive for Texas firms to counter attack by entering India, resulting in *higher* prices in both Texas and India, where consumers are hurt. These two hypothetical scenarios are highly realistic. An OECD study in Australia, Canada, the EU, and the US reports that 90% of the practices found to be unfairly dumping in these countries would never have been questioned under their own antitrust laws if used between domestic firms.[31] In a nutshell, foreign firms are discriminated against by the formal rules of the game.

Discrimination is also evident in the actual antidumping investigation. A case is usually filed by a domestic firm with the relevant government authorities. In the United States, the authorities are the International Trade Administration (a unit of the Department of Commerce) and International Trade Commission (an independent government agency). These government agencies then send lengthy questionnaires to the foreign firms accused of dumping and request comprehensive, proprietary data on their cost and pricing, in English, using US generally accepted accounting principles (GAAP), within 30–45 days. Many foreign defendants fail to provide such data on time because they are not familiar with US GAAP. The investigation can have one of the four following outcomes:

- If no data are forthcoming from abroad, the estimated data provided by the accusing firm become the evidence, and the accusing firm can easily win.

- If foreign firms do provide data, the accusing firm can still argue that these unfair foreigners have lied—"There is no way their costs can be so low!" In the case of Louisiana versus Chinese crawfish suppliers, the authenticity of the $9 per *week* salary made by Chinese workers was a major point of contention.

- Even if the low cost data are verified, US (and EU) antidumping laws allow the complainant to argue that these data are not "fair." In the case of China, the argument goes, its cost data reflect huge distortions due to government intervention because China is still a "nonmarket" economy. Wages may be low, but workers may also be provided with low-cost housing and government-subsidized benefits. Thus the crawfish case boiled down to how much it would cost hypothetically to raise crawfish in a market economy. In this particular case, Spain was mysteriously chosen. Because Spanish costs were about the same as Louisiana costs, despite vehement objections, the Chinese were found guilty of dumping in America by selling below *Spanish* costs. Thus, 110% to 123% import duties were levied on Chinese crawfish.

- The fourth possible outcome is that the defendant wins the case. But this is rare and happens in only 5% of the antidumping cases in the United States.

One study found that simply filing an antidumping petition (regardless of the outcome) may result in a nontrivial 1% increase in the stock price for US listed firms (an average of $46 million increase in market value).[32] Evidently, Wall Street knows that Uncle Sam favors US firms. Globally, this means that governments usually protect their domestic firms in antidumping investigations. Not surprisingly, antidumping cases have proliferated throughout the world. It is ironic that the rising tide of globalization in the past two decades has been accompanied by the rising proliferation of antidumping cases, which are allowed by the World Trade Organization (WTO). The institution-based message to firms defending home markets is clear: Get to know your country's antidumping laws. The institution-based message to firms interested in doing business abroad is also clear: Your degree of freedom in overseas pricing is significantly less than that in domestic pricing. In summary, let's drop the "F" word (free) in "free market" competition.

Overall, institutional conditions such as the availability of antidumping protection are not just the "background." They directly determine what weapons a firm has in its arsenal to wage competitive battles. Next, we outline two main action items.

Attack and Counterattack

attack
An initial set of actions to gain competitive advantage.

counterattack
A set of actions in response to attacks.

thrust
The classic frontal attack with brute force.

feint
A firm's attack on a focal arena important to a competitor, but not the attacker's true target area.

In the form of price cuts, advertising campaigns, market entries, and new product introductions, an **attack** is defined as an initial set of actions to gain a competitive advantage, and a **counterattack** is a set of actions in response to an attack (see Figure 8.6). This section focuses on: (1) What are the main kinds of attacks? (2) What kinds of attacks are more likely to be successful?

Three Main Types of Attack

The three main types of attack are (1) thrust, (2) feint, and (3) gambit.[33] Shown in Figure 8.7, **thrust** is the classic frontal attack with brute forces. A case in point is the smartphone war. In 2008, HTC launched the world's first smartphone powered by Google's Android operating system. Such a thrust made HTC in 2011 become the largest smartphone vendor in the United States with a 25% market share, ahead of Apple iPhone's 20% and Blackberry's 9% (see the Closing Case).

A **feint**, in basketball, is one player's effort to fool his/her defender, pretending he/she would go one way but instead charging ahead another way. Shown in Figure 8.8, in competitive dynamics, a feint is a firm's attack on a focal arena important to a competitor but one that is not the attacker's true target area.[34] The feint is followed by the attacker's commitment of resources to its actual target area. Consider the "Marlboro war" between Philip Morris and R. J. Reynolds (RJR). In the early 1990s, both firms' traditional focal market, the United States, experienced a 15% decline over the previous decade. Both were interested in Central and Eastern Europe (CEE), which grew rapidly. Philip Morris executed a feint in the United States by dropping 20% off the price on its flagship brand, Marlboro, on one *day* (April 2, 1993, which became known as the "Marlboro Friday"). Confronting this ferocious move, RJR diverted substantial resources earmarked for CEE to defend its US market. Philip Morris thus rapidly established its dominance in CEE.

FIGURE 8.6 It's War!

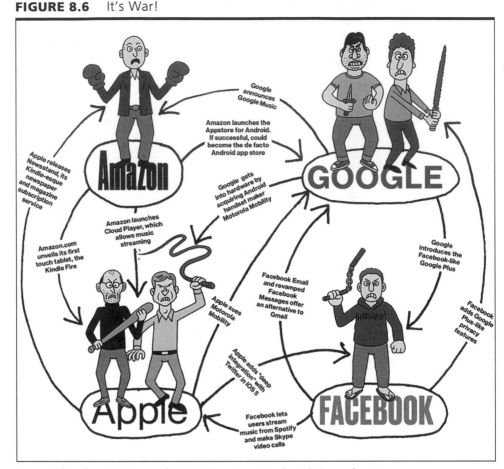

Source: Bloomberg Businessweek, 2011, Year in review (p. 65), December 23.

gambit

A firm's withdrawal from a low-value market to attract rival firms to divert resources into the low-value market so that the original withdrawing firm can capture a high-value market.

A **gambit**, in chess, is a move that sacrifices a low-value piece in order to capture a high-value piece. The competitive equivalent is to withdraw from a low-value market to attract rivals to divert resources into it in order to capture a high-value market (Figure 8.9). For example, Gillette and Bic competed in both razors and lighters. Gillette was stronger in razors and Bic was stronger in lighters. Gillette withdrew *entirely* from lighters and devoted its attention to razors. Bic accepted the gambit and diverted razor resources to lighters. The gambit can be regarded as an exchange of the spheres of influence between Gillette and Bic, each with a stronger position in one market.

Awareness, Motivation, and Capability

Obviously, unopposed attacks are more likely to be successful. Thus, attackers need to understand the three drivers for counterattacks: (1) awareness, (2) motivation, and (3) capabilities.[35]

FIGURE 8.7 Thrust

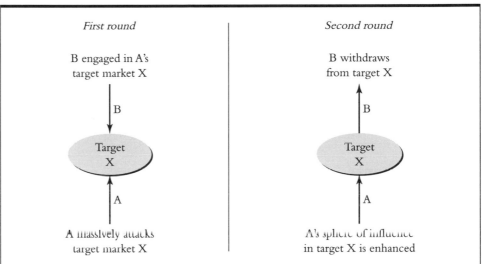

Source: Adapted from R. G. McGrath, M. Chen, & I. C. MacMillan, 1998, Multimarket maneuvering in uncertain spheres of influence: Resource diversion strategies (p. 729), *Academy of Management Review*, 23: 724–740.

FIGURE 8.8 Feint

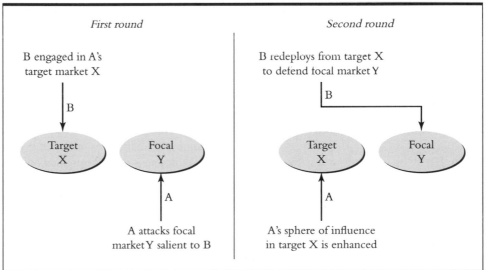

Source: Adapted from R. G. McGrath, M. Chen, & I. C. MacMillan, 1998, Multimarket maneuvering in uncertain spheres of influence: Resource diversion strategies (p. 731), *Academy of Management Review*, 23: 724–740.

FIGURE 8.9 Gambit

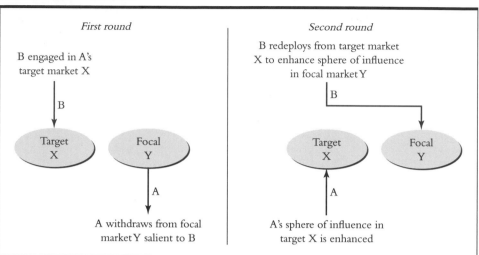

Source: Adapted from R. G. McGrath, M. Chen, & I. C. MacMillan, 1998, Multimarket maneuvering in uncertain spheres of influence: Resource diversion strategies (p. 733), *Academy of Management Review*, 23: 724–740.

blue ocean strategy

A strategy that focuses on developing new markets (or "blue ocean") and avoids attacking core markets defended by rivals, which is likely to result in a bloody price war (or "red ocean").

- If an attack is so subtle that rivals are not *aware* of it, the attacker's objectives are likely to be attained. One interesting idea is the "**blue ocean strategy**" that avoids attacking core markets defended by rivals.[36] A thrust on rivals' core markets is very likely to result in a bloody price war—in other words, a "red ocean." In the 1990s, Netscape drew tremendous publicity by labeling Microsoft the "Death Star" (of the movie *Star Wars* fame) and predicting that the Internet would make Windows obsolete. Such a challenge helped make Netscape Microsoft's number-one enemy, leading to the demise of Netscape (or its drowning in the "red ocean").

- *Motivation* is also crucial. If the attacked market is of marginal value, managers may decide not to counterattack. Consider how China's Haier entered the US white goods market. Although Haier dominates its home country with a broad range of products, it chose to enter the US market in a most non-threatening segment: mini-bars (compact refrigerators) for hotels and dorms. Does anyone remember the brand of the mini-bar in the last hotel room where you stayed? Evidently, not only did you fail to pay attention to that brand, but incumbents such as GE and Whirlpool also dismissed this segment as peripheral and low margin. In other words, they were not motivated to counterattack. Thanks in part to the incumbents' lack of motivation to counterattack, Haier now commands a 50% US market share in compact refrigerators and has built a factory in South Carolina to go after more lucrative product lines.

- Even if an attack is identified and a firm is motivated to respond, it requires strong *capabilities* to carry out counterattacks—as discussed in our earlier section on resources.

Cooperation and Signaling

Some firms choose to compete, and others choose to cooperate. How do firms signal their intention to cooperate in order to *reduce* competitive intensity? Short of illegally talking directly to rivals, firms have to resort to signaling—that is, "While you can't talk to your competitors on pricing, you can always *wink* at them." We outline four means of such winking:

- Firms may enter new markets, not necessarily to challenge incumbents but to seek mutual forbearance by establishing multimarket contact. Thus, MNEs often chase each other, entering one country after another. Airlines that meet in many routes are often less aggressive than airlines that meet in one or a few routes.

- Firms can send an open signal for a truce. As GM faced grave financial difficulties in 2005, Toyota's chairman told the media *twice* that Toyota would "help GM" by raising Toyota prices in the United States. Toyota's signal could not have been more unambiguous, short of talking directly to GM, which would have been illegal.

- Sometimes firms can send a signal to rivals by enlisting the help of governments. Although it is illegal to hold direct negotiations with rivals on what constitutes "fair" pricing, holding such discussions is legal under the auspices of government investigations. Thus, filing an antidumping petition or suing a rival does not necessarily indicate a totally hostile intent but rather a signal to talk. When Cisco sued Huawei, they were able to *legally* discuss a number of strategic issues during settlement negotiations, which were mediated by US and Chinese governments. In the end, Cisco dropped its case against Huawei after both firms negotiated a settlement.

- Firms can organize strategic alliances with rivals for cost reduction. Although price fixing is illegal, reducing cost by 10% through an alliance, which is legal, has the same impact on the financial bottom line as collusively raising price by 10%.

Overall, because of the sensitive nature of interfirm cooperation designed to reduce competition, we do not know a lot about it. However, to the extent that business is both war and peace, strategists need to pay as much attention to making peace with rivals as fighting wars against them.

Local Firms versus Multinational Enterprises

While managers, students, and journalists are often fascinated by MNE rivalries such as between Coca-Cola and Pepsi, GM and Toyota, and SAP and Oracle, much less is known about how local firms cope with MNE attacks. Given the broad choices of competing and/ or cooperating, local firms can adopt one of four strategic postures, depending on (1) the industry conditions and (2) the nature of competitive assets. Shown in Figure 8.10, these factors suggest four strategic actions.[37]

Cell 3 shows how in some industries, the pressures to globalize are relatively low and local firms' strengths lie in a deep understanding of local markets. In this case, local assets where MNEs are weak are leveraged in a **defender** strategy. For example, facing an

defender
A strategy that leverages local assets in areas in which MNEs are weak.

FIGURE 8.10   How Local Firms in Emerging Economies Respond to Multinationals

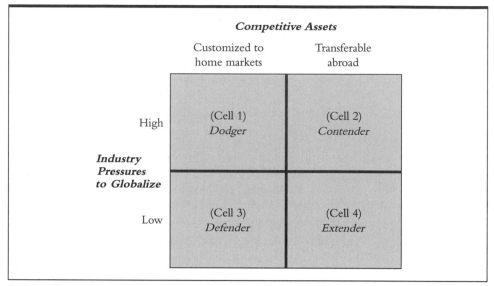

Source: Adapted from N. Dawar & T. Frost, 1999, Competing with giants: Survival strategies for local companies in emerging markets (p. 122), *Harvard Business Review*, March–April: 119–129.

onslaught from MNE cosmetics firms, a number of local Israeli firms turned to focus on products suited to the Middle Eastern climate and managed to defend their turf. Ahava has been particularly successful, partly because of its highly unique components extracted from the Dead Sea that MNEs cannot find elsewhere. In other words, while local firms such as Ahava cede some markets (such as mainstream cosmetics) to MNEs, they build strongholds in narrower but deeper product markets (such as the "Dead Sea mud"). In other words, this is an example of gambit.

Cell 4 shows industries where pressures for globalization are relatively low and local firms may possess some skills that are transferable overseas, thus leading to an **extender** strategy. This strategy centers on leveraging home-grown competencies abroad. For example, Asian Paints controls 40% of the house paint market in India. Asian Paints developed strong capabilities tailored to this environment, characterized by thousands of small retailers serving numerous poor consumers who only want small quantities of paint that can be diluted to save money. Such capabilities are not only a winning formula in India but also in much of the developing world. In contrast, MNEs, whose business model typically centers on affluent customers in developed economies, have had a hard time coming up with profitable low-end products.

Cell 1 depicts local firms that compete in industries with high pressures for globalization. Thus, a **dodger** strategy is necessary. This is largely centered on cooperating through joint ventures (JVs) with MNEs and sell-offs to MNEs. In the Chinese automobile industry, *all* major domestic automakers have entered JVs with MNEs. In the Czech Republic, the government sold Skoda to Volkswagen. In essence, to the extent that local

extender

A strategy that centers on leveraging homegrown competencies abroad by expanding into similar markets.

dodger

A strategy that centers on cooperating through joint ventures with MNEs and/or sell-offs to MNEs.

firms are unable to successfully compete head-on against MNEs, cooperation becomes necessary. In other words, if you can't beat them, join them!

Finally, in Cell 2, some local firms, through a **contender** strategy, engage in rapid learning and then expand overseas. A number of Chinese mobile phone makers such as TCL and Bird rapidly caught up with global heavyweights such as Motorola and Nokia. Domestic firms in China now command more than 50% market share. Following their success at home, TCL and Bird have now entered foreign markets.

Particularly in emerging economies, how domestic firms respond is crucial for managers. For example, in China, despite initial dominance, MNEs do not always stay on top. In numerous industries (such as sportswear, cellular phone, personal computer, and home appliance), many MNEs have found themselves losing market share to domestic firms. While weak domestic players are washed out, some of the stronger domestic firms not only succeed in the competitive domestic environment, but now challenge MNEs overseas. In the process, they become a new breed of MNEs themselves. The upshot is that when facing the onslaught of MNEs, local firms are not necessarily "sitting ducks."

contender
A strategy that centers on rapid learning and then expanding overseas.

Debates and Extensions

Numerous debates revolve around this sensitive area. We outline two of the most significant ones: (1) strategy versus IO economics and antitrust policy, and (2) competition versus antidumping.

Strategy versus IO Economics and Antitrust Policy

Managers deploy strategy to lead their firms to win in the marketplace. But antitrust officials, influenced by IO economics, sometimes get in the way by accusing firms (such as Microsoft) of being "anticompetitive." Most business school students do not study antitrust policy. After they graduate and become managers, they do not care about it. Antitrust officials, on the other hand, tend to study economics and law but not business. A background in economics and law, however, does not give antitrust officials an intimate understanding of how firm-level competition and/or cooperation unfolds, which is something that a business school education provides. These officials often believe that in the absence of government intervention (specifically, antitrust action), competitive advantage of large firms is likely to last forever and monopoly will prevail. Managers know better: Given rapid technological changes, ambitious new entrants, and strong global competition, no competitive advantage lasts forever even in the absence of government intervention (see Chapter 3).[38] It is possible that none of the antitrust officials has ever studied a strategy textbook like this one. But officials who have a static view of the sustainability of competitive advantage end up deciding and enforcing the rules governing competition. Such a disconnect naturally breeds mutual suspicion and frustration on both sides. Business school students and managers will be better off if they arm themselves with knowledge about antitrust concerns and engage in intelligent conversations and debates with officials and policy makers.

Why were large and successful firms such as AT&T, IBM, and Microsoft (Table 8.2) accused of engaging in illegal "anticompetitive" conduct for the very same conduct that made them successful in the first place? Google is now widely rumored to be the next antitrust target. Because the United States has the world's oldest antitrust frameworks (dating back to the 1890 Sherman Act), the US debate is the most watched in the world and so is the focus here. Rather than adopting a US-centric approach, here we treat the US debate as a *case study* that may have global ramifications.

On behalf of managers, strategy and management scholars have made four arguments.[39] First, antitrust laws were often created in response to the old realities of mostly domestic competition—the year 1890 for the Sherman Act is *not* a typo for 1990. However, the largely global competition today means that a large dominant firm in one country (think of Boeing) does not automatically translate into a dangerous monopoly. The existence of foreign rivals (such as Airbus) forces the large domestic incumbent to be more competitive.

Second, the very actions accused to be "anticompetitive" may actually be highly "competitive" or "hypercompetitive." In the 1990s, the hypercompetitive Microsoft was charged with "anticompetitive" behavior. Its alleged crime? *Not* voluntarily helping its competitors. It is puzzling why Microsoft should have voluntarily helped its competitors. Just imagine: If your manager asked you to voluntarily help your firm's competitors, would you just do it or think that your manager was out of his or her mind?

Third, US antitrust laws create strategic confusion.[40] Because the intention to destroy your firm's rivals is the smoking gun of antitrust cases, managers are forced to use milder language. Don't say or write a memo that says "We want to beat our competitors!" Otherwise, managers could end up in court. In contrast, non-US firms often use war-like language: Komatsu is famous for "Encircling Caterpillar!" and Honda for "Annihilate, crush, and destroy Yamaha!" The inability to talk straight creates confusion among lower-level managers and employees in US firms. A confused firm is not likely to be aggressive.

Finally, US antitrust laws may be unfair because these laws discriminate *against* US firms. In 1983, if GM and Ford were to propose to jointly manufacture cars, antitrust officials would have turned them down, citing an (obvious!) intent to collude. The jargon is *per se* (in and of itself) violation of antitrust laws. Ironically, starting in 1983, GM was allowed to jointly make cars with Toyota. Now 30 years later, Toyota is a leading automaker in the United States. The upshot? American antitrust laws have helped Toyota but not Ford or GM. One country's (or region's) antitrust laws may be used against other countries' firms. For example, the EU antitrust authorities have been very harsh on US firms: stopping the merger between GE and Honeywell and severely fining Microsoft and Intel. While these actions provoked protests from the American side, they are at least understandable from a protectionist standpoint (see Emerging Markets 8.2). What is difficult to understand is why US firms are sometimes discriminated against by their own government. The most recent case in point: In 2011, AT&T was forced to abandon its merger with T-Mobile, a wholly owned subsidiary of Deutsche Telekom (DT), and was forced to pay a $3 billion (!) breakup fee to T-Mobile. A US firm was thus forced by the US government to subsidize a foreign firm, which did not even want to compete in the United States anymore.

Far from being theoretical, this institution-based debate has far-reaching ramifications for the future of global competition. Business students and future managers should pay attention to this debate and be prepared to engage in it. As managers rise to assume more strategic, C-level positions (such as CEO, CFO, and CIO), the importance of knowledge about this debate rises.

Competition versus Antidumping

Two arguments exist against the practice of imposing antidumping restrictions on foreign firms. First, because dumping centers on selling "below cost," it is often difficult (if not impossible) to prove the case given the ambiguity concerning "cost." The second argument is that if foreign firms are indeed selling below cost, so what? This is simply a (hyper)competitive action. When entering a new market, virtually all firms lose money on Day 1 (and often in Year 1). Until some point when the firm breaks even, it will lose money because it sells below cost. Domestically, cases abound of such dumping, which are perfectly legal. We all receive numerous coupons in the mail offering free or cheap goods. Coupon items are frequently sold (or given away) below cost. Do consumers complain about such good deals? Probably not. "If the foreigners are kind enough (or dumb enough) to sell their goods to our country below cost, why should we complain?"[41]

A classic response is: What if, through "unfair" dumping, foreign rivals drive out local firms and then jack up prices? Given the competitive nature of most industries, it is often difficult to eliminate all rivals and then recoup losses by charging higher monopoly prices. The fear of foreign monopoly is often exaggerated by special interest groups who benefit at the expense of consumers in the entire country. Joseph Stiglitz, a Nobel laureate in economics, wrote that antidumping duties "are simply naked protectionism" and one country's "fair trade laws" are often known elsewhere as "unfair trade laws."[42]

One solution is to phase out antidumping laws and use the same standards against domestic predatory pricing. Such a waiver of antidumping charges has been in place between Australia and New Zealand, between Canada and the United States, and within the EU. Thus, a Canadian firm, essentially treated as a US firm, can be accused of predatory pricing but cannot be accused of dumping in the United States. Since antidumping is about "us versus them," such harmonization represents essentially an expanded notion of "us." However, domestically, as noted earlier, a predation case is very difficult to make. In such a way, competition can be fostered, aggressiveness rewarded, and "dumping" legalized.

The Savvy Strategist

If capitalism, according to Joseph Schumpeter, is about "creative destruction," then the "strategy as action" perspective highlights how such power of creative destruction is unleashed in the marketplace. Consequently, three implications for action emerge for the savvy strategist (Table 8.3). First, you need to thoroughly understand the nature of your industry that may facilitate competition and/or cooperation. Consider music, software, and film industries, where digital piracy is accelerating thanks to broadband Internet connections and peer-to-peer networks. Table 8.4 advises incumbents (copyright holders) to view pirates as competitors and new entrants. Thus, lower cost and enhanced differentiation, derived from the industry-based view, may prove effective in fighting digital piracy.

Second, you and your firm need to strengthen capabilities to compete and/or cooperate more effectively. In attacks and counterattacks, subtlety, frequency, complexity, and unpredictability are helpful. In cooperation, market similarity and mutual forbearance may be better. As Sun Tzu advised, you not only need to "know yourself," but also "know your opponents" by developing skills and instincts in competitor analysis and thinking like your opponents.

TABLE 8.3 Strategic Implications for Action

- Thoroughly understand the nature of your industry that may facilitate competition and/or cooperation.
- Strengthen resources and capabilities that more effectively compete and/or cooperate.
- Understand the rules of the game governing domestic and international competition around the world.

© Cengage Learning

Third, you need to understand the rules of the game governing competition around the world. Aggressive language such as "Let's beat competitors" may not be allowed in countries such as the United States. Remember, an email, like a diamond, is "forever," and "deleted" emails are still stored on a server and can be recovered. However, carefully crafted ambitions such as Wal-Mart's "We want to be number one in grocery business" are legal, because such wording (at least on paper) shows no illegal intention to destroy rivals. Too bad 31 US supermarket chains declared bankruptcy since Wal-Mart charged into groceries in the 1990s—just a tragic coincidence (!).[43]

The necessity to understand the rules of the game is crucial when venturing abroad. What is legal domestically may be illegal elsewhere. Many Chinese managers are surprised that their low-cost strategy is labeled "illegal" dumping in the very countries advocating "free market" competition. In reality, "free markets" are not free. However, managers well-versed in the rules of the game may launch subtle attacks without incurring the wrath of antidumping officials. Imports commanding less than 3% market share in a 12-month period are regarded by US antidumping laws as "negligible imports" not worthy of investigation.[44] Thus, foreign firms not crossing such a "red line" would be safe. As an exporter, would you like to maintain a steady 3% US market share every year over ten years or a dramatic 30% upsurge in Year 1, which would attract antidumping actions preventing further growth in Year 2 and beyond?

In terms of the four fundamental questions, why firms differ (Question 1) and how firms behave (Question 2) boil down to how the strategy tripod influences competitive

TABLE 8.4 Strategic Responses to Digital Piracy

- Not only compete but also cooperate with pirates by adopting a permissive stance, especially when there are strong network effects and the copyright holder is competing with rivals to get its offering established as a standard.
- Provide free samples, instead of having pirates serve the demand for samples whose quality may be questionable.
- Exercise cost leadership by lowering the price of the legal good in order to deter entry by pirates.
- Enhance differentiation by offering something extra to consumers who pay full price for the legal good.
- Change the incentives of buyers of pirate products (such as music companies' support for Apple's iTune services).
- Influence the norms associated with digital piracy by legally challenging and punishing major offenders.

Source: Based on text in C. Hill, 2007, Digital piracy: Causes, consequences, and strategic responses, *Asia Pacific Journal of Management*, 24: 9–25. For related research, see D. Bryce, J. Dyer, & N. Hatch, 2011, Competing against free, *Harvard Business Review*, June: 104–111.

dynamics. What determines the scope of the firm (Question 3) is driven, in part, by an interest in establishing mutual forbearance with multimarket rivals—in other words, "the best defense is a good offense." Finally, what determines the international success and failure of firms (Question 4), to a large extent, depends on how firms carry out their competitive and cooperative actions. Overall, given that business is simultaneously war *and* peace, a winning formula, as in war and chess, is "Look ahead, reason back."

CHAPTER SUMMARY

1. Articulate the "strategy as action" perspective
- Underpinning the "strategy as action" perspective, competitive dynamics refers to actions and responses undertaken by competing firms.

2. Understand the industry conditions conducive for cooperation and collusion
- Such industries tend to have (1) a small number of rivals, (2) a price leader, (3) homogenous products, (4) high entry barriers, and (5) high market commonality (mutual forbearance).

3. Explain how resources and capabilities influence competitive dynamics
- Resource similarity and market commonality can yield a powerful framework for competitor analysis.

4. Outline how formal institutions affect domestic and international competition
- Domestically, antitrust laws focus on collusion and predatory pricing.
- Internationally, antidumping laws discriminate against foreign firms and protect domestic firms.

5. Identify the drivers for attacks, counterattacks, and signaling
- The three main types of attacks are (1) thrust, (2) feint, and (3) gambit. Counterattacks are driven by (1) awareness, (2) motivation, and (3) capability.
- Without talking directly to competitors, firms can signal to rivals through various means.

6. Discuss how local firms fight MNEs
- When confronting MNEs, local firms can choose a variety of strategic choices: (1) defender, (2) extender, (3) dodger, and (4) contender. They may not be as weak as many people believe.

7. Participate in two leading debates concerning competitive dynamics
- (1) Strategy versus IO economics and antitrust policy, and (2) competition versus antidumping.

8. Draw strategic implications for action
- Thoroughly understand the nature of your industry that may facilitate competition or cooperation.
- Strengthen resources and capabilities to compete and/or cooperate more effectively.
- Understand the rules of the game governing domestic and international competition around the world.

KEY TERMS

Antidumping laws p. 240

Antitrust laws p. 226

Antitrust policy p. 236

Attack p. 241

Blue ocean strategy p. 244

Capacity to punish p. 228

Cartel (trust) p. 226

Collusion p. 225

Collusive price setting p. 237

Competition policy p. 236

Competitive dynamics p. 224

Competitor analysis p. 224

Concentration ratio p. 228

Contender p. 247

Counterattack p. 241

Cross-market retaliation p. 231

Defender p. 245

Dodger p. 246

Dumping p. 238

Explicit collusion p. 226

Extender p. 246

Extraterritoriality p. 238

Feint p. 241

Gambit p. 242

Game theory p. 226

Market commonality p. 231

Multimarket competition p. 225

Mutual forbearance p. 225

Predatory pricing p. 238

Price leader p. 228

Prisoners' dilemma p. 226

Resource similarity p. 232

Tacit collusion p. 226

Thrust p. 241

CRITICAL DISCUSSION QUESTIONS

1. **ON ETHICS:** As a CEO, you feel the price war in your industry is killing profits for all firms. However, you have been warned by corporate lawyers not to openly discuss pricing with rivals, whom you know personally (you went to school with them). How would you signal your intentions?

2. **ON ETHICS:** As a CEO, you are concerned that your firm and the industry in your country are being devastated by foreign imports. Trade lawyers suggest that you file an antidumping case against leading foreign rivals and assure you a win. Would you file an antidumping case or not? Why?

3. **ON ETHICS:** As part of a feint attack, your firm (firm A) announces that in the next year, it intends to enter country X where the competitor (firm B) is very strong. Your firm's real intention is to march into country Y where B is very weak. There is actually *no* plan to enter X. However, in the process of intentionally trying to "fool" B, customers, suppliers, investors, and the media are also being inadvertently misled. What are the ethical dilemmas here? Do the pros of this action outweigh its cons?

TOPICS FOR EXPANDED PROJECTS

1. Find some competitive moves made by some emerging multinationals from emerging economies. How do the two frameworks in Figures 8.4 and 8.10 help you understand these moves?

2. If your country has competition/antitrust laws, find a landmark case, and explain whether you support the plaintiff or the defendant. If your country does not have competition/antitrust laws, explain why.

3. *ON ETHICS:* As a party not directly involved in the (second) *United States v. AT&T* case (in 2011, during which the US government blocked AT&T's proposed merger of T-Mobile), such as a manager at another firm or a student, what do you think is right about antitrust policy? What is wrong about antitrust policy? Why?

CLOSING CASE

Emerging Markets: HTC Fights Apple

Everybody has heard of Apple and its iPhone, which set the smartphone market on fire when it first appeared in 2007. Fast forward to 2012: Which company had the highest smartphone market share in the United States? Not Apple (20% market share), not Samsung (20%), and not Blackberry (9%). The winner was HTC, which commanded a 25% market share. "Apple iPhone's market share was lower than *what*?" some of you may ask.

Founded in Taiwan in 1997, HTC was an "unlikely leader" in the smartphone world infested by global heavyweights, according to *Bloomberg Businessweek*. Founded as High Tech Computer, the firm followed the well-known Taiwanese outsourcing formula of designing and manufacturing gadgets for other companies without a brand name of its own. The plain-vanilla original name (which the firm no longer uses) was as low-profile as a corporate name could be. The firm toiled for a long time in obscurity as an original design manufacturer (ODM), quietly designing and making high-end smartphones for leading Western mobile operators such as Verizon and Orange. HTC's first big contract came when Microsoft asked it to make smartphones. HTC quickly became the world's top producer of Windows phones. It set up its US headquarters in Bellevue, Washington, a Seattle suburb where Microsoft was headquartered. Like many contract manufacturers,

HTC worried that a brandless firm would permanently remain a low-margin manufacturer of commodity products. What was worse was that the already razor-thin margin would be squeezed even further as clients shopped for lower-cost producers (read: China). The solution was usually to launch a firm's own brand to command higher margins and more respect—in other words, to become an original *brand* manufacturer (OBM) just like Apple. However, Taiwanese (and Asian) firms attempting to overcome this hurdle usually had to face a "double whammy:" (1) a lack of capabilities in innovation and branding and (2) the loss of clients, which did not want to do business with an emerging rival. Such a "double whammy" forced many manufacturers to remain on the low-cost treadmill. How did HTC overcome the challenge?

Three things stand out. First, as emphasized by Cher Wang, HTC's chairwoman, in media interviews, HTC never did original *equipment* manufacturing (OEM). From the start, it had always been an ODM—emphasizing the "design" function that was lacking among most OEM manufacturers (such as Foxconn or Hon Hai, the largest Taiwanese OEM). The difference was nontrivial: HTC had developed world-class design and innovation capabilities. It began designing some of the world's first touch screen and wireless handheld devices as early as in 1998.

Second, HTC was very skillful in collaborating with larger firms. Such successful collaborations—in combination with its design prowess—led to a series of enviable first-mover accomplishments in this rapidly developing industry. These accomplishments included creating the world's first touch screen smartphones as the Treo for Palm and the iPAQ for Compaq (2000); the first Microsoft-powered smartphone (2002) and the first Microsoft 3G smartphone (2005); the world's first smartphone powered by Google's Android operating system, which was promoted as a free, open-source system (2008); and the first 4G-capable phone in the United States (2010).

Third, unlike many Asian firms that had a hard time globalizing their operations due to language barriers and cultural constraints, HTC was a "born global" firm. Emails and documents were in English from day one. CEO Peter Chou, according to the *Economist*, sounded more like a Silicon Valley management guru than a typical Asian corporate patriarch. "Instead of telling them what to do, I want people to have the freedom to explore their talent," Chou said. Such an open culture made HTC a more attractive employer for Western talents. In 2006, HTC attracted Horace Luke, a rising star at Microsoft. He had been the creative director of Windows Mobile. At HTC, Luke created an innovation infrastructure of fast-moving development teams. Some of these teams were based in Seattle. In 2011, HTC also opened a research and development (R&D) office in Durham, North Carolina. Chou also proudly noted in a 2010 interview that at the top management level, more than half of the CEO's direct reports were not Taiwanese.

Sticking its neck out as a new OBM, HTC started to develop its own brand in 2006. By 2008 when its first Android phone was marketed, it was branded as "HTC." As Google built an ecosystem based on Android to wage its battle with Apple, HTC as Google's leading Android partner gained tremendous visibility. Since then, HTC took off. In 2011, it displaced Acer and was ranked number one among Taiwan's global brands by Interbrand, which listed its brand as number 98 in the world. In 2011, it was named "Device Manufacturer of the Year" by the Mobile World Congress. Also, its market value surpassed that of Nokia to become the third largest smartphone maker in the world (by market value), behind only Apple and Samsung. When asked about Apple in interviews, Chou acknowledged that despite HTC smartphones' attractive features, they would not attract crowds with "midnight

madness" outside Apple stores to lay their hands on the new gadgets. "HTC is HTC," asserted Chou. "I don't care about the iPhone. I don't even look at it."

Apple, on the other hand, took HTC's challenge very seriously. In addition to vigorously competing on the product dimension, Apple sued HTC for 20 counts of patent violations in 2010. This was part of a broader Apple strategy to slow the ascendance of Android phones, which were not only made by HTC but also by Samsung and Motorola. Led by HTC, Android phones rocketed from less than 3% market share in 2009 to 48% in 2011. In addition to HTC, Apple also sued Samsung, Motorola, as well as Google itself. In response, HTC sued Apple for infringing on five of HTC's patents and sought to ban Apple products imported into the United States from manufacturing facilities in Asia.

As HTC's fight with Apple spilled over from product markets to courts, HTC, the clear underdog, claimed that it had sufficient patents to deal with Apple. "Patent lawsuits are normal," Wang answered the media. "Chinese firms have seldom used this strategic weapon. So we are setting an example." Likewise, Chou said, "if HTC can do a good job and set an example in innovation, we can inspire other companies to try the same."

Sources: Based on (1) *21st Century Business Insights*, 2011, HTC: Can being itself allow it to surpass Apple? October 1: 58–59; (2) *Bloomberg Businessweek*, 2010, A former no-name from Taiwan builds a global brand, November 1: 37–38; (3) *Bloomberg Businessweek*, 2011, Android's dominance is patent pending, August 8: 36–37; (4) *Economist*, 2009, Upwardly mobile, July 11: 68; (5) *Economist*, 2011, Android alert, July 23: 64; (6) Interbrand, 2011, Taiwan top 20 global brands 2011, www.brandingtaiwan.com.

CASE DISCUSSION QUESTIONS

1. From a resource-based view, what are HTC's unique resources and capabilities?

2. From an institution-based view, what are the lessons you can draw from the patent lawsuits between HTC and Apple?

3. What are the lessons that ambitious firms in Asia and other emerging economies can draw when they aspire to upgrade their capabilities, become more innovative, and command more respect as OBMs?

NOTES

[**Journal acronyms**] *AMJ* – *Academy of Management Journal;* ***AMR*** – *Academy of Management Review;* ***BW*** – *BusinessWeek* (before 2010) or *Bloomberg Businessweek* (since 2010); ***HBR*** – *Harvard Business Review;* ***JEP*** – *Journal of Economic Perspectives;* ***JIBS*** – *Journal of International Business Studies;* ***JM*** – *Journal of Management;* ***JMS*** – *Journal of Management Studies;* ***JWB*** – *Journal of World Business;* ***SMJ*** – *Strategic Management Journal*

1. D. Ketchen, C. Snow, & V. Hoover, 2004, Research on competitive dynamics, *JM*, 30: 779–804.
2. L. Capron & O. Chatain, 2008, Competitors' resource-oriented strategies, *AMR*, 33: 97–121; K. Coyne & J. Horn, 2009, Predicting your competitor's reaction, *HBR*, April: 90–97; W. Tsai, K. Su, & M. Chen, 2011, Seeing through the eyes of a rival, *AMJ*, 54: 761–778.
3. V. Rindova, M. Becerra, & I. Contardo, 2004, Enacting competitive wars, *AMR*, 29: 670–686.
4. *BW*, 2011, Dan Akerson is not a car guy, August 29: 56–60.
5. J. Anand, L. Mesquita, & R. Vassolo, 2009, The dynamics of multimarket competition in exploration and exploitation activities, *AMJ*, 52: 802–821; H. Greve, 2008, Multimarket contact and sales growth, *SMJ*, 29: 229–249; Z. Guedri & J. McGurie, 2011, Multimarket competition, mobility barriers, and firm performance, *JMS*, 48: 857–890; G. Markman, P. Gianiodis, & A. Buchholtz, 2009, Factor-market rivalry, *AMR*, 34: 423–441; J. Prince & D. Simon, 2009, Multimarket contact and service quality, *AMJ*, 52: 336–354.
6. T. Yu, M. Subramanian, & A. Cannella, 2009, Rivalry deterrence in international markets, *AMJ*, 52: 127–147.
7. J. Baker, 1999, Developments in antitrust economics, *JEP*, 13: 181–194.
8. S. Brenner, 2011, Self-disclosure at international cartels, *JIBS*, 42: 221–234; Y. Zhang & J. Gimeno, 2010, Earnings pressure and competitive behavior, *AMJ*, 53: 743–768.
9. *United States et al. v. AT&T Inc. et al.*, 2011, Second amended complaint (p. 17), September 30, Washington, DC: US District Court for the District of Columbia.
10. *Economist*, 2011, From Big Three to Magnificent Seven, January 15: 67–68.
11. M. Semadeni, 2006, Minding your distance, *SMJ*, 27: 169–187.
12. M. Benner, 2007, The incumbent discount, *AMR*, 32: 703–720; C. Hill & F. Rothaermel, 2003, The performance of incumbent firms in the face of radical technological innovation, *AMR*, 28: 257–274.
13. J. Barney, 2002, *Gaining and Sustaining Competitive Advantage* (p. 359), Upper Saddle River, NJ: Prentice Hall.
14. M. Chen, 1996, Competitor analysis and interfirm rivalry (p. 106), *AMR*, 21: 100–134.
15. E. Rose & K. Ito, 2008, Competitive interactions, *JIBS*, 39: 864–879.
16. G. Clarkson & P. Toh, 2010, "Keep out" signs, *SMJ*, 31: 1202–1225.
17. G. Kilduff, H. Elfenbein, & B. Staw, 2010, The psychology of rivalry, *AMJ*, 53: 943–969; R. S. Livengood & R. Reger, 2010, That's our turf! *AMR*, 35: 48–66.
18. J. Immelt, V. Govindarajan, & C. Trimble, 2009, How GE is disrupting itself, *HBR*, October: 56–65.
19. D. Spar, 1994, *The Cooperative Edge: The Internal Politics of International Cartels* (p. 5), Ithaca, NY: Cornell UP.
20. D. Sirmon, S. Gove, & M. Hitt, 2009, Resource management in dynamic competitive rivalry, *AMJ*, 51: 919–935.
21. J. R. Baum & S. Wally, 2003, Strategic decision speed and firm performance, *SMJ*, 24: 1107–1129; H. Ndofor, D. Sirmon, & X. He, 2011, Firm resources, competitive actions, and performance, *SMJ*, 32: 640–657.
22. R. Agarwal, M. Ganco, & R. Ziedonis, 2009, Reputations for toughness in patent enforcement, *SMJ*, 30: 1349–1374; M. Chen, H. Lin, & J. Michel, 2010, Navigating in a hypercompetitive environment, *SMJ*, 31: 1410–1430; G. Vroom & J. Gimeno, 2007, Ownership form, managerial incentives, and the intensity of rivalry, *AMJ*, 50: 901–922.
23. J. Boyd & R. Bresser, 2008, Performance implications of delayed competitive responses, *SMJ*, 29: 1077–1096; B. Connelly, L. Tihanyi, S. T. Certo, & M. Hitt, 2010, Marching to the beat of different drummers, *AMJ*, 53: 723–742; V. Rindova, W. Ferrier, & R. Wiltbank, 2010, Value from gestalt, *SMJ*, 31: 1474–1497.
24. B. Golden & H. Ma, 2003, Mutual forbearance, *AMR*, 28: 479–493; A. Kalnins, 2004, Divisional multimarket

contact within and between multiunit organizations, *AMJ*, 47: 117–128.

25. Chen, 1996, Competitor analysis and interfirm rivalry (p. 107). See also W. Desarbo, R. Grewal, & J. Wind, 2006, Who competes with whom? *SMJ*, 27: 101–129; L. Fuentelsaz & J. Gomez, 2006, Multipoint competition, strategic similarity, and entry into geographic markets, *SMJ*, 27: 477–499.

26. N. Kumar, 2006, Strategies to fight low-cost rivals, *HBR*, December: 104–112.

27. E. Graham & D. Richardson, 1997, Issue overview (p. 5), in E. Graham & D. Richardson (eds.), *Global Competition Policy*, Washington: Institute for International Economics.

28. *Economist*, 2009, The unkindest cuts, August 22: 68.

29. J. Clougherty, 2005, Antitrust holdup source, cross-national institutional variation, and corporate political strategy implications for domestic mergers in a global context, *SMJ*, 26: 769–790.

30. R. Lipstein, 1997, Using antitrust principles to reform antidumping law (p. 408, original italics), in E. Graham & D. Richardson (eds.), *Global Competition Policy*, Washington: Institute for International Economics.

31. OECD, 1996, *Trade and Competition: Frictions After the Uruguay Round* (p. 18), Paris: OECD.

32. S. Marsh, 1998, Creating barriers for foreign competitors, *SMJ*, 19: 25–37.

33. R. McGrath, M. Chen, & I. MacMillan, 1998, Multi-market maneuvering in uncertain spheres of influence, *AMR*, 23: 724–740.

34. G. Stalk, 2006, Curveball: Strategies to fool the competition, *HBR*, September: 115–122.

35. M. Chen, K. Su, & W. Tsai, 2007, Competitive tension, *AMJ*, 50: 101–118; T. Yu & A. Cannella, 2007, Rivalry between multinational enterprises, *AMJ*, 50: 665–686.

36. W. C. Kim & R. Mauborgne, 2005, *Blue Ocean Strategy*, Boston: Harvard Business School Press.

37. N. Dawar & T. Frost, 1999, Competing with giants, *HBR*, March: 119–129.

38. R. D'Aveni, G. Dagnino, & K. Smith, 2010. The age of temporary advantage, *SMJ*, 31: 1371–1385.

39. R. D'Aveni, 1994, *Hypercompetition*, New York: Free Press.

40. E. Rockefeller, 2007, *The Antitrust Religion*, Washington, DC: Cato Institute.

41. R. Griffin & M. Pustay, 2003, *International Business*, 3rd ed. (p. 241), Upper Saddle River, NJ: Prentice Hall.

42. J. Stglitz, 2002, *Globalization and Its Discontent* (pp. 172–173), New York: Norton.

43. C. Fishman, 2006, *The Wal-Mart Effect*, New York: Penguin.

44. M. Czinkota & M. Kotabe, 1997, A marketing perspective of the US International Trade Commission's antidumping actions (p. 183), *JWB*, 32: 169–187.

9
Diversifying, Acquiring, and Restructuring

10
Strategizing, Structuring, and Learning Around the World

11
Governing the Corporation Around the World

12
Strategizing with Corporate Social Responsibility

PART **3** | CORPORATE-LEVEL
STRATEGIES

DIVERSIFYING, ACQUIRING, AND RESTRUCTURING

© istockphoto/Alexey Stiop

KNOWLEDGE OBJECTIVES

After studying this chapter, you should be able to

1. Define product diversification and geographic diversification

2. Articulate a comprehensive model of diversification

3. Gain insights into the motives and performance of acquisitions

4. Enhance your understanding of restructuring

5. Participate in two leading debates concerning diversification, acquisitions, and restructuring

6. Draw strategic implications for action

Emerging Markets: Corporate Diversification Strategy in South Korean Business Groups

Large conglomerates (business groups), such as Samsung, Hyundai, and LG, are called *chaebol* in South Korea (hereafter Korea). They dominate the economy, contributing approximately 40% of GDP as of 1996. In 1996, Samsung had 80 subsidiaries, Hyundai 57, LG 49, and Daewoo 30—scattered in different industries such as automobiles, chemicals, construction, electronics, financial services, insurance, semiconductors, shipbuilding, and steel. Why and how did *chaebol*, all from humble roots in focused industries, grow to become such sprawling conglomerates? The chairman of LG shared an intriguing story:

> *My father and I started a cosmetic cream factory in the late 1940s. At that time, no company could supply us with plastic caps of adequate quality for cream jars, so we had to start a plastic business. Plastic caps alone were not sufficient to run the plastic molding plant, so we added combs, toothbrushes, and soap boxes. This plastics business also led us to manufacture electric fan blades and telephone cases, which in turn led us to manufacture electrical and electronic products and telecommunications equipment. The plastics business also took us into oil refining, which needed a tanker shipping company. The oil refining company alone was paying an insurance premium amounting to more than half the total revenue of the then largest insurance company in Korea. Thus, an insurance company was started.*

What the story does not reveal is the visible hand of the Korean government, which channeled financial resources to fund *chaebol*'s growth. In the meantime, the government protected domestic markets from foreign competition. However, the cozy protected environment did not last forever. Because Korea's eagerness to join the OECD prior to its accession in 1996 resulted in external pressures to open the economy, the government gradually removed import restrictions. In addition, capital markets became more open and vibrant. At the same time, labor costs rose sharply. Internationally, *chaebol* products were often stuck in the middle between high-end Japanese offerings and low-cost Chinese merchandise.

Confronting such rising environment turbulence by the 1990s, *chaebol* as a group increased their corporate scope. The average number of affiliates of the top 30 *chaebol* grew from 17 per group in 1987 to 22 in 1996, a 30% increase. In the process, they took on a high level of debt. Banks were happy to provide loans, believing that *chaebol* were "too big to fail." The debt/equity ratio ended up being, on average, 617% for the top 30 *chaebol*s. In some extreme cases, New Core's debt/equity ratio was 1,225%, Halla's was 2,066%, and Jinro's was 3,765%.

Unfortunately, by the time the Asian economic crisis of 1997 struck, *chaebol* took an enormous beating. Their excessive borrowing and reckless growth were sharply criticized. Of the 30 top *chaebol* in 1996, close to half of them went through bankruptcy proceedings or bank-sponsored restructuring programs. Daewoo, ranked number four in 1996, was literally broken up. All surviving *chaebol* sold businesses and substantially reduced their scope.

In retrospect, signs of *chaebol*'s troubles had been like writing on the wall before the crisis. There was indeed a time *chaebol* carried a diversification *premium*, with affiliates outcompeting comparable independent firms (about 10% higher sales during 1984–1987). However, rising environmental turbulence coupled with growing firm size proved to be a lethal combination. By 1994–1996, there was a diversification *discount*, with *chaebol* member firms selling at 5% less than comparable independent firms. Finally, the better developed external capital markets further eroded the *chaebol* advantage to operate an internal capital market.

Prior to 1997, *chaebol* were often applauded as the champions of Korea's economic development and a worthy model for other developing economies to emulate. Since 1997, *chaebol* were often blamed for the country's economic crisis. Korean and Western media called for the dismantling of *chaebol*. Both positions seemed extreme.

Chaebol probably were neither "paragons" nor "parasites." Their roles changed. *Chaebol* as conglomerates did add value during earlier days, but past some point of inflection, their drawbacks started to outweigh their benefits. After the 2008 global crisis, while Korea's exports slid, *chaebol*'s exports gobbled up market share from global competitors. So *chaebol* again were regarded as saviors in Korea. Perhaps one of *chaebol*'s proudest moment came on April 3, 2010, when the *Economist* apologized: "*Chaebol* are certainly due an apology from those, including this newspaper [the *Economist*], who thought they would be too unwieldy for modern business."

Recent corporate diversification strategy in *chaebol* demonstrates both change and continuity. Change is evidenced by the reduced corporate scope and reduced debt loads. Before 1997, Samsung was a mediocre player in many industries. After 1997, Samsung emerged as a world-class leader in LCD screens and mobile phones—one of the key reasons was the reduced corporate scope to focus on these areas of excellence. However, the continued pursuit of a conglomeration (product-unrelated diversification) strategy also seems evident. In recent years, an emboldened Samsung announced a grand scheme of placing a whopping $20 billion in five product-unrelated industries in which it had relatively little presence: solar panels, energy-saving LED lighting, medical devices, biotech drugs, and batteries for electric cars. Despite their lack of obvious product relatedness, Samsung argued that these industries share two things in common: (1) they were about to take off, and (2) they could benefit from a splurge of capital that could scale up manufacturing and thus lower costs—essentially repeating the game that Samsung successfully played in DRAM, LCD, and mobile phones. While Samsung, which contributed 20% of Korea's GDP and 13% of its exports as of 2010, is a shining example, it is not alone. Perhaps, undertaking such a "fast follower" and "scale builder" strategy, supported by stable family ownership and patience, is *chaebol*'s core competence.

Sources: Based on (1) S. Choe & T. Roehl, 2007, What to shed and what to keep, *Long Range Planning*, 40: 465–487; (2) *Economist*, 2010, Return of the overload, April 3: 71–73; (3) *Economist*, 2010, The *chaebol* conundrum, April 3: 14–15; (4) *Economist*, 2011, Asia's new model company, October 1: 14; (5) H. Kim, R. Hoskisson, L. Tihanyi, & J. Hong, 2004, The evolution and restructuring of diversified business groups in emerging markets, *Asia Pacific Journal of Management*, 21: 25–48; (6) K. B. Lee, M. W. Peng, & K. Lee, 2008, From diversification premium to diversification discount during institutional transitions, *Journal of World Business*, 43: 47–65.

corporate-level strategy (corporate strategy)
Strategy about how a firm creates value through the configuration and coordination of its multimarket activities.

business-level strategy
Strategy that builds competitive advantage in a discrete and identifiable market.

Why did Samsung and other *chaebol* groups pursue a conglomeration strategy? Why did reducing their corporate scope after the 1997 Asian economic crisis result in better performance, which enabled them to better cope with the 2008 global economic crisis? What can firms do to improve their odds for successfully diversifying, acquiring, and restructuring? These are some of the key questions driving this chapter.

Starting from this chapter, Part III (Chapters 9, 10, 11, and 12) focuses on **corporate-level strategy** (or, in short, **corporate strategy**), which is how a firm creates value through the configuration and coordination of its multimarket activities. In comparison, Part II (Chapters 5, 6, 7, and 8) has dealt with **business-level strategy**, defined as ways to build competitive advantage in an identifiable market. While business-level strategy is very important, for larger, multimarket firms, corporate-level strategy is equally or perhaps more important.[1] In other words, an understanding of corporate-level strategy helps us see the "forest," whereas business-level strategy focuses on "trees."

In this chapter, we focus on a key aspect of corporate strategy, **diversification**, which is adding new businesses to the firm that are distinct from its existing operations. Diversification is probably the single most researched, discussed, and debated topic in corporate strategy.[2] It can be accomplished along two dimensions. The first is **product diversification**—through entries into different industries. The second is **geographic diversification**—through entries into different countries. Although market entries can entail greenfield investments (see Chapter 6) and strategic alliances (see Chapter 7), our focus here is on mergers and acquisitions (M&As) and restructuring.

We will first introduce product diversification and geographic diversification. Then, we will develop a comprehensive model, drawing on the strategy tripod. Acquisitions and restructuring are examined next, followed by debates and extensions.

Product Diversification

Most firms start as small businesses focusing on a single product or service with little diversification—known as a **single business strategy**. Over time, a product diversification strategy, with two broad categories (related and unrelated), may be embarked upon.

Product-Related Diversification

Product-related diversification refers to entries into new product markets and/or activities that are related to a firm's existing markets and/or activities.[3] The emphasis is on **operational synergy** (also known as **scale economies** or **economies of scale**), defined as increases in competitiveness beyond what can be achieved by engaging in two product markets and/or activities separately. In other words, firms benefit from declining unit costs by leveraging product relatedness—that is, 2 + 2 = 5. The sources of operational synergy can be (1) technologies (such as common platforms), (2) marketing (such as common brands), and (3) manufacturing (such as common logistics).

Product-Unrelated Diversification

Product-unrelated diversification refers to entries into industries that have no obvious product-related connections to the firm's current lines of business.[4] Product-unrelated diversifiers (such as Samsung in the Opening Case) are

---

diversification
Adding new businesses to the firm that are distinct from its existing operations.

product diversification
Entries into new product markets and/or business activities that are related to a firm's existing markets and/or activities.

geographic diversification
Entries into new geographic markets.

single business strategy
A strategy that focuses on a single product or service with little diversification.

Product-related diversification
Entries into new product markets and/or business activities that are related to a firm's existing markets and/or activities.

operational synergy
Synergy derived by having shared activities, personnel, and technologies.

scale economies (economies of scale)
Reductions in per unit costs by increasing the scale of production.

Product-unrelated diversification
Entries into industries that have no obvious product-related connections to the firm's current lines of business.

conglomerate
Product-unrelated diversifier.

conglomeration
A strategy of product-unrelated diversification.

financial synergy
The increase in competitiveness for each individual unit that is financially controlled by the corporate headquarters beyond what can be achieved by each unit competing independently as standalone firms.

scope economies (economies of scope)
Reduction in per unit costs and increases in competitiveness by enlarging the scope of the firm.

internal capital market
A term used to describe the internal management mechanisms of a product-unrelated diversified firm (conglomerate) that operate as a capital market inside the firm.

diversification premium
Increased levels of performance because of association with a product-diversified firm (also known as conglomerate advantage).

diversification discount
Reduced levels of performance because of association with a product-diversified firm (also known as conglomerate discount).

called **conglomerates**, and their strategy is known as **conglomeration**. Instead of operational synergy, conglomerates focus on **financial synergy** (also known as **scope economies** or **economies of scope**)—namely, increases in competitiveness for each individual unit financially controlled by the corporate headquarters beyond what can be achieved by each unit competing independently as stand-alone firms.

The mechanism to obtain financial synergy is different from operational synergy. The key role of corporate headquarters is to identify and fund profitable investment opportunities, such as the five new industries that Samsung Group has entered recently (see the Opening Case). In other words, a conglomerate serves as an **internal capital market** that channels financial resources to high-potential high-growth areas.[5] Given there are active external capital markets that try to do the same, a key issue is whether units affiliated with conglomerates in various industries (such as GE's aircraft engine division) outperform their stand-alone independent competitors in respective industries (such as Snecma). Stated differently, at issue is whether corporate headquarters can do a *better* job in identifying and taking advantage of profitable opportunities than external capital markets. If conglomerate units beat stand-alone rivals (which is something most GE units consistently do), then there is a **diversification premium** (or conglomerate advantage)—in other words, product-unrelated diversification adds value.[6] Otherwise, there can be a **diversification discount** (or conglomerate disadvantage), when conglomerate units are better off by competing as standalone entities (see the Opening Case).

Product Diversification and Firm Performance

Hundreds of studies, mostly conducted in the West, suggest that, on average (although not always), performance may increase as firms shift from single business strategies to product-related diversification, but performance may decrease as firms change from product-related to product-unrelated diversification—in other words, the linkage seems to be an inverted U shape (Figure 9.1).[7] Essentially "putting all your eggs in one basket," a single business strategy can be potentially risky and vulnerable. "Putting your eggs in different baskets," product-unrelated diversification may reduce risk, but its successful execution requires strong organizational capabilities that many firms lack (discussed later). Consequently, product-related diversification, essentially "putting your eggs in *similar* baskets," has emerged as a balanced way to both reduce risk and leverage synergy since the 1970s.

However, important caveats exist. Not all product-related diversifiers outperform unrelated diversifiers. In an age of "core competence," the continuous existence and prosperity of the likes of GE, Siemens, and Virgin Group suggest that for a small group of highly capable firms, conglomeration may still add value in developed economies. Moreover, in emerging economies, a conglomeration strategy seems to be persisting, with some units (such as those affiliated with South Korea's Samsung Group, India's Tata Group, and Turkey's Koc Group) outperforming stand-alone competitors (see the Opening Case).[8] The reason many conglomerates fail is not because this strategy is inherently unsound, but because firms fail to implement it. Conglomeration calls for corporate managers to impose a strict financial discipline on constituent units and hold unit managers accountable—of the sort GE's former chairman and CEO, Jack Welch, famously imposed on all divisions, "Either become

FIGURE 9.1 Product Diversification and Firm Performance

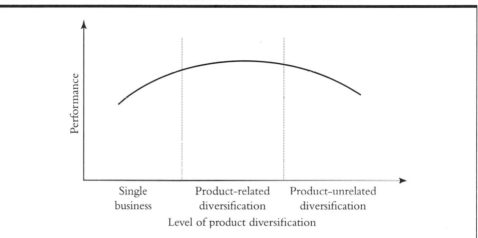

Source: Adapted from R. E. Hoskisson, M. A. Hitt, R. D. Ireland, & J. S. Harrison, 2008, *Competing for Advantage,* 2nd ed. (p. 214), Cincinnati: South-Western Cengage Learning.

the world's top one or two in your industry, or expect your unit to be sold." However, most corporate managers are not so "ruthless," and they may tolerate poor performance of some units, which can be subsidized by better units.[9] By robbing the better units to aid the poor ones, corporate managers in essence practice "socialism." Over time, better units may lose their incentive to do well, and eventually *corporate performance suffers.*

Geographic Diversification

Although geographic diversification can be done within one country (expanding from one city, state, or province to another), in this chapter we focus on **international diversification**, namely, the number and diversity of countries in which a firm competes (see also Chapter 6).

Limited versus Extensive International Scope

Two broad categories of geographic diversification can be identified. The first is limited international scope, such as US firms focusing on NAFTA markets and Spanish firms concentrating on Latin America. The emphasis is on geographically and culturally adjacent countries in order to reduce the liability of foreignness (see Chapters 4 and 6 for details). The second category is extensive international scope, maintaining a substantial presence beyond geographically and culturally neighboring countries. For example, the largest market for Yum! Brands (which operates KFC and Pizza Hut restaurants) is China. While neighboring countries are not necessarily "easy" markets, success in distant countries (such as Yum! Brands' success in China) obviously calls for a stronger set of advantages to compensate for the liability of foreignness there.

international diversification

The number and diversity of countries in which a firm competes.

Geographic Diversification and Firm Performance

In this age of globalization, we frequently hear the calls for greater geographic diversification: All firms need to go "global," non-international firms need to start venturing abroad, and firms with a little international presence should widen their geographic scope. The ramifications for firms failing to heed such calls presumably are grave. However, the evidence is *not* fully supportive of this popular view. As captured by the S curve in Figure 9.2, two findings emerge. First, at a low level of internationalization, there is a U-shaped relationship between geographic scope and firm performance, which suggests an initially negative effect of international expansion on performance before the positive returns are realized. This stems from the well-known hazard of liability of foreignness (see Chapter 6). Second, at moderate to high levels of internationalization, there is an inverted U shape, implying a positive relationship between geographic scope and firm performance—but only to a certain extent, beyond which further expansion is again detrimental. In other words, the conventional wisdom—"the more global, the better"—is actually misleading.

Not all firms have been sufficiently involved overseas to experience the ups and downs captured by the S curve in Figure 9.2. Many studies report a U-shaped relationship, because they only sample firms in the early to intermediate stages of internationalization.[10] Small, inexperienced firms are often vulnerable during the initial phase of overseas expansion. On the other hand, many other studies document an inverted U shape, because their samples are biased for larger firms with moderate to high levels of diversification.[11] Many large multinational enterprises (MNEs) have a "flag planting" mentality, bragging about the number of countries in which they have a presence. However, their performance, beyond a certain limit, often suffers, thus necessitating some withdrawals. Wal-Mart, for example, had to withdraw from Germany and South Korea.

FIGURE 9.2 Geographic Diversification and Firm Performance: An S Curve

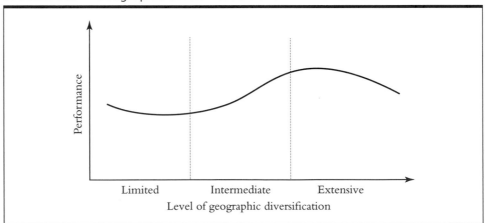

Source: Adapted from (1) F. Contractor, S. K. Kundu, & C.-C. Hsu, 2003, A three stage theory of international expansion: The link between multinationality and performance in the service sector (p. 7), *Journal of International Business Studies*, 34: 5–18; (2) J. Lu & P. Beamish, 2004, International diversification and firm performance: The S-curve hypothesis (p. 600), *Academy of Management Journal*, 47: 598–609.

Given this complexity, it is hardly surprising that there is a great debate about geographic diversification.[12] Shown in Figure 9.2, there indeed is an intermediate range within which firm performance increases with geographic scope, leading some studies that sample firms in this range to conclude that "there is value in internationalization itself because geographic scope is found to be related to higher firm profitability."[13] However, other studies, which sample firms with a high level of geographic scope, caution that "multinational diversification is apparently less valuable in practice than in theory."[14] Consequently, the recent consensus emerging out of the debate is to not only acknowledge the validity of both perspectives, but also to specify conditions under which each perspective (geographic diversification *helps* or *hurts* firm performance) is likely to hold.[15]

Combining Product and Geographic Diversification

Although most studies focus on a single dimension of diversification (product or geographic) that is already very complex, in practice, most firms (except single-business firms with no interest to internationalize) have to entertain both dimensions of diversification *simultaneously*.[16] Figure 9.3 illustrates the four possible combinations. Firms in Cell 3 are **anchored replicators**, because they focus on product-related diversification and a limited geographic scope. They seek to replicate a set of activities in related industries in a small number of countries anchored by the home country.

anchored replicator
A firm that seeks to replicate a set of activities in related industries in a small number of countries anchored by the home country.

Firms in Cell 1 can be called **multinational replicators** because they engage in product-related diversification on the one hand and far-flung multinational expansion on the other

multinational replicator
A firm that engages in product-related diversification on the one hand and far-flung multinational expansion on the other hand.

FIGURE 9.3 Combining Product and Geographic Diversification

		Product Scope	
		Related	Unrelated
Geographic Scope	Extensive	(Cell 1) *Multinational replicator*	(Cell 2) *Far-flung conglomerate*
	Limited	(Cell 3) *Anchored replicator*	(Cell 4) *Classic conglomerate*

hand. Most automakers such as Volkswagen, Renault, and Nissan have pursued this combination.

Firms in Cell 2 can be labeled as **far-flung conglomerates** because they pursue both product-unrelated diversification and extensive geographic diversification. MNEs such as Bombardier, GE, Mitsui, Samsung, Siemens, and Vivendi Universal serve as cases in point.

Finally, in Cell 4 we find **classic conglomerates**, firms that engage in product-unrelated diversification within a small set of countries centered on the home country. Current examples include India's Tata Group, Turkey's Koc Group, and China's Hope Group.

Overall, migrating from one cell to another, although difficult, is possible. For instance, most of the current multinational replicators (Cell 1) can trace their roots as anchored replicators (Cell 3). One interesting migratory pattern in the past two decades is that many classic conglomerates, such as Denmark's Danisco (see Strategy in Action 9.1), Finland's Nokia, and South Korea's Samsung, which formerly dominated multiple unrelated industries in their home countries, have reduced their product scope but significantly expanded their geographic scope—in other words, migrating from Cell 4 to Cell 1.[17] In broad strategic terms, this means that the costs for doing business abroad have declined and that the costs for managing conglomeration have risen. In other words:

Costs in Cell 4 (managing conglomeration while mostly staying at home) > Costs in Cell 1 (doing business extensively abroad but maintaining product relatedness in diversification)

Further, asserting that firms in a particular cell will outperform those in other cells is naïve if not foolhardy. In *every* cell, we can find both highly successful and highly unsuccessful firms. Next, we explore why this is the case.

A Comprehensive Model of Diversification

Why do firms diversify? The strategy tripod suggests a comprehensive model of diversification (Figure 9.4) to answer this complex and important question.

Industry-Based Considerations

A straightforward motivation for diversification is the growth opportunities in an industry. If an industry has substantial growth opportunities (such as biotechnology), most incumbents have an incentive to engage in product-related and/or international diversification. However, if it is a "sunset" industry (think of typewriters), many incumbents may exit and pursue opportunities elsewhere.

In addition to growth opportunities, the structural attractiveness of an industry, captured by the five forces framework, also has a significant bearing on diversification. Intense interfirm rivalry may motivate firms to diversify. PepsiCo diversified into sports drinks. When demand for carbonated beverages, such as Mountain Dew, flattened out

---

far-flung conglomerate
A conglomerate firm that pursues both extensive product-unrelated diversification and extensive geographic diversification.

classic conglomerate
A firm that engages in product-unrelated diversification within a small set of countries centered on the home country.

STRATEGY IN ACTION 9.1

The Evolution of Danisco's Corporate Strategy

When, in 2009, Danisco announced the completion of the sale of its sugar division to its German competitor Nordzucker, many Danes were rubbing their eyes. For them, the name "Danisco" was synonymous with "sugar." What was Danisco doing now? The answer: Danisco had been undergoing a steady transformation over 20 years.

After the transformation, Danisco was positioned as a specialized supplier of food ingredients based on natural raw materials. Its customers included global food giants such as Unilever, Kraft, Danone, and Nestlé, as well as regional and local players in all major economies. Danisco specialized in ingredients that alter the properties of processed foods such as yogurt, ice cream, sauces, and bread. For example, it was involved in the creation of Magnum ice cream, which was successfully marketed by major brand manufacturers around the world.

How did Danisco become a global leader in this niche? It was created in 1989 by a merger of three companies, the oldest of which was Danish Sugar dating back to 1872. The merger was hoped to keep traditional businesses in Danish hands and enhance their viability. The new company was a diversified conglomerate operating mainly in Denmark and other parts of Northern and Western Europe. In the first annual report (1989/1990), the corporate strategy was stated as "to be a first-class supplier to the international food industry on the global market and be a supplier of high quality foods and branded goods on selected European markets." Over the years, the foods, food ingredients, and packaging businesses were grown, while businesses in the machine building segment were sold.

In the sugar sector, Danisco first consolidated its dominant position in Denmark. It then grew by acquisitions around the Baltic Sea in Sweden, (East) Germany, Poland, and Lithuania. The sugar market was shaped by EU regulation that aimed to protect sugar beet farmers, but that also constrained the intensity of competition and limited the scope for aggressive growth.

Liberalization of this market had long been anticipated, and it finally came into effect in 2009.

In 1999, Danisco announced a new strategy focusing solely on food ingredients and acquired Finnish ingredients manufacturer Cultor OY to cement this strategic shift. At the same time, Danisco began to sell its businesses in branded foods and food packaging including iconic Danish brands such as Aalborg Snaps. Two divisions thus remained: Danisco Ingredients focused on emulsifiers, stabilizers, flavors, and enzymes, and Danisco Sugar dominated Northern European sugar markets. The internationalization of sales rapidly increased, with sales outside Denmark rising from 69% in 1995 to 88% in 2004—and over 95% after the sale of the sugar division in 2009. In 2009, Danisco generated €1.7 billion revenue, of which 38% came from Europe, 40% from the Americas, and 17% from the Asia Pacific. Danisco employed 6,800 people in 17 countries, in part to serve local markets (such as China) and in part to process natural ingredients only found in specific locations (such as Chile). Expansion in Europe, North America, and Australia occurred mainly through acquisitions, while business in emerging economies grew to a large extent by greenfield projects.

The sale of the sugar division in 2009 was thus the logical consequence of the two-decade-long evolutionary process of Danisco's corporate strategy. The synergies between the sugar and ingredients sectors had diminished, while liberalization of the EU sugar regime led to the expectation of changing competitive dynamics in the sector. In response, Danisco migrated from Cell 4 to Cell 1 in Figure 9.3 with a reduced product scope and much more extensive geographic scope globally. In 2011, Danisco itself was acquired by DuPont.

Source: Adapted from M. W. Peng & K. Meyer, 2011, *International Business* (pp. 422–423), London: Cengage Learning EMEA.

FIGURE 9.4   A Comprehensive Model of Diversification

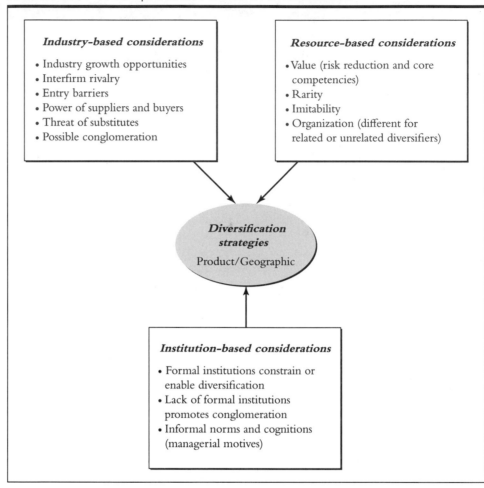

© Cengage Learning

(at least in the United States), PepsiCo's considerable distribution capabilities could find some synergy by adding the newly acquired Gatorade products.

Second, high entry barriers facilitate certain kinds of firms to diversify. For example, most of the industries that Samsung successfully competed in—LCD and mobile phones—are characterized by high entry barriers. The five new industries that Samsung has aggressively entered—solar panels, LED lighting, medical devices, biotech drugs, and batteries for electric cars—share the same characteristics (see the Opening Case). The choices are not random. Samsung has deliberately targeted such high capital intensity industries that would scare away a lot of potential entrants due to high entry barriers.

The bargaining power of suppliers and buyers may prompt firms to broaden their scope by acquiring suppliers upstream and/or buyers downstream. For example, Coca-Cola recently acquired its leading bottlers.

The threat of substitutes also has a bearing on diversification. Kodak and Fuji have been threatened by Canon, Samsung, and HP, which diversified into digital cameras—a substitute for film. None of these electronics firms had been regarded as a rival by Kodak and Fuji until recently.

In summary, the industry-based view, by definition, has largely focused on product-related diversification with an industry focus (often in combination with geographic diversification). Next, we introduce resource-based and institution-based considerations to enrich this discussion.

Resource-Based Considerations

Shown in Figure 9.4, the resource-based view—outlined by the VRIO framework—has a set of complementary considerations underpinning diversification strategies.

VALUE. Does diversification create value? The answer is "Yes," but only under certain conditions.[18] Compared with non-diversified single-business firms, diversified firms are able to spread risk. Even for over-diversified firms that have to restructure, no one is returning to a single business with no diversification. The most optimal point tends to be some moderate level of diversification.

Beyond risk reduction, diversification can create value by leveraging certain core competencies, resources, and capabilities. Honda is renowned for its product related diversification by leveraging its core competence in internal combustion engines. It not only competes in automobiles and motorcycles, but also in boat engines and lawnmowers. HondaJet represents its most recent efforts (see Strategy in Action 9.2).

RARITY. For diversification to add value, firms must have unique skills to execute such a strategy. In 2004, an executive team at China's Lenovo planned to acquire IBM's PC division—a significant move in geographic diversification. The team confronted Lenovo's suspicious board, which raised a crucial question: If a venerable American technology company had failed to profit from the PC business, did Lenovo have what it took to do better when managing such a complex global business? The answer was actually "No." The board only gave its blessing to the plan when the acquisition team agreed to not only acquire the business, but also to recruit top American executives.

IMITABILITY. While many firms undertake acquisitions, a much smaller number of them have mastered the art of post-acquisition integration.[19] Consequently, firms that excel in integration possess *hard-to-imitate* capabilities. At Northrop, integrating acquired businesses has progressed to a "science." Each must conform to a carefully orchestrated plan listing nearly 400 items, from how to issue press releases to which accounting software to use. Unlike its bigger defense rivals such as Boeing and Raytheon, Northrop thus far has not stumbled with any of the acquisitions.

ORGANIZATION. Fundamentally, whether diversification adds value boils down to how firms are organized to take advantage of the benefits while minimizing the

STRATEGY IN ACTION 9.2

Can HondaJet Fly High?

Honda is renowned for leveraging its core competence in internal combustion engines, by not only competing in automobiles and motorcycles but also in boat engines and lawn mowers. And now Honda is taking to the skies. Are you ready for a HondaJet?

Having taken its first maiden flight in 2003, HondaJet is now being introduced to the business jet (corporate aviation) market. Michimasa Fujino, president and CEO of Honda Aircraft Company, Inc., reports that the company will be delivering several aircraft to early customers in 2013, increasing production throughout 2014, and reaching full production capacity—approximately 70 to 100 small jets annually—in 2015.

Currently, however, the HondaJet is still undergoing extensive testing in the process of FAA and EASA certification. These tests are especially important given that Honda is incorporating a number of technological innovations in aviation design. Perhaps the most notable of these is Honda's over-the-wing engine-mount configuration, which Honda claims dramatically improves performance and fuel efficiency by reducing aerodynamic drag. The new design, which gives the HondaJet a distinctive appearance, also reduces noise and increases both cabin and cargo capacity. Another innovation is the "next generation" glass flight deck, which Honda describes as "the most advanced available in any light business jet."

Honda Aircraft Company, a wholly owned subsidiary of American Honda Motors Inc., was founded in 2006. At Honda Aircraft's world headquarters campus in Piedmont Triad International Airport, Greensboro, North Carolina (near the birthplace of aviation where the Wright brothers took their first flight), state-of-the-art R&D and manufacturing work is being performed. In a nutshell, the question now is: "How high can HondaJet fly?"

Sources: Based on (1) K. Arcieri, 2012, Mass production of HondaJet expected later this year, *The Business Journal*, May 14, http://www.bizjournals.com/triad/news/2012/05/14/honda-aircraft-co-to-begin-mass.html (accessed August 14, 2012); (2) R. Goyer, 2012, Honda jet makes progress, *Flying Magazine*, May 15, http://www.flyingmag.com/aircraft/jets/honda-jet-makes-progress (accessed August 14, 2012); (3) http://hondajet.honda.com (accessed February 29, 2012).

costs.[20] Since Chapter 10 will be devoted to organizational issues in geographic diversification, here we focus on product diversification. Given the recent popularity of product-related diversification, many people believe that product-unrelated diversification is an inherently value-destroying strategy. However, this is not true. With proper organization, product-unrelated diversification can add value.

Shown in Table 9.1, product-related diversifiers need to foster a centralized organizational structure with a cooperative culture. The key is to explore operational linkages among various units, and some units may need to be pulled back to coordinate with other units. For example, to maximize corporate profits, Disney's movie division producing the movie *High School Musical* (and its sequels *High School Musical 2* and *3*) had to wait before launching the movie until its merchandise divisions were ready to hawk related merchandise such as books, DVDs, video games, on-stage musicals, ice-skating shows, Valentines' day cards, blankets, and pillow covers. If movie managers' bonuses were linked to the annual box-office receipts, they would obviously be eager to release the movie. But if bonuses were

TABLE 9.1 Product-Related versus Product-Unrelated Diversification

	PRODUCT-RELATED DIVERSIFICATION	PRODUCT-UNRELATED DIVERSIFICATION
Synergy	Operational synergy	Financial synergy
Economies	Economies of scale	Economies of scope
Control emphasis	Strategic (behavior) control	Financial (output) control
Organizational structure	Centralization	Decentralization
Organizational culture	Cooperative	Competitive
Information processing	Intensive rich communication	Less intensive communication

© Cengage Learning

linked with overall corporate profits, then movie managers would be happy to assist and coordinate with their merchandise colleagues and would not mind waiting for a while. Consequently, corporate headquarters should not evaluate division performance solely based on strict financial targets (such as sales). The principal control mechanism is **strategic control** (or **behavior control**), based on largely subjective criteria to monitor and evaluate units' contributions with rich communication between corporate and divisional managers.

However, the best way to organize conglomerates is exactly the *opposite*. The emphasis is on **financial control** (or **output control**), based on largely objective criteria (such as return on investment) to monitor and evaluate units' performance. Because most corporate managers have experience in only one industry (or a few) and none realistically can be an expert in the wide variety of unrelated industries represented in a conglomerate, corporate headquarters is forced to focus on financial control, which does not require a lot of rich industry-specific knowledge. Otherwise, corporate managers will experience a tremendous information overload (too much information to process). Consequently, the appropriate organizational structure is decentralization with substantial divisional autonomy—in other words, structurally separate units. To keep divisional managers focused on financial performance, their compensation should be directly linked with quantifiable unit performance. Thus, the relationship among various divisions is competitive, each trying to attract a larger share of corporate investments. Such competition within an internal capital market is similar to stand-alone firms competing for more funds from the external capital market. The Virgin Group, for example, considers itself as "a branded venture capital firm" whose portfolio includes airlines, railways, beverages, and music. The corporate headquarters supplies a common brand (Virgin) and leaves divisional managers "alone" as long as they deliver sound performance.

Overall, the key to adding value through either product-related or product-unrelated diversification is the appropriate match between diversification strategy and organizational

strategic control (behavior control)

Controlling subsidiary/unit operations based on whether they engage in desirable strategic behavior (such as cooperation).

financial control (output control)

Controlling subsidiary/unit operations strictly based on whether they meet financial/output criteria.

structure and control. Conglomerates often fail when corporate managers impose a more centralized structure undermining lower-level autonomy.

Institution-Based Considerations

Given that it is a combination of formal and informal institutions that drives firm strategies such as diversification, we examine each set of institutions in turn.

FORMAL INSTITUTIONS. Formal institutions affect diversification strategies.[21] The rise of conglomerates in the 1950s and the 1960s in developed economies was inadvertently promoted by formal constraints designed to curtail product-related diversification. In the United States, the post-1950 antitrust authorities viewed product-related diversification (especially mergers), designed to enhance firms' market power within an industry, as "anticompetitive" and challenged them. Thus, firms seeking growth were forced to look beyond their industry, triggering a great wave of conglomeration. By the 1980s, the US government changed its mind and no longer critically scrutinized related mergers within the same industry. It is not a coincidence that the movement to dismantle conglomerates and focus on core competencies has taken off since the 1980s.

Similarly, the popularity of conglomeration in emerging economies is often under-pinned by their governments' protectionist policies. Conglomerates (often called **business groups** in emerging economies) can leverage connections with governments by obtaining licenses, arranging financing (often from state-owned or state-controlled banks), and securing technology. As long as protectionist policies prevent significant foreign entries, conglomerates can dominate domestic economies. However, when governments start to dismantle protectionist policies, competitive pressures from foreign multinationals (as well as domestic non-diversified rivals) may intensify. These changes may force conglomerates to improve performance by reducing their scope (see the Opening Case).[22]

Likewise, the significant rise of geographic diversification undertaken by numerous firms can be attributed, at least in part, to the gradual opening of many economies initiated by formal marketing-supporting and market-opening policy changes.

INFORMAL INSTITUTIONS. Informal institutions can be found along normative and cognitive dimensions. Normatively, managers often seek to behave in ways that will not cause them to be noticed as different and consequently singled out for criticism by shareholders, board directors, and the media. Therefore, when the norm is to engage in conglomeration, more managers may simply follow such a norm. Poorly performing firms are especially under such normative pressures. While early movers in conglomeration (such as GE) may indeed have special skills and insights to make such a complex strategy work, many late movers probably do not have these capabilities and simply jump on the "bandwagon" when facing poor performance. Over time, this explains—at least partially—the massive disappointment with conglomeration in developed economies.

Another informal driver for conglomeration is the cognitive dimension—namely, the internalized beliefs that guide managerial behavior.[23] Managers may have motives to

business group

A term to describe a conglomerate, which is often used in emerging economies.

advance their personal interests that are not necessarily aligned with the interests of the firm and its shareholders.[24] These are called managerial motives for diversification, such as (1) reduction of managers' employment risk and (2) pursuit of power, prestige, and income. Because single-business firms are vulnerable to economy-wide ups and downs (such as recessions), managers' jobs and careers may be at risk. Thus, managers may have an interest to diversify their firms in order to reduce their own employment risk. In addition, since power, prestige, and income are typically associated with a larger firm size, some managers may have self-interested incentives to overdiversify their firms, resulting in value destruction. Such excessive diversification is known as empire building (see Chapter 11).

In summary, the institution-based view suggests that formal and informal institutional conditions directly shape diversification strategy. Taken together, the industry-based, resource-based, and institution-based views collectively explain how the scope of the firm evolves around the world.

The Evolution of the Scope of the Firm[25]

At its core, diversification is essentially driven by economic benefits and bureaucratic costs. **Economic benefits** are the various forms of synergy (operational or financial) discussed earlier. **Bureaucratic costs** are the additional costs associated with a larger, more diversified organization, such as more headcounts and more complicated information systems. Overall, it is the difference between the benefits and costs that leads to certain diversification strategies. Since the economic benefits of the last unit of growth (such as the last acquisition) can be defined as **marginal economic benefits (MEB)** and the additional bureaucratic costs incurred as **marginal bureaucratic costs (MBC)**, the scope of the firm is thus determined by a comparison between MEB and MBC. Shown in Figure 9.5, the optimal scope is at point A, where the appropriate level of diversification should be D_1. If the level of diversification is D_2, some economic benefits can be gained by moving up to D_1. Conversely, if a firm overdiversifies to D_3, reducing the scope to D_1 becomes necessary. Thus, how the scope of the firm evolves over time can be analyzed by focusing on MEB and MBC.[26]

In the United States (Figure 9.6), between the 1950s and 1970s, if we hold MBC constant (an assumption relaxed later), the MEB curve shifted upward, resulting in an expanded scope of the firm on average (moving from D_1 to D_2). This is because (1) growth opportunities within the same industry through product-related diversification, especially for large firms, were blocked by formal institutions such as antitrust policies, (2) the emergence of organizational capabilities to derive financial synergy from conglomeration, and (3) the diffusion of these actions through imitation, leading to an informal but visible norm among managers that such product-unrelated growth was legitimate. During that time, external capital markets, which were less sophisticated, were supportive, believing that conglomerates had an advantage in allocating capital.

However, by the early 1980s, significant transitions occurred along industry, resource, and institutional dimensions. First, M&As within the same industry were no longer critically scrutinized by the government, making it unnecessary to focus on unrelated diversification in different industries. Second, a resource-based analysis suggests that given the VRIO hurdles, it would be extremely challenging—though not impossible—to

---

economic benefits

Benefits brought by the various forms of synergy in the context of diversification.

bureaucratic costs

The additional costs associated with a larger, more diversified organization.

marginal economic benefits (MEB)

The economic benefits of the last unit of growth (such as the last acquisition).

marginal bureaucratic costs (MBC)

The bureaucratic costs of the last unit of organizational expansion (such as the last subsidiary established).

FIGURE 9.5   What Determines the Scope of the Firm?

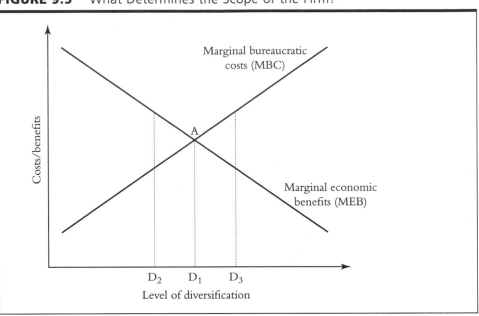

Source: Adapted from G. Jones & C. Hill, 1988, Transaction cost analysis of strategy-structure choices (p. 166), *Strategic Management Journal*, 9: 159–172.

FIGURE 9.6   The Evolution of the Scope of the Firm in the United States: 1950–1970 and 1970–1990

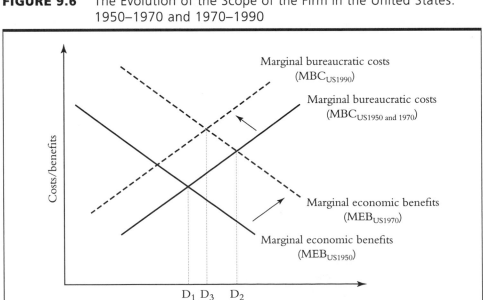

Source: M. W. Peng, S.-H. Lee, & D. Wang, 2005, What determines the scope of the firm over time? A focus on institutional relatedness (p. 627), *Academy of Management Review*, 30: 622–633.

derive competitive advantage from conglomeration (discussed earlier). In other words, with an expanded scope of the firm, MBC also increased, often outpacing the increase in MEB (Figure 9.6). Many firms overdiversified and destroyed value. Consequently, a dramatic reversal in US investor sentiment occurred toward conglomeration: Positive in the 1960s, neutral in the 1970s, and negative in the 1980s. Parallel to these developments, external capital markets became better developed with more analysts and more transparent and real-time reporting, all of which allowed for more efficient channeling of financial resources to high-potential firms. As a result, the conglomerate advantage serving as an internal capital market became less attractive. Finally, informal norms and cognitions changed, as managers increasingly became more disciplined and focused on shareholder value maximization and believed that reducing the scope of the firm was the "right" thing to do. All these combined to push the appropriate scope of the firm from D_2 to D_3 in Figure 9.6 by the 1990s.

Globally, an interesting extension is to understand the puzzle of why conglomeration, which has been recently discredited in developed economies, not only is in vogue but also in some (but not all) cases adds value in emerging economies. Figure 9.7 shows how conglomerates in emerging economies may add value at a higher level of diversification, whereby firms in developed economies are not able to. This analysis relies on two crucial and reasonable assumptions. The first is that at a given level of diversification, $MEB_{EmergingEcon} > MEB_{DevelopedEcon}$. This is primarily because underdeveloped external capital markets in emerging economies make conglomerates as internal capital markets more attractive.

FIGURE 9.7 The Optimal Scope of the Firm: Developed versus Emerging Economies at the Same Time

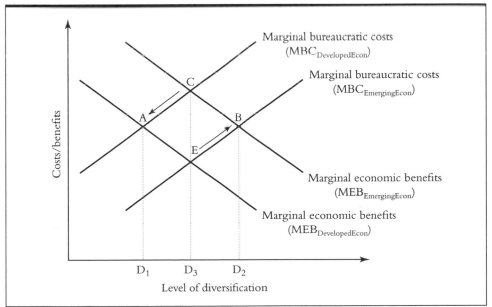

Source: M. W. Peng, S.-H. Lee, & D. Wang, 2005, What determines the scope of the firm over time? A focus on institutional relatedness (p. 628), *Academy of Management Review,* 30: 622–633.

A second assumption is that at a given level of diversification, $MBC_{EmergingEcon} <$ $MBC_{DevelopedEcon}$. In emerging economies, because of the weaknesses of formal institutions, informal constraints rise to play a *larger* role in regulating economic exchanges (see Chapter 4). Most conglomerates in these countries are family firms whose managers rely more on informal personal (and often family) relationships to get things done. Relative to firms in developed economies, firms in emerging economies typically feature a lower level of bureaucratization, formalization, and professionalization, which may result in lower bureaucratic costs.

Consequently, for any scope between D_1 and D_2 (such as D_3) in Figure 9.7, firms in developed economies at point C need to be downscoped toward point A (D_1), whereas there is still room to gain for firms in emerging economies at point E, which can move up to point B (D_2). However, bear in mind that conglomerates in emerging economies confront the same problem that plagues those in developed economies: The wider the scope, the harder it is for corporate headquarters to coordinate, control, and invest properly in different units. It seems evident that for conglomerates in emerging economies, there is also a point beyond which further diversification may backfire. As shown in the Opening Case on South Korean conglomerates, the conglomerate advantage is especially likely to be eroded when external capital markets in emerging economies become better developed. Thus, some reduction of the corporate scope will be a must.

Overall, industry dynamics, resource repertoires, and institutional conditions are not static, nor are diversification strategies. The next two sections describe two primary means for expanding and contracting the scope of the firm—through acquisitions and restructuring, respectively.

Acquisitions

Setting the Terms Straight

Although the term **"mergers and acquisitions"** (**M&As**) is often used, in reality, acquisitions dominate the scene. An **acquisition** is transfer of the control of assets, operations, and management from one firm (target) to another (acquirer), the former becoming a unit of the latter. A **merger** is the combination of assets, operations, and management of two firms to establish a new legal entity. Only approximately 3% of cross-border M&As are mergers. Even many so-called "mergers of equals" turn out to be one firm taking over another (such as DaimlerChrysler). Because the number of "real" mergers is very low, for practical purposes, we can use the two terms "M&As" and "acquisitions" interchangeably. Specifically, we focus on cross-border (international) M&As, whose various types are illustrated by Figure 9.8. Cross-border activities represent approximately 30% of all M&As, and M&As represent the largest proportion (about 70%) of FDI flows.

There are three primary categories of M&As: (1) horizontal, (2) vertical, and (3) conglomerate. **Horizontal M&As** refer to deals involving competing firms in the same industry (such as Nomura's acquisition of Lehman Brothers' assets).[27] Approximately 70% of the cross-border M&As are horizontal. **Vertical M&As**, another form of product-related diversification, are deals that allow the focal firms to acquire (upstream) suppliers and/or (downstream) buyers (such as Coca-Cola's acquisition of its bottler Coca-Cola Enterprises).[28] About 10% of cross-border M&As are vertical ones. **Conglomerate M&As** are

merger and acquisition (M&A)

Merging with or acquiring other firms.

acquisition

The transfer of control of assets, operations, and management from one firm (target) to another (acquirer); the former becomes a unit of the latter.

merger

The combination of assets, operations, and management of two firms to establish a new legal entity.

horizontal M&A

An M&A deal involving competing firms in the same industry.

vertical M&A

An M&A deal involving suppliers (upstream) and/or buyers (downstream).

conglomerate M&A

An M&A deal involving firms in product-unrelated industries.

FIGURE 9.8 The Variety of Cross-Border Mergers and Acquisitions

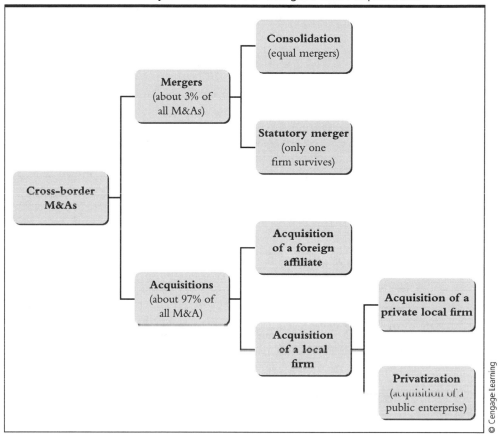

© Cengage Learning

transactions involving firms in product-unrelated industries (such as 3G Capital's acquisition of Burger King—see Emerging Markets 9.1). Roughly 20% of cross-border M&As are conglomerate deals.

The terms of M&As can be friendly or hostile. In **friendly M&As**, the board and management of a target firm agree to the transaction. **Hostile M&As** (also known as **hostile takeovers**) are undertaken against the wishes of the target firm's board and management, who reject M&A offers. In the United States, hostile M&As are more frequent, reaching 14% of all deals in the 1980s (although the number went down to 4% in the 1990s). Internationally, hostile M&As are very rare, accounting for less than 0.2% of all deals and less than 5% of total value. The $19 billion hostile takeover of Cadbury by Kraft in 2010 was a high-profile example of hostile cross-border M&A.

Motives for Mergers and Acquisitions

What drives M&A? Table 9.2 shows three drivers: (1) synergistic, (2) hubris, and (3) managerial motives, which can be illustrated by the three leading perspectives.

friendly M&A

An M&A deal in which the board and management of a target firm agree to the transaction (although they may initially resist).

hostile M&A (hostile takeover)

An M&A deal undertaken against the wishes of target firm's board and management, who reject the M&A offer.

EMERGING MARKETS 9.1 〉 〉

Brazil's Whopper Deal

In 2010, 3G Capital of Brazil, a private equity firm, acquired the Miami-headquartered fast food chain Burger King for $3.3 billion. 3G Capital was supported by three well-known Brazilian investors: Jorge Paulo Lemann, Carlos Alberto Sicupira, and Marcel Telles. Lemann founded one of Brazil's most successful investment banks, Banco de Investimentos Garantia, in the 1970s. Sicupira started in the 1980s at that bank and then grew a single Rio de Janeiro store into Lojas Americanas, one of Brazil's biggest retail chains. In the 1980s, Telles, with Lemann and Sicupira, gained control of a Brazilian brewery that they grew into AmBev, which merged with Belgium's InBev and acquired America's Anheuser-Busch.

In 2011, Alex Behring, a 3G Capital managing partner, became Burger King's chairman and CEO. Behring worked at GP Investmentos, a private equity firm that Sicupira founded. As a result, Brazilians quietly control and manage both Anheuser-Busch and Burger King, two iconic American brands.

As domestic competition in Brazil intensified, it became tougher for Brazilian companies to grow through M&As locally. Therefore, they eyed overseas markets with a great deal of interest. Brazilian companies active in overseas M&As include Gerdau (which picked up Ameristeel); JBS-Friboi (which bought Pilgrim's Pride); Petrobras (which took over the Pasadena refinery and Cascade Field); WEG (which acquired Voltran and Zest Group); and Vale (which invested in White Plains and Fosfertil).

Burger King's new management team must revitalize the 12,000-store, 75-country chain that was a distant number two to McDonald's. This would not be easy. Franchisees resisted the expensive face-lift recommended by Burger King. In an effort to boost sales, some stores in Virginia and Maryland started deliveries. The Latin American connection could help too. Burger King's supply chain could benefit by procuring more meat and grain in South America. Also, the fast food chain could expand across the continent. In the two years after the 3G takeover, Burger King increased the number of restaurants it operated in Latin America by 6%, to about 1,200.

Sources: Based on (1) *Bloomberg Businessweek*, 2010, An expensive face-lift on Burger King's menu, October 11: 21–22; (2) *Bloomberg Businessweek*, 2012, Burger King: A home delivery program, January 23: 26; (3) F. Luzio, 2010, Brazil's Whopper deal, *Harvard Business Review*, September 13: blogs.hbr.org.

In terms of synergistic motives, the most frequently mentioned industry-based rationale is to enhance and consolidate market power.[29] For example, the merger of United and Continental created the world's largest airline.

From a resource-based view, the most important synergistic rationale is to leverage superior resources.[30] Shown in the Closing Case, Indian firms' cross-border acquisitions have primarily targeted high-tech and computer services in order to leverage their superior resources in these industries. Finally, another motive is to gain access to complementary resources, as evidenced by Nomura's interest in Lehman Brothers' worldwide client base.[31]

In terms of synergistic motives, from an institution-based view, acquisitions are often a response to formal institutional constraints and transitions in search of synergy.[32] It is not a coincidence that the number of cross-border M&As has skyrocketed in the past two decades. This is the same period during which trade and investment barriers have gone down and FDI has risen.

TABLE 9.2 Motives behind Mergers and Acquisitions

	INDUSTRY-BASED ISSUES	RESOURCE-BASED ISSUES	INSTITUTION-BASED ISSUES
Synergistic motives	■ Enhance and consolidate market power ■ Overcome entry barriers ■ Reduce risk ■ Leverage scope economies	■ Leverage superior managerial capabilities ■ Access to complementary resources ■ Learning and developing new skills	■ Respond to formal institutional constraints and transitions ■ Take advantage of market openings and globalization
Hubris motives		■ Managers' overconfidence in their capabilities	■ Herd behavior—following norms and chasing fads of M&As
Managerial motives			■ Self-interested actions such as empire-building guided by informal norms and cognitions

© Cengage Learning

hubris

Managers' overconfidence in their capabilities.

acquisition premium

The difference between the acquisition price and the market value of target firms.

While all the synergistic motives, in theory, add value, hubris and managerial motives reduce value. **Hubris** refers to managers' overconfidence in their capabilities. Managers of acquiring firms make two very strong statements. The first is that "We can manage *your* assets better than you [target firm managers] can!" This was essentially what Brazilian executives at 3G Capital who took over Burger King told the former management team (see Emerging Markets 9.1). The second statement is even bolder, because acquirers of publicly listed firms always have to pay an **acquisition premium** (an above-the-market price to acquire another firm).[33] Acquirers of US firms on average pay a 20% to 30% premium, and acquirers of EU firms pay a slightly lower premium (about 18%).[34] This is essentially saying: "We are smarter than the market!" To the extent that the capital market is (relatively) efficient and that the market price of target firms reflects their intrinsic value, there is simply no hope to profit from such acquisitions. Even when we assume the capital market to be inefficient, it is still apparent that when the premium is too high, acquiring firms must have overpaid. This is especially true when multiple firms bid for the same target, the winning acquirer may suffer from the "winner's curse" from auctions—that is, the winner has overpaid. From an institution-based view, many managers join the acquisition "bandwagon" after some first-mover firms start doing deals in an industry. The fact that M&As come in "waves" speaks volumes about such a herd behavior.[35] Eager to catch up, many late movers in such "waves" may rush in, prompted by a "Wow! Get it!" mentality. Not surprisingly, many deals go bust.

While the hubris motives suggest that managers may *unknowingly* overpay for targets, managerial motives posit that for self-interested reasons, some managers may have *knowingly* overpaid the acquisition premium for target firms.[36] Driven by such norms and cognitions, some managers may have deliberately overdiversified their firms through M&As (see Chapter 11 for details).

Overall, synergistic motives add value, and hubris and managerial motives destroy value. They may *simultaneously* coexist. The Closing Case uses emerging multinationals as a new breed of cross-border acquirers to illustrate these dynamics. Next, we discuss the performance of M&As.

Performance of Mergers and Acquisitions

Despite the popularity of M&As, their performance record is rather sobering.[37] As many as 70% of M&As reportedly fail. On average, acquiring firms' performance does not improve after acquisitions and is often negatively affected.[38] Target firms, after being acquired, often perform worse than when they were independent standalone firms.[39] The only identifiable group of winners is shareholders of target firms, who may experience, on average, a 24% increase in their stock value during the period of the transaction (thanks to the acquisition premium). Shareholders of acquiring firms experience a 4% loss of their stock value during the same period. The combined wealth of shareholders of both acquiring and target firms is marginally positive, less than 2%.[40] While these findings are mostly from three decades of M&A data in the United States (where half of the global M&As take place and most of the M&A research is done), they probably also apply to cross-border acquisitions.

Why do many acquisitions fail? Problems can be identified in both pre- and post-acquisition phases (Table 9.3). During the pre-acquisition phase, because of executive hubris and/or managerial motives, acquiring firms may overpay targets—in other words, they fall into a "synergy trap." For example, in 1998, when Chrysler was profitable, Daimler-Benz paid $40 billion, a 40% premium over its market value, to acquire it. Given that Chrysler's expected performance was already built into its existing share price, at a *zero* premium, Daimler-Benz's willingness to pay for such a high premium was indicative of (1) strong managerial capabilities to derive synergy, (2) high levels of hubris, (3) significant managerial self-interests, or (4) *all of the above*. As it turned out, by the time Chrysler was sold in 2007, it only fetched $7.4 billion, destroying four-fifths of the value. In 2010, Microsoft paid $8.5 billion for Skype, which was 400 times greater than Skype's income. Although practically every reader of this book has heard about Skype, Skype has remained an iconic but underachieving Internet firm—how many people have paid money to Skype each other? Not surprisingly, this acquisition, Microsoft's biggest, raised a lot of eyebrows.

TABLE 9.3 Symptoms of Merger and Acquisition Failures

	PROBLEMS FOR ALL M&As	PARTICULAR PROBLEMS FOR CROSS-BORDER M&As
Pre-acquisition: Overpayment for targets	■ Managers overestimate their ability to create value ■ Inadequate pre-acquisition screening ■ Poor strategic fit	■ Lack of familiarity with foreign cultures, institutions, and business systems ■ Inadequate number of worthy targets ■ Nationalistic concerns against foreign takeovers (political and media levels)
Post-acquisition: Failure in integration	■ Poor organizational fit ■ Failure to address multiple stakeholder groups' concerns	■ Clashes of organizational cultures compounded by clashes of national cultures ■ Nationalistic concerns against foreign takeovers (firm and employee levels)

© Cengage Learning

strategic fit

The complementarity of partner firms' "hard" skills and resources, such as technology, capital, and distribution channels.

Another primary pre-acquisition problem is inadequate screening and failure to achieve **strategic fit**, which is the effective matching of complementary strategic capabilities.[41] For example, Bank of America, in a hurry to make a deal, spent only 48 hours in September 2008 before agreeing to acquire Merrill Lynch for $50 billion. Not surprisingly, failure to do adequate homework—technically, due diligence (investigation prior to signing contracts)—led to numerous problems centered on the lack of strategic fit. Consequently, this acquisition was labeled by the *Wall Street Journal* as "a deal from hell."[42]

Acquiring international assets can be even more problematic because institutional and cultural distances can be even larger, and nationalistic concerns over foreign acquisitions may erupt (see the Closing Case). When Japanese firms acquired Rockefeller Center and movie studios in the 1980s and the 1990s, the US media reacted with indignation. In the 2000s, when DP World from the United Arab Emirates and CNOOC from China attempted to acquire US assets, they had to back off due to political backlash.

organizational fit

The complementarity of partner firms' "soft" organizational traits, such as goals, experiences, and behaviors, that facilitate cooperation.

Numerous integration problems may surface during the post-acquisition phase.[43] Defined as similarity in cultures, systems, and structures, **organizational fit** is just as important as strategic fit. Many acquiring firms do *not* analyze organizational fit with targets. For example, when Nomura decided to acquire Lehman Brothers' assets in Asia and Europe in a lightning 24 hours, no consideration was given on the total lack of organizational fit between a hard-charging New York investment bank and a conservative, seniority-based Japanese firm still practicing lifetime employment. Firms may also fail to address the concerns of multiple stakeholders, including job losses and diminished power (see Figure 9.9). Most firms focus on task issues such as

FIGURE 9.9 Stakeholder Concerns During Mergers and Acquisitions

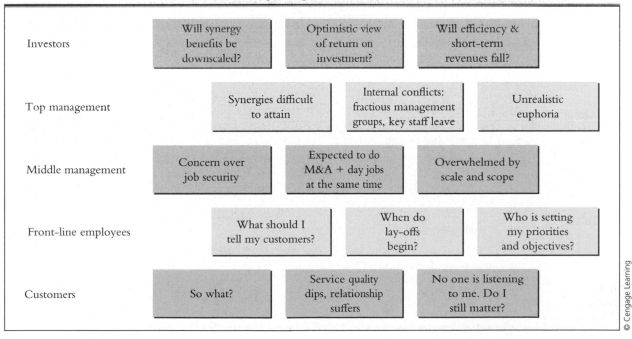

Investors	Will synergy benefits be downscaled?	Optimistic view of return on investment?	Will efficiency & short-term revenues fall?
Top management	Synergies difficult to attain	Internal conflicts: fractious management groups, key staff leave	Unrealistic euphoria
Middle management	Concern over job security	Expected to do M&A + day jobs at the same time	Overwhelmed by scale and scope
Front-line employees	What should I tell my customers?	When do lay-offs begin?	Who is setting my priorities and objectives?
Customers	So what?	Service quality dips, relationship suffers	No one is listening to me. Do I still matter?

© Cengage Learning

standardizing reporting and pay inadequate attention to people issues, which typically results in low morale and high turnover.

In cross-border M&As, integration difficulties may be much worse because clashes of organizational cultures are compounded by clashes of national cultures.[44] Due to cultural differences, Chinese acquirers such as Geely often have a hard time integrating Western firms such as Volvo (see the Closing Case). But even when both sides are from the West, cultural conflicts may still erupt. When Four Seasons acquired a hotel in Paris, the simple American request that employees smile at customers was resisted by French employees and laughed at by the local media as "la culture Mickey Mouse." After Alcatel acquired Lucent, the situation, in the words of *Bloomberg Businessweek*, became "almost comically dysfunctional."[45] At an all-hands gathering at an Alcatel-Lucent European facility, employees threw fruits and vegetables at executives announcing another round of restructuring.

Although acquisitions are often the largest capital expenditures most firms ever make, they frequently are the worst planned and executed activities of all.[46] Unfortunately, while merging firms are sorting out the mess, rivals are likely to launch aggressive attacks. When Daimler struggled first with the chaos associated with the marriage with Chrysler and then was engulfed in the divorce with Chrysler, BMW overtook Mercedes-Benz to become the world's number-one luxury carmaker. Adding all of the above together, it is hardly surprising that most M&As fail.

Restructuring

Setting the Terms Straight

restructuring

(1) Adjusting firm size and scope through either diversification (expansion or entry), divestiture (contraction or exit), or both. (2) Reducing firm size and scope.

Although the term "**restructuring**" normally refers to adjustments to firm size and scope through either diversification (expansion or entry), divestiture (contraction or exit), or both,[47] its most common definition is *reduction* of firm size and scope—we will adopt this more frequently used definition here. There is a historical reason behind this one-sided use of the word "restructuring." By the 1980s and the 1990s when this word surfaced in our vocabulary, many firms suffered from overdiversification and became interested in reducing size and scope. Using this definition, there are two primary ways of restructuring: (1) **downsizing** (reducing the number of employees through lay-offs, early retirements, and outsourcing) and (2) **downscoping** (reducing the scope of the firm through divestitures and spin-offs). The flipside of downscoping is **refocusing**, namely, narrowing the scope of the firm to focus on a few areas (see Strategy in Action 9.1).

downsizing

Reducing the number of employees through lay-offs, early retirements, and outsourcing.

downscoping

Reducing the scope of the firm through divestitures and spin-offs.

Motives for Restructuring

refocusing

Narrowing the scope of the firm to focus on a few areas.

We can draw on the industry-based, resource-based, and institution-based views to understand the motives for restructuring.[48] From an industry-based view, restructuring is often triggered by a rising level of competition within an industry. Given that a primary motivation for M&As is to eliminate redundant assets, industries experiencing a high level of M&As (such as automobiles and banking) not surprisingly often unleash major restructuring efforts.

The resource-based view suggests that while restructuring may bring some benefits, significant costs also arise (such as organizational chaos, anxiety, and low morale). When most rivals restructure, these activities may not generate sustainable value, are not rare, and cause organizational problems. In short, it is "not possible for firms to 'save' or 'shrink' their way to prosperity."[49]

From an institution-based perspective, by the 1980s and the 1990s, firms in developed economies increasingly felt pressure from capital markets to restructure. Managers increasingly accepted restructuring to be a part of legitimate business undertaking.[50] However, strong institutional pressures *against* restructuring also exist. In the United States, restructuring, job losses, and outsourcing have been controversial issues in every recent presidential election. In Germany, all "redundancies" must, by law, be negotiated by workers' councils (unions), whose members understandably are not keen to vote themselves out of jobs. In Asia, restructuring has been slow. Overall, corporate restructuring is not widely embraced around the world.[51]

Debates and Extensions

The two leading debates discussed here are: (1) product relatedness versus other forms of relatedness and (2) acquisitions versus alliances.

Product Relatedness versus Other Forms of Relatedness

What exactly is relatedness? While the idea of product relatedness is seemingly straight-forward (see Strategy in Action 9.2 on HondaJet), it has attracted at least three significant points of contention. First, how to actually measure product relatedness remains debatable.[52] Starbucks now sells music CDs in its coffee shops. Are coffee and music related? The answer would be both "yes" and "no," depending on how you measure relatedness. Amazon not only sells books, but also hawks apparel, furniture, movies, power tools, TVs, and dozens of other product categories. Are these products "related"? From a production standpoint, they certainly are not. But from a distribution/shopping standpoint, a compelling case can be made that these products are related. One interesting quiz is: How do we characterize Sony's product relatedness? Most of us think of Sony as a manufacturer of electronics hardware (such as TV) and software (such as games) as well as a producer of entertainment content (such as movies and music). However, since all of the above make little or lose money in recent years, what has sustained Sony is its seldom-reported and (almost totally) unrelated business in life insurance. So a sarcastic answer to the question, "What is Sony?" can be that Sony is a life insurer that makes TVs as a hobby (!).[53]

Second, beyond measurement issues, an important school of thought, known as the "**dominant logic**" school, argues that it is not the visible product linkages that can only count as product relatedness. Rather, it is a set of common underlying dominant logic that connects various businesses in a diversified firm.[54] Consider Britain's easyGroup, which operates easyJet (airline), easyCinema, and easyInternetcafe, among others. Underneath its conglomerate skin, a dominant logic is to actively manage supply and demand. Early and/or non-peak-hour customers get cheap deals (such as 20 cents a movie), and late and/or peak-hour customers pay a lot more. Charges at the Internet cafés rise as the seats fill

dominant logic
A common underlying theme that connects various businesses in a diversified firm.

up. While many firms (such as airlines) practice such "yield management," none has been so aggressive as the easyGroup. Thus, instead of treating the easyGroup as an "unrelated conglomerate," perhaps we may label it a "related yield management firm."

Finally, from an institution-based view, some "product-unrelated" conglomerates may be linked by **institutional relatedness**, defined as "a firm's informal linkages with dominant institutions in the environment that confer resources and legitimacy."[55] For example, sound informal relationships with government agencies, in countries (usually emerging economies) where such agencies control crucial resources such as licensing, financing, and labor pools, would encourage firms to leverage such relationships by entering multiple industries. In emerging economies, solid connections with banks—a crucial financial institution—may help raise financing to enter multiple industries, whereas stand-alone entrepreneurial start-ups without such connections often have a hard time securing financing. This idea helps explain why in developed economies, e-commerce is dominated by new start-ups (such as Amazon and eBay), whereas in emerging economies it is dominated by new units of old-line conglomerates (such as Hong Kong's Wharf and Singapore's Sembcorp). It seems that despite the Western advice to downscope, some conglomerates in emerging economies have recently *expanded* their scope by entering new industries such as solar panels (see the Opening Case). In other words, a firm, which is classified as a "product-unrelated" conglomerate, may actually enjoy a great deal of institutional relatedness.

institutional relatedness
A firm's informal linkages with dominant institutions in the environment that confer resources and legitimacy.

Acquisitions versus Alliances

Despite the proliferation of acquisitions, their lackluster performance has led to a debate regarding whether they have been overused. Strategic alliances are an alternative to acquisitions (see Chapter 7). However, many firms seem to have plunged straight into "merger mania." Even when many firms pursue both M&As and alliances, they are often undertaken in isolation.[56] While many large MNEs have an M&A function and some have set up an alliance function, few firms have established a combined "mergers, acquisitions, *and* alliance" function. In practice, it may be advisable to explicitly compare and contrast acquisitions vis-à-vis alliances. Compared with acquisitions, alliances, despite their own problems, cost less and allow for opportunities to learn from working with each other before engaging in full-blown acquisitions. Many poor acquisitions (such as Daimler-Chrysler) would probably have been better off had firms pursued alliances first.

The Savvy Strategist

Guided by the three leading perspectives that underpin the strategy tripod, the savvy strategist draws three important implications for action (Table 9.4). First, understand the nature of your industry that may call for diversification, acquisitions, and restructuring. In some "sunset" industries, diversifying out of them is a must. In new hot-growth industries and countries, new entrants often feel compelled to acquire in order to ensure a timely presence (see the Closing Case).

Second, you and your firm need to develop capabilities that facilitate successful acquisitions and restructuring, by following the suggestions outlined in Table 9.5. These would include do not overpay for targets and focus on both strategic and organizational fit.

TABLE 9.4 Strategic Implications for Action

- Understand the nature of your industry that may call for diversification, acquisitions, and restructuring.
- Develop capabilities that facilitate successful acquisitions and restructuring.
- Master the rules of the game governing acquisitions and restructuring around the world.

© Cengage Learning

TABLE 9.5 Improving the Odds for Acquisition Success

AREAS	DO'S AND DON'TS
Pre-acquisition	■ Do not overpay for targets and avoid a bidding war when premiums are too high. ■ Engage in thorough due diligence concerning both strategic fit and organizational fit.
Post-acquisition	■ Address the concerns of multiple stakeholders and try to keep the best talents. ■ Be prepared to deal with roadblocks thrown out by people whose jobs and power may be jeopardized.

© Cengage Learning

Finally, you need to master the rules of the game governing acquisitions around the world. In 2001, GE and Honeywell proposed to merge and cleared US antitrust scrutiny. Yet, they failed to anticipate the power of the EU antitrust authorities to torpedo the deal.[37] These two otherwise highly capable firms should have done more "home work"—known in the jargon as due diligence—on the institutional side. More recently, many Chinese firms failed to complete the overseas M&A deals that they announced, because they did not understand the institutional intricacies of navigating in host countries (see the Closing Case).

In terms of the four most fundamental questions, this chapter directly answers Question 3: What determines the scope of the firm? Industry conditions, resource repertoire, and institutional frameworks shape corporate scope. In addition, why firms differ (Question 1) and how firms behave (Question 2) boil down to why and how they choose different diversification strategies. Finally, what determines the international success and failure of firms (Question 4)? The answer lies in whether they can successfully overcome the challenges associated with diversification, acquisitions, and restructuring.

CHAPTER SUMMARY

1. Define product diversification and geographic diversification
- Product-related diversification focuses on operational synergy and scale economies.
- Product-unrelated diversification (conglomeration) stresses financial synergy and scope economies.
- Geographically diversified firms can have a limited or extensive international scope.
- Most firms pursue product and geographic diversification simultaneously.

2. Articulate a comprehensive model of diversification
  - The strategy tripod suggests industry-based, resource-based, and institution-based factors for diversification.

3. Gain insights into the motives and performance of acquisitions
  - Most M&As are acquisitions.
  - M&As are driven by (1) synergistic, (2) hubris, and/or (3) managerial motivations.

4. Enhance your understanding of restructuring
  - Restructuring involves downsizing, downscoping, and refocusing.

5. Participate in two leading debates concerning diversification, acquisitions, and restructuring
  - (1) Product relatedness versus other forms of relatedness and (2) acquisitions versus alliances.

6. Draw strategic implications for action
  - Understand the nature of your industry that may call for diversification, acquisitions, and restructuring.
  - Develop capabilities that facilitate successful acquisitions and restructuring.
  - Master the rules of the game governing acquisitions and restructuring around the world.

KEY TERMS

Acquisition p. 276

Acquisition premium p. 279

Anchored replicator p. 265

Bureaucratic cost p. 273

Business group p. 272

Business-level strategy p. 260

Classic conglomerate p. 266

Conglomerate p. 262

Conglomerate M&A p. 276

Conglomeration p. 262

Corporate-level strategy (corporate strategy) p. 260

Diversification p. 261

Diversification discount p. 262

Diversification premium p. 262

Dominant logic p. 283

Downscoping p. 282

Downsizing p. 282

Economic benefit p. 273

Far-flung conglomerate p. 266

Financial control (output control) p. 271

Financial synergy p. 262

Friendly M&A p. 277

Geographic diversification p. 261

Horizontal M&A p. 276

Hostile M&A (hostile takeover) p. 277

Hubris p. 279

Institutional relatedness p. 284

Internal capital market p. 262

International diversification p. 263

Marginal bureaucratic cost (MBC) p. 273

Marginal economic benefit (MEB) p. 273

Merger p. 276

Merger and acquisition (M&A) p. 276

Multinational replicator p. 265

Operational synergy p. 261

Organizational fit p. 281

Product diversification p. 261

Product-related diversification p. 261

Product-unrelated diversification p. 261

Refocusing p. 282

Restructuring p. 282

Scale economies (economies of scale) p. 261

Scope economies (economies of scope) p. 262

Single business strategy p. 261

Strategic control (behavior control) p. 271

Strategic fit p. 281

Vertical M&A p. 276

CRITICAL DISCUSSION QUESTIONS

1. M&As are a rare event for most firms. How can they enhance their capabilities for M&As?

2. **ON ETHICS:** As a CEO leading an acquisition of a foreign firm (think of Anheuser-Busch or Cadbury), you are interviewed by a reporter from the host country. The reporter asks: "A lot of people in our country are mad about this foreign takeover of our iconic company. How would you alleviate their concerns?"

3. **ON ETHICS:** CEOs' pay is typically linked to the size of the firms they lead. Therefore, some argue that CEOs have an inherent bias in favor of undertaking M&As using shareholders' money while enriching CEOs' personally. Do you agree or disagree with this view? Explain.

TOPICS FOR EXPANDED PROJECTS

1. Some argue that shareholders can diversify their stockholdings and that there is no need for corporate diversification to reduce risk. The upshot is that any excess earnings (known as "free cash flows"), instead of being used to acquire other firms, should be returned to shareholders as dividends and that firms should pursue more focused strategies. Write a short paper explaining why you agree or disagree with this statement.

2. Unrelated product diversification (conglomeration) is widely discredited in developed economies. However, in some cases it still seems to add value in emerging economies (see the Opening Case). Is this interest in conglomeration likely to hold or decrease in emerging economies over time? Why? Explain your answers in a short paper.

3. **ON ETHICS:** As members of the executive team of a firm, you are trying to decide whether to acquire a foreign firm. The size of your firm will double after this acquisition and it will become the largest in your industry. On the one hand, you are excited about the opportunity to be a leading captain of industry and the associated power, prestige, and income (you expect your income to double next year). On the other hand, you have just read this chapter and are troubled by the 70% M&A failure rate. Working in small groups of three or four, develop a strategy for success. Present your strategy in a short paper or visual presentation.

> CLOSING CASE ETHICAL DILEMMA

Emerging Markets: Emerging Acquirers from China and India

Multinational enterprises (MNEs) from emerging economies, especially from China and India, have emerged as a new breed of acquirers around the world. Causing "oohs" and "ahhs," they have grabbed media headlines and caused controversies. Anecdotes aside, are the patterns of these new global acquirers similar? How do they differ? Only recently has rigorous academic research been conducted to allow for systematic comparison (Table 9.6).

Overall, China's stock of outward foreign direct investment (OFDI) (1.5% of the worldwide total) is about three times India's (0.5%). A visible similarity is that both Chinese and Indian MNEs seem to primarily use M&As as their primary mode of OFDI. Throughout the 2000s, Chinese firms spent $130 billion to engage in M&As overseas, whereas Indian firms made M&A deals worth $60 billion.

From an industry-based view, it is clear that MNEs from China and India have targeted industries to support and strengthen their own most competitive industries at home. Given China's prowess in manufacturing industries at home, Chinese firms' overseas M&As have primarily targeted energy, minerals, and mining—crucial supply industries that feed their manufacturing operations. Indian MNEs' world-class leadership position in high-tech and software services is reflected in their interest in acquiring firms in these industries.

The geographic spread of these MNEs is indicative of the level of their capabilities. Chinese firms have undertaken most of their deals in Asia, with Hong Kong being their most favorable location. In other words, the geographic distribution of Chinese M&As is not global; rather, it is quite regional. This reflects a relative lack of capabilities to engage in managerial challenges in regions distant from China, especially in more developed economies. Indian MNEs have primarily made deals in Europe, with the United Kingdom as the leading target country. For example, acquisitions made by Tata Motors (Jaguar and Land Rover) and Tata Steel (Corus Group) propelled Tata Group to become the number one private-sector employer in the UK. Overall, Indian firms display a more global spread in their M&As, and a higher level of confidence and sophistication in making deals in developed economies.

TABLE 9.6 Comparing Cross-Border M&As Undertaken by Chinese and Indian MNEs

	M&AS UNDERTAKEN BY CHINESE MNES	M&AS UNDERTAKEN BY INDIAN MNES
Top target industries	Energy, minerals, and mining	High-tech and software services
Top target countries	Hong Kong	United Kingdom
Top target regions	Asia	Europe
Top acquiring companies involved	State-owned enterprises	Private business groups
% of successfully closed deals	47%	67%

Source: Extracted from S. Sun, M. W. Peng, B. Ren, & D. Yan, 2012, A comparative ownership advantage framework for cross-border M&As: The rise of Chinese and Indian MNEs, *Journal of World Business*, 47(1): 4–16.

From an institution-based view, the contrasts between the leading Chinese and Indian acquirers are significant. The primary M&A players from China are state-owned enterprises (SOEs), which have their own advantages (such as strong support from the Chinese government) and trappings (such as resentment and suspicion from host country governments). The movers and shakers of overseas M&As from India are private business groups, which generally are not viewed with strong suspicion. The limited evidence suggests that M&As by Indian firms tend to create value for their shareholders. On the other hand, M&As by Chinese firms tend to destroy value for their shareholders—indicative of potential hubris and managerial motives evidenced by empire building and agency problems.

Announcing high-profile deals is one thing, but completing them is another matter. Chinese MNEs have particularly poor records in completing the overseas acquisition deals they announce. Only less than half (47%) of the acquisitions announced by Chinese MNEs were completed, which compares unfavorably to Indian MNEs' 67% completion rate. Chinese MNEs' lack of ability and experience in due diligence and financing is one reason, but another reason is the political backlash and resistance they encounter, especially in developed economies. The 2005 failure of CNOOC's bid for Unocal in the United States and the 2009 failure of Chinalco's bid for Rio Tinto's assets in Australia are but two high-profile examples.

Even assuming successful completion, integration is a leading challenge during the post-acquisition phase. Both Chinese and Indian firms seem to suffer from these challenges. Tata, for example, was famously clawed by Jaguar. In general, acquirers from China and India have often taken the "high road" to acquisitions, in which acquirers deliberately allow acquired target companies to retain autonomy, keep the top management intact, and then gradually encourage interaction between the two sides. In contrast, the "low road" to acquisitions would be for acquirers to act quickly to impose their systems and rules on acquired target companies. Although the "high road" sounds noble, this is a reflection of these acquirers' lack of international management experience and capabilities.

Sources: Based on (1) Y. Chen & M. Young, 2010, Cross-border M&As by Chinese listed companies, *Asia Pacific Journal of Management*, 27: 523–539; (2) L. Cui & F. Jiang, 2010, Behind ownership decision of Chinese outward FDI, *Asia Pacific Journal of Management*, 27: 751–774; (3) P. Deng, 2009, Why do Chinese firms tend to acquire strategic assets in international expansion? *Journal of World Business*, 44: 74–84; (4) S. Gubbi, P. Aulakh, S. Ray, M. Sarkar, & R. Chittoor, 2010, Do international acquisitions by emerging economy firms create shareholder value? *Journal of International Business Studies*, 41: 397–418; (5) M. W. Peng, 2012, The global strategy of emerging multinationals from China, *Global Strategy Journal*, 2: 97–107; (6) M. W. Peng, 2012, Why China's investments aren't a threat, *Harvard Business Review*, February: blogs.hbr.org; (7) H. Rui & G. Yip, 2008, Foreign acquisitions by Chinese firms, *Journal of World Business*, 43: 213–226; (8) S. Sun, M. W. Peng, B. Ren, & D. Yan, 2012, A comparative ownership advantage framework for cross-border M&As: The rise of Chinese and Indian MNEs, *Journal of World Business*, 47(1): 4–16.

CASE DISCUSSION QUESTIONS

1. Why have M&As emerged as the primary mode of foreign market entry for Chinese and Indian MNEs?

2. Drawing on industry-based, resource-based, and institution-based views, outline the similarities and differences between Chinese and Indian multinational acquirers.

3. **ON ETHICS:** As CEO of a firm from either China or India engaging in a high-profile acquisition overseas, shareholders at home are criticizing you of "squandering" their money, and target firm management and unions—as well as host country government and the media—are resisting. Should you proceed with the acquisition or consider abandoning the deal? If you are considering abandoning the deal, under what conditions would you abandon it?

NOTES

[**Journal acronyms**] *AME – Academy of Management Executive;* **AMJ** *– Academy of Management Journal;* **AMP** *– Academy of Management Perspectives;* **AMR** *– Academy of Management Review;* **APJM** *– Asia Pacific Journal of Management;* **BW** *– BusinessWeek* (before 2010) or *Bloomberg Businessweek* (since 2010); **EJ** *–Economic Journal;* **JEP** *– Journal of Economic Perspectives;* **JIBS** *– Journal of International Business Studies;* **JM** *– Journal of Management;* **JMS** *– Journal of Management Studies;* **JWB** *– Journal of World Business;* **MIR** *– Management International Review;* **OSc** *– Organization Science;* **SMJ** *– Strategic Management Journal;* **WSJ** *– Wall Street Journal.*

1. E. Bowman & C. Helfat, 2001, Does corporate strategy matter? *SMJ*, 22: 1–23.
2. M. Nippa, U. Pidun, & H. Rubner, 2011, Corporate portfolio management, *AMP*, November: 50–66.
3. M. Benner & M. Tripsas, 2012, The influence of prior industry affiliation on framing in nascent industries, *SMJ*, 33: 277–302; J. Eggers, 2012, All experience is not created equal, *SMJ*, 33: 315–335; H. Tanriverdi & C. Lee, 2008, Within-industry diversification and firm performance in the presence of network externalities, *AMJ*, 51: 381–397.
4. D. Miller, M. Fern, & L. Cardinal, 2007, The use of knowledge for technological innovation within diversified firms, *AMJ*, 50: 308–326.
5. J. Shackman, 2007, Corporate diversification, vertical integration, and internal capital markets, *MIR*, 47: 479–504.
6. K. B. Lee, M. W. Peng, & K. Lee, 2008, From diversification premium to diversification discount during institutional transitions, *JWB*, 43: 47–65.
7. P. Chen, C. Williams, & R. Agarwal, 2012, Growing pains, *SMJ*, 33: 252–276.
8. M. Carney, E. Gedajlovic, P. Heugens, M. Van Essen, & J. Van Oosterhout, 2011, Business group affiliation, performance, context, and strategy, *AMJ*, 54: 437–460; B. Kedia, D. Mukherjee, & S. Lahiri, 2006, Indian business groups, *APJM*, 23: 559–577; M. Li, K. Ramaswamy, & B. Petitt, 2006, Business groups and market failures, *APJM*, 24: 439–452; Y. Lu & J. Yao, 2006, Impact of state ownership and control mechanisms on the performance of group affiliated companies in China, *APJM*, 23: 485–504; M. W. Peng & A. Delios, 2006, What determines the scope of the firm over time and around the world? *APJM*, 24: 385–405.
9. D. Lange, S. Boivie, & A. Henderson, 2009, The parenting paradox, *AMJ*, 52: 179–198.
10. N. Capar & M. Kotabe, 2003, The relationship between international diversification and performance in service firms, *JIBS*, 34: 345–355.
11. L. Gomes & K. Ramaswamy, 1999, An empirical examination of the form of the relationship between multinationality and performance, *JIBS*, 30: 173–188.
12. M. Chari, S. Devaraj, & P. David, 2007, International diversification and firm performance, *JWB*, 42: 184–197; Y. Fang, M. Wade, A. Delios, & P. Beamish, 2007, International diversification, subsidiary performance, and the mobility of knowledge resources, *SMJ*, 28: 1053–1064; A. Gande, C. Schenzler, & L. Senbert, 2009, Valuation effects of global diversification, *JIBS*, 40: 1515–1532; M. Hitt, L. Tihanyi, T. Miller, & B. Connelly, 2006, International diversification, *JM*, 32: 831–867.
13. A. Delios & P. Beamish, 1999, Geographic scope, product diversification, and the corporate performance of Japanese firms (p. 724), *SMJ*, 20: 711–727.
14. J. M. Geringer, S. Tallman, & D. Olsen, 2000, Product and international diversification among Japanese multinational firms (p. 76), *SMJ*, 21: 51–80.
15. G. Qian, T. Khoury, M. W. Peng, & Z. Qian, 2010, The performance implications of intra- and inter-regional geographic diversification, *SMJ*, 31: 1018–1030.
16. A. Goerzen & S. Makino, 2007, Multinational corporation internationalization in the service sector, *JIBS*, 38: 1149–1169; M. Wiersema & H. Bowen, 2008, Corporate diversification, *SMJ*, 29: 115–132.
17. K. Meyer, 2006, Global focusing, *JMS*, 43: 1109–1144.
18. J. Bercovitz & W. Mitchell, 2007, When is more better? *SMJ*, 28: 61–79; L. Capron & J. Shen, 2007, Acquisitions of private vs. public firms, *SMJ*, 28: 891–911; E. Doving & P. Gooderham, 2008, Dynamic capabilities as antecedents of the scope of related

diversification, *SMJ*, 29: 841–857; S. Karim, 2006, Modularity in organizational structure, *SMJ*, 27: 799–823; K. Ellis, T. Reus, B. Lamont, & A. Ranft, 2011, Transfer effects in large acquisitions, *AMJ*, 54: 1261–1276; J. Macher & C. Boerner, 2006, Experience and scale and scope economies, *SMJ*, 27: 845–865; K. Uhlenbruck, M. Hitt, & M. Semadeni, 2006, Market value effects of acquisitions involving Internet firms, *SMJ*, 27: 899–913.

19. J. Kim & S. Finkelstein, 2009, The effects of strategic and market complementarity on acquisition performance, *SMJ*, 30: 617–646.

20. K. Ellis, T. Reus, & B. Lamont, 2009, The effects of procedural and informational justice in the integration of related acquisitions, *SMJ*, 30: 137–161.

21. C. Moschieri & J. Campa, 2009, The European M&A industry, *AMP*, November: 71–87.

22. M. Dieleman, 2009, Shock imprinting, *APJM*, 27: 481–502.

23. C. Marquis & M. Lounsbury, 2007, Vive la resistance, *AMJ*, 50: 799–820.

24. E. Matta & P. Beamish, 2008, The accentuated CEO career horizon problem, *SMJ*, 29: 683–700; P. Parvinen & H. Tikkanen, 2007, Incentive asymmetries in the M&A process, *JMS*, 44: 759–786.

25. This section draws heavily from M. W. Peng, S. Lee, & D. Wang, 2005, What determines the scope of the firm over time? A focus on institutional relatedness, *AMR*, 30: 622–633.

26. G. Jones & C. Hill, 1988, Transaction cost analysis of strategy-structure choices, *SMJ*, 9: 159–172. See also E. Rawley, 2010, Diversification, coordination costs, and organizational rigidity, *SMJ*, 31: 873–891; Y. Zhou, 2010, Synergy, coordination costs, and diversification choices, *SMJ*, 32: 624–639.

27. J. Clougherty & T. Duso, 2009, The impact of horizontal mergers on rival, *JMS*, 46: 1365–1395.

28. M. Jacobides, 2008, How capability differences, transaction costs, and learning curves interact to shape vertical scope, *OSc*, 19: 306–326.

29. M. Chari & K. Chang, 2009, Determinants of the share of equity sought in cross-border acquisitions, *JIBS*, 40: 1277–1297; D. Iyer & K. Miller, 2008, Performance feedback, slack, and the timing of acquisitions, *AMJ*, 51: 808–822.

30. S. Chen, 2008, The motives for international acquisitions, *JIBS*, 39: 454–471; P. Puranam & K. Srikanth, 2007, What they know vs. what they do, *SMJ*, 28: 805–825.

31. H. Yang, Z. Lin, & M. W. Peng, 2011, Behind acquisitions of alliance partners, *AMJ*, 54: 1069–1080.

32. Z. Lin, M. W. Peng, H. Yang, & S. Sun, 2009, How do networks and learning drive M&As? *SMJ*, 30: 1113–1132; H. Yang, S. Sun, Z. Lin, & M. W. Peng, 2011, Behind M&As in China and the United States, *APJM*, 28: 239–255.

33. H. Krishnan, M. Hitt, & D. Park, 2007, Acquisition premiums, subsequent workforce reductions, and post-acquisition performance, *JMS*, 44: 709–732; T. Laamanen, 2007, On the role of acquisition premium in acquisition research, *SMJ*, 28: 1359–1369.

34. C. Moschieri & J. Campa, 2009, The European M&A industry (p. 82), *AMP*, November: 71–87.

35. G. McNamara, J. Heleblian, & B. Dykes, 2008, The performance implications of participating in an acquisition wave, *AMJ*, 51: 113–130.

36. M. Goranova, T. Alessandri, P. Brandes, & R. Dharwadkar, 2007, Managerial ownership and corporate diversification, *SMJ*, 28: 211–225.

37. T. Laamanen & T. Keil, 2008, Performance of serial acquirers, *SMJ*, 29: 663–672; D. Siegel & K. Simons, 2010, Assessing the effects of M&As on firm performance, *SMJ*, 31: 903–916; G. Valentini, 2012, Measuring the effect of M&A on patenting quantity and quality, *SMJ*, 33: 336–346; M. Zollo & D. Meier, 2008, What is M&A performance? *AMP*, August: 55–77.

38. D. King, D. Dalton, C. Daily, & J. Covin, 2004, Meta-analyses of post-acquisition performance, *SMJ*, 25: 187–200.

39. R. Kapoor & K. Lim, 2007, The impact of acquisitions on the productivity of inventors at semiconductor firms, *AMJ*, 50: 1133–1155.

40. G. Andrade, M. Mitchell, & E. Stafford, 2001, New evidence and perspectives on mergers, *JEP*, 15: 103–120.

41. C. Meyer & E. Altenborg, 2008, Incompatible strategies in international mergers, *JIBS*, 39: 508–525.

42. *WSJ*, 2009, Bank of America-Merrill Lynch: A $50 billion deal from hell, January 22: blogs.wsj.com.

43. J. Allatta & H. Singh, 2011, Evolving communication patterns in response to an acquisition event, *SMJ*, 32: 1099–1118; M. Brannen & M. Peterson, 2009, Merging without alienating, *JIBS*, 40: 468–489; R. Chakrabarti, S. Gupta-Mukherjee, & N. Jayaraman, 2009, Mars-Venus marriages, *JIBS*, 40: 216–236; G. Stahl & A. Voigt, 2008, Do cultural differences matter in M&As? *OSc*, 19: 160–176.

44. T. Reus & B. Lamont, 2009, The double-edged sword of cultural distance in international acquisitions, *JIBS*, 40: 1298–1316; R. Sarala & E. Vaara, 2010, Cultural differences, convergence, and crossvergence as explanations of knowledge transfer in international acquisitions, *JIBS*, 41: 1365–1390.

45. *BW*, 2011, Hi-yah! Alcatel-Lucent chops away at years of failure (p. 29), May 2: 29–31.

46. M. Cording, P. Christmann, & D. King, 2010, Reducing causal ambiguity in acquisition integration, *AMJ*, 51: 744–767.

47. H. Barkema & M. Schijven, 2008, Toward unlocking the full potential of acquisitions, *AMJ*, 51: 696–722; D. Bergh, R. Johnson, & R. DeWitt, 2008, Restructuring through spin-off or sell-off, *SMJ*, 29: 133–148; H. Berry, 2009, Why do firms divest? *OSc*, 21: 380–398; T. Numagami, M. Karube, & T. Kato, 2010, Organizational deadweight, *AMP*, November: 25–37.

48. D. Bergh & E. Lim, 2008, Learning how to restructure, *SMJ*, 29: 593–616.

49. W. Cascio, 2002, Strategies for responsible restructuring (p. 81), *AME, 16: 80–91.* See also J. Guthrie & D. Datta, 2008, Dumb and dumber, *OSc*, 19: 108–123.

50. K. Shimizu, 2007, Prospect theory, behavioral theory, and the threat-rigidity hypothesis, *AMJ*, 50: 1495–1514.

51. E. G. Love & M. Kraatz, 2009, Character, conformity, or the bottom line? *AMJ*, 52: 314–335.

52. A. Pehrsson, 2006, Business relatedness and performance, *SMJ*, 27: 265–282.

53. *BW*, 2011, Sony needs a hit (p. 77), November 21: 72–77.

54. C. K. Prahalad & R. Bettis, 1986, The dominant logic, *SMJ*, 7: 485–501. See also D. Ng, 2007, A modern resource-based approach to unrelated diversification, *JMS*, 44: 1481–1502.

55. Peng, Lee, & Wang, 2005, What determines the scope of the firm over time? (p. 623).

56. X. Yin & M. Shanley, 2008, Industry determinants of the "merger versus alliance" decision, *AMR*, 33: 473–491.

57. N. Aktas, E. Bodt, & R. Roll, 2007, Is European M&A regulation protectionist?, *EJ*, 117: 1096–1121.

CHAPTER 10

STRATEGIZING, STRUCTURING, AND LEARNING AROUND THE WORLD

© istockphoto/Alexey Stiop

LEARNING OBJECTIVES

After studying this chapter, you should be able to

1. Understand the four basic configurations of multinational strategies and structures

2. Articulate a comprehensive model of multinational strategy, structure, and learning

3. Outline the challenges associated with learning, innovation, and knowledge management

4. Participate in three leading debates concerning multinational strategy, structure, and learning

5. Draw strategic implications for action

Emerging Markets: Samsung's Global Strategy Group

Founded in 1938, Samsung Group is South Korea's leading conglomerate. It has 270,000 employees in 470 units in 67 countries, with $227 billion in annual revenues. The flagship company within Samsung Group is Samsung Electronics Corporation (SEC). With $136 billion revenues in 2010 (more than Apple and Sony *combined*), SEC is the largest electronics firm in the world. In addition to SEC, other major Samsung Group companies include Samsung Life Insurance (the 13th largest life insurer in the world), Samsung C&T Corporation (one of the world's largest developers of skyscrapers and solar/wind power plants), and Samsung Heavy Industries (the world's largest shipbuilder). Samsung's performance has been impressive. Despite the Great Recession, SEC's profits have been higher than those of its five largest Japanese rivals (Sony, Panasonic, Toshiba, Hitachi, and Sharp) *combined*. In 2010, SEC achieved record profits of $14 billion, compared with $12 billion profits for Intel and less than $1 billion profits for Panasonic as well as $3.2 billion losses for Sony.

Clearly, Samsung has done something right. However, it has not been easy. To increasingly compete outside Korea, Samsung needs to attract more non-Korean talents. But given its traditionally rigid hierarchical structure and the language barrier, its efforts to attract and retain non-Korean talents had often been disappointing. In response, Samsung Group headquarters in 1997 set up a unique internal consulting unit, the Global Strategy Group, which reports directly to the CEO. Members of the Global Strategy Group are non-Korean MBA graduates from top Western business schools who have worked for leading multinationals such as Goldman Sachs, Intel, and McKinsey. They are required to spend two years in Seoul and study basic Korean. The group's mission, according to its website, is to "(1) develop a pool of global managers, (2) enhance Samsung's business performance, and (3) globalize Samsung."

Global Strategy teams work on various internal strategy projects for different Samsung companies. Each team has a project leader, which gives the individual an opportunity to take on a leadership role in a high-level consulting project much earlier than a typical consulting career provides. Each team has one to two global strategists. It also has a project coordinator, who is a senior Korean manager acting as a

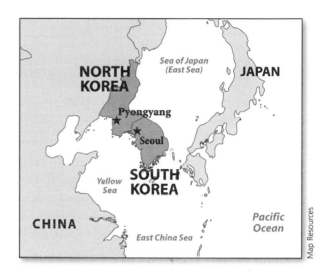

Map Resources

liaison between the team and the management of the (internal) client company. On average, projects last three months and typically involve some overseas travel. Starting with 20 global strategists in the class of 1997, nearly 400 projects have been completed in 15 years. These projects help global strategists form informal ties and expose them to the organizational culture. After two years, global strategists would "graduate" and be assigned to Samsung subsidiaries, many of which are in their home countries.

Despite good-faith efforts by both Korean and non-Korean sides, the success of the Global Strategy Group is anything but assured. Overall, cultural integration is a tough nut to crack. Of the 208 non-Korean MBAs who joined the group since its inception, 135 were still with Samsung as of 2011. The most successful ones are those who have taken the greatest pains to fit into the Korean culture, such as eating kimchi and drinking Korean wine at dinner parties. Before the establishment of the Global Strategy Group, not a single non-Korean MBA lasted more than three years at SEC. With the Global Strategy Group as a cohort group, one-third of the non-Korean MBAs in the first class of 1997 were still with SEC three years later (in 2000). Over the next decade, the retention rate went up to two-thirds. Three experts noted how the non-Korean members of the Global Strategy Group have slowly but surely globalized Samsung's corporate DNA:

The effects of these employees on the organization have been something like that of a steady trickle of water on stone. As more people from the Global Strategy Group are assigned to SEC, their Korean colleagues have had to change their work styles and mind-sets to accommodate Westernized practices, slowly and steadily making the environment more friendly to ideas from abroad. Today, SEC goes out of *its way to ask the Global Strategy group for more newly hired employees.*

Sources: Based on (1) S. Chang, 2008, *Sony vs. Samsung,* Singapore: Wiley; (2) T. Khanna, J. Song, & K. Lee, 2011, The paradox of Samsung's rise, *Harvard Business Review,* July: 142–147; (3) Samsung Global Strategy Group, 2012, gsg.samsung.com.

How can multinational enterprises (MNEs) such as Samsung strategically manage growth around the world? How can they learn country tastes, global trends, and market transitions that may call for structural changes? How can they attract and retain global talents and improve the odds for better innovation? These are some of the key questions driving this chapter. Our focus here is on relatively large MNEs. We start by discussing the crucial relationship between four strategies and four structures. Next, a comprehensive model drawing from the strategy tripod sheds light on these issues. Then, we discuss worldwide learning, innovation, and knowledge management. Debates and extensions follow.

Multinational Strategies and Structures

This section first introduces an integration-responsiveness framework centered on the pressures for cost reductions and local responsiveness. We then outline the four strategic choices and the four corresponding organizational structures that MNEs typically adopt.

Pressures for Cost Reduction and Local Responsiveness

integration-responsiveness framework

A framework of MNE management on how to simultaneously deal with two sets of pressures for global integration and local responsiveness.

local responsiveness

The necessity to be responsive to different customer preferences around the world.

MNEs confront primarily two sets of pressures: cost reduction and local responsiveness. These two sets of pressures are captured in the **integration-responsiveness framework**, which allows managers to deal with the pressures for both global integration and local responsiveness. Cost pressures often call for global integration, while local responsiveness pushes MNEs to adapt locally. In both domestic and international competition, pressures to reduce costs are almost universal. What is unique in international competition is the pressure for **local responsiveness**, which means reacting to different consumer preferences and host-country demands. Consumer preferences vary tremendously around the world. For example, McDonald's beef-based hamburgers would obviously find few customers in India, a land where cows are held sacred by the Hindu majority. Thus, changing McDonald's menu is a must in India. Host-country demands and expectations add to the pressures for local responsiveness. Throughout Europe, Canadian firm Bombardier manufactures an Austrian version of rail-cars in Austria, a Belgian version in Belgium, and so on. Bombardier believes that such local responsiveness, although not required, is essential for making sales to railway operators in Europe, which tend to be state owned.

Taken together, being locally responsive certainly makes local customers and governments happy but unfortunately increases costs. Given the universal interest in lowering cost, a natural tendency is to downplay or ignore the different needs and wants of various local markets and instead market a global version of products and services. The movement to globalize offerings can be traced to a 1983 article by Theodore Levitt: "The Globalization of Markets."[1] Levitt argued that worldwide consumer tastes are converging. As evidence, Levitt pointed to the worldwide success of Coke Classic, Levi Strauss jeans, and Sony color TV. Levitt predicted that such convergence would characterize most product markets in the future.

Levitt's idea has often been the intellectual force propelling many MNEs to globally integrate their offerings while minimizing local adaptation. Ford experimented with "world car" designs. MTV pushed ahead with the belief that viewers would flock to global (essentially American) programming. Unfortunately, most of these experiments are not successful. Ford found that consumer tastes ranged widely around the globe. MTV eventually realized that there is no "global song." In a nutshell, one size does not fit all.[2] This leads us to look at how MNEs can pay attention to *both* dimensions: cost reduction and local responsiveness.

Four Strategic Choices

Based on the integration-responsiveness framework, Figure 10.1 plots the four strategic choices: (1) home replication, (2) localization, (3) global standardization, and (4) transnational. Each strategy has a set of pros and cons outlined in Table 10.1. (Their corresponding structures are discussed in the next section.)

Home replication strategy, often known as international (or export) strategy, duplicates home country–based competencies in foreign countries. Such competencies include production scales, distribution efficiencies, and brand power. In manufacturing, this is usually manifested in an export strategy. In services, this is often done through licensing and franchising. This strategy is relatively easy to implement and usually the first one adopted when firms venture abroad.

On the disadvantage side, home replication strategy often lacks local responsiveness because it focuses on the home country. This strategy makes sense when the majority of a firm's customers are domestic. However, when a firm aspires to broaden its international scope, failing to be mindful of foreign customers' needs and wants may alienate them. For example, when Wal-Mart entered Brazil, the stores had exactly the same inventory as its US stores, including a large number of *American* footballs. Considering that Brazil is the land of soccer that has won the World Cup five times, more wins than any other country, nobody (except a few homesick American expatriates in their spare time) plays American football there.

Localization strategy is an extension of the home replication strategy.[3] **Localization (multidomestic) strategy** focuses on a number of foreign countries/regions, each of which is regarded as a stand-alone local (domestic) market worthy of significant attention and adaptation. While sacrificing global efficiencies, this strategy is effective when differences

home replication strategy

A strategy that emphasizes the international replication of home country–based competencies such as production scales, distribution efficiencies, and brand power.

localization (multi-domestic) strategy

An MNE strategy that focuses on a number of foreign countries/regions, each of which is regarded as a standalone local (domestic) market worthy of significant attention and adaptation.

FIGURE 10.1 Multinational Strategies and Structures: The Integration-Responsive Framework

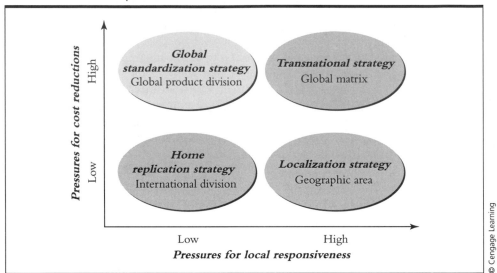

© Cengage Learning

Note: In some other textbooks, "home replication" may be referred to as "international" or "export" strategy, "localization" as "multidomestic" strategy, and "global standardization" as "global" strategy. Some of these labels are confusing, because one can argue that all four strategies here are "international" or "global," thus resulting in some confusion if we label one of these strategies as "international" and another as "global." The present set of labels is more descriptive and less confusing.

TABLE 10.1 Four Strategic Choices for Multinational Enterprises

	ADVANTAGES	DISADVANTAGES
Home replication	■ Leverages home country-based advantages ■ Relatively easy to implement	■ Lack of local responsiveness ■ May result in foreign customer alienation
Localization	■ Maximizes local responsiveness	■ High costs due to duplication of efforts in multiple countries ■ Too much local autonomy
Global standardization	■ Leverages low-cost advantages	■ Lack of local responsiveness ■ Too much centralized control
Transnational	■ Cost efficient while being locally responsive ■ Engages in global learning and diffusion of innovations	■ Organizationally complex ■ Difficult to implement

© Cengage Learning

among national and regional markets are clear and pressures for cost reductions are low. For example, Disney has attempted to localize some of its offerings in its five theme parks in Anaheim, California; Orlando, Florida; Hong Kong; Paris; and Tokyo. Its newest Disneyland in Shanghai, which will open in 2015, will feature traditional Disney rides and those based on Chinese culture. It will drop a standard feature common in all Disney parks: Main Street USA.[4]

In terms of disadvantages, localization strategy has high costs due to duplication of efforts in multiple countries. The costs of producing such a variety of programming for MTV are obviously greater than the costs of producing one set of programming. As a result, this strategy is only appropriate in industries where the pressures for cost reductions are not significant. Another potential drawback is too much local autonomy, which happens when each subsidiary regards its country as so unique that it is difficult to introduce corporate-wide changes. In the 1980s, Unilever had 17 country subsidiaries in Europe. It took four *years* to persuade all 17 subsidiaries to introduce a single new detergent across Europe.

As the opposite of localization strategy, **global standardization strategy** is sometimes referred to simply as global strategy. Its hallmark is the development and distribution of standardized products worldwide in order to reap the maximum benefits from low-cost advantages. While both home replication and global standardization strategies minimize local responsiveness, a crucial difference is that an MNE pursuing a global standardization strategy is not limited to its major operations at home. In a number of countries, the MNE may designate **centers of excellence**, defined as subsidiaries explicitly recognized as a source of important capabilities, with the intention that these capabilities be leveraged by and/or disseminated to other subsidiaries. Centers of excellence are often given a **worldwide** (or **global**) **mandate**—a charter to be responsible for one MNE function throughout the world. HP's Singapore subsidiary has a worldwide mandate to develop, produce, and market all of HP's handheld products.

In terms of disadvantages, a global standardization strategy obviously sacrifices local responsiveness. This strategy makes great sense in industries where pressures for cost reductions are paramount and pressures for local responsiveness are relatively minor (particularly commodity industries such as tires). However, as noted earlier, in industries ranging from automobiles to consumer products, a one-size-fits-all strategy may be inappropriate. Consequently, arguments such as "all industries are becoming global" and "all firms need to pursue a global (standardization) strategy" are potentially misleading.

Transnational strategy aims to capture the best of both worlds by endeavoring to be both cost efficient and locally responsive. In addition to cost efficiency and local responsiveness, a third hallmark of this strategy is global learning and diffusion of innovations. Traditionally, the diffusion of innovations in MNEs is a one-way flow from the home country to various host countries—the label "home replication" says it all (!). Underpinning the traditional one-way flow is the assumption that the home country is the best location for generating innovations. However, given that innovations are inherently risky and uncertain, there is no guarantee that the home country will generate the highest-quality innovations.

MNEs that engage in a transnational strategy promote global learning and diffusion of innovations in multiple ways. Innovations not only flow from the home country to host

global standardization strategy
An MNE strategy that relies on the development and distribution of standardized products worldwide to reap the maximum benefits from low-cost advantages.

center of excellences
MNE subsidiaries explicitly recognized as a source of important capabilities, with the intention that these capabilities be leveraged by and/or disseminated to other subsidiaries.

worldwide (global) mandate
The charter to be responsible for one MNE function throughout the world.

transnational strategy
An MNE strategy that endeavors to be cost efficient, locally responsive, and learning driven simultaneously.

EMERGING MARKETS 10.1 〉

Citroën Designs Cars in Shanghai

For a long time, automakers have been jockeying for position in China, which has recently become the world's largest producer country and buyer country of cars. Obviously automakers have done a great deal in exporting cars to China and producing them locally. But designing cars in China? Not only for the domestic market but also for the world? Unveiled at Auto China 2010, the Citroën Metropolis luxury concept car, designed in Shanghai, has shown how central Chinese tastes now are to global automakers.

Sleek, low, and wide, the Metropolis is a bold statement to signal Citroën's aim to recapture the innovation and individuality embodied in some of its most successful cars in the 20th century. But instead of being designed in France, the Metropolis was designed in the firm's global design studio in Shanghai. Citroën hinted that the Metropolis would become the flagship of the new DS luxury model series. While the production model would not be as avant-garde as the bold concept car, the production model would retain much of the elegant style. Citroën indicated that this car was designed in China for the world. "Our strategy for Citroën is to have the same car for Europe and China," said Citroën's design director.

Sources: Based on (1) Citroën, 2010, Metropolis: A concept car for China, www.citroen.com; (2) *Silkroad*, 2011, Design direction, July: 30.

countries (which is the traditional flow), but also flow from host countries to the home country and flow among subsidiaries in multiple host countries. Citroën not only designs cars in France, but also in China. On a worldwide basis, it intends to produce and market luxury cars such as the Metropolis designed in Shanghai (see Emerging Markets 10.1).

On the disadvantage side, a transnational strategy is organizationally complex and difficult to implement. The large amount of knowledge sharing and coordination may slow down decision making. Trying to achieve cost efficiencies, local responsiveness, and global learning simultaneously places contradictory demands on MNEs (to be discussed in the next section).

Overall, it is important to note that given the various pros and cons, there is no optimal strategy. The new trend in favor of a transnational strategy needs to be qualified with an understanding of its significant organizational challenges. This point leads to our next topic.

Four Organizational Structures

Figure 10.1 also shows four organizational structures that are appropriate for each of the strategic choices: (1) international division, (2) geographic area, (3) global product division, and (4) global matrix.

international division

An organizational structure typically set up when firms initially expand abroad, often engaging in a home replication strategy.

International division is typically used when firms initially expand abroad, often engaging in a home replication strategy. Figure 10.2 shows Starbucks' international division in addition to its four US-centric divisions. Although this structure is intuitively appealing, it often leads to two problems. First, foreign subsidiary managers, whose input

FIGURE 10.2   International Division Structure at Starbucks

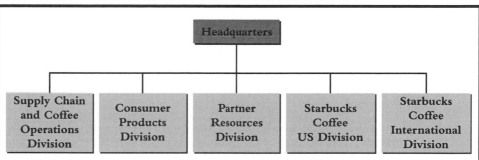

Sources: Adapted from (1) www.cogmap.com and (2) www.starbucks.com. Headquartered in Seattle, Starbucks is a leading international coffee and coffeehouse company.

geographic area structure

An organizational structure that organizes the MNE according to different countries and regions and is the most appropriate structure for a multido-mestic strategy.

country (regional) manager

The business leader in charge of a specific country (or region) for an MNE.

is channeled through the international division, are not given sufficient voice relative to the heads of domestic divisions. Second, by design, the international division serves as a silo whose activities are not coordinated with the rest of the firm, which is focusing on domestic activities. Consequently, many firms phase out this structure after their initial stage of overseas expansion.

Geographic area structure organizes the MNE according to different geographic areas (countries and regions). It is appropriate for a localization strategy. Figure 10.3 illustrates such a structure for Avon. A geographic area can be a country or a region, led by a **country (or regional) manager**. Each area is largely stand-alone. In contrast to the limited voice of subsidiary managers in the international division structure, country (and regional) managers carry a great deal of weight in a geographic area structure. Interestingly and paradoxically, *both* the strengths and weaknesses of this structure lie in its local responsiveness. While being locally responsive can be a virtue, it also encourages the fragmentation of the MNE into fiefdoms.

FIGURE 10.3   Geographic Area Structure at Avon Products

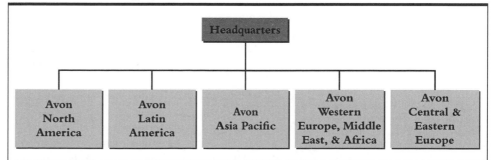

Source: Adapted from avoncompany.com. Headquartered in New York, Avon Products, Inc. is the company behind numerous "Avon ladies" around the world.

FIGURE 10.4 Global Product Division Structure at European Aeronautic Defense and Space Company (EADS)

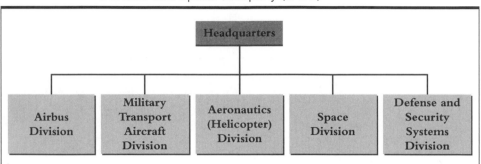

Source: Adapted from www.eads.com. Headquartered in Munich, Germany, and Paris, France, EADS is the largest commercial aircraft maker and the largest defense contractor in Europe.

global product division

An organizational structure that assigns global responsibilities to each product division.

Global product division structure, which is the opposite of the geographic area structure, supports the global standardization strategy by assigning global responsibilities to each product division. Figure 10.4 shows an example from the European Aeronautic Defense and Space Company (EADS), whose most famous unit is Airbus. This structure treats each product division as a stand-alone entity with full worldwide responsibilities. This structure is highly responsive to pressures for cost efficiencies, because it allows for consolidation on a worldwide (or at least regional) basis and reduces inefficient duplication in multiple countries. For example, Unilever reduced the number of soap-producing factories in Europe from ten to two after adopting this structure. Recently, because of the popularity of the global standardization strategy (noted earlier), the global product division structure is on the rise. Its main drawback is that local responsiveness suffers, as Ford discovered when it phased out the geographic area structure.

global matrix

An organizational structure often used to alleviate the disadvantages associated with both geographic area and global product division structures, especially for MNEs adopting a transnational strategy.

A **global matrix** alleviates the disadvantages associated with both geographic area and global product division structures, especially for MNEs adopting a transnational strategy. Shown in Figure 10.5, its hallmark is the coordination of responsibilities between product divisions and geographic areas. In this hypothetical example, the country manager in charge of Japan—in short, the Japan manager—reports to Product Division 1 and Asia Division, both of which have equal power.

In theory this structure supports the goals of the transnational strategy, but in practice it is often difficult to deliver. The reason is simple: While managers (such as the Japan manager in Figure 10.5) usually find dealing with one boss headache enough, they do not appreciate having two bosses who are often in conflict (!). For example, Product Division 1 may decide that Japan is too tough a nut to crack and that there are more promising markets elsewhere, thus ordering the Japan manager to *curtail* her investment and channel resources elsewhere. This makes sense because Product Division 1 cares about its global market position and is not wedded to any particular country. However, Asia Division, which is evaluated by how well it does in Asia, begs to differ. Asia Division argues that it cannot afford to be a laggard in Japan if it expects to be a leading player in Asia. Therefore, Asia Division demands that the

FIGURE 10.5 A Hypothetical Global Matrix Structure

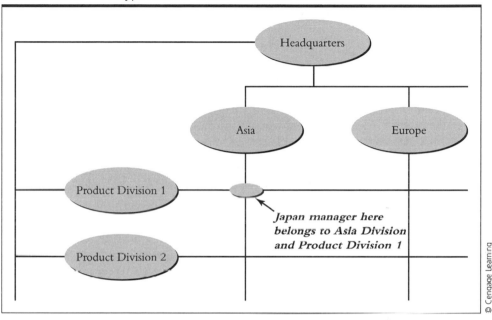

Japan manager *increase* her investment in the country. Facing these conflicting demands, the Japan manager, who prefers to be politically correct, does not want to make any move before consulting corporate headquarters. Eventually, headquarters may provide a resolution. But crucial time may be lost in the process, and important windows of opportunity for competitive actions may be missed.

Despite its merits on paper, the matrix structure may add layers of management, slow down decision speed, and increase costs while not showing significant performance improvement. There is no conclusive evidence for the superiority of the matrix structure. The following quote from the CEO of Dow Chemical, an early adopter of the matrix structure, is sobering:

> *We were an organization that was matrixed and depended on teamwork, but there was no one in charge. When things went well, we didn't know whom to reward; and when things went poorly, we didn't know whom to blame. So we created a global product division structure, and cut out layers of management. There used to be 11 layers of management between me and the lowest level employees, now there are five.*[5]

Overall, the positioning of the four structures in Figure 10.1 is not random. They develop from the relatively simple international division through either geographic area or global product division structures and may finally reach the more complex global matrix stage. Not every MNE experiences all of these structural stages, and the movement is not necessarily in one direction. For example, the matrix structure's poster child, the Swedish-Swiss conglomerate ABB, recently withdrew from this structure.

The Reciprocal Relationship between Multinational Strategy and Structure

In one word, the relationship between strategy and structure is *reciprocal*. Three ideas stand out:

- Strategy usually drives structure.[6] The fit between strategy and structure, as exemplified by the *pairs* in each of the four cells in Figure 10.1, is crucial.[7] A misfit, such as combining a global standardization strategy with a geographic area structure, may have grave consequences.

- The relationship is not one-way. As much as strategy drives structure, structure also drives strategy. The unworkable matrix structure has called into question the wisdom of the transnational strategy.

- Neither strategies nor structures are static. It is often necessary to change strategy, structure, or both. In an effort to move toward a global standardization strategy, many MNEs have adopted a global product division structure while de-emphasizing the role of country headquarters. However, unique challenges in certain countries, especially China, have now pushed some MNEs to revive the country headquarters, such as the China headquarters, so that it can coordinate numerous activities within a large, complex, and important host country.[8] A further experimentation is to have an emerging economies division, which is not dedicated to any single country but dedicated to pursuing opportunities in a series of emerging economies ranging from Brazil to Saudi Arabia. Cisco pioneered this structure, which has been followed by rivals such as IBM.[9]

A Comprehensive Model of Multinational Strategy, Structure, and Learning

Having outlined the basic strategy/structure configurations, let us introduce a comprehensive model that, as before, draws on the strategy tripod (see Figure 10.6).

Industry-Based Considerations

Why are MNEs structured differently? Why do they emphasize different forms of learning and innovation? For example, industrial-products firms (such as semiconductors) tend to adopt global product divisions, and consumer-goods companies (such as cosmetics) often rely on geographic area divisions. Industrial-products firms typically emphasize technological innovations, whereas consumer-goods companies place premiums on learning consumer trends and generating repackaged and recombined products as marketing innovations (such as Heinz's marketing of *green* ketchup that appeals to children). A short answer is that the different nature of their industries provides a clue. Industrial-products firms value technological knowledge that is not location-specific (such as how to most efficiently make *semiconductor* chips). Consumer-goods industries, on the other hand, require deep knowledge about consumer tastes that is location-specific (such as what kinds of *potato* chips consumers in Hungary or Honduras would prefer).[10]

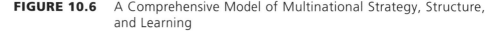

FIGURE 10.6 A Comprehensive Model of Multinational Strategy, Structure, and Learning

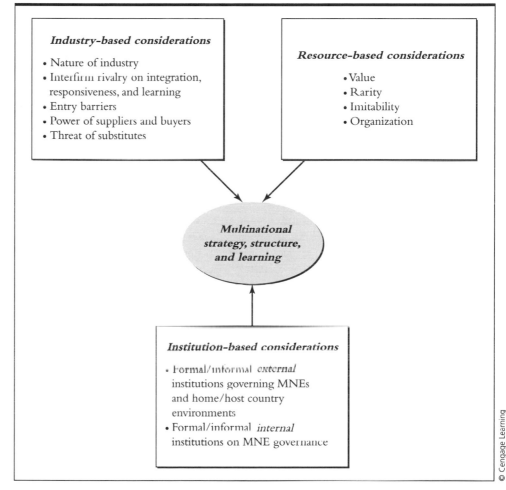

In addition, the five forces framework again sheds considerable light on the issue at hand. Within a given industry, as competitors increasingly match each other in cost efficiencies and local responsiveness, their rivalry naturally focuses on learning and innovation.[11] This is especially the case in oligopolistic industries (such as automobiles and cosmetics) (see Chapter 8).

Entry barriers also shape MNE strategy, structure, and learning. Why do many MNEs phase out the multidomestic strategy and geographic area division structure by consolidating production in a small number of world-scale facilities? One underlying motivation is that smaller suboptimal-scale production facilities, scattered in a variety of countries, are not effective deterrents against potential entrants. Massive, world-scale facilities in strategic locations can serve as more formidable deterrents. For example, Foxconn built a world-scale factory complex employing 300,000 workers in Shenzhen, China.

The bargaining power of suppliers and buyers also has a bearing. When buyer firms move internationally, they increasingly demand integrated offerings from their suppliers—that is, the ability to buy the same supplies at the same price and quality in every country in which they operate. Components suppliers are thus often forced—or at least encouraged (!)—to internationalize. Otherwise, suppliers run the risk of losing a substantial chunk of business. Not surprisingly, as Volkswagen invested in Brazil, *all* of its top suppliers set up factories in adjacent areas at their own expenses.

The threat of substitute products has a direct bearing on learning and innovation. R&D often generates innovative substitutes. 3M's Post-It notes, for example, can partially substitute for glue and tape. Smartphones and mobile devices are now substituting some personal computers.

Resource-Based Considerations

Shown in Figure 10.6, the resource-based view—exemplified by the value, rarity, imitability, and organization (VRIO) framework—adds a number of insights. First, when looking at structural changes, it is critical to consider whether a new structure (such as a matrix) adds concrete *value*. The value of innovation must also be considered. A vast majority of innovations simply fail to reach market, and most new products that do reach market end up being financial failures. The difference between an innovator and a *profitable* innovator is that the latter not only has plenty of good ideas but also lots of complementary assets (such as appropriate organizational structures and marketing muscles) to add value to innovation. Philips, for example, is a great innovator. It invented rotary shavers, video cassettes, and CDs. Still, its ability to profit from these innovations lags behind that of Sony, Matsushita, and Samsung.

A second question is *rarity*. Certain strategies or structures may be in vogue at a given point in time. So, for example, when a company's rivals all move toward a global standardization strategy, this strategy cannot be a source of differentiation. To improve global coordination, many MNEs spend millions of dollars to equip themselves with enterprise resource planning (ERP) packages provided by SAP and Oracle. However, such packages are designed to be implemented widely and appeal to a broad range of firms, thus providing no firm-specific advantage for any adopting firm.

Even when capabilities are valuable and rare, they have to pass a third hurdle—*imitability*. Formal structures are easier to observe and imitate than informal structures. This is one of the reasons why the informal, flexible matrix is in vogue now. It "is less a structural classification than a broad organizational concept or philosophy, manifested in organizational capability and management mentality."[12] Obviously imitating an intangible mentality is much harder than imitating a tangible structure.

The last hurdle is *organization*—namely, how MNEs are organized, both formally and informally, around the world.[13] One elusive but important concept is organizational culture. Recall from Chapter 4 that culture is defined by Hofstede as "the collective programming of the mind which distinguishes the members of one group or category of people from another." We can extend this concept to define **organizational culture** as the collective programming of the mind that distinguishes members of one organization

organizational culture
The collective programming of the mind that distinguishes members of one organization from another.

from another. Huawei, for example, is known to have a distinctive "wolf" culture, which centers on "continuous hunting" and "relentless pursuit" with highly motivated employees who routinely work over time and sleep in their offices. Although rivals can imitate everything Huawei does technologically, their biggest hurdle lies in their lack of ability to wrap their arms around Huawei's "wolf" culture.

Institution-Based Considerations

MNEs face two sets of the rules of the game: Formal and informal institutions governing (1) *external* relationships and (2) *internal* relationships. Each is discussed in turn.

Externally, MNEs are subject to the formal institutional frameworks erected by various home-country and host-country governments. In order to protect domestic employment, the British government taxes the foreign earnings of British MNEs at a higher rate than their domestic earnings. In another example, home-country governments may discourage or ban MNE operations abroad for political reasons. After the Cold War ended, US defense firms such as Boeing and Lockheed Martin were eager to set up R&D subsidiaries in Russia, whose rocket scientists were some of the best (and certainly cheapest!) in the world. The US government warned these firms, however, not to perform any mission critical R&D there.

Host-country governments, on the other hand, often attract, encourage, or coerce MNEs into undertaking activities that they otherwise would not. For example, basic manufacturing generates low-paying jobs, does not provide sufficient technology spillovers, and carries little prestige. Advanced manufacturing, R&D, and regional headquarters, on the other hand, generate better and higher-paying jobs, provide more technology spillovers, and lead to better prestige. Therefore, host-country governments (such as those in China, Hungary, and Singapore) often use a combination of carrots (such as tax incentives and free infrastructure upgrades) and sticks (such as threats to block market access) to attract MNE investments in higher value-added areas (see Strategy in Action 10.1).

In addition to formal institutions, MNEs also confront a series of informal institutions governing their relationships with *home* countries (see Strategy in Action 10.1). In the United States, few laws ban MNEs from aggressively setting up overseas subsidiaries, although the issue is a hot button in public debate and is always subject to changes in political policy. Therefore, managers contemplating such moves must consider the informal but vocal backlash against such activities due to the associated losses in domestic jobs.

Dealing with *host* countries also involves numerous informal institutions. Airbus spends 40% of its procurement budget with US suppliers in 40 states. While there is no formal requirement for Airbus to farm out supply contracts, its sourcing is guided by the informal norm of reciprocity: If one country's suppliers are involved with Airbus, airlines based in that country are more likely to buy Airbus aircraft.

Institutional factors affecting MNEs are not only external. How MNEs are governed *internally* is also determined by various formal and informal rules of the game. Formally, organizational charts, such as those in Figures 10.2 to 10.5, specify the scope of responsibilities for various parties. Most MNEs have systems of evaluation, reward, and punishment in place based on these formal rules.

STRATEGY IN ACTION 10.1 〉〉 ETHICAL DILEMMA

Moving Headquarters Overseas

A number of MNEs have moved headquarters (HQ) overseas. In general, there are two levels of HQ: *business unit* HQ and *corporate* HQ. At the business unit level, examples are numerous. In 2004, Nokia moved its corporate finance HQ from Helsinki, Finland, to New York. In 2006, IBM's global procurement office moved from New York to Shenzhen, China. In 2009, Nomura transferred its investment banking HQ from Tokyo to London. Examples for corporate HQ relocations are fewer, but they tend to be of higher profile. In 1992, HSBC moved corporate HQ from Hong Kong to London. Similarly, Anglo American, Old Mutual, and SAB (later to become SABMiller after acquiring Miller Beer) moved from South Africa to London. In 2004, News Corporation moved corporate HQ from Melbourne, Australia, to New York. In 2005, Lenovo set up corporate HQ in Raleigh, North Carolina, home of IBM's former PC division that Lenovo acquired. The question is: Why?

If you have moved from one house to another in the same city, you can easily appreciate the logistical challenges (and nightmares!) associated with relocating HQ overseas. A simple answer is that the benefits must significantly outweigh the drawbacks. At the business unit level, the answer is straightforward: the "center of gravity" of the activities of a business unit may pull its HQ toward a host country.

At the corporate level, there are at least five strategic rationales. First, a leading symbolic value is the unambiguous statement to various stakeholders that the firm is a global player. News Corporation's new corporate HQ in New York is indicative of its global status, as opposed to being a relatively parochial firm from "down under." Lenovo's coming of age is no doubt underpinned by the establishment of its worldwide HQ in the United States.

Second, there may be significant efficiency gains. If the new corporate HQ is in a major financial center such as New York or London, the MNE can have more efficient and more frequent communication with institutional shareholders, financial analysts, and investment banks. The MNE also increases its visibility in a financial market, resulting in a broader shareholder base and greater market capitalization. Three leading (former) South African firms, Anglo American, Old Mutual, and SABMiller, have now joined FTSE 100—the top 100 UK firms by capitalization.

Third, firms may benefit from their visible commitment to the laws of the new host country. They can also benefit from the higher-quality legal and regulatory regime they now operate under. These benefits are especially crucial for firms from emerging economies where local rules are not world-class. A lack of confidence about South Africa's political stability drove Anglo American, Old Mutual, and SABMiller to London. By coming to London, HSBC likewise deviated from its Hong Kong roots at a time when the political future of Hong Kong was uncertain.

Fourth, moving corporate HQ to a new country clearly indicates a commitment to that country. In addition to political motivation, HSBC's move to London signaled its determination to become a more global player, instead of being a regional player centered on Asia. HSBC indeed carried out this more global strategy since the 1990s. However, in an interesting twist of events, HSBC's CEO relocated back to Hong Kong in 2010. Technically, HSBC's corporate HQ is still in London, and its chairman remains in London. However, the symbolism of the CEO's return to Hong Kong is clear. As China becomes more economically powerful, HSBC is interested in demonstrating its commitment to that part of the world, which was where HSBC started (HSBC was set up in Hong Kong in 1865 as Hongkong and Shanghai Banking Corporation).

Finally, by moving (or threatening to move) HQ, firms enhance their bargaining power vis-à-vis that of their (original) home-country governments. Tetra Pak's 1981 move of its corporate HQ to Switzerland was driven primarily by the owners' tax disputes with the Swedish government. A few years ago, Seagate Technology, formerly registered in Silicon Valley, changed its incorporation to Cayman Islands in search of lower taxes. More US firms may follow such a move. Having already paid overseas taxes, US MNEs naturally resented Obama administration's proposal to extract from them $109 billion additional US taxes. "Doesn't the Obama administration recognize that most big US companies are multinationals that happen to be headquartered in the United States?" asked Duncan Niederauer, CEO of NYSE Euronext in a *BusinessWeek* interview. Likewise, as three of Britain's large banks—Barclays, HSBC, and Standard Chartered, the three best-run ones that didn't need bailouts—now face higher taxes and more government intervention, they too have threatened to move their HQ out of London. The message is clear: If the home-country government treats us harshly, we will pack our bags.

The last point, of course, is where the ethical and social responsibility controversies erupt. According to the *Economist*, Italy "regularly goes into hysteria over whether Fiat will stay." After Fiat's acquisition of Chrysler in 2009, whether the combined group's HQ would be in Turin or Detroit became an emotionally charged debate (Fiat's HQ eventually stayed in Turin). Although the absolute number of jobs lost is not great, these are high-quality (and high-paying) jobs that every government would prefer to see. For that reason, different cities in China, such as Beijing and Shanghai, offered very lucrative packages to attract regional HQ. For MNEs' home country, if a sufficient number of HQ move overseas, there is a serious ramification that other high-quality service providers, such as lawyers, bankers, and accountants, will follow them. In response, proposals are floating to offer tax incentives for these "foot-loose" MNEs to keep HQ at home. However, critics question why these wealthy MNEs (and executives) need to be subsidized (or bribed), while many other sectors and individuals are struggling.

Sources: Based on (1) G. Benito, R. Lunnan, & S. Tomassen, 2011, Distant encounters of the third kind: Multinational companies locating divisional headquarters abroad, *Journal of Management Studies*, 48: 373–394; (2) J. Birkinshaw, P. Braunerhjelm, U. Holm, & S. Terjesen, 2006, Why do some multinational corporations relocate their headquarters overseas? *Strategic Management Journal*, 27: 681–700; (3) *BusinessWeek*, 2009, NYSE chief Duncan Niederauer on Obama and business, 8 June: 15–16; (4) *China Business Review*, 2009, The race for regional headquarters takes off, November: 56–59; (5) *Economist*, 2010, Las Vegas leaving, December 4: 71; (6) *Economist*, 2011, HSBC: Gulliver's travels, April 16: 75–77; (7) IBM, 2006, IBM Procurement headquarters moves to Shenzhen, China, May 22, www 03. ibm.com; (8) T. Laamanen, T. Simula, & S. Torstila, 2012, Cross-border relocations of headquarters in Europe, *Journal of International Business Studies*, 43: 187–210; (9) *Wall Street Journal*, 2009, HSBC re-emphasizes its "H," September 26, www.wsj.com.

What the formal organizational charts do not reveal are the informal rules of the game, such as organizational norms, values, and networks. The nationality of the head of foreign subsidiaries is an example. Given the lack of formal regulations, MNEs essentially can have three choices:

- a home-country national as the head of a subsidiary (such as an American for a subsidiary of a US-headquartered MNE in India)

- a host-country national (such as an Indian for the same subsidiary)

- a third-country national (such as an Australian for the same subsidiary above)

MNEs from different countries have different norms when making these appointments. Most Japanese MNEs follow an informal rule: Heads of foreign subsidiaries, at least initially, need to be Japanese nationals. In comparison, European MNEs are more likely to appoint host-country and third-country nationals to lead subsidiaries. As a group, US MNEs are somewhere between Japanese and European practices. These staffing approaches may reflect strategic differences. Home-country nationals, especially long-time employees of the same MNE at home, are more likely to have developed a better understanding of the informal workings of the firm and to be better socialized into its dominant norms and values. Consequently, the Japanese propensity to appoint home-country nationals is conducive to their preferred global standardization strategy, which values globally coordinated and controlled actions. Conversely, the European comfort in appointing host-country and third-country nationals is indicative of European MNEs' (traditional) preference for a localization strategy.

Beyond the nationality of subsidiary heads, the nationality of top executives at the highest level (such as chairman, CEO, and board members) seems to follow another informal rule: They are almost always home-country nationals. To the extent that top executives are ambassadors of the firm and that the MNE's country of origin is a source of differentiation (for example, a German MNE is often perceived to be different from an Italian MNE), home-country nationals would seem to be the most natural candidates for top positions.

In the eyes of stakeholders such as employees and governments around the world, however, a top echelon consisting of largely one nationality does not bode well for an MNE aspiring to globalize everything it does. Some critics even argue that this "glass ceiling" reflects "corporate imperialism."[14] Consequently, such leading MNEs as BP, Coca-Cola, Electrolux, GSK, Lenovo, Nissan, Nokia, PepsiCo, and Sony have appointed foreign-born executives to top posts. Such foreign-born bosses bring substantial diversity to the organization, which may be a plus. However, such diversity puts an enormous burden on these non-native top executives to clearly articulate the values and exhibit behaviors expected of senior managers of an MNE associated with a particular country. In 2010, Hewlett-Packard (HP) appointed Léo Apotheker, a native of Germany, to be its CEO. Unfortunately, HP lost $30 billion in market capitalization during his short tenure (less than 11 months), thanks to his numerous change initiatives. He was quickly fired in 2011. Since then, the old rule is back: HP is again led by an American executive.

Overall, while formal internal rules on how the MNE is governed may reflect conscientious strategic choices, informal internal rules are often taken for granted and deeply embedded in administrative heritages, thus making them difficult to change.

Worldwide Learning, Innovation, and Knowledge Management

Knowledge Management

knowledge management
The structures, processes, and systems that actively develop, leverage, and transfer knowledge.

Underpinning the recent emphasis on worldwide learning and innovation is the emerging interest in knowledge management.[15] **Knowledge management** can be defined as the structures, processes, and systems that actively develop, leverage, and transfer knowledge.

Many managers regard knowledge management as simply information management. Taken to an extreme, "such a perspective can result in a profoundly mistaken belief that the installation of sophisticated information technology (IT) infrastructure is the be-all and end-all of knowledge management."[16] Knowledge management depends not only on IT but also on informal social relationships within the MNE.[17] There are two categories of knowledge: (1) explicit knowledge and (2) tacit knowledge. **Explicit knowledge** is codifiable—it can be written down and transferred with little loss of richness. Virtually all of the knowledge captured, stored, and transmitted by IT is explicit. **Tacit knowledge** is noncodifiable, and its acquisition and transfer require hands-on practice. For example, reading a driver's manual (a ton of explicit knowledge) without any road practice does not make you a good driver. Tacit knowledge is evidently more important and harder to transfer and learn; it can only be acquired through learning by doing (driving in this case). Consequently, from a resource-based view, explicit knowledge captured by IT may be strategically *less* important. What counts is the hard-to-codify and hard-to-transfer tacit knowledge.[18]

explicit knowledge
Knowledge that is codifiable (that is, it can be written down and transferred without losing much of its richness).

tacit knowledge
Knowledge that is not codifiable (that is, hard to be written down and transmitted without losing much of its richness).

Knowledge Management in Four Types of Multinational Enterprises

Differences in knowledge management among four types of MNEs in Figure 10.1 fundamentally stem from the interdependence (1) between the headquarters and subsidiaries and (2) among various subsidiaries, as outlined in Table 10.2.[19] In MNEs pursuing a

TABLE 10.2   Knowledge Management In Four Types of Multinational Enterprises

STRATEGY	HOME REPLICATION	LOCALIZATION	GLOBAL STANDARDIZATION	TRANSNATIONAL
Interdependence	Moderate	Low	Moderate	High
Role of foreign subsidiaries	Adapting and leveraging parent company competencies	Sensing and exploiting local opportunities	Implementing parent company initiatives	Differentiated contributions by subsidiaries to integrate worldwide operations
Development and diffusion of knowledge	Knowledge developed at the center and transferred to subsidiaries	Knowledge developed and retained within each subsidiary	Knowledge mostly developed and retained at the center and key locations	Knowledge developed jointly and shared worldwide
Flow of knowledge	Extensive flow of knowledge and people from headquarters to subsidiaries	Limited flow of knowledge and people in both directions (to and from the center)	Extensive flow of knowledge and people from center and key locations to subsidiaries	Extensive flow of knowledge and people in multiple directions

Sources: Adapted from (1) C. Bartlett & S. Ghoshal, 1989, *Managing Across Borders: The Transnational Solution* (p. 65), Boston: Harvard Business School Press; (2) T. Kostova & K. Roth, 2003, Social capital in multinational corporations and a micro-macro model of its formation (p. 299), *Academy of Management Review*, 28 (2): 297–317.

home replication strategy, such interdependence is moderate and the role of subsidiaries is largely to adapt and leverage parent company competencies. Thus, knowledge on new products and technologies is mostly developed at the center and flown to subsidiaries, representing the traditional one-way flow. Starbucks, for example, insists on replicating its US coffee shop concept around the world, down to the elusive "atmosphere."

When MNEs adopt a localization strategy, the interdependence is low. Knowledge management centers on developing insights that can best serve local markets. Ford of Europe used to develop cars for Europe, with a limited flow of knowledge to and from headquarters. In MNEs pursuing a global standardization strategy, on the other hand, the interdependence is increased. Knowledge is developed and retained at the headquarters and a few centers of excellence. Consequently, knowledge and people typically flow from headquarters and these centers to other subsidiaries. For example, Yokogawa Hewlett-Packard, HP's subsidiary in Japan, won a coveted Japanese Deming Award for quality. The subsidiary was then charged with transferring such knowledge to the rest of HP, which resulted in a tenfold improvement in *corporate-*wide quality in ten years.

A hallmark of transnational MNEs is a high degree of interdependence and extensive and bi-directional flows of knowledge. For example, Kikkoman first developed teriyaki sauce specifically for the US market as a barbecue glaze. It was then marketed to Japan and the rest of the world. Similarly, Häagen-Dazs developed a popular ice cream in Argentina that was based on a locally popular caramelized milk dessert. The company then took the new flavor and sold it as "dulce de leche" throughout the United States and Europe. Within one year, it became the second most popular Häagen-Dazs ice cream (next only to vanilla). Particularly fundamental to transnational MNEs is knowledge flows among dispersed subsidiaries. Instead of a top-down hierarchy, the MNE thus can be conceptualized as an integrated network of subsidiaries. Each subsidiary not only develops locally relevant knowledge but also aspires to contribute knowledge to benefit the MNE as a whole (see Emerging Markets 10.1).

Globalizing Research and Development (R&D)

R&D represents a crucial arena for knowledge management. Relative to production and marketing, only more recently has R&D emerged as an important function to be internationalized—often known as innovation-seeking investment.[20] The intensification of competition for innovation drives the globalization of R&D. Such R&D provides a vehicle to access a foreign country's local talents and expertise.[21] Recall earlier discussions in Chapter 6 on the importance of *agglomeration* of high-caliber innovative firms within a country. For foreign firms, a most effective way to access such a cluster is to be there through foreign direct investment (FDI)—as Shiseido did in France by setting up a perfume lab there.

From a resource-based standpoint, a fundamental basis for competitive advantage is innovation-based firm heterogeneity (being different).[22] Decentralized R&D performed by different locations and teams around the world virtually guarantees that there will be persistent heterogeneity in the solutions generated.[23] GSK, for example, has aggressively spun off R&D units, because it realizes that adding more researchers in centralized R&D units does not necessarily enhance global learning and innovation.[24] GE's China units have developed low-cost, portable ultrasound machines at a fraction of the cost of existing machines developed in the United States. GE has not only been selling the developed-in-China machines throughout emerging economies, but has also brought them back to the United States and other developed economies, which also benefit tremendously from such low-cost machines (see Emerging Markets 1.2).

Problems and Solutions in Knowledge Management

Institutionally, how MNEs employ the formal and informal rules of the game has a significant bearing behind the success or failure of knowledge management.[25] Shown in Table 10.3, a number of informal "rules" can become problems in knowledge management. In knowledge acquisition, many MNEs prefer to invent everything internally. However, for large firms, R&D actually offers *diminishing* returns.[26] Consequently, a new model, **open innovation**, is emerging.[27] Open innovation is "the use of purposive inflows and outflows of knowledge to accelerate internal innovation and expand the markets for external use of innovation."[28] It relies on more collaborative research among various internal units, external firms, and university labs. Firms that skillfully share research often outperform those that fail to do so.[29]

In knowledge retention, the usual problems of employee turnover are compounded when such employees are key R&D personnel, whose departure will lead to knowledge leakage.[30] In knowledge outflow, there is the "How does it help me?" syndrome. Specifically, managers of the source subsidiary may view the outbound sharing of knowledge as a diversion of scarce time and resources. Further, some managers may believe that "knowledge is power"—monopolizing certain knowledge may be viewed as the currency to acquire and retain power within the MNE.[31]

open innovation

The use of purposive inflows and outflows of knowledge to accelerate internal innovation and expand the markets for external use of innovation.

TABLE 10.3 Problems in Knowledge Management

ELEMENTS OF KNOWLEDGE MANAGEMENT	COMMON PROBLEMS
Knowledge acquisition	Failure to share and integrate external knowledge
Knowledge retention	Employee turnover and knowledge leakage
Knowledge outflow	"How does it help me?" syndrome and "knowledge is power" mentality
Knowledge transmission	Inappropriate channels
Knowledge inflow	"Not invented here" syndrome and absorptive capacity

Source: Adapted from A. Gupta & V. Govindarajan, 2004, *Global Strategy and Organization* (p. 109), New York: Wiley.

global virtual teams

Teams whose members are physically dispersed in multiple locations in the world. They cooperate on a virtual basis.

absorptive capacity

The ability to absorb new knowledge by recognizing the value of new information, assimilating it, and applying it.

social capital

The informal benefits individuals and organizations derive from their social structures and networks.

micro-macro link

The link between micro, informal interpersonal relationships among managers of various units and macro, interorganizational cooperation among various units.

Even when certain subsidiaries are willing to share knowledge, inappropriate transmission channels may still torpedo effective sharing.[32] It is tempting to establish **global virtual teams**, which do not meet face to face, to transfer knowledge. Unfortunately, such teams often have to confront tremendous communication and relationship barriers.[33] Videoconferences can hardly show body language, and Skype often breaks down. Thus, face-to-face meetings—of the sort Samsung's Global Strategy teams often hold (see the Opening Case)—are often still necessary. Finally, for two reasons recipient subsidiaries may block successful knowledge inflows. First, the "not invented here" syndrome creates a resistance to ideas from other units. Second, recipients may have limited **absorptive capacity**—the "ability to recognize the value of new information, assimilate it, and apply it."[34]

As solutions to combat these problems, headquarters can manipulate the formal "rules of the game," such as (1) tying bonuses to measurable knowledge outflows and inflows,[35] (2) using high-powered corporate-based or unit-based incentives (as opposed to individual-based and single-subsidiary-based incentives), and (3) investing in codifying tacit knowledge (such as the codification of the Toyota Way). However, these formal policies fundamentally boil down to the very challenging (if not impossible) task of how to accurately measure inflows and outflows of tacit knowledge. The nature of tacit knowledge simply resists such formal bureaucratic practices. Consequently, MNEs often have to rely on a great deal of informal integrating mechanisms, such as (1) facilitating management and R&D personnel networks among various subsidiaries through joint teamwork, training, and conferences, and (2) promoting strong organizational (that is, MNE-specific) cultures and shared values and norms for cooperation among subsidiaries. Shown in the Opening Case, Samsung's Global Strategy Group has facilitated the establishment of such networks between Korean and non-Korean executives and fostered the sharing of the Samsung culture, by having Global Strategy teams to work on a variety of internal strategy consulting projects interacting with various Samsung subsidiaries in a two-year period.

Instead of using traditional formal command-and-control structures that are often ineffective, knowledge management is best facilitated by informal **social capital**, which refers to the informal benefits individuals and organizations derive from their social structures and networks.[36] Because of the existence of social capital, individuals are more likely to go out of their way to help friends and acquaintances. Consequently, managers of the China subsidiary are more likely to help managers of the Chile subsidiary with needed knowledge if they know each other and have some social relationship. Otherwise, managers of the China subsidiary may not be as enthusiastic to provide such help if the call for help comes from managers of the Canada subsidiary, with whom there is no social relationship. Overall, the micro informal interpersonal relationships among managers of various units may greatly facilitate macro inter-subsidiary cooperation among various units—in short, a **micro-macro link**.[37]

Debates and Extensions

The question of how to manage complex MNEs has led to numerous debates, some of which have been discussed earlier (such as the debate on the matrix structure). Here we outline three of the leading debates not previously discussed: (1) one multinational versus many national companies, (2) corporate controls versus subsidiary initiatives, and (3) customer-focused dimensions versus integration, responsiveness, and learning.

One Multinational versus Many National Companies

We often treat each MNE as one firm. However, from an institution-based view, one can argue that a *multinational* enterprise may be a total fiction that does not exist. Legally, incorporation is only possible under national law. In other words, every so-called MNE is essentially a bunch of *national* companies (subsidiaries) registered in various countries. A generation ago, such firms were often labeled "multi-national companies" with a hyphen. Although some pundits argue that globalization is undermining the power of national governments, little evidence suggests that the modern nation-state system, in existence since the 1648 Treaty of Westphalia, is retreating.

This debate is not just academic hair-splitting fighting over a hyphen. It is very relevant and stakes are high. One case in point concerns taxation. Google Ireland is *not* a branch of the US-based Google Corporation. Google Ireland is a separate, legally independent corporation registered in Ireland. Although Google Corporation intentionally lets Google Ireland earn a lot of profits, the Internal Revenue Service (IRS) cannot tax a dime Google Ireland makes unless it sends back (repatriates) the profits to Google Corporation. Google Corporation does not have just one subsidiary. It has lots around the world. Overall, 54% of Google's profits are parked overseas and are not taxable by the IRS. Google is not alone. The list of leading US firms that have left a *majority* of their profits overseas includes Chevron, Cisco, Citigroup, ExxonMobil, GE, HP, IBM, Johnson & Johnson, Microsoft, P&G, PepsiCo, and Pfizer.[38] These firms claim that they are willing to bring the profits back home to invest and create jobs as long as Congress grants them a tax holiday. Running huge budget deficits, Congress is understandably reluctant.

Another case in point is brought by Indian firm Satyam's scandal. Satyam was listed on the New York Stock Exchange (NYSE), and PricewaterhouseCooper (PwC) endorsed Satyam's books even through $1 billion cash did not exist at all. While such sloppy auditing was done by PwC India, some Satyam shareholders sued PwC International Limited headquartered in New York. But PwC International spokesman argued in interviews that "there is no such a thing as a global firm because we are a membership organization."[39] That is to say: PwC India, registered in India, is a legally independent firm whose conduct has nothing to do with other nationally registered firms such as PwC International or PwC Hong Kong. In court battles, whether the argument that PwC International is not responsible for PwC India's misconduct can repel the allegations remains to be seen.

Corporate Controls versus Subsidiary Initiatives

One of the leading debates on how to manage large firms is centralization versus decentralization (see Strategy in Action 10.2). Within an MNE, the debate boils down to central controls versus subsidiary initiatives. A starting point is that subsidiaries are not necessarily at the receiving end of commands from headquarters. When headquarters promote certain practices (such as quality circles or ethics training), some subsidiaries

STRATEGY IN ACTION 10.2

Centralized and Decentralized Strategic Planning at the Oil Majors

According to some critics, strategic planning is in crisis. Historically top down, bureaucratic, and formalized, strategic planning seems unable to keep up with the turbulent world of modern competition. Many corporate planning departments have been downsized, and critics predict the demise of strategic planning. However, at the world's major oil companies known as the Oil Majors (some of which were formerly known as the Seven Sisters a century ago), such as BP, Chevron, Elf, ENI, ExxonMobil, Shell, and Texaco, such a demise seems unlikely as strategic planning continues to play an important although transformed role.

Usually ranked among the world's largest MNEs, the Oil Majors have complex operations spanning the globe. The uncertainty of their markets and the large capital requirements call for careful planning. As a result, the Oil Majors were among the first group of firms that pioneered the creation of corporate planning departments in the 1960s, and have been leading-edge practitioners of centralized strategic planning.

Since the 1970s, the competitive environment has experienced a great deal of turmoil, because of the Oil Shocks of 1973–74 and 1979–80, tensions in the Middle East, and wars and chaos in major oil-producing countries such as Iraq, Nigeria, Russia, and Venezuela—the most recent case in point: Libya (2011). Thanks to the tremendous fluctuation, the accuracy of crude oil price predictions declines. Thus, the danger of relying on these forecasts becomes apparent.

In response to the heightened uncertainty, strategic planning at the Oil Majors has been transformed in three significant ways. First, forecasting is reduced, whereas scenario planning, based on multiple scenarios with numerous "reference prices," is increasingly used. Planning horizons are shortened from 10–15 years to five years or less. Second, planning is less formal with less emphasis on written documentation and more on open discussions. At Exxon-Mobil, annual planning meetings between divisional and corporate heads have been cut from 3–4 days to a half-day.

Third and perhaps most significantly, all Oil Majors have decentralized their decision making. A more turbulent environment has pushed decision making increasingly down to the subsidiary and divisional level. It is believed that such lower level decision making allows for better, speedier responses to fast-changing circumstances in many different countries. Capital expenditure limits above which subsidiary and divisional managers need corporate approval have all risen—for instance, to $50 million at ExxonMobil and $150 million at BP. On the other hand, subsidiary and divisional managers are increasingly held accountable for performance targets. An inevitable corollary of these changes is that subsidiary and divisional managers must be free to select strategies capable of delivering the required performance. As a result, since the 1990s, strategy formulation has taken place, for the most part, *outside* of the corporate strategic planning systems. Strategic decisions are now typically "bottom up," proposed and made by subsidiary and divisional managers, and are subsequently incorporated into corporate strategic plans.

Overall, there indeed has been some reduction in corporate planning staff since the 1990s. For example, at Shell, the staff has been reduced from 48 to 17. However, the prediction that the planning staff may become an endangered species is premature, because now almost all major subsidiaries and divisions have planning units. The subsidiary and divisional planning staff routinely outnumbers the corporate planning staff—for instance, 416 versus 72 at ENI. Overall, at the Oil Majors, strategic planning has become more decentralized, less corporate staff driven, and more informal, while plans themselves become shorter term, more goal focused, and less specific.

Sources: Based on (1) R. Grant, 2003, Strategic planning in a turbulent environment, *Strategic Management Journal*, 24: 491–517; (2) H. Mintzberg, 1994, *The Rise and Fall of Strategic Planning*, New York: Free Press; (3) M. W. Peng, 2012, Managing political risk in the Middle East (p. 31), *Global*, Cincinnati: South-Western Cengage Learning; (4) D. Simpson, 1998, Why most strategic planning is a waste of time and what you can do about it, *Long Range Planning*, 31: 476–480.

may be in full compliance, others may pay lip service to them, and still others may simply refuse to adopt them, citing local differences.[40]

In addition to reacting to headquarters' demands differently, some subsidiaries may actively pursue their own *subsidiary*-level strategies and agendas.[41] These activities are known as **subsidiary initiatives**, defined as the proactive and deliberate pursuit of new opportunities by a subsidiary. Advocates argue that such initiatives may inject a much-needed spirit of entrepreneurship throughout the larger bureaucratic MNE (see the Closing Case).

However, from the perspective of corporate headquarters, it is hard to distinguish between good-faith subsidiary initiative and opportunistic "empire-building."[42] A lot is at stake when determining which subsidiary initiatives are supported.[43] Subsidiaries whose initiatives fail to receive support may see their roles marginalized and, in the worst case, their facilities closed. Subsidiary managers are often host-country nationals, who would naturally prefer to strengthen their subsidiary. However, these tendencies, although very understandable, are not necessarily consistent with the MNE's *corporate*-wide goals. These tendencies, if not checked and controlled, can surely lead to chaos. According to the title of an influential article authored by Andy Grove, former chairman and CEO of Intel, the challenge for corporate management is:

▌ *Let chaos reign, then rein in chaos—repeatedly.*[44]

Customer-Focused Dimensions versus Integration, Responsiveness, and Learning

As discussed earlier, juggling the three dimensions of integration, responsiveness, and learning has often made the global matrix structure so complex it is unworkable. However, instead of simplifying, many MNEs have added new dimensions. Often, new customer-focused dimensions of structure are placed on top of an existing structure, resulting in a four- or five-dimension matrix.[45]

Of the two primary customer-focused dimensions, the first is a **global account structure** to supply customers (often other MNEs) in a coordinated and consistent way across various countries.[46] Most original equipment manufacturers (OEMs)—namely, contract manufacturers that produce goods *not* carrying their own brands (such as the makers of Nike shoes and Microsoft Xbox)—use this structure. For example, Singapore's Flextronics, one of the world's largest OEMs, has dedicated global accounts for Dell, Palm, and Sony Ericsson. The second customer-focused dimension is the oft-used **solutions-based structure**. For instance, as a "customer solution" provider, IBM will sell whatever combination of hardware, software, and services that customers prefer, whether that means selling IBM products or rivals' offerings.

The typical starting point is to put in place temporary solutions rather than create new layers or units. However, this ad hoc approach can quickly get out of control, resulting in subsidiary managers' additional duties of reporting to three or four "informal bosses" (acting as global account managers) on top of their "day jobs." Eventually, new formal structures may be called for, resulting in more bureaucracy.

So what is the solution when confronting the value-added potential of customer-focused dimensions and their associated complexity and cost? One solution is to *simplify*. For instance, ABB, when facing performance problems, transformed its sprawling "Byzantine" matrix structure to a mere two product divisions.

---

subsidiary initiative

The proactive and deliberate pursuit of new business opportunities by an MNE's subsidiary to expand its scope of responsibility.

global account structure

A customer-focused structure that supplies customers (often other MNEs) in a coordinated and consistent way across various countries.

solutions-based structure

An MNE organizational structure that caters to the needs of providing solutions for customers' problems.

The Savvy Strategist

MNEs are the ultimate large, complex, and geographically dispersed business organizations. To manage effectively, four clear implications emerge for the savvy strategist (Table 10.4). First, understand the nature and evolution of your industry in order to come up with the right strategy-structure configurations. When the Japanese automobile industry was primarily exporting, Honda adopted a home replication strategy supported by an international division. However, as the industry evolved to become more geographically dispersed in terms of production and innovation, Honda's strategy and structure had to adapt to keep up.

Second, managers need to develop learning and innovation capabilities to leverage multinational presence.[47] A winning formula is *think global, act local.*[48] Failing to do so may be costly. Between 1999 and 2000, many Ford Explorer SUVs accidentally rolled over and killed many people in the United States. Most of these accidents were caused by faulty tires made by Japan's Bridgestone and its US subsidiary Firestone. Before the number of US accidents skyrocketed, an alarming number of accidents had already taken place in warmer-weather countries such as Brazil and Saudi Arabia, and local managers dutifully reported them to headquarters in Japan and the United States. Unfortunately, these reports were dismissed by higher-ups as "driver error" or "road conditions." Bridgestone (and Firestone) thus failed to leverage its multinational presence as an asset—it should have learned from these reports and proactively probed into the potential for similar accidents in cooler-weather countries (tires depreciate faster in warmer weather).

Third, mastering the external rules of the game governing MNEs and home/host country environments becomes a must. In 2000, Philips took advantage of home-country rules concerning antidumping (see Chapter 8) by suing Chinese firms for dumping in the EU. However, after Philips upset the host-country government, its sales in China, its second largest market after the United States, immediately dropped by 10% (from $5.5 billion in 2000 to $5 billion in 2001). Getting the message, Philips tried to repair the damage. In 2003 Philips' board held its first meeting outside of Amsterdam in Beijing and visited Chinese officials. It also moved its Asia headquarters from Hong Kong to Shanghai and set up R&D units in Xian.

Finally, managers need to understand and be prepared to change the internal rules of the game governing MNE management. Different strategies and structures call for different internal rules of the game. Some facilitate and others constrain MNE actions. It is impossible for a home replication firm to entertain having a foreigner as its CEO. Yet, as an MNE becomes more global in its operations, its managerial outlook needs to be broadened as well (see the Opening Case).

TABLE 10.4 Strategic Implications for Action

- Understand the evolution of your industry to come up with the right strategy-structure configurations.
- Develop learning and innovation capabilities to leverage multinational presence as an asset—"think global, act local."
- Master the external rules of the game governing MNEs and home/host country environments.
- Be prepared to change the internal rules of the game governing MNE management.

© Cengage Learning

CHAPTER SUMMARY

1. **Understand the four basic configurations of multinational strategies and structures**
   - Governing multinational strategy and structure is an integration-responsiveness framework.
   - There are four strategy/structure pairs: (1) home replication strategy/international division structure, (2) localization strategy/geographic area structure, (3) global standardization strategy/global product division structure, and (4) transnational strategy/global matrix structure.

2. **Articulate a comprehensive model of multinational strategy, structure, and learning**
   - Industry-based considerations drive a number of decisions affecting strategy, structure, and learning.
   - Management of MNE strategy, structure, and learning needs to take into account its VRIO.
   - MNEs are governed by external and internal rules of the game around the world.

3. **Outline the challenges associated with learning, innovation, and knowledge management**
   - Knowledge management primarily focuses on tacit knowledge.
   - Globalization of R&D calls for capabilities to combat a number of problems associated with knowledge creation, retention, outflow, transmission, and inflow.

4. **Participate in three leading debates on multinational structure, learning, and innovation**
   - (1) One multinational versus many national companies, (2) corporate controls versus subsidiary initiatives, and (3) customer-focused dimensions versus integration, responsiveness, and learning.

5. **Draw strategic implications for action**
   - Understand the evolution of your industry to come up with the right strategy-structure configurations.
   - Develop learning and innovation capabilities around the world—"think global, act local."
   - Master the external rules of the game from home/host country environments.
   - Be prepared to change the internal rules of the game governing MNEs.

KEY TERMS

Absorptive capacity p. 314

Center of excellence p. 299

Country (regional) manager p. 301

Explicit knowledge p. 301

Geographic area structure p. 301

Global account structure p. 317

Global matrix p. 302

Global product division p. 302

Global standardization strategy p. 299

Global virtual team p. 314

Home replication strategy p. 297

Integration-responsiveness framework p. 296

International division p. 300

Knowledge management p. 310

Local responsiveness p. 296

Localization (multi-domestic)
strategy p. 297

Micro-macro link p. 314

Open innovation p. 313

Organizational culture p. 306

Social capital p. 314

Solutions-based
structure p. 317

Subsidiary initiative p. 317

Tacit knowledge p. 311

Transnational
strategy p. 299

Worldwide (global)
mandate p. 299

CRITICAL DISCUSSION QUESTIONS

1. In this age of globalization, some gurus argue that all industries are becoming global and that all firms need to adopt a global standardization strategy. Do you agree? Why or why not?

2. From time to time, a manager may be faced with the need to change the internal rules of the game within his/her MNE. What skills and capabilities may be useful in achieving this?

3. *ON ETHICS:* If you were a CEO or a business unit head, under what conditions would you consider moving your headquarters overseas? (see Strategy in Action 10.1)

TOPICS FOR EXPANDED PROJECTS

1. *ON ETHICS:* You are the head of the best-performing subsidiary in an MNE. Because bonuses are tied to subsidiary performance, your bonus is the highest among managers of all subsidiaries. Now headquarters is organizing managers from other subsidiaries to visit and learn from your subsidiary. You worry that if your subsidiary is no longer the star unit when other subsidiaries' performance catches up, your bonus will go down. What are you going to do? State your answer in a one-page paper.

2. *ON ETHICS:* You are a corporate R&D manager at Boeing and are thinking about transferring some R&D work to China, India, and Russia, where the work performed by a $70,000 US engineer reportedly can be done by an engineer in one of these countries for less than $7,000. However, US engineers at Boeing have staged protests against such moves. US politicians are similarly vocal concerning job losses and national security hazards. Write a short paper describing how you've decided to proceed and why.

3. *ON ETHICS:* Working in pairs or small groups, research and review a high-profile case of an MNE moving its headquarters out of your country and the media and political outcry surrounding this move (see Strategy in Action 10.1). Determine whether you are for or against the firm's move, and present your research in a short paper or visual presentation.

CLOSING CASE

A Subsidiary Initiative at Bayer MaterialScience North America

Bayer Group is a $50 billion chemical and health care giant based in Germany. Its three main product divisions are Bayer MaterialScience (BMS), Bayer CropScience, and Bayer HealthCare. In this matrix organization, each of these product divisions has country/regional subsidiaries in major markets. Between 2004 and 2011, the CEO for Bayer MaterialScience North America (BMS NA) was Greg Babe. Contributing 25% of BMS' global revenues, BMS NA delivered highly respected performance. It had strong sales growth in 2005 ($3.5 billion, increasing from $2.7 billion in 2004), and suffered a modest flattening in 2006 ($3.3 billion). However, in early 2007, BMS made a radical decision: to dismantle BMS NA—in other words, to shut down the North America regional headquarters in Pittsburgh. Allegedly undermining cost competitiveness, the regional structure was viewed as too bloated.

Shocked, Babe asked for time to propose another solution. In his own words: "The stakes couldn't have been higher: not only the future of my position but the credibility of the entire regional operation was in question." Cost cutting was nothing unusual in this cyclical industry, and the norm was usually to shave off a certain percentage of overhead (such as 10%). A month into the analysis, Babe and his team had an "aha" moment. The cost structure, they realized, should be dictated by how they grew the business, not by an arbitrary target. With that insight, they looked at the overall picture from a strategic growth lens rather than a tactical cost reduction lens. They set two specific goals: (1) to grow at 1% to 2% above GDP and (2) to save 25% on selling, general, and administrative (SG&A) costs. To deliver that, Babe needed to completely reshape his unit but also needed additional investment of $70 million.

In late 2007, when Babe presented to BMS's global leadership team, everyone expected him to come up with a cost-cutting exercise. Instead, he presented a subsidiary growth initiative. BMS's global leadership team challenged

key concepts of the proposal, many of which deviated from Bayer's global norms. For example, transportation was historically deemed by Bayer as a core competence. Babe proposed to outsource it, which would allow customers to give a 12 (rather than 72) hours' notice for shipping. Overall, Babe promised to turn BMS NA into a lean growth engine. In the end, the bold proposal paid off. Babe left the meeting with $70 million in hand. In his own words:

> *I was excited, but also scared to death, because delivering on it was by no means going to be easy. It would require laying off hundreds of employees and retraining more than 1,000 others, outsourcing many operations, rolling out new IT systems, and modifying our product offerings, all within 18 months—not much time for a project of that scale.*

To make the matters worse, the chemical industry soon entered a severe downturn worldwide, and BMS suffered eight consecutive quarters of declining sales starting in 2008. In such a bleak environment, BMS NA's efforts became more strategically important. By early 2009, BMS NA delivered on everything Babe had promised: it reduced SG&A costs by 25% ($100 million)

and head count by 30%. It actually overdelivered: only $60 million of the $70 million allotted for growth was spent. By 2010, BMS NA's sales turned around and enjoyed double-digit quarterly growth (2010 sales went up to $2.7 billion from the bottom of $2.1 billion in 2009). What was more valuable was that some of the reorganized processes (such as outsourcing transportation), so foreign at the time to BMS, now became implemented by BMS around the world. Overall, by endorsing the regional subsidiary's initiative, BMS's global leadership team took some significant risk. But in the end, the payoff was handsome.

Sources: Based on (1) Bayer AG, 2012, www.bayerus.com; (2) G. Babe, 2011, The CEO of Bayer Corp. on creating a lean growth engine, *Harvard Business Review*, July: 41–45.

Case Discussion Questions

1. While Bayer has a matrix structure, it has maintained some flavor of a geographic area structure. What are the advantages and disadvantages of a geographic area structure as seen in this case?

2. What are the advantages and disadvantages of a matrix structure as seen in this case?

3. **ON ETHICS:** While this is a successful case of subsidiary initiative, from a corporate or division headquarters' standpoint, it is often difficult to ascertain whether the subsidiary is making good-faith efforts acting in the best interest of the MNE or the subsidiary managers such as Babe are primarily promoting their own self-interest, such as protecting their own jobs. How can headquarters differentiate good-faith efforts from more opportunistic maneuvers?

NOTES

[**Journal acronyms**] *AME – Academy of Management Executive;* **AMJ** *– Academy of Management Journal;* **AMP** *– Academy of Management Perspectives;* **AMR** *– Academy of Management Review;* **APJM** *– Asia Pacific Journal of Management;* **ASQ** *– Administrative Science Quarterly;* **BW** *– BusinessWeek (before 2010) or Bloomberg Businessweek (since 2010);* **HBR** *– Harvard Business Review;* **JIBS** *– Journal of International Business Studies;* **JIM** *– Journal of International Management;* **JMS** *– Journal of Management Studies;* **JWB** *– Journal of World Business;* **MIR** *– Management International Review;* **OSc** *– Organization Science;* **SMJ** *– Strategic Management Journal*

1. T. Levitt, 1983, The globalization of markets, *HBR*, May: 92–102.

2. A. Rugman, 2001, *The End of Globalization*, New York: AMACOM.

3. J. Arregle, P. Beamish, & L. Hebert, 2009, The regional dimension of MNEs' foreign subsidiary localization, *JIBS*, 40: 86–107; C. Asmussen, 2009, Local, regional, or global? *JIBS*, 40: 1192–1205; B. Greenwald & J. Kahn, 2005, All strategy is local, *HBR*, September: 95–104.

4. *BW*, 2011, Disney gets a second chance in China, April 18: 21–22.

5. R. Hodgetts, 1999, Dow Chemical CEO William Stavropoulos on structure, *AME*, 13: 30.

6. A. Chandler, 1962, *Strategy and Structure*, Cambridge, MA: MIT Press. See also W. C. Kim & R. Mauborgne, 2009, How strategy shapes structure, *HBR*, September: 73–80; J. Galan & M. Sanchez-Bueno, 2009, The continuing validity of the strategy-structure nexus, *SMJ*, 30: 1234–1243.

7. J. Garbe & N. Richter, 2009, Causal analysis of the internationalization and performance relationship based on neural networks, *JIM*, 15: 413–431; J. Wolf & W. Egelhoff, 2002, A reexamination and extension of international strategy-structure theory, *SMJ*, 23: 181–189.

8. X. Ma & A. Delios, 2010, Home-country headquarters and an MNE's subsequent within-country diversification, *JIBS*, 41: 517–525.

9. *BW*, 2008, Cisco's brave new world, November 24: 56–66.

10. C. Bouquet, A. Morrison, & J. Birkinshaw, 2009, International attention and MNE performance, *JIBS*, 40: 108–131; T. Chi, P. Nystrom, & P. Kircher, 2004, Knowledge-based resources as determinants of MNC structure, *JIM*, 10: 219–238.

11. E. Morgan & F. Fai, 2007, Innovation, competition, and change in IB, *MIR*, 47: 631–638.

12. C. Bartlett & S. Ghoshal, 1989, *Managing Across Borders* (p. 209), Boston: Harvard Business School Press.

13. L. Nachum & S. Song, 2011, The MNE as a portfolio, *JIBS*, 42: 381–405.

14. C. K. Prahalad & K. Lieberthal, 1998, The end of corporate imperialism, *HBR,* August: 68–79.

15. Y. Lu, E. Tsang, & M. W. Peng, 2008, Knowledge management and innovation strategy in the Asia Pacific, *APJM*, 25: 361–374. See also N. Driffield, J. Love, & S. Menghinello, 2010, The MNE as a source of international knowledge flows, *JIBS*, 41: 350–359; N. Foss, K. Husted, & S. Michailova, 2010, Governing knowledge sharing in organizations, *JMS*, 47: 455–482; A. Fransson, L. Hakanson, & P. Liesch, 2011, The underdetermined knowledge-based theory of the MNC, *JIBS*, 42: 427–435; J. Martin & K. Eisenhardt, 2010, Rewiring, *AMJ*, 53: 265–301; H. Yang, C. Phelps, & H. K. Steensma, 2010, Learning from what others have learned from you, *AMJ*, 53: 371–389; J. Zhang & C. Baden-Fuller, 2010, The influence of technological knowledge base and organizational structure on technology collaboration, *JMS*, 47: 679–704.

16. A. Gupta & V. Govindarajan, 2004, *Global Strategy and Organization* (p. 104), New York: Wiley.

17. P. Gooderham, D. Minbaeva, & T. Pedersen, 2011, Governance mechanisms for the promotion of social capital for knowledge transfer in MNCs, *JMS*, 48: 123–150.

18. S. Berman, J. Down, & C. Hill, 2002, Tacit knowledge as a source of competitive advantage, *AMJ*, 45: 13–31.

19. M. Kotabe, D. Dunlap-Hinkler, R. Parente, & H. Mishra, 2007, Determinants of cross-national knowledge transfer and its effect on firm innovation, *JIBS*, 38: 259–282.

20. K. Asakawa & A. Som, 2008, Internationalizing R&D in China and India, *APJM*, 25: 375–394; P. Criscuolo & R. Narula, 2007, Using multi-hub structures for international R&D, *MIR*, 47: 639–660; D. Hillier, J. Pindado, V. de Queiroz, & C. Torre, 2011, The impact of country-level corporate governance on research and development, *JIBS*, 42: 76–98; N. Lahiri, 2010, Geographic distribution of R&D activity, *AMJ*, 53: 1194–1209; A. Minin & M. Bianchi, 2011, Safe nests in global nets, *JIBS*, 42: 910–934; M. Nieto & A. Rodriguez, 2011, Offshoring of R&D, *JIBS*, 42: 345–361.

21. M. W. Peng & D. Wang, 2000, Innovation capability and foreign direct investment, *MIR*, 40: 79–83; J. Penner-Hahn & J. M. Shaver, 2005, Does international R&D increase patent output?, *SMJ*, 26: 121–140.

22. G. Vegt, E. Vliert, & X. Huang, 2005, Location-level links between diversity and innovative climate depend on national power distance, *AMJ*, 48: 1171–1182.

23. F. Sanna-Randaccio & R. Veugelers, 2007, Multinational knowledge spillovers with decentralized R&D, *JIBS*, 38: 47–63; T. Schmidt & W. Sofka, 2009, Liability of foreignness as a barrier to knowledge spillovers, *JIM*, 15: 460–474.

24. A. Witty, 2011, Research and develop (p. 140), *The World in 2011*, London: The Economist Group. Witty is CEO of GSK.

25. This section draws heavily from Gupta & Govindarajan, 2004, *Global Strategy and Organization.*

26. H. Greve, 2003, A behavioral theory of R&D expenditures and innovations, *AMJ*, 46: 685–702.

27. P. Bierly, F. Damanpour, & M. Santoro, 2009, The application of external knowledge, *JMS*, 46: 481–508; H. Hoang & F. Rothaermel, 2010, Leveraging internal and external experience, *SMJ*, 31: 734–758; U. Lichtenthaler, 2011, Open innovation, *AMP*, February: 75–92.

28. H. Chesbrough, W. Vanhaverbeke, & J. West (eds.), 2006, *Open Innovation* (p. 1), Oxford, UK: Oxford University Press.

29. J. Spencer, 2003, Firms' knowledge-sharing strategies in the global innovation system, *SMJ*, 24: 217–233; K. Laursen & A. Salter, 2006. Open for innovation, *SMJ*, 27: 131–150.

30. Q. Yang & C. Jiang, 2007, Location advantages and subsidiaries' R&D activities, *APJM*, 24: 341–358.

31. R. Mudambi & P. Navarra, 2004, Is knowledge power? *JIBS*, 35: 385–406; R. Teigland & M. Wasko, 2009, Knowledge transfer in MNCs, *JIM*, 15: 15–31.

32. T. Ambos & B. Ambos, 2009, The impact of distance on knowledge transfer effectiveness in MNCs, *JIM*, 15: 1–14; A. Dinur, R. Hamilton, & A. Inkpen, 2009, Critical context and international intrafirm best-practice transfers, *JIM*, 15: 432–446; M. Esterby-Smith, M. Lyles, & E. Tsang, 2008, Inter-organizational knowledge transfer, *JMS*, 45: 677–690; D. Gnyawali, M. Singal, & S. Mu, 2009, Knowledge ties among subsidiaries in MNCs, *JIM*, 15: 387–400; J. Hong & T. Nguyen, 2009, Knowledge embeddedness and the transfer mechanisms in MNCs, *JWB*, 44: 347–356; L. F. Monteiro, N. Arvidsson, & J. Birkinshaw, 2008, Knowledge flows within MNCs, *OSc*, 19: 90–107; G. Szulanski & R. Jensen, 2006, Presumptive adaptation and the effectiveness of knowledge transfer, *SMJ*, 27: 937–957.

33. M. Haas, 2010, The double-edged swords of autonomy and external knowledge, *AMJ*, 53: 989–1008; Z. Sharp, 2010, From unilateral transfer to bilateral transition, *JIM*, 16: 304–313; M. Zellmer-Bruhn & C. Gibson, 2006, Multinational organization context, *AMJ*, 49: 501–518.

34. W. Cohen & D. Levinthal, 1990, Absorptive capacity, *ASQ*, 35: 128–152. See also A. Cuervo-Cazurra & C. A. Un, 2010, Why some firms never invest in formal R&D, *SMJ*, 31: 759–779; J. Hong, R. Snell, & M. Easterby-Smith, 2006, Cross-cultural influences on organizational learning in MNCs, *JIM*, 12: 408–429; J. Jansen, F. Bosch, & H. Volberda, 2005, Managing potential and realized absorptive capacity, *AMJ*, 48: 999–1015; P. Lane, B. Koka, & S. Pathak, 2006, The reification of absorptive capacity, *AMR*, 31: 833–863; L. Perez-Nordtvedt, E. Babakus, & B. Kedia, 2010, Learning from international business affiliates, *JIM*, 16: 262–274; G. Todorova & B. Durisin, 2007, Absorptive capacity, *AMR*, 32: 774–786.

35. C. Fey & P. Furu, 2008, Top management incentive compensation and knowledge sharing in MNEs, *SMJ*, 29: 1301–1323.

36. A. Inkpen & E. Tsang, 2005, Social capital, networks, and knowledge transfer, *AMR*, 30: 146–165; N. Noorderhaven & A. Harzing, 2009, Knowledge-sharing and social interaction within MNEs, *JIBS*, 40: 715–741.

37. M. W. Peng & Y. Luo, 2000, Managerial ties and firm performance in a transition economy, *AMJ*, 43: 486–501. See also M. Mors, 2010, Innovation in a global consulting firm, *SMJ*, 31: 841–872; M. Reinholt, T. Pedersen, & N. Foss, 2011, Why a central network position isn't enough, *AMJ*, 54: 1277–1297.

38. *BW*, 2011, Profits on overseas holiday, March 21: 64–69.

39. *BW*, 2009, For accounting giants, nowhere to hide? February 16: 56–57.

40. F. Ciabuschi, M. Forsgren, & O. Martin, 2011, Rationality versus ignorance, *JIBS*, 42: 958–970.

41. A. Bjorkman & R. Piekkari, 2009, Language and foreign subsidiary control, *JIM*, 15: 105–117; C. Garcia-Pont, I. Canales, & F. Noboa, 2009, Subsidiary strategy, *JMS*, 46: 182–214.

42. T. Ambos, U. Andersson, & J. Birkinshaw, 2010, What are the consequences of initiative-taking in multinational subsidiaries? *JIBS*, 41: 1099–1118; C. Bouquet & J. Birkinshaw, 2008, Weight versus voice, *AMJ*, 51: 577–601; F. Ciabuschi, H. Dellestrand, & O. Martin, 2011, Internal embeddedness, headquarters involvement, and innovation importance in MNEs, *JMS*, 48: 1612–1638; A. Delios, D. Xu, & P. Beamish, 2008, Within-country product diversification and foreign subsidiary performance, *JIBS*, 39: 706–724; D. Vora, T. Kostova, & K. Roth, 2007, Roles of subsidiary managers in MNCs, *MIR*, 47: 595–620.

43. J. Balogun, P. Jarzabkowski, & E. Vaara, 2011, Selling, resistence, and reconciliation, *JIBS*, 42: 765–786; H. Dellestrand, 2011, Subsidiary embeddedness as a determinat of divisional headquarters involvement in innovation transfer processes, *JIM*, 17: 229–242; C. Dorrenbacher & J. Gammelgaard, 2010, MNCs, inter-organizational networks, and subsidiary charter removals, *JWB*, 45: 206–216; A. Phene & P. Almeida, 2008, Innovation in multinational subsidiaries, *JIBS*, 39: 901–919; P. Scott, P. Gibbons, & J. Coughlan, 2010, Developing subsidiary contribution to the MNC-subsidiary entrepreneurship and strategy creativity, *JIM*, 16: 328–339; A. Schotter & P. Beamish, 2011, Performance effects of MNC headquarters-subsidiary conflict and the role of boundary spanners, *JIM*, 17: 243–259; C. Williams, 2009, Subsidiary-level determinants of global initiatives in MNCs, *JIM*, 15: 92–104.

44. R. Burgelman & A. Grove, 2007, Let chaos reign, then rein in chaos—repeatedly, *SMJ*, 28: 965–979.

45. S. Segal-Horn & A. Dean, 2009, Delivering "effortless" experience across borders, *JWB*, 44: 41–50.

46. L. Shi, C. White, S. Zou, & S. T. Cavusgil, 2010, Global account management strategies, *JIBS*, 41: 620–638.

47. P. Ghemawat, 2011, The cosmopolitan corporation, *HBR*, May: 92–99.

48. S. Gould & A. Grein, 2009, Think glocally, act glocally, *JIBS*, 40: 237–254.

CHAPTER 11

GOVERNING THE CORPORATION AROUND THE WORLD

© istockphoto/Alexey Stiop

KNOWLEDGE OBJECTIVES

After studying this chapter, you should be able to

1. Differentiate various ownership patterns around the world
2. Articulate the role of managers in both principal–agent and principal–principal conflicts
3. Explain the role of the board of directors
4. Identify voice-based and exit-based governance mechanisms and their combination as a package
5. Acquire a global perspective on how governance mechanisms vary around the world
6. Elaborate on a comprehensive model of corporate governance
7. Participate in three leading debates concerning corporate governance
8. Draw strategic implications for action

High Drama at Hewlett-Packard (HP)

In the late 1990s, something strange happened to HP—the equivalent of a deranged hairy-bellied scientist getting hold of the company's DNA and adding a dangerous dose of Hollywood flakiness. The HP story suddenly acquired some unexpected new ingredients: a board room coup (Carly Fiorina was brought in as the first female chief executive of a Dow-30 company but was tossed out after the company lost half its value); a corporate spying scandal (Patricia Dunn, the company's chairwoman, was also binned after it emerged that she had used a private security firm to spy on board members and journalists); and obscene pay packets (Ms. Fiorina was paid more than $20 million to leave).

The company did its best to rid itself of its new Hollywood DNA by appointing Mark Hurd—a nerdy-looking numbers guy—as chief executive in 2005. But on August 6, 2010, the news broke that Mr. Hurd had more than numbers on his mind. Two more improbable characters entered the HP story. One was Jodi Fisher, a former softcore-porn and B-movie actress who had helped at corporate events for HP. The other was Gloria Allred, a Los Angeles lawyer who had previously locked horns with O. J. Simpson, Britney Spears, and Tiger Woods. Mr. Hurd resigned amid stories of sexual harassment and iffy expense reports—and HP saw $10 billion wiped off its stock market value.

Where does this psychodrama leave the Silicon Valley giant? Pretty much where it was a week ago, said senior figures. Marc Andreessen, a member of the board, said that "HP is not about any one person." Cathie Lesjak, the company's interim chief executive, argued that, although "Mark was a strong leader," he "didn't drive our initiative. The company drove that." But if Mr. Hurd was "only one person" and the company was what mattered, why did HP pay him $30 million in 2009? And why was it reportedly considering paying him $100 million to stay on for another three years?

The problem for HP is that Mr. Hurd deserved his money more than most other chief executives. The company's share price doubled on his watch. HP sped past IBM to become the world's largest information technology (IT) company by revenues. It also became the first IT company to have sales of more than $100 billion. Mr. Hurd restored HP to its former glory as the world's biggest maker of personal computers. He prepared the ground for further growth by putting together a succession of multibillion-dollar deals, snapping up Electronic Data Systems (EDS), 3Com, and Palm. And he did all this while squeezing costs.

HP is now struggling to fill not one but two top positions: Mr. Hurd doubled as chief executive and chairman (despite pointed warnings from corporate reformers). His abrupt departure also leaves HP grappling with innumerable questions. Why exactly is Mr. Hurd leaving? Ms. Fisher says that the two never had sex and that her complaint against him—about which she remains tight-lipped—was settled without a lawsuit. The board's charge sheet on Mr. Hurd focuses on dodgy expense claims. It is all rather confusing. If his ethical lapses were serious, then why is he being given a golden parachute of $12.2 million? And if they weren't serious, then why is the company getting rid of a star chief executive? Larry Ellison, Oracle's chief executive, calls it "the worst personnel decision since the idiots on the Apple board fired Steve Jobs many years ago."

Source: Excerpted from *Economist*, 2010, The curse of HP, August 14: 54.

---

chief executive officer (CEO)
The top executive in charge of the strategy and operations of a firm.

HP's high drama did not end after Mark Hurd's resignation in August 2010. In November 2010, its board hired Léo Apotheker, former **chief executive officer (CEO)** of SAP, as HP's new CEO. But in September 2011 the board fired him after HP lost $30 billion in market capitalization during his short tenure.

FIGURE 11.1   The Primary Participants in Corporate Governance

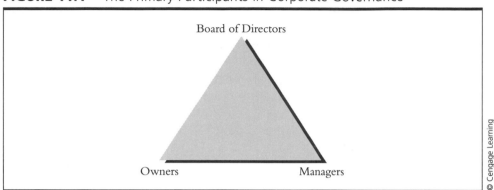

© Cengage Learning

For Apotheker's less than 11 months of service, he walked away with $13 million: severance payment of $7.2 million, HP shares worth $3.4 million, and a performance bonus of $2.4 million. In September 2011, Meg Whitman, an HP board member and eBay's former CEO, was named HP's newest CEO—the fourth CEO since 2005 and the seventh since 1999.

While HP's high drama is an extreme case, it raises a series of questions affecting many firms: What is the most optimal way to govern corporations so that investors will reap returns? What is the proper role of the board of directors? How should CEOs be properly motivated and compensated? These are some of the key questions addressed in this chapter, which focuses on how to govern the corporation around the world. **Corporate governance** is "the relationship among various participants in determining the direction and performance of corporations."[1] The primary participants in corporate governance are (1) owners, (2) managers, and (3) board of directors (Figure 11.1). This chapter first discusses the primary participants. Next, we cover internal and external governance mechanisms from a global perspective, followed by a comprehensive model drawn from the strategy tripod. Debates and extensions follow.

corporate governance
The relationship among various participants in determining the direction and performance of corporations.

Owners

Owners provide capital, bear risks, and own the firm.[2] Three broad patterns exist: (1) concentrated versus diffused ownership, (2) family ownership, and (3) state ownership.

concentrated ownership and control
Ownership and control rights concentrated in the hands of owners.

Concentrated versus Diffused Ownership

Founders usually start up firms and completely own and control them. This is referred to as **concentrated ownership and control**. However, at some point, if the firm aspires to grow and needs more capital, the owners' desire to keep the firm in family hands will have

diffused ownership

An ownership pattern involving numerous small shareholders, none of whom has a dominant level of control.

separation of ownership and control

The dispersal of ownership among many small shareholders, with control of the firm largely concentrated in the hands of salaried, professional managers who own little or no equity.

to accommodate the arrival of other shareholders. Approximately 80% of listed US firms and 90% of listed UK firms are now characterized by **diffused ownership**, with numerous small shareholders but none with a dominant level of control.[3] In such firms, there is a **separation of ownership and control**, in that ownership is dispersed among many small shareholders and control is largely concentrated in the hands of salaried professional managers who own little (or no) equity. In short, this refers to separation of ownership (by dispersed shareholders) and day-to-day control (by managers).

If majority or dominant owners (such as founders) do not personally run the firm, they are naturally interested in keeping a close eye on how the firm is run. However, dispersed owners, each with a small stake, have neither incentives nor resources to do so. Most small shareholders do not bother to show up at annual shareholder meetings. They prefer to free ride and hope that other shareholders will properly monitor and discipline managers. If small shareholders are not happy, they will simply sell the stock and invest elsewhere. However, if all shareholders behave in this manner, then no shareholder would care and managers would end up acquiring significant *de facto* control power.

The rise of institutional investors, such as professionally managed mutual funds and pension pools, has significantly changed this picture.[4] Institutional investors have both incentives and resources to closely monitor and control managerial actions. However, the increased size of institutional holdings limits the ability of institutional investors to dump the stock. This is because when one's stake is large enough, selling out depresses the share price and harms the seller.

While the image of widely held corporations is a reasonably accurate description of most modern large US and UK firms, it is *not* the case in other parts of the world. Outside the Anglo-American world, there is relatively little separation of ownership and control. Most large firms are typically owned and controlled by families or the state.[5] Next, we turn our attention to such firms.

Family Ownership

The vast majority of large firms throughout continental Europe, Asia, Latin America, and Africa feature concentrated family ownership and control. On the positive side, family ownership and control may provide better incentives for the firm to focus on long-term performance. It may also minimize the conflicts between owners and professional managers typically encountered in widely owned firms. However, on the negative side, family ownership and control may lead to the selection of less qualified managers (who happen to be the sons, daughters, and relatives of founders), the destruction of value because of family conflicts, and the expropriation of minority shareholders (discussed later). At present, there is no conclusive evidence on the positive or negative role of family ownership and control on the performance of large firms.[6]

State Ownership

state-owned enterprise (SOE)

A firm owned and controlled by the state (government).

Other than families, the state is another major owner of firms around the world. Since the 1980s, many countries—ranging from Britain to Brazil to Belarus—realized that their **state-owned enterprises (SOEs)** often perform poorly. SOEs typically suffer from an incentive problem. Although in theory all citizens (including employees) are owners, in practice, they have neither the rights to enjoy dividends generated from SOEs (as shareholders would) nor the rights to transfer or sell "their" property. SOEs are *de facto* owned and controlled by government agencies far removed from ordinary citizens and employees. Thus, there is little motivation for SOE managers and employees to improve performance, which they can hardly benefit from personally. In a most cynical fashion, SOE employees in the former Soviet Union summed it up well: "They pretend to pay us and we pretend to work." A wave of privatization hit the world since the 1980s. However, SOEs staged a spectacular comeback recently. In 2008, many governments in developed economies nationalized major firms ranging from General Motors (GM, which reads "Government Motors") to Royal Bank of Scotland (RBS) in order to prevent massive bankruptcies and job losses.

Managers

agency relationship
The relationship between principals and agents.

principals
Persons (such as owners) who delegate authority.

agents
Persons (such as managers) to whom authority is delegated.

agency theory
The theory about principal–agent relationships (or agency relationships in short).

principal–agent conflicts
Conflicts of interests between principals (such as shareholders) and agents (such as professional managers).

agency costs
The costs associated with principal–agent relationships. They are the sum of (1) the principals' costs of monitoring and controlling agents and (2) the agents' costs of bonding.

information asymmetries
Asymmetric distribution of information between two sides.

Managers, especially executives on the top management team (TMT) led by the CEO, represent another important group of players in corporate governance.

Principal–Agent Conflicts

The relationship between shareholders and professional managers is a relationship between principals and agents—in short, an **agency relationship**. **Principals** are persons (such as owners) delegating authority, and **agents** are persons (such as managers) to whom authority is delegated. **Agency theory** suggests a simple yet profound proposition: To the extent that the interests of principals and agents do not completely overlap, there will *inherently* be **principal–agent conflicts**. These conflicts result in **agency costs**, including (1) the principals' costs of monitoring and controlling the agents and (2) the agents' costs of bonding (signaling their trustworthiness).[7] In a corporate setting, when shareholders (principals) are interested in maximizing the long-term value of their stock, managers (agents) may be more interested in maximizing their own power, income, and perks.

Manifestations of agency problems include excessive executive compensation, on-the-job consumption (such as corporate jets), low-risk short-term investments (such as maximizing current earnings while cutting long-term R&D), and empire-building (such as value-destroying acquisitions). Consider executive compensation. In 1980, the average US CEO earned approximately 40 times what the average worker earned. Today, the ratio is 400 times. Despite some performance improvement, it seems difficult to argue that the average firm CEO improved performance 10 times faster than her workers since 1980 and thus deserved the salary of 400 workers today. In other words, one can "smell" some agency costs.

Directly measuring agency costs, however, is difficult. In two most innovative (and hair-raising) studies to directly measure agency costs, scholars find that some sudden CEO *deaths* (plane crashes or heart attacks) are accompanied by an increase in share prices of their firms.[8] These CEOs reduced agency costs that shareholders had to shoulder by dropping dead (!). Conversely, we could imagine how much value these CEOs destroyed when they had been alive. The capital market, sadly, was pleased with such human tragedies.

The primary reason agency problems persist is because of **information asymmetries** between principals and agents—that is, agents such as managers almost always know more about the property they manage than principals do. While it is possible to reduce information asymmetries through governance mechanisms, it is not realistic to completely eliminate agency problems.

Principal–Principal Conflicts

Since concentrated ownership and control by families is the norm in many parts of the world, different kinds of conflicts are at play. One of the leading indicators of concentrated family ownership and control is the appointment of family members as board chairman, CEO, and other TMT members. In East Asia, approximately 57% of the corporations have board chairmen and CEOs from the controlling families.[9] In continental Europe, the number is 68%.[10] The families are able to do so, because they are controlling (although not necessarily majority) shareholders. For example, at News Corporation, neither the board nor angry shareholders can get rid of the Murdochs, who are controlling shareholders (Strategy in Action 11.1).

STRATEGY IN ACTION 11.1 〉　　〉 ETHICAL DILEMMA

The Murdochs versus Minority Shareholders

Founded in Adelaide, Australia, News Corporation (in short, News Corp.) is now headquartered in New York and listed on NASDAQ with secondary listings on the Australian Securities Exchange. While the unethical conduct of its British tabloid operations rocked the world in 2011, this was not the first time News Corp., which enjoys reporting controversies of others, stirred up controversies itself. A consistent theme of controversies is how Rupert Murdoch and his family as controlling shareholders treat minority shareholders.

Exhibit A: In 2003, the 30-year-old James Murdoch became CEO of BSkyB, Europe's largest satellite broadcaster, in the face of loud minority shareholder resistance. The reason? James' father Rupert controlled 35% of BSkyB equity and controlled the board.

Exhibit B: In 2007, Rupert Murdoch pursued a pet project by paying a rich $5.6 billion price to buy Dow Jones, publisher of the *Wall Street Journal*—against the wishes of numerous minority shareholders and the advice of Peter Chernin, News Corp. president and a non-family member. The upshot? After four months, News Corp. wrote down its value by $2.8 billion, and in 2009, Chernin left.

Exhibit C: In 2011, in a related transaction News Corp. announced that it would pay $673 million to buy Shine

Group, a London-based media studio owned by Rupert's daughter Elisabeth Murdoch. While Shine produced some hit shows such as NBC's *The Office* and *The Biggest Loser*, minority shareholders alleged that News Corp. overpaid for Shine with 13.1 times Shine's $45.6 million in earnings before interest, taxes, depreciation, and amortization (EBITDA). In contrast, Apollo Global Management, a leading private equity firm, paid $510 million to purchase *American Idol* owner CKx, a deal valued at 8.5 times CKx's $60.23 million in EBITDA. Frustrated minority shareholders such as Amalgamated Bank and other pension funds filed a lawsuit in Delaware (where News Corp. is registered) to block the sale. The complaint alleged that:

> *Murdoch did not even pretend there was a valid strategic purpose for News Corp. to buy Shine … The transaction is a naked and selfish endeavor by Murdoch to further infuse the upper ranks of News Corp. with his offspring.*

Sources: Based on (1) *Bloomberg Businessweek*, 2011, Will the scandal tame Murdoch? July 25: 18–20; (2) *Economist*, 2011, How to lose friends and alienate people, July 16: 25–27; (3) *Economist*, 2011, Last of the moguls, July 23: 9.

The Murdoch case is a classic example of the conflicts in family-owned and family-controlled firms. Instead of between principals (shareholders) and agents (professional managers), the primary conflicts are between two classes of principals: controlling shareholders and minority shareholders—in other words, **principal–principal conflicts**[11] (Figure 11.2 and Table 11.1). Family managers such as the Murdochs, who represent (or are) controlling shareholders, may advance family interests at the expense of minority shareholders. Controlling shareholders' dominant position as *both* principals and agents (managers) may allow them to override traditional governance mechanisms designed to curtail principal–agent conflicts such as the board of directors.

A manifestation of principal–principal conflicts is that family managers may have the potential to engage in **expropriation** of minority shareholders, defined as activities that enrich

principal–principal conflicts

Conflicts of interests between two classes of principals: controlling shareholders and minority shareholders.

expropriation

Activities that enrich the controlling shareholders at the expense of minority shareholders.

FIGURE 11.2   Principal–Agent Conflicts and Principal–Principal Conflicts

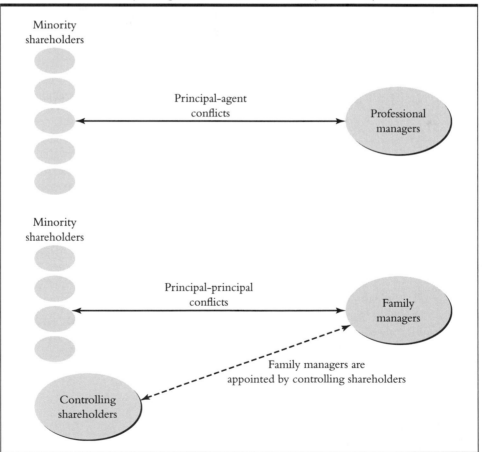

Source: Adapted from M. Young, M. W. Peng, D. Ahlstrom, G. Bruton, & Y. Jiang, 2008, Corporate governance in emerging economies: A review of the principal-principal perspective (p. 200), *Journal of Management Studies*, 45: 196–220.

TABLE 11.1 Principal–Agent versus Principal–Principal Conflicts

	PRINCIPAL–AGENT CONFLICTS	PRINCIPAL–PRINCIPAL CONFLICTS
Ownership pattern	Dispersed—shareholders holding 5% of equity are regarded as "blockholders."	Dominant—often greater than 50% of equity is controlled by the largest shareholders.
Manifestations	Strategies that benefit entrenched managers at the expense of shareholders (such as shirking, excessive compensation, and empire building).	Strategies that benefit controlling shareholders at the expense of minority shareholders (such as minority shareholder expropriation and cronyism).
Institutional protection of minority shareholders	Formal constraints (such as courts) are more protective of shareholder rights. Informal norms adhere to shareholder wealth maximization.	Formal institutional protection is often lacking. Informal norms are typically in favor of controlling shareholders.
Market for corporate control	Active, at least in principle as the "governance mechanism of last resort."	Inactive even in principle. Concentrated ownership thwarts notions of takeover.

Source: Adapted from M. Young, M. W. Peng, D. Ahlstrom, G. Bruton, & Y. Jiang, 2008, Corporate governance in emerging economies: A review of the principal-principal perspective (p. 202), *Journal of Management Studies*, 45: 196–220.

controlling shareholders at the expense of minority shareholders. For example, managers from the controlling family may simply divert resources from the firm for personal or family use. This activity is vividly nicknamed "**tunneling**"—digging a tunnel to sneak resources out.[12] While such "tunneling" (often known as "corporate theft") is illegal, expropriation can be legally done through **related transactions**, whereby controlling owners buy firm assets from another firm they own at above-market prices or spin off the most profitable part of a public firm and merge it with another private firm of theirs (see Strategy in Action 11.1).

Overall, while corporate governance practice and research traditionally focus on how to control professional managers because of the separation of ownership and control in a majority of US and UK firms, how to govern family managers in firms with concentrated ownership and control is of equal or probably higher importance around the world (including in certain US and UK firms, such as News Corporation).

tunneling

Activities of managers from the controlling family of a corporation to divert resources from the firm for personal or family use.

related transaction

Controlling owners sell firm assets to another firm they own at below-market prices or spin off the most profitable part of a public firm and merge it with another of their private firms.

Board of Directors

As an intermediary between owners and managers, the board of directors oversees and ratifies strategic decisions and evaluates, rewards, and if necessary penalizes top managers.

Board Composition

inside director
A director serving on a corporate board who is also a full-time manager of the company.

outside (independent) director
A non-management member of the board.

Otherwise known as the insider/outsider mix, board composition has recently attracted significant attention. **Inside directors** are top executives of the firm. The trend around the world is to introduce more **outside (independent) directors**, defined as non-management members of the board. Often ideally labeled "independent directors," outside directors are presumably more independent and can better safeguard shareholder interests.

Although there is a widely held belief in favor of a higher proportion of outside directors, academic research has *failed* to empirically establish a link between the outsider/insider ratio and firm performance.[13] Even "stellar" firms with a majority of outside directors on the board (on average 74% of outside directors at Enron, Global Crossing, and Tyco before their scandals erupted) can still be plagued by governance problems. In the world's largest financial services firms, the more outside directors on their boards, the *worse* their stock returns during the 2008 crisis.[14]

It is possible that some of these outside directors are *affiliated* directors who may have family, business, and/or professional relationships with the firm or firm management. In other words, such affiliated outside directors are not necessarily "independent."

Leadership Structure

CEO duality
The CEO doubles as chairman of the board.

Whether the board is led by a separate chairman or by the CEO who doubles as a chairman—a situation known as **CEO duality**—is also important. From an agency theory standpoint, if the board is to supervise agents such as the CEO, it seems imperative that the board be chaired by a separate individual. Otherwise, how can the CEO be evaluated by the body that he/she chairs? In other words, can a schoolboy grade his own papers? However, a corporation led by two top leaders (a board chairman and a CEO) may lack a unity of command and experience top-level conflicts. As a powerful executive, a CEO obviously does not appreciate being constantly second-guessed by a board chairman. Not surprisingly, there is significant divergence across countries. For instance, while a majority of the large UK firms separate the two top jobs, many large US firms combine them. A practical difficulty often cited by US boards is that it is very hard to recruit a capable CEO without the board chairman title.

Academic research is inconclusive on whether CEO duality (or non-duality) is more effective.[15] However, pressures have arisen around the world for firms to split the two jobs to at least show that they are serious about controlling the CEO. In 2010, only 12% of the new CEOs around the world were also appointed as chairmen. In 2002, the percentage was 48%. Even in US firms that typically favor CEO duality, Standard & Poor's 500 firms practicing CEO duality fell from 78% in 2002 to 59% in 2010.[16]

Board Interlocks

interlocking directorate
Two or more firms share one director on their boards.

Directors tend to be economic and social elites who share a sense of camaraderie and reciprocity.[17] When one person affiliated with one firm sits on the board of another firm, an **interlocking directorate** has been created. Firms often establish relationships through such board appointments. For instance, outside directors from financial institutions often facilitate financing. Outside directors experienced in acquisitions may help the focal firms engage in these practices.

In the United States, Frank Carlucci, a former Secretary of Defense and chairman of the Carlyle Group (a leading private equity firm), served on 20 boards (!) at one time. In Hong Kong, the most heavily connected director, David Li, chairman of the Bank of East Asia, sat on nine boards.[18] Critics argue that such directors are unlikely to effectively monitor management. In fact, one of the boards David Li served on was Enron's. In the post-Enron environment, such unusual practices are increasingly rare.

The Role of Boards of Directors

In a nutshell, boards of directors perform (1) control, (2) service, and (3) resource acquisition functions. Boards' effectiveness in serving the control function stems from their independence, deterrence, and norms. Specifically:

- The ability to effectively control managers boils down to how *independent* directors are. Outside directors who are personally friendly and loyal to the CEO are unlikely to challenge managerial decisions. Exactly for this reason, CEOs often nominate family members, personal friends, and other passive directors.[19]

- There is a lack of *deterrence* on the part of directors should they fail to protect shareholder interests. Courts usually will not second-guess board decisions in the absence of bad faith or insider dealing.

- When challenging management, directors have few *norms* to draw on. Directors who "stick their necks out" by confronting the CEO in meetings tend to be frozen out of board deliberations.

In addition to control, another important function of the board is service—primarily advising the CEO.[20] Finally, another crucial board function is resource acquisition for the focal firm, often through interlocking directorates.[21]

Overall, until recently, many boards of directors simply "rubber stamped" (approve without scrutiny) managerial actions. Prior to the 1997 economic crisis, many South Korean boards did not bother to hold meetings and board decisions were literally "rubber stamped"—not even by directors themselves, but by corporate secretaries who stamped the seals of all the directors, which were kept in the corporate office. However, change is in the air throughout the world. In South Korea, board meetings are now regularly held and seals are personally stamped by the directors themselves.[22]

Directing Strategically

If boards are to function effectively, being a director is one of the most demanding jobs, calling for an active "nose in but hands off" approach. Given the comprehensive functions of control, service, and resource acquisition and the limited time and resources directors have, directors must strategically prioritize.[23] How they do this differs significantly around the world. In US and UK firms, the traditional focus, which stems from their separation of ownership and control, is on the boards' control function. While the service function is still important, the resource

TABLE 11.2 Outside Directors versus Inside Directors

	PROS	CONS
Outside directors	■ Presumably more independent from management (especially the CEO). ■ More capable of monitoring and controlling managers. ■ Good at financial control.	■ Independence may be illusionary. ■ "Affiliated" outside directors may have family or professional relationships with the firm or management. ■ Not good at strategic control.
Inside directors	■ Have firsthand knowledge about the firm. ■ Good at strategic control.	■ Non-CEO inside directors (executives) may not be able to control and challenge the CEO.

© Cengage Learning

acquisition role, although important in practice, tends to be criticized by policy-makers, activists, and the media, who often regard activities such as interlocking directorates as "collusive." Consequently, recent US regulations, especially the Sarbanes-Oxley (SOX) Act of 2002, emphasize the control function almost to the exclusion of the resource acquisition function. For example, Apple acquired certain resources from Google to power its iPhones, and Google's CEO Eric Schmidt used to serve on Apple's board. However, recently, as the competition between Apple and Google (which launched its own Android phone) heated up, Schmidt had to give up his Apple board membership.

Since outside directors are not likely to have enough firsthand knowledge about the firm, they are thus forced to focus on financial performance targets and numbers—known as financial control (see Table 11.2). Financial control may encourage CEOs to focus on the short term, at the expense of long-term shareholder interests (such as maximizing current earnings by reducing R&D). Therefore, inside directors, who are executives, can bring firsthand knowledge to board deliberations, allowing for a more sophisticated understanding of some managerial actions (such as investing in the future while not maximizing current earnings). A board informed by such inside views is able to exercise strategic control, basing its judgment beyond a mere examination of financial numbers. It seems that a healthy board requires both kinds of control, thus calling for a balanced composition of insiders and outsiders.

voice-based mechanisms
Corporate governance mechanisms that focus on shareholders' willingness to work with managers, usually through the board of directors, by "voicing" their concerns.

exit-based mechanisms
Corporate governance mechanisms that focus on exit, indicating that shareholders no longer have patience and are willing to "exit" by selling their shares.

Governance Mechanisms as a Package

Governance mechanisms can be classified as internal and external ones—otherwise known as voice-based and exit-based mechanisms, respectively. **Voice-based mechanisms** refer to shareholders' willingness to work with managers, usually through the board, by "voicing" their concerns. **Exit-based mechanisms** indicate that shareholders no longer have patience and are willing to "exit" by selling their shares. This section outlines these mechanisms.

Internal (Voice-Based) Governance Mechanisms

The two internal governance mechanisms typically employed by boards can be characterized as (1) "carrots" and (2) "sticks." In order to better motivate managers, increasing executive compensation as "carrots" is often a must. Stock options that help align the interests of managers and shareholders have become increasingly popular.[24] The underlying idea is pay for performance, which seeks to link executive compensation with firm performance.[25] While in principle this idea is sound, in practice it has a number of drawbacks. If accounting-based measures (such as return on sales) are used, managers are often able to manipulate numbers to make them look better. If market-based measures (such as stock prices) are adopted, stock prices obviously are subject to too many forces beyond managers' control. Consequently, the pay-for-performance link in executive compensation is usually not very strong.[26]

In general, boards are likely to use "carrots" before considering "sticks." However, when facing continued performance failures, boards may have to dismiss the CEO.[27] Among the world's largest 2,500 listed firms, CEO tenure has decreased from 8.1 years in 2000 to 6.3 years in 2012. In 2010, 12% of these firms changed CEOs.[28] In brief, boards seem to be more "trigger-happy" recently. Case in point: Léo Apotheker served seven *months* as CEO of SAP and then ten *months* as CEO of HP (see the Opening Case).

Because top managers must shoulder substantial firm-specific employment risk (a fired CEO such as Apotheker is extremely unlikely to run another publicly traded company), they naturally demand more generous compensation—a premium on the order of 30% or more—before taking on new CEO jobs. This in part explains the rapidly rising levels of executive compensation.[29]

External (Exit-Based) Governance Mechanisms

There are three external governance mechanisms: (1) market for product competition, (2) market for corporate control, and (3) market for private equity. Product market competition is a powerful force compelling managers to maximize profits and, in turn, shareholder value. However, from a corporate governance perspective, product market competition *complements* the market for corporate control and the market for private equity, each of which is outlined next.

THE MARKET FOR CORPORATE CONTROL. This is the main external governance mechanism, otherwise known as the takeover market or the mergers and acquisitions (M&A) market (see Chapter 9). It is essentially an arena where different management teams contest for the control rights of corporate assets. As an external governance mechanism, the market for corporate control serves as a disciplining mechanism of last resort when internal governance mechanisms fail. The underlying logic is spelled out by agency theory, which suggests that when managers engage in self-interested actions and internal governance mechanisms fail, firm stock will be undervalued by investors. Under these circumstances, other management teams, which recognize an opportunity to create new value, bid for the rights to manage the firm (see Chapter 9). How effective is the market for corporate control? Three findings emerge:

- On average, shareholders of target firms earn sizable acquisition premiums.

- Shareholders of acquiring firms experience slight but insignificant losses.

- A substantially higher level of top management turnover occurs following M&As.

In summary, while internal mechanisms aim at "fine-tuning," the market for corporate control enables the "wholesale" removal of entrenched managers. As a radical approach, the market for corporate control has its own limitations. It is very costly to wage such financial battles, because acquirers must pay an acquisition premium. In addition, a large number of M&As are driven by acquirers' sheer hubris or empire building, and the long-term profitability of post-merger firms is not particularly impressive[30] (see Chapter 9). Nevertheless, the net impact, at least in the short run, seems to be positive, because the threat of takeovers does limit managers' divergence from shareholder wealth maximization—as recently reported in Japan.[31]

private equity

Equity capital invested in private (non-public) companies.

leveraged buyout (LBO)

A means by which private investors, often in partnership with incumbent managers, issue bonds and use the cash raised to buy the firm's stock.

THE MARKET FOR PRIVATE EQUITY. Instead of being taken over, a large number of publicly listed firms have gone private by tapping into **private equity**—equity capital invested in private (non-public) companies (see the Closing Case). Private equity is primarily invested through **leveraged buyouts (LBOs)**. In an LBO, private investors, often in partnership with incumbent managers, issue bonds and use the cash raised to buy the firm's stock—in essence replacing shareholders with bondholders and transforming the firm from a public to a private entity. As another external governance mechanism, private equity utilizes the bond market, as opposed to the stock market, to discipline managers. LBO-based private equity transactions are associated with three major changes in corporate governance:

- LBOs change the incentives of managers by providing them with substantial equity stakes.

- The high amount of debt imposes strong financial discipline.

- LBO sponsors closely monitor the firms they have invested in.

Overall, evidence suggests that private equity results in relatively small job losses (about 1%–2%) and improves efficiency by about 2%, at least in the short run.[32] The picture is less clear regarding the long run, because LBOs may have forced managers to reduce investments in long-term R&D. However, more recent research reports (1) that private equity-backed firms have more focused patents that generate better economic returns and (2) that such firms do not suffer from a reduction of R&D in the long run.[33]

Internal Mechanisms + External Mechanisms = Governance Package

Taken together, the internal and external mechanisms can be considered a "package."[34] Michael Jensen, a leading agency theorist, argues that in the United States, failures of internal governance mechanisms in the 1970s activated the market for corporate control in the 1980s. Managers initially resisted. However, over time, many firms that are not takeover targets or that have successfully defended themselves against such attempts end up restructuring and downsizing—doing exactly what "raiders" would have done had these firms been taken over. In other words, the strengthened external mechanisms force firms to improve their internal mechanisms.

Overall, since the 1980s, American managers have become much more focused on stock prices, resulting in a new term, "**shareholder capitalism**," which has been spreading around the world. In Europe, executive stock options become popular and M&As more frequent. In Russia, some traces of modern corporate governance have emerged.[35]

shareholder capitalism
A view of capitalism that suggests that the most fundamental purpose for firms to exist is to serve the economic interests of shareholders (also known as capitalists).

A Global Perspective

Illustrated in Figure 11.3, different corporate ownership and control patterns around the world lead to a different mix of internal and external mechanisms. The most familiar type is Cell 4, exemplified by most large US and UK firms. While external governance mechanisms (M&As and private equity) are active, internal mechanisms are relatively weak due to the separation of ownership and control that gives managers significant *de facto* control power.

The opposite can be found in Cell 1, namely, firms in continental Europe and Japan where the market for corporate control is relatively inactive (although there is more activity recently). Consequently, the primary governance mechanisms remain concentrated ownership and control.

FIGURE 11.3   A Global Perspective on Internal and External Governance Mechanisms

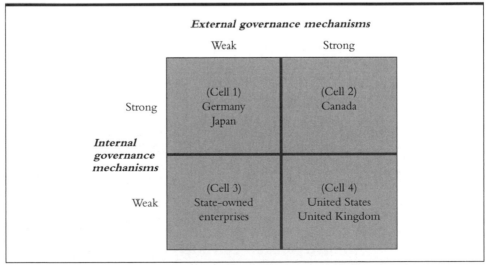

Source: Cells 1, 2, and 4 are adapted from E. R. Gedajlovic & D. M. Shapiro, 1998, Management and ownership effects: Evidence from five countries (p. 539), *Strategic Management Journal*, 19: 533–553. The label of Cell 3 is suggested by the present author.

TABLE 11.3 Two Primary Families of Corporate Governance Systems

CORPORATIONS IN THE UNITED STATES AND THE UNITED KINGDOM	CORPORATIONS IN CONTINENTAL EUROPE AND JAPAN
Anglo-American corporate governance models	German-Japanese corporate governance models
Market-oriented high-tension systems	Bank-oriented network-based systems
Rely mostly on exit-based external mechanisms	Rely mostly on voice-based internal mechanisms
Shareholder capitalism	Stakeholder capitalism

© Cengage Learning

Overall, the Anglo-American and continental European-Japanese (otherwise known as German-Japanese) systems represent the two primary corporate governance families in the world, with a variety of labels (see Table 11.3). Given that both the United States and the United Kingdom as a group and continental Europe and Japan as another group are highly developed successful economies, it is difficult and probably not meaningful to argue whether the Anglo-American or German-Japanese system is better.

Some other systems do not easily fit into such a dichotomous world. Placed in Cell 2, Canada has *both* a relatively active market for corporate control and a large number of firms with concentrated ownership and control—over 380 of the 400 largest Canadian firms are controlled by a single shareholder. Canadian managers thus face powerful internal and external constraints.

Finally, SOEs (of all nationalities) are typically in a position of both weak external and internal governance mechanisms (Cell 3). Externally, the market for corporate control does not exist. Internally, managers are supervised by officials who act as *de facto* "owners" with little control.

Overall, firms around the world are governed by a combination of internal and external mechanisms. For firms in Cells 1, 2, and 4, there is some partial substitution between internal and external mechanisms (for example, weak boards may be partially substituted by a strong market for corporate control).

A Comprehensive Model of Corporate Governance

Figure 11.4 shows a comprehensive model drawn from the strategy tripod. This section discusses these three views in turn.

Industry-Based Considerations

The nature of industry sometimes questions certain widely accepted conventional wisdom regarding (1) outside directors, (2) insider ownership, and (3) CEO duality.[36] Having more outside directors on the board is often regarded as a performance-enhancing

FIGURE 11.4   A Comprehensive Model of Corporate Governance

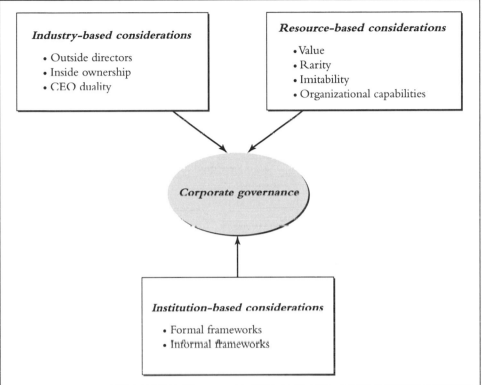

Industry-based considerations

- Outside directors
- Inside ownership
- CEO duality

Resource-based considerations

- Value
- Rarity
- Imitability
- Organizational capabilities

Corporate governance

Institution-based considerations

- Formal frameworks
- Informal frameworks

© Cengage Learning

practice. However, such thinking ignores industry differences. In industries characterized by a rapid pace of innovation requiring significant R&D investments (such as IT), outside directors often have a *negative* impact on firm performance.[37] This is because the necessity for directors to have intimate knowledge about these industries requires more strategic control. Inexperienced outside directors often focus on financial control—inappropriate in these industries.

Another example is the widely noted link between inside management ownership and firm performance. Research finds that for firms in low-growth stable industries, there is *no* such relationship.[38] Only in relatively high-growth turbulent industries has this relationship been found. While increased insider ownership is designed to encourage managers to take more risks, opportunities to profitably take such risks probably are more likely in high-growth turbulent industries.

A third example is the often-criticized practice of CEO duality. In industries experiencing great turbulence, the presence of a single leader may allow a faster and more unified response to changing events. These benefits may outweigh the potential agency costs brought by such duality.

Overall, governance practices need to create a fit with the nature of the industry in which firms are competing. This cautions against universal prescriptions of certain "best" practices.

Resource-Based Considerations

From a corporate governance standpoint, some of the most valuable, rare, and hard-to-imitate firm-specific resources (the first three in the VRIO framework) are the skills and abilities of top managers and directors—often regarded as **managerial human capital**.[39] Some of these capabilities are highly unique, such as international experiences. Executives without such firsthand experience are often handicapped when they try to expand overseas. In addition, the social networks of these executives, often through board interlocks, are highly unique and likely to add value.[40] Also, top managerial talents are hard-to-imitate—unless they are hired away by rival firms.

managerial human capital

The skills and abilities acquired by top managers.

In another example, the ability to successfully list on a high-profile exchange such as the New York Stock Exchange (NYSE) and London Stock Exchange (LSE) is valuable, rare, and hard to imitate. In 1997, the valuations of foreign firms listed in New York were 17% higher than their domestic counterparts in the same country that were either unable or unwilling to list abroad.[41] Now, despite hurdles such as SOX, the select few that are able to list in New York are rewarded more handsomely: Their valuations are now 37% higher than comparable groups of domestic firms in the same country.[42] London-listed foreign firms do not enjoy such high valuations.[43] This is classic resource-based logic at work: Precisely because it is much more challenging to list in New York in the SOX era, the small number of foreign firms that are able to do this are truly exceptional. Thus, they deserve much higher valuations.

The last crucial component in the VRIO framework is O: organizational. It is within an organizational setting (in TMTs and boards) that managers and directors function.[44] Overall, the few people at the top of an organization can make a world of difference—Steve Jobs at Apple was a great example. Governance mechanisms need to properly motivate and discipline them to make sure they make a positive impact.

Institution-Based Considerations

FORMAL INSTITUTIONAL FRAMEWORKS. A fundamental difference is between the separation of ownership and control in (most) Anglo-American firms and the concentration of ownership and control in the rest of the world. Why is there such a difference? While explanations abound, a leading answer is an institution-based one. In brief, better formal legal protection of shareholder rights, especially those held by *minority* shareholders, in the United States and the United Kingdom encourages founding families to dilute their equity to attract minority shareholders and delegate day-to-day management to professional managers. Given reasonable investor protection, founding families themselves (such as the Rockefellers) may, over time, feel comfortable becoming minority shareholders of the firms they founded. On the other hand, when formal legal and regulatory institutions are dysfunctional, founding families *must* run their firms directly. In the absence of investor protection, inviting outside professional managers may invite abuse and theft.

Strong evidence exists to point out that the weaker the formal legal and regulatory institutions protecting shareholders, the more concentrated ownership and control rights become—in other words, there is some substitution between the two. Common-law countries generally have the strongest legal protection of investors and the lowest concentration of corporate ownership.[45] Among common-law countries, such ownership concentration is higher for firms in emerging economies (such as Hong Kong, India, and Israel) than developed economies (such as Australia, Canada, Ireland, and New Zealand). In short, concentrated ownership and control is an answer to potentially rampant principal–agent conflicts in the absence of sufficient legal protection of shareholder rights.

However, what is good for controlling shareholders is not necessarily good for minority shareholders and for an economy. As noted earlier, the minimization of principal–agent conflicts through concentration of ownership and control, unfortunately, introduces more principal–principal conflicts (see Strategy in Action 11.1). Consequently, many potential minority shareholders may refuse to invest. "How to avoid being expropriated as a minority shareholder?" one popular saying suggests, "Don't be one!" If minority shareholders are informed enough to be aware of these possibilities and still decide to invest, they are likely to discount the shares floated by family owners. For example, thanks to the "Murdoch discount," News Corporation's stock performance has trailed behind that of its rivals such as Time Warner, Walt Disney, and Viacom (see Strategy in Action 11.1). Overall, such principal–principal conflicts can result in lower valuations, fewer publicly traded firms, inactive and smaller capital markets, and, in turn, lower levels of economic development in general.

Given that almost every country desires vibrant capital markets and economic development, it seems puzzling why strong investor protection is not universally embraced. It is important to note that at its core, corporate governance ultimately is a choice about *political* governance. For largely historical reasons, most countries have made hard-to-reverse political choices. For example, the German practice of "codetermination" (employees control 50% of the votes on supervisory boards) is an outcome of political decisions made by postwar German governments.[46] If German firms had US/UK-style dispersed ownership and still allowed employees to control 50% of the votes on supervisory boards, these firms would end up becoming *employee*-dominated firms. Thus, concentrated ownership and control become a natural response.

Changing political choices, though not impossible, will encounter significant resistance, especially from incumbents (such as German labor unions or Asian families) who benefit from the present system. Some of the leading business families not only have great connections with the government, sometimes they *are* the government. Two recent prime ministers of Italy and Thailand—Silvio Berlusconi and Thaksin Shinawatra, respectively—came from leading business families and were the richest men in these countries.

Only when extraordinary events erupt would some politicians muster sufficient political will to initiate major corporate governance reforms.[47] The spectacular corporate scandals in the United States (such as Enron) are an example of such extraordinary events prompting more serious political reforms such as SOX. The 2008 financial crisis resulted in the enactment of the Dodd-Frank Act in 2010, which for the first time allows shareholders to cast proxy votes on executive compensation—in short, "say on pay."

INFORMAL INSTITUTIONAL FRAMEWORKS. In the past two decades around the world, why and how have informal norms and values concerning corporate governance changed to such a great extent?[48] From the United States and the United Kingdom, the idea of shareholder capitalism is rapidly spreading. At least three sources of these changes can be identified: (1) the rise of capitalism, (2) the impact of globalization, and (3) the global diffusion of "best practices."

First, recent changes in corporate governance around the world are part of the greater political, economic, and social movement embracing capitalism. The triumph of capitalism naturally boils down to the triumph of *capitalists* (otherwise known as shareholders). However, "free markets" are not necessarily free. Even some of the most developed countries have experienced significant governance failures, calling for a sharper focus on shareholder value.

Second, at least three aspects of recent globalization have a bearing on corporate governance.

- Thanks to more trade and investment, firms with different governance norms increasingly come into contact and expose their differences. Being aware of alternatives, shareholders as well as managers and policymakers are no longer easily persuaded that "our way" is the best way of corporate governance.[49]

foreign portfolio investment (FPI)

Foreigners' purchase of stocks and bonds in one country.

- **Foreign portfolio investment (FPI)**—foreigners purchasing stocks and bonds—has scaled new heights. These investors naturally demand better shareholder protection before committing their funds.

- The global thirst for capital has prompted many firms to pay attention to corporate governance. Foreign firms that list their stock in New York and London have to be in compliance with US and UK listing requirements.

Third, the changing norms and values are also directly promoted by the global diffusion of "best practices" in the form of corporate governance codes.[50] A lot of codes are advisory and not legally binding. However, strong pressures exist for firms to "voluntarily" adopt these codes. For example, in Russia, although adopting the 2002 Code of Corporate Conduct is voluntary, firms not adopting it have to publicly explain why, essentially naming and shaming themselves.

In addition, the Organization for Economic Cooperation and Development (OECD) has spearheaded efforts to globally diffuse "best practices" through the *OECD Principles of Corporate Governance* (1999). The *Principles* are non-binding even for the 34 OECD member countries. Nevertheless, the global norms seem to be moving toward the *Principles*. For example, China and Taiwan, both non-OECD members, have recently taken a page from the *Principles* and allowed for class action lawsuits brought by shareholders.

Slowly but surely, change is in the air. But such change is not necessarily in one direction. The ferociousness of the 2008 global financial crisis has caused tremendous resentment toward fat executive pay packages, income inequality, and the financial services industry in general. Movements such as Occupy Wall Street and Occupy London are a tangible indication of the changing informal sentiments as the swing of the pendulum (see Chapter 1), which has triggered or intensified formal regulatory changes.

Debates and Extensions

This section discusses three major debates: (1) opportunistic agents versus managerial stewards, (2) global convergence versus divergence, and (3) state ownership versus private ownership.

Opportunistic Agents versus Managerial Stewards

Agency theory assumes managers to be agents who may engage in self-serving opportunistic activities if left to their own devices. However, critics contend that most managers are likely to be honest and trustworthy. Managerial mistakes may be due to a lack of competence, information, or luck, and not necessarily due to self-serving motives. Thus, it may be unfair to characterize all managers as opportunistic agents. Although very influential, agency theory has been criticized as an "anti-management theory of management."[51] A "pro-management" theory, **stewardship theory** has emerged recently. It suggests that most managers can be viewed as owners' stewards. Safeguarding shareholders' interests and advancing organizational goals will maximize (most) managers' own utility functions.

If all principals view all managers as self-serving agents with control mechanisms to put managers on a "tight leash," some managers, who initially view themselves as stewards, may be so frustrated that they end up engaging in the very self-serving behavior agency theory seeks to minimize. In other words, as a self-fulfilling prophecy, agency theory may *induce* such behavior.

stewardship theory
A theory that suggests that managers should be regarded as stewards of owners' interests.

Global Convergence versus Divergence

Another leading debate is whether corporate governance is converging or diverging globally. Convergence advocates argue that globalization unleashes a "survival-of-the-fittest" process by which firms will be forced to adopt globally best (essentially Anglo-American) practices. Global investors are willing to pay a premium for stock in firms with Anglo-American-style governance, prompting other firms to follow.

One interesting phenomenon often cited by convergence advocates is **cross-listing**, namely, listing shares on foreign stock exchanges. Cross-listing is primarily driven by the desire to tap into larger pools of capital. Foreign firms thus must comply with US and UK securities laws and adopt Anglo-American governance norms. For instance, Japanese firms listed in New York and London, compared with those listed at home, are more concerned about shareholder value. A US or UK listing can be viewed as a signal of the firm's commitment to strengthen shareholder value, resulting in higher valuations.

cross-listing
Firms list their shares on foreign stock exchanges.

Critics contend that governance practices will continue to diverge throughout the world.[52] For example, promoting more concentrated ownership and control is often recommended as a solution to combat principal–agent conflicts in US and UK firms. However, making the same recommendation to reform firms in the rest of the world may be counterproductive or even disastrous.[53] The main problem there is that controlling shareholders typically already have too much ownership and control. Finally, some US and UK practices differ significantly. In addition to the split on CEO duality (the UK against, the US for) discussed earlier, none of the US anti-takeover defenses (such as "poison pills") is legal in the UK.

In the case of cross-listed firms, divergence advocates make two points. First, despite some convergence on paper (such as having more outside directors), cross-listed foreign firms do not necessarily adopt US governance norms before or after listing. Second, despite the popular belief that US and UK securities laws would apply to cross-listed foreign firms, in practice, these laws have rarely been effectively enforced against foreign firms' "tunneling."[54]

At present, complete divergence is probably unrealistic, especially for large firms in search of capital from global investors. Complete convergence also seems unlikely. What is more likely is "cross-vergence," balancing the expectations of global investors and those of local stakeholders.[55]

State Ownership versus Private Ownership[56]

Private ownership is good. State ownership is bad. Although crude, these two statements fairly accurately capture the intellectual and political reasoning behind three decades of privatization around the world between 1980 and 2008. Table 11.4 summarizes the key differences between private ownership and state ownership. Obviously, both forms of ownership have their own pros and cons. So the debate boils down to which form of ownership is better—whether the pros outweigh the cons.

The debate on private versus state ownership underpins much of the global economic evolution in the 20th century. The Great Depression (1929–1933) was seen as a failure of capitalism and led numerous elites in developing countries and a nontrivial number of scholars in developed economies to favor the Soviet-style socialism centered on state

TABLE 11.4 Private Ownership versus State Ownership

	PRIVATE OWNERSHIP	STATE OWNERSHIP
Objective of the firm	Maximize profits for private owners who are capitalists (and maximize shareholder value for shareholders if the firm is publicly listed).	Optimal balance for a "fair" deal for all stakeholders. Maximizing profits is not the sole objective of the firm. Protecting jobs and minimizing social unrest are legitimate goals.
Establishment of the firm	Entry is determined by entrepreneurs, owners, and investors.	Entry is determined by government officials.
Financing of the firm	Financing is from private sources (and public shareholders if the firm is publicly traded).	Financing is from state sources (such as direct subsidiaries or banks owned or controlled by governments).
Liquidation of the firm	Exit is forced by competition. A firm has to declare bankruptcy or be acquired if it becomes financially insolvent.	Exit is determined by government officials. Firms deemed "too big to fail" may be supported by taxpayer dollars indefinitely.
Appointment and dismissal of management	Management appointments are made by owners and investors largely based on merit.	Management appointments are made by government officials who may also use noneconomic criteria.
Compensation of management	Managers' compensation is determined by competitive market forces. Managers tend to be paid more under private ownership.	Managers' compensation is determined politically with some consideration given to a sense of fairness and legitimacy in the eyes of the public. Managers tend to be paid less under state ownership.

Sources: Based on (1) M. W. Peng, 2000, *Business Strategies in Transition Economies* (p. 19), Thousand Oaks, CA: Sage; (2) M. W. Peng, G. Bruton, & C. Stan, 2012, Theories of the (state-owned) firm, working paper, University of Texas at Dallas.

ownership. As a result, the postwar decades saw an increase in state ownership and a decline in private ownership. State ownership was not only extensive throughout the former Eastern bloc (the former Soviet Union, Central and Eastern Europe, China, and Vietnam), but was also widely embraced throughout developed economies in Western Europe. By the early 1980s, close to half of the GDP in major Western European countries such as Britain, France, and Italy was contributed by SOEs.

Experience throughout the former Eastern bloc and Western Europe indicated that SOEs typically suffer from a lack of accountability and a lack of economic efficiency. SOEs were known to feature relatively equal pay between managers and the rank and file. Since extra work did not translate into extra pay, employees had little incentive to improve the quality and efficiency of their work.

As Britain's prime minister, Margaret Thatcher privatized a majority of British SOEs in the 1980s. Very soon, SOEs throughout Central and Eastern Europe followed suit. After the Soviet Union collapsed, the new Russian government unleashed some of the most aggressive privatization schemes in the 1990s. Eventually, the privatization movement became global, reaching Brazil, India, China, Vietnam, and most countries in Africa. In no small part, such a global movement was championed by the **Washington Consensus**, spearheaded by two Washington-based international organizations: the International Monetary Fund (IMF) and the World Bank. A core value of the Washington Consensus is the unquestioned belief in the superiority of private ownership over state ownership. The widespread privatization movement suggested that the Washington Consensus had clearly won the day—or so it seemed.

But in 2008, the pendulum suddenly swung back (see Chapter 1). During the unprecedented recession, major governments in developed economies, led by the US government, bailed out numerous failing private firms using public funds, effectively turning them into SOEs. As a result, all the arguments in favor of private ownership and "free market" capitalism collapsed. Since SOEs had such a dreadful reputation (essentially a "dirty word"), the US government has refused to acknowledge that it has SOEs. Instead, the US government refers to them as "government-sponsored enterprises" (GSEs).

Conceptually, what are the differences between SOEs and GSEs? Hardly any! The right column in Table 11.4 is based on research on the "classical" SOEs in pre-reform China and Russia published more than a decade ago. This column also accurately summarizes what is happening in developed economies featuring GSEs now. For example, protecting jobs is one of the stated goals behind bailouts. Entry and exit are determined by government officials, and some firms that have been clearly run to the ground, such as AIG, GM, and RBS, are deemed "too big to fail" and are bailed out with taxpayer dollars. The US government forced the exit of GM's former chairman and CEO and is now directly involved in the appointment and compensation of executives at GM and other GSEs.

One crucial concern is that despite noble goals to rescue the economy, protect jobs, and fight recession, government bailouts serve to heighten **moral hazard**—recklessness when people and organizations (including firms and governments) do not have to face the full consequences of their actions.[57] In other words, capitalism without the risk of failure becomes socialism. It is long known that managers in SOEs face a "soft budget constraint" in that they can always dip into state coffers to cover their losses. When managers in private firms make risky decisions that turn sour, but their firms do not go under—thanks to generous bailouts—they are likely to embrace *more* risk in the future.

Washington Consensus
A view centered on the unquestioned belief in the superiority of private ownership over state ownership in economic policy making, which is often spearheaded by two Washington-based international organizations: the International Monetary Fund and the World Bank.

moral hazard
Recklessness when people and organizations (including firms and governments) do not have to face the full consequences of their actions.

Beijing Consensus

A view that questions Washington Consensus' belief in the superiority of private ownership over state ownership in economic policy making, which is often associated with the position held by the Chinese government.

sovereign wealth fund (SWF)

A state-owned investment fund composed of financial assets such as stocks, bonds, real estate, or other financial instruments funded by foreign exchange assets.

Although the worst fear about the recession is now over, debates continue to rage. In the ashes of the Washington Consensus emerged a **Beijing Consensus**, which centers on state ownership and government intervention. Anchored by SOEs, China over the past 30 years has grown its GDP by 9.5% a year and its international trade volume by 18% a year. SOEs represent 80% of China's stock market capitalization. But China is not alone. In Russia, the figure is 62%, and in Brazil 38%.[58] Overall, nine of the top 15 largest IPOs since 2006 are SOEs (Table 11.5). For policymakers in developed economies, an important dimension of this debate is about how to view the incoming investments from state-owned entities such as **sovereign wealth funds (SWFs)** from emerging economies (see Emerging Markets 11.1).

TABLE 11.5   State-Owned Enterprises Represent Nine of the 15 Largest IPOs since 2005

COMPANY	INDUSTRY	YEAR	VALUE ($ BILLION)
Agricultural Bank of China (SOE)	Finance	2010	22.1
Industrial & Commercial Bank of China (SOE)	Finance	2006	21.9
AIA (Hong Kong)	Insurance	2010	20.5
Visa (United States)	Finance	2008	19.7
General Motors (United States) (SOE)	Automotive	2010	18.1
Bank of China (SOE)	Finance	2006	11.2
Dai-ichi Life Insurance (Japan)	Insurance	2010	11.1
Rosneft (Russia) (SOE)	Oil & gas	2006	10.7
Glencore International (Switzerland)	Mining	2011	10.0
China Construction Bank (SOE)	Finance	2005	9.2
Electricité de France (SOE)	Utility & energy	2005	9.0
VTB Group (Russia) (SOE)	Finance	2007	8.0
Banco Santander Brasil	Finance	2009	7.5
China State Construction Engineering Corporation (SOE)	Construction	2009	7.3
Iberdrola Renovables (Spain)	Utility & energy	2007	6.6

Source: Adapted from *Economist*, 2012, New masters of universe (p. 8), Special Report: State Capitalism, January 21: 8.

Welcoming versus Restricting Sovereign Wealth Fund Investments

A sovereign wealth fund (SWF) is a state-owned investment fund composed of financial assets such as stocks, bonds, real estate, or other financial instruments funded by foreign exchange assets. Investment funds that we now call SWFs were first created in 1953 by Kuwait. Both the United States and Canada have had their own SWFs (at least at the state and provincial level, such as the Alaska Permanent Fund and Alberta Heritage Fund).

In the recent crisis, SWFs came to the rescue. They now represent approximately 10% of global investment flows. For example, in 2007, the Abu Dhabi Investment Authority injected $7.5 billion (4.9% of equity) into Citigroup. In 2008, China Investment Corporation (CIC) invested $5 billion for a 10% equity stake in Morgan Stanley. While most SWFs make relatively passive investments, some have become more active, direct investors as they hold larger stakes in recipients.

Such large-scale investments have ignited the debate on SWFs. On the one hand, SWFs have brought much-needed cash to rescue desperate Western firms. On the other hand, concerns are raised by host countries, which are typically developed economies. A primary concern is national security in that SWFs may be politically (as opposed to commercially) motivated. Another concern is SWFs' inadequate transparency. Governments in several developed economies, in fear of the "threats" from SWFs, have been erecting anti-SWF measures to defend their companies.

Foreign investment certainly has both benefits and costs to host countries. However, in the absence of any evidence that the costs outweigh benefits, the rush to erect anti-SWF barriers is indicative of protectionist (or, some may argue, even racist) sentiments. For executives at hard-pressed Western firms, it would not seem sensible to ask for government bailouts on the one hand and to reject cash from SWFs on the other hand. Most SWF investment is essentially free cash with little strings attached. For example, CIC, which now holds 10% of Morgan Stanley equity, did not demand a board seat or a management role. For Western policymakers, it makes little sense to spend taxpayers' dollars to bail out failed

firms, run huge budget deficits, and then turn away SWFs. Commenting on inbound Chinese investment in the United States (including SWF investment), leading scholars Steve Globerman and Daniel Shapiro note:

It seems feckless on the part of US policymakers to stigmatize Chinese investment in the United States based upon imprecise and likely exaggerated estimates of the relevant costs and risks of that investment.

At least some US policymakers agree. In the September/October 2008 issue of *Foreign Affairs*, then-Secretary of the Treasury Henry Paulson commented:

These concerns [on Chinese investment] are misplaced ... the United States would do well to encourage such investment from anywhere in the world—including China—because it represents a vote of confidence in the US economy and it promotes growth, jobs, and productivity in the United States.

Lastly, thanks to the financial crisis in 2008–2009, recent SWF investment in developed economies suffered major losses. Such a "double whammy"—both the political backlash and the economic losses—has severely discouraged SWFs. As a result, the recession put a premium on maintaining a welcoming climate. As part of the efforts to foster such a climate in times of great political and economic anxiety, both US and Chinese governments confirmed the following in the US-China Strategic and Economic Dialogue (S&ED) on July 28, 2009:

The United States confirms that the Committee on Foreign Investment in the United States (CFIUS) process ensures the consistent and fair treatment of all foreign investment without prejudice to the place of origin. The United States welcomes sovereign wealth fund investment, including that from China. China stresses that investment decisions by its state-owned investment firms will be based solely on commercial grounds.

Beyond bilateral negotiations such as the US-China S&ED, in September 2008, major SWFs of the world at a summit in Santiago, Chile, agreed to a voluntary code of conduct known as the Santiago Principles. These principles are designed to alleviate some of the concerns for host countries of SWF investment and to enhance the transparency of such investment. These principles represent an important milestone of SWFs' evolution.

Sources: Based on (1) V. Fotak & W. Megginson, 2009, Are SWFs welcome now? *Columbia FDI Perspectives*, No. 9, July 21, www.vcc.columbia.edu; (2) S. Globerman & D. Shapiro, 2009, Economic and strategic considerations surrounding Chinese FDI in the United States (p. 180), *Asia Pacific Journal of Management*, 26: 163–183; (3) H. Paulson, 2008, The right way to engage China, *Foreign Affairs*, September/October, www.foreignaffairs.org; (4) Sovereign Wealth Fund Institute, 2012, About sovereign wealth fund, www.swfinstitute.org; (5) United Nations (UN), 2010, *World Investment Report 2010* (p. xviii), New York and Geneva: UN; (6) US Department of the Treasury, 2009, *The First US-China Strategic and Economic Dialogue Economic Track Joint Fact Sheet*, July 28, Washington.

The Savvy Strategist

In the corporate governance arena, the savvy strategist capitalizes on three strategic implications for action (Table 11.6). First, understand the nature of principal–agent and principal–principal conflicts to create better governance mechanisms. For example, the rise of private equity is a direct response to principal–agent conflicts typically found in publicly listed firms (see the Closing Case). Amazingly, private equity typically makes the *same* managers, managing the *same* assets, perform much more effectively. In terms of mechanisms to alleviate principal–principal conflicts, one practice is to introduce a second controlling (dominant) shareholder that may monitor and constrain the action of the first controlling shareholder.[59]

Second, savvy strategists need to develop firm-specific capabilities to differentiate on governance dimensions. In India, the leading IT firm Infosys has emerged as an exemplar.[60] It is the first Indian firm to follow US generally accepted accounting principles (GAAP), the first to offer stock options to all employees, and one of the first to introduce outside directors. Since its listings in Mumbai in 1993 and NASDAQ in 1999, it has gone far beyond disclosure requirements mandated by both Indian and US standards. On NASDAQ, Infosys *voluntarily* behaves like a US domestic issuer, rather than subjecting itself to the less stringent standards of a foreign issuer.

Third, savvy strategists need to understand the rules and anticipate changes.[61] In the first year that shareholders were granted a "say on pay" in US firms (2011), median pay for CEOs at Standard & Poor's 500 firms *jumped* 35% to $8.4 million.[62] While

TABLE 11.6   Strategic Implications for Action

- Understand the nature of principal–agent and principal–principal conflicts to create better governance mechanisms.
- Develop firm-specific capabilities to differentiate a firm on corporate governance dimensions.
- Master the rules affecting corporate governance and anticipate changes.

shareholders only rejected executive pay at less than 2% of public firms, this practice of significantly increasing CEO compensation seemed to deviate from the spirit—if not the letter—of the Dodd-Frank Act that unleashed "say on pay." As a result, more tightening of the rules can be expected down the road.

Overall, a better understanding of corporate governance can help us answer the four fundamental questions in strategy. First, why do firms differ? Firms differ in corporate governance because of the different nature of industries, different abilities to motivate and discipline managers, and different institutional frameworks. Second, how do firms behave? Given that most corporations throughout the world have similar basic components of corporate governance (owners, managers, and boards), the primary sources of differences stems from how these components relate and interact with each other to set the direction of the corporate ship. Third, what determines the scope of the firm? From a corporate governance standpoint, a wide scope may be indicative of managers' empire-building and risk reduction. Finally, what determines the success and failure of firms around the globe? Although research is still inconclusive, there is reason to believe—in the aggregate and in the long run—that better governed firms will be rewarded with a lower cost of capital and consequently better firm performance.[63]

CHAPTER SUMMARY

1. **Differentiate various ownership patterns (concentrated/diffused, family, and state ownership)**
   - In the US and UK, firms with separation of ownership and control dominate.
   - Elsewhere, firms with concentrated ownership and control in the hands of families or governments are predominant.

2. **Articulate the role of managers in both principal–agent and principal–principal conflicts**
   - In firms with separation of ownership and control, the primary conflicts are principal–agent conflicts.
   - In firms with concentrated ownership, principal–principal conflicts prevail.

3. **Explain the role of the board of directors**
   - The board of directors performs (1) control, (2) service, and (3) resource acquisition functions.
   - Around the world, boards differ in composition, leadership structure, and interlocks.

4. **Identify voice-based and exit-based governance mechanisms and their combination as a package**
   - Internal voice-based mechanisms and external exit-based mechanisms combine as a package to determine corporate governance effectiveness.
   - The market for corporate control and the market for private equity are two primary external mechanisms.

5. **Acquire a global perspective on how governance mechanisms vary around the world**
   - Different combinations of internal and external governance mechanisms lead to four main groups.
   - Privatization around the world represents efforts to enhance governance effectiveness.

6. **Elaborate on a comprehensive model of corporate governance**
   - Industry-based, institution-based, and resource-based views shed considerable light on governance issues.

7. **Participate in three leading debates concerning corporate governance**
   - (1) Opportunistic agents versus managerial stewards, (2) global convergence versus divergence, and (3) state ownership versus private ownership.

8. **Draw strategic implications for action**
   - Understand the nature of principal–agent and principal–principal conflicts.
   - Develop firm-specific capabilities to differentiate on corporate governance dimensions.
   - Master the rules affecting corporate governance and anticipate changes.

KEY TERMS

Agency cost p. 330

Agency relationship p. 330

Agency theory p. 330

Agent p. 330

Beijing Consensus p. 348

CEO duality p. 334

Chief executive officer (CEO) p. 327

Concentrated ownership and control p. 328

Corporate governance p. 328

Cross-listing p. 345

Diffused ownership p. 329

Exit-based mechanism p. 336

Expropriation p. 332

Foreign portfolio investment (FPI) p. 344

Information asymmetries p. 330

Inside director p. 334

Interlocking directorate p. 334

Leveraged buyout (LBO) p. 338

Managerial human capital p. 342

Moral hazard p. 347

Outside (independent) director p. 334

Principal p. 330

Principal–agent conflict p. 330

Principal–principal conflict p. 332

Private equity p. 338

Related transaction p. 333

Separation of ownership and control p. 329

Shareholder capitalism p. 339

Sovereign wealth fund (SWF) p. 348

State-owned enterprise (SOE) p. 329

Stewardship theory p. 345

Tunneling p. 333

Voice-based mechanism p. 336

Washington Consensus p. 347

CRITICAL DISCUSSION QUESTIONS

1. Some argue that the Anglo-American-style separation of ownership and control is an inevitable outcome in corporate governance. Others contend that this is one variant (among several) on how large firms can be effectively governed and that it is not necessarily the most efficient form. What do you think?

2. Recent corporate governance reforms in various countries urge (and often require) firms to add more outside directors to their boards and separate the jobs of board chairman and CEO. Yet, academic research has not been able to conclusively support the merits of both practices. Why?

3. **ON ETHICS:** You are 30 years old and obtained your MBA from a top business school two years ago. You are being promoted to be CEO of a multibillion-dollar firm that is publicly listed in your country. There is loud minority shareholder resistance to your appointment because you are too young. Too bad, your father and your family are the controlling shareholders and you get the job. What are you going to say at your first press conference as CEO, knowing that there will be some tough questions from reporters?

TOPICS FOR EXPANDED PROJECTS

1. Given that you can choose where to register and list your firm anywhere in the world, which country's securities and corporate governance laws would you prefer? Working in small groups, research and compare at least five possible locations, and then make a final selection. Present your research findings, selection criteria, and explanation of final choice in a short paper or visual presentation.

2. How do you side in the debate on state ownership versus private ownership? State your position in a short paper.

3. **ON ETHICS:** As a chairman/CEO, you are choosing between two candidates for one outside director position on your board. One is another CEO, a long-time friend whose board you have served on for many years. The other is a known shareholder activist whose tag line is "No need to make fat cats fatter." Placing him on the board will earn you kudos among analysts and journalists for inviting a leading critic to scrutinize your work. However, he may try to prove his theory that CEOs are overpaid. Who would you choose? Explain your rationale for your choice in a short paper.

CLOSING CASE — ETHICAL DILEMMA

Emerging Markets: The Private Equity Challenge

Private equity is one of the hottest and most controversial buzzwords in corporate governance. Private equity firms often take an underperforming publicly listed company off the stock exchange, add some heavy dose of debt, throw in sweet "carrots" to incumbent managers, and trim all the "fat" (typically through layoffs). Private equity firms get paid by (1) the fees and (2) the profits reaped when they take the private firms public again through a new IPO.

Private equity first emerged in the 1980s, with a stream of deals peaked by Kohlberg Kravis Robert's (KKR) $25 billion takeover of RJR Nabisco in 1988—then the highest price paid for a public firm. While KKR disciplined dead-wood managers who destroyed shareholder value, it received a ton of bad press, cemented in a best-selling book *Barbarians at the Gate* that portrayed KKR as a greedy and barbarous raider.

After the RJR Nabisco deal, the private equity industry stagnated during the 1990s. However, in the 2000s, private equity scaled new heights. In 1991, just 57 private equity firms existed. In 2007, close to 700 chased deals. Private equity deals now routinely represent 25% of all mergers and acquisitions (M&As) in the world (and 35% in the United States). Since 2005, Europe has had more actions (measured by deal values) than the United States. In 2007, Cerberus, a private equity firm, purchased Chrysler from DaimlerChrysler for $7.4 billion. APAX Partners spent $7.75 billion to buy Thomson Learning—the publisher of *this book*—from The Thomson Corporation listed in New York and Toronto. However, private equity suffered a tremendous setback since 2008. Many deals struck in the easy credit environment of 2006–2007 collapsed, resulting in severe losses. In a record-breaking $43 billion deal in 2007, Texas Pacific Group (now known as TPG Capital) and KKR jointly took over Dallas-based utility TXU, which is now called Energy Future Holdings. However, by 2011, KKR valued its investment at only ten cents on the dollar.

Private equity has always been controversial. Proponents argue that private equity is a response to the corporate governance deficiency of the public firm. Private equity excels in four ways:

- Private owners, unlike dispersed individual shareholders, care deeply about the return on investment. Private equity firms always send experts to sit on the board and are hands-on in managing.

- A high level of debt imposes strong financial discipline to minimize waste.

- Private equity turns managers from agents to principals with substantial equity (typically 5% equity for the CEO and 16% for the whole top management team). Private equity firms pay managers more generously, but also punish failure more heavily. Managers' compensation at firms under private ownership, according to leading expert Michael Jensen, is *20 times* more sensitive to performance than at firms listed publicly. On average, private equity makes the *same* managers, managing the *same* assets, perform much more effectively. On average there is a 2% boost in productivity and efficiency.

- Finally, privacy is fabulous. For managers, no more short-term burden to "meet the numbers" for Wall Street, no more burdensome paperwork from regulators (an especially crushing load thanks to SOX), and better yet, no more disclosure in excruciating detail of their pay (an inevitable invitation to be labeled "fat cats"). Top

managers under private ownership are indeed *fatter* cats. It is not surprising that more managers prefer a quieter but far more lucrative life. In 1997, over 7,000 firms were listed on US stock exchanges. In 2012, thanks to private equity only over 4,000 bothered to be listed.

All of the above, according to critics, are exactly what is wrong with private equity. Other than "barbarians," private equity has also been labeled "asset strippers" and "locusts." As high executive compensation at public firms has already become a huge controversy, private equity has further increased the income inequality between the high financiers and top managers as one group and the rest of us as another group. Private equity has rapidly proliferated around the world. Some of the fuss reflects the shock in countries suddenly facing the full rigor of Anglo-American private equity. In Germany, some politicians labeled foreign private equity groups as "locusts who feast on German firms for profit before spitting them out." In South Korea, Lone Star Funds of Dallas was initially hailed in 2003 as a brave outsider willing to save troubled Korean firms. However, in 2006, when Lone Star tried to cash out by selling its 51% equity of Korea Exchange Bank, unions took to the street to protest and prosecutors issued a warrant to arrest its co-founder for alleged financial manipulation.

To be sure, private equity results in job cuts (about 1%–2% of the jobs at the firms that were taken over were lost). But the same would happen if targets were acquired by public firms. In other words, private equity buyers are no more barbaric than public firms. In terms of financial returns, private equity investors earn slightly more than the Standard and Poor's (S&P) 500 before the fees are charged. However, after the fees are charged, private equity performs slightly below S&P. In other words, outside investors would do as well or better with their money in an S&P index fund. In summary, while private equity is under attack for destroying jobs, its real problem is that returns to investors are low.

Private equity is inherently global. As the homeland of private equity is now engulfed in economic recession and widespread resentment (think of Occupy Wall Street), the outlook is grim. Is private equity "Monsters, Inc.?" asked an *Economist* editorial. Thus, private equity firms have increasingly targeted emerging economies, especially China, for future growth. The following quote is from a speech in 2010 given by David Rubenstein, co-founder and managing director of one of the largest private equity firms, Carlyle Group:

> *When I'm in Washington, DC, people are barraging me, saying that I'm not paying enough taxes, I'm not worried enough about labor concerns. I've got labor unions protesting me. I've got everybody telling me that I didn't do something right. In China, people want my autograph. In China, private equity professionals are like rock stars. Because China has taken the view that private equity is a value-adding technique and a value-added resource, they encourage it ... Honestly, I tell people ... the center of capitalism is Beijing, and the center of non-capitalism is Washington, DC. Now obviously, that's an exaggeration to make a point, but there's no doubt that in China, what private equity people do is very much welcomed and not criticized.*

Sources: Based on (1) *Bloomberg Businessweek*, 2011, The people vs. private equity, November 28: 90–93; (2) *Bloomberg Businessweek*, 2012, You're so Bain, January 16: 6–8; (3) G. Bruton, I. Filatotchev, S. Chahine, & M. Wright, 2010, Governance, ownership structure, and performance of IPO firms: The impact of different types of private equity investors and institutional environments, *Strategic Management Journal*, 31: 491–509; (4) D. Cumming & U. Walz, 2010, Private

equity returns and disclosure around the world, *Journal of International Business Studies*, 41: 727–754; (5) *Economist*, 2012, Bain or blessing? January 28: 73–74; (6) *Economist*, 2012, Monsters, Inc.? January 28: 10–11; (7) M. Jensen, 1989, Eclipse of the public corporation, *Harvard Business Review*, September: 61–74; (8) S. Kaplan & P. Stromberg, 2009, Leveraged buyouts and private equity, *Journal of Economic Perspectives*, 23: 121–146; (9) L. Phalippou, 2009, Beware of venturing into private equity, *Journal of Economic Perspectives*, 23: 147–166; (10) Wharton Private Equity Review, 2010, *The Storm Clouds Begin to Clear* (p. 19), Wharton School.

CASE DISCUSSION QUESTIONS

1. If you were a private equity specialist, what kind of target firms would you look for?

2. If you were CEO of a publicly traded firm and were approached by a private equity firm, how would you proceed?

3. If you were a Chinese regulator, how concerned should you be after you have learned about the criticisms against private equity in the United States, Germany, South Korea, and elsewhere?

NOTES

[**Journal acronyms**] *AER – American Economic Review; AMJ – Academy of Management Journal; AMP – Academy of Management Perspectives; AMR – Academy of Management Review; APJM – Asia Pacific Journal of Management; BW – BusinessWeek* (before 2010) or *Bloomberg Businessweek* (since 2010); *CG – Corporate Governance; JAE – Journal of Accounting and Economics; JEP – Journal of Economic Perspectives; JF – Journal of Finance; JFE – Journal of Financial Economics; JIBS – Journal of International Business Studies; JMS – Journal of Management Studies; JWB – Journal of World Business; MOR – Management and Organization Review; OSc – Organization Science; OSt – Organization Studies; RES – Review of Economics and Statistics; RFS – Review of Financial Studies; SMJ – Strategic Management Journal*

1. R. Monks & N. Minow, 2001, *Corporate Governance* (p. 1), Oxford, UK: Blackwell. See also M. Benz & B. Frey, 2007. Corporate governance, *AMR*, 32: 92–104; S. Globerman, M. W. Peng, & D. Shapiro, 2011, Corporate governance and Asian companies, *APJM*, 28: 1–14.
2. B. Connelly, R. Hoskisson, L. Tihanyi, & S. T. Certo, 2010, Ownership as a form of corporate governance, *JMS*, 47: 1561–1589.
3. R. Stulz, 2005, The limits of financial globalization (p. 1618), *JF*, 60: 1595–1638.
4. K. Schnatterly, K. Shaw, & W. Jennings, 2008, Information advantages of large institutional owners, *SMJ*, 29: 219–227.
5. R. La Porta, F. Lopez-de-Silanes, & A. Shleifer, 1999, Corporate ownership around the world, *JF*, 54: 471–517.

6. Y. Jiang & M. W. Peng, 2011, Are family ownership and control in large firms good, bad, or irrelevant? *APJM*, 28: 15–39; M. W. Peng & Y. Jiang, 2010, Institutions behind family ownership and control in large firms, *JMS*, 47: 253–273; W. Schulze & E. Gedajlovic, 2010, Whither family business? *JMS*, 47: 191–204.

7. M. Jensen & W. Meckling, 1976, Theory of the firm, *JFE*, 3: 305–360.

8. J. Combs, D. Ketchen, A. Perryman, & M. Donahue, 2007, The moderating effect of CEO power on the board-composition-firm performance relationship, *JMS*, 44: 1309–1322; W. Johnson, R. Magee, N. Nagarajan, & H. Newman, 1985, An analysis of the stock price reaction to sudden executive deaths, *JAE*, 7: 151–174.

9. S. Claessens, S. Djankov, & L. Lang, 2000, The separation of ownership and control in East Asian corporations, *JFE*, 58: 81–112.

10. M. Faccio & L. Lang, 2002, The ultimate ownership of Western European corporations, *JFE*, 65: 365–395.

11. M. Young, M. W. Peng, D. Ahlstrom, G. Bruton, & Y. Jiang, 2008, Corporate governance in emerging economies, *JMS*, 45: 196–220.

12. S. Johnson, R. La Porta, F. Lopez-de-Silanes, & A. Shleifer, 2000, Tunneling, *AER*, 90: 22–27.

13. D. Dalton, C. Daily, A. Ellstrands, & J. Johnson, 1998, Meta-analytic reviews of board composition, leadership structure, and financial performance, *SMJ*, 19: 269–290; M. Kroll, B. Walters, & S. Le, 2007, The impact of board composition and top management team ownership structure on post-IPO performance in young entrepreneurial firms, *AMJ*, 50: 1198–1216; M. W. Peng, T. Buck, & I. Filatotchev, 2003, Do outside directors and new managers help improve firm performance? *JWB*, 38: 348–360.

14. D. Erkins, M. Hung, & P. Matos, 2012, Corporate governance in the 2007–2008 financial crisis, working paper, University of Southern California.

15. V. Chen, J. Li, & D. Shapiro, 2011, Are OECD-prescribed "good corporate practices" really good in an emerging economy? *APJM*, 28: 115–138; M. W. Peng, S. Zhang, & X. Li, 2007, CEO duality and firm performance during China's institutional transitions, *MOR*, 3: 205–225.

16. *Economist*, 2012, The shackled boss, January 21: 76.

17. M. Geletkanycz & B. Boyd, 2011, CEO outside directorships and firm performance, *AMJ*, 54: 335–352.

18. K. Au, M. W. Peng, & D. Wang, 2000, Interlocking directorates, firm strategies, and performance in Hong Kong (p. 32), *APJM*, 17: 29–47.

19. J. Tang, M. Crossan, & W. G. Rowe, 2011, Dominant CEO, deviant strategy, and extreme performance, *JMS*, 48: 1479–1502; J. Westphal & I. Stern, 2007, Flattery will get you everywhere, *AMJ*, 50: 267–288.

20. A. Gore, S. Matsunaga, & P. E. Yeung, 2011, The role of technical expertise in firm governance structure, *SMJ*, 32: 771–786; M. Kroll, B. Walters, & P. Wright, 2008, Board vigilance, director experience, and corporate outcomes, *SMJ*, 29: 363–382; M. McDonald, J. Westphal, & M. Graebner, 2008, What do they know? *SMJ*, 29: 1155–1177.

21. M. W. Peng, 2004, Outside directors and firm performance during institutional transitions, *SMJ*, 25: 453–471.

22. A. Chizema & J. Kim, 2010, Outside directors on Korean boards, *JMS*, 47: 109–129.

23. R. Adams, A. Licht, & L. Sagiv, 2011, Shareholders and stakeholders, *SMJ*, 32: 1331–1355; S. Graffin, M. Carpenter, & S. Boivie, 2011, What's all that (strategic) noise? *SMJ*, 32: 748–770.

24. C. Devers, R. Wiseman, & R. M. Holmes, 2007, The effects of endowment and loss aversion in managerial stock option valuation, *AMJ*, 50: 191–208; M. Goranova, T. Alessandri, P. Brandes, & R. Dharwadkar, 2007, Managerial ownership and corporate diversification, *SMJ*, 28: 211–225; W. G. Sanders & A. Tuschke, 2007, The adoption of institutionally contested organizational practices, *AMJ*, 50: 33–56.

25. C. Cadsby, F. Song, & F. Tapon, 2007, Sorting and incentive effects of pay for performance, *AMJ*, 50: 387–405; T. Cho & W. Shen, 2007, Changes in executive compensation following an environmental shift, *SMJ*, 28: 747–754; M. Larraza-Kintana, R. Wiseman, L. Gomez-Mejia, & T. Welbourne, 2007, Disentangling compensation and employment risks using the behavioral agency model, *SMJ*, 28: 1001–1019.

26. L. Bebchuk & J. Fried, 2004, *Pay without Performance*, Cambridge, MA: Harvard University Press; J. Wade, J. Porac, T. Pollock, & S. Graffin, 2006, The burden of celebrity, *AMJ*, 49: 643–660; X. Zhang, K. Bartol, K. Smith, M. Pfarrer, & D. Khanin, 2008, CEOs on the edge, *AMJ*, 51: 241–258.

27. A. Cowen & J. Marcel, 2011, Damaged goods, *AMJ*, 54: 509–527; M. Wiersema & Y. Zhang, 2011, CEO dismissal, *SMJ*, 32: 1161–1182.

28. *Economist*, 2012, The shackled boss, January 21: 76.

29. R. Hoskisson, M. Castleton, & M. Withers, 2009, Complementarity in monitoring and bonding, *AMP*, May: 57–74.

30. V. Bodolica & M. Spraggon, 2009, The implementation of special attributes of CEO compensation contracts around M&A transactions, *SMJ*, 30: 985–1011; N. Hiller & D. Hambrick, 2007, Conceptualizing executive hubris, *SMJ*, 26: 297–319; R. Masulis, C. Wang, & F. Xie, 2007, Corporate governance and acquirer returns, *JF*, 62: 1851–1889.

31. M. Nakamura, 2011, Adoption and policy implications of Japan's new corporate governance practices after the reform, *APJM*, 28: 187–213; T. Yoshikawa & J. McGuire, 2008, Change and continuity in Japanese corporate governance, *APJM*, 25: 5–24.

32. S. Kaplan & P. Stromberg, 2009, Leveraged buyouts and private equity, *JEP*, 23: 147–166; L. Phalippou, 2009, Beware of venturing into private equity, *JEP*, 23: 147–166; P. Phan & C. Hill, 1995, Organizational restructuring and economic performance in leveraged buyouts, *AMJ*, 38: 704–739.

33. J. Lerner, P. Stromberg, & M. Sorensen, 2008, Private equity and long-run investment, in J. Lerner & A. Gurung (eds.), *The Global Economic Impact of Private Equity Report 2008* (pp. 27–42), Geneva, Switzerland: World Economic Forum.

34. R. Aguilera, I. Filatotchev, H. Gospel, & G. Jackson, 2008, An organizational approach to comparative corporate governance, *OSc*, 19: 475–492; B. Boyd, K. Haynes, & F. Zona, 2011, Dimensions of CEO-board relations, *JMS*, 48: 1892–1923; G. Dowell, M. Shackell, & N. Stuart, 2011, Boards, CEOs, and surviving a financial crisis, *SMJ*, 32: 1025–1045; B. Hermalin, 2005, Trends in corporate governance, *JF*, 60: 2351–2384.

35. D. McCarthy & S. Puffer, 2008, Interpreting the ethicality of corporate governance decisions in Russia, *AMR*, 33: 11–31.

36. A. Henderson, D. Miller, & D. Hambrick, 2006, How quickly do CEOs become obsolete? *SMJ*, 27: 447–460.

37. Y. Kor & V. Misangyi, 2008, Outside directors' industry-specific experience and firms' liability of foreignness, *SMJ*, 29: 1345–1355.

38. M. Li & R. Simerly, 1998, The moderating effect of environmental dynamism on the ownership-performance relationship, *SMJ*, 19: 169–179.

39. S. Kaplan, 2008, Cognition, capabilities, and incentives, *AMJ*, 51: 672–695; J. Tian, J. Haleblian, & N. Rajagopalan, 2011, The effects of board human and social capital on investor reactions to new CEO selection, *SMJ*, 32: 731–747; J. Westphal & M. Clement, 2008, Sociopolitical dynamics in relations between top managers and security analysts, *AMJ*, 51: 873–897.

40. A. Alexiev, J. Jansen, F. Van den Bosch, & H. Volberda, 2010, Top management team advice seeking and exploratory innovation, *JMS*, 47: 1343–1364.

41. C. Doidge, A. Karolyi, & R. Stulz, 2004, Why are foreign firms listed in the US worth more? *JFE*, 71: 205–238.

42. A. Karolyi, 2010, Corporate governance, agency problems, and international cross-listings, working paper, Cornell University.

43. C. Doidge, A. Karolyi, & R. Stulz, 2009, Has New York become less competitive than London in global markets? *JFE*, 91: 253–277; N. Fernandes, U. Lel, & D. Miller, 2010, Escape from New York, *JFE*, 95: 129–147.

44. S. Boivie, D. Lange, M. McDonald, & J. Westphal, 2011, Me or we, *AMJ*, 54: 551–576; J. He & Z. Huang, 2011, Board informal hierarchy and firm financial performance, *AMJ*, 54: 1119–1139; A. Mackey, 2008, The effect of CEOs on firm performance, *SMJ*, 29: 1357–1367; S. Nadkarni & P. Herrmann, 2010, CEO personality, strategic flexibility, and firm performance, *AMJ*, 53: 1050–1073; A. Raes, M. Heijltjes, U. Glunk, & R. Roe, 2011, The interface of the top management team and middle managers, *AMR*, 36: 102–126; Z. Simsek, 2007, CEO tenure and organizational performance, *SMJ*, 28: 653–662; C. Tuggle, K. Schnatterly, & R. Johnson, 2010, Attention patterns in the boardroom, *AMJ*, 53: 550–571; Y. Zhang & M. Wiersema, 2009, Stock market reaction to CEO certification, *SMJ*, 30: 693–710.

45. A. Bris & C. Cabolis, 2008, The value of investor protection, *RFS*, 21: 605–648; C. Doidge, A. Karolyi, & R. Stulz, 2007, Why do countries matter so much for corporate governance? *JFE*, 86: 1–39.

46. T. Buck & A. Shahrim, 2005, The translation of corporate governance changes across national cultures, *JIBS*, 36: 42–61.

47. G. Davis, 2009, The rise and fall of finance and the end of the society of organizations, *AMP*, August: 27–44.

48. S. Estrin & M. Prevezer, 2011, The role of informal institutions in corporate governance, *APJM*, 28: 41–67.

49. P. David, T. Yoshikawa, M. Chari, & A. Rasheed, 2006, Strategic investments in Japanese corporations, *SMJ*, 27: 591–600.

50. R. Aguilera & A. Cuervo-Cazurra, 2009, Codes of good governance, *CG*, 17: 376–387; I. Haxhi & H. van Ees, 2010, Explaining diversity in the worldwide diffusion of codes of good governance, *JIBS*, 41: 710–726.

51. L. Donaldson, 1995, *American Anti-management Theories of Management*, Cambridge, UK: Cambridge University Press.

52. M. Lubatkin, P. Lane, S. Collin, & P. Very, 2005, Origins of corporate governance in the USA, Sweden, and France, *OSt*, 26: 867–888; Y. Shi, M. Magnan, & J. Kim, 2012, Do countries matter for voluntary disclosure? *JIBS*, 43: 143–165.

53. M. van Essen, J. van Oosterhout, & P. Heugens, 2012, Competition and cooperation in corporate governance, *OSc* (in press).

54. J. Siegel, 2003, Can foreign firms bond themselves effectively by renting US securities laws? *JFE*, 75: 319–359.

55. A. Chizema & Y. Shinozawa, 2012, The "company with committees," *JMS*, 49: 77–101; C. Crossland & D. Hambrick, 2007, How national systems differ in their constraints on corporate executives, *SMJ*, 28: 767–789; T. Khanna, J. Kogan, & K. Palepu, 2006, Globalization and similarities in corporate governance, *RES*, 88: 69–90; C. Kwok & S. Tadesse, 2006, National culture and financial systems, *JIBS*, 37: 227–247.

56. State ownership is also often referred to as "public ownership." However, since a lot of privately owned firms are publicly listed and traded (which can cause confusion), I have decided to use "state ownership" here to minimize confusion.

57. P. Bernstein, 2009, The moral hazard economy, *HBR*, July–August: 101–102.

58. *Economist*, 2012, The rise of state capitalism, January 21: 11.

59. Y. Jiang & M. W. Peng, 2011, Principal-principal conflicts during crisis, *APJM*, 28: 683–695.

60. T. Khanna & K. Palepu, 2004, Globalization and convergence in corporate governance, *JIBS*, 35: 484–507.

61. R. G. Bell, I. Filatotchev, & A. Rasheed, 2012, The liability of foreignness in capital markets, *JIBS*, 43: 107–122; L. Capron & M. Guillen, 2009, National corporate governance institutions and post-acquisition target reorganization, *SMJ*, 30: 803–833; J. Kang & J. Kim, 2010, Do foreign investors exhibit a corporate governance disadvantage? *JIBS*, 41: 1415–1438; A. Pe'er & O. Gottschalg, 2011, Red and blue, *SMJ*, 32: 1356–1367; H. Zou & M. Adams, 2008, Corporate ownership, equity risk, and returns in the People's Republic of China, *JIBS*, 39: 1149–1168.

62. *BW*, 2011, After much hoopla, investor "say on pay" is a bust, June 20: 23–24.

63. O. Gottschalg & M. Zollo, 2007, Interest alignment and competitive advantage, *AMR*, 32: 418–437; J. Ho, A. Wu, & S. Xu, 2011, Corporate governance and returns on information technology investment, *SMJ*, 32: 595–623.

CHAPTER 12

STRATEGIZING WITH CORPORATE SOCIAL RESPONSIBILITY

© istockphoto/Alexey Stiop

KNOWLEDGE OBJECTIVES

After studying this chapter, you should be able to

1. Articulate what a stakeholder view of the firm is
2. Develop a comprehensive model of corporate social responsibility
3. Participate in three leading debates concerning corporate social responsibility
4. Draw strategic implications for action

Launching the Nissan Leaf: The World's First Electric Car

An electric car that does not burn a single drop of gasoline—technically called an "electric vehicle" (EV)—is the "dream car" of many environmentalists. Known as a "plug-in" vehicle, an EV is totally based on battery power, has no tailpipe, and thus has zero emission. It would be more revolutionary than Toyota's hybrid Prius, which drives on battery power before its gasoline engine kicks in and recharges the battery.

The million-dollar question is: Are car buyers ready for the EV? The environmental benefits are clear, yet the technological, social, psychological, and economic forces working against the EV are formidable. Technologically, the most advanced EV can only run between 60 and 100 miles (between 96 and 160 kilometers) per charge. It takes about seven hours to fully charge. The EV is clearly not as convenient as the conventional car. Socially, the EV, like the Prius, may be a hit in a niche market, but it is questionable whether the LV can penetrate the mainstream. Psychologically, since public charging stations are few and far between (and nonexistent in many communities), drivers will experience "range anxiety"—will the EV run out of battery before it reaches the next charging station? Finally, the economics of the EV is not too enticing. Hybrids such as the Prius cost about $4,000 more than a comparable conventional car. The EV is likely to cost $10,000 to $20,000 more. Owners preferably will also need a special charger installed at home, which would cost another $2,000. Simply plugging into the standard household power outlet is advised for emergency charging only; the local utility circuit may collapse if so much electricity is suddenly sucked out by an EV.

Against such significant odds, Nissan in December 2010 launched a mid-size five-door hatchback, the Leaf, which is the world's first mass-produced EV. The world's very first customer, in San Francisco, drove home the Leaf on December 11, 2010. The first delivery in Japan took place at Kanagawa Prefecture on December 22, 2010. Portugal, Ireland, and the UK are the first European markets the Leaf entered. While Americans may be shocked by the $32,780 list price, the Leaf in the United States is the least expensive globally (see Table 12.1). Elsewhere, the EV costs between $44,600 to $49,800 (!). Even adding all the incentives dished out by governments, the Leaf is still not a cheap car. So what did Nissan do to prepare the launch of this pioneering car?

At least three areas of Nissan's preparation stand out. First, from an institution-based view, Nissan has a sharp awareness of the emerging regulatory requirements that would necessitate the EV. While the car industry fought the tightening of emission standards for years, the 2007 Energy Independence and Security Act raised fuel economy averages of all cars made by any single automaker to 35 miles per gallon by 2020, a 40% improvement over current levels. Instead of shying away from the EV, having a zero-emission car like the Leaf has become a smart way to balance out the fuel-thirsty gas guzzlers such as SUVs. All of a sudden, most automakers are rushing to develop the EV, but none—not even Prius' maker, Toyota—can beat Nissan in the race to introduce the first EV.

Second, from a resource-based view, Nissan has accumulated significant capabilities in the crucial lithium-ion

TABLE 12.1 The Nissan Leaf's Prices and Launch Times in the First Five Markets

	LIST PRICE (US$)	NET PRICE AFTER INCENTIVES (US$)	MARKET LAUNCH
United States	$32,780	$25,000	December 2010
Japan	$44,600	$35,500	December 2010
Portugal	$45,500	$39,325	January 2011
Ireland	$45,100	$39,000	February 2011
United Kingdom	$49,800	$38,400	March 2011

© Cengage Learning

battery technology. As early as in 1997, it introduced its first prototype EV. In 1999, when Renault took over Nissan and Carlos Ghosn became in charge, Nissan was dangerously close to bankruptcy. In the gut-wrenching restructuring initiated by Ghosn, 60% of the R&D projects were slashed. Yet, the costly and uncertain battery project was kept and nurtured, which ultimately led to the Leaf.

Third, to ensure a successful launch, Nissan embraced a stakeholder approach by meticulously working with a variety of stakeholders, such as government officials, utilities, activists, and customers, in highly innovative ways. In 2008, Nissan set up a Zero Emission Mobility Team, whose members were not only executives from sales and marketing, but also from government affairs, product planning, and communications. In the United States, the team focused on seven environmentally progressive states: Arizona, California, Hawaii, Oregon, Tennessee, Texas, and Washington (state). By limiting the launch to just seven states, Nissan can achieve a critical mass of charging stations. The team visited government officials to urge them to offer more incentives to buyers and utilities to encourage them to install public charging stations, and worked to streamline the permitting and installation process for home chargers. The team also called on the utilities to get ready and made presentations at utility conferences, which was something automakers had never done before. The Nissan team also reached out to activists. It invited a total of 1,400 people in 307 cities in 27 states to participate in focus group meetings. Leading activists were invited to Yokohama, Japan, where the Leaf was being built, to test drive the EV.

The moment of truth came in April 2010, when Nissan invited interested buyers to pre-order by putting down a refundable $99 fee. Within the first 24 hours, Nissan received 6,000 (!) reservations. By September, Nissan no longer accepted any more reservations for the remainder of 2010. Customers had to wait four to seven months. It seemed that Nissan would have no problem selling the first 50,000 Leafs produced in its Yokohama factory. Production will ramp up, involving its Smyrna, Tennessee, plant in 2012 and its Sunderland, UK, plant in 2013.

Map Resources

Officially ranked as the most fuel efficient vehicle (99 miles per gallon gasoline *equivalent*) in the United States, the Leaf costs about 2 cents per mile to drive, far more economical than the 13 cents per mile for an average conventional car. While the Chevy Volt and the Toyota Prius Plug-In will enter the foray soon, they remain hybrids. As the only full EV, the Leaf has enjoyed a great deal of attention and grabbed numerous awards, such as the 2010 Green Car Vision Award, 2011 European Car of the Year, 2011 World Car of the Year, 2011 Eco-Friendly Car of the Year, and 2012 Car of the Year Japan. While the Leaf earns a lot of kudos for its contributions to a cleaner environment, from a competitive standpoint, Nissan is especially pleased that so much of the "green car" conversation now revolves around the Leaf, instead of the Prius.

Sources: Based on (1) *Bloomberg Businessweek*, 2011, Charged for battle, January 3: 49–56; (2) *Bloomberg Businessweek*, 2010, Green cars still need training wheels, December 6: 37–38; (3) Economist, 2012, *The World in 2012* (p. 134), London: The Economist Newspaper Group; (4) www.2011nissanleaf.net; (5) www.nissanusa.com.

W hy is an EV the "dream car" for many environmentalists? Why do many automakers not bother to offer it? Why does Nissan, the first firm that has mass produced an EV, earn so many kudos? The simple answer is that Nissan's decision to take the risk to develop the first EV is indicative of Nissan's interest in **corporate social responsibility (CSR)**, which refers to "consideration of, and response to, issues beyond the narrow economic, technical, and legal requirements of the firm to accomplish social benefits along with the traditional economic gains which the firm seeks."[1] Historically, CSR issues have been on the back burner for many managers, but these issues are increasingly being brought to the forefront of corporate agendas. While this chapter is positioned as the last in this book, by no means do we suggest that CSR is the least important topic. Instead, we believe that this chapter is one of the best ways to *integrate* previous chapters drawing on the strategy tripod.[2] The comprehensive nature of CSR is evident in our Opening Case.

At the heart of CSR is the concept of *stakeholder*, which is "any group or individual who can affect or is affected by the achievement of the organization's objectives."[3] Shown in Figure 12.1, while shareholders certainly are an important group of stakeholders, other stakeholders include managers, non-managerial employees (hereafter "employees"), suppliers, customers, communities, governments, and social and environmental groups. Since Chapter 11 has already dealt with shareholders at length, this chapter focuses on *non-shareholder stakeholders*, which we term

corporate social responsibility (CSR)

The social responsibility of corporations. It pertains to consideration of, and response to, issues beyond the narrow economic, technical, and legal requirements of the firm to accomplish social benefits along with the traditional economic gains that the firm seeks.

FIGURE 12.1 A Stakeholder View of the Firm

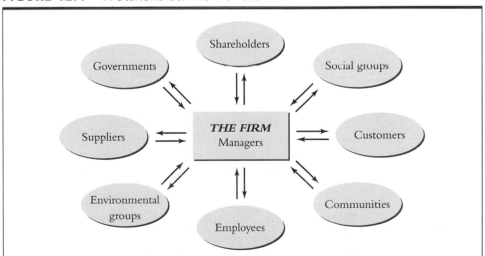

Source: Adapted from T. Donaldson & L. Preston, 1995, The stakeholder theory of the corporation: Concepts, evidence, and implications (p. 69), *Academy of Management Review*, 20: 65–91.

"stakeholders" here for compositional simplicity. A leading debate on CSR is whether managers' efforts to promote the interests of these stakeholders are at odds with their fiduciary duty (required by law) to safeguard shareholder interests.[4] To the extent that firms are *not* social agencies and that their primary function is to serve as economic enterprises, it is certainly true that firms should not (and are unable to) take on all the social problems of the world. Yet on the other hand, failing to heed to certain CSR imperatives may be self-defeating in the long run. Therefore, the key is how to strategize with CSR.

The remainder of this chapter introduces a stakeholder view of the firm and discusses a comprehensive model of CSR drawn from the strategy tripod. Debates and extensions then follow.

A Stakeholder View of the Firm

A Big Picture Perspective

global sustainability
The ability to meet the needs of the present without compromising the ability of future generations to meet their needs.

A stakeholder view of the firm, with a quest for global sustainability, represents a "big picture." A key goal for CSR is **global sustainability**, which is defined as the ability "to meet the needs of the present without compromising the ability of future generations to meet their needs."[5] It not only refers to a sustainable social and natural environment, but also sustainable capitalism (see the Closing Case).[6] Globally, at least three sets of drivers are related to the urgency of sustainability:

- Rising levels of population, poverty, and inequity associated with globalization call for new solutions. The repeated protests staged around the world are but tips of an iceberg of such sentiments.

- Compared with the relatively eroded power of national governments in the wake of globalization, nongovernmental organizations (NGOs) and other civil society stakeholders have increasingly assumed the role of monitor and in some cases enforcer of social and environmental standards.[7]

- Industrialization has created irreversible effects on the environment.[8] Global warming, pollution, soil erosion, and deforestation have become problems demanding solutions.[9]

Drivers underpinning global sustainability are complex and multidimensional. For multinational enterprises (MNEs) with operations spanning the globe, their CSR areas seem mind-boggling. This bewilderingly complex "big picture" forces managers to *prioritize*.[10] To be able to do that, primary and secondary stakeholders must be identified.

Primary and Secondary Stakeholder Groups

primary stakeholder groups
Constituents on which the firm relies for its continuous survival and prosperity.

Primary stakeholder groups are constituents the firm relies on for its continuous survival and prosperity. Shareholders, managers, employees, suppliers, customers—together with governments and communities whose laws and regulations must be obeyed and to whom taxes and other obligations may be due—are typically considered primary stakeholders.

Secondary stakeholder groups are defined as "those who influence or affect, or are influenced or affected by, the corporation, but they are not engaged in transactions with the corporation and are not essential for its survival."[11] Environmental groups (such as Greenpeace) often take it upon themselves to fight pollution. Fair labor practice groups (such as Fair Labor Association) frequently challenge firms that allegedly fail to provide decent labor conditions for employees. While the firm does not depend on secondary stakeholder groups for its survival, such groups may have the potential to cause significant embarrassment and damage—think of Nike in the 1990s.

A key proposition of the stakeholder view of the firm is that instead of only pursuing the economic bottom line, such as profits and shareholder returns, firms should pursue a more balanced set, called the triple bottom line. First introduced in Chapter 1, the triple bottom line consists of *economic*, *social*, and *environmental* performance.[12] To the extent that some competing demands obviously exist, it seems evident that the CSR proposition represents a dilemma. In fact, it has provoked a fundamental debate, which is introduced next.

A Fundamental Debate

The CSR debate centers on the nature of the firm in society. Why does the firm exist? Most people would intuitively answer: "To make money." Milton Friedman, a former University of Chicago economist and Nobel laureate, eloquently argued: "The business of business is business."[13] The idea that the firm is an economic enterprise seems uncontroversial. At issue is whether the firm is *only* an economic enterprise. Although Friedman passed away in 2006, his ideas continue to be influential.[14]

One side of the debate argues that "the social responsibility of business is to increase its profits," which is the title of Friedman's influential article mentioned earlier that was published in 1970. This free market school of thought draws upon Adam Smith's idea that pursuit of economic self-interest (within legal and ethical bounds) leads to efficient markets. Free market advocates believe that the first and foremost stakeholder group is shareholders, whose interests managers have a fiduciary duty to look after. To the extent that the hallmark of our economic system remains capitalism, the providers of capital—namely, capitalists or shareholders—deserve a commanding height in managerial attention. Since the 1980s, a term that explicitly places shareholders as the single most important stakeholder group, *shareholder capitalism*, has become increasingly influential around the world (see Chapter 11).

Free market advocates argue that if firms attempt to attain social goals, such as providing employment and social welfare, managers will lose their focus on profit maximization (and its derivative, shareholder value maximization). Consequently, firms may lose their character as capitalistic enterprises and become *socialist* organizations. This perception of socialist organization is not a pure argumentative point, but an accurate characterization of numerous state-owned enterprises (SOEs) throughout the pre-reform Soviet Union, Central and Eastern Europe, and China, as well as other developing countries in Africa, Asia, and Latin America. Privatization, in essence, is to remove the social function of these firms and restore their economic focus through private ownership (see Chapter 11). Overall, the free market school is influential around the world. It has also provided much of the intellectual underpinning for globalization spearheaded by MNEs.

It is against such a formidable and influential school of thought that the CSR movement has emerged. CSR advocates argue that a free market system that takes the pursuit of self-interest and profit as its guiding light—although in theory constrained by rules, contracts, and property rights—may in practice fail to constrain itself, thus often breeding greed, excesses, and abuses. Firms and managers, if left to their own devices, may choose self-interest over public interest. The financial meltdown in 2008–2009 is often fingered as a case in point. While not denying that shareholders are important stakeholders, CSR advocates argue that all stakeholders have an *equal* right to bargain for a "fair deal." Given stakeholders' often conflicting demands, the very purpose of the firm, instead of being a profit-maximizing entity, is argued to serve as a vehicle for coordinating their interests. Of course, a very thorny issue in the debate is whether all stakeholders indeed have an equal right and how to manage their (sometimes inevitable) conflicts.[15]

Starting in the 1970s as a peripheral voice in an ocean of free market believers, the CSR school of thought has slowly but surely made progress in becoming a more central part of strategy discussions.[16] Strategy guru Michael Porter has been vehemently advocating the importance of creating shared value, "which involves creating economic value in a way that also creates value for society by addressing its needs and challenges" (see Strategy in Action 12.1). The CSR school has two driving forces. First, even as free markets march around the world, the gap between the haves and have-nots has *widened*. Although many emerging economies have been growing by leaps and bounds, the per capita income gap between developed economies and much of the developing world has widened.[17] While 2% of the world's children living in America enjoy 50% of the world's toys, one-quarter of the children in Bangladesh and Nigeria are in their countries' work force. Even within developed economies such as the United States, the income gap between the upper and lower echelons of society has widened. In 1980, the average American CEO was paid 40 times more than the average worker. The ratio is now above 400. Although American society accepts a greater income inequality than many others do, aggregate data of such widening inequality, which both inform and numb, often serve as a stimulus for reforming the "leaner and meaner" capitalism. Participants in the Occupy Wall Street movement in 2011 argued that the 1% have gained at the expense of the 99%.[18] However, the response from free market advocates is that to the extent there is competition, there will always be *both* winners and losers. What CSR critics describe as "greed" is often translated as "incentive" in the vocabulary of free market advocates.

A second reason behind the rise of the CSR movement seems to be waves of disasters and scandals.[19] In 1989, the oil tanker *Exxon Valdez* spilled a tanker-load of oil in the pristine waters of Alaska. In 2002, scandals of Enron, WorldCom, Royal Ahold, and Parmalat rocked the world. In 2009, excessive amounts of Wall Street bonuses distributed by financial services firms receiving government bailout funds were criticized of being socially insensitive and irresponsible. In 2010, BP made a huge mess in the Gulf of Mexico. In 2011, a Japanese earthquake triggered the meltdown of the Fukushima nuclear power station. Not surprisingly, new disasters and scandals often propel CSR to the forefront of public policy and management discussions.

STRATEGY IN ACTION 12.1 〉   〉 ETHICAL DILEMMA

Michael Porter on Creating Shared Value

The capitalist system is under siege. In recent years business increasingly has been viewed as a major cause of social, environmental, and economic problems. Companies are widely perceived to be prospering at the expense of the broader community.

Even worse, the more business has begun to embrace CSR, the more it has been blamed for society's failures. The legitimacy of business has fallen to levels not seen in recent history. This diminished trust in business leads political leaders to set policies that undermine competitiveness and sap economic growth. Business is caught in a vicious circle.

A big part of the problem lies with companies themselves, which remain trapped in an outdated approach to value creation that has emerged over the past few decades. They continue to view value creation narrowly, optimizing short-term financial performance in a bubble while missing the most important customer needs and ignoring the broader influences that determine their long-term success. How else could companies overlook the well-being of customers, the depletion of natural resources vital to their businesses, the viability of key suppliers, or the economic distress of the communities in which they produce and sell? How else could companies think that simply shifting activities to locations with even lower wages was a sustainable "solution" to competitive challenge? Government and civil society have often exacerbated the problem by attempting to address social weaknesses at the expense of business. The presumed trade-offs between economic efficiency and social progress have been institutionalized in decades of policy choices.

Companies must take the lead in bringing business and society back together. The recognition is there among sophisticated business and thought leaders, and promising elements of a new model are emerging. Yet we still lack an overall framework for guiding these efforts, and most companies remain stuck in a "CSR" mind-set in which societal issues are at the periphery, not the core.

The solution lies in the principles of shared value, which involves creating economic value in a way that *also* creates value for society by addressing its needs and challenges. Businesses must reconnect company success with social progress. Shared value is not CSR, philanthropy, or even sustainability, but a new way to achieve economic success. It is not on the margin of what companies do but at the center. We believe that it can give rise to the next major transformation of business thinking.

A growing number of companies known for their hard-nosed approach to business—such as GE, Google, IBM, Intel, Johnson & Johnson, Nestlé, Unilever, and Wal-Mart—have already embarked on important efforts to create shared value by reconceiving the intersection between society and corporate performance. Yet our recognition of the transformative power of shared value is still in its genesis. Realizing it will require leaders and managers to develop new skills and knowledge—such as a far deeper appreciation of societal needs, a greater understanding of the true bases of company productivity, and the ability to collaborate across profit/nonprofit boundaries. Government must learn how to regulate in ways that enable shared value rather than work against it.

Capitalism is an unparalleled vehicle for meeting human needs, improving efficiency, creating jobs, and building wealth. But a narrow conception of capitalism has prevented business from harnessing its full potential to meet society's broader challenges. The opportunities have been there all along but have been overlooked. Businesses acting as businesses, not as charitable donors, are the most powerful force for addressing the pressing issues we face. The moment for a new conception of capitalism is now; society's needs are large and growing, while customers, employees, and a new generation of young people are asking business to step up.

The purpose of the corporation must be redefined as creating shared value, not just profit per se. This will drive the next wave of innovation and productivity growth in the global economy. It will also reshape capitalism and its relationship to society. Perhaps most important of all, learning how to create shared value is our best chance to legitimate business again.

Source: Excerpts from M. E. Porter & M. R. Kramer, 2011, Creating shared value, *Harvard Business Review*, January–February: 62–77. Michael Porter is a professor at Harvard Business School, and Mark Kramer is managing director of FSG, a global social impact consulting firm that he co-founded with Porter.

Overall, managers as a stakeholder group are unique in that they are the only group that is positioned at the center of all these relationships.[20] It is important to understand how they make decisions concerning CSR, as illustrated next.

A Comprehensive Model of Corporate Social Responsibility

While some people do not view CSR as an integral part of strategy, a comprehensive model of CSR drawn from the strategy tripod (Figure 12.2) shows that the three traditional perspectives on strategy can shed considerable light on CSR with relatively little adaptation and extension. This section articulates why this is the case.

Industry-Based Considerations

The industry-based view, exemplified by the five forces framework, can be extended to help understand the emerging competition on CSR.

RIVALRY AMONG COMPETITORS. The more concentrated an industry is, the more likely competitors will recognize their mutual interdependence based on old ways of doing business that are not up to the higher CSR standards (see Chapter 8). Under such circumstances, it is easier for incumbents to resist CSR pressures. For example, when facing mounting pressures to reduce emission levels, the automobile industry lobbied politicians, challenged the science of global climatic change, and pointed to the high costs of reducing emissions—until some first-mover firms deviated from such norms in order to score competitive points with game-changing new products such as the Nissan Leaf (see the Opening Case).

THREAT OF POTENTIAL ENTRY. How can incumbents raise entry barriers to deter potential entrants? Experience accumulated from being first movers in pollution control technologies can create entry barriers that favor incumbents. The two major types of pollution control technologies have their differences. The first is for more proactive *pollution prevention*. Like defects, pollution typically reveals flaws in product design or production. Pollution prevention technologies reduce or eliminate pollutants by using cleaner alternatives, often resulting in superior products (such as the Nissan Leaf in the Opening Case). The second pollution control area is more reactive, "end-of-pipe" *pollution reduction*, often added as a final step to capture pollutants prior to their

FIGURE 12.2 A Comprehensive Model of Corporate Social Responsibility

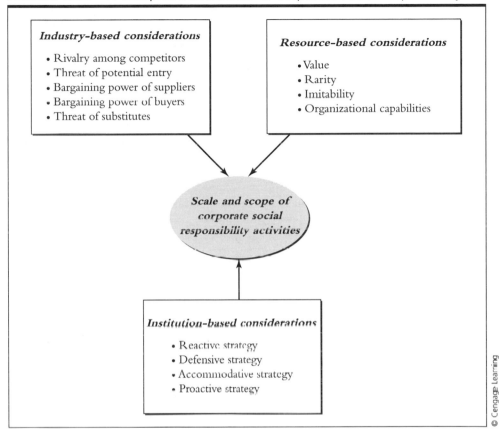

discharge. Their effectiveness is not equal. The technologies likely to give incumbents the most effective entry barrier are in the area of proactive pollution prevention.

BARGAINING POWER OF SUPPLIERS. If socially and environmentally conscious suppliers provide unique differentiated products with few or no substitutes, their bargaining power is likely to be substantial. For example, Coca-Cola is the sole provider of Coke syrup to its bottlers around the world, most of which are independently owned by franchisees. Coca-Cola is thus able to assert its bargaining power by requiring that all its bottlers certify that their social and environmental practices are responsible. Coca-Cola also encourages its bottlers to support social programs, such as financing start-up kiosks in South Africa and Vietnam, donating free drinks to earthquake victims in China and Japan, and promoting reading among school children in 42 countries, including the United States.

BARGAINING POWER OF BUYERS. By leveraging their bargaining power, individual and corporate buyers interested in CSR may extract substantial concessions from the focal firm. An example of the power of individual consumers is the controversy regarding Shell's 1995 decision to sink an oil platform in the North Sea. It led to strong protests organized by Greenpeace in Germany, which caused an 11% drop in Shell gas station sales in one month. Such pressures forced Shell to reverse its decision and dismantle the oil platform on shore at great cost.

An example of how corporate buyers extract concessions is the recent efforts made by Nike, which acted in response to criticisms for its failure to eradicate "sweatshops" throughout its supply chain. Although Nike does not own its supplier factories, Nike is able to enact a worldwide monitoring program for all supplier factories, using both internal and third-party auditors. For "clean" contractors that have never engaged in "sweatshop" practices, this simply adds a ton of work such as documentation and hosting of auditors as well as extra costs. For "sweatshop" operators, this requires some fundamental and costly change to the way they do business. Not surprisingly both groups initially resisted Nike's efforts. Nevertheless, Nike has been able to "just do it" by throwing its weight around.

Finally, buyers can increase bargaining power when they are in great difficulties. Dying HIV/AIDS patients in Africa, Asia, and Latin America, backed by their governments and CSR groups, often demand that pharmaceutical firms headquartered in rich developed economies (1) donate free drugs, (2) lower drug prices, and (3) release patents to allow for local manufacturing of cheaper generic versions of the same drugs. While pharmaceutical firms have resisted these attempts, they may eventually give in.

THREAT OF SUBSTITUTES. If substitutes are superior to existing products and costs are reasonable, they may attract more customers. For example, wind power, which is much more environmentally friendly than fossil-fuel sources of power (such as oil and coal) and safer than nuclear power, may have great potential. It is true that at present, wind power requires heavy government subsidies in order to become commercially viable. However, its future is likely to be promising, given the increasing depletion of fossil fuel, the skyrocketing oil prices, and the growing awareness of the risks associated with conventional technologies (such as the risk of terrorism at nuclear power plants). Overall, the possible threat of substitutes requires firms to vigilantly scan the larger environment, instead of narrowly focusing on the focal industry.

TURNING THREATS TO OPPORTUNITIES. Taken together, the five forces framework suggests two lessons. First, it reinforces the important point that not all industries are equal in terms of their exposure to CSR challenges. Energy- and materials-intensive industries (such as chemicals) are more vulnerable to environmental scrutiny. Labor-intensive industries (such as apparel) are more likely to be challenged on fair labor practice grounds. However, despite varying degrees of exposure, no industry may be completely immune from CSR. Table 12.2 shows the widening list of industries challenged by environmentalists, one of the core CSR groups, over the past four decades.

Given the increasingly inescapable responsibility to be good corporate citizens, the second lesson is that industries and firms may want to selectively but proactively turn some of these threats into opportunities. For example, instead of treating NGOs as threats, Dow Chemical, Home Depot, Lowe's, and Unilever work with them. Many managers

TABLE 12.2 Industries Challenged by Environmentalists

1960s	1970s	1980s	1990s
Coal mining and pollution	Aerosols	Aerosols	Aerosols
Detergents	Airports	Agriculture	Agriculture
Mining	Asbestos	Airports	Air conditioning
Pesticides	Automobiles	Animal testing	Airlines and airports
Water (dams)	Biotechnology	Automobiles	Animal testing
	Chemicals	Biotechnology	Armaments
	Coal mining and pollution	Chemicals	Automobiles
	Deep sea fishing	Coal mining and pollution	Banking
	Detergents	Computers	Biotechnology
	Heavy trucks	Deep sea fishing	Catering
	Metals	Detergents	Chemicals
	Nuclear power	Fertilizers	Coal mining and pollution
	Oil tankers	Forestry	Computers
	Packaging	Incineration	Detergents
	Passenger jets	Insurance	Dry cleaning
	Pesticides	Landfill	Electricity supply
	Pulp mills	Nuclear power	Electrical equipment
	Tobacco	Oil tankers	Fashion
	Toxic waste	Onshore oil and gas	Fertilizers
	Transport	Packaging	Fish farming
	Water	Paints	Fishing
	Whaling	Pesticides	Forestry
		Plastics	Incineration
		Pulp and paper	Insurance
		Refrigeration	Landfill
		Supermarkets	Meat processing
		Tobacco	Mining
		Toxic waste	Motorways
		Tropical hardwoods	Nuclear power
		Tuna fishing	Office supplies
		Water	Oil tankers
		Whaling	Onshore oil and gas
			Packaging
			Paints
			Pesticides
			Plastics
			Property
			Pulp and paper
			Refrigeration
			Shipping
			Supermarkets
			Textiles
			Tobacco
			Tourism
			Toxic waste
			Transport
			Tropical hardwoods
			Tires
			Water

Sources: Adapted from J. Elkington, 1994, Towards the sustainable corporation: Win-win-win business strategies for sustainable development (p. 95), *California Management Review,* winter: 90–100.

traditionally treat CSR as a nuisance, involving heavy regulation, added costs, and unwelcome liability. Such an attitude may underestimate strategic business opportunities associated with CSR. The most proactive managers and the companies they lead (such as Nissan in the Opening Case, Whole Foods in the Closing Case, and Dow Chemical in Emerging Markets 12.1) are far-sighted enough to embrace CSR challenges through selective but preemptive investments and sustained engagement—in essence, making their CSR activities a source of *differentiation*, as opposed to an additional item of cost.

Resource-Based Considerations

CSR-related resources can include *tangible* technologies and processes as well as *intangible* skills and attitudes.[21] The VRIO framework can shed considerable light on CSR.

VALUE. Do CSR-related resources and capabilities add *value*? This is the litmus test for CSR work (see Strategy in Action 12.1). Many large firms, especially MNEs, can apply their tremendous financial, technological, and human resources toward a variety of CSR causes. For example, firms can choose to appease environmental groups by purchasing energy only from power plants utilizing green sources, such as wind-generated power. Or firms can respond to human rights groups by not doing business in or with countries accused of human rights violations. These activities can be categorized as **social issue participation**, which refers to a firm's participation in social causes not directly related to the management of its primary stakeholders. Research suggests that these activities may actually *reduce* shareholder value.[22] Overall, although social issue participation may create some remote social and environmental value, it does not satisfy the economic leg of the triple bottom line, so these abilities do not qualify as value-adding firm resources.

social issue participation
Firms' participation in social causes not directly related to managing primary stakeholders.

RARITY. CSR-related resources are not always *rare*. Remember that even a valuable resource is not likely to provide a significant advantage if competitors also possess it. For example, both Home Depot and Lowe's have NGOs such as the Forest Stewardship Council certify that suppliers in Brazil, Indonesia, and Malaysia use only material from renewable forests. These complex processes require strong management capabilities such as negotiating with local suppliers, undertaking internal verification, coordinating with NGOs for external verification, and disseminating such information to stakeholders. Such capabilities are valuable. But since both competitors possess capabilities to manage these processes, they are common (but not rare) resources.

IMITABILITY. Although valuable and rare resources may provide some competitive advantage, the advantage will only be temporary if competitors can *imitate* it. Resources must be not only valuable and rare but also hard to imitate in order to give firms a sustainable (not merely temporary) competitive advantage. At some firms, CSR-related capabilities are deeply embedded in idiosyncratic managerial and employee skills, attitudes, and interpretations. The socially complex way of channeling their energy and conviction toward CSR at Whole Foods, led by John Mackey, a guru on conscious capitalism, cannot be easily imitated (see the Closing Case).

ORGANIZATION. Does the firm have *organizational* capabilities to do a good job on CSR? Is the firm organized to exploit the full potential of CSR? Numerous components within a firm, such as formal management control systems and informal relationships between managers and employees, may be relevant. These components are often called complementary assets (see Chapter 3), because, by themselves, they typically do not generate advantage. However, complementary assets, when combined with valuable, rare, and hard-to-imitate capabilities, may enable a firm to fully utilize its CSR potential.

For example, assume that Firm A is able to overcome the three hurdles mentioned above (V, R, I) by achieving a comprehensive understanding of some competitors' best practices in pollution prevention. Although Firm A has every intention to implement such best practices, chances are that they may not work unless Firm A also possesses a number of complementary assets. Process-focused best practices of pollution prevention are not in isolation and are often difficult to separate from a firm's other activities. These best practices require a number of complementary assets, such as a continuous emphasis on process innovation and a dedicated workforce. These complementary assets are not developed as part of new environmental strategies; rather, they are grown from more general business strategies, such as differentiation. If such complementary assets are already in place, they can be leveraged in the new pursuit of best environmental practices. Otherwise, single-minded imitation is not likely to be effective.

THE CSR-ECONOMIC PERFORMANCE PUZZLE. The resource-based view helps solve a major puzzle in the CSR debate: the CSR economic performance puzzle. The puzzle—a source of frustration to CSR advocates—is why there is no conclusive evidence on a direct, positive link between CSR and *economic* performance such as profits and shareholder returns. Although some studies do indeed report a *positive* relationship,[23] others find a *negative* relationship[24] or *no* relationship.[25] Viewed together, "CSR does not hurt [economic] performance, but there is no concrete support to believe that it leads to supranormal [economic] returns."[26] While there can be a number of explanations for this intriguing mess, a resource-based explanation suggests that because of the capability constraints discussed above, many firms are not cut out for a CSR-intensive (differentiation) strategy.[27] Since all studies have some sampling bias (no study is perfect), studies that over-sample firms not yet ready for a high level of CSR activities are likely to report a negative relationship between CSR and economic performance. Likewise, studies that over-sample firms ready for CSR may find a positive relationship. Also, studies with more balanced (more random) samples may fail to find any statistically significant relationship. In summary, since each firm is different (a basic assumption of the resource-based view), not every firm's economic performance is likely to benefit from CSR.

Institution-Based Considerations

The institution-based view sheds considerable light on the gradual diffusion of the CSR movement and the strategic responses of firms.[28] At the most fundamental level, regulatory pressures underpin *formal* institutions, whereas normative and cognitive pressures support *informal* institutions.[29] The strategic response framework consists of (1) reactive,

TABLE 12.3 The US Chemical Industry Responds to Environmental Pressures

PHASE	STRATEGIC RESPONSE	REPRESENTATIVE STATEMENTS FROM THE INDUSTRY'S TRADE JOURNAL, *CHEMICAL WEEK*
1962–70	Reactive	Denied the severity of environmental problems and argued that these problems could be solved independently through the industry's technological prowess.
1971–82	Defensive	"Congress seems determined to add one more regulation to the already 27 health and safety regulations we must answer to. This will make the EPA [Environmental Protection Agency] a chemical czar. No agency in a democracy should have that authority" (1975).
1983–88	Accommodative	"The EPA has been criticized for going too slow … Still, we think that it is doing a good job" (1982). "Critics expect an overnight fix. The EPA deserves credit for its pace and accomplishments" (1982).
1989–present	Proactive	"Green line equals bottom line—The Clean Air Act (CAA) equals efficiency. Everything you hear about the 'costs' of complying with the CAA is probably wrong … Wiser competitors will rush to exploit the Green Revolution" (1990).

Sources: Extracted from text from A. Hoffman, 1999, Institutional evolution and change: Environmentalism and the US chemical industry, *Academy of Management Journal*, 42: 351–371. Hoffman's last phase ended in 1993; its extension to the present is done by the present author.

(2) defensive, (3) accommodative, and (4) proactive strategies, as first introduced in Chapter 4 (see Table 4.5). This framework can be extended to explore how firms make CSR decisions, as illustrated in Table 12.3.

reactive strategy
A strategy that is passive about corporate social responsibility. Firms do not act in the absence of disasters and outcries. When problems arise, denial is usually the first line of defense.

A **reactive strategy** is indicated by relatively little or no support by top management of CSR causes. Firms do not feel compelled to act in the absence of disasters and outcries. Even when problems arise, denial is usually the first line of defense. Put another way, the need to accept some CSR is neither internalized through cognitive beliefs nor does it result in any norms in practice. That leaves only formal regulatory pressures to compel firms to comply. For example, in the United States, food and drug safety standards that we take for granted today were fought by food and drug companies in the first half of the 20th century. The basic idea that food and drugs should be tested before being sold to customers and patients was bitterly contested even as unsafe foods and drugs killed thousands of people. As a result, the Food and Drug Administration (FDA) was progressively granted more powers. This era is not necessarily over. Today, many dietary supplement makers, whose products are beyond the FDA's regulatory reach, continue to sell untested supplements and deny responsibility.

defensive strategy
A strategy that is defensive in nature. Firms admit responsibility, but often fight it.

A **defensive strategy** focuses on regulatory compliance. Top management involvement is piecemeal at best, and the general attitude is that CSR is an added cost or nuisance. Firms admit responsibility but often fight it. After the establishment of the Environmental Protection Agency (EPA) in 1970, the US chemical industry resisted the EPA's intrusion (see Table 12.3). The regulatory requirements were at significant odds with the norms and cognitive beliefs held by the industry at that time.

How do various institutional pressures change firm behavior? In the absence of informal normative and cognitive beliefs, formal regulatory pressures are the only feasible way to push firms ahead. A key insight of the institution-based view is that individuals and organizations make *rational* choices given the right kind of incentives. For example, one efficient way to control pollution is to make polluters pay some "green" taxes—ranging from gasoline retail taxes to landfill charges. But how demanding these regulatory pressures should be remains controversial. One side of the debate argues that tough environmental regulation may lead to higher costs and reduced competitiveness, especially when competing with foreign rivals not subject to such demanding regulations. Others argue, however, that "green" taxes simply force firms to pay real costs that they otherwise place on others. If a firm pollutes, it is imposing a cost on the surrounding community that must either live with the pollution or pay to clean it up. By imposing a pollution tax that roughly equals the cost to the community, the firm has to account for pollution as a real cost. Economists refer to this as "internalizing an externality."

CSR advocates, endorsed by former vice president and Nobel laureate Al Gore, further argue that stringent environmental regulation may force firms to innovate, however reluctantly, thus benefiting the competitiveness of both the industry and country.[30] For example, a Japanese law set standards to make products easier to disassemble. Although Hitachi initially resisted the law, it responded by redesigning products to simplify disassembly. The company reduced the parts in its washing machines by 16% and in vacuum cleaners by 30%. The products became not only easier to disassemble but also easier and cheaper to *assemble* in the first place, thus providing Hitachi with a significant cost advantage.

accommodative strategy
A strategy that tries to accommodate corporate social responsibility considerations into decision making.

The **accommodative strategy** is characterized by some support from top managers, who may increasingly view CSR as a worthwhile endeavor. Since formal regulations may be in place and informal social and environmental pressures may be increasing, a number of firms themselves may be concerned about CSR, leading to the emergence of some new industry norms. Further, new managers who are passionate about or sympathetic toward CSR causes may join the organization, or some traditional managers may change their outlook, leading to increasingly strong cognitive beliefs that CSR is the right thing to do. In other words, from both normative and cognitive standpoints, it becomes legitimate or a matter of social obligation to accept responsibility and do all that is required.[31] For example, in the US chemical industry, such a transformation probably took place in the early 1980s (see Table 12.3). More recently, Burger King, Kraft, Nestlé, and Unilever were pressured by Greenpeace to be concerned about the deforestation practices undertaken by their major palm oil supplier Sinar Mas in Indonesia. Eventually, the food giants accommodated Greenpeace's demands and dumped Sinar Mars as a supplier, leading to a new industry norm that is more earth-friendly.[32]

Adopting a code of conduct is a tangible indication of a firm's willingness to accept CSR. A code of conduct (sometimes called a code of ethics) is a set of written policies and standards outlining the proper practices for a firm. The global diffusion of codes of conduct is subject to intense debate. First, some argue that firms adopting these codes may not necessarily be sincere. This *negative* view suggests that an apparent interest in CSR may simply be window dressing. Some firms feel compelled to appear sensitive to CSR, following what others are doing, but have not truly and genuinely internalized CSR concerns.[33] For example, in 2009, BP implemented a new safety-oriented operating management system.[34] But after the 2010 oil spill, it became apparent that this system had not been seriously implemented, and the result was a huge catastrophe. Second, an *instrumental* view suggests that CSR activities simply represent a useful instrument to make good profits.[35] Firms are not necessarily becoming more ethical. For example, after the 2010 oil spill, BP reshuffled management and created a new worldwide safety division. The instrumental view would argue that these actions did not really mean that BP became more ethical. Finally, a *positive* view believes that (at least some) firms and managers may be self-motivated to do it right regardless of social pressures.[36] Codes of conduct tangibly express values that organizational members view as central and enduring.

The institution-based view suggests that all three perspectives are probably valid. This is to be expected given how institutional pressures work to instill value. Regardless of actual motive, the fact that firms are practicing CSR is indicative of the rising *legitimacy* of CSR on the management agenda.[37] Even firms that adopt a code of conduct simply as window dressing open doors for more scrutiny by concerned stakeholders because they have publicized a set of CSR criteria against which they can be judged. Such pressures are likely to transform the firms internally into more self-motivated, better corporate citizens. Thus, it probably is fair to say that Nike is a more responsible corporate citizen in 2014 than it was in 1994.

proactive strategy

A strategy that focuses on proactive engagement in corporate social responsibility.

From a CSR perspective, the best firms embrace a **proactive strategy** when engaging in CSR, constantly anticipating responsibility and endeavoring to do more than is required.[38] Top management at a proactive firm not only supports and champions CSR activities, but also views CSR as a source of differentiation that permeates throughout the corporate DNA. For example, Whole Foods' co-founder and co-CEO John Mackey commented (see the Closing Case for details):

> *When people are really happy in their jobs, they provide much higher degrees of service to the customers. Happy team members result in happy customers. Happy customers do more business with you. They become advocates for your enterprise, which results in happy investors. That is a win, win, win, win strategy. You can expand it to include your suppliers and the communities where you do business, which are tied in to this prosperity circle.*

Similarly, Starbucks since 2001 has voluntarily published an annual report on CSR, which embodies its founder, chairman, and CEO Howard Schultz's vision that "we must balance our responsibility to create value for shareholders with a social conscience."[39]

Proactive firms often engage in three areas of activity. First, some firms such as Swiss Re and Duke Energy actively participate in regional, national, and international policy and standards discussions.[40] To the extent that policy and standards discussions today may become regulations in the future, it seems better to get involved early and (hopefully) steer the course toward a favorable direction. Otherwise—as the saying goes—if you're not at the table, you're on the menu. For example, Duke Energy operates 20 coal-fired power plants in five states. It is the third largest US emitter of CO_2 and the 12th largest in the world. But its CEO Jim Rogers has proactively worked with green technology producers, activists, and politicians to engage in policy and legislative discussions. These are not merely defensive moves to protect his firm and the power utility industry. Unlike his industry peers, Rogers has been "bitten by the climate bug" and is genuinely interested in reducing greenhouse gas emissions.[41]

Second, proactive firms often build alliances with stakeholder groups. For example, many firms collaborate with NGOs.[42] Because of the historical tension and distrust, these "sleeping-with-the-enemy" alliances are not easy to handle. The key lies in identifying relatively short-term, manageable projects of mutual interests. For instance, Starbucks collaborated with Conservation International to help reduce deforestation practices.

Third, proactive firms often engage in *voluntary* activities that go beyond what is required by regulations.[43] While examples of industry-specific self-regulation abound, an area of intense global interest is the pursuit of the International Standards Organization (ISO) 14001 certification of the environment management system (EMS). Headquartered in Switzerland, the ISO is an influential NGO consisting of national standards bodies in 111 countries. Launched in 1996, the ISO 14001 EMS has become the gold standard for CSR-conscious firms. Although not required by law, many MNEs, such as Ford and IBM, have adopted ISO 14001 standards in all their facilities worldwide. Firms such as Toyota, Siemens, and General Motors have demanded that all of their top-tier suppliers be ISO 14001 certified.

From an institutional perspective, these proactive activities are indicative of the normative and cognitive beliefs held by many managers on the importance of doing the right thing.[44] While there is probably a certain element of window dressing and a quest for better profits, it is obvious that these efforts provide some tangible social and environmental benefits.

MAKING STRATEGIC CHOICES. The typology of (1) reactive, (2) defensive, (3) accommodative, and (4) proactive strategies is an interesting menu provided for different firms to choose from. At present, the number of proactive firms is still a minority. While many firms are compelled to do something, a lot of CSR activities probably are still window dressing. Only sustained pressures along regulatory, normative, and cognitive dimensions may push and pull more firms to do more. After publicizing its corporate-wide CSR plan for one year, British retailer Marks & Spencer (M&S) reported interesting data on the distribution of its consumers and employees along these four dimensions (Table 12.4). Since

TABLE 12.4 Distribution of Marks & Spencer's Consumers and Employees

CONCEPTUAL CATEGORY	M&S'S LABEL	PERCENTAGE OF CONSUMERS	PERCENTAGE OF EMPLOYEES
Reactive	"Not my problem"	24%	1%
Defensive	"What's the point"	38%	21%
Accommodative	"If it's easy"	27%	54%
Proactive	"Green crusaders"	11%	24%

Source: Based on text in Marks & Spencer, 2008, *Plan A: Year 1 Review* (p. 16), January 15, plana. marksandspencer.com.

CSR cannot be embarked upon in a vacuum, a firm's particular strategy needs to have some alignment with the CSR propensity of its consumers, employees, and other stakeholders. In other words, it is not realistic to implement a proactive strategy when the firm has numerous reactive employees and consumers.

Debates and Extensions

Without exaggeration, the entire subject of CSR is about debates. It is not far-fetched to suggest that there is a big debate between this chapter (focusing on stakeholder capitalism) and Chapter 11 (focusing on shareholder capitalism). Here, we discuss three recent, previously unexplored debates particularly relevant for international operations: (1) domestic versus overseas social responsibility, (2) active versus inactive CSR engagement overseas, and (3) race to the bottom ("pollution haven") versus race to the top.

Domestic versus Overseas Social Responsibility

Given that corporate resources are limited, devoting resources to overseas CSR often means fewer resources left to devote to domestic CSR. Consider two *primary* stakeholder groups: domestic employees and communities. Expanding overseas, especially toward emerging economies, may not only increase corporate profits and shareholder returns, but also provide employment to host countries and develop these economies at the "base of the pyramid," all of which have noble CSR dimensions (see Chapter 1). However, this is often done at the expense of domestic employees and communities. One can vividly appreciate the devastation of job losses on such employees and communities by watching the 1998 movie *The Full Monty*. The movie takes place in Sheffield, England, the former steel capital of Europe and the world. In the movie, the local economy has been so decimated by plant closures that laid-off steel mill workers eventually take up an "alternative" line of work (male strip dancing). To prevent such a possible fate, in the 2000s, DaimlerChrysler's German unions had to scrap a 3% pay raise and endure an 11% increase in work hours (from 35 to 39 hours) with no extra pay in exchange for promises that 6,000 jobs would be kept in Germany for eight years—otherwise, their jobs would go to the Czech Republic, Poland, and South Africa. However, such labor deals will probably only slow down, not stop, the outgoing tide of jobs from developed economies. The wage differentials are just too great.[45]

To the extent that few (or no) laid-off German employees would move to the neighboring Czech Republic and Poland to seek work (and forget about moving to China, India, or South Africa), most of them end up being social welfare recipients in Germany. Thus, one may argue that MNEs shirk their CSR by increasing the social burdens of their home countries. Executives making these decisions are often criticized by the media, unions, and politicians. However, from a corporate governance perspective, especially the "shareholder capitalism" variant, MNEs are doing nothing wrong by maximizing shareholder returns (see Chapter 11).

Although framed in a domestic versus overseas context, the heart of this debate boils down to a fundamental point that frustrates CSR advocates: In a capitalist society, it is shareholders (otherwise known as *capitalists*) who matter at the end of the day. According to Jack Welch, GE's former chairman and CEO:

> *Unions, politicians, activists—companies face a Babel of interests. But there's only one owner. A company is for its shareholders. They own it. They control it. That's the way it is, and the way it should be.*[46]

When firms have enough resources, it would be nice to take care of domestic employees and communities. However, when confronted with relentless pressures for cost cutting and restructuring, managers have to prioritize. Given the lack of a clear solution, this politically explosive debate is likely to heat up in the years to come.

Active versus Inactive CSR Engagement Overseas

Active CSR engagement is now increasingly expected of MNEs.[47] MNEs that fail to do so are often criticized by NGOs. In the 1990s, Shell was harshly criticized for "not lifting a finger" when the Nigerian government brutally cracked down on rebels in the Ogoni region where Shell operated. In 2009 Shell settled a long-running case brought by Ogoni activists with $15.5 million.[48] However, such well-intentioned calls for greater CSR engagement are in direct conflict with a long-standing principle governing the relationship between MNEs and host countries: *non*-intervention in local affairs.

The non-intervention principle originated from concerns that MNEs may engage in political activities against the national interests of the host country. Chile in the 1970s serves as a case in point. After the democratically elected socialist President Salvador Allende had threatened to expropriate the assets of MNEs, ITT (a US-based MNE), allegedly in connection with the Central Intelligence Agency (CIA), promoted a coup that killed President Allende. Consequently, the idea that MNEs should not interfere in the domestic political affairs of the host country has been enshrined in a number of codes of MNE conduct sponsored by international organizations such as the United Nations (UN).

However, CSR advocates have been emboldened by some MNEs' actions during the apartheid era in South Africa, when local laws required racial segregation of the workforce. While many MNEs withdrew, those that remained (such as BP) challenged the apartheid system by desegregating their employees and thus undermining the government's base of power. Emboldened by the successful removal of the apartheid regime in South Africa in 1994, CSR advocates have unleashed a new campaign, stressing the necessity for MNEs to engage in actions that often constitute political activity, in particular in the human rights area. Shell, after its widely criticized (lack of) action in Nigeria, has explicitly endorsed the UN Declaration on Human Rights and supported the exercise of such rights "within the legitimate role of business."

But what exactly is the "legitimate role" of CSR initiatives in host countries? In almost every country, there are local laws and norms that some foreign MNEs may find objectionable. In Estonia, ethnic Russians are being discriminated against. In many Arab countries, women do not have the same legal rights as men. In the United States, a number of groups (ranging from Native Americans to homosexuals) claim to be discriminated against. At the heart of this debate is whether foreign MNEs should spearhead efforts to remove some of these discriminatory practices or should remain politically neutral by conforming to current host country laws and norms. This obviously is a nontrivial challenge.

Race to the Bottom ("Pollution Haven") versus Race to the Top

One side of this debate argues that because of heavier environmental regulation in developed economies, MNEs may have an incentive to shift pollution-intensive production to developing countries with lower environmental standards. To attract investment, developing countries may enter a "race to the bottom" by lowering (or at least not tightening) environmental standards and some may become "pollution havens."

The other side argues that globalization does not necessarily have negative effects on the environment in developing countries to the extent suggested by the "pollution haven" hypothesis. This is largely due to many MNEs' *voluntary* adherence to environmental standards higher than those required by host countries.[49] Most MNEs reportedly outperform local firms in environmental management. The underlying motivations behind MNEs' voluntary "green practices" can be attributed to (1) worldwide CSR pressures in general, (2) CSR demands made by customers in developed economies, and (3) requirements of MNE headquarters for worldwide compliance of higher CSR standards (such as ISO 14001). Although it is difficult to suggest that the "race to the bottom" does not exist, MNEs as a group do not necessarily add to the environmental burden in developing countries.[50] Some MNEs, such as Dow, may facilitate the diffusion of better environmental technologies to these countries (see Emerging Markets 12.1).

The Savvy Strategist

Concerning CSR, the strategy tripod suggests three clear implications for action (Table 12.5). First, the industry-based view points out that while managers in certain industries may have stronger CSR challenges, savvy managers in all industries need to be prepared to confront these challenges. Given the increasingly inescapable responsibility to be good corporate citizens, managers may want to integrate CSR as part of the core activities of the firm—instead of "faking it" and making cosmetic changes. Many managers traditionally treat CSR as a nuisance, involving regulation, added costs, and liability. Such an attitude may underestimate potential business opportunities associated with CSR. Table 12.6 outlines some suggestions made by Porter (see Strategy in Action 12.1), and the Closing Case illustrates an exemplary firm.

Second, savvy managers need to pick CSR battles carefully. The resource-based view suggests an important lesson, which is captured by Sun Tzu's timeless teaching: "Know yourself, know your opponents." While your opponents may engage in high-profile CSR activities that allow them to earn bragging rights while contributing to their triple bottom line, blindly imitating these practices, while not knowing enough about "yourself" (you as a manager and the firm/unit you lead), may lead to some disappointment. Instead of

TABLE 12.5 Strategic Implications for Action

- Integrate CSR as part of the core activities and processes of the firm—faking it doesn't last very long.
- Understand the rules of the game, anticipate changes, and seek to shape and influence such changes.
- Pick your CSR battles carefully—don't blindly imitate other firms' CSR activities.

EMERGING MARKETS 12.1

Dow Chemical Company in China

Dow Chemical Company is a leading US-based MNE that has a presence in more than 175 countries. Dow has paid considerable attention to CSR. Since 1999, it has advocated the Guiding Principles of Responsible Care, a voluntary initiative within the chemical industry to safely handle its products from inception to ultimate disposal.

China naturally has become an increasingly important market for Dow. However, beyond Dow's immediate market reach, the general deterioration of the environment in China, an unfortunate byproduct of the strong economic growth, is visible and getting worse. For example, on a "sunny" day, pedestrians in Beijing have a hard time seeing through the smog to actually see the sun. As a result, China's leadership is putting increasing focus on environmental sustainability as a key national policy.

Aspiring to serve as a multinational role model fully aligned with Dow's own CSR commitment and with the government's concern to reduce pollution, Dow partnered with the State Environmental Protection Administration (SEPA) of China to launch a SEPA-Dow National Cleaner Production Pilot Project in 2005. Dow agreed to contribute $750,000 over the first three years. Cleaner Production is the continuous application of an integrated preventive environmental strategy to processes, products, and services to increase efficiency and reduce risks and possible damage to humans and the environment. The Pilot Project has focused on training local environmental protection agencies and officials as well as managers at

small and medium-sized enterprises (SMEs), a category of firms in China that, on average, tend to be less professional and more reckless in environmental management.

In the Pilot Project's first year, 19 SMEs in the chemical, dyeing, electronics, brewery, and food industries participated. The Project generated a combined reduction of waste water by 3.3 million cubic meters, of exhaust gas emissions by 554 tons, and of solid waste by 487 tons. This resulted in 538 cleaner production measures and an annual economic profit of approximately $130,000 for the 19 participating firms. Overall, these achievements, in Dow's own words, "confirm Dow's belief that Cleaner Production not only reduces waste in the production processes, it also increases the efficiency of energy resources and ultimately improves competitiveness of enterprises." Further, Dow intends to diffuse such "best practices" in China and beyond.

Sources: Based on (1) *China Business Review*, 2007, Dow partners with China's SEPA, May–June: 17; (2) Dow, 2006, SEPA-Dow Cleaner Production National Pilot Project achieves strong start and outstanding results, news.dow.com; (3) E. Economy & K. Lieberthal, 2007, Scorched earth: Will environmental risk in China overwhelm its opportunities, *Harvard Business Review*, June: 88–96; (4) M. W. Peng, 2011, *Global Business*, 2nd ed. (p. 568), Cincinnati: South-Western Cengage Learning.

always chasing the newest best practices, firms are advised to select CSR practices that fit with their *existing* resources, capabilities, and especially complementary assets.

Third, savvy managers need to understand the formal and informal rules of the game, anticipate changes, and seek to shape such changes. Although the US government refused to ratify the 1997 Kyoto Protocol and only signed the nonbinding 2009 Copenhagen Accord, many US firms (such as Duke Energy) voluntarily participate in CSR activities not (yet) mandated by law, in anticipation of more stringent environmental requirements down the road.

TABLE 12.6 From Corporate Social Responsibility to Creating Shared Value

(RELATIVELY ISOLATED) CORPORATE SOCIAL RESPONSIBILITY	CREATING SOCIAL VALUE (VIA ECONOMIC VALUE CREATION)
Value: Doing good	Value: Economic and societal benefits relative to cost
Citizenship, philanthropy, and sustainability	Joint company and community value creation
Discretionary or in response to external pressure	Integral to competing
Separate from profit maximization	Integral to profit maximization
Agenda is determined by personal preferences	Agenda is company specific and internally generated
Impact limited by corporate footprint and CSR budget	Realigns the entire company budget

Source: Adapted from M. E. Porter & M. R. Kramer, 2011, Creating shared value (p. 76), *Harvard Business Review*, January–February: 62–77. For details, see Strategy in Action 12.1 for an excerpt of this article.

For current and would-be strategists, this chapter has clearly shown that from a CSR perspective, we can revisit the four fundamental questions. First, why do firms differ in CSR activities? Firm differences can be found in (1) industry structures, (2) resource repertoire, and (3) formal and informal institutional pressures. Second, how do firms behave in the CSR arena? Some are reactive and defensive, others are accommodative, and still others are proactive. Third, what determines a firm's CSR scope? While industry structures, resource bases, and formal institutional pressures are likely to ensure some minimal involvement, firms with a broad range of CSR engagements are likely to be characterized by a large percentage of managers and employees who intrinsically feel the need to "do it right" (see Table 12.4). In other words, it fundamentally boils down to differences in informal normative and cognitive beliefs held by managers and employees. Finally, what determines the success and failure of firms around the world? No doubt, CSR will increasingly become an important part of the answer. The best performing firms are likely to be those that can integrate CSR activities into the core economic functions of the firm while addressing social and environmental concerns.

The globally ambiguous and different CSR standards, norms, and expectations make many managers uncomfortable. Many managers continue to relegate CSR to the "back burner." However, this does not seem to be the right attitude for current and would-be strategists who are studying this book—that is, *you.* It is important to note that we live in a dangerous period of global capitalism. In the post–Great Recession and post–Occupy Wall Street world, managers, as a unique group of stakeholders, have an important and challenging responsibility to safeguard and advance capitalism (see Strategy in Action 12.1 and the Closing Case). From a CSR standpoint, this means building more humane, more inclusive, and fairer firms that not only generate wealth and develop economies, but also respond to changing societal expectations concerning the social and environmental role of the firm around the world.[51]

CHAPTER SUMMARY

1. **Articulate what a stakeholder view of the firm is**
   - A stakeholder view of the firm urges companies to pursue a more balanced triple bottom line, consisting of economic, social, and environmental performance.
   - Despite the fierce defense of the free market school, especially its shareholder capitalism variant, the CSR movement has now become a more central part of strategy discussions around the globe.

2. **Develop a comprehensive model of CSR**
   - The industry-based view argues that the nature of different industries drives different CSR strategies.
   - The resource-based view posits that not all CSR activities satisfy the VRIO requirements.
   - The institution-based view suggests that when confronting CSR pressures, firms may employ (1) reactive, (2) defensive, (3) accommodative, and (4) proactive strategies.

3. **Participate in three leading debates concerning CSR**
   - (1) Domestic versus overseas social responsibility, (2) active versus inactive CSR engagement overseas, and (3) race to the bottom versus race to the top.

4. **Draw strategic implications for action**
   - Integrate CSR as part of the core activities and processes of the firm.
   - Pick your CSR battles carefully—don't blindly imitate other firms' CSR activities.
   - Understand the rules of the game, anticipate changes, and seek to influence such changes.

KEY TERMS

Accommodative strategy p. 375

Corporate social responsibility (CSR) p. 363

Defensive strategy p. 374

Global sustainability p. 364

Primary stakeholder groups p. 364

Proactive strategy p. 376

Reactive strategy p. 374

Secondary stakeholder groups p. 365

Social issue participation p. 372

CRITICAL DISCUSSION QUESTIONS

1. **ON ETHICS:** Between the two opposing views (CSR does not create value versus CSR can create value), which view do you support? Why?

2. **ON ETHICS:** Your CPA firm is organizing a one-day-long CSR activity using company time, such as cleaning up a dirty road or picking up trash on the beach. A colleague tells you: "This is so stupid. I already have so much unfinished work. Now to take a *whole* day away from work? Come on! I don't mind CSR. If the company is serious about CSR, why

don't they donate one day of my earnings, which I am sure will be more than the value I can generate by cleaning up the road or picking up trash? With that money, they can just hire someone to do a better job than I would." What are you going to say to her? (Your colleague makes $73,000 a year and on a per-day basis she makes $200.)

3. ***ON ETHICS:*** As CEO of a leading bank in Wall Street or the City of London, you have decided to directly meet participants in the Occupy Wall Street movement or the Occupy London movement, respectively. What will you say?

TOPICS FOR EXPANDED PROJECTS

1. ***ON ETHICS:*** In the landmark *Dodge v. Ford* case in 1919, the Michigan State Supreme Court determined whether Henry Ford could withhold dividends from the Dodge brothers (and other shareholders of the Ford Motor Company) to engage in what today would be called CSR activities. With a resounding "No," the court opined that "A business organization is organized and carried on primarily for the profits of the stockholders." If the court in your country were to decide on this case this year (or in 2019), what do you think would be the likely outcome?

2. ***ON ETHICS:*** Some argue that investing in emerging economies greatly facilitates economic development at the base of the global economic pyramid. Others contend that moving jobs to low-cost countries not only abandons CSR for domestic employees and communities in developed economies, but also exploits the poor in these countries and destroys the environment. If you were (1) CEO of an MNE headquartered in a developed economy, (2) the leader of a labor union in the home country of the MNE mentioned here that is losing a lot of jobs, or (3) the leader of an environmental NGO in the low-cost country in which the MNE invests, how would you participate in this debate?

3. ***ON ETHICS:*** Hypothetically, your MNE is the largest foreign investor in (1) Vietnam where religious leaders are being prosecuted or (2) Estonia where ethnic Russian citizens are being discriminated against by law. As the country manager there, you are being pressured by NGOs of all stripes to help the oppressed groups in these countries. But you also understand that the host government could be upset if your firm is found to engage in local political activities deemed inappropriate. These activities, which you personally find distasteful, are not directly related to your operations. How would you proceed?

CLOSING CASE   **ETHICAL DILEMMA**

Whole Foods' John Mackey on Conscious Capitalism

After dropping out of the University of Texas at Austin, John Mackey co-founded Safer Way Natural Foods store in Austin in 1978. In 1980, Safer Way merged with a competitor to become Whole Foods, one of the country's first natural foods supermarkets. Thirty years and 15 acquisitions later, Whole Foods dominates natural foods retailing and has become an iconic brand in the United States. It is expanding in the United Kingdom as well. Its purchasing standards and priorities shape agricultural practices around the world. The outspoken Mackey, who is a self-styled guru on conscious capitalism, was interviewed by *Harvard Business Review*:

❚ *What is conscious capitalism?*

First, you have to understand the basic principles that help capitalism flourish. One is property rights. You need the ability to trade your property, and to trade it to pretty much whoever you want. Another is the rule of law—laws and regulations that are well understood so that you can factor them into your business decisions. The rule of law has to be applied equally to everyone. For example, if Whole Foods goes into a city and is told our cheese has to be refrigerated, it's fundamentally unjust if that rule isn't applied to our competitors as well—which, I might add, does sometimes happen in New York City. You also need to have conscious businesses—that is, businesses that become conscious of their higher purpose, which is not just about maximizing profits and shareholder value.

Second, you have to recognize the stakeholder model: Customers, employees, investors, suppliers, larger communities, and the environment are all interdependent. You operate the business in such a way that it's not a zero-sum game.

Third, you need what we call conscious leadership. You could also call it servant leadership. Leaders identify their own flourishing with the flourishing of the organization. They're trying to serve the organization and its purpose.

Fourth, you have to create a conscious culture—a culture that allows the organization to fulfill its higher purpose, implements the stakeholder model, and enables conscious leadership to flourish.

❚ *So, what are the core principles of Whole Foods, and where do they come from?*

I think business enterprises are like any other communities. They can aspire to the highest values that have inspired humans throughout time. You can use different value models, but I like Plato's the good, the true, and the beautiful. Add the heroic to that—meaning changing and improving the world and standing up for what you believe is true and right and good. I think Whole Foods's highest purpose is a heroic one: to try to change and improve our world. That is what animates me personally. That is what animates the company. I resisted that purpose for a long time, by the way. I actually thought we were in some variant of service—that was really about fulfilling the good. The team members consistently told me I was wrong, that we had a different purpose. It was this more heroic purpose.

❚ *In terms of the age-old debate about whether companies exist for the shareholders or for something else, is there one group? Is it customers? Is it employees? Or is it purpose?*

That gets back to the second principle of conscious capitalism—the stakeholder model. I think it's deep in human nature to think in terms of the zero sum. If one stakeholder is winning, someone else must be losing. It comes from sports, where there is one winner and lots of losers, and this idea of a fixed pie, where if someone is getting a bigger share, someone else has to be getting a smaller piece, and what's needed for social justice is to make sure people get equal pieces. But a conscious business recognizes that you can have an expanding pie, and potentially everyone can get a larger piece.

I'll give you a simple example: management's job at Whole Foods is to make sure that we hire good people, that they are well trained, and that they flourish in the workplace, because we found that when people are really happy in their jobs, they provide much higher degrees of service to the customers. Happy team members result in happy customers. Happy customers do more business with you. They become advocates for your enterprise, which results in happy investors.

That is a win, win, win, win strategy. You can expand it to include your suppliers and the communities where you do business, which are tied in to this prosperity circle. A metaphor I like is the spiral, which tends to move upward but doesn't move in a straight line.

> *HBR's pages are full of discussions about how sustainability is becoming a competitive advantage. Do you believe that?*

I do think sustainability is a way to compete. I don't think it's the most important way. I see it as more of a niche. It reflects the consciousness of your customers, and the truth is that most customers don't care about it. Most customers at the end of the day care mostly about price. That consciousness is still dominant out there. But there is a growing consciousness about things like environmental sustainability and animal welfare. When we started out, 30 years ago, organic was a niche, and most people didn't know what it was. But I would say that partly because of Whole Foods' success, organic is now very much in the national consciousness.

More recently, Whole Foods has gotten behind the emphasis on local agriculture and has helped to popularize it. Wal-Mart is beginning to pay attention to this also, so in a lot of ways Whole Foods is helping to evolve the agricultural system in the United States.

Source: Excerpts from J. Mackey, 2011, What is it that only I can do? *Harvard Business Review*, January: 119–123.

CASE DISCUSSION QUESTIONS

1. What are Whole Foods' firm-specific resources and capabilities that underpin its success?

2. From an institution-based view, how would you characterize Whole Foods' strategy featuring its "heroic" purpose to "try to change and improve our world"?

3. Why does Mackey acknowledge that most customers don't care about consciousness, and yet he and his firm emphasize so much of it?

NOTES

[**Journal acronyms**] *AMJ – Academy of Management Journal; **AMP** – Academy of Management Perspectives; **AMR** – Academy of Management Review; **APJM** – Asia Pacific Journal of Management; **BSR** – Business and Society Review; **BW** – BusinessWeek (before 2010) or Bloomberg Businessweek (since 2010); **HBR** – Harvard Business Review; **JBE** – Journal of Business Ethics; **JIBS** – Journal of International Business Studies; **JIM** – Journal of International Management; **JMS** – Journal of Management Studies; **JWB** – Journal of World Business; **NYTM** – New York Times Magazine; **OSt** – Organization Studies; **SMJ** – Strategic Management Journal; **WSJ** – Wall Street Journal.*

1. K. Davis, 1973, The case for and against business assumption of social responsibilities (p. 312), *AMJ*, 16: 312–322. See also R. Aguilera, R. Rupp, C. Williams, & J. Ganapathi, 2007, Putting the S back in CSR, *AMR*, 32: 836–863; P. Cappelli, H. Singh, J. Singh, & M. Useem, 2010, The India way, *AMP*, May: 624; J. Campbell, L. Eden, & S. Miller, 2012, Multinationals and CSR in host countries, *JIBS*, 43: 84106; C. Egri & D. Ralston, 2008, Corporate responsibility, *JIM*, 14: 319–339; D. Matten & J. Moon, 2008, "Implicit" and "explicit" CSR, *AMR*, 33: 404–424.

2. Y. He, Z. Tian, & Y. Chen, 2007, Performance implications of nonmarket strategy in China, *APJM*, 24: 151–169; K. O'Shaughnessy, E. Gedajlovic, & P. Reinmoeller, 2007, The influence of firm, industry, and network on the corporate social performance of Japanese firms, *APJM*, 24: 283–304; A. Scherer & G. Palazzo, 2011, The new political role of business in a globalized world, *JMS*, 48: 899–931.

3. E. Freeman, 1984, *Strategic Management: A Stakeholder Approach* (p. 46), Boston: Pitman. See also M. Barnett, 2007, Stakeholder influence capacity and the variability of financial returns to CSR, *AMR*, 32: 794–816; S. Brickson, 2007, Organizational identity orientation, *AMR*, 32: 864–888; D. Crilly, 2011, Predicting stakeholder orientation in the MNE, *JIBS*, 42: 694–717; T. Jensen & J. Sandstrom, 2011, Stakeholder theory and globalization, *OSt*, 32: 473–488; A. Kacperczyk, 2009, With greater power comes greater responsibility? *SMJ*, 30: 261–285.

4. P. David, M. Bloom, & A. Hillman, 2007, Investor activism, managerial responsiveness, and corporate social performance, *SMJ*, 28: 91–100; J. Harrison, D. Bosse, & R. Phillips, 2010, Managing for stakeholders, stakeholder utility functions, and competitive advantage, *SMJ*, 31: 58–74.

5. World Commission on Environment and Development, 1987, *Our Common Future* (p. 8), Oxford: Oxford University Press.

6. S. Hart, 2005, *Capitalism at the Crossroads*, Philadelphia: Wharton School Publishing; R. Rajan, 2010, *Fault Lines*, Princeton, NJ: Princeton University Press.

7. J. Doh & T. Guay, 2006, CSR, public policy, and NGO activism in Europe and the United States, *JMS*, 43: 47–73.

8. P. Romilly, 2007, Business and climate change risk, *JIBS*, 38: 474–480.

9. C. Seelos & J. Mair, 2007, Profitable business models and market creation in the context of deep poverty, *AMP*, November: 49–63; A. Scherer & G. Palazzo, 2007, Toward a political conception of corporate responsibility, *AMR*, 32: 1096–1120.

10. B. Husted & D. Allen, 2006, CSR in the MNE, *JIBS*, 37: 838–849.

11. M. Clarkson, 1995, A stakeholder framework for analyzing and evaluating corporate social performance (p. 107), *AMR*, 20: 92–117. See also F. den Hond & F. de Bakker, 2007, Ideologically motivated activism, *AMR*, 32: 901–924; C. Marquis, M. Glynn, & G. Davis, 2007, Community isomorphism and corporate social action, *AMR*, 32: 925–945; S. Waddock, 2008, Building a new institutional infrastructure for corporate responsibility, *AMP*, August: 87–109.

12. T. Donaldson & L. Preston, 1995, The stakeholder theory of the corporation, *AMR*, 20: 65–91; J. Elkington, 1997, *Cannibals with Forks: The Triple Bottom Line of 21st Century Business*, New York: Wiley.

13. M. Friedman, 1970, The social responsibility of business is to increase its profits, *NYTM*, *September* 13: 32–33.

14. D. Ahlstrom, 2010, Innovation and growth, *AMP*, August: 11–24; A Karnani, 2010, The case against corporate social responsibility, *WSJ*, August 23.

15. A. Delios, 2010, How can organizations be competitive but dare to care? *AMP*, August: 25–36.

16. A. Mackey, T. Mackey, & J. Barney, 2007, CSR and firm performance, *AMR*, 32: 817–835.

17. G. Bruton, 2010, Business and the world's poorest billion, *AMP*, August: 6–10.

18. *Economist*, 2011, Rage against the machine, October 22: 13.

19. Y. Mishina, B. Dykes, E. Block, & T. Pollock, 2010, Why "good" firms do bad things, *AMJ*, 53: 701–722; A. Muller & R. Kraussl, 2011, Doing good deeds in times of need, *SMJ*, 32: 911–929; C. Oh & J. Oetzel, 2011, Multinationals' response to major disasters, *SMJ*, 32: 658–681.

20. K. Basu & G. Palazzo, 2008, Corporate social responsibility, *AMR*, 33: 122–136.

21. A. Kolk & J. Pinkse, 2008, A perspective on MNEs and climate change, *JIBS*, 39: 1359–1378.

22. A. Hillman & G. Keim, 2001, Shareholder value, stakeholder management, and social issues, *SMJ*, 22: 125–139.

23. R. Chan, 2010, Corporate environmentalism pursuit by foreign firms competing in China, *JWB*, 45: 80–92; Y. Eiadat, A. Kelly, F. Roche, & H. Eyadat, 2008, Green and competitive? *JWB*, 43: 131–145; P. Godfrey, C. Merrill, & J. Hansen, 2009, The relationship between CSR and shareholder value, *SMJ*, 30: 425–445; B. Lev, C. Petrovits, & S. Radhakrishnan, 2010, Is doing good good for you? *SMJ*, 31: 182–200; S. Ramchander, R. Schwebach, & K. Staking, 2012, The informational relevance of CSR, *SMJ*, 33: 303–314; M. Sharfman & C. Fernando, 2008, Environmental risk management and the cost of capital, *SMJ*, 29: 569–592; H. Wang & C. Qian, 2011, Corporate philanthropy and corporate financial performance, *AMJ*, 54: 1159–1181.

24. S. Ambec & P. Lanoie, 2008, Does it pay to be green? *AMP*, November: 45–62; D. Vogel, 2005, The low value of virtue, *HBR*, June: 26.

25. S. Brammer & A. Millington, 2008, Does it pay to be different? *SMJ*, 29: 1325–1343; J. Surroca, J. Tribo, & S. Waddock, 2010, Corporate responsibility and financial performance, *SMJ*, 31: 463–490.

26. T. Devinney, 2009, Is the socially responsible corporation a myth? *AMP*, May: 53.

27. J. Choi & H. Wang, 2009, Stakeholder relations and the persistence of corporate financial performance, *SMJ*, 30: 895–907; C. Hull & S. Rothenberg, 2008, Firm performance, *SMJ*, 29: 781–789.

28. J. Campbell, 2007, Why would corporations behave in socially responsible ways? *AMR*, 32: 946–967; J. Murillo-Luna, C. Garces-Ayerbe, & P. Rivera-Torres, 2008, Why do patterns of environmental response differ? *SMJ*, 29: 1225–1240; A. Terlaak, 2007, Order without law? *AMR*, 32: 968–985; D. Waldman et al., 2006, Cultural and leadership predictions of CSR values of top management, *JIBS*, 37: 823–837.

29. B. Gifford, A. Kestler, & S. Anand, 2010, Building local legitimacy into CSR, *JWB*, 45: 304–311.

30. A. Gore, 2006, *An Inconvenient Truth,* Emmaus, PA: Rodale Press.

31. A. Muller & A. Kolk, 2010, Extrinsic and intrinsic drivers of corporate social performance, *JMS,* 47: 1–26.

32. *Economist,* 2010, The other oil spill, June 26: 71–73.

33. J. Janney & S. Gove, 2011, Reputation and CSR aberrations, trends, and hypocrisy, *JMS,* 48: 1562–1584.

34. *BW,* 2010, Nine questions (and provisional answers) about the spill, June 14: 62.

35. D. Siegel, 2009, Green management matters only if it yields more green, *AMP,* August: 5–16.

36. A. Marcus & A. Fremeth, 2009, Green management matters regardless, *AMP,* August: 17–26.

37. V. Hoffmann, T. Trautmann, & J. Hemprecht, 2009, Regulatory uncertainty, *JMS,* 46: 1227–1253.

38. N. Darnall, I. Henriques, & P. Sadorsky, 2010, Adopting proactive environmental strategy, *JMS,* 47: 1072–1094.

39. *Starbucks Global Responsibility Report 2010,* 2011, Message from Howard Schultz, www.starbucks.com.

40. G. Unruh & R. Ettenson, 2010, Winning in the green frenzy, *HBR,* November: 110–116.

41. *BW,* 2010, The smooth-talking king of coal—and climate change, June 7: 65.

42. A. King, 2007, Cooperation between corporations and environmental groups, *AMR,* 32: 889–900; A. Kourula, 2010, Corporate engagement with NGOs in different institutional contexts, *JWB,* 45: 395–404; J. Nebus & C. Rufin, 2010, Extending the bargaining power model, *JIBS,* 41: 996–1015.

43. M. Barnett & A. King, 2008, Good fences make good neighbors, *AMJ,* 51: 1150–1170; M. Delmas &

M. Montes-Sancho, 2010, Voluntary agreements to improve environmental quality, *SMJ,* 31: 575–601.

44. B. Arya & G. Zhang, 2009, Institutional reforms and investor reactions to CSR announcements, *JMS,* 46: 1089–1112; M. Delmas & M. Toffel, 2008, Organizational responses to environmental demands, *SMJ,* 29: 1027–1055; E. Reid & M. Toffel, 2009, Responding to public and private politics, *SMJ,* 30: 1157–1178; E. Wong, M. Ormiston, & P. Tetlock, 2011, The effects of top management team integrative complexity and decentralized decision making on corporate social performance, *AMJ,* 54: 1207–1228.

45. *BW,* 2004, European workers' losing battle (p. 41), August 9: 41.

46. J. Welch & S. Welch, 2006, Whose company is it anyway? *BW,* October 9: 122.

47. S. Brammer, S. Pavelin, & L. Porter, 2009, Corporate charitable giving, MNCs, and countries of concern, *JMS,* 46: 575–596; B. Scholtens, 2009, CSR in the international banking industry, *JBE,* 86: 159–175.

48. *Economist,* 2009, Spilling forever, June 13: 51.

49. P. Christmann & G. Taylor, 2006, Firm self-regulation through international certifiable standards, *JIBS,* 37: 863–878.

50. P. Madsen, 2009, Does corporate investment drive a "race to the bottom" in environmental protection? *AMJ,* 52: 1297–1318.

51. R. Bies, J. Bartunek, T. Fort, & M. Zald, 2007, Corporations as social change agents, *AMR,* 32: 788–793; N. Gardberg & C. Fombrun, 2006, Corporate citizenship, *AMR,* 31: 329–346; T. Hemphill, 2004, Corporate citizenship, *BSR,* 109: 339–361.

INTEGRATIVE
CASES

3i Group's Private Equity Investment in China's Little Sheep[1]

How and why was an unlikely yet productive relationship forged between a large, well-established global private equity firm and a rapidly growing Chinese restaurant chain?

Lily Fang, *INSEAD*
Roger Leeds, *Johns Hopkins University, School of Advanced International Studies*

"Many people grow a company like raising a pig. The pig gets fat, you kill it and make money. I grow my company like raising a son. The average life of a restaurant is less than three years in China. I want Little Sheep to last a century."

—Zhang Gang, Founder, Little Sheep Catering Chain Co.

"Helping a great business to realize its potential takes a lot more than just capital. It is ultimately about the people, thus your relationship with the management team and the sort of support you can provide, such as introductions to key industry expertise and relevant operational best practice, is very important."

—Anna Cheung, 3i Partner, China

3i Group PLC

3i Group plc is one of the oldest private equity firms in the world, with a track record dating back to 1945 when the British government and a consortium of banks founded two organizations—the Industrial and Commercial Finance Corporation (ICFC) and the Finance Corporation for Industry (FCI)—to bridge the financing gap afflicting small and medium-sized enterprises (SMEs) in the aftermath of World War II.[2] In 1975, these two corporations merged, and in 1983, the combined entity was renamed 3i—"investors in industry." In 1994, 3i was listed on the London Stock Exchange, becoming the first large private equity fund to go public and have access to permanent capital. 3i invests in a wide variety of businesses through its five lines: buyouts, growth capital, venture capital, infrastructure, and quoted private equity (see Exhibit 1).

Expanding its geographic footprint beyond the UK and Europe, 3i today has offices in 14 countries across Europe, Asia, and the US and has made investments in more than 30 countries. The firm opened its first Asia office in Singapore in 1997, followed by a second office in Hong Kong four years later and offices in Shanghai, Mumbai, and Beijing subsequently. During fiscal year 2006, 16% of the group's new investments were in Asia. Alongside the geographic shift, 3i's investment strategy has also evolved, with an emphasis on making fewer, larger, and more sector-focused investments. In Asia, the group's average investment size has been about $40 million to $50 million, and sectors in focus included consumer-related goods and services, healthcare, and energy.

These changes in investment strategy were consistent with a decision to become more actively involved

---

1 This case was written by Lily Fang (INSEAD) and Roger Leeds (SAIS, Johns Hopkins University). It was originally published in 2008 as "3i Group plc and Little Sheep" by the World Economic Forum USA, Inc., as part of *Globalization of Alternative Investments Working Papers, Volume 1 The Global Economic Impact of Private Equity Report 2008* (http://www3.weforum.org/docs/WEF_IV_PrivateEquity_Report_2008.pdf). The authors express their appreciation for the research and editing support provided by Brian DeLacey. © World Economic Forum, Lily Fang, and Roger Leeds. Reprinted with permission.
2 The perceived funding gap—the "Macmillan gap"—was scrutinized back in 1929 in a report by a committee under the chairmanship of Lord Macmillan. The founding of ICFC, predecessor of 3i, was closely linked to one suggestion in the Macmillan Report.

EXHIBIT 1 Summary Information on 3i's Business Lines

Note: Figures in millions £						
	Buyouts	Growth Capital	Venture Capital	Infrastructure	Quoted Public Equity	Total
3i's own capital	1,281	1,460	741	469	20	3,971
Third-party funds	2,129	227	15	385	0	2,756
TOTAL	3,410	1,687	756	854	20	6,727

Source: 3i Annual Report 2007; http://www3.weforum.org/docs/WEF_IV_PrivateEquity_Report_2008.pdf.

in its portfolio companies, returning to the firm's original *modus operandi* as an "investor in industry." To better serve its portfolio companies, 3i developed two unique programs: People Program and Business Development Practice. People Program is a highly sophisticated approach to cultivating relationships internationally with seasoned executives and industry experts whom 3i regularly calls upon to assist the deal team at various stages of the investment process, from due diligence to post-investment operational support. While many private equity groups rely upon industry experts, 3i's People Program is unique in its scale and 20-year history of building an enviable rolodex. Chris Rowlands, 3i's managing director for Asia, explained: "At 3i, this is not a nice-to-have, or an afterthought. This is at the heart of our investment model."

The second distinctive 3i program, the Business Development Practice, is a dedicated resource to help 3i's portfolio companies expand their operations internationally. Initially this grew out of a demand from European firms wanting to gain entry to Asia, but the team is increasingly working with Asian firms seeking to tap into the European and US markets, and Rowlands believes it "is not only a service for our portfolio companies, but we believe it directly increases our investment value as well."

Entrepreneurial Beginnings of Inner Mongolia Little Sheep Catering Chain Co., Ltd.

In 1999, an entrepreneur called Zhang Gang founded Little Sheep Catering Chain Co. in Inner Mongolia, one of the most remote and underdeveloped corners of the world. One of the five autonomous regions in China, Inner Mongolia's economy was primarily agrarian and until the 1990s had ranked among the country's poorest regions. But this began to change dramatically with the economic reform programs initiated by Deng Xiaoping in the 1980s. The combination of a reform-minded regional government and rich natural resources provided strong impetus for Inner Mongolia's economic growth. By 2006, Inner Mongolia had been transformed into one of the wealthiest regions in terms of GDP per capita.[3]

Although with no formal business education, Zhang (ethnic Han Chinese) was an opportunistic and intuitive businessman long before he founded Little Sheep. A short stint as a factory worker in Baotou Steel Factory at an early age led Zhang to conclude that a career as a worker in a state-owned factory would be "very repressive." He then ventured into clothes retailing while still a teenager and, by the early 1990s, had accumulated enough capital to enter the cell phone

---

3 In 2006, Inner Mongolia's GDP per capita ranked number ten among Chinese regions, behind only nine wealthy coastal provinces (GDP per capita ranking data from wikipedia.com, November 2007).

business, eventually rising to become the sole distributor of cell phone equipment in Inner Mongolia.

Zhang initially thought about entering the food business as a hobby. He focused on a popular dish in Northern China called "hot pot"—a pot of boiling soup that sits atop a small, table-top stove to which diners add thinly sliced meat and vegetables. Traditionally, the cooked food is then dipped in flavored sauces. Zhang wanted to improve the soup base so that there would be no need to dip the cooked food in sauces—he wanted to create a healthier and more naturally flavored hot pot. After many trials and tastings, he finally settled on a unique recipe containing over 60 spices and herbs. Only then did he begin thinking about it as a business. "It made sense—I always wanted to have a basic business, selling something simple that people wanted," he recalled.

Zhang named his venture Little Sheep because locally raised lamb is a staple in the Mongolian diet and thinly sliced lamb would be the specialty in his new restaurant. He opened the first Little Sheep restaurant in Baotou, a large city in Inner Mongolia on August 8, 1999, and it was an instant success. By the second day, long lines of customers lined up outside the restaurant, an unprecedented phenomenon in a city where people were unaccustomed to waiting in line for supper. Based on this early success, Zhang managed to open two additional restaurants in Baotou within two months, with an equally enthusiastic customer response.

The Trademark Battle

As Zhang witnessed the surprising popularity of Little Sheep, his business intuition immediately set in. Once word spread about the phenomenal early success of the restaurants, he knew others would try to replicate his business model and even use the Little Sheep name, undermining the brand value. As early as October 1999, just as he was opening his second and third restaurants, Zhang submitted his first application to the National Trademark Office, the official government agency in charge of intellectual property matters. This proved to be the start of a battle that would drag on for nearly seven years, until Little Sheep was finally awarded trademark protection in June 2006. Ironically, it took Little Sheep longer to be granted trademark protection in China than in several overseas markets.

Reflecting on this drawn-out experience with the government authorities, Zhang lamented that this was his "single biggest headache" during the entire history of the firm. Not only would this have an unexpected impact on Little Sheep's growth strategy, it also would sow the seeds in Zhang's mind to bring Little Sheep to the public market.

Rapid Growth and Strategic Re-orientation

The extraordinary success of the first three restaurants spurred Zhang to expand with lightening speed throughout the country. By the end of 2002, just over three years after opening the doors to his first restaurant in Baotou, the company had established a nationwide chain of more than 500 restaurants. Ironically, the lack of trademark protection was as much a driver of rapid expansion as the founder's ambition and entrepreneurial talent. "I didn't have the luxury to wait. I had to move fast to grab market. Otherwise, anyone could start a Little Sheep and we had no legal recourse to fight back," Zhang explained.

But this success came at a high cost, and by the end of 2002, the company was suffering from serious growing pains. While the rapid expansion had been primarily driven by an aggressive franchise strategy, the company's thin management ranks resulted in very weak oversight of the franchisees. The problems were aggravated when media reports began to appear claiming substandard quality and service in certain Little Sheep franchise stores, inevitably damaging the brand.

At the end of 2002, Zhang faced a critical decision: Should the company curtail growth and scale back the franchises until the management team could be strengthened, even though this would result in the immediate loss of substantial franchise fees? Moreover, Zhang would risk alienating a growing roster of franchise applicants who were waiting to capitalize on the brand and open Little Sheep restaurants. Resisting the temptation to maximize short-term profit, Zhang decided to temporarily halt the awarding of new franchises in the following year. In addition, he initiated efforts to more closely monitor the performance of the existing franchises and designated one of his long-time lieutenants, Zhang Zhan Hai, to be in charge of the task.

Management's Goal

Gradually, Zhang's decision to scale back the expansion began to pay off. In 2004, the company strengthened its management ranks significantly by hiring as senior vice president of finance, industry veteran Lu Wen Bing, former vice president of Meng Niu (Mongolian Cow), a well-known Inner Mongolia–based dairy company. Lu brought much-needed financial discipline and internal control to the company, and by 2005, Little Sheep's performance had clearly rebounded as the company collected a number of prestigious regional and national business awards, including the Little Sheep brand being ranked 95th by the World Brand Lab among "The 500 Most Valuable Chinese Brands." According to Ministry of Commerce statistics, the company had the second largest market share among China's restaurants chains, behind only the fast-food giant KFC. (See Exhibit 2 for a major-events time line in Little Sheep's corporate history up to the 3i investment and Exhibit 3 for the company's footprint in China at the end of 2005, just before the 3i investment.)

Notwithstanding this renewed success, Zhang recognized that sustaining the company's growth would require not only financial resources but, more importantly, additional industry expertise. Like many Chinese entrepreneurs, Zhang came to believe that the ultimate validation for Little Sheep's success would be a public listing, preferably on an overseas exchange.[4] This would give the company a diversified source of capital as well as brand recognition and subject it to market discipline. His preference for an overseas listing was rooted in his concern about the lax listing standards on the domestic Chinese exchanges. But to prepare for an initial public offering (IPO), he believed that the company needed to attract not only additional capital, but also a partner with the capability to provide much-needed industry knowledge and expertise. "What we lacked were high level professionals from the food and beverage industry who could help take Little Sheep

to the next, higher level…We needed a partner that could help us prepare for an IPO outside China," explained Zhang.

Origin of 3i's Private Equity Deal with Little Sheep

Little Sheep's extraordinary growth and brand name recognition attracted many willing investors, including such prestigious investment banks as Morgan Stanley and Goldman Sachs. At 3i, Little Sheep was spotted by an associate director, Daizong Wang, a Wharton MBA who had recently joined the group after a four-year stint with Goldman Sachs in Hong Kong. As 3i's investment strategy in Asia was becoming more sector focused, Wang was assigned to study the food and beverage sector, which had been growing at a rate twice as fast as China's GDP for over 15 years. As the Chinese economy began to shift toward more consumption-led growth, Wang believed that consumer-related sectors such as restaurants would offer tremendous upside (see Exhibit 4).

Wang also noticed that even though the sector was experiencing rapid growth, prior to 2005, there had been no private equity investments due to the lack of scale in typical restaurant businesses. Unfazed, he began to analyze the market share rankings of restaurant chains in China to screen for investment targets. Little Sheep ranked second, occupying 6.2% of the entire restaurant and catering market, behind KFC.[5] Intrigued by Little Sheep's ability to achieve scale unlike most other restaurants, Wang realized that the key was the simplicity of Little Sheep's business model: "The Chinese restaurant business is fragmented because it is difficult to standardize. In most restaurants the largest cost component is the chef, but it is difficult to achieve consistency. Little Sheep is different because customers cook their own food in the hot pot, which eliminates the need for a chef. This do-it-yourself style of dining and the ease of standardization made this business capable of scale." In fact, these characteristics made hot pot restaurants a significant subsector of the total restaurant industry, accounting

---

4 At the time, the Chinese A-share market was closed for new public listing.
5 According to *Euromonitor*, Little Sheep had a higher, 9.9% market share among China's full-service restaurant chains, excluding fast food.

EXHIBIT 2   Major Events in Little Sheep's Corporate History

DATE	EVENT
August 1999	Little Sheep opens first restaurant
October 1999	Little Sheep becomes a chain with two more restaurants opened
May 2001	Subsidiary company in Shanghai established
January 2002	Little Sheep sets up subsidiary companies in Beijing and Shenzhen
August 2002	Little Sheep receives both the China national "Green Food" certification and ISO 9001 certification
January 2003	Research and development (R&D) facility for seasonings established by Little Sheep
January 2004	Subsidiary company in Hong Kong established
May 2004	First Hong Kong Little Sheep restaurant opened
November 2004	Little Sheep becomes the only restaurant to break into the "China Top 500 Businesses" list at #451; the company is also awarded the Chinese "Prestigious Brand" label
May 2005	The "Inner Mongolia Top 50 Private Business" list ranks Little Sheep at #2
August 2005	Little Sheep ranks #95 on the "China Top 500 Most Valuable Brands" list, with an estimated value of 5.5 billion RMB; on the "China Top 500 Service Business" list, Little Sheep ranks #1 among food companies and #160 overall
September 2005	Little Sheep ranks #2 on the "China Top 100 Food Businesses" list
October 2005	Little Sheep establishes its first overseas direct-ownership restaurant in Toronto, Canada
December 2005	The company enters the "China Food and Beverages Top 10 Quality" list and the "China Top 500 Quality" list
May 2006	Little Sheep is awarded a spot on "Inner Mongolia's Most Respected 50 Businesses" list
June 2006	Little Sheep receives its official trademark

Source: Compiled from company documents; http://www3.weforum.org/docs/WEF_IV_PrivateEquity_Report_2008.pdf.

for more than 20% of all consumer spending on restaurants, with Little Sheep the clear market leader with one-third of total hot-pot revenue (see Exhibit 5).

Based on this analysis, Daizong Wang concluded, "From the very beginning, I wanted to invest in this business."

EXHIBIT 3 Little Sheep's Footprint in China (as of the end of 2005)

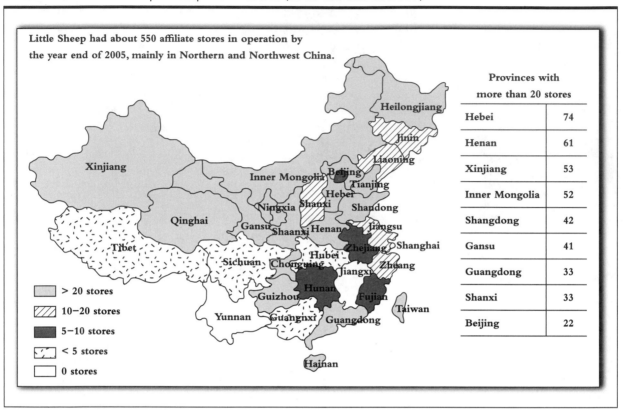

Little Sheep had about 550 affiliate stores in operation by the year end of 2005, mainly in Northern and Northwest China.

Provinces with more than 20 stores	
Hebei	74
Henan	61
Xinjiang	53
Inner Mongolia	52
Shangdong	42
Gansu	41
Guangdong	33
Shanxi	33
Beijing	22

Source: Company documents; http://www3.weforum.org/docs/WEF_IV_PrivateEquity_Report_2008.pdf.

His next step, in August 2005, was to cold-call Little Sheep's senior vice president of finance, Lu Wen Bing. After making his pitch to Lu, whom Wang found "surprisingly open minded [about private equity]," he was invited to a formal meeting in Baotou, Little Sheep's headquarters. Reflecting on the initial exchange, Wang said: "At a time when few in China understood the difference between private equity and investment banking, Lu was very sophisticated and ahead of the curve." It turned out that earlier in his career, Lu had worked on the senior management team of Meng Niu when it received a widely publicized investment from Morgan Stanley and CDH, a well-known Chinese private equity fund. Based on this previous experience, he was *predisposed* to working with a private equity investor.

Winning the Mandate

After the initial meeting in August, 3i engaged in a four-month competition with other private equity suitors, including Goldman Sachs and Morgan Stanley, before finally being awarded the Little Sheep mandate. During this period, Anna Cheung, a 3i partner based in Hong Kong, was assigned as the senior member on the team working with Wang to secure the mandate. The investment team flew to Baotou frequently, getting to know Little Sheep's senior management team and explaining 3i's investment philosophy. At the same time, the team spoke with a number of research analysts covering the Hong Kong and Chinese restaurant sector to learn more about the sector and shared its findings with Little Sheep senior management. The team also

EXHIBIT 4   Growth Statistics for the Chinese Restaurant Industry

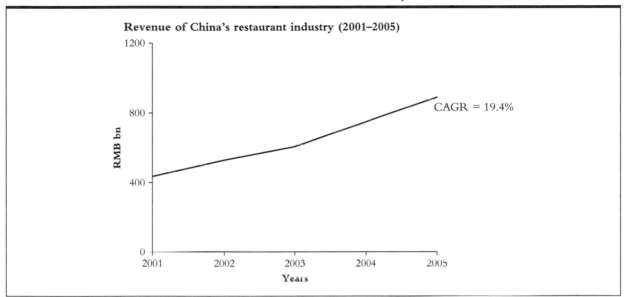

Source: Company documents; http://www3.weforum.org/docs/WEF_IV_PrivateEquity_Report_2008.pdf.

EXHIBIT 5   Hot Pot Restaurant as a Sub-sector of the Dining Industry

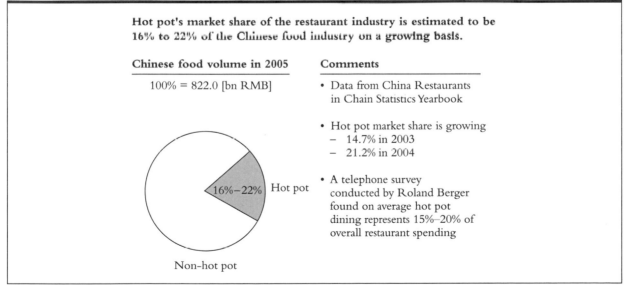

Source: Company documents; http://www3.weforum.org/docs/WEF_IV_PrivateEquity_Report_2008.pdf.

tapped into 3i's network of industry experts (via 3i's People Program) and identified Nish Kankiwala, former president of Burger King International, as a suitable advisor for Little Sheep. As the top executive at one of the world's largest fast-food restaurant chains, Kankiwala would bring a wealth of sorely needed knowledge about the franchise business. At the request of the 3i team, Kankiwala flew to Beijing and spent a number of days meeting with Little Sheep's entire senior management team, learning the ups and downs of the company's performance and discussing the relevance of his own experience to Little Sheep's future strategy. This was the first time that Little Sheep managers had direct access to a world-class expert with a deep understanding of their business, and they were impressed by 3i's commitment and ready access to this caliber of expertise.

But the specter of Goldman Sachs continued to lurk in the background. Wang heard that his former Goldman colleagues were visiting Little Sheep in Baotou in late 2005, so he immediately flew there and was "prepared to sit there until we signed the term sheet." His persistence paid off, and four months after Wang's August cold call, 3i signed a term sheet with Little Sheep, agreeing to a $25 million equity investment for a minority stake in the company. (Prax Capital, a private equity fund focused on Chinese investments, invested $5 million as a co-investor.) The transaction closed six months later in June 2006, and 3i's real value-add to the company began to take shape.

Forming a Strategic Blueprint

During the six-month period between the signing of the mandate in late 2005 and the final closing in June 2006, 3i worked closely with Little Sheep management to clarify a number of strategic questions that the company needed to address, and an agreement was reached to engage Roland Berger, a strategy consulting company, to provide fact-based analysis as a basis for resolving some of the most pressing issues.

Based on extensive data collection and analysis, the consultants made a number of specific recommendations, such as optimal store size and location in different sub-markets[6] and how the company should overhaul its existing franchises (as described in the next section). These findings and recommendations became the basis of a blueprint that outlined a step-by-step effort to professionalize and improve the company's operations. When the analysis and recommendations

were presented to the Little Sheep board, the response was highly favorable.

Mapping Strategy to Operations: The 180-Day Plan

Aided by the strategic insights gained from Roland Berger's report, 3i's Wang drafted a "180-day plan," a detailed work plan of tasks that the company needed to address in the ensuing six months, including specific financial, legal, operational, and HR issues (see Exhibit 6). After discussing the plan with the management and obtaining full commitment to executing it, its progress was then continuously tracked and updated. 3i partner Anna Cheung explained: "The 180-day plan helped to provide structure and a time frame that gave all parties involved a goal to work towards."

This detailed level of post-investment involvement is standard for all 3i investments, and it confirmed for the Little Sheep management team that 3i was willing and able to provide the non-financial benefits that it had been seeking from its private equity investor.

Strengthening the Management Team and the Board

Both 3i and Little Sheep understood clearly that a critical task for the company prior to a public listing was strengthening the management team and board structure. Little Sheep's management team had a high level of integrity and drive but lacked depth: the entire top management team consisted of founder and CEO, Zhang, a senior vice president of finance, and three regional vice presidents (see Exhibit 7). Even more significantly, as Wang remarked, "the company lacked systems such as centralized operation management, new store development and marketing teams which were crucial for the company to continue to grow in a coordinated manner." Through the years, the company had been carried forward almost entirely by a small team of managers united and motivated by the founder's sheer personal strength and charm. "The founder, Mr Zhang, is an inspirational person," remarked Cheung. As one of Zhang's lieutenants would confirm, Zhang was "the heart

---

6 For example, Roland Berger found that the optimal store sizes for tier-1, tier-2, and tier-3 cites were 1200 m^2, 600 m^2, and 300 m^2, respectively, and that the reason for most under-performing stores (profitability < 5% of sales) was due to a wrong store location.

EXHIBIT 6   Highlights from the "180-Day Plan"

#	ISSUES	TIMING	ACTION / OUTPUT
I.	**Legal**		
...			
g.	Lease agreement	Within 6 months	- Renew lease agreements by 31 July 2006 - Revise certain lease agreements (identified in legal due diligence) by 31 July 2006 - ...
...			-
i.	Other permits and certificates	Within 12 months	- Obtain compliance with fire safety and environmental protection within 12 months
II.	**Financial**		
a.	Internal System	Within 3 months— report and recommendations; within 12 months— adoption of recommendations	- ... - Engage a leading accounting firm to examine systems, processes, and controls to ensure speedy and accurate information flow - Recommendations for improvements to be presented at first Board meeting post-completion. Satisfactory system in place in 12 months - ...
...			
III.	**Business and Operations**		
...			
c.	New site selection	By 31 September 2006	- Standardize and formalize location assessment process - Set up a dedicated team responsible for new site selection for the whole group - Establish a set of criteria such as those in the Roland Berger report - ...
...			
e.	Store-level operational improvement	Assign responsibilities and agree on action plan within 3 months	- Refine operations manual - Step up staff training and communications - Enhance internal audit and increase frequency of store checks - Implement KPI benchmark at city/provincial, regional, and national levels
...			-

Source: Company documents; http://www3.weforum.org/docs/WEF_IV_PrivateEquity_Report_2008.pdf.

EXHIBIT 7 Little Sheep's Management Team before 3i's Investment

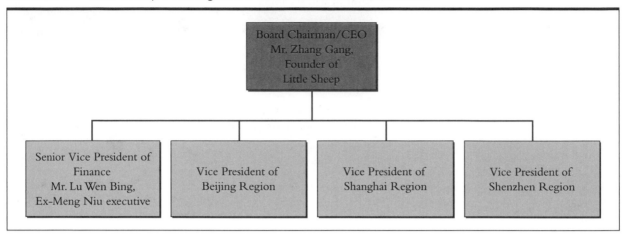

Source: http://www3.weforum.org/docs/WEF_IV_PrivateEquity_Report_2008.pdf.

and soul" of the business. But there was a pressing need to recruit additional professional managers, install management information systems, and revamp the structure and responsibilities of the board.

In this regard, 3i was instrumental in helping Little Sheep gradually put a strong team and a governance system in place. Once 3i made the investment, Cheung and Wang both joined the board as non-executive directors. 3i also recruited two additional independent directors with strong industry experience: Nish Kankiwala, the former president of Burger King International who played a part in the deal initiation process, and Yuka Yeung, CEO of the KFC franchise in Hong Kong. Both individuals had extensive experience in the food industry and were exactly the type of high-level industry people that Little Sheep had been looking for.

Instead of viewing these new directors as outsiders, however, Little Sheep's top management enthusiastically welcomed them as partners capable of adding considerable value to the company. When 3i proposed four board meetings per year, Little Sheep came back and asked for more. "Little Sheep is the only company I have worked with that has asked for more board meetings… Zhang is an extraordinary entrepreneur, but he was very humble and eager to learn. This is one of the most impressive things about the company," Cheung commented.

The newly constituted board immediately began to focus on adding depth to the management team. Up to this point, Zhang had served as both the board chairman and CEO and had tended to delegate much of routine management to members of his senior management team. One of the first 3i recommendations was to recruit a full-time CEO dedicated to overseeing day-to-day management of the business. "We practically insisted on it," recalled Wang. In addition, based on 3i's recommendation, the board agreed to create new positions for a COO and a CFO, but emblematic of China's thin supply of professional managers, it would take more than a year to recruit the right candidates. (See Exhibit 8 for Little Sheep's organization chart as of October 2007.)

Creating a Standards Committee

Until these three new senior executives could be recruited, an interim management solution was needed. 3i proposed—and the board agreed—to create a Standards Committee consisting of Little Sheep's existing management team, plus Wang. The committee's purpose was to serve as interim CEO, focusing especially on enhancing the communication and coordination among the three regional operations until a proper headquarters could be set up. For the first three months between June and September 2006, the committee met bi-weekly to

EXHIBIT 8   Little Sheep's Management Team after 3i's Investment

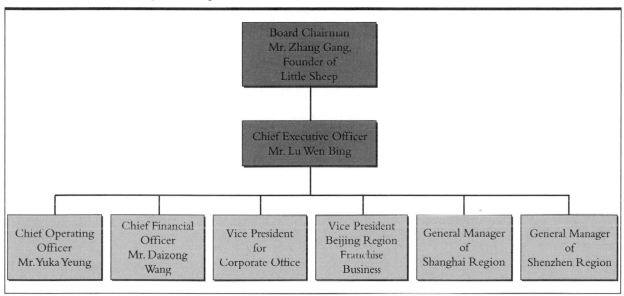

Source: http://www3.weforum.org/docs/WEF_IV_PrivateEquity_Report_2008.pdf.

discuss detailed operational matters and make decisions to be carried out by the three regional VPs. Gradually, as internal communication improved and key headquarters functions were established, the Standard Committee evolved to become a series of monthly meetings focused more on long-term strategic issues, such as new-store developments, marketing, and budgeting. Finally, in November 2007, with the establishment of Little Sheep's new national operation headquarters in Shanghai, the committee was formally dissolved.

Creating and Executing a New Franchise Strategy

Although Little Sheep had taken the initiative to halt the awarding of new franchises in 2003, the existing sprawling network of over 500 franchises was not systematically addressed prior to 3i's involvement. Symptomatic of the problem was the fact that management had actually lost count of the exact number of stores in the Little Sheep network. Cleaning up the existing franchise system and designing a new franchise strategy thus became a top priority for the newly constituted board. Based on the insights from the Roland Berger

report, the board came to the conclusion that the new strategy should focus on quality rather than quantity and that the franchise system should become more centrally managed. Not only was this consistent with protecting and strengthening the Little Sheep brand, it was also made feasible by the strengthened management and headquarters capabilities. The following three-phased overhaul of the franchise system was agreed on and carried out:

- *Phase 1: Cleaning up the existing franchise system.* A systematic effort was taken to visit and catalogue every franchise in the country. These visits generated store-by-store information that was fed into a database created to track critical performance indicators and served as a basis for making decisions about the future status of each franchise. More than 200 franchises that had clearly violated the franchise agreement or did not meet Little Sheep's quality standards were closed. Others that were performing reasonably well had their franchise agreements renewed, and the best-performing stores were bought back by Little Sheep to become directly owned as part of the new, more centralized strategy. This task was complete by the end of 2006.

- *Phase 2: Enhancing training and support to remaining franchise stores.* Phase 2 involved stepping up the training for all franchise personnel through an elaborate new program consisting of various stages of training at headquarters, on site, and during regular national and regional franchisee meetings. In addition, headquarters staff members continued to provide on-site training during their regular store visits.

- *Phase 3: Developing new franchise stores.* The final phase in the new franchise strategy was to proactively develop new stores and grow the franchise fee base. In contrast to the traditional, passive expansion method of responding when potential franchisees called, Little Sheep's new, active approach began with research into the local business environment, which then led to a choice of locations. The company then actively sought out restaurant operators with good reputations to run the franchise stores.

In little more than a year, this new proactive strategy transformed the profile of Little Sheep's franchise system. The company moved from having 40 directly owned stores to over 500 franchises before the 3i investment to a more balanced mix of 101 to 260 by late 2007. Even with a dramatically decreased total store count, these fundamental changes resulted in year-on-year revenue growth of close to 40%, double the industry average of about 20%.

Shelving the International Expansion Plan

Prior to 3i's investment, Little Sheep had an ambitious plan for international expansion. With successful restaurants already operating in Toronto and Hong Kong, management was eager to accelerate the pace of overseas growth and establish the Little Sheep brand name globally. Each regional VP was designated to lead expansion efforts in different overseas regions—North America, North Asia, and South East Asia—even though they were already stretched thin managing their domestic operations.

Little Sheep's overseas ambitions were quite common among the new generation of Chinese private enterprises. On this issue, however, 3i and Little Sheep management had different views. Even though 3i was well placed to provide introductions and on-the-ground

support for an overseas expansion, it strongly recommended that Little Sheep initially focus on strengthening domestic operations rather than rushing into overseas expansion. "Given the vast and yet untapped opportunities in China's restaurant industry, it is strategically important for Little Sheep to leverage the leading market share and brand name it has already established to secure a dominant market position at home before expanding its operations overseas," Cheung explained.

Although management initially resisted this 3i recommendation, Zhang later conceded that this was a sensible approach. Looking back on the incident, one of the independent directors viewed the outcome as one more example of the company's fundamental strength: "They [Little Sheep management] are open-minded, and very willing to listen," remarked Yuka Yeung, "which is really remarkable. It is a learning company."

Early Results

From the time of 3i's investment in mid-2006 until the end of 2007, Little Sheep opened 37 new stores and achieved year-on-year revenue growth of 40%, far in excess of the 15%–20% average growth in China's food sector. The strong revenue growth was also fueled by the evolution of Little Sheep from a pure restaurant business into a more diversified food and beverages group with two meat processing facilities, a packaged-seasoning plant, a logistics company, and a number of regional subsidiary companies. Little Sheep also completed its search for new senior executive talent: Daizong Wang validated his confidence in Little Sheep by resigning from 3i in October 2007 to become Little Sheep's new CFO, and Yuka Yeung, one of the independent directors and the former CEO of KFC's Hong Kong franchise, became the new COO.

Conclusions

At first glance, the pairing of 3i, a global private equity group with almost no track record in China, and a restaurant chain with origins in remote Inner Mongolia might seem like an odd and unlikely match. But the story of their relationship conforms to many of the fundamental characteristics of successful private equity transactions, especially in emerging markets. First, the initial driver that allowed 3i to win the mandate after an intense contest with better-known competitors was chemistry, or the ability to make the founder comfortable with its industry expertise, commitment to the company, and approach to post-investment value creation. Money was secondary. Second, Little Sheep's founder had the foresight and self-confidence to recognize the value of accepting an *active* investor into his company. Even though he had never heard of 3i before meeting Daizong Wang, he and his senior management team exhibited an openness and eagerness to learn from outsiders, which is not always the case, especially with closely held family-run firms in emerging markets. Third, this is a textbook case of the positive results that stem from closely aligned interests between a private equity investor and the management of a portfolio company. From the beginning, the 3i team was exceptionally hands on, working closely with the company's senior management team on a continuous basis to make significant changes in the company, always with an eye to building value and moving closer to the day when Little Sheep would be positioned to successfully execute an IPO. The combination of these three factors go far to explain the ingredients required for successful private equity transactions in emerging markets—or anywhere.

CASE DISCUSSION QUESTIONS

1. From an industry-based view, identify some of the competitive forces affecting the Chinese restaurant industry.

2. What are the key factors that explain the success of Little Sheep? What are the main obstacles associated with its continued growth?

3. From a resource-based view, explain the non-financial benefits that 3i can bring to Little Sheep. In other words, why did 3i win the competition against other private equity suitors such as Goldman Sachs and Morgan Stanley?

4. Compare and contrast the similarities and differences between the typical mid-size private equity investments in the West and such investments in China (as captured by this case). If you were a manager working for a Western private equity firm (such as 3i), what lessons would you draw from this case?

5. If you were an entrepreneur at a firm in China (such as Little Sheep) or in emerging economies in general, what lessons would you draw from this case?

TeliaSonera: A Nordic Investor in Eurasia[1]

How did TeliaSonera grow from being a local telecom provider in the Nordic region to a trend-setting international player in Eurasia markets?

Canan Mutlu, *University of Texas at Dallas*

Today, climbers can have 3G access on Mount Everest to brag about their experience on top of the world. However, not many people know that it is a Nordic company providing this service in such an alien environment. The company is TeliaSonera, which provides telecommunications (hereafter "telecom") services in a wide geographic area from Nordic countries to Nepal that includes the emerging and highly valued Eurasia markets. TeliaSonera is the fifth largest telecom operator in Europe and has operations in Azerbaijan, Belarus, Denmark, Estonia, Finland, Georgia, Kazakhstan, Latvia, Lithuania, Moldova, Nepal, Norway, Russia, Spain, Sweden, Tajikistan, Turkey, Ukraine, and Uzbekistan.

As a Swedish-Finnish company, TeliaSonera launched the world's first 4G network. Spanning from the Nordic and Baltic countries to the Himalayas, TeliaSonera serves more than 150 million customers in total. Listed on NASDAQ OMX Stockholm and NASDAQ OMX Helsinki, TeliaSonera had net sales of around US$15.9 billion and EBITDA of US$5.6 billion, and enjoyed a market value of US$31 billion as of April 2010. How did TeliaSonera grow from being a local telecom provider in the Nordic region to a trend-setting international player in Eurasia markets (see Exhibit 1)?

Merger of Telia & Sonera

TeliaSonera emerged as a company after the merger of Telia of Sweden and Sonera of Finland in 2002. Telia's history goes back to the early 1900s, when the Swedish government established a state-owned monopoly telephone company in the name of Royal Telegraph Service, which became Televerket in 1953. How could a state-owned monopoly evolve into a modern, private, and competitive company?

The rules of the game began to change for the telecom industry toward the end of the 20th century. First, accelerated technologies in the form of cordless and mobile phones forced Televerket to re-evaluate its organizational capabilities. Second, new private players started to enter the Swedish telecom market. Third, the fall of the Berlin Wall in 1989 presented new investment opportunities in Eastern Europe markets. With an urge to modernize the company and respond to these opportunities and challenges, Televerket was privatized and removed from the national budget in 1984. After investing in several Eastern Europe countries, Televerket converted into Telia AB in 1993, a private and competitive company that operated both in Sweden and Europe's liberalized telecom market.

Finland was governed by Russia between 1809 and 1917, and its telegraph operations had been part of the Russian state telegraph system since 1855. However, as Finland declared independence in 1917, the country's telephone system went under the control of private parties, unlike the early state monopoly of Sweden. However, the government still controlled the expansion of telecom systems in rural and international areas. In 1921, about 850 private telecom companies united into a federation, which was named Finnet later in 1996. Eventually, the Finnish telecom market had two major players, one state-owned and one private. The telephone part of the state-owned company turned into a commercial company in 1994 in the name of Telecom Finland. Introduced in the stock exchange in 1998, the company's name changed to Sonera.

---

1 This case was written by Canan Mutlu (University of Texas at Dallas) under the supervision of Professor Mike Peng. © Canan Mutlu. Reprinted with permission.

EXHIBIT 1   TeliaSonera's Eurasia Operations

COUNTRY	POPULATION	GDP GROWTH	BRAND NAME	TELIASONERA OWNERSHIP	MARKET POSITION	SUBSCRIPTION RATE	MARKET SHARE
Azerbaijan	9 million	2.8%	Azercell	51.3%	1	4 million	55%
Georgia	4.4 million	5.5%	Geocell	100.0%	1	2 million	44%
Kazakhstan	16.5 million	5.9%	Kcell	51%	1	9 million	50%
Moldova	3.6 million	4.5%	Moldcell	100%	2	907,000	32%
Nepal	28.5 million	4.5%	Ncell	80.0%	2	4.1 million	42%
Russia	141.9 million	4.8%	MegaFon	43.8%	2	57 million	26%
Tajikistan	7.1 million	5.8%	Tcell	60%	1	1.7 million	36%
Turkey	73.7 million	4.6%	Turkcell	38%	1	34 million	55%
Uzbekistan	27.8 million	7%	Ucell	94%	2	7 million	32%

Source: TeliaSonera website, http://www.teliasonera.com.

The fall of the Berlin Wall in 1989 and the EU's new telecom policies presented both challenges and opportunities. Financial restrictions and the necessity to face new opportunities with a stronger cooperation led Telia of Sweden and Sonera of Finland to merge in 2002. In the Baltic countries, Telia and Sonera joined forces to build fixed and mobile networks. They were on the scene even before the collapse of the former Soviet Union in the early 1990s. Telia already had experience operating mobile companies in various countries in Asia, Africa, Latin America, and Europe. The most significant aspect of this collective power was displayed in its Eurasia expansion.

Eurasia Expansion

Distinguishing its markets as mature and growth markets, TeliaSonera identified its operations under three business areas: mobility services, broadband services, and Eurasia (see Exhibit 2). Mature markets especially consisted of the Northern Europe countries, where customers demand value-added services that can best be used with smartphones. The leading growth market, Eurasia, was named as its growth engine by TeliaSonera.

TeliaSonera developed aggressive goals for its Eurasia operations: (1) double-digit revenue growth, (2) defending the EBITDA margin, (3) taking a leading position in mobile data, and (4) increasing ownership in core holdings. What are the underlying reasons that led to the successful expansion of TeliaSonera in these challenging yet attractive markets? TeliaSonera's operations in Eurasia, where the institutional frameworks are either in transition from planned to market economy or relatively weak compared to Europe, can be examined under the lens of the strategy tripod in terms of the resource-based, institution-based, and industry-based views.

First, TeliaSonera leveraged its decades of telecom expertise developed in Nordic countries in the developing countries of Eurasia region. The technical know-how and deep customer understanding of the company as unique resources enabled operations in difficult areas to be smoother and less problematic. TeliaSonera utilized its know-how specifically in infrastructure investments in the region. The highly technological and better quality network investments provided TeliaSonera a leading edge in the region compared to local competitors. This high

EXHIBIT 2 TeliaSonera's Business Areas

MOBILITY SERVICES	Mobile communication services. The business area is composed of mobile operations in Sweden, Finland, Norway, Denmark, Lithuania, Latvia, Estonia, and Spain.
BROADBAND SERVICES	Communication and entertainment services to corporate and individual customers. The business area is composed of operations in Sweden, Finland, Norway, Denmark, Lithuania, Latvia, Estonia, and international carrier operations.
EURASIA	TeliaSonera is the biggest telecom investor in Eurasia. The business area is composed of mobile operations in Kazakhstan, Azerbaijan, Uzbekistan, Tajikistan, Georgia, Moldova, and Nepal. The business area is also responsible for developing TeliaSonera's shareholding in Russian MegaFon and Turkish Turkcell.

Source: TeliaSonera website, http://www.teliasonera.com.

investment cost turned into a larger and more satisfied customer base, upgrading TeliaSonera into the leading positions in most countries. Moreover, the technology expertise reflected in infrastructure investments expedited the government relations and related bureaucratic issues.

Second, TeliaSonera faced certain challenges due to weak institutional settings, especially in former Soviet Union countries in Eurasia. Although each country is in a different phase of transition to market economy, the economic, legal, and regulatory systems are still highly bureaucratic and risky. The ambiguity in the institutional frameworks brings additional risks for businesses, significantly increasing the costs of investments. The telecom industry has further liabilities in terms of infrastructure spending and related fix costs. TeliaSonera's success in its Eurasia expansion lay in utilization of strong business and government ties that were developed in decades throughout the company's history in the region.

Third, the market conditions in Eurasia countries present many opportunities for technology companies. In contrast to developed European countries, fixed networks are not as developed, which in turn makes these countries rely more on mobile networks. This in fact means a jump into a higher technology for consumers. Moreover, mobile network penetration is lower in Eurasia than in TeliaSonera's mature markets, offering a great deal of potential for TeliaSonera's mobile operations. There are fewer competitors, which enables higher margins to be reaped. Moreover, many Eurasia markets welcome foreign direct investments (FDI) as a source of economic development. These market conditions not only increased

the attractiveness of the region for TeliaSonera but also the likelihood of future investments.

Another significant aspect of market conditions is a larger and younger population that is the number one customer group of new technologies and telecom services in Eurasia countries. This provided a huge sales opportunity for TeliaSonera's telecom services in the region. For example, although it is below the level of developed economies, the use of mobile data services showed an increasing trend and constituted a big share in total revenues in Eurasia markets (see Exhibit 3). Moreover, improved macroeconomic situations and growing economies led to strong subscription intake, which increased revenues by 16% in 2010. By further leveraging its capabilities, TeliaSonera set its target to become the number one player in Eurasia and neighboring region, which has a population of more than 380 million.

Alliances and Acquisitions in Eurasia

How could a Nordic company with roots in highly developed markets in Europe expand in such politically risky and institutionally ambiguous settings? Savvy use of alliances and acquisitions in Eurasia appeared to be a key. Itself the result of a merger between Telia of Sweden and Sonera of Finland in 2002, TeliaSonera certainly understood the importance of alliances and acquisitions. Its alliances and acquisitions throughout Eurasia resulted in enviable performance in many host countries, often commanding either the number one or number two positions (see Exhibit 1).

EXHIBIT 3 TeliaSonera's Mobile Data Potential and Revenues

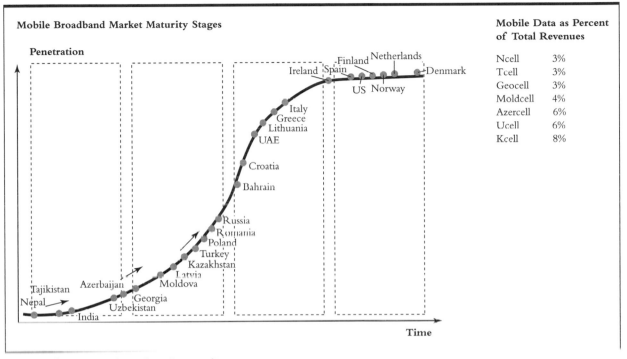

Mobile Data as Percent of Total Revenues	
Ncell	3%
Tcell	3%
Geocell	3%
Moldcell	4%
Azercell	6%
Ucell	6%
Kcell	8%

Source: TeliaSonera website, http://www.teliasonera.com.

Nepal is an interesting case study for TeliaSonera's challenges in Eurasia. After TeliaSonera's acquisition of 80% equity of Nepalese youth brand MeroMobile in 2008, the start-up company, which was now called Ncell, grew into a GSM leader in the whole country. However, the road to success had serious difficulties. There was an ongoing political and security crisis involving terrorist attacks and union strikes, which negatively affected multinationals. TeliaSonera contributed to the efforts to overcome such host country difficulties by offering world-class technologies to this country traditionally suffering from poor telecommunications and also by generating local jobs and employment opportunities. The base stations (cell transmission towers) increased from 300 to 1500 in three years. As a result, the percentage of the population covered by mobile TeliaSonera networks increased from 44% to 80%. Another significant contributor was the use of local employees. Other than employing 25 expatriates, Ncell created 500 solid jobs for locals in a variety of positions.

TeliaSonera's operations in Eurasia aimed to be the trendsetter in these highly dynamic and low penetration markets. For example, its alliance with a local player, Kcell (in which TeliaSonera held a 51% share), was the first company to launch GPRS technologies that provided Kazakhstan people the opportunity to access Mobile Internet, WAP, and MMS services. Kcell owed its reputation to providing the best network coverage and also distribution systems in the whole country. In addition, the young and dynamic population generated a promising customer base for mobile data services, which already made 8% of total Kcell revenues.

New Branding Strategy

Operating in such a broad geographic area, TeliaSonera refined its branding strategy to identify its operations under one brand image in 2009. Eighteen brands of TeliaSonera from Nordics to Nepal began to use the same brand image to convey the customers the message of unity under a strong, multinational brand. At the same time, the local brand names were not altered. Lars Nyberg, CEO and president of TeliaSonera, explained:

> *Our strength lies in the combination of two features: leading and local. We are one of Europe's leading operators with international strength and reach. At the same time, we have strong local brands and operate very close to our customers on each market. Therefore, it is natural to keep the name of the strong local brands but adding a unifying visual brand symbol. This strategy also clearly differentiates us from our competitors.*

The most interesting aspect of this change was that the new branding strategy was first tested in the Eurasia markets in Kcell (Kazakhstan), Geocell (Georgia), Ncell (Nepal), Tcell (Tajikistan), Azercell (Azerbaijan), Moldcell (Moldova), and lastly in Ucell (Uzbekistan) as seen in Exhibit 4. The new brand identity united the local companies under the same umbrella and turned out to be a success in the region that led the companies to protect their leading market positions. Defined as "the next step on our journey to unify the company" by Lars Nyberg, the new branding strategy took off from Eurasia and spread to the Nordic and Baltic region. This harmonization in branding enabled TeliaSonera to further spread and better defend its extensive telecommunication technology in risky but high opportunity markets.

Sources: Based on publicly available information and press releases of TeliaSonera. The following sources were primarily helpful: (1) TeliaSonera CEO's speech Annual General Shareholders Meeting April 6, 2011; (2) TeliaSonera Annual Report 2010; (3) TeliaSonera Investor Day, 2011.

EXHIBIT 4 TeliaSonera's Eurasian Brands

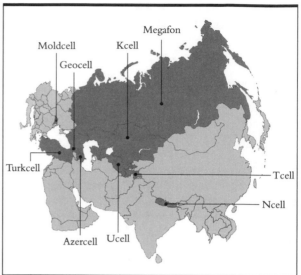

Source: © 1999 Cartesia Software. All rights reserved. Map Resources is a trademark of Cartesia Software.

CASE DISCUSSION QUESTIONS

1. How would you characterize the competitive intensity and attractiveness of the telecom industry in Eurasia by using Porter's Five Forces?

2. Many multinational companies fail in their expansion in emerging economies. What are the main capabilities and resources that drive TeliaSonera's successful growth in Eurasian markets?

3. Given the institutional differences between European and Eurasian markets, what are the main challenges faced by TeliaSonera in its international expansion strategy? Which strategies enable TeliaSonera to minimize the risks of these challenges?

4. How does TeliaSonera differentiate itself from its competitors in Eurasian markets?

The Indian Business Process Offshoring Industry[1]

How has the Indian BPO industry evolved? What are its recent trends after the global recession?

Debmalya Mukherjee, *University of Akron*

The global business process offshoring (BPO) industry is estimated at more than $50 billion in 2012. India accounts for more than 30% of the worldwide BPO market and remains the world's most attractive destination for BPO services delivery. Recent estimates suggest that the BPO sector in India directly and indirectly employs over 4.5 million people, with 50% of these employees younger than 25 years.

Industry Evolution

BPO as a strategic device gained popularity among companies in developed economies chiefly due to its cost attractiveness. In addition, a vast pool of English-speaking graduates who can perform the BPO activities at a fraction of the cost in developed economies makes India a popular destination for companies worldwide. The BPO industry has evolved dramatically in the past two decades. It first gained impetus in the early 1990s when Western companies, driven by increasing cost pressures, started to offshore routine information technology (IT) activities such as testing, simple coding, and data entry to countries such as India, China, and the Philippines. The next wave of offshoring involved business processes that are more knowledge intensive than low-complexity IT activities. As offshoring service providers scaled up their operations and became more specialized, an increasing number of multinationals began to offshore more knowledge-intensive IT and BPO functions including R&D, product design, analytical research, and engineering services.

Genpact, Aegis, Tata Consultancy Service (TCS), WNS Global services, Wipro BPO, Infosys BPO, Mphasis, HCl

Technologies, and Sparsh are some of the key players in this fiercely competitive and increasingly growing industry. Their clients include most Fortune 500 companies. Two retail giants, the UK-based Tesco and the US-based Home Depot, have been outsourcing projects to Indian third-party service providers, including TCS and Infosys, apart from Tesco's and Home Depot's own captive centers. Tesco, for instance, saves over $100 million every year by outsourcing some of its IT projects to India and primarily drives projects from its own captive center in Bangalore.

---

1 © Debmalya Mukherjee. Reprinted with permission.

BPO providers such as TCS BPO, Wipro, Genpact, Infosys, and WNS are global players capable of offering a diversified portfolio of services and also possessing the capabilities to deliver globally. TCS, one of Target's BPO partners, supports the retailer's operations from its delivery centers in Uruguay and Chile, in addition to India. TCS recently bagged a multi-year BPO deal of $2.2 billion from the UK-based Friends Life, a provider of pensions, investments, and insurance. Small and mid-sized players offering a more focused portfolio of services represent over 60% of the market.

Interestingly, a recent trend for client firms has been to divest their non-core captive centers to the top BPO players in exchange for better outsourcing rates and long-term contracts. In 2008, Citibank sold its Indian back-office business to TCS for $505 million and Citi Technology Services sold its own in-house captive center for $127 million to Wipro. These transactions were coupled with the assurance of $3 billion in business for TCS and Wipro. In a win-win situation, Citigroup benefited from freed-up financial resources that had been tied to its non-core business. The close partnerships with firms in developed economies have helped the Indian BPO companies to scale up their service offerings. The industry players have invested heavily to reinforce their relationship management with the client firms and develop capabilities to serve newer industries (such as healthcare) and also across the full range of the product development value chain. In 2011, the engineering design and products development segments grew by 13.6% to generate revenues of $9 billion.

The Impact of the Global Recession

The global recession and the careful spending of North American and European companies have also impacted the dynamics of the Indian BPO industry in at least two ways. First, several BPO providers have started addressing newer and mostly untapped markets in Europe, Asia, and Latin America. Wipro, for instance, has expanded its existing operations in Germany by setting up centers in six German cities. Infosys is also expanding its European operations. TCS has recently set up a global delivery center in Buenos Aires, Argentina. In an effort to better serve the US market, the former GE spin-off Genpact acquired Headstrong, a Virginia-based consulting and IT services company with a specialized focus in financial services, for $550 million. In 2011, Genpact also acquired EmPower Research, a New York-based integrated media and business research company that has strong capabilities in social media research and measurement with office locations in New York, Bangalore, Cincinnati, New Jersey, San Francisco, and London.

Second, huge opportunities for growth lie in the domestic market itself. Infosys entered the domestic market in 2008. It has entered into a partnership with Airtel and is actively trying to grab big government projects as the Indian economy continues to grow despite the global recession. Recently, Infosys concluded a $45.3 million deal to help Indian Railways, the largest railway network in the world, to build an integrated coach management system. Indian IT firms are also increasing their focus on the domestic market to enhance their skill sets. More opportunities exist in the utilities industries, including power, oil, gas, and water distribution projects. Handling such big projects may also help these providers develop capabilities that can be successfully exploited in other emerging markets.

Sources: Based on (1) *BusinessWeek*, 2009, Indian outsourcing companies: Look for new markets, October 12: http://www.businessweek.com/globalbiz/content/oct2009/gb20091012_021104.htm; (2) *IndiaTechOnline*, 2011, India BPO still rules: Nasscom, October: http://indiatechonline.com/nasscom-bpo-summit-2011-543.php; (3) B. Kedia & D. Mukherjee, 2009, Understanding offshoring: A research framework based on disintegration, location, and externalization advantages, *Journal of World Business*, 44: 250–261; (4) S. Lahiri, B. Kedia, & D. Mukherjee, 2012, The impact of management capability on the resource-performance linkage: Examining Indian outsourcing providers, *Journal of World Business*, 47: 145–155; (5) www.nasscom.in.

CASE DISCUSSION QUESTIONS

1. How would you characterize the competition in the Indian BPO industry?

2. What unique resources and capabilities help Indian BPO firms to compete globally and also enter new markets?

3. What formal and informal institutions may accelerate or constrain the growth of the Indian BPO industry?

4. ***ON ETHICS:*** As CEO of any of the leading Indian BPO providers, how do you answer a US reporter who asks: "Many Americans believe outsourcing IT/ BPO work has destroyed a lot of US jobs. What do you think?"

Wynn Macau: Gambling on the Edge of China[1]

Las Vegas-based Wynn Resorts entered Macau in 2002. How did it emerge to become the leader in Macau's gaming industry in ten years? What are its future challenges?

Javier C. Cuervo, *University of Macau*

The liberalization of the gaming industry in Macau, a Special Administrative Region (SAR) of the People's Republic of China, attracted eager bidders to operate casinos in the former Portuguese enclave. In 2001, the year before the casino monopoly of Stanley Ho's S.T.D.M. ended in Macau, gross gaming revenues (GGR) were US$2.3 billion. By 2011, GGR increased to US$33.5 billion. Macau's 29.7 square kilometer area attracted a record-breaking 28 million visitors in 2011—a big leap from the 10 million visitors in 2001.

In January 2012, visitor arrivals increased by 18.6% year on year, with those coming from mainland China representing 60.7% of the total of 2,461,640 visitors.

Visitors from other major markets came from Hong Kong (26%), Taiwan (3.5%), South Korea (1.9%), Japan (1.3%), and Southeast Asia.

The GGR pie is now shared by six players: (1) Sociedade de Jogos de Macau, S. A. ("SJM")—a subsidiary of S.T.D.M.; (2) Galaxy Casino, S.A. ("Galaxy"); (3) Wynn Resorts (Macau), S.A. ("Wynn"); (4) Venetian Macau S.A. ("Venetian"); (5) MGM Grand Paradise, S.A. ("MGM"); and (6) Melco PBL Jogos (Macau), S.A. ("Melco"). There were 34 casinos operated by the six players in Macau by year-end 2011 (Exhibit 1). In 2011, the Wynn Macau casino was reported by *Macau Business* to be the most productive single casino property with gross gaming revenues at US

EXHIBIT 1   Number of Casinos in Macau

PLAYERS	2002	2003	2004	2005	2006	2007	2008	2009	2010	2011
SJM	11	11	13	15	17	18	19	20	20	20
Galaxy	—	—	1	1	5	5	5	5	5	6
Venetian	—	—	1	1	1	2	3	3	3	3
Wynn	—	—	—	—	1	1	1	1	1	1
Melco	—	—	—	—	—	1	2	3	3	3
MGM	—	—	—	—	—	1	1	1	1	1
TOTAL	11	11	15	17	24	28	31	33	33	34

Source: Direcção de Inspecção e Coordenação de Jogos (DICJ) or Gaming Inspection and Coordination Bureau, 2012, Information, http://www.dicj.gov.mo/web/en/information/index.html, accessed on February 24, 2012.

---

1 This case was written to provide material for class discussion and learning. The author does not intend to illustrate either effective or ineffective handling of a managerial situation. The views in this case are those of the author alone and do not represent those of the University of Macau. The author thanks Mr. Richie Chiu for research assistance and Prof. Mike Peng for his support. © Javier C. Cuervo. Reprinted with permission.

$4.375 billion. How did Wynn emerge as the industry leader in ten years? What are its future challenges?

The Stage for Competition

The arena where competition takes place in Macau's gaming market has to be viewed in perspective. Macau is the only jurisdiction within China where casinos are legal. Equally important are the entry requirements of mainland Chinese citizens who visit Macau. Before July 2003, mainland Chinese citizens were allowed to visit Macau only on a group tour visa or on business. With the introduction of the Individual Visit Scheme (IVS) in July 2003, the number of mainland tourists visiting Macau was given a boost. Added to this are factors such as the Chinese penchant for games of fortune, the rise of the Chinese currency relative to the pataca (the Macau currency), and the increasing number of wealthier Chinese, all of which create opportunities for Macau's privileged position.

Supply-side dynamics of gaming operations in Macau are initially determined by institutional factors, such as by Law no. 16/2001 and Administrative Regulation no. 26/2001. The concession contracts by the Macau SAR government for the operation of casinos were signed in March 2002 with SJM and in June 2002 with Galaxy and Wynn. Following the issuance of a sub-concession contract in December 2002 by Galaxy with the Venetian, SJM also signed a sub-concession contract with MGM in April 2005, while Wynn signed a sub-concession contract with Melco in September 2006. These concession contracts are for a 20-year period, after which they are subject to renewal—or the government may award a concession to a new casino operator.

The other limiting factor in competition is the number of gaming tables that casinos are allowed to provide—a main source of gaming revenues. Gaming tables have significantly increased from 339 in 2002 to 5,302 in 2011 (see Exhibit 2). A cap has been set by the Macau SAR government at 5,500 gaming tables until 2013 and thereafter to be increased between 3% to 5% annually. The table cap signals the need to develop further the contribution of the non-gaming revenues in Macau, which is currently trivial, compared to Las Vegas where only 26% of revenues are based on gaming.

The importance of gaming tables is described by McCartney (2010, pp. 176–177): "In 2008, 835 of the

EXHIBIT 2   Number of Gaming Tables and Slot Machines

YEAR	GAMING TABLES	SLOT MACHINES
2002	339	808
2003	424	814
2004	1,092	2,254
2005	1,388	3,421
2006	2,762	6,546
2007	4,375	13,267
2008	4,017	11,856
2009	4,770	14,363
2010	4,791	14,050
2011	5,302	16,056

Source: Direcção de Inspecção e Coordenação de Jogos (DICJ) or Gaming Inspection and Coordination Bureau, 2012, Information, http://www.dicj.gov.mo/web/en/information/index.html, accessed on February 24, 2012.

casino tables were VIP tables, generating around 70% of casino revenues. Historically, the majority of gaming revenues are from casino tables (or VIP tables), and mostly from the game of baccarat. These are through junket operators who receive commission payments." More recently, the VIPs are estimated to have contributed 72% of Macau's gaming revenues in 2010.

It has been reported by a source to *Macau Business* that two out of every five gaming tables are VIP tables. Moreover, the same source also noted the following market share of VIP tables as of the end of September 2011: SJM (28%), Venetian (17%), Melco (17%), Galaxy (16%), Wynn (13%), and MGM (9%).

Legalized in 2010, junket operators play an important role in securing gaming revenues for VIP tables in Macau's casinos. They serve as middlemen who lend high-rollers money to play at the VIP tables and are paid 40% of the casinos' take in return. The junket operators commit a minimum amount of rolling chip purchases set by the casino with which they are associated and then enter into agreements with their representatives, who make the credit checks on the high-rollers and bring them in to play at the VIP gaming tables. The government has imposed an agreed VIP commission cap to avert any commission war among the casinos.

The dynamics of competition take place in various locations within Macau SAR. These include the Macau peninsula of 9.3 square kilometers, which is geographically contiguous south of mainland China and where the border gate and the old ferry terminal are located. South of the Macau peninsula and connected by three bridges is the 6.8 square kilometers of Taipa, where the international airport and the new ferry terminal are located. Finally, the southern tip of Macau SAR is Coloane, which is 7.6 square kilometers. The swamp land that was reclaimed between Coloane and Taipa was termed Cotai by combining the first syllables of these two words—an estimated area of 6 square kilometers. The land in Cotai is where future expansion is being eyed by the incumbents to up the ante in competition.

The casino properties of the six players are located throughout Macau SAR. SJM has 16 properties in the Macau peninsula and four properties in Taipa. Galaxy has six properties with four in the Macau peninsula, one in Taipa, and the largest land bank in Cotai. Venetian has one property in Macau and two properties in Cotai. Wynn has one casino property in the Macau peninsula. Melco has two properties in Taipa and one in Cotai. MGM has a single casino property on the waterfront of the Macau peninsula. Based on a recent Standard Chartered report on Macau's gaming industry published at year-end 2011, the six players' performance metrics are presented in Exhibit 3.

Wynn Is Winning

Based on the metrics of performance, the most productive and profitable single property casino sector player is Wynn. This was analyzed in the same Standard Chartered report: "The key to Wynn's success is the high yield it generates in its mass, VIP, slots and non-gaming businesses. In the

EXHIBIT 3 Performance Metrics on Macau's Six Gaming Concessionaires and Sub-concessioners

PLAYER/METRIC	VENETIAN	MELCO	MGM	SJM	WYNN	GALAXY	TOTAL
VIP tables Dec 2011E	213	341	193	586	286	498	2,117
Mass tables Dec 2011E	909	314	226	1,153	212	452	3,266
Slot handles Dec 2011E	3,515	3,068	1,142	4,147	943	1,254	14,069
Mass market net win (HK $m) Dec 2011E	14,660	6,512	4,595	21,360	6,207	5,656	58,990
VIP net win (HK$m) Dec 2011E	22,335	30,201	21,239	53,349	28,114	35,402	190,641
Slot net win (HK$m) Dec 2011E	2,928	2,048	1,534	1,461	2,278	878	11,127
Total GGR (HK$m) Dec 2011E	39,923	38,761	27,368	76,170	36,600	41,936	260,758
Adjusted EBITDA (HK$m) Dec 2011E	11,770	6,131	4,919	6,984	8,014	5,443	43,261
Adjusted EBITDA margin (% of net revenues)	31.5	20.4	24.5	12.0	27.1	21.8	23.9
Net debt/(cash) HK$m 30 June 2011	11,913	9,997	1,173	-14,161	-4,446	4,996	n.a.
Retail GFA (sq ft) Dec 2011E	1,216,900	175,000	0	0	49,200	0	1,441,100
Hotel keys Dec 2011E	3,439	1,616	587	1,097	1,004	2,522	10,265

Source: Standard Chartered Bank Ltd., 2011, *Macau Gaming*, December 6, Figure 25, p. 14. "E" refers to estimates.

gaming segment, Wynn's fair share ratio (gross gaming revenue market share divided by table count market share) is the highest of any operator or property in 2011." The profitability performance of Wynn is even more outstanding when considering its relatively lower number of gaming tables, retail space, and hotel rooms—compared with the Venetian, for example. Finally, Wynn Macau has a strong balance sheet position of HK$4 billion net cash (i.e., total debt—cash and cash equivalent) in June 2011. What were the underlying factors or reasons behind Wynn's successful performance in Macau?

In 2005, *BusinessWeek* reported that Wynn's "timing couldn't be better" in working out detailed plans to plug into the booming Chinese market in Macau. Indeed, as *Macau Business* pointed out, "Even before opening its doors, Wynn Macau was three-quarters paid for, thanks to the sale of its sub-concession… More than that, it elevated Stanley Ho's second son, Lawrence, the Melco chairman, to gaming business stardom."

Wynn Macau, Limited, is traded on the Main Board of the Hong Kong Stock Exchange and is a subsidiary of Nevada-based and S&P 500/NASDAQ-100 listed Wynn Resorts, Limited. Wynn Macau broke ground in June 2004, and the first phase was completed in September 2006. The approximate cost of the first phase of the property development in Macau (including the expansion completed in December 2007) was US$1.1 billion featuring 380 gaming tables, 1,270 slot machines in 205,000 square feet of casino space, and 46,000 square feet of retail space. Wynn Macau is successfully positioned to cater to the upper end of the market.

With the benefit of hindsight or prudence—a year before the financial crisis took its toll on the US economy and US-based casinos—Stephen A. Wynn, chairman and CEO of Wynn Macau, Limited, commented that "management recognizes and will continue to monitor the effect on our business of the dramatic expansion in supply represented by the openings of the Venetian Cotai in August and the MGM Grand Paradise in November. In light of this uncertainty in the marketplace, we have elected to open only a portion of our Wynn Macau expansion in the third quarter of 2007 and to opportunistically provide the additional supply available in the remainder of the expansion."

Wynn Macau approved to pay dividends on December 3, 2010, and considered paying recurring dividends to shareholders of the company. Moreover, Wynn Macau has also contributed social dividends through the preservation and appreciation of Chinese art through generous donations of Buccleuch vases displayed at the Wynn Macau hotel lobby and Chinese vases that Wynn purchased for US$12.8 million at Christie's London auction for the future Cotai property. Mr. Wynn proudly said, "I am delighted to announce that we are returning an extraordinary collection of porcelain vases from the Qing Dynasty to the People's Republic of China."

In November 2008, Wynn Macau won two prestigious Mobile Five-Star ranking awards and is the only hotel in Macau to do so, reinforcing its leadership role in the transformation of Macau into an international travel and leisure destination for the most discerning guests.

The Cotai Challenge

The Venetian is the largest multi-use integrated resort in Macau with a first-mover advantage in the Cotai area. Its dominant presence in the area will be further strengthened when in March 2012 the first phase of Sands Cotai Central opens with approximately 600 five-star Conrad rooms/suites, 1,200 four-star Holiday Inn rooms/suites, and 300,000 square feet of meeting space, retail outlets, and gaming space. The third quarter of 2012 will also bring in 2,000 Sheraton-branded rooms and more space for entertainment, retail, and meeting facilities.

The Venetian is positioned to take the leading position in the non-gaming segment in Macau as 30% of its hotel guests are families and business travelers. Its announced strategy is "to develop Cotai and to leverage our integrated resort business model to create Asia's premier gaming, leisure and convention destination. Our ultimate plans for Cotai include five interconnected integrated resorts, which leverage a wide range of branded hotel and resort offerings to attract different segments of the market. When complete, we expect our Cotai Strip development to contain over 20,000 hotel rooms, approximately 1.6 million square feet of MICE space, over 2.0 million square feet of retail malls, six theaters and other amenities."

Another major player in Cotai is Galaxy, which has the largest confirmed land bank in the area and is positioned as an integrated "Asian Centric Resort" with world-class hospitality and global standard for the Asian market. Galaxy is the recipient of two prestigious international awards at the International Gaming Awards ceremony held in London: the Casino Operator of the

Year Australia/Asia award and the World's Best Casino/ Integrated Resort of the Year award. The Galaxy has delivered 12 consecutive quarters of EBITDA growth as of the third quarter 2011 and a solid balance sheet with cash on hand of HK$7.0 billion as of September 30, 2011.

Melco's City of Dreams in Cotai is another integrated urban casino resort, which recently won the Best Customer Experience of the Year Award from International Gaming Awards (IGA) 2012, announced at the ceremony held in London on January 23, 2012. The award recognized City of Dreams' outstanding customer service and unique world-class entertainment experience, such as the successful spectacular "The House of Dancing Water," a Franco Dragone Entertainment Group creation.

Proud of the achievements, Mr. Lawrence Ho, co-chairman and CEO of Melco Crown Entertainment Limited, commented: "I am pleased to report our results for the fourth quarter of 2011, completing a remarkable year for the Company where we delivered full year net revenue and EBITDA growth of 45% and 88%, respectively, demonstrating strong top line growth together with impressive operating leverage. Our strong results in the fourth quarter of 2011 further demonstrate our ability to build on the meaningful improvements made earlier in the year, while at the same time executing on a range of strategically important milestones." Long-term growth and increased presence for Melco were given a boost with the successful acquisition of a 60% interest in the Studio City project in the Cotai area. The Studio City project is 32 acres with an expected gross floor area of 465,000 square meters and is aimed at delivering a unique, entertainment-driven experience through innovative attractions in Macau.

As competition heats up in Macau, a "wait-and-see" or "patience may be the path to victory" attitude may be called for by Wynn, MGM, and SJM as they seek the Macau SAR government's approval of their Cotai land applications. Moreover, further expansion by some players in Cotai (such as Sands) will certainly bring pressures in recruitment given Macau's tight labor market. The unemployment rate in Macau was 2.2% in the period October–December 2011.

Given the Cotai Challenge, the future will tell what opportunities the casino operators will face, how they will deal with such opportunities, what obstacles they will encounter, and, most importantly, how they will address these challenges.

Sources: Based on (1) P. Azevedo, 2004, Nice bet, Wynn, www.macaubusiness.com, Issue 8, accessed on December 29, 2011; (2) Direcção dos Serviços de Estatística e Censos (DSEC) or Statistics and Census Service, Macau SAR Government, 2012a, http://www.dsec.gov.mo/Statistic.aspx, accessed on February 24, 2012; (3) DSEC, 2012b, Employment survey for November 2011–January 2012, February 7, http://www.dsec.gov.mo/Statistic/LabourAndEmployment/EmploymentSurvey/Employment Survey2011M11.aspx, accessed on February 29, 2012; (4) Direcção de Inspecção e Coordenação de Jogos (DICJ) or Gaming Inspection and Coordination Bureau, 2012, Information, http://www.dicj.gov.mo/web/en/information/index.html, accessed on February 24, 2012; (5) *Economist,* 2009, Gambling in Macau, June 6: 64; (6) *Economist,* 2011, A window on China, December 10: 61–62; (7) Galaxy Entertainment Group Limited, 2010a, Galaxy Entertainment Group won top awards at International Gaming Awards, http://www.galaxyentertainment.com/en/ir-release.html?view=investorrelation, accessed on February 22, 2012; (8) Galaxy Entertainment Group Limited, 2010b, Selected unaudited 2011 third quarter financial data, October 20, http://www.galaxyentertainment.com/en/financial-reports.html?view=investor relation, accessed on February 22, 2012; (9) A. Lages, 2010, Gaming table cap to remain unchanged, *Macau Daily Times* online, November 15; (10) N. Lam & I. Scott (Eds.), 2011, *Gaming, Governance and Public Policy in Macao* (pp. 225–241), Hong Kong University Press and University of Macau Press; (11) L. Leitão, 2012, Very important promoters, *Macau Business,* February: 75–76; (12) *Macau Business,* 2011a, Wynn Macau buys Chinese vases for Cotai property, July 8, www.macaubusiness.com, accessed on December 29, 2011; (13) *MacauBusiness*, 2011b, Buccleuch vases arrive at Wynn Macau, October 28, www.macaubusiness.com, accessed on December 29, 2011; (14) *Macau Business,* 2012, The money spinners, February: 67; (15) *Macau Daily Times,* 2012, Sands new recruitment campaign pressures SMEs, February 27, http://www.macaudailytimes.com.mo/macau/34035-Sands-new-recruitment-campaign-pressures-SMEs.html, accessed on February 29, 2012; (16) G. McCartney, 2010, Stanley Ho Hung-sun: The "King of Gambling," in R. Butler & R. Russel (Eds.), *Giants of Tourism*, Cambridge, MA: CABI Publishing; (17) Melco Crown Entertainment Limited, 2012a, City of Dreams garnered Best Customer Experience of the Year Award from International Gaming Awards 2012, January 26, http://www.melco-crown.com/eng/ir_pr.php, accessed on February 22, 2012; (18) Melco Crown Entertainment Limited, 2012b, Melco Crown Entertainment announces unaudited Fourth Quarter 2011 earnings, February 9, http://www.melco-crown.com/eng/ir_pr.php, accessed on February 22, 2012; (19) Melco Crown Entertainment Limited, 2012c, Melco Crown Entertainment: Your winning hand, http://www.melco-crown.com/eng/bg.php, accessed on February 29, 2012; (20) Melco Crown Entertainment Limited, 2012d, Our properties: The Studio City Project, http://www.melco-crown.com/eng/tsc.php, accessed on February 29, 2012; (21) C. Palmeri, 2005, The revenge of Steve Wynn, *BusinessWeek*, April 11: 74–75; (22) Sands China Ltd., 2010a, *2010 Annual Report*, http://www.sandschinaltd.com/sands/en/financial_information/, accessed on February 29, 2012; (23) Sands China Ltd., 2010b, *2011 Interim Report*, http://www.sandschinaltd.com/sands/en/financial_information/, accessed on February 29, 2012; (24) Sands China Ltd., 2010c, The company, http://www.sandschinaltd.com/sands/en/company/, accessed on February 29, 2012, (25) Standard Chartered Bank Ltd., 2011, *Macau Gaming*, 6 December; (26) University of Macau, 2010, *About Responsible Gambling*, The Institute for the Study of Commercial Gaming, http://www.umac.mo/iscg/Events/RG_symposium/rg_home.html, accessed on February 29, 2012; (27) Wynn Resorts, Limited, 2006, Wynn Resorts, Limited reports third quarter results, November 7, (28) Wynn Resorts, Limited, 2007, Wynn Resorts, Limited announces equity repurchase program, June 7; (29) Wynn Resorts, Limited, 2008a, Wynn Resorts, Limited reports fourth quarter results, February 12; (30) Wynn Resorts, Limited, 2008b, Wynn Macau celebrates Five-Star Awards from Mobil Travel Guide, November 10; (31) Wynn Resorts, Limited, 2010, Wynn Resorts, Limited reports third quarter results, November 2.

CASE DISCUSSION QUESTIONS

1. How would you characterize competition in the gaming industry in Macau?

2. From the institution-based view, what institutional developments have facilitated the development of this industry?

3. What resources and capabilities were behind the performance of Wynn Macau?

4. Retrieve and analyze recent information concerning Wynn's operations in Macau. Are there any recent developments that may significantly affect Wynn's future performance? How does the updated assessment of performance differ from your assessment of Wynn's performance answered in Question 3? What factors may be able to explain the change in its recent performance?

5. ***ON ETHICS:*** Responsible gaming is promoted by various stakeholders in various gambling capitals of the world, such as Macau. The government in your city or country is soliciting views from stakeholders on the issues concerning the introduction of gambling. Discuss the various stakeholders' positions that will most likely be presented to the government, and debate the pros and cons of introducing gambling in your city or country. What conclusions can you make about gambling and its impact on society?

Ryanair[1]

From industry-based, resource-based, and institution-based views, how can we understand the drivers behind Ryanair's success? From an ethical standpoint, is CEO Michael O'Leary a loose cannon or an astute strategist?

Charles M. Byles, *Virginia Commonwealth University*

Always in the news and not shy of adverse publicity, Ryanair has been soaring in profits for the past few years. In November 2011, CEO Michael O'Leary announced a 20% increase in profits that in his words was "a testament to the strength of Ryanair's lowest fare/lowest cost model." Ryanair did not start with this model, however. Founded in 1985 with its headquarters in Dublin, Ireland, Ryanair began flights between Ireland and the UK and later launched services on the lucrative Dublin-London route after challenging the British Airways-Aer Lingus duopoly. But its initial foray into the airline business was not profitable. As a result of severe financial losses in 1990, Ryanair changed its strategy, adopting the Southwest Airlines business model and becoming the pioneer of low fares in Europe. The next two decades showed growth from 745,000 passengers in 1990 to 73.5 million in 2010. Based on passengers carried, the airline is now Europe's largest low-cost carrier and second largest airline.

Resources and Strategy

While Ryanair competes primarily on low cost, it also differentiates (through certain aspects of customer service) and raises revenues on non-ticket items (through ancillary services) as a means of offsetting the lower fares. Although successful, this strategy has been controversial. The airline has been accused of concealing its ancillary fees and offering customer services that are only available for a fee. How does Ryanair deliver on its low-cost strategy? Five value chain activities are key to its low-cost advantage: (1) operations, (2) human

resource management, (3) customer service, (4) use of the Internet, and (5) ancillary revenues.

Operations

Use of a single model of aircraft (the Boeing 737-800) is the primary method of cost control because it allows minimization of training and maintenance costs, efficient management of spare parts inventory, and more flexible scheduling of flight crews. The popularity of the 737 model also means that flight crews are more readily available for hire. Finally, because Ryanair purchases a large number of aircraft from Boeing, it can negotiate price concessions.

Other cost savers are the use of secondary and regional airports that offer competitive prices, the use of outdoor boarding stairs instead of jetways, having all passengers check in on the Internet, and the introduction of a checked bag fee, which reduces the number of bags carried by passengers (hence reducing handling costs and the number of check-in desks). Airports are chosen because of their low fees rather than for market reasons. Some agreements with secondary and regional airports base the airline's fees on traffic volume.

The short-haul flights operate without the costs of meals, movies, and other in-flight services expected by passengers on longer flights. While the distance of the secondary airport from the main cities and the charge for checked baggage are inconvenient, a benefit is more frequent on-time arrivals, quicker turnarounds (fewer bags to check), and more frequent on-time departures because these airports are less congested. Quicker turnarounds and more frequent on-time departures are also

---

1 © Charles M. Byles. Reprinted with permission. As of February 2012, the exchange rates were approximately €1 = £0.83 = US$1.32.

enhanced because the airline offers neither connecting flights nor the transfer of baggage to other flights, whether operated by Ryanair or not.

Human Resource Management

The productivity-based incentive system is another activity contributing to greater ancillary revenues and efficiency. Flight attendants receive commissions for onboard sales and, along with pilots, payments based on the number of hours or sectors flown. For the 2010 fiscal year, productivity-based incentives accounted for approximately 39% of a typical flight attendant's total earnings and 37% of a typical pilot's total compensation. The cost of customer service is reduced by outsourcing ticketing and other services at airports. For these services, Ryanair has been successful in negotiating fixed-price multi-year contracts.

Customer Service

Although Ryanair has a reputation for poor customer service, the airline states that customer service is an important aspect of its strategy. Ryanair's stated approach to customer service is the deliberate reduction of services in some areas (e.g., free checked bags, meals, flights to major airports) while raising it in others (e.g., on-time departures and arrivals, fewer lost bags). Its December 2011 customer service statistics (published on the Ryanair website) state that 89% of flights arrived on time, complaints were less than one per 1,000 passengers, and mislaid bag claims were fewer than one per 2,000 passengers.

The airline believes that customers prefer fewer services plus extra fees as needed for meals and other items in exchange for low fares. The Air Transport Users' Council, however, claims that in 2009, easyJet and Ryanair had the most complaints of any major European airlines. Cancellations, missing bags, and denied boardings were top complaints. In a recent *Bloomberg Businessweek* article titled "Ryanair's O'Leary: The Duke of Discomfort," even CEO O'Leary suggests that customer service is poor:

> In exchange for cheap fares, he [O'Leary] says, passengers will put up with just about anything. On Ryanair, that can include high luggage fees; relentless in-flight sales pitches for smokeless

> cigarettes and scratch-off lottery games; minimal customer service; bad, expensive food; cramped seats; and flights to secondary city airports that are sometimes hours from the actual city.

In the same article, O'Leary criticizes competitors for treating budget travelers with a level of courtesy that they do not receive elsewhere nor expect when traveling. O'Leary believes that customers will endure discomfort and indignity as long as they get to their destination cheaply and with their suitcases.

Ancillary Revenues

Ancillary revenues (revenues beyond the sale of a ticket and including sales of related items such as hotel reservations or car rental, as well as charges for food, checked baggage, priority boarding, and other items) allow the airline to make up income lost through lower ticket prices. Ryanair has been particularly creative in coming up with new means of generating ancillary revenues. For example, in 2009, the company announced the sale of smokeless cigarettes to ensure that passengers get their "fix" of nicotine without lighting up.

The company's website contains offers for car hire, travel insurance, hotels, airport transfer, credit cards, hostels and bed and breakfasts, cruise holidays, villas and apartments, campsite holidays, and others. Ancillary revenues are also generated by charging fees for priority boarding, reserved seats, airport boarding card reissue, checked baggage, excess baggage, infant equipment, sports equipment, musical instruments, and many others. One controversial fee is the boarding pass reissue fee (charging €40/£40 for a passenger who fails to print out his boarding pass) that has been ruled illegal by a judge in Barcelona, Spain. Without the charge, Ryanair argues that it would have to employ numerous handling agents to issue boarding passes for passengers who forget to print them.

The Irish Examiner newspaper reported that Ryanair's ancillary revenues for 2009 were €663 million, more than any European airline, and in the top five ranking of airlines around the world (the top three are United, American, and Delta). For the half-year ended September 30, 2011, ancillary revenues increased by 15% to €486.5 million, faster than the increase in passenger volume.

Use of the Internet: Booking, Check-in, and Boarding

Passengers must book and pay for fares on the Ryanair website or through the call center. An administrative fee applies to all bookings made through the call center and also to web bookings made without using Ryanair's free payment method (MasterCard Prepaid Debit Card). Flights are booked one-way only, and tickets may be changed for a fee but cannot be cancelled. Passengers must check in online starting 15 days before the flight and up to 4 hours before departure time. An online check-in fee applies to all tickets booked (€6/£6 for flights booked online and €12/£12 for those made via the call center or at the airport). After checking in, the boarding pass must be printed and presented at boarding. No changes can be made to passenger name(s), flight dates, times, or route once the check-in is completed. Seating is not assigned unless "Reserved Seating" has been purchased (on the website) or where passengers have indicated that they need special assistance. Passengers who have purchased "Priority Boarding" (also from the website) may board before others provided they arrive at the gate no later than 30 minutes before boarding. Refunds are possible only in the event of a flight cancellation or the death of an immediate family member (within 14 days of the travel date).

Loose Cannon or Astute Strategist

CEO Michael O'Leary has served as a director since November 1988, deputy chief executive from 1991 to 1994, and CEO since January 1, 1994. In 1991, he went to Dallas to meet Southwest executives and took the lessons back to Ryanair. While O'Leary embraced a few central aspects of Southwest's model (e.g., a single aircraft model, secondary airports), he went much further with the constant drive to keep costs down. In particular, the extensive use of ancillary fees to balance the low ticket prices became a trademark of Ryanair and now forms a core element of its low-cost strategy.

Known for his aggressiveness, outrageous public statements, and insults to almost any group or individual who gets in the way of Ryanair—including customers who complain about poor service—O'Leary has been accused of making outlandish suggestions (for example, to have standing passengers on aircraft or to replace one of the pilots with a computer) to gain publicity. One recent proposal is to remove two of the three toilets on each aircraft in order to add six seats.

O'Leary referred to the decision to close Scottish airspace in May 2011 because of the volcano eruption in Iceland as "bureaucratic incompetence." To demonstrate that there was no safety threat to aircraft and the designation of it as a "red zone" by the UK's Civil Aviation Office was flawed, Ryanair deliberately flew an aircraft (without passengers) through that closed airspace.

Despite giving the impression of being a loose cannon, however, industry experts say O'Leary is an astute strategist who has created a singular focus on cost control that competitors have been unable to imitate. He leads by example—staying in budget motels, having no smartphone, and flying on Ryanair. His office is sparse and the company headquarters in Dublin is a drab 15,000-square-foot building.

Operating and Financial Performance

For the half-year ended September 30, 2011, total operating expenses increased 26% to €2.06 billion as a result of increased fuel prices, an increased level of activity, and costs associated with the growth of the airline. Fuel remains the main cost (€907.0 million or 44%), but airport and handling charges are also significant (€316.3 million or 15%), as well as route charges (€271.5 million or 13%) and staff costs (€222.5 million or 11%). Fuel costs increased by 37%, while route charges increased by 22% and airport and handling charges increased by 18%. Ryanair aggressively tries to hold costs in check through fuel hedging and negotiation with airports over their charges. Adjusted profit after taxes increased 20% to €543.5 million compared with €451.9 million in the previous half-year. The increase was primarily due to increases in fares and strong ancillary revenues of €486.5 million, an increase of 15% over the previous year.

Government Regulation

Ryanair owes much of its success to the liberalization of air transportation in Europe, starting first with air transportation between Ireland and the UK. In 1992, the Council of Ministers of the EU adopted measures to liberalize air transportation. EU carriers were allowed to set fares provided they created access to routes throughout the EU. A licensing procedure was also established. Beginning in April 1997, EU carriers have generally been able to provide service on domestic routes within any EU member state outside the home country in which the airline is based. Ryanair is subject to both Irish and EU regulation.

The Irish Department of Transportation (DOT) is responsible for implementation of EU and Irish legislation and international standards relating to air transportation. Of importance to Ryanair, in 2005, the DOT enacted legislation in response to EU legislation requiring compensation and assistance to passengers in the event of denied boarding, flight cancellation, and long delays (EU 261).

Ryanair views the EU 261 regulations as "unfair and discriminatory" because they require airlines to pay compensation to passengers as well as cover other costs in circumstances beyond the control of the airline such as air traffic control strikes or failure by airports to clear snow from runways. Ryanair argues that compensation in such circumstances be limited to the ticket price paid as is required for train, coach, and ferry operations. (The regulation itself states that airlines are not responsible for passenger compensation for events beyond the airline's control.) In the case of denied boarding, cancellation, or a long delay (which is deemed the same as a cancellation), short-haul airlines such as Ryanair would be required to pay €250 per passenger (for inconvenience to that passenger). Airlines are also required to reroute or refund the ticket and may be required to provide meals, accommodation, and other amenities to passengers.

Questionable Practices

Ryanair has been accused of a number of questionable practices, particularly the use of controversial or misleading advertisements. Several complaints have been filed against Ryanair with the Advertising Standards Authority (ASA), the UK's independent regulator of advertising. BBC News reported that, in 2008, Ryanair faced an ASA probe asserting that it made exaggerated claims about the availability of flights at advertised prices that did not include taxes and fees.

Even Ryanair acknowledges its controversial advertisements by a statement on its website that it engages in "punchy advertising that sometimes gets us in trouble." In 2011, the ASA criticized a Ryanair advertisement featuring a bikini-clad woman promoting trips to a "place in the sun." The ASA argued that some of these places had as little as three hours of sunshine per day. Many of these advertisements appear to violate Ryanair's own policy against "misrepresentation of the facts" (part of the airline's published ethics code).

Industry and Competition

The European airline industry is highly competitive with a number of low-fare (e.g., easyJet, Air Berlin, and Germanwings), traditional (e.g., British Airways, Lufthansa, and Air France), and charter airlines (e.g., Monarch Airlines and Titan Airways). Charter flights are offered by low-fare as well as traditional airlines, and some charter airlines (e.g., Monarch) offer scheduled services. Airlines compete on fares, time and frequency of services, service quality (e.g., number of on-time departures and arrivals, frequency of lost baggage, and frequency of involuntary denied boardings), amenities such as frequent flyer programs, and reputation. Ryanair believes that state-owned competitors have advantages because of subsidies and other state aid provided to them. In addition, the EU-US Open Skies Agreement that took effect in 2008 allows US carriers to offer services in the intra-EU market that result in increased competition. The increasing consolidation in the industry (for example, the recent acquisition of BMI by International Airlines Group, the parent company of the merged British Airways and Iberia) poses additional threats for Ryanair as these airlines control large percentages of short-haul slots at major airports.

Although Ryanair boasts having the lowest fares, a survey in May 2011 by *The Telegraph* showed how the cost of a flight on a low-cost carrier can escalate when all fees are added, making prices on a traditional carrier such as British Airways more competitive. The survey was of return flights for a family of four from London to Madrid traveling on the same dates in August with two checked bags, golf clubs, and a cot (baby crib) and paying with a debit card. The base fares were: Ryanair

£271.92; easyJet £275.92; and British Airways £476.20. While Ryanair had the lowest fare, the costs went up substantially once all fees were added. To Ryanair's ticket cost would be added an online check-in fee (£48), luggage fees (£80 plus £80 for golf clubs and £20 for the travel cot), administration fees (£48), and the new delay/cancellation fee (£16) for a total cost of £563.92, the highest of the three carriers. While this survey represents a snapshot of a particular trip and may not be applicable to all trips, it makes the point that Ryanair is not always the cheapest way to travel; passengers must consider the added fees before making the ticket purchase. To the extent that passengers become more familiar with the complex Ryanair fee structure, Ryanair may be placed at a disadvantage compared to low-fare and traditional airlines as illustrated in this survey.

Airlines also face competition from substitutes such as high-speed rail systems and sea transportation (which in Ryanair's case would be more relevant to travel between the UK, Ireland, and continental Europe, as well as travel to Morocco). Finally, the industry faces cost pressure from monopoly suppliers such as airports and air traffic control services as well as revenue pressures from buyers with low switching costs.

Future Risks and a Bold Idea

Ryanair's recent financial performance shows growth, profitability, and strong returns to shareholders. CEO O'Leary attributes this success to the company's strategy. But the company also faces risks of cost increases from suppliers (primarily fuel) and regulatory agencies that may impose additional costs associated with environmental, safety, and security measures. Fuel prices are expected to rise in 2012. Increasing legislation, in particular EU 261, could have continuing adverse effects on Ryanair. One new piece of legislation that took effect in January 2012 is the European Union's emissions trading scheme. Under this requirement, airlines must pay for the carbon dioxide they emit. Estimates are that airlines are likely to pay about €1.4 billion for carbon permits in 2012, rising to €7 billion by 2020. A certain number of permits will be issued free to each airline, but they will have to buy permits on the open market for emission beyond the allowed amount.

Could other airlines successfully imitate Ryanair's strategy much as it imitated Southwest's strategy?

Should Ryanair raise the competitive stakes? One bold strategic idea is to offer free flights in perpetuity (the airline already has some free flights) given Ryanair's remarkable success with ancillary revenues. Ken Fisher, founder of Fisher Investments (and a Ryanair shareholder), told CNBC in an interview, "You get on the plane; they sell you stuff; the stuff they sell you is what pays for you going." Is this idea a realistic possibility? The most recent financial data show that while ancillary revenues had record growth in the previous six months, they make up only 18% of total operating revenues. Ryanair would have to generate significantly large increases in revenues to cover its expenses and generate a profit, especially given the cost increases cited earlier.

Sources: Based on (1) Airlines to spend estimated €1.4bn on carbon permits in 2012, *The Guardian,* January 3, 2012; (2) Ancillary charges account for 20% of Ryanair income, *Belfast Telegraph,* September 11, 2012; (3) *Annual Report,* Ryanair Holdings PLC, (Form 20F filed with US Securities and Exchange Commission), July 20, 2010; (4) Careers: Working for Ryanair, Ryanair website, 2011; (5) S. P. Chan, Monarch to compete with Ryanair and easyJet as it steers away from package holidays, *The Telegraph,* June 1, 2011; (6) Child free flights from October 2011, *Ryanair News,* April 1, 2011 (website); (7) easyJet and Ryanair top complaints league, *guardian.co.uk,* 12 March, 2010; (8) N. Emerson, Ryanair challenges Spanish court over boarding passes, *BBC News,* 21 January, 2011; (9) N. Erlich, Bullish on Ryanair's free flights: Investor, *CNBC Stock Blog,* 19 April, 2011; (10) F. Gillette, Ryanair's O'Leary: The Duke of Discomfort, *Bloomberg Businessweek,* September 2, 2010; (11) N. Hennessy, Baggage, credit card charges driving Ryanair's €663 million ancillary revenue haul, *Irish Examiner.com,* July 23, 2010; (12) History of Ryanair, Ryanair website, 2011; (13) M. Leroux & A. Schaefer, Ryanair fights to reduce passenger luggage, *The Times,* February 25, 2009; (14) S. Lyall, No apologies from the boss of a no-frills airline, *The New York Times,* August 1, 2009; (15) R. Massey, Cross your legs and prepare for takeoff: Ryanair reveals plan to have just one toilet on each plane to make room for more seats, *Mail Online,* 13 October, 2011; (16) M. Maier, A radical fix for airlines: Make flying free, *CNNMoney,* March 31, 2006; (17) D. Milmo, Ryanair to charge for seat reservations, *guardian.co.uk,* April 19, 2011; (18) Ryanair faces probe over adverts, *BBC News,* September 4, 2008; (19) Ryanair flies plane through Icelandic volcano ash cloud, *The Telegraph,* May 24, 2011; (20) Ryanair half year profits rise 20% to €544m, traffic grows 12%, full year guidance raised 10% to €440m, half year results 2012, Ryanair website; (21) Ryanair No 1 customer service stats—December 2011, *Ryanair News*, January 18, 2012 (website); (22) Ryanair's bikini advert banned by ASA, *BBC News*, 27 April, 2011; (23) Ryanair's Michael O'Leary: Outrageous success story, *Travel Sentry*, August 2, 2009; (24) Ryanair to allow passengers to 'smoke' on board, *Ryanair News*, September 20, 2009 (website); (25) Ryanair will comply with unfair EU 261 regulations, *Ryanair News*, April 22, 2010 (website).

CASE DISCUSSION QUESTIONS

1. From an industry-based view, assess the strength of the five forces and determine the extent to which Ryanair is positioned against those forces.

2. From a resource-based view, what explains Ryanair's success?

3. From an institution-based view, assess the opportunities and threats presented by the current and future institutional environment (both formal and informal). How should Ryanair respond?

4. What is your evaluation of the proposal that Ryanair offer free flights in perpetuity? Draw on the three views in your answer.

5. *ON ETHICS:* Evaluate Ryanair's ethical (or unethical) behavior, especially in light of the questionable practices discussed in the case. What changes, if any, would you recommend to CEO Michael O'Leary?

SolarWorld USA[1]

> *SolarWorld USA, a subsidiary of Germany's SolarWorld AG, is the largest US-based manufacturer of solar products. In the face of intense Chinese competition, SolarWorld USA's revenue has declined and margins are in free fall. How can it survive?*

David Darling, *University of Texas at Dallas*
Fabia Bourda, *University of Texas at Dallas*

Gordon Brinser, president of SolarWorld USA (a subsidiary of Germany's SolarWorldAG), reviewed the quarterly financial statements from his office in Hillsboro, Oregon. It was a bright, sunny afternoon in June 2011. Although the clear sunny day was perfect for the production of electricity from the solar panels his company produced, the financial reports provided a stormy forecast. Brinser had just come back to his office from the quarterly business meeting with his top management team, and the results were troubling. The sales forecasts showed declining sales, deteriorating gross margin, and a rapid reduction in market share. He desperately needed to find a way to reverse this downward trend in sales volume and to increase sales margins in the face of serious market competition.

Particularly troubling was the pressure from Chinese solar panel makers. These low-cost suppliers came from relative obscurity and were now the dominant players globally. Thousands of US jobs, hundreds of millions of dollars, and the future of SolarWorld were at stake. As Brinser intently studied the financial documents, he recounted how rapidly the situation had changed in the solar panel industry.

Just three short years before, riding the waves of political support, recent financial success, and anticipating bright growth prospects in North America, SolarWorld had dramatically increased its US investment. The future had seemed bright due to the dramatic growth in the sales

forecasts and SolarWorld's leading market share position. With the sun setting, knowing that he had to face shareholders and reporters with the quarterly financial report tomorrow, Brinser began to write down the strategic options and plans for SolarWorld. In the back of his mind, he was wondering: "How can SolarWorld survive in a world of intense Chinese competition?"

SolarWorld History

From the austere beginnings as Solar Technology International in 1975, SolarWorld AG emerged in 1998 to enter Germany's rapidly increasing solar market. The dramatic growth of the German solar industry was driven by the German government through wide-ranging

---

1 This case was written by David Darling and Fabia Bourda (University of Texas at Dallas EMBA 2012) under the supervision of Professor Mike Peng. The purpose of the case is to serve as a basis for class discussion rather than to illustrate the effective or ineffective handling of an administrative situation. The views expressed are those of the authors (in their private capacity as EMBA students) and do not necessarily reflect those of the individuals and organizations mentioned. © David Darling and Fabia Bourda. Reprinted with permission.

regulations and initiatives like the "100,000 Roofs Initiative." The programs included regulated wholesale and retail pricing of electricity and significant incentives for manufacturers and large-scale solar power production facility operators.

On this foundation, SolarWorld built a business whose principal activities include research, development, production, and marketing of products for solar power generation as well as the installation of complete solar power stations. The company is fully vertically integrated, combining all aspects of the solar product cycle from the raw material silicon to turnkey solar power plants, as well as the development of proprietary solar systems and power solutions. Controlling all the stages of the product design and production cycle allows the company to uphold high quality and environmental standards throughout the process.

The SolarWorld group of companies operates in Germany, Europe, Asia, the US, and other countries. It is also involved in the planning, construction, and operation of wind energy and solar energy parks as well as other power stations based on renewable energies.

In 2008, SolarWorld purchased a 480,000-square-foot production facility in Hillsboro, Oregon, and added 1,000 employees, making it the largest US-based solar manufacturer as well as one of the largest in the world. Just like the expansion in Germany a decade earlier, this US expansion was also largely driven and supported by government initiatives. These included regulations, tax incentives, low-interest loans, and multiple other federal programs. The Obama administration's green initiatives and "Buy American" programs were consistent with the desire to expand the US demand for solar products and to create US jobs.

Corporate Financial Performance

SolarWorld is struggling with serious financial problems. Shown in Exhibit 1, revenue has decreased by 21% between 2Q2010 and 2Q2011. In addition, the declining gross margin due to sales price erosion has resulted in a 66% decrease in consolidated net income. Investors and creditors rely heavily on the quarterly performance reports in making their investment decisions. The company's stock price, also shown in Exhibit 1, has been taking a beating based upon earnings rumors. These new financial results, to be released tomorrow, will further erode the stock price. In addition to these pressures, many of the subsidized loans and tax incentives are based upon revenue performance targets and sustained employment commitments for the US employees. Therefore, cost cutting through US production or job reductions is not an option.

Solar Technology

Solar energy is a 100% renewable form of energy that is generated by radiant sunlight. It is a secondary energy source categorized alongside wind, ocean wave power, hydroelectricity, and biomass. Only a very small amount of total electrical power in the world is generated using solar energy.

Solar technologies are broadly characterized as either passive solar or active solar depending on the way they capture, convert, and distribute the solar energy. Active solar technology includes the use of photovoltaic panels and is the primary product of SolarWorld. The core objective of solar panels is to efficiently capture the photons of sunlight and convert them into useable electrical power.

US Solar Power Utilization

The United States has multiple sources of fuel energy for the production of electricity. Coal is the predominant fuel used, and the US has large coal reserves. Coal is followed by nuclear power and then natural gas. The average retail price paid for electricity in the US in 2010 was $0.1046 per kilowatt-hour. The reasonable price for electricity in the US provides very little incentive for producers or consumers to quickly move to alternative forms of energy.

Renewable energy makes up 8% of the total power production and consumption in the US with photovoltaic generation supplying 1% of the total renewable energy. The primary reason for the small percentage of utilization is the high comparative cost of solar power and the capital investment required. Actual performance and financial data proved difficult to obtain from public sources, so as part of this case research, a quotation for a roof-mounted photovoltaic system was

EXHIBIT 1   SolarWorld AG Financial Data

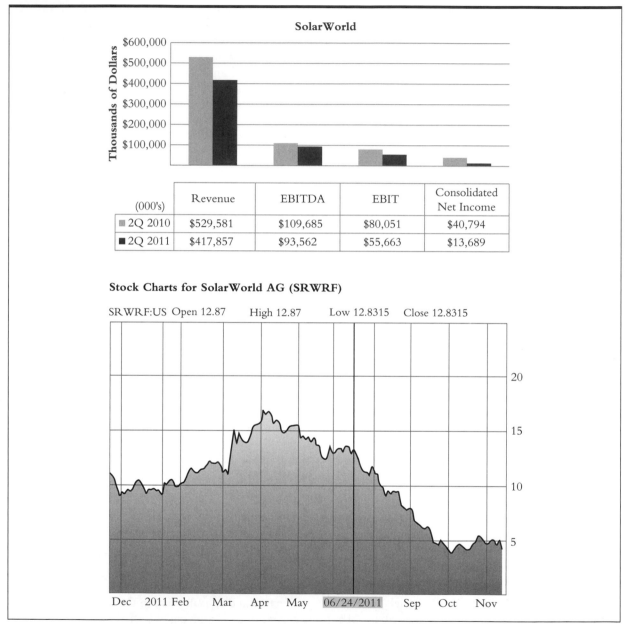

(000's)	Revenue	EBITDA	EBIT	Consolidated Net Income
■ 2Q 2010	$529,581	$109,685	$80,051	$40,794
■ 2Q 2011	$417,857	$93,562	$55,663	$13,689

Sources: SolarWorld.com (currency conversion done November 15, 2011); Bloomberg.com.

sourced from a national provider of solar energy solutions. The system included 224 240-watt solar modules and a non-penetrating ballasted roof mounting structure. The DC power produced would be fed through one 50kW, 480-volt inverter and connected to the main building power. Solar performance as well as federal and state utility tax incentive information was also provided with the quotation. The results are provided

EXHIBIT 2 Solar Photovoltaic Project Proposal

Fujitsu—Photovoltaic Proposal 2011
- Proposed 54 kW DC system
- Roof mounting on light framing
- 50 kW, 480 VAC inverter
- No batteries
- Connected to main service

Photovoltaic Solution: 54 KW, no batteries	
System Costs	$309,120
Federal Incentives	− 92,736
Utility Incentives	− 94,080
Net Initial Investment	$122,304

Return on Investment

	78,948 kWh at $0.08/kWh	78,948 kWh at $0.08/kWh
Yearly Production		
Yearly Profit	$6,316	$7,895
Simple Payback	19.4 years	15.5 years
IRR	2%	4%

Source: Fujitsu Network Communications, Facilities Department, Dallas.

in Exhibit 2, which illustrates that with more than 60% of the capital cost paid for by federal and state incentives, the system still requires 15 to 20 years to achieve a simple payback. The internal rate of return is very low, ranging from 2% to 4% based upon a 25-year expected life of the system.

US Solar Energy Trade

In 2010, the United States remained a significant net exporter of solar energy products. The total net exports were $1.9 billion. The US solar energy products segment maintained a net positive trade balance of $247 million to $540 million with China. The largest single export product is polysilicon at $2.5 billion, and it is used in the production of photovoltaic cells abroad. The largest solar energy imported product was photovoltaic modules. Additional information is available in Exhibit 3.

SolarWorld Products

In addition to polysilicon and other industrial products in support of photovoltaic technology manufacturing for power generation, SolarWorld makes Sunmodule™ and Sunkits® solar products for the US consumer market.

Sunmodule™ solar panels are designed and manufactured to the highest standards of quality, guaranteed performance, and durability. Sunkits® are custom-designed complete solar electric systems. A new and innovative solar carport is also offered. These products are supported by a 25-year linear electrical output performance guarantee and 10-year product workmanship warranty. The mono-crystalline and poly-crystalline products from SolarWorld come in a variety of sizes, making them suitable for all applications—from a residential rooftop to a large-scale facility.

International Market Conditions

China is currently the largest solar energy–related trading partner with the United States. At this time, the US maintains a net positive trade balance with China. The US provides capital equipment and raw materials, and China sells back the completed solar modules. The dynamics are rapidly changing, however, as China begins to flex its economic muscle. Chinese companies have led the way toward reducing the price of solar modules by nearly 50% in 2009, and the economic battle is raging.

Much like the US government, the Chinese government sees a dramatic opportunity in the growth of solar energy products. However, China has a significant institutional advantage: It has tens of billions of dollars to invest. In 2010 alone, the Chinese Development Bank provided $30 billion in low-cost loans to the top five solar module producers. The magnitude of this capital infusion has some people in the solar industry calling it "predatory financing."

The stage is currently being set for a charge by US solar companies against Chinese firms for the dumping of solar modules on the US and world markets. Chinese firms are often the focus of US antidumping accusations, but these accusations also occur between many countries. The typical claim is that the foreign company is using an unfair advantage or government

EXHIBIT 3 US Solar Imports and Exports

Imports from Selected Country to the United States (in millions of dollars)	Exports from the United States to Selected Country (in millions of dollars)
China: 1,431	China: 1,671–1,963
Mexico: 480	Germany: 865
Japan: 322	Japan: 609
Taiwan: 264	Norway: 258
Germany: 215	Canada: 223
Austria: 24	Italy: 126
Canada: 22	France: 74
Korea: 20	Spain: 23
Italy: 12	All Other: 912
All Other: 194	Undisclosed*: 561–853
Undisclosed*: 695	

$3,679M TOTAL IMPORTS

$5,614M TOTAL EXPORTS

$1,934M NET EXPORTS

*Some estimates provided as a range due to corporate confidentiality policies.

Source: GTM Research.

funding to engage in dumping in order to benefit in the foreign market and drive out the domestic competition.

SolarWorld's Resources and Capabilities

SolarWorld has several significant resources that are available to help combat their sagging performance. It is a fully vertically integrated provider, which creates a long and resilient value chain. This can be demonstrated using value (V), rarity (R), imitability (I), and organization (O)—or the VRIO framework.

Multiple opportunities for additional focus and revenue generation are available. For example, new technology development and fully integrated solutions are opportunities to enhance value. Value can also be exploited through bundling of products and services, such as SolarWorld's dual-purpose solar carport.

As solar modules are becoming commoditized, SolarWorld continues to have other strong product segments that provide advantages in the area of rarity including polysilicon production. Polysilicon is a very

specialized product and requires considerable time and capital to establish a production facility.

A primary area of concern is imitability. The Chinese are close on the heels of SolarWorld, and China has demonstrated the financial capability and the staying power to keep driving the industry.

Finally, organizational structure and experienced management resources are also tremendous assets to SolarWorld due to its long history in the solar industry and the experience gained from operations through multiple business cycles.

Institutional Considerations

The dominant threat posed by the influx of Chinese solar modules is best evaluated from the institution-based view. Institutions played a key role in the original founding of SolarWorld and its early success in Germany, as well as the expansion and success in the US from 2008 to present.

The entire US solar power industry is largely funded and propelled by federal and state support and receives enthusiastic public support from multiple constituencies. These provide an excellent strategic advantage for SolarWorld. The institutional framework in the US is a dominant market force. In a recent research study on the American Jobs Creation Act of 2004, government action provided companies that lobbied for these laws a return of $220 for every $1 invested in lobbying for its passage. These same forces were at work in the Economic Recovery Bill of 2009 in which $100 billion was invested in clean energy and environmental projects.

Lastly, SolarWorld has an advantage due to the US antidumping laws and the sentiment among constituents and lawmakers that favor US-produced solar products.

Business Decision

Over the previous three years, the US government during the Obama presidency has provided an excellent opportunity for green energy providers. With billions of tax dollars invested in green energy initiatives in the past three years, the US solar power industry received a huge upward boost. These funds were invested in research, development, and federally guaranteed low-interest business loans. They provided federal funding for procuring renewal energy sources including solar panels for use in state and federal properties.

During this same time period of dramatic federal investment, however, another dramatic change was occurring. According to SustainableBusiness.com, the US global market share of solar modules had decreased from 50% to about 6%. Even more surprising, the Chinese had captured more than 50% of the global market, and the importation of Chinese panels into the US grew by more than 300%.

In the face of the challenging market conditions and intense market competition particularly from Chinese manufacturers, SolarWorld is determined to create a strategy to adapt. As Brinser reviewed his notes, he began to formulate a strategy based upon the firm's resources and capabilities as he wondered: "Which strategy should I pursue, and is it possible for SolarWorld to survive?"

Sources: Based on (1) US Energy Information Administration, *2010 Annual Review* (n.d.), retrieved November 16, 2011, http://www.eia.gov/forecasts/aeo/sector_electric_power.cfm; (2) US Energy Information Administration, 2011, *Average Retail Prices,* October 19, retrieved November 16, 2011, http://38.96.246.204/totalenergy/data/annual/showtext.cfm?t=ptb0810; (3) K. Bradsher, 2011, China charges protectionism in call for solar panel tariffs, *New York Times*, October 21, retrieved November 6, 2011, http://www.nytimes.com/2011/10/22/business/global/china-warns-of-bad-effects-if-us-turns-protectionist.html?pagewanted=all; (4) K. Bradsher, 2009, China racing ahead of US in the drive to go solar, *New York Times*, August 24, retrieved November 6, 2011, http://www.nytimes.com/2009/08/25/business/energy-environment/25solar.html; (5) K. Bradsher, 2011, Chinese trade case has clear targets, not obvious goals, *New York Times*, October 20, retrieved November 6, 2011, http://www.nytimes.com/2011/10/21/business/chinese-solar-trade-case-has-clear-targets-not-obvious-goals.html?pagewanted=all; (6) A. Carey, 2010, Obama's green initiatives lobbied for by the same people who profit from them, *Daily Caller*, August 26, retrieved November 16, 2011, http://dailycaller.com/2010/08/26/obamas-green-initiatives-lobbied-for-by-the-same-people-who-profit-from-them/; (7) Coalition for American Solar Manufacturing, 2011, *Fact Sheet,* November 6, retrieved November 6, 2011, http://www.americansolarmanufacturing.org/; (8) R. Gaertner, 2001, Germany embraces the sun, *Wired*, July 9, retrieved November 16, 2011, http://www.wired.com/science/discoveries/news/2001/07/45056?currentPage=all; (9) A. Giegerich, 2011, Salem, Hillsboro got in "the zone" for solar jobs, *Sustainable Business Oregon*, May 23, retrieved November 16, 2011, http://sustainablebusinessoregon.com/articles/2011/05/salem-hillsboro-got-in-the-zone-for.html; (10) S. Lacey, 2011, How China dominates solar power, *Guardian*, September 12, retrieved November 6, 2011, http://www.guardian.co.uk/environment/2011/sep/12/how-china-dominates-solar-power; (11) M. W. Peng, 2009, *Global Strategy*, 2nd ed., Mason, OH: South-Western Cengage Learning; (12) S. Alexander, 2009, Measuring rates of return for lobbying expenditures, *SSRN*, retrieved November 16, 2011, http://ssrn.com/abstract=1375082; (13) B. Stuart, 2010, SolarWorld to Create 350 Jobs, retrieved November 16, 2011, from http://www.pv-magazine.com/news/details/beitrag/solarworld-to-create-350-jobs-_100000110/; (14) Sustainable Business.com News, 2011, US solar companies call for stiff tariffs on Chinese solar imports, October 20, retrieved November 16, 2011, www.sustainablebusiness.com/index.cfm/go/news.display/id/23056.

CASE DISCUSSION QUESTIONS

1. How would you characterize the competition in this industry?

2. What resources and capabilities underpin Solar-World's competitive advantage? Why is such advantage eroding?

3. From an institution-based view, why do antidumping tariffs emerge as a weapon of choice?

4. What is Brinser going to tell shareholders and reporters tomorrow?

5. Predict the likely response from Chinese rivals after SolarWorld files antidumping charges against them.

SnowSports Interactive: A Global Start-up's Challenges[1]

SnowSports Interactive executives confronted a number of challenges: Could they attract investors who could share their dream? Which countries could they spread their wings to? How should they spread their wings, i.e., what global strategy should they implement? Could a Brisbane, Australia-based start-up expand globally? If so, how?

Marilyn L. Taylor, *University of Missouri at Kansas City*
Xiaohua Yang, *University of San Francisco*
Diaswati (Asti) Mardiasmo, *Queensland University of Technology*

"The best trick this season won't be done on skis or a board, it will be worn." SnowSports Interactive (hereafter, SSI) executives felt that phrase appropriately described the new technology they were planning to introduce to the world of skiing in the winter of 2006–2007. However, in late June 2006, the company confronted a number of challenges. What, they wondered, did they need to do to maximize the potential for their company?

History of the Company

SSI was born over a beer at a conference in Melbourne, Australia, in January 2004. Company founders Steve Kenny and Shubber Ali quickly envisioned their initial product as a skier tracker system. During 2004, Kenny completed an analysis of the global ski industry. He identified key gaps in the market and the combination of technologies available to fill them. In May 2005, SSI was legally born with Kenny as CEO and Ali as Chairman.

The company's core intellectual property combined the latest positioning, wireless, and identification technologies with proprietary tracking and analysis software. In simple English, SSI technology could locate people and assets at any ski resort in the world where the company's technology was installed.

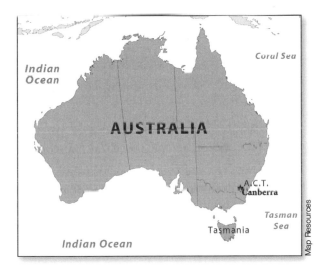

The company was located in Brisbane, Australia, and became an i.Lab member in November 2005. The i.Lab was part of the Queensland Government's new Statewide Technology Incubation Strategy. Location in the i.Lab provided the company with the opportunity to work with some of the leading business minds in Queensland and Australia. Nurturing, mentoring, and resources from i.Lab helped the company reach the next stage/level.

1 The case was developed based on face-to-face interviews with the company executives and publicly available sources. The authors wish to express thanks to the SSI executives and other associates who continue to contribute to the ongoing development of this case study. © Marilyn L. Taylor, Xiaohua Yang, and Diaswati (Asti) Mardiasmo. Reprinted with permission.

The Product/Services

From 2004 through spring 2006, SSI associates concentrated on product design and technology development. The company called its initial product, a small lightweight tag worn by skiers and snowboarders, the Flaik. The Flaik device included multiple technologies, including Global Positioning System (GPS) units to continuously monitor the position and time of users and GSM Communications units to transmit position and time data to a Network Operating Centre.

In March 2006, SSI and Mt. Buller Alpine Resort agreed to a beta test of SSI technology. Located near Melbourne, the Mt. Buller Alpine Resort was the fourth largest among Australia's five major ski resorts. SSI provided both tracking technology and the firm's wireless Internet service called whispar™ at Mt. Buller. The partners used a significant proportion of available funds to install the wireless system. SSI established an on site office for company personnel who dealt directly with customers and observed first-hand how the technology operated on the slopes. The system came into operation on June 9, 2006, and the beta test ran successfully during the 2006 season. Sales of the whispar system increased daily during the first month of operation and continued a favorable growth pattern.

SSI executives wanted to dramatically enhance the experience of skiers, snowboarders, and downhill sliders worldwide. The company had developed extensive intellectual property combining the latest in GPS, Wi-Fi, and RFID technologies with proprietary tracking and analysis software. When asked what the company's competitive advantage was, an SSI representative responded, "The SSI advantage is simple. We provide a simple, compelling user experience through the integration of the latest technology with unique, proprietary applications and services, all in a sleek package with a simple user interface."

The Flaik would be another accessory offering for the skier. Accessories, apparel, and apparel accessories were a must on the slopes. Among items that had been popular in recent years were anti-outerwear, urban influences for edgy looks, hip in the city, hip on the slopes, denim in snowboard pants, synthetic leather pants, prints like zebra, military fatigues, great fitting clothes for women, pockets with CD players, and avalanche devices in garments for the backcountry.

The Industry

The snow sports industry was composed of many facets including manufacturing, retailing, resort development, and tourism. The industry's success was dependent on often-fickle Mother Nature—i.e., on whether the season had sufficient snow. The snow season was different on the five populated continents, and SSI would need to adapt its business model accordingly.

Snow depth was considered very important in the skiing industry as it determined whether a ski resort stayed open or not, the amount of operational days within a season, and the number of lifts operating within the season. The industry reported that the 2003–2004 ski season was the third best season ever in terms of skier visits, despite persistent negative factors such as a slowly rebounding international economy, a jobless recovery in many sectors of the economy, high gas prices, muted consumer confidence levels, and international tensions.

The snow sports industry was primarily known for its downhill and cross-country skiing and snowboarding. In the US, the demand for alpine ski lessons had increased, with a 1.1% increase between 2002–2003 (17,935 lessons) and 2003–2004 (18,135 lessons). The number of snowboard lessons had a smaller increase of 0.2% (from 6,101 in 2002–2003 to 6,113 in 2003–2004).

A new sport that had become recently popular was New School—a youth movement about music, festivals, and action sports. The movement was a fusion of snowboarding, skiing, skateboarding, bike stunt riding, motocross, and surfing. It was "hot" with 12- to 16-year-olds. Another sport that had become popular was Telemark Skiing, where downhill skiers "floated" down the mountain with their heels un-attached. Telemark skiers mostly accessed the backcountry, as it offered freedom and untouched powder for advanced skiers who wanted to push their limits.

The industry had created many innovative products and experienced significant gains in women's and children's equipment and apparel stores. The industry recognized that it relied heavily on affluent but aging baby boomers. However, the industry was also marketing itself to GEN Y, a group defined as those born immediately after GEN X. GEN Y included people in their early to mid-20s, teenagers, and children over the age of five. The term *GEN Y* was most popular in the

US, but its use had gone far beyond the US to refer to the youth throughout the anglophone world. The GEN Y age group was more diverse than previous "generations." For example, 40% of 16- to 24-year-olds were not Caucasian.

In the US, the snow sports industry was governed by SnowSports Industries America (SIA). SIA was a national, not-for-profit, member-owned trade association of competing snow sports companies. Its membership was open to product manufacturers, distributors, suppliers, and retail shops. Service providers, including web designers, could be involved through limited memberships. SIA was known for its comprehensive report on the global skiing market.

The industry also included manufacturers, importers, distributors, and retail suppliers of equipment, apparel, and accessories. Some of these companies were divisions of major corporations listed on the New York Stock Exchange. Others were small, independent companies. The greatest strength of the independent companies lay in their ability to innovate in design of new products, which were constantly giving skiers and riders fresh reasons to hit the slopes

In the US alone, there were 8,500 retailers and other companies offering winter sports products for sale, rent, use as promotions, or use for professional purposes. Of that number, about 2,000 were specialty and chain stores that sold apparel or accessories related to winter sports but not what would be called a "ski/snowboard shop."

The consumer profile of the snow sports industry had continued to exhibit stability on many visitor characteristics and a gradual shift on others. Among the most prominent shifts were the continued aging of the visitor base and a related increase in experience in snow sports. There were also signs of gradual increase in participation by children in the 10–14 and 15–17 age groups, first-timers and beginners, and different ethnicities.

At that time, SSI's main competitors for the Flaik included NASTAR, Slope Tracker, Suunto, and NAVMAN. SSI identified its competitive advantage in real-time remote monitoring, the ability to locate friends, and safety applications. SSI's potential competition came from two main streams, namely, recreational GPS receiver and sports tool manufacturers and recreational snow sports analysis service providers. However, SSI executives felt they were differentiating themselves as a company that would provide customers a low-cost, easy-to-use service with functionality that far outstripped that provided by existing manufacturers and service providers.

The Financial Situation

One of the challenges SSI as a global start-up continued to face in mid-2006 was how to finance growth and capitalize on its current greenfield opportunity presented by the lack of dedicated ski tracking companies. SSI was initially funded by Kenny and Ali. The two founders then relied on a round of financing provided by "three Fs" (family, friends, and fools). In mid-2006, SSI was in the process of placing a round for US$1.5 million at US$3.50 a share (i.e., a company valuation of US$6.06 million). The company had recruited Mike Wallas, CEO of Enterprise Growth Solutions, to secure this round from a combination of high net worth individuals, investment groups, and venture capitalists. The company had also secured government funding through Commercialising Emerging Technologies (COMET) and was preparing grant applications for Commercial Ready, the Queensland Innovation Start-up Scheme, and the (Australian) Federal Government's Export Market Development Grant.

Most experts identify financial issues as among global start-ups' major challenges. SSI executives agreed. The company's five-year profit and loss forecast is presented in Exhibit 1.

The Company Strategy

SSI identified five potential revenue sources in its business model. These sources were: ski school applications, user applications, resort management applications, sponsorship and advertising, and wireless Internet.

A tentative global strategy SSI had adopted to raise funds involved creating partnerships with ski resorts. SSI executives envisioned approaching target markets for expressions of interest. Each partnership would involve creating a limited liability company with a ski resort company. The limited liability company would be operated by a combination of the existing SSI Australian team and a local team. SSI executives

EXHIBIT 1 SSI Five-Year Profit and Loss Forecast

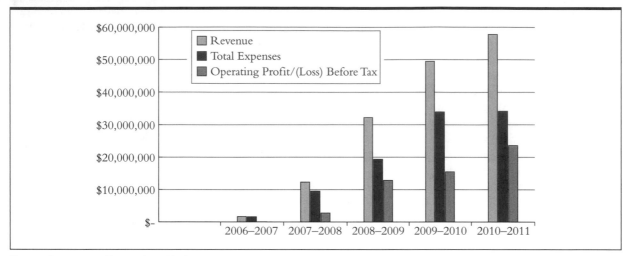

Source: Snowsports Interactive, 2006.

identified the benefits offered to the resort itself as well as to the users of the system, including:

- Improved efficiency of ski school operations resulting in increased utilization of resort assets, including the ski runs, and thus increased revenue.

- Increased safety for ski school participants.

- Improved peace of mind for participants who could locate current positions of friends and family anywhere on the mountain—an aspect deemed to be especially useful to parents in trying to keep track of children, ski schools instructors tracking the whereabouts of their students, or the ski patrol trying to locate missing skiers.

- Enhanced skier experiences on the slopes by keeping score of performance statistics and enabling the skier to compare rankings with friends, family, and competitors.

- Extension of the skiing experience beyond the slopes by creating an online memory of their time on the mountain to share at a later date.

As an SSI partner, each resort would have two options for the infrastructure deployment. The infrastructure would support the range of applications that SSI would provide to the resort operators and guests. The options were: (1) resort purchasing infrastructure that included a three-year life span with license and services contract charges yearly, or (2) resort leasing infrastructure for three years with the license and services contract charged yearly.

The partnership agreement called for SSI to provide a user-friendly process for customers through three elements: (1) integrating Flaik into existing point-of-sale systems in order to simplify the rental process for users, (2) providing upselling of data to parents of ski school participants, and (3) providing optimal placement locations for interactive kiosks in congregation areas such as lodges for customers to use across the resort.

Revenue sharing opportunities between SSI and its resort partners included the upselling of performance data to parents of ski school participants, provision of wireless access to customers using the whispar service, and rental of Flaik devices to non-ski school participants during the first phase of deployment.

The infrastructure and supporting technologies utilized by SSI were sourced from leading technology providers around the world and, where necessary, adapted to the alpine environmental conditions. SSI's current ecosystem of network partners included: Wireless Tech Group, CMD, Power Converter Technologies, Strix Systems Inc, MassMedia Studios, and Abuzz Technologies.

SSI believed that its primary competitive advantages lay in continual innovation through an evergreen research and development (ERD) program, which would allow SSI to update the functionality, flexibility, and interactivity of its front-end user software on a seasonal basis and its hardware every 12 to 18 months. The company planned to protect its intellectual property through a variety of means including patents, trademarks, and copyrights, as well as trade secrets of its designs and circuit layouts. The company also planned to use and enforce confidential non-disclosure agreements.

SSI identified the company's business activities as subject to relatively high risk factors, risks that were related to its business activities and were also of a general business nature. SSI executives fully acknowledged that the company's risks were higher than those generally faced by other companies. These risks included: limited operating history and forecasted losses, intellectual property, national and international regulations, specific country laws, dependence on third-party suppliers, schedule delays, seasonal market fluctuations, and competition. To manage such risks, SSI managers prepared a risk management plan detailing both preventive and contingency actions.

A Global Market for SSI?

SSI executives recognized that signing the agreement with Mt. Buller was "just baby steps" on a long road; the only way to grow the business was to expand into international markets given the seasonality of the ski industry. The company's executives had identified several countries as target markets including the US, Canada, Japan, European countries, China, and New Zealand.

In-house market research suggested that the North American market was the most promising, owing in part to the abundance of information SSI had been able to acquire on it. Although there was more limited information on other target market countries, the executives aimed to spend time investigating them to identify and aggressively address areas with snow skiing activities. As Kenny put it in June 2006:

> We currently have one location, i.e., Mt. Buller. And, we need to be in more resorts in Australia but there are only five major ski resorts and four minor ones here in this country. The most lucrative market, of course, is the USA where there are 493 ski resorts. We could focus on Japan, but that takes a different protocol and we would have to redesign our technology. However, we have had inquiries from Japan and there are a couple of people associated with Hoikkaido resorts. We need to think this through.

Sources: Based on (1) authors' interviews, (2) SnowSports Interactive, 2006, *SnowSports Interactive Information Memorandum*, Brisbane, Australia; (3) SnowSports Interactive, 2006, *Resort Visitor Statistics*, Brisbane, Australia

CASE DISCUSSION QUESTIONS

1. Assess the company as a potential investor. Use a thorough SWOT analysis as a basis for your assessment. Utilize the RBV and VIRO analytical tools to assess SSI's core competences.

2. What are the major risks the company faces as it implements

   a. its domestic market strategy?
   b. a "born global" strategy?

3. What advice do you have for SSI founders for future international expansion? Which market(s) should SSI expand into first?

Wikimart: Building a Russian Version of Amazon[1]

How does a Russian Internet start-up grow? How does it line up financing? How promising are its prospects?

Daniel J. McCarthy, *Northeastern University*
Sheila M. Puffer, *Northeastern University*

Wikimart was founded in 2008 by Stanford MBA students Maxim Faldin and Kamil Kurmakayev as an online marketplace for Russia and Russian-speaking countries. Its focus was a B2C platform for Russian retailers who listed goods at no charge but initially paid a minimum 3% fee to Wikimart on each transaction, later reduced to 1.5%. Wikimart also provided services to these retailers including order fulfillment, accounting and legal support, and e-commerce marketing tools. The company's objective was to become a dominant e-commerce marketplace in Russia and other countries of the former Soviet Union.

Time Line of Financing and Growth

In the first half of 2009, financing of $700,000 was secured from a number of sophisticated angel investors, including Michael van Swaaij who had invested in Skype and eBay Europe; Mark Zaleski and Robert Dighero who had invested in QXL Ricardo; Alec Oxenford, founder of OLX, DineroMail.com, and DeRemate; Jose Marin, founder of DeRemate; and Kerim Baran, founder of Yonja.com. By mid-2009, Wikimart's website was attracting 5,000 daily visitors and had more than 1,000 online merchants offering over 370,000 products.

In early 2010, Series A financing was secured from Tiger Global Management, a successful US-based private equity investor specializing in technology start-ups, often in emerging economies. The deal raised $5 million for Wikimart and resulted in 50% ownership for Tiger, according to a filing with the US Securities and Exchange Commission. In August 2010, Wikimart secured Series B financing of $7 million, again from Tiger Global.

By mid-2010, the company website had 2,000 online merchants generating $1.5 million in monthly revenues for Wikimart that by 2011 had increased to 2,500 merchants and $3 million in monthly revenues. Of course, online sales were a significant order of magnitude larger. Company revenues would have been greater if the order completion rates could have been

1 This case was written by Daniel J. McCarthy (McKim d'Amore Distinguished Professor of Global Management and Innovation, Northeastern University) and Sheila M. Puffer (University Distinguished Professor and Cherry Family Senior Fellow of International Business, Northeastern University). The authors would like to acknowledge the excellent research assistance provided by Northeastern University College of Business student Maxim Russkikh. © Daniel J. McCarthy and Sheila M. Puffer. Reprinted with permission.

improved beyond the 68% level prevailing in 2011. Achieving such an increase, however, would remain a major challenge to implementing the company's strategy as retailers often had insufficient inventories to fulfill customer orders.

By March 2011, the company had signed up 2,200 retailers that listed more than 528,000 products through Wikimart's website. The company reported that the site was attracting 2 million visitors per month, although one of the founders stated that the number could be as large as 3 million. Among the products prominent on its website were home goods and appliances, consumer electronics, wine and tobacco, and virtually any product that could be found on Amazon's website, with the best-selling categories being clothing, sporting goods, and children's products. The vast majority of the products were familiar, internationally known brands.

Why Tiger?

One of Wikimart's founders, Kurmakayev, explained in 2011 why the company had chosen Tiger Global from among various potential core investors: "We chose Tiger because they did not impose their views and did not seek to participate in the business management, but are ready for the long-term partnership." Other potential core investors included Accel Partners, a firm based primarily in the US, with offices in Palo Alto, CA, and New York, that had invested in companies like Groupon and Veritas. Accel also had offices in London, China, and India. Another potential core investor was Index Ventures, a US investor with successful investments in technology start-ups like Skype and Dropbox. It seemed that all of these investment firms might have been looking for the next Google, the hugely successful Internet giant cofounded a decade earlier by Russian-born University of Maryland and Stanford University graduate Sergei Brin.

Business Model

Wikimart's business model centered around creating an Amazon-like online retail platform and business model in the Russian-speaking countries of the former Soviet Union. Similar models had been developed in Korea by Gmarket and in Japan by Rakuten Ichiba. The company's business model offered free space online to merchants while collecting a minimum of 1.5% of each transaction once sales began.

Company Strategy and Organization

The company's strategy included reaching a younger, tech-savvy segment of customers in the Russian-speaking world. The company was headquartered in Moscow, and merchants selling on its site delivered goods only within Russia as of early 2011. One of the partners stressed that Wikimart's objective was to continue developing the Russian market even after it moved to new markets. The company planned to expand overall services to other Russian-speaking countries of the former Soviet Union such as Ukraine and Kazakstan. The partner reasoned that Russia was the tenth largest European country in terms of GDP but had even greater promise in terms of Internet users. Although Wikimart seemed to have vast potential, the company had not turned a profit by early 2012. However, the founders believed that 2013 could be a profitable year. With an objective of eventually attaining 20% to 30% share of the fast growing online retail market, company executives saw the possibility of annual revenues reaching as high as $15 billion by 2018.

The two founders initially assumed separate responsibilities, with Kurmakayev being in charge of maintaining relations with retailers and developing the company's technology and Faldin being responsible for sales, marketing, and business development. As the company grew, the founders recognized early that they had to change to a more corporate-like structure. Faldin became CEO responsible for the operational aspects of the business, such as developing metrics and achieving goals. Kurmakayev took on a strategic role incorporating forecasting and budgeting, as well as developing the company's competitive strategy.

One of the founders claimed that a significant percentage of company costs stemmed from intensive development efforts. Wikimart, although an online retail business, was basically a technology company. The vast majority of the 260 employees in 2011 were programmers who wrote software code to support the company's online business. They were guided in their development work with Silicon Valley expertise provided by their investors and consultants.

Russia's Internet Industry and Wikimart's Competition

The overall Russian e-commerce market was estimated at $7 billion to $9 billion in 2011, a substantial increase over the $6 billion in 2010, growth that attracted many competitors. Exponential future growth, with forecasts of 40% annually, saw estimates of up to a $50 billion market by 2018. Such forecasts added luster to the already attractive Russian online retail market. Wikimart's largest competitor was Ozon.ru, the oldest e-commerce giant of the Russian Internet. Sites like Groupon and KupiVip offering group discounts on products and services were also substantial competitors, and both had attracted relatively large investments from US firms. The order fulfillment challenge for Wikimart noted earlier was due to retailers relying on relatively poor IT technologies. One of Wikimart's founders noted that the online retail industry in Russia required huge investments in IT and supply chain. In 2012, only 1.5% of all Russian retail purchases took place online, but the founders believed that the number would grow to 10% to 20% within five to 10 years.

Some Russian companies, such as mail.ru, had already become powerful Internet players within Russia. That firm's parent, the mail.ru Group, was formerly known as Digital Sky Technologies and was an early-stage investor in Facebook, owning 5%–10% of that company by 2011 according to various reports. It had invested $200 million in 2009 and an additional $500 million in 2011. This is another example of the globalization of private investments; this time, however, the participants were a Russian investment group taking a stake in a US online venture. Mail.ru itself was an extremely successful publicly traded Internet company. Other successful Russian online companies included Vkontakte and Rambler. Vkontakte was a private company that offered social network services and was notable for design and functionality that mimicked Facebook. As of February 2012, Vkontakte reportedly had 116.6 million user accounts and was the fourth most popular Russian Internet website. Rambler was a search engine that offered Web 2.0 services such as e-mail aggregation and e-commerce, with its main competitors being mail.ru and Yandex. Yandex had a reported 64% market share of the Russian search provider space and was the fifth largest search engine worldwide with 1.7% of global searches as of September 2011. The company had enjoyed a decade of success before going public in 2011 on NASDAQ in the US. Its IPO raised $1.3 billion, and its stock price soon traded up by 55%. The price of $1.3 billion valued the company at about $8 billion.

Wikimart's Future

Analysts noted that start-ups like Wikimart had become attractive for strategic investors as the Internet expansion in Russia accelerated. In 2012, the number of Internet users in Russia was not large but was expected to grow by approximately 10% per year. Some analysts expected that if Wikimart continued to increase revenues and profits, it could soon be targeted by strategic investors such as Amazon or eBay. Having US investors like Tiger Global that were very familiar with the Russian Internet market could help attract others, including strategic investors who might invest funds with the intention of acquiring Wikimart at some point. Wikimart's founders and other major shareholders, such as Tiger Global, might eventually have to decide between selling the company to a strategic investor or continuing to maintain control while growing the company to its full potential. As is typical in such cases, timing would be a key factor.

Sources: Based on (1) DST smenila nazvanie (DST changes its name), 2010, http://www.vedomosti.ru/companies/news/1103680/dst_smenila_nazvanie; (2) A. Hesseldahl, 2012. Zuckerberg is the billion-share man: Who owns what, who makes what in the Facebook IPO, *AllThingsD*, February 1, http://allthingsd.com/20120201/facebooks-ipo-filing-who-owns-what-who-makes-what/; (3) *Forbes*, 2011, My stroim Amazon in Russia (We are building Amazon in Russia), July 20, http://www.forbes.ru/tehno-opinion/internet-i-telekommunikatsii/70954-my-stroim-amazon-v-rossii; (4) *RT*, 2011, Tiger Global ups the ante on Wikimart, March 2, http://rt.com/business; (5) http://bloomberg.com/news/2011-05-24/yandex-jumps-after-raising-1-3-billion-in-biggest-technology-ipo-of-the-year.html; (6) http://en.wikipedia.org/wiki/Yandex.

CASE DISCUSSION QUESTIONS

1. From an industry-based view, given the fragmented, rapidly growing nature of online retail space in the Russian-speaking world, how would you characterize the competition in this industry?

2. Why was Wikimart able to secure financing during its early stages of growth? Put differently, if you were an angel investor or private equity investor, what special qualities of Wikimart would attract you?

3. While Wikimart's objective is to become a dominant e-commerce marketplace in Russia and other countries of the former Soviet Union, given the existing competition (such as Ozon.ru), is such ambition realistic?

4. What are some of the viable exit strategies for the two founders?

Texas Instruments in South Korea: An Educational Opportunity[1]

The South Korean Ministry of Education (MOE) recently announced plans to spend $2 billion providing tablet PCs with digital textbooks to a vast majority of students in South Korea by 2015. How can Texas Instruments' Education Technology division tap into these opportunities? What are the challenges?

Kris Baker, *University of Texas at Dallas*
Harold Burman, *University of Texas at Dallas*
Andrew Cyders, *University of Texas at Dallas*
Ben Wilson, *University of Texas at Dallas*
Yanmin Wu, *Texas Instruments*

The South Korean Ministry of Education (MOE) recently announced plans to spend $2 billion providing tablet PCs with digital textbooks to a vast majority of students in South Korea (hereafter "Korea") by 2015.[2] With an average of fewer than eight students per PC in 2007, the Korean education system already boasts one of the most technologically enabled student bodies in the world, and this initiative will advance its cutting-edge use of computers in the classroom even further. This effort, in conjunction with the ongoing digital textbook initiative undertaken by the MOE in 2007, will push the Korean education system to the forefront of industrialized nations and presents a huge opportunity for educational device suppliers.

Based in Dallas, Texas Instruments (TI) has long been a leader in producing and marketing education solutions for students and teachers. TI offers both hardware solutions (including calculators, scientific instruments, and docking stations) and software solutions (including teacher–student interface programs, math and science modules, and class interconnectivity applications), providing a multitude of value-add products for educators and students alike. Given TI's

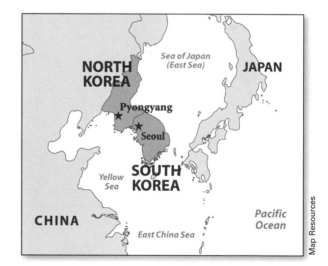

prominent position in the education marketplace and its broad product portfolio, the Korean market represents an intriguing prospect for future business.

The questions for TI are quite simple: What opportunities does the Korean tablet initiative provide for TI?

---

1 This case was written by Kris Baker, Harold Burman, Andrew Cyders, and Ben Wilson (University of Texas at Dallas MBA 2011) and Yanmin Wu (Texas Instruments) under the supervision of Professor Mike Peng. The team thanks Ashwin Joshi for his collaboration. The purpose of the case is to serve as a basis for class discussion rather than to illustrate the effective or ineffective handling of an administrative situation. The views expressed are those of the authors (in their private capacity) and do not necessarily reflect those of the individuals and organizations mentioned.
© Kris Baker, Harold Burman, Andy Cyders, Ben Wilson, and Yanmin Wu. Reprinted with permission.
2 Socyberty.com, 2010, Koreans substitute books with PC tablets.

How can TI effectively communicate the value of its education solutions to its Korean constituents? Perhaps most importantly, how can TI ensure that its products have all of the attributes necessary to meet the needs of the Korean education system?

Textbooks: From Paper to Pixels

The ubiquitous paper textbook is an item that most modern students know quite well. The multi-billion dollar industry boasts a number of large international players including Cengage Learning (publisher of *this* textbook), McGraw-Hill, and Pearson Education. While such textbooks are deeply ingrained in traditional classroom instruction, recent studies into the feasibility of digital textbooks and the massive increase in personal computing access have pushed both educators and textbook publishers to examine the future of the industry, which appears to be digital.[3] The combination of interactivity, reduced marginal cost, and personalized content have positioned digital textbooks at the precipice of worldwide adoption, and many educational institutions worldwide are beginning to incorporate digital textbooks into their curriculum.

Removing the textbook from the written page offers a number of significant benefits to both students and teachers. Far beyond basic PDF versions of traditional text, modern digital textbooks apply technology to enrich the student experience, including audio, video, and interactive features like quizzes and note-sharing tools. Digital textbooks complement the multimedia and interactive functions with links to references such as articles, primary sources, workbooks, and dictionaries. Furthermore, they allow students the convenience of accessing the textbook on the same computer that they use to complete their homework assignments. Digital textbooks also offer significant benefits to educators, as they allow teachers to monitor student activity, identify areas of improvement, and facilitate interaction between students. Exhibit 1 illustrates the benefits of digital textbooks.

Many textbook publishers are also beginning to identify the massive opportunity that digital textbooks provide. Margins for digital textbooks are quite high. Although they are typically priced lower than print versions, they avoid the production cost of paper textbooks, which currently eats up a large portion of publishers' margins. "Printing and distribution of traditional books account for more than 20 percent of the cost of the book."[4] With commodity prices expected to continue rising, that share stands to grow. Publishers may also benefit from a larger customer base since digital textbooks can be easily divided and sold in portions. Further, additional revenue streams are presented to publishers through both licensing of books (allowing customers to use the content for a limited period of time) and dissemination of content update patches (a process with minimal distribution costs due to the digital nature of the content).

While publishers certainly face challenges in adapting and developing content for digital textbooks, the most compelling reason to enter this market is quite simple: increasing demand. The recent rise of tablet PCs and digital media devices, such as Amazon's Kindle and Apple's iPad, has led to an explosion in the electronic book market. The digital textbook market has been slow to catch on, representing "only 2.8 percent of total US textbook sales in 2010,"[5] but is already experiencing large growth, with expected US sales of $267.3 million in 2011—up 44.3% from the year before.[6] However, with students increasingly turning to personal computing for help both inside and outside of the classroom, sales are expected to grow considerably in the near term, "[doubling] over the next four years to $1.5 billion by 2015, [and accounting] for 25 percent market share."[7] Publishers can expect to face stiff competition as software programmers, device manufacturers, and content developers push for a piece of this market. With global trends mirroring the US market, competition will only intensify.

---

3 C. Schuetze, 2011, Textbooks finally take a big leap to digital, *New York Times*, November.

4 B. Coombs, 2011, Tablets make digital textbooks cool on campus, *USA Today*, June 17, http://www.usatoday.com/tech/news/2011-06-17-digital-textbooks_n.htm.

5 N. Rachlin, 2011, Digital textbooks slow to catch on, *New York Times*.

6 C. Schuetze, 2011, Textbooks finally take a big leap to digital, *New York Times*, November.

7 Coombs, 2011, Tablets make digital textbooks cool on campus, *USA Today*.

EXHIBIT 1   The Benefits of Digital Textbooks

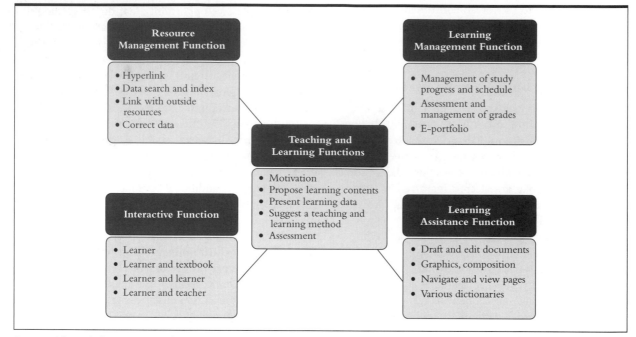

Source: Adapted from Korea Education & Research Information Service, 2007, *Research on the Standardization of Digital Textbooks,* Seoul.

South Korea: Modernizing Education

As a nation with limited natural resources but high population density and a rising standard of living, the Korean government has long recognized the importance of maintaining a well-educated, technologically enabled workforce. To this end, the Korean government has taken a number of measures, from facilitating the fastest residential broadband network in the world[8] to investing heavily in applying information and communications technology (ICT) in Korean classrooms. Additionally, the Korean culture highly values education, seeing it as a measure of both social status and economic differentiation. While Americans may view secondary education as an investment, "in Korea, high school students and their parents sustain a constant demand for higher education, even following significant declines in both the relative lifetime earnings advantages for college graduates and the expected rate of return on higher education."[9]

The combination of economic incentive and cultural demand for access to quality education has led the Korean government to devote significant resources to improving education nationwide. Responding to recent studies showing that traditional methods of lecture- and text-based learning are not adequately preparing students for careers in a "multitasking, multifaceted, technology-driven, diverse, and vibrant world,"[10] the Korean Ministry of Education, Science and Technology (MEST) initiated the Digital Textbook project in 2007. With a goal of studying the benefits and challenges associated with implementing digital textbooks in Korean classrooms, the project began with 5th and 6th

---

8 J. Sutter, 2010, Why Internet connections are fastest in South Korea, CNN.com, March 31, http://articles.cnn.com/2010-03-31/tech/broadband. south.korea_1_broadband-plan-south-korea-broadband-internet/2?_s=PM:TECH.

9 D. Kim, 2002, Expectations from education, *Journal of Higher Education Policy and Management, 24*(2), p. 2.

10 D. Kim, 2002, Expectations from education, p. 2.

graders in a test group of 20 schools, later expanded to 100 schools.[11]

The conclusions drawn from this pilot program were striking. First, students showed significant improvement in "interest, comprehension, satisfaction, and self-efficacy as well as in their level of academic achievement after using differentiated instruction with digital textbooks."[12] Second, low-achievement students in test groups showed marked improvement over control groups using printed textbooks. While results varied by region, socioeconomic status, and family status, test groups responded favorably overall.[13] Third, and perhaps most importantly, teachers responded extremely well to the implementation of digital textbooks. Teachers spent less time preparing instructional props to align with printed textbooks, allowing them to focus on "designing and developing instructional strategies" and "concentrate on providing more significant instructional feedback than simply checking homework."[14]

Despite these clear benefits, the study went on to identify a number of potential challenges in the implementation of digital textbooks in Korean classrooms. A lack of clear design parameters led to complex textbook packages that were "difficult to develop and maintain,"[15] and integration of the multitude of additional features was costly and time consuming. Without significant upfront training and experience with the digital textbooks, teachers struggled to smoothly integrate them into the classroom environment. Further, while digital textbooks were shown to be effective for teaching mathematics, teachers still felt that additional effort was needed to align the digital textbooks used in the study with specific academic subjects. "For instance, science classes often require various laboratory activities; however, digital textbooks cannot

support them."[16] After reviewing the results of this study, the Korean MOE and MEST viewed these challenges as temporary gaps in quality that will be overcome as publishers collaborate with software developers to improve content delivery. Expanding the study each year following the pilot in 2007, the Korean government has recently announced plans to provide tablet PCs with digital textbooks for each student in K–12 education and is set to implement this plan in 2015.

TI: A Pioneer in Education

Founded in 1930, TI is a manufacturing, design, and sales leader that produces a variety of products including communications equipment, computing hardware, industrial supplies, consumer electronics, automotive components, and education solutions (see Exhibit 2).[17] With 2010 net income of $3.2 billion on roughly $14 billion in revenue, TI is one of the largest and most profitable manufacturers in the United States. TI also has a significant global presence. In 2010, over 88% of its revenue was generated outside the US (see Exhibit 3).[18]

To students in the United States, TI's most visible products are its lineup of calculators and other education solutions, which come from the TI Education Technology (TI ET or Ed Tech) division and generate 3% of TI's overall revenue.[19] TI ET offers a multitude of hardware products and software applications to help improve learning in the classroom. Assuming the MOE will continue to source tablets from LG as it did during the pilot tests,[20] there may not be a market for TI's lower-level graphing calculators. Therefore, the following discussion will examine attributes of the *high-end* hardware and software applications most applicable to the Korean market: the Nspire calculator product line and the software/online content products offered by TI to educators.

11 J. Kim & H. Jung, 2010, *South Korean Digital Textbook Project*, Taylor & Francis Group, LLC, p. 6.
12 Kim & Jung, 2010, South Korean Digital Textbook Project, p. 11.
13 Kim & Jung, 2010, South Korean Digital Textbook Project, p. 12.
14 Kim & Jung, 2010, South Korean Digital Textbook Project, p. 12.
15 Kim & Jung, 2010, South Korean Digital Textbook Project, p. 13.
16 Kim & Jung, 2010, South Korean Digital Textbook Project, p. 14.
17 TI Form 10-K, http://investor.ti.com/sec.cfm?DocType=Annual&Year=2011, Edgar Online, 2011, p. 4.
18 TI Form 10-K, Edgar Online, 2011, p. 59.
19 TI Form 10-K, Edgar Online, 2011, p. 4.
20 T. Kim, 2009, Digital textbook plan hits snag, *Korea Times*, November 12.

EXHIBIT 2   Texas Instruments Product Portfolio

END MARKET	APPLICATIONS	TI PRODUCTS
Communications (42% of product revenue)	Phones and infrastructure equipment Mobile connectivity solutions (including wireless LAN, global positioning systems, Bluetooth®, NFC) Video conferencing	Analog, Embedded Processing, Wireless, Other
Computing (22% of product revenue)	Printers Hard disk drives Monitors and projectors Notebooks, netbooks, desktop computers and servers Tablet computers	Analog, Embedded Processing, Wireless, Other

Industrial (14% of product revenue)	Digital power controls:
	    Switch mode power supplies
	    Uninterruptible power supplies
	Motor controls:
	    Heating/ventilation/air conditioning
	    Industrial control motor drives
	    Power tools
	    Printers/copiers
	Security:
	    Biometrics (fingerprint identification and authentication)
	    Intelligent sensing (smoking and glass-breakage detection)
	    Video analytics (surveillance)
	Smart metering
	Test and measurement
	Point of service/portable data terminals
		Analog, Embedded Processing, Other

Consumer Electronics (11% of product revenue)	Digital cameras, gaming and audio/visual equipment Portable and car audio Home appliances Personal navigation devices eBook readers	Analog, Embedded Processing, Wireless, Other
Automotive (8% of product revenue)	Body systems Chassis systems Driver information/telemetrics Entertainment Powertrain Safety systems Security systems	Analog, Embedded Processing, Other
Education (3% of product revenue)	Handheld graphing and scientific calculators Educational software	Others

Source: Texas Instruments 2010 Annual Report, http://investor.ti.com/sec.cfm?DocType=Annual&Year=2011.

EXHIBIT 3   Texas Instruments Revenue by Region and Product Segment ($ Million)

Revenue by Region

	US	ASIA	EUROPE	JAPAN	REST OF WORLD	TOTAL
Revenue						
2010	$ **1,539**	$ **8,903**	$ **1,760**	$ **1,366**	$ **398**	$ **13,966**
2009	1,140	6,575	1,408	976	328	10,427
2008	1,551	7,387	1,875	1,268	420	12,501
Property, plant and equipment, net						
2010	$ **1,694**	$ **1,575**	$ **139**	$ **249**	$ **23**	$ **3,680**
2009	1,727	1,013	161	244	13	3,158
2008	1,785	988	200	314	17	3,304

Revenue by Product Segment

	ANALOG	EMBEDDED PROCESSING	WIRELESS	OTHER	TOTAL
Revenue					
2010	$ **5,979**	$ **2,073**	$ **2,978**	$ **2,936**	$ **13,966**
2009	4,202	1,471	2,626	2,128	10,427
2008	4,789	1,631	3,451	2,630	12,501
Operating profit					
2010	$ **1,876**	$ **491**	$ **683**	$ **1,464**	$ **4,514**
2009	770	194	315	712	1,991
2008	1,074	268	323	772	2,437

Source: Texas Instruments 2010 Annual Report, http://investor.ti.com/sec.cfm?DocType=Annual&Year=2011.

TI Nspire

Nspire is TI's premium educational package and consists of a combination of powerful graphing calculators, sophisticated software, and a network interface that allows students and teachers to be linked wirelessly. The calculators come in four product types: CX, CX-CAS, Nspire Handheld, and CAS Handheld, all of which contain standard software modules with a variety of hardware and software upgrades focused primarily on science and math education. Standard software modules include basic scientific calculator functions, lists and spreadsheets, data analysis and statistics, geometry modules, and document viewing software.

The Nspire product line also has two additional software features that are particularly relevant for classroom use: Vernier DataQuest and the Question application. DataQuest allows Nspire devices to interface with external sensors that conduct readings on motion, temperature, PH, light, and gas pressure, and automatically produces a graphical or table readout on the calculator screen, allowing for easy scientific experimentation. As an additional benefit, the USB interface of the DataQuest equipment makes it compatible with most other hardware available on the market today. The Question application allows teachers to ask subject-specific questions tailored to a student's level of proficiency and embed those questions within the calculator for the student to answer.

There are a number of additional product attributes that make Nspire a premier selection for classroom instructors in the United States. Most important are the Nspire Teacher and Student Software packages that can be purchased in addition to the calculator units. The Teacher Software allows instructors to browse ready-made lessons, customize documents using the PublishView application, manage lessons digitally, and transmit interactive lessons to the students' devices using the TI Smartview emulator. The Student Software packages contain "all the same functionality as TI-Nspire handhelds,"[21] but also allow students to begin assignments on their Nspire units and then transfer the files to their personal computers for completion at home.

The Nspire solution also offers connectivity solutions that enrich the student experience, fostering classroom interaction and monitoring of individual activity by the instructor. The Nspire Navigator system provides adaptors that enable wireless communication between the Nspire units and a central router, and the Navigator for Network Computers solution allows schools to operate the Nspire modules through their existing computer platform. Features of Navigator include Screen Capture, which allows instructors to monitor their students' activity in real time; Live Presenter, which transmits the image on one student's screen to the whole class; and Quick Poll, which allows the teacher to ask the entire student group a question through their devices and collect responses. The Nspire solution also comes with a docking station that charges the devices and simultaneously allows the teacher to transfer student files to the instructor's computer.

Software and Content

In addition to the comprehensive hardware and software package offered by Nspire, TI has worked to develop additional education solutions that are not reliant on its hardware components. These include software modules that run on existing networks, such as the network-enabled version of Navigator mentioned above, and educational content including fully developed lessons, activity modules, explanatory videos, and exams and quizzes. Examining TI's software products in further detail identifies a number of potential opportunities for expansion within the Korean market.

As mentioned in the previous section, two of the most easily transferrable solutions offered by TI are the Math Nspire and Science Nspire software packages. These products not only offer students the aforementioned benefits, but also provide subject-specific guidance for instructors tasked with teaching the material. As part of these packages, video tutorials and professional development webinars give teachers the tools and knowledge to best deliver the content, providing teachers with a rewarding way to develop their skill as educators.

Additional software and supplementary online content, such as the Activities Exchange and TI-Math.com, deliver a superior level of service to teachers implementing these solutions. Activities Exchange is an online database of free math and science lessons that teachers can browse and download for use in their classrooms. TI-Math.com is a subscription-based service that sends subject-specific lessons directly to

---

21 *Texas Instruments Education Product Catalog*, 2010, p. 7.

teachers' computers, allowing teachers to shift their preparation time from content development to content integration and delivery. Through workshops such as TI-MathForward and Teacher Leader Cadre, TI works with teachers to develop their proficiency in using TI products and provides feedback on how to integrate those tools into their lessons. Lastly, and perhaps most importantly, TI works with textbook publishers to integrate its hardware, software, and digital content with the textbook in order to enrich the student experience.

Conclusion

Both within Korea and globally, the digital textbook market represents a significant opportunity for TI. As publishers, students, schools, and teachers continue to develop this market, companies that have lengthy experience integrating educational software with technology interfaces have a significant advantage over tablet manufacturers that attempt to develop proprietary educational software on an in-house basis. As textbooks go digital, TI's brand identity, reputation for quality, and integration-ready software platform facilitate a much smoother transition than firms attempting

to develop education software from scratch. TI's history of hardware enablement allows it to differentiate its software from competitors offering mere simulations of fully interactive programs. Furthermore, TI's existing solutions are primarily targeted at math and science. These two subjects can be particularly enriched by the use of digital textbooks and tablets, positioning TI even further ahead of the competition. Much like a classroom, there is a learning process associated with entering new markets and developing new applications for existing products, and much like its customers, TI will truly be taking its own education digital.

CASE DISCUSSION QUESTIONS

1. What opportunities does the Korean tablet initiative provide for TI?

2. How can TI effectively communicate the value of its education solutions to its Korean constituents?

3. How can TI ensure that its products have all of the attributes necessary to meet the needs of the Korean education system?

Jobek do Brasil's Joint Venture Challenges[1]

Jobek do Brasil's joint venture with a US partner, Hatteras Hammocks, is in trouble. The environmentally conscious Jobek do Brasil insists on using certified (sustainable) wood to make hammocks, but Hatteras has demanded uncertified wood products at more competitive prices. The troubled relationship has been compounded by the global economic crisis, which has reduced customers' willingness to pay a premium for socially and environmentally responsible products. Will the joint venture survive?

Dirk Michael Boehe, *Insper Institute of Education and Research, Brazil*
Luciano Barin Cruz, *HEC Montréal, Canada*

Barny Köpf had just returned from Spoga, the international trade fair for outdoor equipment and furniture held in Germany. Despite the global economic crisis, the results achieved at the fair were very positive for his company, Jobek, a Brazil-based multinational manufacturer of leisure furniture and hammocks. However, Barny must resolve some issues before he can relax and enjoy the magical sunset from the patio of his beach house in Iguape, located 50 kilometers from the city of Fortaleza on Brazil's Northeast Coast. The main issue is what to do with the international joint venture (IJV) forged seven years ago with the US company Hatteras Hammocks. The IJV, which began with the sale of a 49.5% interest in his company, was causing him to lose sleep. Jobek had always maintained a focus on environmental protection. The wood used to make its hammocks came from certified sources, a fact that the company had always used as a competitive advantage. The owners of Hatteras, however, had never been concerned with environmental matters. Historically, their clients were large chains such as Wal-Mart, and the focus was low prices.

What worried Barny was the fact that Jobek had adopted a strategy to enter international markets that

had little or nothing in common with Hatteras' strategy. This difference had become apparent over the years of the partnership, which led to the initial terms of the IJV agreement not being fully observed. If the IJV agreement had been complied with to the letter, Hatteras would not be buying from China, but from Jobek. At the same time, the contract for the exclusive distribution of Jobek products in the US market by Hatteras prevented Barny from selling to other US retailers and distributors he had met at the last trade fair. An ideal move would be to terminate the partnership, but how? Barny quickly dialed the number of his brother, Josef, the co-owner of Jobek.

The Hammock and Leisure Furniture Industry

In Brazil, production is concentrated in a few centers of small-scale manufacturers located in the Northeast, especially in the state of Ceará. In Latin America, there are several such centers in Mexico and Colombia. In Asia, especially in India and China, there are various producers of diversified outdoor leisure furniture products, including sun umbrellas, tables, chairs, swing chairs, hammocks, and other textile products for the export market. In developed economies (such as Europe and the United States), companies have emerged with strong brands. They often outsource production to or operate manufacturing plants in developing countries.

It is worth noting that in recent years the sector has been undergoing change on a global scale. In the 1970s and the 1980s, developed economies were responsible for most of production, as well as exports of the final product. As of 1980, however, emerging economies began to play a more important role due to their cheaper labor and raw materials. As a result, companies in developed economies began to specialize in design, product development, distribution, and sales, handing over production to producers in emerging economies. In this process, the importance of agencies that verify product quality and conformity began to increase.

Social and Environmental Certifications

Preoccupation over the environment and sustainability has become increasingly apparent in the media and in public policies. Companies have come under increasing pressure to adopt the path of sustainability. However, a new problem arises. What does being responsible mean, and how does it add value to a company that uses sustainability as a competitive advantage? It is well known that the cost of being environmentally responsible can be extremely high and that consumers around the world respond to sustainability concerns in different ways.

As a result, more certifications have been created to support a reliable sustainability and social responsibility seal. They include the well-known ISO series, international reporting standards (such as the Global Reporting Initiative [GRI]), and certifications in specific areas and sectors (such as those granted by the Forest Stewardship Council [FSC]). The FSC is an international and independent NGO, and its seal is the most widely recognized by other international NGOs (including the WWF, Greenpeace, and Friends of the Earth) and by the consumer market. The FSC fosters responsible forest management, aiming to preserve the forests' main economic, environmental, and social characteristics.

The FSC provides two types of certification: Forest Management certifies organizations or agents that manage the forest in a sustainable manner in accordance with international standards and technical, economic, environmental, and social requirements. The main Chain of Custody Certificate requirement is the traceability of raw material from the forest(s) in question (in every stage of production, from extraction to the final product sold to the customer). Jobek possesses the FSC Chain of Custody Certificate, granted after an audit to ensure that only certified wood was used in its products. The certification is valid for five years, during which time the firm is subject to annual inspections to ensure compliance.

Despite the FSC's initiatives to reduce certification costs, it is still up to the contracting company to pay for the annual audits and inspections, in addition to an annual fee whose precise amount is determined by the size of the operation to be certified. Nevertheless, sustainability certificates are increasingly valued by consumers, especially in developed countries. Consequently, obtaining the FSC seal is an attractive option for Jobek do Brasil in that it adds value to its products through the green seal and a guarantee of high quality.

History of Jobek do Brasil

At the end of the 1980s, Jobek's founders, two German brothers named Barny and Josef Köpf, put their enterprising idea into practice. Barny recalls:

> In 1989, we started with the traditional Latin hammock, as we call it here: the hammock of Brazil and Mexico, hammocks without a rope, without a wooden framework. And so we started to import 400 hammocks as a test (from Ceará, Brazil, to Germany). We had no idea how it was going to work out but [...] our neighbors liked them, since we started selling them straight from our garage [...] Later we added support, accessories, etc.

Today Jobek is a multinational manufacturer of hammocks and leisure furniture based in two countries. The first base was established in 1992 in Schwangau, Germany, where Barny and Josef Köpf were born. The second was founded in 2000 in Maracanaú, in the metropolitan region of Fortaleza, Ceará, in Brazil. Today they run the Maracanaú facility, which is also where the products are manufactured. The German headquarters is in charge of quality management and product sales. In Brazil, Jobek has 250 employees in the high season and 80 in the low season. The German facility has a staff of 25. Between 2005 and 2007, Jobek's annual export revenue averaged more than US$5 million. In 2008, however, it was less. Export profitability varies between 1% and 10% of revenue. Germany is the main export destination, followed by France and Spain (see Exhibit 1).

Product Design

Due to growing competition for mass-produced, low-added-value products, Jobek do Brasil has been

EXHIBIT 1 Jobek's Key Markets

COUNTRY	2005	2006	2007	2008	2009
Germany	47%	47%	45%	47%	66%
Canada	7%	5%	5%	5%	5%
US		5%	10%	3%	
France	30%	30%	28%	32%	17%
Switzerland	1%	1%	1%		
Spain	10%	10%	9%	10%	7%
Other	5%	2%	2%	3%	5%
TOTAL EXPORTS	**100%**	**100%**	**100%**	**100%**	**100%**
DOMESTIC MARKET (BRAZIL)					
% of Total Produced	**1%**	**1%**	**2%**	**3%**	**5%**

Source: Jobek

focusing more on the premium niche. Some hammocks with accessories sell for more than €1,500 (US$2,000) each, thanks to innovative and exclusive design, rapid renewal of the product range, and possession of FSC certification, international safety certification (GS), and quality certification (ISO). In addition, some of the products' attributes are beneficial for health. Hatteras Hammocks supplies a synthetic yarn called DuraCord exclusively to Jobek do Brasil, replacing the old cotton-based yarn. In addition to being cheaper than cotton, DuraCord is more resistant and durable while maintaining cotton's soft texture. Jobek usually protects its more innovative products by patenting them. According to the quality and purchasing manager at the south German facility, the company is concerned with the continuous development of new products and is constantly striving to stay ahead of its competitors: "We are always two years ahead of the Asians because we're continuously coming up with new products."

Jobek's global value chain formed in the past few years encompasses suppliers in Brazil and China, production in Brazil, and distributors in Canada, the United States, and several countries in Europe, among others.

The Adoption of the FSC Certification Standard and the Supply of Certified Wood

Although the FSC seal is only one certification among many, its name, brand, and reputation have become established in several markets, and it is the most widely recognized and respected in Europe. In order to promote the seal, the FSC attends trade shows and also communicates its proposal through television and magazines. Given the characteristics of the hammock production sector and the growing tendency of seeking environmental and social certifications, companies need to ensure the sustainability of the global value chain within which they operate in order to maintain the global and general consistency of their differentiation based on social and environmental responsibility. However, this is no easy task. Although Jobek do Brasil has been attempting to do precisely this, its JV with Hatteras Hammocks has raised certain issues that merit some reflection.

Certified wood suppliers are few in number and in a position to impose payment conditions almost unilaterally. In 2008, the FSC's representatives in Brazil admitted that "there is a problem of wood supply and, at the moment, certified forests have stopped increasing." While Jobek do Brazil's distributors and retailers can make use of a 180-day credit line, the company has to pay for its certified wood in cash. Barny comments on the reasons for this imbalance:

> *Like everything else, there are two sides to the story. The bad side is [that] today we are dependent on FSC suppliers, which is very difficult, since we are not the only ones seeking FSC-certified wood. The Chinese, the Vietnamese, the entire world is after this wood. Unfortunately, Brazil's rules put us at a disadvantage. When it arrives here, from the interior of Pará (Brazil), our wood is already loaded with taxes, and freight is also very expensive. The Chinese go there, to Belém (Brazil) or Curitiba (Brazil), pay for their wood for export and get it tax-free. For us, buying wood is very complicated, not to mention frustrating. We currently have only one FSC supplier. One! We are in the hands of a single supplier.*

Due to growing demand for certified wood, Jobek's quality and purchasing manager in Germany and Jobek do Brasil's export manager admit that the company has had to turn down orders. In fact, it has been suffering legal problems due to the bottlenecks in the supply of certified wood to a major German retail chain.

> *Jobek has been trying to obtain alternative suppliers, in addition to certification from Brazilian agencies. However, this new certification has limited potential, since it is much less well-known than the FSC's, which hinders the penetration of international markets.*

Jobek's owners visit their suppliers regularly in order to verify the quality of the wood and the volume produced, which has helped increase the company's credibility with its international distributors and clients. The wood certification auditor firm considers Jobek even as a pioneer in its sector.

International Marketing

The success of Jobek's international hammock sales depends heavily on public awareness of the company's FSC certification. Barny points out that Brazilian products with a dubious ecological pedigree cannot take part in trade fairs in Europe, given that Europe keeps a very close eye on what is happening in the Amazon region. "If you sell an uncertified product, there's a good chance you'll have Greenpeace protesting in front of your store and no one wants that."

In this sense, the FSC's disclosure efforts are already producing results worldwide. Jobek's Canadian distributor believes that consumers are changing and that the green seal constitutes a definite advantage for the product. "Previously, it was the sellers who used to tell clients about the certification, but today it's the customers who are demanding the FSC seal." However, Jobek's US distributor believes that certified wood products have no market there, since both retailers and customers regard price as the most important factor in purchasing decisions. As a result, Hatteras Hammocks began to demand *uncertified* wood products at more competitive prices. A Hatteras representative leaves us with no doubt regarding his opinion of certified wood:

> Personally, I think it's a great idea and everyone should support it. The problem is that the people who go to Walmart or stores of that type are not willing to pay more. It's all or nothing. You can't have a company that's competitive just because it's sustainable if there's no market for it. The thing is that everyone wants to be environmentally correct, but they don't realize the cost and they're not willing to pay for it.

Obviously, the emphasis on FSC certification is not enough in itself to promote Jobek's product abroad. The product is closely associated with the Latin American culture—think of the lifestyle of Latin American people, life in tropical regions, and beaches surrounded by palm trees. Because many people in the Northern hemisphere envy such a lifestyle, it makes perfect sense to exploit these concepts when promoting the product internationally. According to Barny, this is part of the strategy:

> We associated Brazilian culture with the product, which I personally think is very important, and I used this strategy in Europe and at the trade fair. I said: in Brazil the culture is hammocks, the culture is coffee. What comes from Brazil? Fruit, caipirinha, exuberance—a hammock can't come from India or China. And we used this as a marketing tool; we put it on the packaging. These products are the most expensive line we have, they use a lot of wood, 100% certified wood of course. The packaging with the coffee sack stamp [...] was a great success.

Production and Distribution

In June 2000, following investments of R$3.5 million (US$2 million), Jobek do Brasil Indústria Têxtil opened a 6,900-square-meter factory in Maracanaú, which produces the entire line of hammocks, hanging chairs, and accessories. After peaking in 2004, when the facility turned out 500,000 items, production plunged in 2008 and 2009 due to dwindling US demand and the global economic crisis. As a result, Jobek reduced its direct workforce to around 80 in the low season and outsourced part of production.

Until 2008, Jobek exported almost its entire output. It is the sector leader in Europe, with a market share of around 80%, but competition from Asia has begun to threaten its performance. Currently, it exports to more than 40 countries: more than three-quarters of production goes to Europe, while 15% goes to the US and 5% to Asia. Only 1% of output is sold in Brazil itself, mostly in the south and southeast. Exports exceed 200,000 hammocks per year.

The International Joint Venture with Hatteras

Walter R. Perkins, Jr., the founder and current CEO of Hatteras, acquired Pawleys Island and became the world's largest hammock producer. Pawleys Island Hammocks was the oldest hammock manufacturer in the United States, which had been handcrafting cotton hammocks since its founding in 1889. Pawleys Island Rope Hammock stood for high-quality material, mixing comfort and art. One of Hatteras' competitive advantages is the DuraCord yarn that was specially created for it.

In view of the stronger competition, Jobek sought to increase its strength by forming a JV. The partnership with Hatteras started in a curious way, as Barny explains:

> At the beginning of 2001 and 2002, we began to take part in trade fairs in the US, in Chicago, and apparently Hatteras had heard about us. They came to our stand, talked [...]. In 2002, we began selling to Walmart and Sam's, and Hatteras folks were seriously upset, because someone had broken their monopoly and they lost a major client.

Hatteras' response caught Barny and his brother by surprise:

> Hatteras' CEO told me he thought we should talk instead of becoming competitors. Then they invited me to come to Greenville, in North Carolina, so I did, and we were really interested in establishing a partnership with them, with production in Brazil, and so were they. The two biggest companies in the US and Europe were going to get together. To create more! Two times two doesn't make four, it makes five. That was the idea. In 2002 and 2003, the dollar was exceptionally strong, almost four reais (Brazilian currency), so it was cheap for them to produce here (in Brazil). At the time, we had very little working capital, so we decided: "let's sell 49.5% of Jobek to them." And they promised to transfer all their production to Brazil, expand the factory here, the infrastructure, everything. We drew up the agreement, sold 49.5% to them and began to build a larger factory.

In addition to building the new factory, the JV agreement also established that Hatteras would have the exclusive right to distribute Jobek's products in the United States, while Jobek would distribute Hatteras and Pawleys Island brand products in Europe. Jobek products would be sold in the United States under the Jobek do Brasil name, aiming to associate Brazil's image with the Latin hammock made of fabric, thus differentiating it from the typical American hammocks. The Americans were visibly committed to the new venture. The son of Hatteras' founder, Walter Perkins III, spent four weeks in Maracanaú to help implement the basis for Hatteras hammock production, whose process is completely different from that used for the production of Jobek hammocks. In fact, the JV got off to an excellent start. The Americans trained the Brazilian workers, who learned extremely quickly. For the Americans, who already had business ties with Chinese suppliers, Brazil was also ideal from the logistics point of view. Proximity with the US shortened sea transport significantly: from 35 days from China to only 12 days from Pecém, Ceará, to Norfolk, Virginia.

However, much to Barny and Josef's surprise, in the course of the JV, Jobek's annual US sales plunged from US$3 million to just US$100,000. Initially, Jobek employees did not realize what was happening. Barny recalls: "We weren't aware of it. Since they sold through a distributor, we never got the correct figure. Unfortunately, that was a mistake." The experience left Jobek's owners with a bitter taste because they were expecting to double the company's revenue through the partnership. After all, they had changed the company's entire infrastructure in Maracanaú and reserved "2,500 square meters of the factory just for them."

But in 2003, the exchange rate started to worsen, moving from 3.6 Brazilian Reais per US$ in January 2003 to 1.75 Brazilian Reais per US$ in January 2008 (see Exhibit 2). It did not take long for Brazil-based production of hammocks to lose its allure for Hatteras, which ordered more products from India and China. In hindsight, Barny remarks:

> They cut down on their orders and their idea was always to produce as little as possible—it wasn't to sell our products in the US—and we began to realize that. They were not bad partners in the beginning. When you are a partner with almost 50%, when things become difficult, I expect you to remain a partner because the company is yours. Three years ago I called them and we had a meeting: "You have to place the orders or we're going to have to change the infrastructure here…" "No, but the orders are coming…" And they continued acting like that [...] they had come through the door but had never really entered.

The situation got so bad that Hatteras has not placed a single order since May 2008. Barny concludes: "We

EXHIBIT 2   Exchange Rate Real (R$)/US$

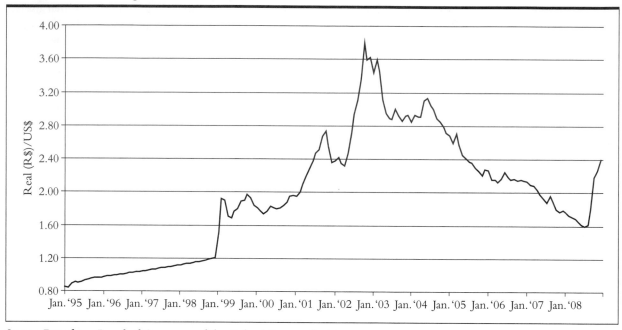

Source: Data from Board of Governors of the Federal Reserve System

have the infrastructure, their things are completely idle here and we no longer communicate with Hatteras." On the other hand, European sales of Hatteras products through Jobek's distribution channels were not very significant, either. Analyzing the Hatteras JV in hindsight, Barny observes:

> *I think it was a big cultural problem. I'm German, they are Americans, and we are in Brazil. As a German, I see everything from a long-term perspective. Like this warehouse, which was built to last a lifetime. I think it's a very different culture. And I saw a little of the difference between idealism and capitalism. I understood that it was no longer working with the Americans, not with that exchange rate. But maybe we could have come up with an alternative for another product line, adding more value. With a cheaper product I can't produce more due to labor and infrastructure costs; I have to manufacture a product with greater added value or I have to rationalize more [...]*

The Crisis and Future Challenges

The impasse in the Hatteras–Jobek partnership was compounded by the global economic crisis, which affected people's willingness to pay a premium for socially and environmentally responsible products, in turn penalizing those companies committed to such products. As a result, many certified wood suppliers (such as Precious Wood in Belém, Brazil) have gone out of business. Others (such as El Dorado) are in the process of doing so. "How can we honor our commitments to our clients abroad?" Barny wonders, "We only have a few orders, but we still have to fill a container with FSC-certified wood products by the end of the season." As if that were not enough, the crisis also affected the other side of the global value chain: "On December 22, 2008, our largest French distributor, Interproduct, went under," Barny recalls.

It is Hatteras that is keeping Jobek's owners awake at night. Barny and Josef both know that they would have been able to easily weather the crisis if they had not formed a JV with the Americans and expanded the company's infrastructure. "High fliers have the most to lose; now we have no working capital. In addition to being stuck for capital, there is also the agreement giving Hatteras the exclusive right to distribute Jobek's products in the US. If it were not for that, we could capitalize on our advantages with sustainable products," Barny declares. A possible change in US environmental policy could help Jobek. "Last night, the new American president Obama said on TV that the US economy would have to grow with [...] renewable energy. In this case we are two steps ahead of Hatteras, who will be our competitor because they never cared about the issue."

At that moment, Barny remembers everything he learned from the Americans when they were in the factory in Maracanaú: "from products to how they estimated the costs. Nevertheless, it wouldn't make any sense to compete with the same products. The products that Hatteras buys from China are cheaper. It would be smarter to compete with design, quality, innovation, with products that are not yet sold in the US. And we learned a lot from the Americans. If it weren't for this exclusivity agreement [...] they wanted to sell us their share, but since we don't have enough working capital, how can we pay them?" Barny questions, "Working capital is hard to come by because of the global crisis. They offered to sell their 49.5% for the same price they paid when they entered the partnership. That's absurd," he exclaims, outraged. "Because in the meantime they caused us a huge loss due to the lack of orders. So, how am I going to buy at the same price? You come in with no risk and you get out with no risk? Perfect, isn't it?"

Sources: Based on (1) authors' interviews; (2) L. Barin Cruz & D. M. Boehe, 2008, CSR in the global market place: Towards sustainable global value chains, *Management Decision*, 46(1): 1187–1209; (3) Forst Stewardship Council, http://www.fsc.org; (4) Internal documents provided by Jobek GmbH, http://www.jobek.com.br.

CASE DISCUSSION QUESTIONS

1. How would you evaluate the IJV between Jobek and Hatteras?

2. What was the international market strategy of Jobek? And of Hatteras?

3. What are the differences between the concepts of corporate social responsibility used by Hatteras and Jobek?

4. Based on your evaluation, what should Jobek do?

5. Describe Jobek's current competitive environment. What changes do you foresee in the future? How do you think they will influence Jobek?

The Antitrust Case on the AT&T–T-Mobile Merger[1]

In 2011, the second largest US mobile wireless carrier, AT&T (with a 25% market share), proposed to merge with the fourth largest carrier, T-Mobile, which had a 15% market share and was a wholly owned subsidiary of Deutsche Telekom. Antitrust authorities blocked this merger. Why?

Mike W. Peng, *University of Texas at Dallas*

The Merger

In March 2011, Dallas-based AT&T announced that it reached an agreement with Deutsche Telekom (DT) to purchase DT's wholly owned US subsidiary, T-Mobile USA, for $39 billion. The top-four concentration in mobile wireless telecommunications services in the United States accounted for more than 90% of market share. Of the Big Four, the second-ranked AT&T had about 25% market share, and the fourth-ranked T-Mobile had 15%. The largest player was Verizon (31%), and the third was Sprint Nextel (20%). Although some small carriers competed in certain regions, no carriers other than the Big Four competed nationally. After the proposed merger, the combined AT&T/T-Mobile would become the nation's largest wireless carrier, commanding over 40% of market share with 132 million customers and $72 billion in revenues. The scale and scope of the merger would require regulatory approval. AT&T indicated its willingness to sell off certain assets if necessary and planned to complete the merger in one year.

AT&T argued that the merger would allow AT&T to expand 4G LTE broadband to another 55 million Americans, reaching a total of 97% of the population and especially benefitting rural areas currently without broadband coverage. Because T-Mobile was losing money and suffered from its poor economies of scale, it (and its parent company DT) had been unable to upgrade its networks and invest in 4G broadband. While AT&T was booming and adding customers, T-Mobile was losing customers—it was the only major

carrier that did not offer the iPhone. But T-Mobile possessed some hard-to-substitute resources: spectrum. Spectrum was finite resources auctioned by the Federal Communications Commission (FCC). Exhausting its own spectrum, AT&T could benefit from tapping into T-Mobile's underutilized spectrum. Accelerating 4G wireless deployment would not only generate new jobs due to AT&T's own investment, but also stimulate broader job creation and civil engagement due to better access to more affordable and more widespread wireless broadband services.

A variety of labor, environmental, and business groups supported the merger. These groups pointed to AT&T's record and commitments to labor and environmental standards and appreciated the investment and the jobs the merger would bring. Also, civil rights groups applauded the additional boost in civil engagement that could be facilitated by more widespread broadband. Governors of 26 states wrote letters to support the merger.

However, other diverse groups were opposed to this merger. Not surprisingly, Verizon and Sprint did not like this deal because it would make them weaker. Sprint would become a distant third, so clearly it would not appreciate the outcome. Verizon would lose its top position, but it would still be a strong player in a new duopoly. Internet companies did not like the merger either, because it would leave them with fewer service providers to negotiate with for getting their content and applications to customers. The Computer and Communication Industry Association, which included eBay, Google, Microsoft, and Yahoo as its members,

---

1 This research was supported by the O. P. Jindal Chair at the Jindal School of Management, University of Texas at Dallas. All views and errors are those of the author. © Mike W. Peng. Reprinted with permission.

was opposed to the merger. Consumer groups argued that the merger would raise prices and stifle innovation by consolidating so much of the wireless industry in one firm.

On the core issue of whether increasing AT&T's market power would hurt consumers, AT&T pointed out that the average inflation-adjusted price for wireless services in the United States *fell* by 50% from 1999 to 2009, according to the Government Accounting Office. AT&T also argued that in many local markets AT&T would still be competing with four or more rivals, so taking T-Mobile (which was losing customers anyway) out of the mix would not dent competition. If AT&T could not acquire T-Mobile (which had sizable infrastructure such as cellular towers and significant spectrum), then AT&T might be forced to build its own infrastructure, which would be an unnecessarily costly undertaking and social waste, especially in crowded urban areas such as San Francisco. But even if AT&T went head to head with infrastructure building, it would still suffer from a shortage of spectrum, while T-Mobile, at the same time, could not fully utilize its spectrum—clearly a waste of finite resources.

The Antitrust Case

In August 2011, the US Department of Justice (DOJ) filed a lawsuit alleging that this merger would reduce competition and violate antitrust law. DOJ alleged that the "anticompetitive harm" of this merger would include:

> *(a) actual and potential competition between AT&T and T-Mobile will be eliminated; (b) competition in general likely will be lessened substantially; (c) prices are likely to be higher than they otherwise would; (d) the quality and quantity of services are likely to be less than they otherwise would due to reduced incentives to invest in capacity and technology improvements; and (e) innovation and product variety likely will be reduced.*

In particular, given T-Mobile's positioning as a self-styled "Disruptive Pricing" provider, "AT&T's acquisition of T-Mobile," alleged DOJ, "would eliminate the important price, quality, product variety, and innovation

competition that an independent T-Mobile brings to the marketplace." In addition, DOJ argued:

> *The substantial increase in concentration that would result from this merger, and the reduction in the number of nationwide providers from four to three, likely will lead to lessened competition due to an enhanced risk of anticompetitive coordination. Certain aspects of mobile wireless communications services markets, including transparent pricing, little buyer-side market power, and high barriers to entry and expansion, make them particularly conductive to coordination.*

In conclusion, DOJ argued that the proposed merger would violate Section 7 of the Clayton Act and that it should be stopped. In the lawsuit, DOJ also sued T-Mobile and DT as co-defendants. On behalf of the US government, DOJ was the sole plaintiff in its first complaint filed on August 31, 2011. In its first amended complaint filed on September 16, DOJ was joined by the states of New York, Washington, California, Illinois, Massachusetts, Ohio, and Pennsylvania as co-plaintiffs. In its second amended complaint filed on September 30, Puerto Rico joined as a co-plaintiff. The case was officially the *United States et al. v. AT&T Inc. et al.*

AT&T was not a stranger to antitrust lawsuits. Today's AT&T is the direct result of the first *United States v. AT&T* antitrust lawsuit. Because of its monopoly in long-distance (land-line) telephone, the *original* AT&T ("Ma Bell") was forced by DOJ to break up into seven regional Bell operating companies (known as "Baby Bells") in 1983. Between 1983 and 2005, today's AT&T was one of these Baby Bells—named Southwestern Bell Corporation between 1983 and 1995 and shortened to SBC between 1995 and 2005. Due to its successful market performance, SBC emerged as a leading offspring of the original AT&T (Verizon was another leading offspring). In 2005, SBC spent $16 billion to purchase its former parent company, AT&T Corporation—a Baby Bell acquiring Ma Bell. Quitting the SBC name, the merged entity named itself AT&T Inc. and took on the iconic AT&T branding (including its logo and its stock ticker "T," which simply stands for "telephone"). Before the filing of the second *United States v. AT&T* case, the *Economist* asked: "Could the bid for T-Mobile be a sign that monopoly Ma is trying to return from her grave?"

The Outcome

In November 2011, the FCC issued its opinion and joined DOJ in opposing the merger. In December 2011 (before the antitrust case went on trial), AT&T gave up the merger and DOJ dismissed the case. A triumphant DOJ announced:

> *Consumers won today… Had AT&T acquired T-Mobile, consumers in the wireless market place would have faced higher prices and reduced innovation. We sued to protect consumers who rely on competition in this important industry. With the parties' abandonment, we achieved that result.*

A frustrated AT&T noted in its press release:

> *[Dallas, Texas, December 19, 2011] AT&T Inc. (NYSE: T) said today that after a thorough review of options it has agreed with Deutsche Telekom AG to end its bid to acquire T-Mobile USA, which began in March of this year.*
>
> *The actions by the Federal Communications Commission and the Department of Justice to block this transaction do not change the realities of the US wireless industry. It is one of the most fiercely competitive industries in the world, with a mounting need for more spectrum that has not diminished and must be addressed immediately. The AT&T and T-Mobile USA combination would have offered an interim solution to this spectrum shortage. In the absence of such steps, customers will be harmed and needed investment will be stifled*
>
> *"AT&T will continue to be aggressive in leading the mobile Internet revolution," said Randall Stephenson, AT&T chairman and CEO. "Over the past four years we have invested more in our networks than any other US company. As a result, today we deliver best-in-class mobile broadband speeds—connecting smartphones, tablets, and emerging devices at a record pace—and we are well underway with our nationwide 4G LTE deployment.*
>
> *"To meet the needs of our customers, we will continue to invest," Stephenson said. "However,*

> *adding capacity to meet these needs will require policymakers to do two things. First, in the near term, they should allow the free markets to work so that additional spectrum is available to meet the immediate needs of the US wireless industry, including expeditiously approving our acquisition of unused Qualcomm spectrum currently pending before the FCC. Second, policymakers should enact legislation to meet our nation's longer-term spectrum needs.*
>
> *"The mobile Internet is a dynamic industry that can be a critical driver in restoring American economic growth and job creation, but only if companies are allowed to react quickly to customer needs and market forces," Stephenson said.*

The fine print in the deal included DOJ's *blessing* of AT&T and T-Mobile's collaboration in roaming. The more significant (or, if you will, the more bizarre) outcome was that as per AT&T's original deal with DT, in the event of merger failure, AT&T would pay T-Mobile $3 billion as a break-up fee and give T-Mobile $1 billion worth of AT&T-held wireless spectrum. In short, the US government reduced the competitiveness of a US firm by forcing a US firm to subsidize the wholly owned subsidiary of a foreign firm.

In the name of preserving (domestic) competition, the US government preserved a (foreign) competitor. "The problem is," noted one expert at *Slate*, "T-Mobile doesn't want to be a competitor anymore. Its parent company DT wants out of the US market." As the weakest among the Big Four, T-Mobile only added 89,000 new customers between 2009 and 2011, while the industry took in 33 million new customers. By essentially giving up since March 2011, T-Mobile lost 467,000 lucrative contract customers during the merger process. By focusing on its terms of exit, T-Mobile turned its attention away from network upgrades and improvements. DOJ and FCC cannot force T-Mobile to be in business, just like no one can force customers to sign up for plans they do not want. By breathing a new lease on life into T-Mobile, that was exactly what DOJ and FCC did: forcing T-Mobile to be in business against its (and its parent company's) own wishes. The same expert at *Slate* continued:

> *Sure, companies like T-Mobile and Sprint can offer cheaper plans, but the success of Verizon and AT&T shows price is not our primary concern when it comes to wireless service. We want shiny smartphones and big, powerful, reliable networks ... Rather than stifle competition, the merger would have intensified the war between the two giants, AT&T and Verizon. And for those people for whom price is paramount, there would remain not only Sprint, but a slew of smaller, regional providers like Leap and MetroPCS.*

Sources: Based on (1) the author's interviews, 2011; (2) AT&T, 2011, AT&T ends bid to add network capacity through T-Mobile USA purchase, December 19, www.att.com; (3) AT&T, 2011, AT&T statement on Department of Justice action, August 31, www.att.com; (4) *Bloomberg Businessweek*, 2011, Behind AT&T's epic lobbying failure, December 12: 40–42; (5) *Bloomberg Businessweek*, 2011, For wireless giants, reception may get spotty, July 18: 35–36; (6) CBS News, 2011, What the AT&T-T-Mobile breakup means for you, December 20, www.cbsnews.com; (7) *Economist*, 2011, An audacious merger with a poor reception, March 26: 71–72; (8) *Economist*, 2011, Tripped at the altar, September 3: 62; (9) W. Oremus, 2011, Truth, justice, and terrible mobile service, *Slate*, December 21, www.slate.com; (10) *United States of America v. AT&T, T-Mobile USA, Inc., and Deutsche Telekom AG*, 2011, Complaint, Case 1:11-cv-01560, August 31, Washington, DC: US District Court for the District of Columbia; (11) *United States of America et al. v. AT&T Inc. et al.*, 2011, Amended complaint, Civil Action No. 11-01560 (ESH), September 16, Washington, DC: US District Court for the District of Columbia; (12) *United States of America et al. v. AT&T Inc. et al.*, 2011, Second amended complaint, Civil Action No. 11-01560 (ESH), September 30, Washington, DC: US District Court for the District of Columbia; (13) *United States of America et al. v. AT&T Inc. et al.*, 2011, Stipulation of dismissal, Civil Action No. 11-01560 (ESH), December 20, Washington, DC: US District Court for the District of Columbia; (14) *Wall Street Journal*, 2012, T-Mobile will focus on network quality in wake of deal failure, January 11, online.wsj.com.

CASE DISCUSSION QUESTIONS

1. Defend AT&T's position as its CEO.

2. Defend this merger as T-Mobile's or Deutsche Telekom's CEO (both firms were co-defendants in this case).

3. Provide an expert testimonial as Verizon's or Sprint Nextel's CEO.

4. Challenge AT&T's position as an antitrust lawyer working for the government.

5. *ON ETHICS:* As a party not directly involved in the case (such as a manager at another firm not in this industry or a student), what do you think is right about antitrust policy? What is wrong about antitrust policy? Why?

Ocean Park Fights Hong Kong Disneyland[1]

Before and immediately after Hong Kong Disneyland's opening in 2005, many people believed that Hong Kong's homegrown amusement park, Ocean Park, might not be able to survive. Would Ocean Park become a "sitting duck" when Donald Duck came?

Michael N. Young, *Hong Kong Baptist University*

The Arrival of Hong Kong Disneyland

The arrival of Hong Kong Disneyland in 2005 had caused many pundits to predict the demise of Hong Kong's homegrown amusement park, Ocean Park. Several of Disney's characters, such as Mickey Mouse, Donald Duck, and Winnie the Pooh, were household names all over the world. With its legendary "Imagineering," Disney was cranking out new animated characters that debuted in movies, making them well known by the time visitors encountered them in Disney parks.

In comparison, few people outside of Hong Kong had even heard of Ocean Park. Founded in 1977, Ocean Park had been the only amusement park in town. The lack of competition did not push it to strengthen its brand image, symbolized by its Seahorse logo. The nonsmiling seahorse was far from warm and cuddly to the impressionable younger customers—it was hard for children to imagine snuggling with a seahorse. "You could say that we had no brand image at all at that time," conceded one manager. Hearing that Disney would be coming, Ocean Park introduced a sea lion named Whiskers as its new mascot. Whiskers was bigger and cuter with a big smile, triggering a much warmer and easily approachable feeling to customers. Soon after Whiskers was introduced, he became a household name in Hong Kong, particularly with children and families. In addition to stronger brand building, Ocean Park also geared up to prepare for Disney's onslaught by installing new attractions, upgrading existing rides, and enhancing interactive activities with animals (including Hong Kong's only pandas). Yet the dazzling commencement ceremony of Hong Kong

Disneyland made Ocean Park look relatively tired and dated by comparison.

Most local people were sympathetic to Ocean Park, as it seemed like a classic David versus Goliath competition. Ocean Park, the clear underdog, had become a fixture of Hong Kong's cultural heritage. Disneyland, playing the part of Goliath, represented the quintessential multinational giant set out to destroy the local icon. But the fact was that despite some improvement, Ocean Park was beginning to look and feel tired and shabby, and its attractions paled when compared with the glitz and glamour of Disney. Would Ocean Park be able to survive? In other words, when Donald Duck came, would Ocean Park become a "sitting duck"?

Leveraging Ocean Park's Strengths

While Ocean Park did have thrill rides, its primary focus was on nature and wildlife with many animal-related

---

1 © Michael N. Young. Reprinted with permission. All dollar figures used in this case are US dollars.

activities. Its Ocean Theater staged dolphin and sea lion shows. Its world-class Atoll Reef, Shark Aquarium, Bird Aviary, and Pacific Pier gave visitors opportunities to view wild animals and beautiful scenery up close—a rarity in urban Hong Kong. In addition, Ocean Park had distinct Chinese characteristics that reflected its roots in Hong Kong.

"The only way we can survive is to make our park world class," stated Allan Zeman, Ocean Park's Board Chairman. Early on, Ocean Park made a clear decision that it would not try to beat Disneyland at its own game. Zeman stated: "We do not want to try to 'out-Disney' Disney." The result was an ambitious $700 million master plan, including schemes for a new roller coaster that would be operating by 2012, a subzero Ice Palace, and a 7.6-million-liter aquarium with an underwater restaurant. An extra 33 animal species would be brought in, and the number of rides was doubled to 70. Ocean Park hoped to position itself as a world-class marine-based attraction with real animals in this ambitious overhaul. The park would further strengthen its core competencies in "real" nature rather in contrast to Disney's strengths in cartoon characters, castles, virtual reality, and fantasy. It was hoped that Ocean Park could differentiate itself more clearly from Disneyland. However, the huge $700 million investment would put a severe financial burden on Ocean Park as half of the investment would come from bank loans. Ocean Park's profit in 2005 was only $15 million. Despite the high cost of the redevelopment plan, management kept Ocean Park's admission fee at 30% lower than Disney's: $36 versus $51 for adults in 2011.

To boost attendance of local visitors, Ocean Park introduced an annual pass with unlimited admissions for an entire year. It hoped that annual pass holders might also bring along other visitors. Besides the new pricing campaign, seasonal holiday themes were another field of battle between Ocean Park and Hong Kong Disneyland. This battle highlighted the different approaches taken by East and West. For instance, for Halloween 2009, a creative campaign was laid out. While Hong Kong Disneyland was fashioning a sinister, dark world, like the one in Hollywood blockbusters, Ocean Park tapped into the local psyche, derived from old tales like the madness at the high street police station and the long-haired girl who was said to haunt a university laboratory. There was a clear contrast between Ocean Park that played the Hong Kong card and Disneyland that deployed strong Western elements.

Turning a Threat into an Opportunity

By 2010, Ocean Park had not only overcome Disney's challenges, but had even managed to turn a threat into an opportunity. Far from being the death knell as predicted by many analysts, Disney's arrival in Hong Kong had been a *boon* for Ocean Park. Disney's opening spurred Ocean Park into action with a dramatic turnaround. In 2010, Ocean Park achieved the highest recorded attendance (5.1 million) in its history, surpassing Disneyland's 5 million visitors. Some commentators suggested that Ocean Park was a bigger benefactor from Disneyland than was Disney itself. The opening of Disneyland had rejuvenated local interest in amusement parks. Furthermore, Hong Kong Disneyland increased the number of tourists from China and Southeast Asia to Hong Kong—particularly families interested in amusement parks. In addition to seeing Disney, it was natural for them to want to see Ocean Park. As a result, Ocean Park enjoyed increasing profits, while Hong Kong Disneyland struggled—with missing attendance goals and doubtful profitability.

CASE DISCUSSION QUESTIONS

1. How was Ocean Park able to turn a threat into an opportunity?

2. Ocean Park made the decision not to compete head to head with Disneyland. Will this strategy always work when local companies face multinational giants? Explain.

3. How can Ocean Park further capitalize on Disneyland's presence? (Hint: Check out how other parks surrounding Disney, such as Sea World and Universal Studios, survive and thrive in Anaheim, California, and Orlando, Florida.)

4. How can Hong Kong Disneyland turn around its lackluster performance?

Nomura's Integration of Lehman Brothers' Assets in Asia and Europe[1]

Is there strategic fit between Nomura and Lehman? Is there organizational fit? Does Nomura have what it takes to successfully integrate these two companies with contrasting management styles?

Mike W. Peng, *University of Texas at Dallas*

The Opportunity of a Lifetime

In September 2008, Lehman Brothers went bankrupt. Britain's Barclay Capital bought Lehman's North America operations for $3.75 billion. Lehman's assets in Asia and Europe were purchased by Nomura for the bargain-basement price of $200 million. Founded in 1925, Nomura is the oldest and largest securities brokerage and investment banking firm in Japan. Although Nomura had operated in 30 countries prior to the Lehman deal in 2008, it had always been known as a significant but still primarily regional (Asian) player in the big league of the financial services industry. In addition to Lehman, the list of elite investment banking firms in early 2008 would include Goldman Sachs, Morgan Stanley, Bear Stearns, JP Morgan, and Citigroup of the United States; Credit Suisse and UBS of Switzerland; and Deutsche Bank of Germany. No one would include Nomura in this group. Nomura viewed itself primarily as an Asian version of Merrill Lynch.

The tumultuous 2008 left Bear Stearns dead first, Lehman second, and all of the firms in the big league named above in deep financial trouble. To Nomura, this became the opportunity of a lifetime. Within a lightning 24 hours, CEO Kenichi Watanabe decided to acquire Lehman's remnants in Asia and Europe. Some of the Lehman assets were dirt cheap. For example, its French investment banking operations were sold to Nomura for only one euro (that is, €1!). Overall, by cherry-picking Lehman's Asia and Europe operations and adding 8,000 employees who tripled Nomura's size outside Japan, Nomura transformed

itself into a global heavyweight overnight. The question was: Does Nomura have what it takes to make this acquisition a success?

Integration Challenges

The answer was a decisive "No!" from Nomura's investors, who drove its shares down by 70% by 2012. Since the purchase price seemed reasonable and there was little evidence that Nomura overpaid, the biggest challenge was postacquisition integration, merging a hard-charging New York investment bank with a

---

1 This research was supported by the O. P. Jindal Chair at the Jindal School of Management, University of Texas at Dallas. All views and errors are those of the author. © Mike W. Peng. Reprinted with permission.

hierarchical Japanese firm that still largely practices lifetime employment.

Clearly, Lehman's most valuable, rare, and hard-to-imitate assets are its talents. To ensure that Nomura retained most of the ex-Lehman talents, Nomura set aside a compensation pool of $1 billion (five times the acquisition price) and guaranteed all ex-Lehman employees who chose to stay with Nomura not only their jobs, but also their 2007 pay level (including bonuses) for three years. About 95% of them accepted Nomura's offer. Given the ferociousness of the financial meltdown in 2008–2009 (which, if you remember, was triggered by Lehman's collapse), many employees at other firms that were not bankrupt lost their jobs. The fact that Nomura guaranteed both jobs and pay levels was widely appreciated by ex-Lehman employees who otherwise would have been devastated.

Instead, acquiring Lehman introduced significant stress to Nomura's long-held traditions. A leading challenge was pay level. Most senior executives at Lehman made on average $1 million in 2007. On average, Nomura employees only received *half* the pay of their Lehman counterparts. Not surprisingly, guaranteeing ex-Lehman employees at such an astronomical pay level (viewed from a Nomura perspective) created a major problem among Nomura's Japanese employees. In response, Nomura in 2009 offered its employees in Japan higher pay and bonuses that would start to approach the level ex-Lehman employees were commanding, in exchange for less job security—in other words, they could be fired more easily if they underperformed. So far, about 2,000 Japanese employees accepted the offer, which would link pay to individual and departmental performance rather the firm as a whole.

Another challenge was the personnel rotation system. Like many leading Japanese firms, Nomura periodically rotated managers to different positions. For example, Yoshihiro Fukuta, who served as head of Nomura International Hong Kong Ltd. in 2008, was rotated back to Tokyo as head of the Internal Audit Division in 2009. While these practices produced well-rounded generalist managers, they generated a rigid hierarchy: a manager in a later cohort year, no matter how superb his (always a male) performance was, was unlikely to supervise a manager in an earlier cohort year. These Nomura practices directly clashed with

Western norms: (1) work was increasingly done by specialists who developed deep expertise and (2) super stars were typically on a fast track rocketing ahead. Although the personnel rotation system largely did not apply to Nomura's overseas employees, it resulted in a top echelon that consisted entirely of Japanese executives who went through the rotations. In an effort to globalize, Nomura's top echelon needed to attract diverse talents, especially those from Lehman. Could the rotation system accommodate the arrival of ex-Lehman employees who had neither experience with nor stomach for it?

Postacquisition Performance

Four years after the acquisition, the performance was disappointing. In 2009, Nomura moved its investment banking headquarters to London to demonstrate its commitment to break into the top tier. In 2011, in Europe, Nomura was No. 13 in underwriting equities and No. 15 in advising on mergers. In Asia outside of Japan and in the United States, it was a distant No. 24 and No. 22, respectively, in underwriting equity offerings. Its dominance in Japan was indeed strengthened by the Lehman deal. Nomura's market share in advising Japanese acquirers that made deals overseas shot up from 10% in 2007 to 25% in 2011.

Integration continued to be Nomura's number-one headache. Outside Japan, the deal turned out to be a "reverse" takeover with *gaijin* (foreigners) running most of the show. Nomura undertook a campaign to expunge the long shadows of the Lehman hangover. Both symbolically and comically, mentioning the "L" word (such as "This is how we did it at Lehman") during senior executive meetings in London would cost executives £5 every time—they had to toss the money into a box as a penalty. In 2012, Jesse Bhattal, who was the former Asia Pacific CEO of Lehman, the deputy president of the Nomura group, and the CEO of Nomura's investment banking group (the highest ranked non-Japanese executive at Nomura), resigned amid heavy losses. Bhattal failed to see eye to eye with the board and was frustrated by his inability to undertake much-needed cost cutting. His departure was regarded as "the culmination of a clash with Nomura's old guard," according to Bloomberg. The dark clouds over Nomura thickened…

Sources: Based on (1) Bloomberg, 2012, Nomura reeling from Lehman hangover, February 28, www.bloomberg.com; (2) *BusinessWeek*, 2009, Nomura is starting to flex its Lehman muscles, September 28; (3) E. Choi, H. Leung, J. Chan, S. Tse, & W. Chu, 2009, How can Nomura be a true global financial company? Case study, University of Hong Kong; (4) *Economist*, 2009, Numura's integration of Lehman, July 11; (5) A. Huo, E. Liu, R. Gampa, & R. Liew, 2009, Nomura's bet on Lehman, case study, University of Hong Kong; (6) Reuters, 2012, Ex-Lehman's Bhattal quits Nomura amid deep losses, January 10: www.reuters.com.

CASE DISCUSSION QUESTIONS

1. What is the strategic fit between Nomura and Lehman?

2. Is there any organizational fit? How can the gaps between the cultures of these two firms be bridged?

3. How does Nomura alleviate the concerns of multiple stakeholders?

4. How would you predict the effectiveness of Nomura's transformation after this acquisition?

Baosteel Europe[1]

How does a leading Chinese steelmaker manage its European headquarters in Germany?

Bernd Michael Linke, *Friedrich Schiller University of Jena, Germany*
Andreas Klossek, *Technical University of Freiberg, Germany*

The Making of a Global Corporation

The name "Baosteel" combines Baoshan, a district in Shanghai, China, and the English word "steel." "Baosteel" stands for a Chinese company with global outreach. However, experts in Asia think that there is an additional twist at play, as is often the case with company names in this region. In Chinese, "bao" also signifies "valuable" or "precious," and a literal translation of Baosteel may be "premium steel"—certainly something to which the company aspires.

Baosteel's home market is staggering. On the demand side, the market reflects the sheer and insatiable needs of the largest and most successful emerging economy in the world. However, on the supply side, it is fragmented unlike any other market in the world. Currently, the Chinese steel market is divided by 260 steelmakers of various sizes, and some sources say this number could be greater than 1,000. While some of these firms are profitable, most are not. Thus, it is not surprising that the Chinese government is urging them to turn themselves into large steelmaking corporations following the lead of Baosteel.

Baosteel Group was founded in Shanghai in 1978 under the name of Baoshan Iron and Steel Complex. Skipping some of the historical details, it suffices to say that the current-day corporation is the result of a large merger between Shanghai Metallurgical Holding Group Corporation and Shanghai Meishan Group Co., Ltd., carried out in 1998 on the basis of a government decree. With continued growth, the most recent acquisition took place in April 2008, when Baosteel acquired the Bayi Steel Group in the province of Xinjiang.

Baosteel Group is a holding company consisting of five divisions: (1) financial, (2) steel trading, (3) equipment and spare parts engineering, (4) steel products, and (5) Shanghai headquarters office (administrative and service). The company produces and sells steel primarily to carmakers, shipbuilders, electronics and household appliances makers, oil drilling and pipeline companies, and construction companies. Baosteel has further diversified into areas such as financial services, trading, and logistics services. In sum, the company's operational philosophy is to continue to "diversify trading functions and operation products" while "gradually expanding non-Baosteel trading business."[2]

In comparison to international rivals, Baosteel displays a high degree of diversification. However, this is typical for many large Asian firms. Baosteel is a wholly owned state-owned enterprise (SOE). The largest business unit, Baoshan Iron and Steel Co., Ltd. (Baosteel Co., Ltd.), has been listed on the Shanghai Stock Exchange since 2000. Currently, 78% of the shares are held by Baosteel Group and thus ultimately by the Chinese government.

In recent years, the turnover of Baosteel has risen annually by 10%, from $19.5 billion in 2004 to $26.3 billion in 2007. During the same period, steel production has risen from 21.4 million to 28.6 million tons.

1 This case was written by Bernd Michael Linke (Friedrich Schiller University of Jena, Germany) and Andreas Klossek (Technical University of Freiberg, Germany). It was first published in the authors' study *Chinese Companies in Germany: Chances and Challenges*, which was sponsored by Bertelsmann Foundation and Deloitte (the full study can be accessed at http://www.bertelsmann-stiftung.de/cps/rde/xbcr/SID-12ED87F3-5090242B/bst_engl/xcms_bst_dms_27517_27534_2.pdf). The authors would like to thank both for granting the permission to reprint this case. © Bertelsmann Foundation. Reprinted with permission. Case discussion questions were added by Mike Peng.
2 Baosteel, 2009, Address by the President, Accessed November 11, 2009, www.baosteel.eu.

Baosteel, which currently employs 122,780 workers, is China's largest producer of steel. It has worked on prestigious and complex building projects such as the principal venue of the 2008 Summer Olympic Games (the national stadium nicknamed "Bird's Nest" in Beijing), the headquarters of CCTV state television in Beijing, and the terminals of international airports in Beijing and Shanghai. In international terms, the company is also one of the largest corporations of its kind. Since 2006, Baosteel has been in fifth place in the global steelmaker category. In 2004, Baosteel was the first Chinese manufacturing company to be included in the *Fortune* 500 list at 372—by 2008, it had climbed to 259. Baosteel aims to become one of the three largest steel producers in the world as soon as possible and is well on its way to achieving this goal.

Strategic Positioning and Global Activities

Many experts believe that Baosteel's goal is attainable. Its accomplishments, which the Western media traditionally would not have thought possible in the case of a Chinese SOE, speak for themselves. Over the course of the most recent merger, the workforce was cut 43% from 176,000 to 122,780. Baosteel believes that its future success is no longer going to be based on cheap labor, but instead on automated production. The main plant in Shanghai is considered to be one of the most modern and most efficient manufacturing sites for steel products in the *world*. At Baosteel, the new management focus is visible in many areas. For example, the "Six Sigma" quality management system was successfully introduced in 2005. Further, Baosteel engages in strategic planning and has an integrated management system designed to regulate and assign responsibilities, executive order powers, and communication channels between business entities.

Corporate social responsibility (CSR) has also become increasingly important in recent years. Baosteel is ahead of this social trend, embracing CSR and bankrolling numerous social projects as early as in 1990. For example, the establishment of Baosteel Education Fund

is one of the most visible education awards nationwide. Its foundation has set up 38 Hope elementary schools[3] and provides support for sustainability and environmental projects. To further substantiate its dedication to CSR, Baosteel is the first Chinese company to publish annual sustainability reports, which have appeared since 2005. Moreover, in 2006, the management announced a new slogan and goal centered around CSR. The slogan, "Green Baosteel, our common home," is aligned with its goal of turning Baosteel into the cleanest and most sustainable steelmaker in the world.

The preconditions for turning the company into a global player are in place. First, Baosteel, since its founding, has never been a typical Chinese SOE. Second, it dates back only to 1978, which coincides with the exact point at which the Chinese economic reforms got off the ground. Thus, unlike many SOEs, it was not burdened with the legacy of the Chinese communist past. Finally, it has been shaped by the cosmopolitan tradition of Shanghai, which is reflected in the long-lasting relationships and numerous joint ventures that the Baosteel Group holds with other global players.

Baosteel is prepared to confront the future and recognizes the enormous challenges it will bring. Special market segments in China have, for some time, seen higher growth rates and much higher demand levels than in other emerging markets such as India and Russia. To some extent, they have even caught up with those of industrialized countries such as the United States. The latest OECD research suggests that this trend is visible in every segment of the Chinese steel market and is projected to become more pronounced. At the same time, exports continue to grow despite the gigantic demand in China. In 2004, Chinese steel exports exceeded imports for the first time in history.

Endeavoring to meet the high demand at home, more than 90% of Baosteel's turnover is in China. Additionally, to enhance its negotiating position in the competition for scarcer natural resources, it is planning further mergers and acquisitions at home and abroad, both horizontally and vertically (upstream and downstream) across the value chain. The current consolidation of the Chinese steel market and open

---

3 In Chinese jargon, Hope schools refer to schools set up in poor rural areas where children would not have been educated had these schools not been set up. These schools are known to offer "hope."

access to international markets are making this strategy of acquiring new plants and integrating important mining sites possible. For example, currently, Baosteel imports 80% of the iron ore it needs. However, as early as in 2001, the company took a 50% share in the Brazilian iron ore mine Água Limpa, and in 2003, it acquired shares in Hamersley Iron, an Australian subsidiary of Rio Tinto. These equity positions are examples of Baosteel's vertical movement on the value chain. Moreover, loose partnerships and numerous meetings with other steel giants in Asia, such as Nippon Steel in Japan and Posco in Korea, nurture rumors that a merger may emerge.

Of decisive importance for the Baosteel Group's strategic planning are not only the economic goals, but also the acquisition of international management experience. As such, internationalization efforts, such as those detailed in the remainder of the case with a focus on Baosteel Europe, are crucial.

Setting Up a Subsidiary in Hamburg, Germany

Baosteel has been conducting business in Germany for a long time, though its activities have changed significantly over the years. In the beginning, it was impossible to think about selling steel products; rather, its main task was to supply Chinese companies with vital replacement parts sourced in Germany for domestic production. This changed in 1993, when senior management decided to expand and founded Baosteel Europe GmbH with $6.64 million. Baosteel selected Germany for a very specific reason: the local courts provide European customers and suppliers with more legal protection than if business were to be conducted in Hong Kong or China. In other words, using the institution-based view, Baosteel considered the "rules of the game" regarding the legal infrastructure and enforcement across countries and made its location decision.

After deciding to locate in Germany, Baosteel also evaluated a number of German cities. Its decision to locate the business in the Hamburg metropolis was based on both economical motives (such as direct access to shipping routes) and cultural aspects. For example, Ye Meng, the current President of Baosteel Europe, states, "Hamburg and China can look back on a long history of partnership. There really are quite a lot of Chinese companies and trading entities here. The parent of Baosteel Europe GmbH comes from Hamburg's sister city, Shanghai, which is also a port city. Both from a cultural perspective and for geographical reasons Hamburg in our opinion provides us with favorable conditions for the development of our company." Additionally, the workforce, technology, and infrastructure in Germany are known to be world class. Further, Meng believes that earning the trust of German clients and selling "Made in Germany" steel parts in China have benefited the company greatly.[4]

Indeed, Baosteel Europe's business has been booming. In the past three years, turnover increased to $732 million. This means that Baosteel Europe is among the largest Chinese companies in Germany. While making a profit, Baosteel Europe is certainly not resting on its laurels. Not only is Baosteel Europe strategizing to increase its share of the global market, it is also seeking to expand in Germany and Europe with new products and innovations. As such, the Hamburg subsidiary is due for expansion with new specialists recruited. Under Meng, the structure of Baosteel Europe GmbH has changed considerably in the past few years. For example, in 2004, there were 30 Baosteel employees in Germany, and today there are 55—with additional employees in other offices throughout Europe, the Middle East, and Shanghai. The finance department and the Shanghai office are responsible for the internal organization of what happens in Hamburg. Looking after customers and suppliers is the task of each business area (i.e., steel trading, spare parts and equipment, and metal products). Recently, the new business department has been given the mandate of expanding into new business areas. In order to manage a variety of tasks, the company employs individuals from a number of countries. In Hamburg, Chinese expatriates work side by side with Germans. In other subsidiaries in Europe, employees from the various host countries are in the majority. Taken

---

4 "Hamburg provides Chinese company with link to Germany, Europe, and the world," accessed November 12, 2009, http://www.gtai.com/homepage/info-service/publications/our-publications/germany-investment-magazine/vol-2008/vol-032008/foreign-direct-investment1/.

together, it is apparent that Baosteel is a transnational company with a global outlook.

Business Areas of the Baosteel Subsidiary in Germany

Procurement, which was of considerable importance at the start of Baosteel's activities in Germany, continues to play an important role today. The transactions involved are complicated and interculturally demanding, requiring good coordination. The procurement process is set in motion by a firm in a given location—for example, a Chinese steelmaker in a province that needs spare parts obtainable only from Europe. This requirement is relayed to the Baosteel head office in Shanghai, which subsequently transmits an inquiry to Baosteel Europe. The inquiry is received by a Chinese or German employee in Hamburg, who then places an order with a local (German) supplier. After the spare parts arrive, another Chinese or German Baosteel employee arranges for them to be sent to China. Inquiry, order processing, and transport are dealt with in Chinese, German, and English, meaning that employees of both nations transact on many tasks together and must engage in an ongoing dialogue. Thus, at the Hamburg location, business success absolutely depends on Sino-German cooperation, which is based on years of experience and mutual understanding. A Chinese department head supervises four tandems, each consisting of a Chinese and a German employee, who know each other and work together in a coordinated manner.

Steel trading, however, has a fundamentally different procurement process, wherein ten Chinese co-workers—most of whom are engineers—work under the direction of the internationally experienced deputy managing director, Guo Zheng. The working language is Chinese, and in keeping with international business practices, English is used when communicating with the "outside" world. In steel trading, the German market plays a subordinate role. Sales orders are sent via Hamburg, where the contracts are concluded, to the whole of Europe and the rest of the world. The majority of customers value Baosteel's quality, reliability, punctual delivery, and service. Although price is important in certain countries, Baosteel does not position itself in the lower price segment, preferring to have a price level akin to that of ThyssenKrupp and ArcelorMittal. In order to increase its market share in Europe, Baosteel is pinning its hopes on premium quality and customer orientation. The turnover volume, currently about 500,000 to 600,000 tons annually, is still a very small percentage of the total output.

The new business department is also managed by a Chinese expatriate with international experience. "New" refers both to new regions (such as the Middle East, Eastern Europe, and Africa) and to new activities (such as investments in sectors other than the steel industry). The current planning phase involves conducting feasibility studies (with the help of external expertise) and studying market entry methods.

Corporate Culture and Work Atmosphere

In recent years, Baosteel's senior management has come to realize the importance of a common corporate culture—for both Chinese and foreign employees. In 2004, Baosteel implemented a program that stresses "good faith" and "synergy" as basic values and emphasizes the significance of culture as the basis of all economic action. It has been said that "Baosteel's culture is the soul of management, while Baosteel's management is the vehicle of culture." The executives at Baosteel Europe emphasize words such as "integrity," "teamwork," and "loyalty," and are thus transferring to all employees the essence and level of their cooperation with the head office in Shanghai. To stress the high opinion and importance of the local workforce, all German employees of Baosteel Europe were invited to stay in Shanghai for a week. There they were shown the organization of the head office, met their counterparts with whom they often telephoned or exchanged emails, and experienced Chinese hospitality—along with gratitude for their achievement and loyalty to the company. The German employees have also been included in the Chinese bonus system in order to encourage their participation in the success of the company.

At the biannual meeting involving all Baosteel Europe employees, management reports at length about the success and goals of the parent company and the Hamburg subsidiary, hoping to foster a community spirit. The German employees were also pleasantly surprised that the Chinese executives clearly try to respect German habits and customs by not expecting German employees to stay in the office until late in the evening, as is often the case with Chinese expatriates. Baosteel has come to understand and acknowledge that despite different work habits, in the end, the efficiency is the same.

The German employees are also particularly appreciative of the respect with which Chinese superiors treat their subordinates. The experience of working together on a daily basis means that German employees at Baosteel certainly do not share the typically negative picture of China that is often painted by the media. Instead, most have developed a far more positive picture of China.

Apart from the good atmosphere in the workplace, employees have additional motivations. Specifically, a large and expanding company is synonymous with safe jobs. This is especially true for Chinese companies, where protection against dismissal is based on the Chinese and Confucian belief that one has a duty to look after the well-being of others. The high one-off bonuses for special accomplishments confirm the appreciative attitude of the senior management. Therefore, employee turnover is quite low in comparison with other companies within this industry.

To advance within Baosteel, it is necessary to occupy a position of responsibility at the head office. As such, it is important for individuals to possess not only professional qualifications, but also have the ability to speak fluent Chinese. Thus, many German employees who do not speak Chinese find it extremely difficult to reach the senior management level at Baosteel Europe. Overall, while challenges remain, Baosteel has overcome many of the cultural differences by taking time to understand those differences and finding ways to embed both the German and Chinese cultures within its organizational culture.

Human Resource Management (HRM)

In China, Baosteel enjoys a good reputation for its excellent compensation and career opportunities. To maintain its reputation and recruit top talent, Baosteel implements a very thorough recruiting process. Candidates for its comprehensive examination procedure are selected from a large number of applicants—all of whom are university graduates. Unlike most companies in East Asia, Baosteel rarely recruits candidates jumping ship from other employers or at job fairs. However, once candidates are selected, the successful applicants are introduced to and trained in Baosteel's corporate culture, which is a customary practice in Chinese firms. If the candidate does well over the course of the year, the company may cover the cost of further education—for example, a one-year higher education program at home or abroad. After this, the individual is likely to be promoted within the company and employed as a senior executive, alternating between China and other countries. Interestingly, until recently it had been considered a welcome opportunity for Chinese employees to be offered the opportunity to work abroad for a number of years, since it coincided with good pay and enhanced qualifications. However, because income and career opportunities have developed enormously within China in recent years, many consider this same "opportunity" or assignment to be a burden, especially since the quality of life in Shanghai is now higher than that in many Western cities.

In other words, Chinese expatriates now experience the same types of burdens as expatriates from developed countries, such as separation from their family or problems with their children's schools overseas. Although Baosteel takes into account these reservations and offers its Chinese expatriates numerous incentives such as increased compensation and job guarantees for spouses, the willingness to work in other countries is declining. However, for individuals trying to climb the career ladder, successful stints abroad considerably facilitate access to the senior management level and to executive posts in the subsidiaries and at the head office.

More recently, Baoteel has expanded the scope of its HRM, becoming more strategic in nature. In addition to regular assessments, the skills of its employees are continually being enhanced by means of systematic training. Further, preparatory country-specific or culture-specific instruction for foreign assignments is now available, as are returnees' programs. Finally, the mentoring system is well organized and highly valued. Talented young executives are watched over and given advice by mentors appointed to look after and guide them. As mentors rise in the company hierarchy, it will eventually lead to advancement for their "mentees," who may also receive recommendations for employment elsewhere. This network system not only leads to good professional work, but is indispensable if one wishes to advance to a decision-making position.

Baosteel Europe Paves the Way for Integration and Expansion

For Baosteel, numerous economic and cultural aspects were of decisive importance when it chose Hamburg as its European location. Endeavoring for a win-win outcome, Baosteel Europe has developed a great relationship with the Hamburg city government, especially with its departments involved in economic development. Baosteel continuously manages this relationship by staying in touch with the media and having company representatives participate in and sponsor public events. Interestingly, Baosteel has also incorporated its German-oriented practices of external representation back in China, demonstrating its dedication to learning from global best practices. Baosteel has also begun to develop ideas regarding networking strategies with other Chinese organizations in Germany geared toward the joint promotion of their interests and maintained loose partnerships with two other large Chinese corporations also located in Hamburg—COSCO and Bank of China.

Baosteel Europe is said to exemplify the "large Chinese corporation abroad," and it occupies a front-runner role in two senses—being both a "test case" and a "model."[5] Many Chinese companies still find it difficult to be internationally competitive, and there is often a discrepancy between an impressive success story told at home and the hesitant progress overseas that may be marred by setbacks. This could change quickly if "pilot projects," such as the internationalization of Baosteel, are a success and the senior management of other companies draws the right conclusions. However, it is not only the views within an industry that are of importance. Chinese companies, especially those with international ambitions, must assume that they are being watched intently by the public both at home and abroad and must behave in a responsible manner.

After a rough start, Baosteel has made significant progress in recent years. Admittedly, the situation has been rather auspicious for the steel industry. An essential basis for further expansion in the international sector is a systematic development of HR beginning with recruiting and leading to career planning and further education. Baosteel aims to use the talents of both German and third-country specialists and to form international leadership teams that will be in a position to meet the challenges of international management. Further, in the case of international customer–supplier relationships, it is important to preempt cross-cultural conflicts by increasing the level of intercultural competence and strengthening an overarching corporate culture.

Baosteel is well on its way to mastering these challenges, having already united a variety of very different companies in Shanghai and developing a distinct corporate culture among its employees. When discussing Baosteel's "hard skills," the former chairwoman Qihua Xie once coined the slogan "quality, not quantity." The same can just as well be applied to Baosteel's "soft skills." Overall, the Baosteel Group is an exemplary company from which other Chinese companies can learn.

CASE DISCUSSION QUESTIONS

1. What location-specific advantages did Hamburg, Germany, provide Baosteel? Evaluate other European locations that might offer similar advantages.

2. How did Baosteel manage its entry into Europe? What factors have enhanced its success?

3. How did Baosteel Europe overcome the challenges of managing a subsidiary?

4. What are the lessons on how to manage human resources in a subsidiary that we can draw based on Baosteel Europe's experience in Germany?

5. Why does Baosteel devote considerable resources to corporate social responsibility?

---

5 Handelsblatt no. 43, March 1, 2007.

Bank of America's Corporate Social Responsibility and the Occupy Wall Street Movement[1]

> *Although Bank of America invested $268.8 billion in CSR-related activities in 2010, it was a leading target for the Occupy Wall Street protestors in 2011. In the middle of the Occupy Wall Street movement, two executives were trying to figure out how to formulate CSR plans for 2012.*

Cathy Benjamin, *University of Texas at Dallas*
Vivian Brown, *University of Texas at Dallas*
James Buchanon, *University of Texas at Dallas*
Grace Crane, *University of Texas at Dallas*
Michele Harkins, *University of Texas at Dallas*

"What do these people want from us?" Mary Turner, Global Strategy and Marketing Executive for Bank of America, looked outside her fourth floor window as Occupy Wall Street protesters marched on the sidewalk in front of the bank in October 2011. Anne was preparing to meet with Mark Smith, Global Corporate Social Responsibility (CSR) and Consumer Policy Executive, to discuss their recommendations to the board regarding 2012 CSR plans.

Public outcry demanded more and more from the bank, as it was repeatedly blamed for causing the 2008 mortgage crisis. Occupy Wall Street protesters marched with signs stating "We are the 99%" as a reminder of the distribution of wealth between the wealthiest 1% and the remainder of the population. Wealth distribution had become a growing and heated debate in 2011. The week before, a group of protestors had briefly taken over a Los Angeles branch demanding that Bank of America help resolve state budget deficits. The bank was forced to call in police to protect its customers, employees, and property. Trash recovered from a foreclosed home was dumped on the lawn of some bank executives.

Consumers were being encouraged to close accounts at big banks and open accounts at credit unions. Protestors seemed to believe that corporate greed was the root cause

1 This case was written by Cathy Benjamin, Vivian Brown, James Buchanon, Grace Crane, and Michele Harkins (University of Texas at Dallas EMBA 2012) under the supervision of Professor Mike Peng. The purpose of the case is to serve as a basis for class discussion rather than to illustrate the effective or ineffective handling of an administrative situation. The views expressed are those of the authors (in their private capacity as EMBA students) and do not necessarily reflect those of the individuals and organizations mentioned. © Cathy Benjamin, Vivian Brown, James Buchanon, Grace Crane, and Michele Harkins. Reprinted with permission. Case discussion questions were added by Mike Peng.

of America's financial crisis. This public outcry for the banks to be more socially responsible was threatening their ability to do business.

Bank of America's CSR Activities

Bank of America considered itself to be a socially responsible company. Its 2010 CSR activities included investments of $268.8 billion (see Exhibit 1), including:

- $168.5 billion in community development (see Exhibit 2)
- $92 billion in small and medium-sized businesses
- $4.1 billion spent with thousands of small, medium, and diverse suppliers
- $4 billion in environmental business initiatives

- $207.9 million in philanthropy (see Exhibit 3)
- 1.3 million employee volunteer hours

Despite the challenging economic environment, the bank launched its Emergency Safety Net Strategy. The program was designed to meet pressing community needs stemming from the poor economy. It provided direct funding to enable health and human service nonprofit organizations to continue delivering health care, job training, childcare programs, shelter, hunger relief, and other services to help stabilize the communities it served. At a time of government cutbacks and failing service providers, the bank continued to support education and youth development, community development and neighborhood preservation, health and human services, and arts and culture.

EXHIBIT 1 Bank of America 2010 CSR Highlights

BIG GOALS FOR 2010	ACHIEVEMENTS IN 2010
Invest and lend **$1.5 trillion** in community development projects by 2019.	Invested **$168.5 billion** in community development, increasing total investment since 2009 to $336.7 billion.
Increase loans to small and medium-sized businesses by **$5 billion** in 2010.	Increased lending to more than **$92 billion** to small and medium-sized businesses, $10.5 billion more than in 2009.
Spend **$10 billion** with small, medium-sized, and diverse suppliers by 2015.	Spent **$4.1 billion** with thousands of small, medium-sized and diverse suppliers, including $2.3 billion with diverse suppliers alone.
Invest **$20 billion** in environmentally friendly businesses by 2017.	Invested nearly **$4 billion** toward environmental business initiative in 2010, reaching the $11.6 billion mark on three-year-old initiative to address climate change through lending, investing products and services, and operations.
Reduce total greenhouse gas emissions by **9%** between 2004 and 2009.	Surpassed goal to achive an overall emissions reduction of **18%** within the legacy Bank of America portfolio between 2004 and 2010; reduced Scope 1 and 2 emissions by 8 percent in 2010 alone.
Invest **$2 billion** through philanthropy by 2019, including at least $200 million in 2010.	Invested **$207.9 million** in philanthropy in 2010.
Volunteer **one million** employee hours of service in 2010.	Volunteered nearly **1.3 million** hours of employee service.

Source: Bank of America, Opportunity in Motion Corporate Responsibility Report 2010, http://webmedia.bankofamerica.com/ aheadbankofamerica/v4/video_files/CSR/Bank%20of%20America%202010%20Corporate%20Social%20Responsibility%20 Report.pdf

EXHIBIT 2   Bank of America 2010 Community Development Efforts

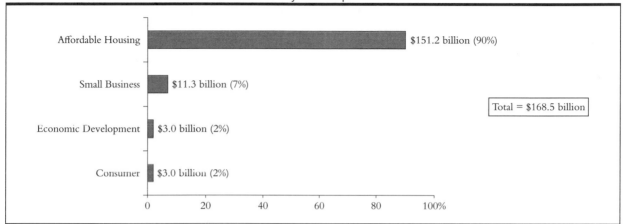

Source: Bank of America, Opportunity in Motion Corporate Responsibility Report 2010, http://webmedia.bankofamerica.com/ aheadbankofamerica/v4/video_files/CSR/Bank%20of%20America%202010%20Corporate%20Social%20Responsibility%20 Report.pdf

EXHIBIT 3   Bank of America 2010 Philanthropic Investments

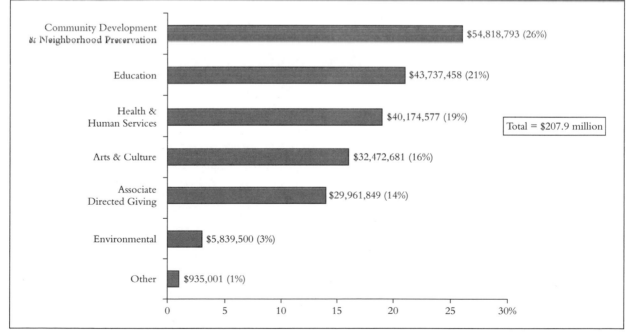

Source: Bank of America, Opportunity in Motion Corporate Responsibility Report 2010, http://webmedia.bankofamerica.com/ aheadbankofamerica/v4/video_files/CSR/Bank%20of%20America%202010%20Corporate%20Social%20Responsibility%20 Report.pdf

Turner doubted that the protesters were aware of the sacrifice the bank was making at a time when she believed it should focus more on its bottom line. She knew it would be tough to convince Smith to cut back on corporate giving. But the bank was under scrutiny at every turn. Every morning when she turned on MSNBC, she dreaded the moment the bank's name would be mentioned. A new story about the bank and its robo-signing practices was on the front page of the Mortgage Servicing News on her desk. She glanced at the articles in her inbox—Bloomberg, *American Banker*, *ABA Banking Journal*, *Wall Street Journal*, and *New York Times*. She began to wonder if Bank of America had a reserved spot on the front page of every financial news vehicle. She reached for her BlackBerry and shook her head as she read the latest tweet about how many homeowners the bank had forced to be homeless. She had recently shut down her LinkedIn and Facebook accounts due the flood of negative comments she was receiving. Since she agreed to the interview on *Good Morning America*, she had begun to receive personal messages. "Aren't banks in the business to make a profit for their shareholders?" she wondered out loud as Smith stuck his head in her door.

History

Bank of America is one of the largest financial institutions in the world with offices in more than 40 countries. Its Global Capital Markets and Global Corporate & Investment Banking divisions work to structure and underwrite capital raising transactions in the debt and equity markets. In the United States, the bank serves individual consumers, small- and middle-market businesses, and large corporations. Its services include banking, investing, asset management, and other products and services, including consumer mortgage lending and servicing.

In July 2008, Bank of America acquired Countrywide Financial and became the largest mortgage lender and consumer bank in the US, making it the lender in one of every four US home loans. In 2007, Countrywide and its CEO, Angelo Mozilo, came under scrutiny for the large number of defaults and foreclosures of subprime loans. Although several other mortgage lenders were also under scrutiny, Countrywide was the nation's largest lender and carried with it a history of predatory lending practices. Starting in the 1990s, the company borrowed from Wall Street, quickly closed the loans, and sold them on the secondary market. Although originally a profitable situation for both sides, the increased number of mortgage defaults created a breakdown of this cycle. By 2007, the threat of bankruptcy as a result of predatory lending practices was looming, and Mozilo agreed to the Bank of America buyout. Mozilo's exit package was approximately $72 million, even though he was under investigation for his accelerated sale of stock from 2006 to 2007.

The 2008 subprime mortgage crisis was triggered when over 20% of these high-risk borrowers defaulted on primarily adjustable-rate mortgages. By the end of 2007, Americans had also increased their debt to personal income ratio to over 120%, home prices declined, mortgage-backed securities lost their value, foreclosures increased, banks tightened credit, interest rates increased, and banks were forced to foreclose on homes. In October 2008, Congress passed the Troubled Asset Relief Program (TARP) designed to allow banks and other mortgage financers to regain stability and to resume consumer lending. Bank of America was deemed "too big to fail" and received $45 billion in TARP funds, which it repaid in December 2009.

2010 CSR Report: Conflict Between Social and Financial Responsibility

Bank of America released its 2010 CSR Report in early 2011 amid controversy as to how the bank should repay the public for the legacy Countrywide issues. The report emphasized the bank's commitment to its core values and operating principles and its continued struggles in the mortgage arena. The company was not shy about discussing how it would clean up its legacy issues and outlined its mortgage retention solutions, including home loan modifications, customer assistance programs, and improved clarity in the lending process. The report indicated that 76% of foreclosed borrowers had not made a mortgage payment for at least one year. Through its self-identified audit practices, the bank evaluated the integrity of its foreclosure practices and responded with additional staffing, controls, and quality checks.

Bank of America committed to prepare for and participate in upcoming mortgage industry reforms, to introduce a new loan modification program, to dispatch a dedicated mortgage servicing team, and to deploy the newly formed Legacy Asset Servicing division with a dedicated staff and executive leadership. The bank supports employee volunteerism by granting two volunteer hours per week per employee during business hours. Philanthropy is supported by up to $5,000 in matching funds for employee donations to non-profit organizations.

Turner believed in the bank's approach to CSR. However, she had to convince Smith, and the board, that the economic downturn demanded that the bank sharpen its focus on its shareholders. She began her discussion with Smith by reminding him of the losses the bank had suffered since the Countrywide purchase. The midyear report indicated the bank's $6.78 billion loss in net income, excluding goodwill impairment charge. Although the bank had realized a slight reduction in nonperforming loans, leases, and foreclosed properties, 2011 financial reports indicated the bank had a need to reduce debt and increase capital.

Last year, Moody's, Standard & Poor's, and Fitch had each downgraded the bank's credit rating. In June 2011, Moody's placed the bank on review for an additional downgrade. These agencies reminded the bank of the systemic damage legacy issues have on the economy. Slow US job growth, supply chain impacts due to the Japanese natural disaster, concern over the European financial crisis, inflation pressures in China, and the US federal debt issues contributed to an environment that reduced the public's confidence in Bank of America.

In 2011, the Financial Accounting Standards Board (FASB) introduced new guidelines affecting loan modifications, repurchase agreements, fair value measurement principles, and the presentation of comprehensive income. In June, BAC Home Loans Servicing and certain Countrywide affiliates entered a $8.6 billion settlement agreement. Bank of New York Mellon acted as trustee to resolve outstanding and potential claims regarding warranty breaches and other historical loan servicing claims associated with legacy Countrywide activities. Bank of America was under investigation by the Department of Justice for alleged irregularities in foreclosure practices, including compliance with FHA HUD requirements. Regulatory reform resulting from the 2010 Financial Reform Act threatened to increase the cost of doing business. FDIC deposit insurance assessments of large and complex financial institutions threatened the bank's cash reserves. Scrutiny by the Consumer Financial Protection Bureau, BASEL II capital requirement rules, and changes to Market Risk Rules continued to threaten the financial services industry. Other threats to the bank's solvency included new rules surrounding how non-sufficient fund fees, overdraft charges, and ATM fees could be charged.

The Dilemma Bank of America Faced for 2012 CSR Plan

Smith was well aware of the state of the economy, including the state of the financial services environment. He understood all of the threats to the solvency of the bank and was clear on the potential impact to the communities in which it served. Turner was delivering a haunting speech that made him seriously rethink his 2012 CSR plans. He began to wonder if the bank could afford its current commitments. He had always vowed to treat the bank's funds as if they were his own. However, he had already reduced his personal financial commitments by 25% over the past two years. He continued his philanthropic giving, but reduced it to health and human services, reasoning that necessities such as food and shelter were most important during this financial downturn. He received disappointing calls and letters from the arts and cultural organizations to which he traditionally donated. A few of his friends at the country club tried to persuade him that he had no reason to feel personally responsible for the mortgage crisis. Even his family taunted him after he announced he would be reducing spending. Perhaps it was time for the bank to do likewise.

Smith listened intently as Turner detailed the state of the bank. Although she agreed that corporate giving promoted the company's brand, she could not ignore the need for deeper financial cuts. In September, the bank announced that it would reduce its 288,000 workforce by 30,000 over the next few years, citing attrition and freezes of job opening as the primary manner of reduction. However, by early October, layoffs were occurring throughout the company. Was the bank in a worse shape than Turner realized?

Smith thought about the upcoming meeting with the board and realized that he had no options. The bank could no longer afford to continue its level of giving. Something had to change quickly in order to meet stakeholder demands. But how could Bank of America change its CSR strategy without further damaging the brand? Already, Wells Fargo was being criticized for reducing its commitment to green building. Citigroup was battling the SEC over mortgage fraud charges. Goldman Sachs paid millions last year in an SEC settlement related to subprime loans.

Bank of America was looking for more cash. The CEO, Brian Moynihan, announced in early 2011 the bank was looking to improve its fortress balance sheet amid questions on whether the bank had sufficient capital to sustain itself through the economic downturn. Rumors were surfacing around the bank's likelihood of further reducing its holdings in China Construction Bank. Since becoming CEO in 2010, Moynihan had already sold a Canadian credit-card portfolio, an insurance unit, and a private bank. The week before, the bank agreed to sell its stake in the Pizza Hut franchisee, including its debt, for $755 million to Olympus Partners. The deal would result in a net gain of over $375 million for the bank.

Smith realized that shareholder value should be the most immediate concern of the bank. He was suddenly exhausted as he looked over his list of corporate commitments. Slowly he pulled out his highlighter and started a lengthy review that would take him and Turner the next four hours to complete.

Sources: Based on (1) *Bank of America and Countrywide*, June 2010, retrieved October 15, 2011, from RealtyTrac: http://www.realtytrac.com/foreclosure/reo/bank-of-america-countrywide-foreclosure.html; (2) *Bank of America Finishes TARP Repayment*, December 10, 2009, retrieved October 29, 2011, from DealBook: http://dealbook.nytimes.com/2009/12/10/bank-of-america-finishes-tarp-repayment/; (3) *Bank of America Investor Relations*, September 13, 2011, retrieved November 5, 2011, from Bank of America: http://investor.bankofamerica.com/phoenix.zhtml?c=71595&p=irol-reports other; (4) *Bank of America Investor Relations*, September 13, 2011, retrieved November 7, 2011, from Bank of America Investor Fact Book - Midyear 2011: http://investor.bankof america.com/phoenix.zhtml?c=71595&p=irol-reportsother; (5) *Bank of America Releases First Corporate Social Responsibility Report*, July 12, 2011, retrieved October 15, 2011, from Bank of America, Inside Our Company: http://ahead.bankofamerica.com/featured/bank-of-america-releases-corporate-social-responsibility-report/; (6) *Bank of America* (n.d.), retrieved from http://investor.bankofamerica.com/phoenix.zhtml?c=71595&p=irol-reportsother; (7) *Wall Street Journal*, BofA Hunts for More Cash, November 8, 2011, retrieved November 8, 2011, http://online.wsj.com/article/SB10001424052970204190704577023890083609800.html?KEYWORDS=pizza+hut.

CASE DISCUSSION QUESTIONS

1. ***ON ETHICS:*** Despite such significant contributions to CSR causes, why is Bank of America so resented, not only by the Occupy Wall Street crowd but also by large segments of the general public?

2. ***ON ETHICS:*** Did or should Bank of America communicate to the Occupy Wall Street crowd about its CSR work?

3. ***ON ETHICS:*** What should Turner and Smith recommend to the board?

GLOSSARY

A

absorptive capacity The ability to absorb new knowledge by recognizing the value of new information, assimilating it, and applying it.

accommodative strategy A strategy that tries to accommodate corporate social responsibility considerations into decision making.

acquisition The transfer of control of assets, operations, and management from one firm (target) to another (acquirer); the former becomes a unit of the latter.

acquisition premium The difference between the acquisition price and the market value of target firms.

agency costs The costs associated with principal–agent relationships. They are the sum of (1) the principals' costs of monitoring and controlling agents and (2) the agents' costs of bonding.

agency relationship The relationship between principals and agents.

agency theory The theory about principal–agent relationships (or agency relationships in short).

agents Persons (such as managers) to whom authority is delegated.

agglomeration Clustering economic activities in certain locations.

ambidexterity Ability to use one's both hands equally well. In management jargon, this term has been used to describe capabilities to simultaneously deal with paradoxes (such as exploration versus exploitation).

anchored replicator A firm that seeks to replicate a set of activities in related industries in a small number of countries anchored by the home country.

antidumping laws Laws that punish foreign companies that engage in dumping in a domestic market.

antitrust laws Laws that attempt to curtail anti-competitive business practices such as cartels and trusts.

antitrust policy Competition policy designed to combat monopolies, cartels, and trusts.

arm's-length transactions Transactions in which parties keep a distance (see also formal, rule-based, impersonal exchange).

attack An initial set of actions to gain competitive advantage.

B

backward integration Acquiring and owning upstream assets.

balanced scorecard A performance evaluation method from the customer, internal, innovation and learning, and financial perspectives.

bargaining power of buyers The ability of buyers to reduce prices and/or enhance the quality of goods and services.

bargaining power of suppliers The ability of suppliers to raise prices and/or reduce the quality of goods and services.

base of the pyramid (BOP) The vast majority of humanity, about five billion people, who make less than $2,000 a year.

Beijing Consensus A view that questions Washington Consensus' belief in the superiority of private ownership over state ownership in economic policy making, which is often associated with the position held by the Chinese government.

benchmarking Examination as to whether a firm has resources and capabilities to perform a particular activity in a manner superior to competitors.

blue ocean strategy   A strategy that focuses on developing new markets (or "blue ocean") and avoids attacking core markets defended by rivals, which is likely to result in a bloody price war (or "red ocean").

born global firm (international new venture)   A start-up company that attempts to do business abroad from inception.

bounded rationality   The necessity of making rational decisions in the absence of complete information

BRIC   Brazil, Russia, India, and China.

BRICS   Brazil, Russia, India, China, and South Africa

build-operate-transfer (BOT) agreement   A special kind of turnkey project in which contractors first build facilities, operate them for a period of time, and then transfer them back to clients.

bureaucratic costs   The additional costs associated with a larger, more diversified organization.

business group   A term to describe a conglomerate, which is often used in emerging economies.

business process outsourcing (BPO)   Outsourcing of business processes such as loan origination, credit card processing, and call center operations.

business-level strategy   Strategy that builds competitive advantage in a discrete and identifiable market.

C

capability   The tangible and intangible assets a firm uses to choose and implement its strategies.

capacity to punish   Having sufficient resources to deter and combat defection.

captive sourcing   Setting up subsidiaries to perform in-house work in foreign location. Conceptually identical to foreign direct investment (FDI).

cartel   An entity that engages in output- and price-fixing, involving multiple competitors. Also known as a trust.

causal ambiguity   The difficulty of identifying the causal determinants of successful firm performance.

center of excellences   MNE subsidiaries explicitly recognized as a source of important capabilities, with the intention that these capabilities be leveraged by and/or disseminated to other subsidiaries.

CEO duality   The CEO doubles as chairman of the board.

chief executive officer (CEO)   The top executive in charge of the strategy and operations of a firm.

classic conglomerate   A firm that engages in product-unrelated diversification within a small set of countries centered on the home country.

co-marketing   Agreements among a number of firms to jointly market their products and services.

code of conduct (code of ethics)   Written policies and standards for corporate conduct and ethics.

cognitive pillar   The internalized, taken-for-granted values and beliefs that guide individual and firm behavior.

collectivism   The perspective that the identity of an individual is most fundamentally based on the identity of his or her collective group (such as family, village, or company).

collusion   Collective attempts between competing firms to reduce competition.

collusive price setting   Monopolists or collusion parties setting prices at a level higher than the competitive level.

commoditization   A process of market competition through which unique products that command high prices and high margins generally lose their ability to do so—these products thus become "commodities."

competition policy   Policy governing the rules of the game in competition, which determine the institutional mix of competition and cooperation that gives rise to the market system.

competitive dynamics   Actions and responses undertaken by competing firms.

competitor analysis   The process of anticipating rivals' actions in order to both revise a firm's plan and prepare to deal with rivals' responses.

complementary assets Numerous noncore assets that complement and support the value-adding activities of core assets.

complementor A firm that sells products that add value to the products of a focal industry.

concentrated ownership and control Ownership and control rights concentrated in the hands of owners.

concentration ratio The percentage of total industry sales accounted for by the top four, eight, or 20 firms.

conduct Firm actions such as product differentiation.

conglomerate Product-unrelated diversifier.

conglomerate M&A An M&A deal involving firms in product-unrelated industries.

conglomeration A strategy of product-unrelated diversification.

constellation A multipartner strategic alliance (also known as strategic network).

contender A strategy that centers on rapid learning and then expanding overseas.

contractual (non-equity-based) alliance A strategic alliance that is based on contracts and does not involve the sharing of ownership

corporate governance The relationship among various participants in determining the direction and performance of corporations.

corporate social responsibility (CSR) The social responsibility of corporations. It pertains to consideration of, and response to, issues beyond the narrow economic, technical, and legal requirements of the firm to accomplish social benefits along with the traditional economic gains that the firm seeks.

corporate-level strategy (corporate strategy) Strategy about how a firm creates value through the configuration and coordination of its multimarket activities.

corruption The abuse of public power for private benefit usually in the form of bribery.

cost leadership A competitive strategy that centers on competing on low cost and prices.

counterattack A set of actions in response to attacks.

country (regional) manager The business leader in charge of a specific country (or region) for an MNE.

country-of-origin effect The positive or negative perception of firms and products from a certain country.

cross-listing Firms list their shares on foreign stock exchanges.

cross-market retaliation Retaliation in other markets when one market is attacked by rivals.

cross-shareholding Both partners invest in each other to become cross-shareholders.

cultural distance The difference between two cultures along some identifiable dimensions.

culture The collective programming of the mind that distinguishes the members of one group or category of people from another.

currency hedging A transaction that protects traders and investors from exposure to the fluctuations of the spot rate.

currency risks Risks stemming from exposure to unfavorable movements of the currencies.

D

defender A strategy that leverages local assets in areas in which MNEs are weak.

defensive strategy A strategy that is defensive in nature. Firms admit responsibility, but often fight it.

differentiation A strategy that focuses on how to deliver products that customers perceive as valuable and different.

diffused ownership An ownership pattern involving numerous small shareholders, none of whom has a dominant level of control.

direct exports Directly selling products made in the home country to customers in other countries.

dissemination risks The risks associated with the unauthorized diffusion of firm-specific assets.

diversification   Adding new businesses to the firm that are distinct from its existing operations.

diversification discount   Reduced levels of performance because of association with a product-diversified firm (also known as conglomerate discount).

diversification premium   Increased levels of performance because of association with a product-diversified firm (also known as conglomerate advantage).

dodger   A strategy that centers on cooperating through joint ventures with MNEs and/or sell-offs to MNEs.

domestic demand   Demand for products and services within a domestic economy.

dominance   A situation whereby the market leader has a very large market share.

dominant logic   A common underlying theme that connects various businesses in a diversified firm.

downscoping   Reducing the scope of the firm through divestitures and spin-offs.

downsizing   Reducing the number of employees through lay-offs, early retirements, and outsourcing.

downstream vertical alliance   A strategic alliance with firms in distribution (downstream).

due diligence   Investigation prior to signing contracts

dumping   An exporter selling below cost abroad and planning to raise prices after eliminating local rivals.

duopoly   A special case of oligopoly that has only two players.

E

economic benefits   Benefits brought by the various forms of synergy in the context of diversification.

economies of scale   Reduction in per unit costs by increasing the scale of production.

emergent strategy   A strategy based on the outcome of a stream of smaller decisions from the "bottom up."

emerging economies (emerging markets)   A label that describes fast-growing developing economies since the 1990s.

entrepreneur   An individual who identifies and explores previously unexplored opportunities.

entrepreneurship   The identification and exploitation of previously unexplored opportunities.

entry barriers   The industry structures that increase the costs of entry.

equity modes   Modes of foreign market entry that involve the use of equity.

equity-based alliance   A strategic alliance that involves the use of equity.

ethical imperialism   The imperialistic thinking that one's own ethical standards should be applied universally around the world.

ethical relativism   The relative thinking that ethical standards vary significantly around the world and that there are no universally agreed upon ethical and unethical behaviors.

ethics   The norms, principles, and standards of conduct governing individual and firm behavior.

excess capacity   Additional production capacity currently underutilized or not utilized.

exit-based mechanisms   Corporate governance mechanisms that focus on exit, indicating that shareholders no longer have patience and are willing to "exit" by selling their shares.

explicit collusion   Firms directly negotiate output, fix pricing, and divide markets.

explicit knowledge   Knowledge that is codifiable (that is, it can be written down and transferred without losing much of its richness).

exploitation   Actions captured by terms such as refinement, choice, production, efficiency, selection, and execution.

exploration   Actions captured by terms such as search, variation, risk taking, experimentation, play, flexibility, discovery, and innovation.

export intermediary   A firm that performs an important middleman function by linking domestic sellers and foreign buyers that otherwise would not have been connected.

expropriation (1) of foreign assets: Activities that enrich the controlling shareholders at the expense of minority shareholders. (2) of minority shareholders: Confiscation of foreign assets invested in one country.

extender A strategy that centers on leveraging home-grown competencies abroad by expanding into similar markets.

extraterritoriality The reach of one country's laws to other countries.

F

factor endowments The endowments of production factors such as land, water, and people in one country.

far-flung conglomerate A conglomerate firm that pursues both extensive product-unrelated diversification and extensive geographic diversification.

feint A firm's attack on a focal arena important to a competitor, but not the attacker's true target area.

femininity A relatively weak form of societal-level sex role differentiation whereby more women occupy positions that reward assertiveness and more men work in caring professions.

financial control (output control) Controlling subsidiary/unit operations strictly based on whether they meet financial/output criteria.

financial synergy The increase in competitiveness for each individual unit that is financially controlled by the corporate headquarters beyond what can be achieved by each unit competing independently as standalone firms.

firm strategy, structure, and rivalry How industry structure and firm strategy interact to affect interfirm rivalry.

first-mover advantages The advantages that first movers enjoy and later movers do not.

five forces framework A framework governing the competitiveness of an industry proposed by Michael Porter. The five forces are (1) the intensity of rivalry among competitors, (2) the threat of potential entry, (3) the bargaining power of suppliers, (4) the bargaining power of buyers, and (5) the threat of substitutes.

flexible manufacturing technology Modern manufacturing technology that enables firms to produce differentiated products at low costs (usually on a smaller batch basis than the large batch typically produced by cost leaders).

focus A strategy that serves the needs of a particular segment or niche of an industry.

Foreign Corrupt Practices Act (FCPA) A US law enacted in 1977 that bans bribery of foreign officials.

foreign direct investment (FDI) A firm's direct investment in production and/or service activities abroad.

foreign portfolio investment (FPI) Foreigners' purchase of stocks and bonds in one country.

formal institutions Institutions represented by laws, regulations, and rules.

formal, rule-based, impersonal exchange A way of economic exchange based on formal transactions in which parties keep a distance (see also arm's-length transactions).

forward integration Acquiring and owning downstream assets.

franchising Firm A's agreement to give Firm B the rights to use A's proprietary technology (such as a patent) or trademark (such as a corporate logo) for a royalty fee paid to A by B. This term is typically used in service industries.

friendly M&A An M&A deal in which the board and management of a target firm agree to the transaction (although they may initially resist).

G

gambit A firm's withdrawal from a low-value market to attract rival firms to divert resources into the low-value market so that the original withdrawing firm can capture a high-value market.

game theory A theory that focuses on competitive and cooperative interaction (such as in a prisoners' dilemma situation).

generic strategies Strategies intended to strengthen the focal firm's position relative to the five competitive forces, including (1) cost leadership, (2) differentiation, and (3) focus.

geographic area structure An organizational structure that organizes the MNE according to different countries and regions and is the most appropriate structure for a multidomestic strategy.

geographic diversification Entries into new geographic markets.

global account structure A customer-focused structure that supplies customers (often other MNEs) in a coordinated and consistent way across various countries.

global matrix An organizational structure often used to alleviate the disadvantages associated with both geographic area and global product division structures, especially for MNEs adopting a transnational strategy.

global product division An organizational structure that assigns global responsibilities to each product division.

global standardization strategy An MNE strategy that relies on the development and distribution of standardized products worldwide to reap the maximum benefits from low-cost advantages.

global strategy (1) Strategy of firms around the globe. (2) A particular form of international strategy, characterized by the production and distribution of standardized products and services on a worldwide basis.

global sustainability The ability to meet the needs of the present without compromising the ability of future generations to meet their needs.

global virtual teams Teams whose members are physically dispersed in multiple locations in the world. They cooperate on a virtual basis.

globalization The close integration of countries and peoples of the world.

greenfield operation Building factories and offices from scratch (on a proverbial piece of "greenfield" formerly used for agricultural purposes).

H

home replication strategy A strategy that emphasizes the international replication of home country–based competencies such as production scales, distribution efficiencies, and brand power.

horizontal alliance A strategic alliance formed by competitors.

horizontal M&A An M&A deal involving competing firms in the same industry.

hostile M&A (hostile takeover) An M&A deal undertaken against the wishes of target firm's board and management, who reject the M&A offer.

hubris Managers' overconfidence in their capabilities.

hypercompetition A way of competition centered on dynamic maneuvering intended to unleash a series of small, unpredictable, but powerful actions to erode the rivals' competitive advantage.

I

in-group Individuals and firms regarded as part of "us."

incumbents Current members of an industry that compete against each other.

indirect exports Exporting indirectly through domestic-based export intermediaries.

individualism The perspective that the identity of an individual is most fundamentally based on his or her own individual attributes (rather than the attributes of a group).

industrial organization (IO) economics A branch of economics that seeks to better understand how firms in an industry compete and then how to regulate them.

industry A group of firms producing products (goods and/or services) that are similar to each other.

industry positioning Ways to position a firm within an industry in order to minimize the threats presented by the five forces.

informal institutions Institutions represented by norms, cultures, and ethics.

informal, relationship-based, personalized exchange A way of economic exchange based on informal relationships among transaction parties. Also known as relational contracting.

information asymmetries Asymmetric distribution of information between two sides.

information overload Too much information to process.

initial public offering (IPO) The first round of public trading of company stock.

inside director A director serving on a corporate board who is also a full-time manager of the company.

institution Humanly devised constraints that structure human interaction—informally known as the "rules of the game."

institution-based view A leading perspective of strategy that argues that in addition to industry- and firm-level conditions, firms also need to take into account wider influences from sources such as the state and society when crafting strategy.

institutional distance The extent of similarity or dissimilarity between the regulatory, normative, and cognitive institutions of two countries.

institutional framework A framework of formal and informal institutions governing individual and firm behavior.

institutional relatedness A firm's informal linkages with dominant institutions in the environment that confer resources and legitimacy.

institutional transitions Fundamental and comprehensive changes introduced to the formal and informal rules of the game that affect organizations as players.

intangible resources and capabilities Hard-to-observe and difficult-to-codify resources and capabilities.

integration-responsiveness framework A framework of MNE management on how to simultaneously deal with two sets of pressures for global integration and local responsiveness.

intended strategy A strategy that is deliberately planned for.

interlocking directorate Two or more firms share one director on their boards.

internal capital market A term used to describe the internal management mechanisms of a product-unrelated diversified firm (conglomerate) that operate as a capital market inside the firm.

internalization The process of replacing a market relationship with a single multinational organization spanning both countries.

internalization advantage The advantage associated with internalization, which is one of the three key advantages of being a multinational enterprise (the other two are ownership and location advantages).

international diversification The number and diversity of countries in which a firm competes.

international division An organizational structure typically set up when firms initially expand abroad, often engaging in a home replication strategy.

international entrepreneurship A combination of innovative, proactive, and risk-seeking behavior that crosses national borders and is intended to create wealth in organizations.

J

joint venture (JV) A "corporate child" that is a new entity given birth and jointly owned by two or more parent companies.

K

knowledge management The structures, processes, and systems that actively develop, leverage, and transfer knowledge.

L

late-mover advantages Advantages associated with being a later mover (also known as first-mover disadvantages).

learning by doing A way of learning not by reading books but by engaging in hands-on activities.

learning race A race in which alliance partners aim to outrun each other by learning the "tricks" from the other side as fast as possible.

leveraged buyout (LBO) A means by which private investors, often in partnership with incumbent managers, issue bonds and use the cash raised to buy the firm's stock.

liability of foreignness   The inherent disadvantage foreign firms experience in host countries because of their nonnative status.

liability of newness   The inherent disadvantage that entrepreneurial firms experience as new entrants.

licensing   Firm A's agreement to give Firm B the rights to use A's proprietary technology (such as a patent) or trademark (such as a corporate logo) for a royalty fee paid to A by B. This term is typically used in manufacturing industries.

LLL advantages   Linkage, leverage, and learning advantages, which are typically associated with MNEs from emerging economies.

local content requirements   Government requirements that certain products be subject to higher import tariffs and taxes unless a given percentage of their value is produced domestically.

local responsiveness   The necessity to be responsive to different customer preferences around the world.

localization (multi-domestic) strategy   An MNE strategy that focuses on a number of foreign countries/regions, each of which is regarded as a standalone local (domestic) market worthy of significant attention and adaptation.

location-specific advantages   Advantages associated with operating in a specific location.

long-term orientation   A perspective that emphasizes perseverance and savings for future betterment.

M

managerial human capital   The skills and abilities acquired by top managers.

marginal bureaucratic costs (MBC)   The bureaucratic costs of the last unit of organizational expansion (such as the last subsidiary established).

marginal economic benefits (MEB)   The economic benefits of the last unit of growth (such as the last acquisition).

market commonality   The degree to which two competitors' markets overlap.

masculinity   A relatively strong form of societal-level sex role differentiation whereby men tend to have occupations that reward assertiveness and women tend to work in caring professions.

mass customization   Mass produced but customized products.

merger   The combination of assets, operations, and management of two firms to establish a new legal entity.

merger and acquisition (M&A)   Merging with or acquiring other firms.

micro-macro link   The link between micro, informal interpersonal relationships among managers of various units and macro, interorganizational cooperation among various units.

microfinance   A practice to provide microloans ($50–$300) to start small businesses with the intention of ultimately lifting the entrepreneurs out of poverty.

mobility barrier   Within-industry differences that inhibit the movement between strategic groups.

monopoly   A situation whereby only one firm provides the goods and/or services for an industry.

moral hazard   Recklessness when people and organizations (including firms and governments) do not have to face the full consequences of their actions.

multimarket competition   Firms engage the same rivals in multiple markets.

multinational enterprise (MNE)   A firm that engages in foreign direct investment (FDI) by directly controlling and managing value-adding activities in other countries.

multinational replicator   A firm that engages in product-related diversification on the one hand and far-flung multinational expansion on the other hand.

mutual forbearance   Multimarket firms respect their rivals' spheres of influence in certain markets and their rivals reciprocate, leading to tacit collusion.

N

network centrality   The extent to which a firm's position is pivotal with respect to others in the interfirm network.

network externalities   The value a user derives from a product increases with the number (or the network) of other users of the same product.

non-equity modes   Modes of foreign market entries that do not involve the use of equity.

non-scale-based advantages   Low-cost advantages that are not derived from the economies of scale.

nongovernmental organization (NGO)   Organization advocating causes such as the environment, human rights, and consumer rights that are not affiliated with government.

nontariff barriers   Trade and investment barriers that do not entail tariffs.

norm   The prevailing practice of relevant players that affect the focal individuals and firms.

normative pillar   How the values, beliefs, and norms of other relevant players influence the behavior of individuals and firms.

O

obsolescing bargain   A deal struck by an MNE and a host government, which change the requirements after the entry of the MNE.

offshoring   International/foreign outsourcing.

OLI advantages   Ownership, location, and internalization advantages, which are typically associated with MNEs.

oligopoly   A situation whereby a few firms control an industry.

onshoring   Outsourcing to a domestic firm.

open innovation   The use of purposive inflows and outflows of knowledge to accelerate internal innovation and expand the markets for external use of innovation.

operational synergy   Synergy derived by having shared activities, personnel, and technologies.

opportunism   Self-interest seeking with guile.

organizational culture   The collective programming of the mind that distinguishes members of one organization from another.

organizational fit   The complementarity of partner firms' "soft" organizational traits, such as goals, experiences, and behaviors, that facilitate cooperation.

original brand manufacturer (OBM)   A firm that designs, manufactures, and markets branded products.

original design manufacturer (ODM)   A firm that both designs and manufactures products.

original equipment manufacturer (OEM)   A firm that executes design blueprints provided by other firms and manufactures such products.

out-group   Individuals and firms not regarded as part of "us."

outside (independent) director   A non-management member of the board.

outsourcing   Turning over all or part of an activity to an outside supplier to improve the performance of the focal firm.

ownership advantage   Advantage associated with directly owning assets overseas, which is one of the three key advantages of being a multinational enterprise (the other two are location and internalization advantages).

P

partner rarity   The difficulty to locate partners with certain desirable attributes.

perfect competition   A competitive situation in which price is set by the "market," all firms are price takers, and entries and exits are relatively easy.

performance   The result of firm conduct.

power distance   The degree of social inequality.

predatory pricing   (1) Setting prices below costs in the short run to destroy rivals and (2) intending to raise prices to cover losses in the long run after eliminating rivals.

price leader   A firm that has a dominant market share and sets "acceptable" prices and margins in the industry.

primary stakeholder groups   Constituents on which the firm relies for its continuous survival and prosperity.

principals Persons (such as owners) who delegate authority.

principal–agent conflicts Conflicts of interests between principals (such as shareholders) and agents (such as professional managers).

principal–principal conflicts Conflicts of interests between two classes of principals: controlling shareholders and minority shareholders.

prisoners' dilemma In game theory, a type of game in which the outcome depends on two parties deciding whether to cooperate or to defect.

private equity Equity capital invested in private (non-public) companies.

proactive strategy A strategy that focuses on proactive engagement in corporate social responsibility.

product differentiation The uniqueness of products that customers value.

product diversification Entries into new product markets and/or business activities that are related to a firm's existing markets and/or activities.

product proliferation Efforts to fill product space in a manner that leaves little "unmet demand" for potential entrants.

product-related diversification Entries into new product markets and/or business activities that are related to a firm's existing markets and/or activities.

product-unrelated diversification Entries into industries that have no obvious product-related connections to the firm's current lines of business.

R

reactive strategy A strategy that is passive about corporate social responsibility. Firms do not act in the absence of disasters and outcries. When problems arise, denial is usually the first line of defense.

real option An option investment in real operations as opposed to financial capital.

refocusing Narrowing the scope of the firm to focus on a few areas.

regulatory pillar How formal rules, laws, and regulations influence the behavior of individuals and firms.

regulatory risks Risks associated with unfavorable government regulations.

related and supporting industries Industries that are related to and/or support the focal industry.

related transaction Controlling owners sell firm assets to another firm they own at below-market prices or spin off the most profitable part of a public firm and merge it with another of their private firms.

relational (collaborative) capabilities The capabilities to successfully manage interfirm relationships.

relational contracting Contracting based on informal relationships (see also informal, relationship-based, personalized exchange).

replication Repeated testing of theory under a variety of conditions to establish its applicable boundaries.

research and development (R&D) contracts Outsourcing agreements in R&D between firms (that is, Firm A agrees to perform certain R&D work for Firm B).

resource The tangible and intangible assets a firm uses to choose and implement its strategies.

resource similarity The extent to which a given competitor possesses strategic endowments comparable to those of the focal firm.

resource-based view A leading perspective of strategy that suggests that differences in firm performance are most fundamentally driven by differences in firm resources and capabilities.

restructuring (1) Adjusting firm size and scope through either diversification (expansion or entry), divestiture (contraction or exit), or both. (2) Reducing firm size and scope.

reverse innovation Low-cost innovation from emerging economies that has potential in developed economies.

risk management The identification and assessment of risks and the preparation to minimize the impact of high-risk, unfortunate events.

S

scale economies (economies of scale) Reductions in per unit costs by increasing the scale of production.

scale of entry The amount of resources committed to foreign market entry.

scale-based advantages Advantages derived from economies of scale (the more a firm produces some products, the lower the unit costs become).

scenario planning A technique to prepare and plan for multiple scenarios (either high or low risk).

scope economies (economies of scope) Reduction in per unit costs and increases in competitiveness by enlarging the scope of the firm.

secondary stakeholder groups Stakeholders who influence or affect, or are influenced or affected by, the corporation, but they are not engaged in transactions with the corporation and are not essential for its survival.

semiglobalization A perspective that suggests that barriers to market integration at borders are high but not high enough to completely insulate countries from each other.

separation of ownership and control The dispersal of ownership among many small shareholders, with control of the firm largely concentrated in the hands of salaried, professional managers who own little or no equity.

serial entrepreneur An entrepreneur who starts, grows, and sells several businesses throughout his/her career.

shareholder capitalism A view of capitalism that suggests that the most fundamental purpose for firms to exist is to serve the economic interests of shareholders (also known as capitalists).

single business strategy A strategy that focuses on a single product or service with little diversification.

small and medium-sized enterprise (SME) A firm with fewer than 500 employees in the United States or with fewer than 250 employees in the European Union.

social capital The informal benefits individuals and organizations derive from their social structures and networks.

social complexity The socially complex ways of organizing typical of many firms.

social issue participation Firms' participation in social causes not directly related to managing primary stakeholders.

solutions-based structure An MNE organizational structure that caters to the needs of providing solutions for customers' problems.

sovereign wealth fund (SWF) A state-owned investment fund composed of financial assets such as stocks, bonds, real estate, or other financial instruments funded by foreign exchange assets.

stage model Model that suggests firms internationalize by going through predictable stages from simple steps to complex operations.

stakeholder Any group or individual who can affect or is affected by the achievement of the organization's objectives.

state-owned enterprise (SOE) A firm owned and controlled by the state (government).

stewardship theory A theory that suggests that managers should be regarded as stewards of owners' interests.

strategic alliance A voluntary agreement of cooperation between firms

strategic ambidexterity Firms' dynamic capabilities to simultaneously manage influences from both governments and markets.

strategic control (behavior control) Controlling subsidiary/unit operations based on whether they engage in desirable strategic behavior (such as cooperation).

strategic fit The complementarity of partner firms' "hard" skills and resources, such as technology, capital, and distribution channels.

strategic groups Groups of firms within a broad industry.

strategic hedging Spreading out activities in a number of countries in different currency zones to offset any currency losses in one region through gains in other regions.

strategic investment One partner invests in another as a strategic investor.

strategic management A way of managing the firm from a strategic, "big picture" perspective.

strategic network A strategic alliance formed by multiple firms to compete against other such groups and against traditional single firms (also known as a constellation).

strategy A firm's theory about how to compete successfully.

strategy as action A perspective that suggests that strategy is most fundamentally reflected by firms' pattern of actions.

strategy as integration A perspective that suggests that strategy is neither solely about plan nor action and that strategy integrates elements of both schools of thought.

strategy as plan A perspective that suggests that strategy is most fundamentally embodied in explicit, rigorous formal planning as in the military.

strategy formulation The crafting of a firm's strategy.

strategy implementation The actions undertaken to carry out a firm's strategy.

strategy tripod A framework that suggests that strategy as a discipline has three "legs" or key perspectives: industry-based, resource-based, and institution-based views.

strong ties More durable, reliable, and trustworthy relationships cultivated over a long period of time.

structure Structural attributes of an industry such as the costs of entry/exit.

structure-conduct-performance (SCP) model An industrial organization economics model that suggests that industry structure determines firm conduct (strategy), which in turn determines firm performance.

subsidiary initiative The proactive and deliberate pursuit of new business opportunities by an MNE's subsidiary to expand its scope of responsibility.

substitutes Products of different industries that satisfy customer needs currently met by the focal industry.

sunk costs Irrevocable costs incurred and investments made.

SWOT analysis A strategic analysis of a firm's internal strengths (S) and weaknesses (W) and the opportunities (O) and threats (T) in the environment.

T

tacit collusion Firms indirectly coordinate actions to reduce competition by signaling to others their intention to reduce output and maintain pricing above competitive levels.

tacit knowledge Knowledge that is not codifiable (that is, hard to be written down and transmitted without losing much of its richness).

tangible resources and capabilities Observable and more easily quantified resources and capabilities.

tariff barriers Taxes levied on imports.

thrust The classic frontal attack with brute force.

top management team (TMT) The team consisting of the highest level of executives of a firm led by the CEO.

trade barriers Barriers blocking international trade.

transaction costs Costs associated with economic transaction—or more broadly, costs of doing business.

transnational strategy An MNE strategy that endeavors to be cost efficient, locally responsive, and learning driven simultaneously.

Triad Three primary regions of developed economies: North America, Europe, and Japan.

triple bottom line A performance yardstick consisting of economic, social, and environmental performance.

tunneling Activities of managers from the controlling family of a corporation to divert resources from the firm for personal or family use.

turnkey projects Projects in which clients pay contractors to design and construct new facilities and train personnel.

U

uncertainty avoidance   The extent to which members in different cultures accept ambiguous situations and tolerate uncertainty.

upstream vertical alliance   A strategic alliance with firms on the supply side (upstream).

V

value chain   Goods and services produced through a chain of vertical activities that add value.

venture capitalist (VC)   An investor who invests capital in early-stage, high-potential start-ups.

vertical M&A   An M&A deal involving suppliers (upstream) and/or buyers (downstream).

voice-based mechanisms   Corporate governance mechanisms that focus on shareholders' willingness to work with managers, usually through the board of directors, by "voicing" their concerns.

VRIO framework   A resource-based framework that focuses on the value (V), rarity (R), imitability (I), and organizational (O) aspects of resources and capabilities.

W

Washington Consensus   A view centered on the unquestioned belief in the superiority of private ownership over state ownership in economic policy making, which is often spearheaded by two Washington-based international organizations: the International Monetary Fund and the World Bank.

weak ties   Relationships that are characterized by infrequent interaction and low intimacy.

wholly owned subsidiary (WOS)   Subsidiary located in a foreign country that is entirely owned by the MNE.

worldwide (global) mandate   The charter to be responsible for one MNE function throughout the world.

INDEX OF ORGANIZATIONS

3Com, 327
3G Capital, 278
3i, 235, 401
3i Group PLC, 391–403
3M, 306

A

AAR, 205, 206, 215–217
ABB, 303
ABC, 39, 49, 234
ABN Amro, 179
Abuzz Technologies, 434
Accel Partners, 437
Accenture, 202
Access, 215
Acer, 63, 85
ADM, 239
Aegis, 409
Aer Lingus, 418
Agricultural Bank of China, 348
Água Limpa, 467
Ahava, 246
AIG, 347
Air Berlin, 421
Air Canada, 190, 192
Air France-KLM, 190, 192, 421
Air India, 164
Airbus, 5, 38, 41, 43, 50, 72, 130, 164, 302, 307
Alaska Permanent Fund, 235, 349
Alberta Heritage Fund, 349
Alcatel, 282
Alcatel-Lucent, 165, 282
Alfa Group, 197, 215
All Nippon Airways (ANA), 73
Aluminum Company of America (ALCOA), 237
Amalgamated Bank, 332
Amanah, 170
Amazon, 3, 6, 38, 49, 50, 54, 127, 194, 204, 284, 436–438, 441
AmBev, 278
American Airlines (AA), 190, 192, 198–199, 232, 236
American Honda Motors Inc., 269
Ameristeel, 278
Amtrak, 156
Android alliance, 194
Anglo American, 308
Anheuser Busch (Budweiser), 38, 239, 278
Apax Partners, 3

APAX Partners, 354
Apollo Global Management, 332
Apple, 6, 41, 49, 63, 76, 139, 160, 168, 211, 223, 232, 236, 241, 250, 253–254, 327, 336, 342, 441
ArcelorMittal, 468
Asian Paints, 246
AT&T, 49, 165, 199, 228, 237, 247–248, 456–459
AT&T/T-Mobile, 456–459
Australian Securities Exchange, 332
Avon Products, 301
Azul, 143

B

BAE Systems, 177, 199
Baidu, 28, 143, 195
Bain, 355
Banco de Investimentos Garantia, 278
Banco Santander Brasil, 348
Bank of America, 281
Bank of China, 348, 470
Baosteel Europe, 465–470
Baosteel Europe GmbH, 467
Baosteel Group, 465, 466, 467
Baotou Steel Factory, 392
Barclays, 309
Baring Vostok Private Equity Fund, 127
Barnes and Noble, 38, 50
Bath & Body Works, 80
Bayer Group, 321
Bayer MaterialScience, 321, 322
Bayi Steel Group, 465
BBC, 131
Bear Stearns, 462
Bearing Point, 202
BenQ, 80
Bentley, 48
Best Price, 33
Bharti, 33, 199
Bic, 242
Bing, 28
Bird, 247
Blackwater, 132. See also Xe Services LLC
BMI, 421
BMW, 40, 42, 47, 112–113, 116, 166, 194, 282
Boashan Iron and Steel Complex, 465
Boeing, 5, 39, 41, 43, 69, 72, 73, 130, 164, 238, 269, 307

Bombardier, 266, 297
Borders, 50
Boston Consulting Group, 127
BP, 161, 196, 197, 205, 206, 215–217, 310, 316, 366, 376, 379
Bridgestone, 318
British Aerospace, 177
British Airways (BA), 46, 50, 164, 190, 192, 198–199, 236, 418, 421–422
British Petroleum (BP), 177
British Telecom (BT), 177
BSkyB, 332
Burberry, 58
Burger King, 277, 278, 375, 398, 400
BYD, 85

C

Cadbury, 277
Calvin Klein, 131
Cambridge, 4
Canon, 160, 178, 269
Capgemini, 202
Cardinal Distribution, 44
Cardinal Foods, 44
Cardinal Health, 44
Carlesberg, 231
Carlyle Group, 335, 355
Carnival cruise line, 39
Carrefour, 33, 80, 158, 197
Cascade Field, 278
Caterpillar, 160
Cathay Pacific, 190, 192
CBS, 234
CDH, 396
Cemex, 5, 85
Cengage Learning, 3, 4, 441
CFM International, 198
Checkpoint, 134
Chevrolet, 362
Chevron, 131, 315, 316
China Dow Chemical, 382
China Construction Bank, 348
China Investment Corporation (CIC), 349
China National Offshore Oil Corporation (CNOOC), 179
China Petroleum and Chemical Corporation. *See* Sinopec
China State Construction Engineering Corporation, 348
Christian Lacroix, 58
Chrysler, 72, 170, 228, 280, 282, 354
Cisco, 6, 49, 169, 197, 202, 232, 245, 303, 315
Citi Technology Services, 410
Citibank, 410
Citibank Islamic Bank, 170
Citigroup, 110, 168, 169, 197, 315, 349, 462
Citroën, 300
CKx, 332

CMD, 434
CNN, 49, 234
CNOOC, 281
Coach, 58, 236
Coach USA, 155
Coca-Cola Company, 5, 9, 40, 42, 156, 162, 178, 194, 210, 213, 239, 245, 268, 276, 297, 310, 369
Colgate, 168
Commercial Ready, 433
Compaq, 254
Condé Nast Traveler, 67
Conrad, 415
Continental Airlines, 278
Continental Lite, 236
COSCO, 470
COSTCO, 42
Credit Suisse, 462
Croma, 33
Cultor OY, 267

D

Daewoo, 259
Dai-ichi Life Insurance, 348
Daimler-Benz, 280
DaimlerChrysler, 210, 276, 284, 354, 378
Danisco, 266, 267
Danish Sugar, 267
Danone, 206, 267
DataQuest, 445–446
De Beers, 36, 167, 229, 238
Dell, 6, 41, 49, 63, 71, 75, 80, 235, 317
Delta, 190, 192, 236
DeRemate, 436
Deutsche Bank, 462
Deutsche Telekom, 199, 248, 456–459
DHL, 69, 160
Diamond Syndicate, 229
Diamond Trading Company (DTC), 229
Dicos, 189
Didata, 167
Digital Sky Technologies, 438
DineroMail.com, 436
Discovery, 47
Disney, 47, 269, 299, 460–461
Disneyland, 460–461
Dow Chemical, 95, 303, 370, 372, 381
Dow Jones, 332
DP World, 281
Dropbox, 437
Dubai International Airport (DXB), 164
Dubai Ports World (DP World), 179
Dubai World Central-Al Maktoum International (DWC), 164
Duke Energy, 376, 381

E

EADS, 209
East Dawning, 189
easyCinema, 283
easyGroup, 283
easyInternetcafe, 283
easyJet, 283, 421, 422
eBay, 284, 327, 438, 456
eBay Europe, 436
EDS, 202
El Dorado, 454
Electricité de France, 348
Electrolux, 108, 310
Electronic Data Systems (EDS), 327
Elf, 316
Eli Lily, 206, 212
Embraer, 5, 85, 209
EMC, 202
EMI, 169
Emirates Airlines, 163
eModeration, 131, 132
EmPower Research, 410
Energy Future Holdings, 354
ENI, 316
Enron, 95, 334, 335, 343, 369
Enterprise Growth Solutions, 433
Epson, 168, 169
Ericsson, 6, 165, 168, 169
Ermenegildo Zegna, 47, 58
Escada, 58
ESPN, 131
Expedia, 194
ExxonMobil, 161, 315, 316

F

Facebook, 11, 99, 112, 119–120, 127, 131, 134, 144, 195, 438
FedEx, 127, 135, 160, 168
Ferrari, 36
Fiat, 309
Finnet, 404–408
Firefox/Mozilla, 195
Firestone Tires, 112–113
Fisher Investments, 422
Flextronics, 80, 178
Ford, 42, 69, 112, 197, 199, 228, 248, 318, 377
Fox, 49
Fox News Channel, 234
Foxconn, 5–7, 13, 69, 80, 85, 253
Friends Life, 410
Frito-Lay, 42
Fuji, 160, 269
Fujitsu, 165, 202

G

Galaxy Casino, 412, 413, 414, 415
Game, 167
Gazprom, 41
GE, 7–8
Geely, 7, 85, 282
General Electric (GE), 7–9, 38, 85–86, 157, 169, 198, 203, 231, 238–239, 244, 262, 266, 269, 272, 285, 313, 315, 367, 410
General Motors (GM), 7, 38, 49, 53, 69, 72, 144, 165, 168, 170, 213, 228, 230, 245, 248, 330, 347, 348, 377
Genpact, 409, 410
Geocell, 408
Gerdau, 278
Germanwings, 421
Gillette, 231, 242
Glencore International, 348
Global Crossing, 334
Goldman Sachs, 295, 394, 398, 462
Goldwind, 85
Google, 28, 49, 119, 143, 144, 168, 179
194, 195, 211, 223, 248, 254, 315, 336
367, 437, 456
GP Investmentos, 278
Grameen Bank, 149–150
Greyhound, 155, 168, 169
Groupon, 437, 438
GSK, 194, 310, 312–313
Gucci Group, 58, 80, 177

H

Häagen-Dazs, 177, 312
Haier, 244
Hamersley Iron, 467
Hatteras Hammocks, 448–455
HCl Technologies, 409
Headstrong, 410
Heinekin, 231
Heinz, 304
Hewlett-Packard (HP), 41, 49, 80, 198, 202, 269, 310, 315, 327, 337
Hitachi, 295, 376
Holiday Inn, 415
Home Depot, 370, 372, 409
Honda, 5, 38, 51, 85, 168–170, 230, 269, 318
Honda Aircraft Company, 269
HondaJet, 269, 283
Honeywell, 238, 239, 285
Hong Kong Disneyland, 460–461
Hongkong and Shanghai Banking Corporation. *See* HSBC
Hongzhuangyuan, 189
HonHai, 253
Hope Group, 266
HP. *See* Hewlett Packard (HP)
HSBC, 5, 131, 170, 179, 308, 309

HTC, 80, 85, 194, 223, 241, 253–254
Huawei, 5, 49, 80, 165, 232, 235, 245, 307
Huiyuan, 239
Hyundai, 52, 170, 259
Hyundai/Kia, 230

I

Iberdrola Renovables, 348
Iberia, 421
IBM, 49, 63–64, 69, 72–73, 76, 82, 86, 135, 178, 202, 237, 247, 269, 303, 308, 315, 327, 367, 377
ICUC Moderation, 131, 132
IKEA, 80, 139, 144
InBev, 239, 278
Index Ventures, 127, 437
Industrial & Commercial Bank of China, 348
Infosys, 69, 79, 350, 409, 410
Infosys BPO, 409
ING Group, 179
Intel, 6, 131, 134, 178, 202, 238, 295, 317, 367
Intelligentsia, 47
International Airlines Group, 421
International Monetary Fund (IMF), 347
Italtel, 202

J

Japan Airlines (JAL), 190, 192
JBS-Friboi, 278
JetBlue, 143
Jobek do Brasil, 448–455
Johnson & Johnson, 42, 315, 367
Jolibee, 189
Joyo, 127
JP Morgan, 462
JP Morgan Chase, 168, 169

K

K-Mart, 236
Kcell, 407, 408
Kentucky Fried Chicken (KFC), 189, 239, 263, 394, 400
Kimberly-Clark (Kleenex), 38
KLM, 236
Koc Group, 262, 266
Kodak, 80, 160, 269
Komatsu, 160
Korea Exchange Bank, 354
Korean Air, 190, 192
Kraft, 38
Kraft Foods, 48, 267, 277, 375
Kroger, 42
KupiVip, 438

L

Lamborghini, 36
Lego, 131

Lehman Brothers, 276, 278, 462–463
Lenovo, 41, 63, 72, 85, 269, 308
Lexmark, 63
LG, 259, 443
Limited Brands, 80
LINUX, 28, 130
Little Sheep Catering
    Chain Co., 391–403
Little Sheep Hot Pot, 239, 393
Lockheed Martin, 307
Logitech, 144
Lojas Americanas, 278
London Heathrow Airport, 164
Lone Star Funds, 354
L'Oreal, 166
Lowe's, 370, 372
Lucent, 282
Lufthansa, 164, 190, 192, 421
LVMH, 58, 59, 80, 178

M

Macy's, 58
Magnum, 267
Mahindra, 85
Mail.ru, 127
mail.ru Group, 438
Manpower, 69
Marks & Spencer, 42, 377
Massmart, 167
MassMedia Studios, 434
Matsushita, 169, 306
Mattel, 223
Maxwell House, 48
Mazda, 52
McDonald's, 21, 47, 141, 172, 175, 189–190, 195, 197, 233, 278, 296
McDonnell Douglas, 238
McGraw-Hill Irwin, 3, 4, 441
McKinsey, 295
Megabus, 130, 155–156, 168, 169
Melco PBL Jogos, 412, 413, 416
Meng Niu (Mongolian Cow), 394, 396
Mercedes-Benz, 166, 194, 282
MeroMobile, 407
Merrill Lynch, 281, 462
Metro, 33, 158
Mettalurgical Corporation of China, 168, 169
MGM Grand Paradise, 412, 413, 416
Microsoft, 14, 16, 27–28, 28, 40, 41, 49, 63, 130, 169, 195, 202, 232, 236–239, 244, 247, 254, 280, 315, 317, 456
Miller Beer, 167
Minor Group, 142
Mirabilis, 134
Mitsui, 266
Moldcell, 408
Molson, 131

Monarch Airlines, 421
Morgan Stanley, 349, 394, 396, 462
Morris Air, 143
Motorola, 6, 202, 203, 247
Mozilla, 239
Mphasis, 409
MTN, 167
MTV, 5, 131, 297

N

NASDAQ, 332
NASTAR, 433
National Foods, 96
National Public Radio, 131
Naver, 178
NAVMAN, 433
NBC, 49, 234, 332
Ncell, 407, 408
NEC, 160, 169
Nestlé, 131, 158, 194, 267, 367, 377
Netscape, 169, 239
New Core, 259
New York Post, 234
News Corporation, 234, 332, 333, 342
Nike, 33, 69, 112, 317, 365, 370, 376
Nintendo, 6
Nippon Steel, 467
Nissan, 52, 169, 230, 266, 310, 361–362, 363, 368, 372
Nokia, 6, 33, 63, 80, 160, 178, 195, 202, 223, 247, 266, 308, 310
Nokia Siemens Networks, 202
Nomura, 276, 278, 281, 308, 462–463
Nordzucker, 267
Noriba, 170
Northrop, 269
Norwegian Cruise Line, 39
Nspire, 443, 445–446
Nutrasweet, 43
NYSE Euronext, 309

O

Ocean Park, 460–461
Old Mutual, 167, 308
OLX, 436
OMERS Capital Partners, 3
Oneworld, 175, 190, 192, 198–199
Opera Software, 239
Oprah, 131
Oracle, 223, 245, 306, 327
Oxford University Press, 4
Oyak (Turkish Armed Forces Pension Fund), 195
Ozon, 127–128
Ozon.ru, 438

P

Palm, 327
Panasonic, 295
Paris Disneyland, 177
Parmalat, 369
Pawleys Island Hammocks, 452
Pearl River, 172, 174, 176, 177, 178, 182, 236
Pearl River Piano Group (PRPG), 182–183
Pearson Education, 441
Pearson Prentice Hall, 4
PepsiCo, 5, 42, 245, 266, 268, 310, 315
Petrobras, 163, 278
Peugeot, 170
Pfizer, 44, 194, 315
Philip Morris, 241
Philips, 178, 318
Pilgrim's Pride, 278
Pizza Hut, 142, 172, 175, 189, 239, 263
Posco, 467
Power Converter Technologies, 434
Prax Capital, 398
Precious Wood, 454
Priceline, 194
PricewaterhouseCoopers (PwC), 63, 72, 315
Proctor & Gamble (P & G), 15, 42, 45, 210, 213, 231, 315

Q

Qantas, 190, 192
QXL Ricardo, 436

R

Rakuten, 127
Rambler, 438
Ranbaxy, 206
Raytheon, 165, 269
RCA, 79
RealNetworks, 239
Reebok, 38
Reksoft, 127
Reliance Group, 33
Renault, 195, 213, 266, 362
Renova, 215
Research in Motion (RIM), 195, 223
Richemont, 58
Ritmuller, 173, 176, 177, 178, 183
R.J. Reynolds, 241
RJR Nabisco, 353
Rolls Royce, 36
Rosneft, 205, 216–217, 348
Royal Ahold, 369
Royal Bank of Scotland (RBS), 330
Royal Caribbean, 39
Royal Telegraph Service, 404
Ryanair, 45, 46, 54, 76, 232, 418–422

S

SAB, 308
SABMiller, 167, 308
SABRE, 63
Sabre Travel Network, 200
Safer Way Natural Foods. *See* Whole Foods
Safeway, 42
Samsung, 160, 194, 223, 253–254, 259, 261–262, 266, 268–269, 306, 314
Samsung C&T Corporation, 295
Samsung Electronics Corporation (SEC), 295
Samsung Group, 295
Samsung Heavy Industries, 295
Samsung Life Insurance, 295
Sands Cotai Central, 415
SAP, 135, 202, 245, 306, 327, 337
SAS, 190, 192, 236
SASOL, 167
Satyam, 315
Scotiabank, 131
Seagate Technology, 308–309
Sealy, 38
Seattle Coffee, 142
Sembcorp, 284
Shanghai Disneyland, 177
Shanghai Meishan Group Co., Ltd., 465
Shanghai Metallurgical Holding Group Corporation, 465
Shanghai Volkswagon, 172
Sharp, 295
Shell, 316, 370, 379
Shine Group, 332
Shoprite, 167
Siemens, 85, 165, 262, 266, 377
Sinar Mas, 375
Singapore Airlines, 50, 54, 232
Sinopec, 189, 190, 195
Skoda, 246
Skype, 280, 314, 436, 437
SkyTeam, 190, 192
SkyTV, 49
Slope Tracker, 433
Snecma, 203
SnowSports Industries America (SIA), 433
SnowSports Interactive (SSI), 431, 431–435
Sociedade de Jogos de Macau (SJM), 412, 413, 414, 416
SolarWorld AG, 424–430
SolarWorld USA, 424–430
Sonera, 404
Sony, 6, 49, 63, 168–169, 178, 283, 295, 306, 310
Sony Ericsson, 131, 317
South African Breweries (SAB), 167
South-Western Cengage Learning, 3, 18, 40
Southwest Airlines, 46, 54, 76, 232, 235, 236, 418, 420, 422
Southwestern Bell Corporation (SBC), 457
h, 409

Sprint, 456
Stagecoach Group, 155–156, 161
Standard & Poor, 95, 334, 350, 354
Standard Bank, 167
Standard Chartered, 309
Standard Oil, 237
Star Alliance, 175, 190, 192
Starbucks, 33, 47, 48, 80, 131, 142, 233, 283, 300, 312, 376, 377
Steinway, 182, 236
STMicroelectronics, 165
Strix Systems Inc, 434
Stumptown, 47
Subway, 142
Suntory, 194
Suunto, 433
Suzlon, 85
Swiss Re, 376

T

T-Mobile, 199, 238, 456–459
Taj Mahal Palace Hotel, 66, 66–67, 108
Target, 236, 410
Tata, 5
Tata Consultancy Service (TCS), 409
Tata Group, 33, 266
Tata Motors, 7, 9, 85, 262, 285
Tata Nano, 75
Tata Setel (Corus Group), 285
Tcell, 408
TCL, 247
TCS, 409, 410
TCS BPO, 410
Televerket, 404
Telia, 404
TeliaSonera, 404–408
Tesco, 33, 42, 409
Tetra Pak, 308
Texaco, 316
Texas Instruments (TI), 160, 165, 440–447
Texas Pacific Group (TPG Capital), 354
Thales, 209
The Bistro, 197
The Economist, 131
The New York Times, 132
The Pizza Company, 142
Thomson Corporation, 354
Thomson Learning, 354
ThyssenKrupp, 468
Tiffany, 58
Tiger Global Management, 436, 437, 438
Time Warner, 234, 342
Ting Hsin International Group, 189
Titan Airways, 421
TNK-BP, 196, 197, 205, 206, 215–217
Tokyo Disneyland, 177

Toshiba, 160, 295
Toyota, 5, 42, 45, 49, 51, 53–54, 163, 168–169, 213, 230, 245, 248, 314, 361–362, 377
Travelocity, 194
Trump Holdings, 95
Twitter, 119
TXU, 354
Tyco, 334

U

UBS, 170, 462
Unilever, 66, 168, 267, 299, 367, 370, 375
United Airlines, 50, 190, 192, 236, 278
United Colors of Benetton, 80
UPS, 127

V

Vale, 278
Venetian Macau, 412, 413
Veritas, 437
Verizon, 165, 253, 456
Viacom, 342
Victoria's Secret, 47, 80
ViiV Healthcare, 194
Virgin Group, 131, 262, 270
Visa, 348
Vivendi Universal, 266
Vkontakte, 134, 438
VMware, 49
Volkswagon, 5, 246, 266
Voltran, 278
Volvo, 282

W

Wahaha, 131, 206
Walgreens, 44
Wall Street Journal, 332
Walmart, 13, 14, 19, 33, 39, 41, 45, 50, 80, 158, 163, 199, 235–236, 250, 264, 297, 367, 386, 448

WEG, 278
WestJet, 143
Wharf, 284
Whirlpool, 244
Whole Foods, 372, 376, 385–386
Wikimart, 436–438
Wikipedia, 131
Wipro, 79, 202, 410
Wipro BPO, 409
Wireless Tech Group, 434
WNS Global Services, 409, 410
Woolworths, 33
WorldCom, 369
Wynn Macau, 412–417
Wynn Resorts, 412, 413, 414, 416

X

Xe Services LLC, 132
Xerox, 168

Y

Yahoo!, 195, 456
Yamaha, 182, 183
Yamakawa Corp., 91
Yandex, 127, 438
YKK, 139
Yokogawa Hewlett-Packard (HP), 312
Yonghe King, 189
Yonja.com, 436
Yoshinoya, 189
Yoshinoya Holdings, 189
YouTube, 49
Yum! Brands, 189, 190, 195, 239, 263

Z

Zara, 80
Zest Group, 278
ZTE, 235

INDEX OF NAMES

A

Abdelnour, S., 120
Acs, Z., 150
Adams, G., 89
Adams, M., 358
Adams, R., 356
Adegbesan, J., 218
Adner, R., 88, 152
Afuah, A., 60, 220
Agarwal, R., 151, 218, 255, 290
Aggarwal, V., 152, 218
Aguilera, R., 184, 357, 386
Ahlstrom, D., 152–153, 332–333, 356, 387
Ahmadjian, C., 60
Ahuja, G., 218
Aime, F., 88, 89
Ainuddin, R. Z., 218
Akerson, Dan, 255
Akremi, A., 185
Aktas, N., 292
Aldrich, H., 151
Alessandri, T., 121, 291, 356
Alexiev, A., 357
Ali, Mahummad Azhar, 96
Ali, Shubber, 431
Allata, J., 291
Allen, D., 387
Allen, J., 30
Allende, Salvador, 379
Allred, B., 90
Allred, Gloria, 327
Almeida, P., 324
Altenborg, E., 291
Ambec, S., 387
Ambos, B., 123, 323
Ambos, T., 323–324
Amit, R., 59
Anand, J., 218, 219, 255
Anand, S., 387
Anderson, B., 185
Anderson, E., 30
Andersson, U., 324
Andrade, G., 291
Andreessen, Marc, 327
Ang, S., 218
Anokhin, S., 151
Ansoff, I., 29
Apotheker, Léo, 310, 327–328, 337

Apud, S., 123
Ariely, D., 121
Arikan, A., 151, 184
Arino, A., 218, 219
Armington, C., 150
Arnold, M., 184
Arora, A., 151
Arregle, J., 87, 322
Arthurs, J., 152
Arvidson, N., 323
Arya, B., 388
Asaba, S., 89
Asakawa, K., 323
Asmussen, C., 322
Ataay, A., 218
Au, K., 150, 152, 356
Aulakh, P., 86, 185, 289
Autio, E., 151, 152
Avolio, B., 120

B

Babakus, E., 324
Babe, Greg, 321, 322
Bachrack, M., 239
Baden-Fuller, C., 323
Baker, J., 255
Baker, Kris, 440–447
Baker, T., 150
Balasubramanian, N., 89
Balogun, J., 324
Bals, L., 88
Banalieva, E., 185
Baran, Kerim, 436
Barden, J., 121, 219
Barkema, H., 184, 185, 292
Barker, R., 29
Barnes, B., 151
Barnett, M., 386, 388
Barney, J., 31, 59, 71, 87–89, 153
    255, 387
Barr, P., 120
Barry, D., 151
Barthelemy, J., 60, 185
Bartlett, C., 29, 311, 323
Bartol, K., 356
Bartunek, J., 388
Basu, K., 387
Baum, J., 219, 220

Baum, J. R., 255
Beamish, P., 87, 122, 217, 218, 219, 220, 264, 290–291, 322, 324
Bebchuk, L., 356
Becerra, M., 255
Beethoven, 183
Behring, Alex, 278
Belderbos, R., 184
Bell, J., 152
Bell, R. G., 153, 358
Bell, S., 184
Ben, R., 29
Benito, G., 185, 309
Benjamin, Cathy., 471–476
Benner, M., 255, 290
Benz, M., 355
Bercovitz, J., 290
Berger, Roland, 398
Bergh, D., 292
Bergh, R., 121
Berlusconi, Silvio, 343
Berman, S., 89, 323
Bernstein, A., 24
Bernstein, P., 358
Berry, H., 123, 184, 292
Bettis, R., 292
Beugelsdijk, S., 88, 184
Bezos, Jeffrey, 127
Bhagat, R., 31, 87, 122
Bhardwaj, A., 122
Bhattal, Jesse, 462
Bhaumik, S., 30, 184
Bianchi, M., 323
Bierly, P., 323
Bies, R., 388
Bigley, G., 121
Bilous, Keith, 131
Bing, Lu Wen, 394, 396
Bingham, C., 152
Birkinshaw, J., 309, 322, 323, 324
Bjorkman, A., 324
Blavatnik, Len, 215
Blevins, D., 31, 104
Block, E., 387
Bloom, M., 386
Bloom, N., 30
Boal, K., 185
Boddewyn, J., 31, 90
Bodolica, V., 357
Bodt, E., 292
Boehe, Dirk Michael, 448–455
Boeker, W., 218
Boerner, C., 291
Boiset, M., 153
Boivie, S., 290, 356, 357
Boone, C., 61

Bosch, F., 324
Bosse, D., 386
Bou, J., 61
Bouquet, C., 322, 324
Bourda, Fabia, 424–430
Bourdeau, B., 218
Bowen, H., 31, 151, 185, 290
Bower, J., 30
Bowman, E., 290
Boyd, B., 356, 357
Boyd, J., 255
Boyd, N., 89
Bradley, S., 151
Brammer, S., 387, 388
Brandenburger, A., 220
Brandes, P., 291, 356
Brannen, M., 91, 122, 291
Branzai, O., 120
Braunerhjelm, P., 309
Brenner, S., 255
Bresser, R., 255
Brettel, M., 89
Brickson, S., 386
Bridoux, F., 88
Brin, Sergei, 437
Brinser, Gordon, 424
Bris, A., 357
Brousseau, K., 152
Brouthers, K., 31
Brouthers, L., 31, 185, 220
Brown, S., 60
Brown, Vivian, 471–476
Brush, T., 218
Bruton, G., 30, 150, 152–153, 332–333, 346, 355–356, 387
Bryce, D., 250
Buchan, N., 122
Buchanon, James, 471–476
Buchholtz, A., 255
Buck, T., 356, 357
Budhwar, P., 122
Bunyaratavej, K., 88
Burgelman, R., 324
Burgess, S., 167
Burman, Harold, 440–447
Burrus, D., 90
Burt, R., 152, 220
Bygrave, W., 152
Byles, C., 46
Byles, Charles M., 418–422

C

Cabolis, C., 357
Cadsby, C., 356
Cainkota, M., 120
Calabrese, T., 220

Cameron, K., 30
Camillus, J., 30
Camp, S. M., 150
Campa, J., 291
Campbell, B., 151
Campbell-Hunt, C., 60
Campbell, J., 87, 386, 387
Canales, I., 324
Cannella, A., 255, 256
Cannella, B., 121
Cantwell, J., 184
Capaldo, A., 88
Capar, N., 290
Capelleras, J., 151
Cappelli, P., 386
Capron, L., 121, 255, 290, 358
Cardinal, L., 185, 290
Cardon, M., 151
Caringal, C., 89
Carlucci, Frank, 335
Carmeli, A., 29, 87
Carney, M., 30, 121, 290
Carpenter, M., 356
Carr, C., 30
Carter, N., 91
Cascio, W., 292
Cassar, G., 152
Castaner, X., 218
Castellucci, F., 218
Castleton, M., 356
Cavusgil, S. T., 220, 324
Certo, S. T., 255, 355
Chacar, A., 121, 219
Chachine, S., 152
Chahine, S., 355
Chakrabarti, R., 291
Challagalla, G., 184
Chan, C., 31, 184, 219
Chan, J., 464
Chan, R., 387
Chandler, Alfred, 11, 30, 322
Chandra, Y., 150
Chang, K., 291
Chang, S., 31, 87, 219, 296
Chari, M., 89, 90, 290, 291, 357
Chatain, O., 88, 121, 255
Chatterji, A., 151
Chattopadhyay, P., 121
Chavez, H., 150
Chen, C., 122, 123
Chen, D., 218
Chen, E., 89
Chen, G., 152
Chen, H., 30
Chen, M., 30, 243–244, 255, 256, 289

Chen, P., 290
Chen, S., 59, 152, 219, 233, 291
Chen, Tim, 28
Chen, V., 356
Chen, Y., 386
Cheng, K., 184
Chernin, Peter, 332
Chesbrough, H., 323
Chester, Jeff, 119
Cheung, Anna, 391, 396, 400
Cheung, M., 185, 219
Chi, T., 89, 220, 322
Child, J., 121, 218
Chintakananda, A., 121, 185, 218
Chittour, R., 86, 289
Chizema, A., 356, 358
Cho, M., 184
Cho, T., 356
Choe, S., 260
Choi, B., 184
Choi, C., 220
Choi, E., 464
Choi, J., 123, 387
Choi, T., 60
Chou, Peter, 254
Chow, R., 30
Christensen, C., 30, 151
Christmann, P., 292, 388
Chu, W., 464
Chua, R., 218
Chun, H., 120
Chun, R., 87
Chung, W., 184
Ciabuschi, F., 324
Ciravegna, L., 153
Claessens, S., 356
Clarke, J., 151
Clarkson, G., 255
Clarkson, M., 387
Clement, M., 357
Clougherty, J., 122, 239, 256, 291
Cockburn, A., 230
Coeurderoy, R., 88, 121
Cohen, W., 324
Collin, S., 358
Collis, D., 30, 76, 89
Colombo, M., 151
Combs, J., 356
Connelly, B., 88, 255, 290, 355
Connors, John, 28
Contardo, I., 255
Contractor, F., 88, 264
Cool, K., 59, 60
Cooper, B., 122
Cooper, J., 121

Copernicus, 14
Corbett, A., 152
Cording, M., 292
Corredoira, R., 121
Corsten, D., 218
Coucke, K., 88
Coughlan, J., 324
Coviello, N., 150
Covin, J., 150, 291
Cowen, A., 356
Coyne, K., 255
Crane, Grace, 471–476
Crilly, D., 386
Criscuolo, P., 323
Cronin, J., 218
Crook, T., 121
Crosen, R., 218
Crossan, M., 356
Crossland, C., 30
Cruz, Luciano Barin, 448–455
Cuervo-Cazurra, A., 87, 121, 122, 184, 324, 357
Cuervo, J., 185
Cuervo, Javier C., 412–417
Cui, L., 289
Cullen, J., 122
Cumming, D., 150, 355
Cuypers, I., 218
Cyders, Andrew, 440–447
Czinkota, M., 256

D
Dacin, M. T., 121, 153, 219
Dagnino, G., 90, 256
Daily, C., 291, 356
Dalsace, F., 60
Dalton, D., 291, 356
Dalziel, T., 152
Damanpour, F., 123, 323
Danneels, E., 87
Darling, David, 424–430
Darnall, N., 388
Das, T., 217
Datta, D., 152, 292
Dau, L., 87, 121
D'Aunno, T., 121
D'Aveni, R., 89, 90, 256
David, P., 89, 90, 290, 357, 386
Davies, G., 87
Davies, H., 121
Davis, G., 122, 357, 387
Davis, K., 386
Dawar, N., 246, 256
de Bakker, F., 387
De Castro, J., 121
De Clercq, D., 151

de Fontenay, C., 60
de Quieroz, V., 323
de Rond, M., 30
de Soto, H., 120
Dean, A., 324
Decker, C., 61
Deeds, D., 31, 60, 152
Deeg, R., 30
Delios, A., 185, 290, 322, 324, 387
Dell, Michael, 43, 63
Dellestrand, H., 324
Delmas, M., 388
Delmestri, G., 184
Demil, B., 61
Demirbag, M., 88, 184
den Hond, F., 387
Deng, P., 289
Desarbo, W., 60, 256
Deshpandé, R., 67
Dess, G., 151
Devaraj, S., 290
Devarjai, S., 89
Devers, C., 356
Devinney, T., 31, 387
Dew, N., 30, 150
DeWitt, R., 292
Dhanaraj, C., 152, 219
Dharwadkar, R., 291, 356
Dieleman, M., 291
Dietz, J., 122
Dighero, Robert, 436
Dikova, D., 220
Dinur, A., 323
Dixit, A., 90
Djankov, S., 356
Dobrev, S., 185
Doh, J., 31, 88, 387
Doidge, C., 357
Domoto, H., 60
Donahue, M., 356
Donaldson, L., 358
Donaldson, T., 363
Donaldson, Thomas, 110, 122, 387
Dorfman, P., 122
Dorrenbacher, C., 324
Doving, E., 290
Dow, D., 123
Dow, S., 60
Dowell, G., 59, 357
Dowling, P., 108
Down, J., 89, 323
Doz, Y., 29
Dranove, D., 60
Driffield, N., 323
Driver, M., 152

Drnovsek, M., 151
Droge, C., 88, 185
Drogendijk, R., 184
Drucker, Peter, 11, 30
Du, J., 122
Dudley, Robert, 215, 216
Dunlap-Hinkler, D., 323
Dunn, Patricia, 327
Dunning, J., 29
Dunning, John, 173, 184, 185
Durand, R., 88, 120
Durisin, B., 324
Duso, T., 291
Dussuage, P., 218
Dyer, J., 60, 151, 210, 218, 220
Dykes, B., 291, 387

E

Easterby-Smith, M., 324
Economy, E., 381
Eddleston, K., 185
Eden, L., 218, 386
Egelhoff, W., 60, 322
Eggers, J., 290
Egri, C., 386
Eiadat, Y., 387
Einav, L., 59
Einstein, 14
Eisenhardt, K., 78, 89, 151, 152, 323
Eisenmann, T., 59
Elango, B., 184
Elbanna, S., 121
Elfenbein, H., 255
Elkington, J., 371, 387
Ellis, K., 291
Ellis, P., 121
Ellison, Larry, 327
Ellstrands, A., 356
Erez, M., 122
Eriksson, T., 88
Erkins, D., 356
Ertug, G., 218
Eskin, E., 60
Esterby-Smith, M., 323
Estrin, S., 30, 184, 357
Ethiraj, S., 89
Ettenson, R., 388
Eunni, R., 151
Evangelista, F., 219
Eyadat, H., 387

F

Faccio, M., 356
Faems, D., 219
Fai, F., 322

Fails, D., 88
Faldin, Maxim, 436, 437
Falllieres, M., 399
Fang, E., 218, 219
Fang, Lily, 391–403
Fang, T., 122
Fang, Y., 290
Farrell, D., 79
Fern, M., 290
Fernando, C., 387
Fernhaber, S., 152
Ferrier, W., 255
Fey, C., 184, 324
Field, J., 88
Filatotchev, I., 121, 151–153, 355, 356, 357, 358
Finkelstein, S., 291
Fiorina, Carly, 327
Fisher, Jodi, 327
Fisher, Ken, 422
Fishman, C., 256
Fladmoe-Lindquist, K., 87
Flores, R., 184
Fombrun, C., 87, 388
Ford, Henry, 6
Forsgren, M., 324
Forster, W., 150
Fort, T., 388
Foss, N., 323, 324
Fotak, F., 350
Francis, J., 151
Franco, A., 151
Fransson, A., 323
Frazier, G., 184
Freeman, E., 386
Freene, F., 151
Fremeth, A., 388
Frese, E., 60
Frey, B., 355
Fridman, Mikhail, 197, 215–217
Fried, J., 356
Friedman, Milton, 365, 387
Frost, T., 246, 256
Frynas, J. G., 185
Fuentelsaz, L., 256
Fujita, J., 185
Fukata, Yoshihiro, 462
Fukuyama, F., 122
Furu, P., 324

G

Galan, J., 185, 322
Galileo, 14
Gammelgaard, J., 324
Gampa, R., 464
Ganapathi, J., 386

Ganco, M., 151, 255
Gande, A., 290
Gang, Zhang, 391, 392, 393, 394, 400
Gannon, M., 108
Gans, J., 60
Gao, G., 31, 185
Garbe, J., 322
Garces-Ayerbe, C., 387
Garcia-Canal, E., 184
Garcia-Pont, C., 324
Gardberg, N., 87, 388
Garrette, B., 218
Garung, A., 357
Gates, Bill, 27, 28
Gau, G., 184
Gaur, A., 151, 185
Gaur, S., 151
Gavet, Maelle, 127–128
Gavetti, G., 30
Gedajlovic, E., 30, 121, 150, 290, 338, 356, 386
Geletaknycz, M., 356
Genakos, C., 30
George, B., 151
George, E., 121
George, G., 151, 152
Geringer, J. M., 290
Germann, K., 30
Geroski, P., 151
Ghauri, P., 220
Ghemawat, P., 29, 31, 324
Ghoshal, S., 29, 122, 311, 323
Ghosn, Carlos, 362
Ghuari, P., 219
Gianiodis, P., 255
Giarratana, M., 152
Gibbons, P., 324
Gibson, C., 122, 324
Gifford, B., 387
Gilbert, B., 152
Gilbert, C., 30
Gimeno, J., 233, 255
Glaister, K., 88, 184
Globerman, S., 122
Globerman, Steve, 349, 350, 355
Glunk, U., 357
Glynn, M., 387
Gnyawali, D., 120, 218, 323
Godfrey, P., 89, 387
Goerzen, A., 87, 219, 290
Golden, B., 255
Golden-Biddle, K., 30
Goldstein, D., 31
Golovko, E., 151
Gomes, L., 290
Gomez, J., 185, 256

Gomez-Mejia, L., 356
Gonzalez-Benito, J., 185
Gooderham, P., 290, 323
Goranova, M., 291, 356
Gordon, B., 59
Gore, A., 356, 375, 388
Gospel, H., 357
Gotsopoulos, A., 185
Gottfredson, M., 90
Gottschlag, O., 358
Gou, 6
Gould, S., 324
Gove, S., 88, 255, 388
Govindarajan, V., 29, 86, 152, 255, 313, 323
Gozubuyuk, R., 218
Graebner, M., 152, 356
Graffin, S., 356
Graham, E., 256
Graham, J., 122
Grahovac, J., 88
Grajek, M., 122
Grant, R., 316
Greenwald, B., 31, 322
Gregerson, H., 151
Gregorio, D., 88, 151, 152
Grein, A., 324
Greve, H., 122, 218, 219, 255, 323
Grewal, R., 60, 256
Griffin, D., 150
Griffith, D., 60, 88, 123, 185
Griffiths, A., 121
Grilli, L., 151
Grimm, C. M., 225
Grimpe, C., 88
Grove, Andrew, 50, 60, 316, 324
Gruber, M., 89
Guar, A., 220
Guay, T., 387
Gubbi, S., 289
Guedri, Z., 255
Guillen, M., 121, 123, 184, 358
Gulati, R., 59, 219
Gupta, A., 29, 152, 313, 323
Gupta-Mukherjee, S., 291
Gupta, V., 122
Guthrie, J., 292
Gyoshev, B., 151

H
Haas, M., 324
Habib, M., 122
Hahn, E., 88
Hakanson, L., 123, 323
Haleblian, J., 357
Hambrick, D., 30, 31, 152, 357

Hamilton, R., 60, 323
Hammes, T., 132
Hanges, P., 122
Hannah, S., 120
Hansen, J., 387
Harkins, Michele, 471–476
Harmancioglu, N., 88
Harrison, J., 386
Harrison, J. S., 263
Hart, B. Liddell, 30
Hart, Liddell, 11
Hart, S., 122, 387
Hartmann, E., 88
Harzing, A., 324
Hashai, N., 152
Hatch, N., 250
Hatonen, J., 88
Hau, L., 219
Haxhi, I., 357
Hayden, 183
Haynes, K., 357
Hayward, M., 87, 150
He, J., 357
He, X., 255
He, Y., 386
Heath, C., 224
Hebert, L., 322
Heide, J., 184
Heijltjes, M., 357
Heine, K., 89
Heinemann, F., 89
Heleblian, J., 291
Helfat, C., 87, 290
Hellman, J., 122
Hemphill, T., 388
Hemprecht, J., 388
Hendel, J., 224
Henderson, A., 290, 357
Henderson, J., 59, 60
Hennart, J., 122, 184, 185
Henriques, I., 388
Heracleous, L., 60
Hermalin, B., 357
Hermelo, F., 75
Herrmann, P., 152, 357
Hess, A., 89
Heugens, P., 30, 290, 358
Higgins, M., 218
Hill, A., 88
Hill, C., 60, 89, 153, 250, 255, 291, 323, 357
Hiller, N., 357
Hillier, D., 323
Hillman, A., 121, 386, 387
Hines, J., 104

Hinings, C., 184
Hirst, G., 122
Hitt, M., 71, 87, 88, 150, 218, 255, 263, 290, 291
Ho, J., 358
Ho, Lawrence, 416
Ho, Stanley, 412
Hoang, H., 323
Hodgetts, R., 322
Hoegl, M., 122
Hoffman, A., 374
Hoffman, W., 219
Hoffmann, V., 388
Hofstede, Geert, 105, 106, 107, 122, 306
Holburn, G., 121
Holcomb, T., 88
Holm, U., 309
Holmes, M., 88
Holmes, R. M., 356
Holmqvist, M., 152
Holzinger, I., 121
Hong, J., 260, 323, 324
Hong, S., 122
Hoopes, D., 60
Hoover, V., 255
Hope, D., 152
Horn, J., 255
Hoskisson, R., 30, 71, 121, 150, 260, 263, 355–356
Hough, J., 89
House, R., 122
Hrivnak, G., 152
Hsieh, L., 218
Hsu, C.-C., 264
Hsu, D., 152
Huang, K., 121
Huang, X., 323
Huang, Y., 151
Huang, Z., 121, 357
Huckman, R., 60
Hull, C., 387
Hulland, J., 218
Hult, G. T., 60
Hung, M., 356
Hungeling, S., 89
Hunter, L., 121
Huo, A., 464
Hurd, Mark, 327
Huselid, Mark, 91
Husted, B., 387
Husted, K., 323
Hutzschenreuter, T., 184

I

Imelt, Jeff, 231
Immelt, Jeffrey, 8, 255
Ingram, P., 121

Inkpen, A., 323, 324
Ireland, R. D., 71, 87, 150, 153, 218, 263
Isobe, T., 31, 219
Ito, K., 185, 255
Iyer, B., 89, 291

J

Jack, S., 151
Jackson, G., 30, 357
Jacobides, M., 60, 291
Jagad, Mallika, 66
Janney, J., 388
Jansen, J., 89, 324, 357
Janssens, M., 219
Jap, S., 185
Jarzabkowski, P., 324
Javagli, R., 90
Javidan, M., 122
Jayaraman, N., 291
Jennings, W., 355
Jensen, M., 218, 356
Jensen, Michael, 354
Jensen, P., 88
Jensen, R., 323, 337–338
Jensen, T., 386
Jiang, C., 218, 323
Jiang, F., 289
Jiang, M., 185
Jiang, Y., 30–31, 120, 332–333, 356, 358
Jintao, Hu, 27
Jobs, Steve, 139, 211, 327, 342
Johanson, J., 184
Johnson, D., 60
Johnson, J., 122, 123, 356
Johnson, R., 150, 292, 357
Johnson, S., 88, 151, 356
Johnson, W., 356
Jones, G., 122, 291
Jonsson, S., 89
Joshi, A., 218
Julian, S., 30, 121
Justis, R., 121

K

Kabanoff, B., 60
Kacperczyk, 386
Kahn, J., 31, 322
Kaiser, U., 88
Kale, P., 210, 217, 218, 219, 220
Kalnins, A., 255
Kalotay, K., 157
Kamins, M., 87
Kamprad, Ingvar, 139
Kang, J., 358
Kang, Karambir Singh, 66–67

Kang, R., 31
Kankiwala, Nish, 398, 400
Kaplan, R., 19, 219
Kaplan, S., 355, 357
Kapoor, R., 88, 291
Karim, S., 291
Karnani, A., 387
Karolyi, A., 357
Karube, M., 292
Karunaratna, A., 123
Katila, R., 89, 151
Kato, T., 292
Kaufmann, D., 122
Ke, Y., 31
Kedia, B., 88, 290, 324, 410
Kedia, J., 88
Keil, M., 218
Keil, T., 291
Keim, G., 387
Kelly, A., 387
Kenney, M., 88
Kenny, Steve, 431, 435
Kestler, A., 387
Ketchen, D., 60, 151, 153, 255, 356
Ketkar, S., 184
Khanin, D., 356
Khanna, T., 30, 121, 296, 358
Khavul, S., 150
Khoury, T., 30, 120, 185, 290
Kilduff, G., 255
Kim, D., 151
Kim, H., 260
Kim, J., 291, 356, 358
Kim, K., 90
Kim, S., 122
Kim, W. C., 256, 322
King, A., 89, 388
King, D., 291, 292
Kirca, A., 184
Kircher, P., 322
Kirkman, B., 122
Kistruck, G., 153
Kleinberg, J., 123
Kliesch-Eberl, M., 87
Klossek, Andreas, 465–470
Knight, G., 120, 151
Knott, A., 153
Kochan, T., 121
Kogan, J., 358
Kogut, B., 218
Koka, B., 218, 324
Kolk, A., 388
Köpf, Barny, 448, 450, 452
Köpf, Josef, 450
Kor, Y., 357

Kostova, T., 89, 121, 311, 324
Kotabe, M., 31, 60, 89, 184, 218, 256, 290, 323
Kotha, S., 151
Kourula, A., 388
Koveos, P., 122
Koza, M., 218
Kraatz, M., 292
Kramer, M. R., 368, 382
Kraussl, R., 387
Krishnan, H., 291
Krishnan, M., 89
Kroll, M., 89, 152, 356
Kronborg, D., 185
Kruse, G., 121
Kuilman, J., 60
Kuma, V., 88
Kumar, K., 88
Kumar, N., 235, 256
Kumar, V., 184
Kunar, M., 220
Kunc, M., 88
Kundu, S., 88, 153, 264
Kurmakayev, Kamil, 436, 437
Kuznetsov, A., 104
Kwak, M., 60
Kwan, H., 152
Kwok, C., 122, 358

L

La, V., 88
La Porta, R., 355, 356
Laamanen, T., 291, 309
Lado, A., 89
Lafley, A. G., 15
Lages, L., 185
Lahiri, S., 88, 290, 323
Lai, J., 219
Lam, K., 123
Lamin, A., 88
Lamont, B., 89, 291, 292
Lane, P., 324, 358
Lang, L., 356
Lange, D., 290, 357
Lanoie, P., 387
Lanzolla, G., 185
Larraza-Kintana, M., 356
Larsson, R., 152
Lau, V., 150
Laursen, K., 323
Lavie, D., 59, 219, 220
Lawrence, P., 59
Lawrence, T., 59
Lazzarini, S., 217
Le, S., 356
Leask, G., 60

Lechner, C., 219
Lecocq, X., 61
Lee, B., 121
Lee, C., 89, 290
Lee, G., 185, 219
Lee, J., 30
Lee, K., 30, 122, 260, 290, 296
Lee, K. B., 30, 260, 290
Lee, S., 30–31, 59, 121–123, 153, 184–185, 274–275, 291–292
Leeds, Roger, 391–403
Leiblein, M., 60, 88
Lemak, D., 185
Lemann, Jorge Paulo, 278
Lemelson, Jerome, 223
Lenartowicz, T., 123
Lenox, M., 89
Lepak, D., 151
Lerner, J., 357
Lester, R., 121
Leung, H., 464
Leung, K., 122
Lev, B., 387
Levie, J., 151
Levinthal, D., 324
Levitt, T., 31, 297, 322
Levy, D., 88
Lewin, A., 88, 89, 184
Lewis, D., 31
Li, D., 218
Li, David, 335
Li, H., 121, 153
Li, J., 60, 123, 184, 219, 356
Li, M., 290, 357
Li, P., 185
Li, Y., 75, 88
Licht, A., 356
Lichtenthaler, U., 323
Lieberman, M., 89, 219
Lieberthal, K., 323, 381
Liesch, P., 87, 120, 185, 323
Liew, R., 464
Liker, J., 60
Lim, E., 292
Lim, K., 291
Lin, H., 255
Lin, W., 184
Lin, Y., 218
Lin, Z., 30, 218, 220, 291
Lincoln, J., 60
Linke, Bernd Michael, 465–470
Liou, F., 89
Lioukas, S., 89
Lipstein, R., 256
Liu, C., 219
Liu, E., 464

Liu, R., 88
Liu, Y., 88, 184
Livengood, R. S., 255
Loane, S., 152
Lockett, A., 218
Long, C., 122
Looy, B., 219
Lopez-de-Silanes, F., 355, 356
Lopez, L., 153
Lorsch, J., 30
Lounsbury, M., 122, 291
Lovallo, D., 89
Love, E. G., 292
Love, J., 323
Lowe, K., 122
Lowe, R., 150
Lu, J., 31, 152, 184, 219, 264
Lu, Y., 30, 151, 183, 290, 323
Lubatkin, M., 59, 150, 358
Luce, R., 60
Lui, S., 219
Luk, C., 30
Luke, Horace, 254
Lukey, Bernard, 127
Lumpkin, G. T., 151
Luo, Y., 30, 86, 122–123, 152
        218, 219, 324
Lupton, N., 217
Lux, S., 121
Lyles, M., 219, 220, 323

M

Ma, H., 255
Ma, R., 151
Ma, X., 322
Macaulay, C., 75
Macaulay, L., 31
Macharzina, K., 29
Macher, J., 291
Mackay, P., 31
Mackenzie, W., 89
Mackey, A., 387
Mackey, John, 372, 376, 385, 386
Mackey, T., 387
MacMillan, I. C., 243–244, 256
Madhok, A., 219–220
Madsen, P., 388
Madsen, T., 88
Magee, R., 356
Magnan, M., 358
Mahoney, J., 218
Maicas, J., 185
Mainkar, A., 59
Mair, J., 387
Makhija, M., 31, 184

Makino, S., 31, 184, 185, 219, 290
Malhotra, N., 184
Maloney, M., 184
Manev, I., 151
Manigart, S., 218
Manning, S., 184
Manolova, T., 151
Manrakhan, S., 184
Marcel, J., 356
March, James, 203, 219
Marcus, A., 388
Mardiasmo, Diaswati, 431–435
Marginson, D., 31
Marin, Jose, 436
Markman, G., 29, 255
Marquis, C., 121, 291, 387
Marsh, L., 87
Marsh, S., 256
Martin, J., 78, 89, 323
Martin, K., 122
Martin, O., 324
Martin, X., 60, 89, 218
Martinez-Fernandez, M., 218
Martinez, Z., 90
Marvel, M., 151
Mas-Ruiz, F., 60
Maseland, R., 122
Mason, P., 30
Massini, S., 88
Masulis, R., 357
Mata, J., 151
Mathews, J., 29, 59, 87, 152
Mathews, John, 178
Matos, P., 356
Matsunaga, S., 356
Matta, E., 291
Matten, D., 386
Mauborgne, R., 256, 322
May, D., 120
Maznevski, M., 184
McCann, B., 184
McCarter, M., 218
McCarthy, D., 121, 122, 153, 357
McCarthy, Daniel J., 436–438
McCarthy, I., 59
McDermott, G., 121
McDonald, M., 356, 357
McDonald, R., 89
McDougall, P., 150, 152
McGahan, A., 60, 61
McGrahan, A., 151
McGrath, R. G., 243–244, 256
McGuire, J., 60, 255, 357
McIntyre, D., 218
McKinsey, 79

McMullen, J., 150, 152
McNamara, G., 60, 89, 291
McNaughton, R., 152
Meckling, W., 356
Megginson, W., 350
Meier, D., 291
Mellahi, K., 185
Mellewigt, T., 61
Menghinello, S., 323
Mentzer, J., 219
Merrill, C., 387
Mesquita, L., 218, 255
Meuleman, M., 218
Meyer, C., 291
Meyer, K., 30
Meyer, Klaus, 40, 184, 185, 219, 267, 290
Michaels, M., 60
Michailova, S., 323
Michel, J., 255
Mignonac, K., 185
Milanov, H., 218
Miller, C. C., 185
Miller, D., 88, 89, 290, 357
Miller, K., 291
Miller, S., 386
Miller, T., 290
Millington, A., 387
Minbaeva, D., 323
Minford, P., 121
Minin, A., 323
Minniti, M., 152
Minnow, N., 355
Mintzberg, H., 30, 316
Mishina, Y., 387
Mishra, H., 323
Missangyi, V., 357
Mitchell, M., 291
Mitchell, R., 151
Mitchell, W., 218, 290
Mitsuhashi, H., 218, 219
Moeller, S., 31
Mole, K., 151
Molina-Morales, F., 218
Moliterno, T., 89
Monks, R., 355
Monteiro, L. F., 323
Montes-Sancho, M., 388
Moon, J., 386
Moore, C., 153
Moore, K., 31
Moran, P., 89, 122
Morecroft, J., 88
Morgan, E., 322
Morrison, A., 322
Mors, M., 324

Morse, E., 151
Moschieri, C., 291
Mu, S., 323
Mudambi, R., 88, 151, 323
Mudambi, S., 88
Muhanna, W., 89
Mukherjee, D., 88, 151, 290
Mukherjee, Debmayla, 409–410
Mukhopadhyay, S., 185
Muller, A., 387
Mundie, Craig, 28
Murdoch, Elisabeth, 332
Murdoch, James, 331–332
Murdoch, Rupert, 234, 331–332, 342
Murillo-Luna, J., 387
Murray, F., 121
Murray, G., 121
Murray, J., 31, 89, 184, 218
Murtha, T., 88
Murtinu, S., 151
Musteen, M., 88, 151
Mutlu, Canan, 404–408
Myers, M., 60, 185, 219

N

Nablebutt, B., 220
Nachum, L., 31, 123, 184, 323
Nadkarni, S., 60, 120, 152, 357
Nadolska, A., 185
Nagarajan, N., 356
Nakamura, M., 357
Nambisan, S., 217
Nandkumar, A., 151
Narayanan, V., 60
Narula, R., 323
Nasra, R., 153
Navarra, P., 323
Ndofor, H., 255
Nebus, J., 388
Neeleman, David, 143
Nelson, K., 122
Nelson, R., 75
Nerkar, A., 218
Ness, H., 219
Newbert, S., 87
Newburry, W., 121
Newman, H., 356
Ng, D., 292
Nguyen, T., 323
Niederauer, Duncan, 309
Nielsen, B., 219
Nielsen, S., 219
Nielsen, T., 152
Nieto, M., 323
Nifadkar, S., 123

Noble, C., 89
Noboa, F., 324
Nohria, N., 30
Noorderhaven, N., 324
North, Douglass, 94, 120, 121
Northcraft, G., 218
Norton, D., 19, 219
Numagami, T., 292
Nyberg, Lars, 408
Nystrom, P., 322

O

Obama, Barack, 309, 424–430
Oetzel, J., 184, 387
Ofori-Dankwa, J., 30, 121
Oh, C., 184, 387
Oh, K., 122
O'Leary, Michael, 46, 418–422
Olffen, W., 184
Oliver, C., 121, 219
Olsen, D., 290
O'Mahony, S., 121
O'Neill, H., 185
Ormiston, M., 388
Orr, R., 123
Osborne, J. D., 60
Osegowitsch, T., 185
O'Shaughnessy, K., 386
Oster, S., 60
Ou, A., 123
Oviatt, B., 150, 152
Oxenford, Alec, 436
Ozcan, P., 152

P

Pacheco-de-Almeida, G., 60, 90
Paik, Y., 218
Pajunen, K., 121
Palazzo, G., 386, 387
Palepu, K., 358
Palich, L., 185
Palmer, T., 60
Pan, Y., 185
Pande, A., 88
Pangarkar, N., 219
Panibratov, A., 157
Parboteeah, K., 122
Parente, R., 89, 184, 323
Park, D., 291
Park, H., 151, 219
Park, S., 123, 218
Parker, D., 60
Parker, G., 59
Parmigiani, A., 88
Parvinen, P., 291

Pathak, S., 324
Patterson, P., 88
Paul, D., 184
Paulson, Henry, 349, 350
Pavelin, S., 388
Pearce, J., 121
Pedersen, T., 31, 88, 184, 323, 324
Peeters, C., 88
Pehrsson, A., 292
Peng, M. W., 24, 29–31, 44, 46, 52, 59–60, 75, 87–88, 97–99, 102, 104, 120–122, 132, 152–153, 184–185, 205, 212, 218, 219, 220, 260, 267, 274–275, 289–292, 316, 323–324, 332–333, 346, 355–356, 358, 381, 456–459, 462–463
Peng, W., 59
Penner-Hahn, J., 323
Perez-Nordtvedt, L., 324
Perez, P., 152
Perkins, Walter R., 452
Perrigot, R., 185
Perryman, A., 356
Peteraf, M., 60, 121
Petersen, B., 88, 185
Petersen, M., 291
Petitt, B., 290
Petrovits, C., 387
Pettigrew, A., 30
Pfarrer, M., 356
Phalippou, L., 355
Phan, P., 357
Phelps, C., 218, 323
Phene, A., 87, 218, 324
Pheng, L., 185
Philippe, D., 120
Philips, S., 90
Phillips, R., 386
Piekkari, R., 324
Piesse, J., 151
Pigman, G., 185
Pindado, J., 323
Pinkham, B., 30, 120
Pinkham, C., 97
Pinkse, J., 387
Pisano, G., 78
Piscitello, L., 151
Piva, E., 151
Ployhart, R., 89
Polidoro, F., 89, 218
Pollock, T., 87, 152, 356, 387
Porac, J., 356
Porter, L., 388
Porter, M., 30
Porter, Michael, 35, 43, 50, 54, 59–61, 88, 99–100, 121, 130, 366, 367, 368, 380, 382
Portugal, P., 151

Posen, H., 153
Pothukuchi, V., 123
Powell, T., 89
Prahalad, C. K., 292, 323
Prashantham, S., 152
Prescott, J., 218
Presley, Elvis, 82
Preston, L., 363, 387
Prevezer, M., 357
Prince, Erik, 132
Prince, J., 255
Puffer, S., 121, 122, 153, 357
Puffer, Shiela M., 436–438
Puranam, P., 59, 89, 291
Puryear, R., 90

Q

Qian, C., 387
Qian, G., 30, 123, 185, 290
Qian, I., 185
Qian, Z., 30, 185, 290
Qinghou, Zong, 131

R

Radhakrishnan, S., 387
Raes, A., 357
Ragozzino, R., 219
Raina, A., 67
Rajagopalan, N., 219, 357
Rajan, R., 387
Ralston, D., 386
Ramamurti, R., 86
Ramaprasad, A., 60
Ramasubba, N., 89
Ramaswamy, K., 290
Ramchander, S., 387
Ranft, A., 89, 291
Rangan, S., 152
Rasheed, A., 357, 358
Rawley, E., 291
Ray, G., 89
Ray, S., 86, 289
Raynor, M., 30
Read, S., 30
Reay, T., 30
Redding, G., 121, 122
Reed, R., 121, 185
Reger, R., 255
Regner, P., 89
Reid, E., 388
Reinmoeller, P., 386
Reitzig, M., 90, 224
Ren, B., 87, 220, 289
Reuer, J., 60, 121, 217, 218, 219

Reus, T., 89, 291–292
Rhodes, Cecil, 229
Ricart, J., 184
Rich, Al, 183
Richardson, D., 256
Richter, N., 322
Ricks, D., 108
Riddle, L., 152
Ridge, J., 88
Rindova, V., 87, 151, 255
Ring, P., 121, 218
Rique, M., 184
Ritmuller, Willhelm, 183
Ritzman, L., 88
Rivera-Torres, P., 387
Rivkin, J., 30
Robert, Kohlberg Kravis (KKR), 353, 354
Robertson, C., 122
Roche, F., 387
Rockart, S., 89
Rockefeller, E., 256
Rockefellers, 342
Rodkin, D., 31
Rodrigues, S., 218
Rodriguez, A., 323
Roe, R., 357
Rochl, T., 260
Rogers, Jim, 376–377
Roll, R., 292
Rometty, Ginni, 72
Romilly, P., 387
Rose, Charlie, 30, 220
Rose, E., 185, 255
Rosenkopf, L., 219
Rosenzweig, P., 121
Roth, K., 89, 121, 311, 324
Rothaermel, F., 89, 218, 255, 323
Rothenberg, S., 387
Rouse, M., 218
Rowe, W. G., 356
Rowlands, Chris, 392
Rowley, T., 219
Roy, A., 218
Roy, J., 219
Rubenstein, David, 355
Ruckstad, M., 30
Ruddock, A., 46
Rufin, C., 388
Rugelsjoen, B., 219
Rugman, A., 29
Rugman, Alan, 177, 322
Rui, H., 289
Ruiz-Moreno, F., 60
Rukstad, M., 76

Rumelt, R., 30, 61
Rupp, R., 386
Russell, C., 123

S

Sadorsky, P., 388
Sadun, R., 30
Safizadeh, H., 88
Sagiv, L., 356
Salk, J., 122, 219
Salter, A., 323
Sammartino, A., 185
Sampson, R., 218
Sanchez-Bueno, M., 322
Sanders, W. G., 356
Sandstrom, J., 386
Sanna-Randaccio, F., 323
Santoro, M., 323
Santos, F., 151
Santos, J., 29
Saparito, P., 122
Sapienza, H., 150, 152
Sarala, R., 292
Sarasvathy, S., 150
Saravathy, S., 30
Sarkar, M., 86, 88, 289
Satorra, A., 61
Sawhney, M., 217
Schendel, D., 30, 61
Schenzler, C., 290
Scherer, A., 386, 387
Scherer, R., 90
Schijven, M., 292
Schilling, M., 184
Schmid, F., 151
Schmidt, Eric, 211, 220, 336
Schmidt, T., 323
Schnatterly, K., 355, 357
Scholnick, B., 88
Scholtens, B., 388
Schomaker, M., 123
Schotter, A., 324
Schreiner, M., 218
Schreyogg, G., 87
Schultz, Howard, 376, 388
Schulze, W., 356
Schumpeter, Joseph, 146
Schwartz, M., 132
Schwebach, R., 387
Scott, P., 324
Scott, Richard, 94
Scott, W. R., 120, 123
Seawright, K., 151
Seelos, C., 387
Segal-Horn, S., 324

Seko, Mobuto, 229
Semadeni, M., 185, 255, 291
Senbert, L., 290
Senor, Dan, 135
Seth, A., 89
Shackell, M., 357
Shackman, J., 290
Shaffer, M., 150
Shah, R., 218
Shahrim, A., 357
Shakespeare, William, 145
Shamsie, J., 38
Shane, S., 150, 151
Shaner, J., 184
Shanley, M., 60, 218, 292
Shapiro, D., 122
Shapiro, D. M., 338
Shapiro, Daniel, 349, 350, 355, 356
Sharfman, M., 387
Sharp, Z., 324
Shaver, J. M., 59, 323
Shaw, K., 355
Shen, J., 290
Shen, W., 356
Shenkar, O., 87, 122–123, 151, 184, 201, 205, 212, 219
Shepherd, D., 150–152
Shervani, T., 184
Shi, L., 324
Shi, W., 218
Shi, Y., 358
Shimizu, K., 292
Shin, H., 24
Shin, S., 185
Shinawatra, Thaksin, 343
Shinozawa, Y., 358
Shipilov, A., 219
Shipton, H., 122
Shleifer, A., 355, 356
Short, J., 60
Shulze, W., 59
Sicupira, Carlos Alberto, 278
Siegel, D., 150, 291, 388
Siegel, J., 358
Siggelkow, N., 218
Silva, C., 91
Silverman, B., 121, 220
Simerly, R., 357
Simester, D., 30
Simon, D., 59, 255
Simons, K., 291
Simons, R., 31
Simpson, D., 316
Simpson, O. J., 327
Simsek, Z., 151, 357
Simula, T., 309

Sin, L., 30
Singal, M., 323
Singer, Saul, 135
Singh, H., 60, 210, 217, 218, 219, 220, 291, 386
Singh, J., 151, 386
Singh, K., 122
Sinha, R., 89
Sinkovics, R., 219
Sirmon, D., 87, 88, 150, 255
Sitkin, S., 121
Slangen, A., 184, 185
Sleuwaegen, L., 88
Smith, Adam, 34, 225, 365
Smith, K., 90, 151, 256, 356
Smith, K. G., 225
Snell, R., 324
Snow, C., 255
Sofka, W., 323
Som, A., 323
Sonderegger, P., 152
Song, F., 356
Song, J., 296
Song, S., 323
Sorensen, M., 357
Souder, D., 59, 151
Spanos, Y., 89
Spar, D., 255
Spears, Britney, 327
Spencer, J., 323
Spitznagel, M., 31
Spraggon, M., 357
Srikanth, K., 89, 291
Srivastava, M., 218
Stafford, E., 291
Stahl, G., 291
Staking, K., 387
Stalk, G., 256
Stan, C., 346
Stanislaw, J., 31
Staw, B., 255
Steen, J., 87, 120, 185
Steensma, H. K., 151, 219, 220, 323
Stephenson, Randall, 458
Stern, I., 356
Stevenes, C., 121
Stglitz, J., 256
Stieglitz, N., 89
Stiglitz, J., 31
Stiglitz, Joseph, 249
Storey, D., 151
Stromberg, P., 355, 357
Stuart, N., 357
Stubbart, C., 60
Stulz, R., 355, 357
Styles, C., 88

Su, K., 255, 256
Suarez, F., 185
Subramani, M., 88
Subramanian, M., 255
Suharto, 110
Sull, D., 151
Sullivan, D., 151
Summers, Tim, 215
Sun, J., 86
Sun, M., 88
Sun, S., 29–31, 104, 120, 218, 220, 289, 291
Surroca, J., 387
Swaminathan, V., 218
Swan, S., 90
Szulanski, G., 323

T

Tadesse, S., 122, 358
Taleb, N., 31
Tallman, S., 29, 31, 88, 201, 218, 219, 290
Tan, D., 219
Tan, H., 59
Tan, J., 30, 52, 59, 60, 185, 219
Tang, J., 356
Tang, L., 122
Tang, Y., 89
Tanriverdi, H., 89, 290
Tao, Z., 152
Tapon, F., 356
Tarnovskaya, V., 152
Tatoglu, E., 184
Taube, F., 152
Taylor, G., 388
Taylor, M. S., 151
Taylor, Marilyn, 431–435
Teece, D., 30, 60, 61, 87
Telles, Marcel, 278
Teng, B., 217
Terjesen, S., 309
Terlaak, A., 387
Terziovski, M., 151
Tetlock, P., 388
Teva, 235
Thatcher, Margaret, 347
Thietart, R., 30
Thomas, D., 88, 151, 152
Thomsen, S., 185
Thornhill, S., 60
Tian, J., 357
Tian, X., 184
Tian, Z., 386
Tiberius, 20
Tiegland, R., 323
Tihanyi, L., 123, 219, 255, 260, 290, 355

Tikkanen, H., 291
Timmons, J., 137
Tishler, A., 87
Tiwana, A., 218
Todorova, G., 324
Toffel, M., 388
Toh, P., 89, 255
Tomassen, S., 309
Tompson, G., 60
Tong, T., 52, 60, 121, 218, 219
Torre, C., 323
Torrisi, S., 152
Torsila, S., 309
Townsend, J., 220
Toyne, B., 90
Tracey, P., 184
Trahms, C., 150
Trautmann, G., 88
Trautmann, T., 388
Trevino, L., 122
Tribo, J., 387
Trimble, C., 255
Tripsas, M., 290
Tsai, W., 90, 255, 256
Tsang, E., 184, 185, 323, 324
Tse, A., 30
Tse, D., 185
Tse, E., 88
Tse, S., 464
Tsui, A., 123
Tuchman, B., 12
Tuggle, C., 357
Tung, R., 122
Turner, Ted, 234
Tuschke, A., 356
Tyler, B., 120
Tzabbar, D., 88
Tzu, Sun, 10, 11, 23, 29, 224
        249, 380

U

Uhlenbruck, K., 291
Un, C. A., 324
Unruh, G., 388
Useem, M., 386

V

Vaaler, P., 89, 152
Vaara, E., 292, 324
Vahlne, J., 184
Valentini, G., 151, 291
Van Alstyne, M., 59
Van den Bosch, F., 89, 357
van Ees, H., 357
Van Essen, M., 30, 290, 358

van Fenema, P., 88
van Hoom, A., 122
Van Iddekinge, C., 89
Van Oosterhout, J., 30, 290, 358
Van Reenen, J., 30
van Swaaij, Michael, 436
Van Witteloostujin, A., 61
Vanhaverbeke, W., 323
Vardi, Yossi, 135
Varghese, Thomas, 66
Vassolo, R., 75, 255
Vasudeva, G., 219
Vegt, G., 323
Vekselberg, Viktor, 215
Venkataraman, S., 150
Venkatraman, N., 89
Venzin, M., 88
Verbeke, A., 122
Very, P., 358
Veugelers, R., 323
Vining, A., 60
Vissa, B., 121, 151
Vliert, E., 323
Vogel, D., 387
Voigt, A., 291
Volberda, H., 89, 150, 184, 324, 357
Von Clausewitz, Carl, 10, 12, 30
von Glinow, M., 88
Von Nordenflycht, A., 89
Voorhees, C., 218
Vora, D., 324
Vroom, G., 184, 255
Vyas, D., 152

W

Waddock, S., 387
Wade, J., 356
Wade, M., 290
Wagner, S., 90
Waldman, D., 387
Wallas, Mike, 433
Wally, S., 255
Walter, Robert, 44
Walters, B., 152, 356
Walz, U., 355
Wang, C., 357
Wang, Cher, 253
Wang, D., 30, 120, 153, 274–275, 291–292, 323, 356
Wang, Daizong, 394, 396, 401, 403
Wang, H., 387
Wang, L., 220
Wang, R., 60
Wang, S., 86
Wasko, M., 323

Watanabe, Kenichi, 462
Watson, A., 122
Webb, J., 153
Weber, K., 122
Wei, S., 122
Wei, Z., 88
Weigelt, C., 88
Weiss, J., 110
Welbourne, T., 356
Welch, D., 108
Welch, Jack, 190, 262–263, 380, 388
Welch, L., 185
Welch, S., 388
Werner, S., 31
Wernerfelt, B., 89
West, J., 323
West, M., 122
Westphal, J., 356, 357
Wezel, F., 184
White, C., 324
White, R., 60, 152
White, S., 219
Whitley, R., 30
Whitman, Meg, 327
Wiersema, M., 31, 89, 185, 290
    356, 357
Wiklund, J., 151
Wilkinson, T., 185
Williams, C., 290, 324, 386
Williamson, O., 60, 89, 95, 120
Williamson, P., 29
Wilson, Ben, 440–447
Wiltbank, R., 30, 255
Wincent, J., 151
Wind, J., 256
Winter, S., 87
Wirtz, J., 60
Wiseman, R., 356
Withers, M., 356
Witt, M., 121
Witty, A., 323
Wixted, B., 59
Woehr, D., 121
Wolf, J., 322
Wong, E., 388
Woo, C. Y., 233
Woo, J., 185
Woodman, R., 30
Woods, Tiger, 327
Wooster, P., 184
Wright, M., 121, 150, 152, 153
    218, 355
Wright, P., 89, 152, 356
Wu, A., 358
Wu, Yanmin, 440–447

X
Xia, J., 185, 220
Xiaoping, Deng, 392
Xie, F., 357
Xie, Q., 184
Xie, Qihua, 470
Xie, Y., 184
Xu, C., 122
Xu, D., 123, 184, 219, 324
Xu, S., 358

Y
Yafeh, Y., 30
Yagi, N., 123
Yakova, N., 185
Yamakawa, Y., 31, 60, 152, 153
Yamamoto, Mineo, 73
Yan, D., 29, 87, 220, 289
Yang, G., 122
Yang, H., 30, 218, 220, 291, 323
Yang, J., 184
Yang, Q., 323
Yang, X., 30, 31, 121
Yang, Xiaohua, 431–435
Yao, J., 290
Yau, O., 30
Yeaple, S., 184
Yeh, K., 152
Yeniyurt, S., 220
Yergin, D., 31
Yeung, P. E., 356
Yeung, Yuka, 400, 401
Yildiz, H., 184
Yin, X., 218, 292
Yip, G., 29, 289
Yip, P., 185
Yiu, D., 30
Yoffie, D., 60
Yoheskel, O., 123
York, A., 88, 152, 185
Yoshida, Tadao, 139
Yoshikawa, T., 357
Young, M., 289, 332, 333, 356
Young, Michael N., 460–461
Yu, J., 152
Yu, T., 255, 256
Yue, D., 184
Yunus, Muhammad, 149, 150

Z
Zacharakis, A., 152
Zaheer, S., 31, 88, 123, 184, 218
Zahra, S., 151, 152, 153

Zajac, E., 219, 220
Zald, M., 388
Zammuto, R., 121
Zander, I., 152
Zaralis, G., 89
Zardari, Asif Ali, 96
Zardkoohi, A., 121
Zellmer-Bruhn, M., 324
Zeman, Allan, 461
Zemsky, P., 88
Zeng, M., 122
Zhang, G., 388
Zhang, J., 323
Zhang, S., 356
Zhang, X., 356
Zhang, Y., 121, 219, 356, 357
Zhao, H., 184
Zhao, J. H., 122
Zheng, Guo, 468

Zhou, C., 219
Zhou, J., 121, 122, 185
Zhou, L., 151
Zhou, N., 123
Zhou, Y., 88, 291
Ziedonis, A., 150, 224
Ziedonis, R., 255
Zinner, D., 60
Zocco, Giueppe, 127
Zollo, M., 219, 220, 291, 358
Zona, F., 357
Zoogah, D., 218
Zook, C., 30
Zott, C., 59
Zou, H., 358
Zou, J., 184
Zou, S., 218, 219, 324
Zuckerberg, Mark, 30, 78, 119–120
Zurawicki, L., 122

INDEX OF SUBJECTS

2W1H foreign market entry model
how, 170–176
when, 168–170
where, 163–166
5 forces framework, 35–37, 130
bargaining power of buyers, 41–42
bargaining power of suppliers, 41
foreign market entries and, 160
intensity of rivalry among competitors, 35–38
threat of potential entry, 38–41
threat of substitutes, 42–43

A

Absorptive capacity, 314
Abu Dhabi Investment Authority, 349
Accommodative strategies, 112, 375
Acquisition premiums, 279
Acquisitions, 276. *See also* Diversification, acquisition and
restructuring versus alliances, 204
establishing WOSs, 176
versus market transactions, 200
Active CSR engagement overseas, 379
Afghan National Army, 132
Afghanistan, 132
Africa, 167
diamond industry, 229
trade and, 167
Agency costs, 330
Agency relationships, 330
Agency theory, 330
Agglomeration, 164
Air Transport Users Council, 419
Airline industry, 46, 73, 191, 226, 235, 418–422
Alliance dissolution, 205, 215–217
Alliance formation, 200–202, 207, 404–408
Alliances. *See* Strategic alliances and networks
American Jobs Creation Act of 2004, 429
Anchored replicators, 265
Anglo-American capitalism, 15–16
Anglo-American governance systems, 345
Anna Karenina (Tolstoy), 198
Anti-failure bias, 144–146
Antidumping, 237–241, 249
Antiglobalization protests, 21, 23
Antitrust issues, 226, 236, 239, 456–459
Arab Spring, 28
Arm's-length transaction, 99
The Art of War (Sun Tzu), 10

Attack on hotel in Mumbai, 66–67
Attacks, 241–242
Australia, 6, 33, 433
snow-sports industry, 431–435
Statewide Technology Incubation Strategy, 431
Austria, 111
Automobile industry
bailout of, 72
electric cars, 361–362
mass market cars, 51
strategic groups, 51

B

Backward integration, 42
Balanced scorecard, 18
Bankruptcy, 145
Baosteel Education Fund, 466
Barbarians at the Gate, 353
Barclay Capital, 462
Bargaining power
of buyers, 41–42, 130
of suppliers, 41, 130
Base of the pyramid (BOP), 7–8
Behavior controls, 271
Beijing Consensus, 348
Belgium, 12
Benchmarking, 68
Berlin Wall, fall of, 404, 405
Best practices, 343
Beyer CropScience, 321
Big ticket items, 38
Binding international commercial arbitration
(BICA), 97
Blue ocean strategy, 244
Blurred boundaries, 48–49
Boards of directors, 398, 400
composition of, 334
directing strategically, 335–336
interlocks, 334–335
leadership structure, 334
role of, 335
Born global firms, 140, 435
BOT (build-operate-transfer)
agreements, 175
Bounded rationality, 104
Branding, 408
Brazil, 5–6, 97, 105, 278, 448–455, 467
airline industry, 209–210

BRIC, 7, 17, 102–103
politics of, 75
bribes, 111
BRIC (Brazil, Russia, India, China), 7, 17, 102–103
Britain, 42, 97
Build-operate-transfer (BOT) agreement, 175
Bureaucratic costs, 273
Burundi, 133
Business groups, 259–260, 272
Business-level strategies, 260
    for competitive dynamics
        attacks and counterattacks, 241–244
        comprehensive model for, 225–241
        cooperation and signaling, 245
        debates and extensions for, 247–249
        implications for action, 249–251
        local firms versus multinational enterprises, 245–247
        strategy as action concept, 224–225
    for entrepreneurial firm growth and internationalization
        comprehensive model for, 129–132
        debates and extensions for, 142–146
        entrepreneurial firms and, 128–129
        financing and governance, 136–137
        growth, 134
        harvest and exit, 138–139
        implications for action, 146
        innovation, 134–135
        internationalization, 140–142
        network, 136
    for foreign market entries
        2W1H model, 163–176
        comprehensive model for, 159–163
        debates and extensions for, 177–179
        implications for action, 179–180
        liability of foreignness, 156–157
        propensity to internationalize, 158–159
    for strategic alliances and networks
        comprehensive model for, 191–200
        debates and extensions for, 208–211
        defined, 190
        evolution of, 200–206
        formation of, 200–203
        implications for action, 211–213
        performance of, 206–208
Business process outsourcing (BPO), 79, 409–410
Business unit HQ, 308
"Buy American" policy, 21
Buyers, bargaining power, 41–42, 130

C

Canada, 131
Capabilities. *See* Resource capabilities and leverage
Capacity to punish concept, 228
Capitalism, 367, 382

Captive sourcing, 70
Cartels, 226, 229–230
Causal ambiguity, 73
Center for Digital Democracy, 119
Centers of excellence, 299
Central Intelligence Agency, 379
CEO duality, 334
CEOs (chief executive officer), 327, 400
Chapter 11 bankruptcy, 146, 155, 191, 192
Chief executive officers (CEOs), 327, 400
China, 16, 20–21, 97, 103, 110, 157, 288, 381, 412
    Antimonopoly Law (2008), 239
    automobile industry, 7–8, 86, 170, 199, 300
    BRIC, 7, 17, 102–103
    computer industry, 27–28
    corporate social responsibility (CSR), 466
    electronics industry, 7–8, 52
    global strategy in, 5–6
    human rights in, 28
    luxury goods industry, 58
    mergers and acquisitions (M&As), 189–190, 199
    mobile phones, 247
    multinational enterprises (MNEs) and, 288, 349
    outward foreign direct investment (OFDI), 103
    piano companies, 182
    restaurant industry, 189, 391–403
    solar power industry, 424–430
    state-owned enterprises (SOEs), 347, 466
    steel industry, 465–470
    textbook industry, 16
"Chinatown buses," 155
Classic conglomerates, 266
Clayton Act (1914), 237, 457
Clear boundaries, 48–49
Co-marketing, 175, 191
Code of Corporate Conduct 2002, 344
Codes
    of conduct, 108, 344, 375–376
    of corporate governance, 344
Cognitive pillars, 95, 199–200
Collaborative capabilities, 196
Collectivism, 91, 92, 106
Collusion, 225–226, 228, 237
Commercialising Emerging Technologies (COMET), 433
Committee on Foreign Investment in the United
    States (CFIUS), 349
Commoditization, 68
Commonwealth of Independent States (CIS), 157
Competition management, 413, 421, 424–430
    vs. antidumping, 238–240
    vs. collusion, 225–226
    debates and extensions for, 49
        clear vs. blurred boundaries of industry, 48–49
        five forces vs. a sixth force, 50
        industry rivalry vs. strategic groups, 48–49, 51

industry-specific vs. firm-specific and institution-specific
  determinants of performance, 54
integration vs. outsourcing, 52–54
stuck in the middle vs. all rounder, 50–51
threats vs. opportunities, 49
five forces framework, 35–37
  bargaining power of buyers, 41–42
  bargaining power of suppliers, 41
  intensity of rivalry among competitors, 35–38
  lessons from, 43, 43T
  threat of potential entry, 38–41
  threat of substitutes, 42–43
generic strategies, 45–48
  cost leadership, 45
  differentiation, 47
  focus, 47–48
  lessons from, 48
Competition policy, 236
Competitive dynamics management
  attacks and counterattacks, 241–244
  comprehensive model for
    industry-based considerations, 225–231
    institution-based considerations, 236–241
    resource-based considerations, 231–236
  cooperation and signaling, 245
  debates and extensions for
    competition versus antidumping, 249
    strategy versus IO economics and antitrust policy, 247–248
  defined, 224
  implications for action, 249–251
  local firms versus multinational enterprises, 245–247, 460–461
  strategy as action, 224–225
Competitor analysis, 224, 233
Competitor rivalry, 35–36, 368
Complementary assets, 74
Complementors, 50
Computer and Communication Industry Association, 456
Concentrated ownership, 328
Concentration ratios, 228
Conduct codes, 35, 344
Conglomerates and conglomeration, 259–260, 262, 276–277
Conscious capitalism, 372, 385–386
Conscious leadership, 385
Constellations, 190
Contender strategies, 247
Contractual agreements, 172, 175
Contractual alliances, 190, 191
Cooperation and signaling, 245
Copenhagen Accord, 381
Corporate culture, 468
Corporate divorce, 205, 215–217
Corporate governance (CG), 400
  boards of directors
    composition of, 334
    directing strategically, 335–336

interlocks, 334–335
    leadership structure, 334
    role of, 335
  comprehensive model for
    industry-based considerations, 340–341
    institution-based considerations, 342–344
    resource-based considerations, 342
  debates and extensions for
    convergence versus divergence, 345–346
    opportunistic agents versus managerial stewards, 345
    overview, 344
    state ownership versus private ownership, 346–348
  defined, 328
  governance
    combination of mechanisms, 338–339
    external mechanisms, 337–338
    global perspective on, 339–340
    internal mechanisms, 337
    overview, 336–337
  implications for action, 350–351
  managers
    principle-agent conflicts, 330–331
    principle-principle conflicts, 331–332, 331–333
  ownership
    concentrated versus diffused ownership, 328–329
    family ownership, 329
    state ownership, 329–330
  private equity, 338
  privatization, 346–347
Corporate headquarters (HQ), 308–309
Corporate-level strategies, 260
  for corporate governance
    boards of directors, 334–336
    comprehensive model for, 340–344
    debates and extensions for, 345–358
    governance, 336–340
    implications for action, 350–351
    managers, 330–332
    ownership, 328–330
    private equity, 338
    privatization, 346–347
  for corporate social responsibility
    comprehensive model for, 368–378
    debates and extensions for, 378–380
    implications for action, 380–382
    stakeholders and, 364–368
  for diversification, acquisition, and restructuring, 284–285
    combinatorial diversification, 265–266
    comprehensive model for, 269–273
    debates and extensions for, 283–284
    evolution of, 273
    geographic diversification, 263–265
    implications for action, 284–285
    motives for, 277–279
    performance of, 280–282

product diversification, 261–263
terminology, 273, 282
for multinational strategies and structures
comprehensive model for, 304–307
cost reduction and local responsiveness, 296–297
debates and extensions for, 314–318
implications for action, 318
knowledge management, 310–314
organizational structures, 300–303
reciprocal relationship between strategy and structure, 304
research & development (R&D), 312–313
strategic choices, 297–300
Corporate marriage, 201, 207
Corporate Rehabilitation Law, 191
Corporate social responsibility (CSR), 448–455, 466
comprehensive model for
industry-based considerations, 368–372
institution-based considerations, 373–378
resource-based considerations, 372–373
debates and extensions for
active versus inactive CSR engagement overseas, 379
domestic versus overseas social responsibility, 378–379
pollution haven debate, 380
economic performance puzzle, 373
implications for action, 380–382
stakeholders and
big picture perspective, 363
debate, 365–369
primary stakeholder groups, 364
secondary stakeholder groups, 365
Corruption, 110
Cost leadership, 45
Counterattacks, 241–244
Country managers, 301
Country-of-origin effect, 177
Cross-border M&As, 277, 282, 288–289
Cross-cultural blunders, 108T
Cross-listing, 345
Cross-market retaliation, 231
Cross-shareholding, 190, 191
Cruise industry, 39
CSR. *See* Corporate social responsibility (CSR)
Cultural distance, 114–115, 166–167
Cultural emphases. *See* Institutional, cultural, and ethical emphases
Currency hedging, 163
Currency risks, 163
Czech Republic, 6, 8

D
Debates and extensions, 48–54
for business-level strategies
competitive dynamics management, 247–249
entrepreneurial firm growth and internationalization, 142–146
foreign market entries, 177–179
strategic alliances and networks, 208–211

for corporate-level strategies
corporate governance, 344–348
corporate social responsibility, 378–380
diversification, acquisition, and restructuring, 283–284
for foundation-level strategies
industry competition management, 48–54
institutional, ethical, and cultural emphases, 113–116
resource capabilities and leverage, 76–81
for multinational strategies and structures
multinational strategies and structures, 315–318
Decision model, 68, 170–171
Defender strategies, 245
Defensive strategies, 112, 374
Diamond industry, 229–230
"Diamond model" by M. Porter, 100
Differentiation, 47
Diffused ownership, 329
Digital piracy, 250
Digital textbooks, 440–447
Direct exports, 141, 172, 174
Dissemination risks, 161
Distance, cultural vs. institutional, 114–115
Diversification, acquisition and restructuring, 258, 261, 282
combining product and geographic, 265–266
comprehensive model for
industry-based considerations, 266–269
institution-based considerations, 272–273
resource-based considerations, 269–272
debates and extensions for
acquisitions versus alliances, 284
product relatedness versus other forms, 283–284
evolution of, 273
geographic diversification
firm performance and, 264–265
limited versus extensive international scope, 263
implications for action, 284–285
motives for, 277–279, 282–283
performance of, 280–282
product diversification
firm performance and, 262–263
product-related, 261
product-unrelated, 261–262
terminology, 276–277, 282
Diversification discount, 262
Diversification premium, 262
Dodd-Frank Act of 2010, 343
Dodger strategies, 246
Doing Business (World Bank Survey), 133
Domestic demands, 101
Domestic in-house activity, 69, 70
Domestic markets, 158–159
Dominance, 36
Dominant logic, 283
Downscoping, 282
Downsizing, 282

Downstream vertical alliances, 194
Dubai, 163, 164
Due diligence, 199
Dumping, 238
Duopolies, 35
Dynamic capabilities, 78

E

E-commerce, 436–438
EBITDA (earnings before interest, taxes, depreciation, and amortization), 332, 405, 416
Economic benefits, 273
Economic Recovery Bill of 2009, 429
Economies of scale, 39, 261
Economies of scope, 262
The Economist, 16, 33, 110
Educational software, 445–446
Educational technology, 440–447
Efficiency seeking firms, 165
Electric vehicle (EV), 361–362, 363
Electronic books (e-books), 38, 440–447
Emergent strategy, 11
Emerging economies, 5–11, 27–28, 32–34, 66, 75, 97, 403, 404–408
    China, 58
    India, 57 59
    piracy, 85
Emerging markets. *See* Emerging economies
Energy Independence and Security Act (2007), 361
Entering foreign markets *See* Foreign market entries
Enterprise resource planning (ERP), 135
Entrepreneur-friendly bankruptcy laws, 144 146
Entrepreneurial firm growth and internationalization, 126–153
    comprehensive model for, 129f
        industry-based considerations, 130
        institution-based considerations, 133–134
        resource-based considerations, 130–132
    debates and extensions for
        anti failure biases vs. entrepreneur-friendly bankruptcy laws, 144–146
        slow internationalizers vs. born global start-ups, 143–144
        traits vs. institutions, 142–143
    entrepreneurial firms, 128–129
    five strategies
        financing and governance, 136–137
        growth, 134
        harvest and exit, 138–139
        innovation, 134–135
        network, 136
    implications for action, 146
    internationalization
        strategies for entering foreign markets, 141
        strategies for staying in domestic markets, 141–142
        transaction costs, 140

Entry barriers, 38, 130
Environmentalist challenges, 371
Environment management system (EMS), 377
Environmental Protection Agency (EPA), 374
Equity-based alliances, 190, 191, 202
Equity modes, 170–174
Ethical emphases. *See* Institutional, cultural, and ethical emphases
Ethical imperialism, 110
Ethical relativism, 110
EU-US Open Skies Agreement, 421
Eurasia, 404–408
Eurasian markets
    telecom industry, 408
Europe
    Eurozone, 163
European Aeronautic Defense and Space Company (EADS), 302
European Union (EU), 5, 16, 128
    euro crisis, 23
Evergreen Research and Development (ERD) program, 435
Excess capacity, 40
Exit-based governance mechanisms, 336
Explicit collusion, 226
Explicit knowledge, 311
Exploitation, 204
Exploration, 204
Export intermediaries, 142
Exports, 172, 174
Expropriation, 162, 331
Extender strategies, 246
Extensions. *See* Debates and extensions
External governance mechanisms, 338
Extraterritoriality, 238
Exxon Valdez, 366

F

Factor endowments, 100
Fair Labor Association, 365
Family ownership, 331, 332
Far-flung conglomerate, 266
Fashion industry, 57–59
Fast-moving industries, 78
FCPA (Foreign Corrupt Practices Act), 111
FDA (Food and Drug Administration), 374
(FDI) foreign direct investment, 5
Federal Communications Commission (FCC), 456, 458
Federal Trade Commission, 112
Feints, 241, 243f
Femininity, 106–107
Feng-GUI, 135
Finance Corporation for Industry (FCI), 391
Financial control, 271, 336
Financial resources and capabilities, 65

Financial synergy, 262
Finland
   telecom industry, 404–408
Firm-specific determinants of
    performance, 54
Firm strategy, structure, and rivalry, 100
Firms, 15–18
   behavior of, 16–17
   scope of, 17
   strategic choices, 102
   success and failure of, 18
   why differ, 15–16
First-mover advantages, 168
Five dimensions of culture, 104
Five forces framework, 35–43, 50, 130
   bargaining power of buyers, 41–42
   bargaining power of suppliers, 41
   foreign market entries and, 160
   intensity of rivalry among competitors, 35–38
   threat of potential entry, 38–41
   threat of substitutes, 42–43
Flexible manufacturing technology, 51
Focus, 47–48
Food and Drug Administration (FDA), 374
Forbearance, mutual, 225
Foreign Corrupt Practices Act (FCPA), 111
Foreign direct investment (FDI), 5, 33, 70, 97, 103, 141, 157, 174, 406
Foreign market entries, 154–185
   2W1H aspects
    how, 170–176
    when, 168–170
    where, 163–166
   comprehensive model for
    industry-based considerations, 160
    institution-based considerations, 161–163
    overview, 159
    resource-based considerations, 160–161
   debates and extensions
    global vs. regional geographic diversification, 177–178
    liability vs. asset of foreignness, 177
    old-line vs. emerging multinationals
     (OLI vs. LLL), 178–179
   implications for action, 179–180
   liability of foreignness, 156–157
   propensity to internationalize, 158–159
   strategic goals and, 165
Foreign portfolio investment (FPI), 344
Foreignness liability concept, 156
Forest Stewardship Council (FSC), 372, 449, 451, 452
Formal institutions, 94
   competitive dynamics management, 236–241
   corporate governance, 342–343
   corporate social responsibility, 373
   diversification, 272
   foreign market entries, 166

multinational strategies and
    structures, 307
   strategic alliances and networks, 198–199
Formal, rule-based, impersonal
   exchanges, 99
Fortune 500, 44
Forward integration, 41
Foundation, 54
Foundation-level strategies. *See also* Five forces framework
   fundamental topics for
    21st century, 23–24
    firms, 15–18
    global nature of, 4–9
    global strategy, 19–20
    globalization, 20–21
    strategy issues, 9, 9–14
   for industry competition management
    debates and extensions, 48–54
    defined, 34–35
    generic strategies, 45–48
    implications for action, 54–55
   for institutional, cultural, and ethical emphases
    corruption and, 110, 110–111
    debates and extensions for, 113–115
    defined, 94
    five dimensions of, 105–107
    implications for action, 115–116
    managing overseas, 93, 109
    reduction of uncertainty, 98–100
    role of, 95
    strategic choices and, 104–105, 107–108, 111–112
    strategic response framework for, 111–113
    view of business strategy, 100–101
   for resource capabilities and leverage
    debates and extensions for, 76–81
    implications for action, 81–83
    understanding, 64–65
    value chain and, 67–71
    VRIO framework, 71–76
Four Tigers, 21
FPI (foreign portfolio investment), 344
France, 12, 16, 42, 111
Franchising, 141, 175, 191
Franco-Prussian War, 12
Fukushima nuclear power station, 366
The Full Monty, 378

G

GAAP (generally accepted accounting principles), 240
Gambits, 242, 244f
Game theory, 226
Gaming industry, 412–417
Generally accepted accounting principles (GAAP), 240
Generic strategies, 45–48
   cost leadership, 45

differentiation, 47
focus, 47–48
lessons from, 48
Geographic area structures, 301
Geographic diversification, 261, 263–265
Germany, 12, 14, 16, 40, 111, 467
bankruptcy in, 38, 145
solar technology industry, 424–430
Global account structures, 317
Global activities, 466
Global mandate, 299
Global matrix, 302–303
Global Positioning System (GPS), 432
Global product division, 302
Global recession, 410
Global Reporting Initiative (GRI), 449
Global standardization strategy, 298–299, 311
Global start-ups, 431–435
Global strategies, 3, 5, 9, 19, 435
business-level strategies
for competitive dynamics, 224–230
for entrepreneurial firm growth and internationalization, 126–147
for strategic alliances and networks, 190–213
corporate-level strategies
for corporate governance, 324–348
for corporate social responsibility, 363–382
for diversification, acquisition, and restructuring, 265–284
corporate-level strategies (corporate strategy)
for multinational strategies and structures, 296–318
for foreign market entries, 159–179
foundation-level strategies
fundamental topics for, 4–24
for industry competition management, 32–61
for institutional, cultural, and ethical emphases, 94–116
for resource capabilities and leverage, 64–83
Global Strategy Group, 295
Global sustainability, 364
Global virtual teams, 314
Globalization, 20
in the 21st century, 23–24
debate about, 23
overview, 20–21
pendulum view on, 20–21
semiglobalization, 22
views of, 24T
Golden parachute, 327
Government sponsored enterprises (GSEs), 347
Grameen Project, 149
Great Depression, 346
Great Recession, 21, 46, 47, 57–58, 63, 95, 144, 157, 179, 295, 382
Greece, 197
Green energy, 429
Greenfield operations, 173, 176, 182–183
Greenpeace, 365, 370, 375, 449
Growth strategies, 134

H

Hammock and leisure furniture industry, 449
Hart-Scott-Rodino (HSR) Act of 1976, 237
Harvest strategies, 138–139
Hawaii, 43
Headquarters (HQ), 308–309
Health care industry, 44
Hedging, 163
High School Musical, 100, 269
High-volume low-margin approach, 45
HIV/AIDS drugs, 192, 370
Hofstede dimensions of cultures, 104–106
Home replication strategies, 297–298, 311
Hong Kong, 6, 21
Disneyland in, 460–461
Hope schools, 466
Horizontal alliances, 194
Horizontal M&As, 276
Hostile M&A's, 277
HQ (Headquarters), 308–309
HSR (Hart-Scott-Rodino) Act of 1976, 237
Hubris, 279
Human resource management (HRM), 65, 419, 469
The Hunt for Red October, 203
Hypercompetition, 78

I

ICQ instant messaging software, 134
i.Lab, 431
Imitability
competitive dynamics management, 232
corporate social responsibility, 372
diversification, 269
foreign market entries and, 161
multinational strategies and structures, 306
resource capabilities and leverage, 72–74
strategic alliances and networks, 197–198
Imperialism, ethical, 110
Implications for action, 54–55
for business-level strategies
strategic alliances and networks, 211–213
competitive dynamics management, 224–225
for corporate-level strategies
corporate governance, 350–351
diversification, acquisition, and restructuring, 284–285
multinational strategies and structures, 318
entrepreneurial firm growth and internationalization, 146
foreign market entries and, 179–180
for foundation-level strategies
industry competition management, 54–55
resource capabilities and leverage, 81–83
for institutional, cultural, and ethical emphases, 115–116
In-group members, 114
In-house production, 69
Inactive CSR engagement overseas, 379

Incumbents, 38, 54
Independent directors, 334
India, 5–7, 86, 103, 288
    automobile market in, 7
    BRIC, 7, 17, 102–103
    business acquisitions in, 288–289
    business process offshoring (BPO) industry, 409–410
    multinational enterprises (MNEs) and, 288
    offshoring to, 79
    retail industry in, 32–34, 41
Indirect exports, 142, 174
Individualism, 106
Indonesia, 110
Industrial and Commercial Finance Corporation (ICFC), 391
Industrial organization (IO) economics, 34, 247–248
Industry, 34
Industry-based considerations
    for business-level strategies
        competitive dynamics management, 225–231
        entrepreneurial firm growth and internationalization, 130
        foreign market entries, 160
        strategic alliances and networks, 193–194
    for corporate-level strategies
        corporate governance, 340–341
        corporate social responsibility, 368–372
        diversification, acquisition and restructuring, 266–269
        multinational strategies and structures, 304–306
Industry-based view, 49
    debates and extensions for
        five forces vs. a sixth force, 50
        industry-specific vs. firm-specific and institution-specific determinants of performance, 54
        integration vs. outsourcing, 52–54
        stuck in the middle vs. all rounder, 50–51
        threats vs. opportunities, 49
Industry competition management, 32–61, 48–49
    debates and extensions for, 49
        clear vs. blurred boundaries of industry, 48–49
        five forces vs. a sixth force, 50
        industry rivalry vs. strategic groups, 51
        industry-specific vs. firm-specific and institution-specific determinants of performance, 54
        integration vs. outsourcing, 52–54
        stuck in the middle vs. all rounder, 50–51
        threats vs. opportunities, 49
    five forces framework, 35–37
        bargaining power of buyers, 41–42
        bargaining power of suppliers, 41
        intensity of rivalry among competitors, 35–38
        lessons from, 43, 43T
        threat of potential entry, 38–41
        threat of substitutes, 42–43
    generic strategies, 45, 45–48
        cost leadership, 45
        differentiation, 47
        focus, 47–48
        lessons from, 48
Industry positioning, 43
Industry rivalry, 51
Industry-specific determinants of performance, 54
Industry-specific restrictions, 33
Informal institutions, 94
    corporate governance, 343–344
    corporate social responsibility, 373
    diversification, acquisition and restructuring, 272–273
    entrepreneurial firm growth and internationalization, 130
    institutional, ethical, and cultural emphases, 93
    multinational strategies and structures, 307
    strategic alliances and networks, 199–200
Informal, relationship-based, personalized exchange, 98, 98f
Information asymmetries, 330
Information overload, 18
Initial public offerings (IPOs), 139, 394
Inner Mongolia, 392
Innovation, 85, 86
Innovation entrepreneurship strategies, 134–135
Innovation resources and capabilities, 65
Innovation seeking firms, 165
Inside directors, 334, 335
Insourcing, 70
Institution-based considerations, 418–422, 428–429
    for business-level strategies
        competitive dynamics management, 236–241
        entrepreneurial firm growth and internationalization, 133–134
        foreign market entries, 161–163
        strategic alliances and networks, 199–200
    for corporate-level strategies
        corporate governance, 342–344
        corporate social responsibility, 368–372
        diversification, acquisition and restructuring, 272–273
        multinational strategies and structures, 307, 309–310
Institution-based views, 94, 102f
Institution-specific determinants of performance, 54
Institutional, cultural, and ethical emphases
    corruption and, 110, 110–111
    debates and extensions for
        cultural distance vs. institutional distance, 114–115
        opportunism vs. individualism/collectivism, 113–114
        origin of unethical business behavior, 115
    defined, 94
    five dimensions of, 105–107
    implications for action, 115–116
    institution-based views
        core propositions of, 102, 104–105
        overview, 100–101
    managing overseas, 109, 110
    reduction of uncertainty, 98–100
    role of, 95

strategic choices and, 104–105, 107–108
strategic response framework for, 111–113
Institutional distance, 115, 165
Institutional framework, 94
Institutional relatedness, 284
Institutional transactions, 100
Institutions, 94
    dimensions of, 95T
    reduction of uncertainty, 98–100
    strategic choices, 102
    vs. traits, 142–143
Intangible resources and capabilities, 65
Integration, 52–54, 462
Integration-responsiveness framework, 296, 298
Intellectual property rights (IPR), 27, 161, 392, 431, 435
Intended strategies, 11
Intercity bus travel, 154–155
Interfirm rivalry, 130
Interlocking directorates, 334–335
Internal capital markets, 262
Internal governance mechanisms, 338
Internalization, 173
Internalization advantage, 173
International diversification, 263
International division structure, 300–301
International entrepreneurship, 128
International Gaming Awards (IGA), 416
International joint venture (IJV), 448–455, 452
International marketing, 452
International safety certification (GS), 451
International Standards Organization (ISO), 377
Internationalization. *See* Entrepreneurial firm growth and
    internationalization
Internet, 131, 420, 436–438
Intra-African trade, 167
IO (industrial organization) economics, 34, 247–248
IPOs (initial public offerings), 139, 149
IPR (intellectual property rights), 27, 161
Iraq, 40, 132
Irish Department of
    Transportation (DOT), 421
Islamic finance, 170
ISO (International Standards
    Organization), 377
Israel, 134, 135
IT industry, 63, 70, 409
Italy, 16
ITT, 379

J

Japan, 5–6, 16, 39, 40, 53, 105, 462
    airline industry, 73, 191
    automobile industry, 193
    bankruptcy in, 38, 145
    bookselling industry in, 54

collectivism, 92
    earthquake in, 23, 366, 369
    internet commerce in, 127
    layoffs and, 91
    luxury goods industry, 58
Jasmine Revolution, 28
Joint ventures (JVs), 171, 175, 190, 191
    246, 448–455

K

keiretsu, 16, 53, 168, 193
Knowledge management, 310–311
Korea, 16, 39
Korean Ministry of Education, Science and Technology (MEST), 443
Kung Fu Panda, 86
Kyoto Protocol (2007), 381

L

Late-mover advantages, 168–169
Latin America, 21
Learning. *See* Multinational strategies and structures
Learning by doing, 200
Learning race view, 196
Leveraged buyouts (LBOs), 338
Licensing, 141, 175, 191
Linkage, leverage, and learning (LLL) framework, 178, 179
Local content requirements, 162
Local firms, 245–247, 460–461
Local responsiveness, 296
Localization strategies, 297–298, 311
Location-specific advantages
    and goals, 163–166
London Stock Exchange, 127
Long-term orientation, 107
Love Boat (ABC), 39
Low-cost rivals, 46, 234–236, 253–254
Low-volume high-margin approach, 47
Luxury automobiles, 51
Luxury goods industry, 57–59

M

M&As. *See* Mergers and acquisitions (M&As)
Macau, 412–417
Managerial human capital, 342
Managerial stewards, 345
Marginal bureaucratic costs (MBCs), 273
Marginal economic benefits (MEBs), 273
Market commonalities, 231
Market seeking firms, 165
Masculinity, 106–107
Mass customization, 51
MBCs (marginal bureaucratic costs), 273
MEBs (marginal economic benefits), 273
Merchant of Venice (Shakespeare), 145

Mergers and acquisitions (M&As), 191, 276, 337–338, 354, 404–408, 465–470
  in China, 288–289
  defined, 277
  mobile phone industry, 456–459
  performance of, 280–283, 464
Mexico, 6, 19
Micro-macro link, 314
Microfinance, 138, 149–150
Microfinance institutions (MFIs), 149
Middle-of-the-road approaches, 110
Military strategy, 12
Minority shareholders, 331, 332, 342–343
MNEs. *See* Multinational enterprises (MNEs)
Mobile phone industry, 456–459
Mobility barriers, 52
Modes of entry, 170–176
Monopolies, 35
Moral hazard, 347
Moscow Municipality Government, 198
Multi-brand stores, 33
Multidomestic strategies, 297–298, 311
Multimarket competition, 225
Multinational enterprises (MNEs), 9, 21, 85, 86T, 103–104, 157, 174, 264, 288–289, 379, 380, 404–408
  defined, 5
  emerging, 85–86
  geographic diversification by sales, 178
  versus local firms, 245–247, 460–461
  outward foreign direct investment (OFDI), 103
Multinational replicators, 265
Multinational strategies and structures
  comprehensive model for
    industry-based considerations, 304–306
    institution-based considerations, 307, 309–310
    resource-based considerations, 306–307
  cost reduction and local responsiveness, 296–297
  debates and extensions for
    corporate controls versus subsidiary initiatives, 315–316
    integration, responsiveness, and learning, 317–318
    one multinational versus many national companies, 315
    overview, 314–315
  implications for action, 318
  knowledge management, 310–312, 313–314
  organizational structures, 300–303
  reciprocal relationship between strategy and structure, 304
  research & development (R&D), 312–313
  strategic choices, 297–300
Music industry, 43
Mutual forbearance, 225

N

NAFTA markets, 263
NASDAQ, 6, 127, 143, 350, 404, 438

National Medal of Science, 63
National Medals of Technology, 63
Natural resource seeking firms, 165
Nepal, 407
Netherlands, 6, 42, 111
Network centrality, 197
Network externalities, 40
Networks. *See* Strategic alliances and networks
New York Stock Exchange, 315, 342, 433
New Zealand, 43
Newness liability concept, 136
NGOs (nongovernmental organizations), 23, 370, 372, 377, 379
Non-equity based alliances, 190, 191, 202T
Non-equity modes, 171
Non-operating entities (NOEs), 223
Non-scale-based advantages, 40
Non-shareholder stakeholders, 363
Nongovernmental organizations (NGOs), 23, 370, 372, 377, 379
Nontariff barriers, 162
Normative pillars, 94, 199–200

O

Obsolescing bargain, 161
Occupy London, 344
Occupy Wall Street, 23, 344, 354, 366, 382
OECD (Organization for Economic Cooperation and Development), 111, 259, 344
OEMs (original equipment manufacturers), 80
OFDI, 103
Offshoring, 70, 79, 409–410
Oil Majors, 316
Oil Shocks of 1973-74 and 1979-80, 316
OLI (ownership-location-internalization) advantages, 173–174
Oligopolies, 35
Online media, 43
Online moderators, 131
Onshoring, 70
OPEC, 160
Open innovation, 313
Operational synergy, 261
Opportunism, 97, 196, 203
Organization
  competitive dynamics management, 232
  corporate social responsibility, 373
  diversification, 269
  multinational strategies and structures, 306
  resource capabilities and leverage, 74–76
  strategic alliances and networks, 198
Organization for Economic Cooperation and Development (OECD), 344
Organizational culture, 306–307
Organizational fit, 281, 462–463
Origin of strategy, 10
Original brand manufacturers (OBMs), 80

Original design manufacturers (ODMs), 80
Original equipment manufacturers (OEMs), 80
Out-group, 114
Output control, 271, 336
Outside directors, 334, 335
Outsourcing, 6, 9, 69–70, 175
    defined, 69
    versus integration, 52–54
Outward foreign direct investment (OFDI), 103, 104
Ownership, 52
Ownership advantage, 173
Ownership-location-internalization (OLI) advantages, 173–174

P

Pakistan, 95, 96, 107
Partner opportunism, 196
Partner rarity, 196
Patenting, 223–224, 253–254, 435
Pendulum view on globalization, 21
Pentium chip, 134
Perfect competition, 34
Performance, 19, 35, 207, 414–415, 420
Pharmaceutical industry, 44
Physical resources and capabilities, 65
Piano companies, 182
Piracy, digital, 250
PMCs (private military companies), 132–133
Poland, 168–169
Political deadlocks, 95
Politics, 75
Pollution, 368–369, 373, 375, 380, 381
Porter diamond model, 100, 101
Power distance, 104
Predatory pricing, 238
Price leaders, 228
Primary stakeholder groups, 364
Principals, 330
Principle-agent conflicts, 330
Principle-principle conflicts, 331
Prisoner's dilemma, 225–227
Privacy issues, 119–120
Private equity, 338, 346, 353–355, 391–403, 436
Proactive strategies, 112, 376
Product differentiation, 40
Product diversification, 261
    combining with geographic diversification, 265–266
    defined, 261
    firm performance and, 262–263
    product-related, 261
    product-unrelated, 261–262
Product proliferation, 40
Product-related diversification, 261
Product-related versus unrelated diversification, 261–262
Proprietary technology, 40
PRPG America, 173

Public opinion of globalization, 23–24
Pyramid, base of the (BOP), 7, 7–8

Q
Quality certification (ISO), 451

R
Race to the bottom debate, 380
Races, learning, 194
Rarity
    competitive dynamics management, 232
    corporate social responsibility, 372
    diversification, 269
    multinational strategies and structures, 306
    resource capabilities and leverage, 72
    strategic alliances and networks, 196–197
Reactive strategies, 112, 374
Real options, 195
Rebranding, 177
Reduction of uncertainty, 95
Refocusing, 282
Regional geographic diversification, 177–178
Regional managers, 301
Regulatory pillars, 94, 198–199
Regulatory risks, 161
Related and supporting industries, 100
Related transactions, 333
Relational capabilities, 196
Relational contracting, 98
Relationships. See Strategic alliances and networks
Relativism, ethical, 110
Renewable energy, 425
Replication, 13
Reputation resources and capabilities, 65
Research and development (R&D), 47
Research and development (R&D)
    contracts, 175, 191
Resource-based considerations, 418–422
    for business-level strategies
        competitive dynamics management, 231–236
        entrepreneurial firm growth and internationalization, 130–132
        foreign market entries, 160–161
        strategic alliances and networks, 194–195, 197–198
    for corporate-level strategies
        corporate governance, 342
        corporate social responsibility, 372–373
        diversification, acquisition and restructuring, 269–272
        multinational strategies and structures, 306–307
Resource-based view, 64
Resource capabilities and leverage
    debates and extensions for
        domestic resources vs. international (cross-border) capabilities, 81
        firm-specific vs. industry-specific determinants of performance, 76–77

offshoring vs. non-offshoring, 79, 79–81
static resources vs. dynamic capabilities, 77–78
implications for action, 81–83
understanding, 64–65
value chain and, 67–71
VRIO framework
imitability, 72–74
organization, 74–76
rarity, 72
value, 71–72
Resource similarity, 231–232
Resources, 64
Restaurant industry, 391–403
Restructuring. *See* Diversification, acquisition and restructuring
Reverse innovation, 7–9
RFID technologies, 432
Risk management, 22, 435
Rule of law, 97
Russia, 6, 16, 97–98, 103, 198
BRIC, 7, 17, 102–103
Code of Corporate Conduct 2002, 344
internet commerce in, 127–128, 436–438
oil industry, 199
state-owned enterprises (SOEs), 347

S
Santiago Principles, 350
Sarbanes-Oxley (SOX) Act of 2002, 336, 342–343, 354
SARS epidemic, 46
Scale-based advantages, 39
Scale economies, 261
Scale of foreign market entries, 170–171
Scenario planning, 22
Schlieffen Plan, 12
Scope economies, 262
Secondary stakeholder groups, 365
Semiglobalization, 22
SEPA-Dow National Cleaner Production Pilot, 381
Separation of ownership and control, 329
September 2001 terrorist attacks, 21, 113–114
Serial entrepreneurs, 143
Servant leadership, 386
Sex role differentiation, 105–106
Shanghai Stock Exchange, 465
Shareholder capitalism, 339, 343, 365
Shareholders, 332
Sherman Act of 1890, 226, 237, 248
Sierra Leone, 133
Singapore, 6, 21
Single business strategies, 261
"Six Sigma" quality management system, 466
Ski resorts, 431
Slovakia, 6
Slow-moving industries, 78
Small and medium-sized enterprises (SMEs), 128, 135, 142

Smartphones, 43, 253–254
SMEs (small and medium-sized enterprises), 135, 142
Snow sports industry, 431–435
Social complexity, 74
Social issue participation, 372
Social networking, 119–120
SOEs (state-owned enterprises), 162, 289, 329–330, 346–348
Solar power industry, 428
Solar technology industry, 424–430
Solar Technology International, 425
Solutions-based structures, 317
South Africa, 7, 167
diamond industry, 229
emerging multinationals from, 167
internationalization of firms from, 167
South Korea, 14, 21, 259–260, 440–447
digital tablets, 440, 445–446
modernizing education, 443–444
South Korean Ministry of Education (MOE), 440, 443
Sovereign wealth funds (SWFs), 348, 349
Soviet Union (former), 21
collapse of, 405. *See also* Russia
SOX (Sarbanes-Oxley) Act of 2002, 336, 342–343, 354
Spain, 42
Spiderman, 100
Stage models, 144
Stakeholders, 18
Start-up business, 431–435, 436–438
The Start-Up Nation (Senor and Singer), 135
State Environmental Protection Administration (SEPA) of China, 381
State-owned enterprises (SOEs), 162, 289, 329–330, 346–348, 465, 466
Steel industry, 465–470
Stewardship theory, 345
Stockholm Chamber of Commerce (SCC), 97
Strategic alliances and networks, 190
comprehensive model for
industry-based considerations, 192–194
institution-based considerations, 198–199
resource-based considerations, 195–198
debates and extensions for
acquiring vs. not acquiring alliance partners, 211
alliances vs. acquisitions, 209–210
majority vs. minority JVs, 208–209
defined, 190–191
evolution of
combating opportunism, 203
from corporate marriage to divorce, 189, 205–206, 212
overview, 200
from strong ties to weak ties, 203–205
formation of
contract or equity, 200–202
market transactions vs. acquisitions, 200
positioning relationships, 202–203

implications for action, 211–213
performance of
  overview, 206–207
  parent firms, 207–208
Strategic ambidexterity, 75
Strategic choices, 102, 107
Strategic control, 271
Strategic fit, 281, 462–463
Strategic groups, 51, 52
Strategic implications for action. *See* Implications for action
Strategic investment, 190, 191
Strategic management, 10
Strategic networks, 190
Strategic planning, 316, 398, 399
Strategic positioning, 466
Strategic response framework, 111–112
Strategies, 10. *See also names of specific strategies*
  fundamental questions in, 15
  localization, 297–298, 311
  overview, 14f
  tripod of, 11, 16, 16f
  versus IO economics and antitrust policy, 247–248
Strategy as action school, 11, 225f
Strategy as integration school, 11
Strategy as plan school, 10
Strategy as theory, 11, 12
Strategy formulation, 11
Strategy implementation, 11
Strong ties, 136
Structure-conduct-performance
  (SCP) model, 35
Sub-Saharan Africa, 167
Subsidiaries, 424–430, 467, 468
  partially owned, 172
  wholly owned, 173
Subsidiary initiatives, 316, 317, 321–322
Substitutes, 42, 130, 422
  threat of, 42–43, 57
Suicides, 6
Sunk costs, 162
Suppliers, bargaining power of, 41
Survival rates, start-up businesses, 137
Sustainable capitalism, 364
Sweden, 406
Switzerland, 158
SWOT analysis, 11, 34, 64
Synergy
  financial, 262
  operational, 261

T

Tablet PCs, 440–447
Tacit collusion, 226
Tacit knowledge, 311

Taiwan, 5, 6, 21
Tangible resources and capabilities, 65
Tariff barriers, 162
Technological resources and capabilities, 65
Technology start-ups, 436, 437
Telecom industry, 404–408
Television broadcasting industry, 234
Terrorism, 21, 66–67, 113–114
Textbook publishing industry, 4, 16, 440
Threats (T)
  of potential entry, 38
  of substitutes, 42–43
  turning to opportunities, 49, 460–461
Thrusts, 241, 243f
Top management teams (TMTs), 15, 330–331, 398, 400, 401
Trade barriers, 162
Traits, 142–143
Transaction costs, 95
Transnational strategy, 298, 299–300, 311
Treaty of Westphalia, 315
Triad, 5
Triple bottom line, 18
Tunneling, 333
Turnkey projects, 175, 191

U

Ultra-luxury car market, 51
UN Declaration on Human Rights, 379
Uncertainty, 95, 98–100, 107
Unethical business behavior, 110
United Arab Emirates, 164
United Kingdom, 9, 15
United Nations, 379
United States, 6, 8, 15, 42, 97, 105
  antitrust laws, 456–459
  antitrust laws in, 230, 237
  automobile market in, 7
  bankruptcy in, 191
  chemical industry, 374, 375
  Congress, 132
  Department of Commerce, 240
  Department of Justice, 228
  environmental policies, 455
  Federal Trade Commission (FTC), 119
  intercity bus travel in, 155–156
  International Trade Administration, 240
  International Trade Commission, 240
  snow-sports industry, 433
  solar power industry, 425, 427, 428
  State Department, 132, 215
  television broadcasting industry, 234
United States et al. v. AT&T Inc. et al., 457, 458
Universal Product Code (UPC), 63
Upstream vertical alliances, 193

US-China Strategic and Economic Dialogue (S&ED), 349
US Department of Justice (DOJ), 457, 458
US Securities and Exchange Commission, 436

V

Value, 130
    competitive dynamics management, 231–232
    corporate social responsibility, 371, 372, 376, 382
    creating shared, 367
    diversification, 269
    foreign market entries, 160
    multinational strategies and structures, 306
    resource capabilities and leverage, 71–72
    strategic alliances and networks, 195–196
Value chains, 67–71, 467
Venture capitalists (VCs), 137
Vertical M&As, 276
Voice-based mechanisms, 336
VRIO framework, 71, 71f, 76, 82, 130, 342
    competitive dynamics management, 231–232
    corporate social responsibility, 372–373
    diversification, acquisition and restructuring, 269, 269–272
    foreign market entries, 160–161
    multinational strategies and structures, 306
    resource capabilities and leverage, 71–76
    strategic alliances and networks, 194–198
VTB Group, 348

W

"Wal-Mart effect," 34
Wall Street Journal, 16
Washington Consensus, 347, 348
Watson artificial intelligence, 63
Weak ties, 136
Wealth of Nations (Smith), 225
Wholly owned subsidiary (WOS), 176, 456–459
Wi-Fi, 432
World Bank, 21, 133, 347
World War I, 12
World War II, 21
Worldwide mandate, 299

Y

Y2K problem, 85